Law for
Social Workers

Law for
Social Workers

13th edition

Hugh Brayne | Helen Carr |
David Goosey

OXFORD
UNIVERSITY PRESS

OXFORD
UNIVERSITY PRESS

Great Clarendon Street, Oxford, OX2 6DP,
United Kingdom

Oxford University Press is a department of the University of Oxford.
It furthers the University's objective of excellence in research, scholarship,
and education by publishing worldwide. Oxford is a registered trade mark of
Oxford University Press in the UK and in certain other countries

Tenth edition 2008
Eleventh edition 2010
Twelfth edition 2013

Impression: 1

Published in the United States of America by Oxford University Press
198 Madison Avenue, New York, NY 10016, United States of America

British Library Cataloguing in Publication Data

Data available

Library of Congress Control Number: 2014947490

ISBN 978–0–19–968568–4

Printed in Great Britain by Bell & Bain Ltd., Glasgow

The pace of change, always fast when it comes to the legal framework of social work, has accelerated since the last edition of *Law for Social Workers* was published in 2012. The Coalition Government has been determined to implement a range of changes in relation to children and adult social care, changes which reflect their particular priorities. As a result, several chapters of the book have had major rewrites. Part 1 of the book, which has been fully updated, continues to provide you with a clear and precise focused explanation of the broader legal environment in which you practise as social workers. We would encourage you to spend some time reading this part—the chapter on human rights is particularly useful in helping you to understand and protect the dignity and rights of your service users and to minimize the risk to you of legal challenges. It also seeks to engage with current debates surrounding human rights law, in particular the misgivings that the current government appears to have about the role of human rights. Part 2 of the book has probably seen the most changes. David Goosey, who has joined me as co-author, and has taken particular responsibility for this part, has had a baptism of fire! However, his expertise in children's law and his firm grasp of the challenges of practising as a social worker mean that you gain a clear and helpful statement of the current position. The Care Act 2014, which received Royal Assent in May, is central to Part 3 of the book. The Act will, as it is implemented over the next couple of years, transform the legal landscape of adult social care. We have given you what we hope is a useful outline of the statute, which will enable you to understand the new regulations as they are published. The *McDonald* case, which we covered fully in the last edition, has now reached Europe. The decision, although not particularly positive for Ms McDonald herself, does open up some limited possibilities for giving legal force to concepts of dignity.

As usual a range of people have helped us with this edition. We are grateful to Kevin Jackson, a barrister specializing in children's law, who has provided us with some good practice points for social workers appearing in court which we have included in the Toolkit. I must particularly thank Richard Alcock whose enthusiasm for clear and useful legal writing and up-to-date legal knowledge remains unabated. David would like to thank Sandra Duhaney for her comments on the youth justice chapter.

Helen Carr
David Goosey
July 2014

Law for Social Workers is full of features designed to help you to continuously develop and improve your legal skills, from the first stages of your degree through to placements, your first job, and beyond. This guide to the book shows you how to fully utilize its key features, whether you're a student new to the subject or a qualified professional.

OVERVIEW AND OBJECTIVES

The aim of this chapter is to look at the c
Act 1989 and at some common definiti
describes the Safeguarding and Interage
sider in some detail the agencies whic
children and other vulnerable people a
the range of problems which vulnerabl

Overview and objectives

Key learning objectives are set out at the beginning of each chapter to enable you to draw out the main themes. They provide a helpful signpost to what you can expect to learn from the chapter and offer a recap of the key issues discussed, making them ideal for revision.

CASE STUDY

A and another v Essex County Council (2003

Mr A and Mrs B were married in 1985. Both
from his first marriage. They had no children
prospective adoptive parents. Their local au
as defined under the Act then in force, the A
social worker and adoption adviser, emplo

Case study

Each chapter opens with a discussion of a significant case or inquiry, helping you to learn the facts of key cases and demonstrating how the law applies in practice. Each case study is followed by an explanation of its key themes and relevance to your studies and career.

Private family law	176
Marriage, civil partnership,	
and other couple	
relationships	176
Parental responsibility	178
Private disputes involving	
children—section 8 orders	178
Changing the Safeguarding and	

Chapter content lists

These quick-reference lists at the beginning of each chapter allow you to find information easily—perfect for quick advice and fact-finding on practice placements and in the workplace.

EXERCISES

1. Read the whole of this chapter carefully a
will need to consider before recommendin
respect of an individual child.
2. Locate and read one of the articles listed
article in 100–150 words.
3. Try to construct a time line of events leadi

Exercises

Chapter exercises help you to consider how to approach real-life issues and give you the opportunity to practise advising the service user. Guidance on how to approach these scenarios can be found on the Online Resource Centre, allowing you to check your ideas and prepare for exams.

WHERE DO WE GO FROM HERE?

In this chapter we have considered a numbe
its philosophy, structure, overarching princi
by the courts. This chapter serves as an intro
sibilities to children. However, it is more than
the principles upon which the Act is based,
stand your role within the Act. In addition

Where do we go from here?

These sections provide a useful review of what has been covered in each chapter and demonstrate how topics link together, ideal for planning essays and revision as well as considering how the law relates to your role as a social worker.

Annotated further reading and web links

Further reading suggestions and useful websites are provided at the end of each chapter with author advice to help you to direct your research and find more detailed information.

Extracts and key point boxes

Essential information and extracts from significant judgments or inquiries are reproduced in coloured boxes to help to provide useful context for key issues and recap important information.

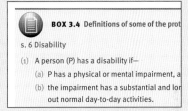

Figures and tables

Useful information and key processes are distilled into easy-to-follow figures and flowcharts, while essential points are summarized in tables for quick reference and exam preparation.

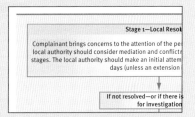

THE SOCIAL WORKER'S TOOLKIT

The Social Worker's Toolkit offers unrivalled practical support for your social work career. Full of practical information and tips from the authors it offers more detailed advice on areas such as giving evidence, report writing, and dealing with lawyers.

Written by a qualified social worker, it is the ideal quick-reference tool for practice placements and work experience, and provides a recap of essential information and advice which will be invaluable throughout your studies and career.

The Toolkit is also supported by a range of online resources including video footage and checklists from a social work professional on preparing for court, giving evidence, cross-examination, and what to do after the hearing. See the **Guide to the Online Resource Centre** for more details.

Evidence FAQ

Can anyone help me with my evidence?

The simple answer is 'No'. Once in the witness box, you are on your own. Preparation of your evidence gives some assistance, as long as it is still your own evidence and truthful. There is nothing to prevent you discussing what you will say (so long as no one coaches you).

Can I refuse to answer questions?

No, unless the answer would incriminate you—ie leave you personally vulnerable to criminal charges. Since the Children Act, s. 98, you are unlikely to see a witness being allowed to refuse to answer a question on this ground, for the rule of self-incrimination

The Online Resource Centre which accompanies this book provides extra resources which are free to use and designed to help support your legal learning and development as a social work student and professional.

 www.oxfordtextbooks.co.uk/orc/socialwork13e/

For students:

Guidance on answering exercises in the book

Ideal for checking your knowledge on a particular subject or preparing for exams, this online guidance provides the extra support needed to give you confidence when applying the law to real-life situations.

Court skills and advice

Video footage and checklists from Michael Griffith-Jones, a qualified social worker and trainer, offering practical tips and advice on a range of topics including preparing for court, giving evidence, cross-examination, and what to do after the hearing. Ideal for use in practice placements and throughout your career, this advice will be invaluable in calming last-minute nerves and ensuring you are well prepared for court.

Human rights video discussion

Social worker Leon Taylor offers advice on the Human Rights Act and its impact on the work of social workers, taking you through the key articles and how they may relate to service users. Great for revision and as a recap on this wide-ranging area of legislation.

Further reading

Suggested sources for more information on the topics covered in each chapter help you to prepare for assessments and continue your studies once qualified.

Glossary

An online glossary allows you to check your understanding of key terms and provides clear explanations of the legal jargon you may encounter as a social work student or professional.

Updates

Regular updates on new cases, legislation, and proposals affecting social workers allow you to keep up to date with developments in this fast-moving area.

For lecturers:

Password protected to ensure only those involved in teaching social work can access these resources; each registration is personally checked to ensure the security of the site. Registering is easy: click on 'Lecturer Resources' on the Online Resource Centre, complete a simple registration form and access will be granted within 72 hours (subject to verification).

Test bank of multiple-choice questions

A fully customizable resource containing 200 interactive multiple-choice questions accompanied by answers and feedback with which to test your students. Offers versatile testing tailored to the contents of the book.

Lecture outlines

PowerPoint slides for each chapter of the book are provided, which can be downloaded and adapted for your own use in class notes and lecture materials.

Lecture notes

Each set of slides is accompanied by a short discussion on issues which you might like to consider when teaching this area of law.

- Children and Families Act 2014
- Public Law Outline 2014
- Updated *Working Together to Safeguard Children*, 2013 guidance
- *Re B* [2013] UKSC 33
- *Re B-S* [2013] EWCA Civ 1146
- Care Act 2014
- New decisions on the Deprivation of Liberty Safeguards
- *McDonald v UK* (4241/12) (2014) European Court of Human Rights

CONTENTS

DETAILED CONTENTS

ADSS	Association of Directors of Adult Social Services
AMHP	Approved Mental Health Practitioner
ASBO	Anti-social behaviour order
BASW	British Association of Social Workers
Cafcass	Children and Family Court Advisory and Support Service
CC(DD)A 2003	Community Care (Delayed Discharges) Act 2003
CC(DP)A 1996	Community Care (Direct Payments) Act 1996
CCG	clinical commissioning group
CCTV	closed circuit television
CDA	Crime and Disorder Act 1998
CDCA	Carers and Disabled Children Act 2000
C(EO)A	Carers (Equal Opportunities) Act 2004
CJA	Criminal Justice Act 2003
CP plan	child protection plan
CPS	Crown Prosecution Service
CQC	Care Quality Commission
C(RS)A	Carers (Recognition and Services) Act 1995
CSA 2000	Care Standards Act 2000
CSDPA 1970	Chronically Sick and Disabled Persons Act 1970
CTO	Community Treatment Order
CYPA	Children and Young Persons Act
CYPP	Children and Young People's Plans
DoH	Department of Health
DoLS	Deprivation of Liberty Safeguards
DP(SCR)A 1986	Disabled Persons (Services, Consultation and Representation) Act 1986
DWP	Department for Work and Pensions
ECHR	European Convention on Human Rights
ECM	Every Child Matters
ECtHR	European Court of Human Rights
EHRC	Equality and Human Rights Commission
EIA	Equality Impact Assessment
EINA	Equality Impact Needs Assessment
EPA	Enduring Power of Attorney
ERRA	Enterprise and Regulatory Reform Act 2013
EU	European Union
FACS	*Fair Access to Care Services*
FCWO	Family Court Welfare Service

FTT	First Tier Tribunal
HASSASSA	Health and Social Services and Social Security Adjudications Act 1983
HCPC	Health and Care Professions Council
HRA	Human Rights Act
HSCA	Health and Social Care Act
HSPHA 1968	Health Services and Public Health Act 1968
IB	individual budget
ILF	Independent Living Fund
IMHA	independent mental health advocates
IRO	independent reviewing officer
ISA	Independent Safeguarding Authority
ISS	intensive supervision and surveillance
LA	local authority
LADO	Local Authority Designated Officer
LASPO	Legal Aid, Sentencing and Punishment of Offenders Act 2012
LASSA	Local Authority Social Services Act 1970
LAC	Local Authority Circular
LPA	Lasting Power of Attorney
LSCB	Local Safeguarding Children Board
MAPPA	Multi-Agency Public Protection Arrangements
MCA	Mental Capacity Act 2005
MHA	Mental Health Act 1983
MHRT	Mental Health Review Tribunal
MIAM	family mediation, information and assessment meeting
MP	Member of Parliament
NAA 1948	National Assistance Act 1948
NACRO	National Association for the Care and Resettlement of Offenders
NAM	New Asylum Model
NASS	National Asylum Support Service
NCB	National Children's Bureau
NCSWD	National Council for the Single Woman and her Dependants
NHS	National Health Service
NHSCCA 1990	National Health Service and Community Care Act 1990
NIAA 2002	Nationality, Immigration and Asylum Act 2002
NSPCC	National Society for the Prevention of Cruelty to Children
Ofsted	Office for Standards in Education, Children's Services and Skills
ONS	Office for National Statistics
PACE	Police and Criminal Evidence Act 1984
PCA	Protection of Children Act 1999
PCCSA	Powers of Criminal Courts (Sentencing) Act 2000

PCT	primary care trust
PEP	personal education plan
PIDA	Public Interest Disclosure Act 1998
PSED	public sector equality duty
RAS	research allocation system
RC	responsible clinician
SAB	safeguarding adults board
SAQ	self-assessment questionnaire
SCIE	Social Care Institute for Excellence
STC	secure training centre
SVGA	Safeguarding Vulnerable Groups Act 2006
UBC	Upper Banding Calculator
UNCRC	United Nations Convention on the Rights of the Child
VCS	Voluntary and community sector
YJB	Youth Justice Board
YOT	Youth Offending Teams
YRO	Youth Rehabilitation Order

Part 1

The legal context of social work

Part 1 The legal context of social work

You have chosen a career assisting vulnerable or socially excluded members of society. Your motivation probably includes both altruism and idealism. Social workers want to do their best for the people who use their services.

For a person wanting to make a difference, it can be tempting to see law, with its complexity, its language, its procedures, its institutions, as bit of an irrelevance, or worse, an obstacle to achieving these ideals. But you must not underestimate its importance. It is integral to your chosen career.

Law is the product of Parliament, judges, international agreements, and ancient legal tradition. In the area of social services it defines what services should be provided and the rights and responsibilities of providers and users of those services. Legislation establishes what agencies (eg social work departments of local authorities) will provide the services, which services will be obligatory and which discretionary (a matter of whether a local authority wishes to or can afford to provide them), and sets out procedures for delivering those services. If you are a social worker, the law establishes rules for when it is appropriate or when it is necessary for action to be taken. The law sets out your obligations—requiring you to act—but also sets out the restraints on your actions when you try to fulfil those obligations. Laws provide a framework for holding you, the social worker, to account.

This book aims to be about law rather than about social work. The context you work in is the English/Welsh legal system.

Chapter 1 describes where law comes from and examines the institutions you will encounter or which make and apply the law you will use. **Chapter 2** describes the regulation of social work and the relationship between the law and different roles of the social worker. It also looks at important issues such as consent and capacity. **Chapter 3**, human rights, looks at the European Convention on Human Rights and the Human Rights Act 1998, as well as considering anti-discrimination law. **Chapter 4**, information sharing, focuses on the legal framework which governs when you can and when you cannot share confidential information about service users.

The legal system in England and Wales

1

OVERVIEW AND OBJECTIVES

Lawyers talk of the Rule of Law. This is the principle that we are all equal before the law; none of us above it, particularly not the government or those who work for the government, whether police, civil servants, Inland Revenue staff, or social workers. So even when these people are doing the work required of them by law or under the orders of government, they must do that work within the law.

Courts are required to administer the law without bias towards the government, the powerful, or anyone else. In our democracy, law-makers in Parliament are expected to make laws balancing the wishes of the electorate, the good of the country, and the need to protect the vulnerable. These are then interpreted by judges on the basis of the real-world cases that come before them. Neither Parliaments nor the courts and tribunals always get things right, but you are required to follow the law even if you think they have got it wrong.

The state in many cases establishes public institutions or makes use of private bodies to act on its policies, delivering services that the law says must or may be made available to people. They include the police, education authorities, health authorities under the National Health Service (NHS), and, of course, social services departments within local authorities.

Parliament has also passed laws to establish what powers and obligations social workers have and what limitations are placed on their work. It is important to note that social workers are also governed by the general law of the land. They cannot break the law by restraining people or breaching their privacy, for example, even if it is to achieve the duties placed on them by Parliament, unless Parliament has given them specific powers to do so. Social workers are not above the law any more than police officers or government ministers.

This book is designed to make the law familiar to you. We therefore use extracts from statutes and case studies to illustrate our points. No one can possibly know or describe all the laws, but each professional person needs to know the core elements of the law that dictate how they carry out their profession, and then, through their own research or knowing whom to ask, to know how to find out more when the need arises. As a social worker you need to know enough about the law to ensure that your decisions are lawful. When decisions are particularly complex you need to know that you should consult lawyers to help you to make those decisions.

In order to practise successfully you must go beyond what we provide in this book, which is based on what we think you must understand. We provide some further reading suggestions at the end of each chapter. We try to remind you at all stages that the principles we are dealing with derive, above all, from statute and from court and tribunal cases, so we quote directly from the important statutory materials and we mention important or illustrative cases throughout. We refer to other materials, such as the findings of inquiries, where useful.

We also, after this chapter, give you a case study as your route into each topic at the beginning of the chapter. If you have to think about a real-life issue, and how the law dealt with it, you then have a context for the issues you will be looking at yourself. We hope to expose you to the full range of materials that are relevant to law for social workers, so even if you do not always agree with our interpretation, you will know where we got our information.

Our own thinking on how to approach the law can be summarized as follows:

- law must be obeyed, by individuals and professionals, including law you may consider to be wrong;
- law indicates what social workers *must* do and what they *may* do (areas of work that are discretionary and may depend on the policies of your local authority);
- law tells social workers how they should go about their work, including what powers they have. You should *know* this part of the law, not just be able to look it up;
- other laws affect the lives of service users including their rights in relation to social workers. It is essential at least to know the broad principles of these laws;
- lawyers, particularly those employed by the authority for which you work, are paid to know the rest (or to find it), so know your limits and use the lawyers when you reach that limit.

Sources of law in England and Wales

Common law

Common law is most simply explained as the law that has been established by the law courts over centuries to solve the problems brought before them. Principles are developed by looking at previous decisions by judges, known as precedents, and trying to arrive at new decisions that are consistent with the precedents, or at least with the principles that appear to underpin them. Fairness and pragmatism dictate that principles used to decide cases in the past should apply in the present in similar cases. Common law has evolved (and continues to evolve) slowly, sometimes too slowly to deal with new problems and certainly in a way that cannot create entirely new rights and obligations.

Common law is still very relevant in England and Wales. Much criminal law, such as the law against murder, is derived from the common law. Common law is also the foundation of civil law, in which monetary claims are made against individuals, companies, or state agencies. Social workers could face negligence cases, for example where a person or organization is sued for compensation because they failed to act with sufficient care.

Equity

This developed centuries ago as a branch of law in which judges could use discretion, within certain limits and according to certain long-standing rules, to remedy unfairness in the rigidity of the common law, particularly in financial disputes. Equity is still important in family law work. It is principles derived from equity, for instance, that decide how the family home of an unmarried couple is divided when the house is in the man's name, but both partners have contributed to it. The principles of equity are used in certain legal remedies, such as injunctions—a temporary ban at the judge's discretion on one person acting to the detriment of another prior to a court hearing on the issue—thus freezing the status quo until one side or the other wins a subsequent court case. For example, if a tenant alleges harassment against a landlord, a judge might, at his or her discretion, grant an injunction to prevent further acts of harassment. That would be temporary pending a full court case at which the claims against the landlord are heard and dealt with. Equitable principles also underlie domestic violence injunctions (non-molestation orders), though judges have statutory powers to issue these under the Family Law Act 1996 and Domestic Violence, Crime and Victims Act 2004. If an allegation of assault or some form of harassment is made, an order might be issued against, say, the accused husband (or cohabiting partner—the law calls spouses of cohabitees in this context 'associated persons'). But it is at the discretion of the judge and temporary (though renewable).

Statute law

This is law that has been passed by Parliament. Almost every aspect of child protection, assisting children in need, and community care is based on detailed statutory provisions. According to legal theory, statute law is supreme. Parliament is able to create any new laws or amend or repeal previous statutes—however modern or ancient they may be. It can also enshrine in statute legal principles established by judges under the common law system—and also change, redefine, or abolish those principles. It does so by passing statutes, or Acts of Parliament. These set out mandatory legal provisions, which must be followed by everyone, including the judges. The judges' role is to work out what the words in a statute actually mean (or what the intention of Parliament was) and how the statutes apply in particular cases. Often judges disagree. Lawyers may appeal against a judgment to a higher court such as the Court of Appeal or the Supreme Court. It is the judgment of the higher courts that trump the lower courts and is taken as the correct interpretation of the statute or any legal principle involved.

It is therefore often necessary to look at court case decisions to establish the meaning of a law. If Parliament does not like the way judges are interpreting the law or Members of Parliament (MPs) decide the law is wrong after all, they can change it through new statutes. We discuss how you locate, read, and understand statutes in the next chapter.

International law

Rulers have always made agreements with other rulers. This system of agreement, or treaties, between different states has evolved into what is known as international law. The UK has agreed to be bound by many international treaties agreed with other states. These are agreements between governments and so require governments to enforce them. The pressure is moral, political, or economic—and sometimes military.

Parliament can, however, pass legislation saying that an international treaty is law and must be applied directly in the UK courts. Most significantly for social workers, Parliament decided that the European Convention on Human Rights would have legal force in the UK. It gives people in the many nations signing up to it (all of the European Union (EU) but other European and non-European nations as well) rights against their governments. The Convention was established in 1952. It starts by asserting that 'everyone's right to life shall be protected by law' then lists many rights—against torture and slavery, in favour of liberty, privacy, and a right to a family life, for example. Although the intention was to try to avoid a renewed rise in totalitarian states after the Second World War, many of these rights have a day-to-day application in quite ordinary circumstances. Social workers, for example, since they are 'agents' of the state (set up by the state and given powers and direction by the state) have to abide by the Convention. One can imagine cases in which social workers or those setting policy in a social work department might restrict people's liberty or intervene in family life or put someone's privacy at risk.

Convention court cases are heard by judges in Strasbourg who are drawn from all the signatory nations. For years it was a complex and costly process to pursue rights in Strasbourg. The Human Rights Act 1998 embeds all Convention rights in UK law and allows people to use UK courts to pursue those rights. The law also required all parliamentary legislation to be 'Convention-compliant'—always adhering to the Convention's principles. In this way, European human rights law has become part of the UK law with the Strasbourg court becoming a final court of appeal.

(Note that the European Convention on Human Rights and the Strasbourg court are not European Union entities; the EU has its own Court of Justice in Luxembourg regulating legal relations between the EU nations.)

Procedural rules

These are rules that cover court and tribunal processes—how cases are dealt with, the documentation required, and what must happen at each stage before, during, and after the hearing. For example, if a local authority intends to take a child into care, this requires a court order which must be applied for. Certain requirements will have to be met before the court will issue the order. Procedural rules are derived from the principles underpinning natural justice and due process.

Is 'good practice' a form of law?

Good practice describes the ideal way that social work principles should be put into day-to-day practice. It is not law, and much of what amounts to good practice is not issued in the form of either regulations ('secondary' legislation issued by ministers usually setting out practical details of the statute) or statutory guidance (which expands on the legalistic words of statutes, explaining how, for example, particular powers or responsibilities given to social workers should be acted on in practice). Therefore, good practice must always give way to the requirements of statute, regulations, guidance, and case law on the rare occasions when the requirements conflict.

We have now completed our overview of the sources of law. See **Box 1.1** for a summary, and some additional terms you may come across.

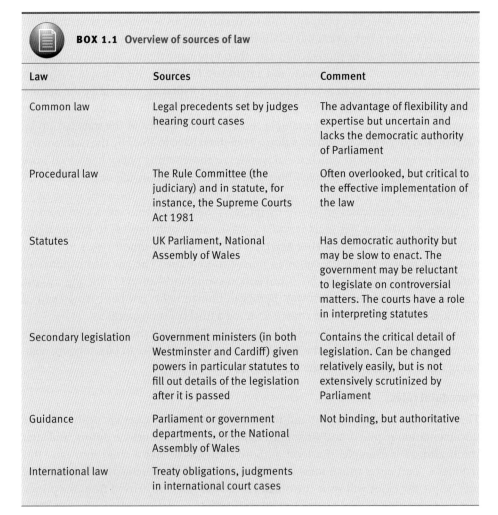

BOX 1.1 Overview of sources of law

Law	Sources	Comment
Common law	Legal precedents set by judges hearing court cases	The advantage of flexibility and expertise but uncertain and lacks the democratic authority of Parliament
Procedural law	The Rule Committee (the judiciary) and in statute, for instance, the Supreme Courts Act 1981	Often overlooked, but critical to the effective implementation of the law
Statutes	UK Parliament, National Assembly of Wales	Has democratic authority but may be slow to enact. The government may be reluctant to legislate on controversial matters. The courts have a role in interpreting statutes
Secondary legislation	Government ministers (in both Westminster and Cardiff) given powers in particular statutes to fill out details of the legislation after it is passed	Contains the critical detail of legislation. Can be changed relatively easily, but is not extensively scrutinized by Parliament
Guidance	Parliament or government departments, or the National Assembly of Wales	Not binding, but authoritative
International law	Treaty obligations, judgments in international court cases	

Some conceptual issues relevant to law for social workers

All law, to be valid in England and Wales, will derive from one of the sources listed in **Box 1.1**. Now we need to explore some legal concepts that do not depend on where the law comes from. The exploration will provide a framework for understanding the areas of law relevant to social workers.

The distinction between private and public law

We have already highlighted the distinction between courts and Parliament, between common law and statute, and between common law and equity. There is another distinction which is important for your work, the distinction between public law and private law. Private law cases involve private disputes between private individuals or between organizations or between individuals and organizations. Private law, perhaps through a civil case in the County Court, might assist in a dispute between a car owner and a garage over the quality of a repair.

Public law regulates the actions of bodies exercising public functions—government, government agencies, local authorities, but also many private organizations tasked with duties by the government such as privately run prisons or care homes.

Because public authorities or their private agents (organizations, sometimes private companies, which the authorities use to do their work) often intervene in people's lives, they are required to conform to certain standards. Care proceedings, for example, are an area of public law. The state must ensure that it has powers to remove children from their parents; establish the circumstances in which it can remove those children; ensure that its agents (those working for the state) follow proper procedures in doing so; and that when it interferes in liberty and family life in this way, it can offer legal justification for doing so if challenged on human rights grounds.

Individuals with a grievance against such bodies may bring a civil law case perhaps through a specialist tribunal or the High Court.

The particular area of the law which performs this function of ensuring that public bodies act according to those standards is administrative law. Sometimes both public law and private law proceedings will arise from a particular situation that has reached the courts. For example, divorce proceedings are private law. However, under the provisions of the Children Act 1989 there are powers during divorce proceedings to require the local authority to carry out an investigation if the court is concerned about the welfare of the children. One outcome of this investigation can be the local authority commencing care proceedings, which as we have stated, are public law.

Administrative law

The state is very powerful and well resourced in comparison with any individual. Administrative law, in principle, attempts to ensure that justice is done between the state and the individual. It seeks to apply principles that operate to restrain arbitrary or wrong or corrupt decision making by the state. It can also be seen as restraining well-meaning state agents (eg social workers) with power over individuals' lives who might overstep the limits of their lawful powers or threaten an individual's rights or liberties. Administrative law can also be seen as enabling beneficial intervention by the state. For example, if there had been no legislation about rights and protections for children then there would have been no role for social workers in child protection. Thus the Children Act 1948 identified the duties of local authorities over children and in providing for orphans. The Local Authority Social Services Act 1970 makes provision for 'the organisation, management and administration of local authority social services'.

The principles underlying administrative law have developed in common law cases. They are:

- openness (often described as transparency);
- fairness;
- rationality (including giving reasons for decisions);
- lawfulness (meaning the state and its agents are not above the law);
- impartiality (which means that decision-makers should be independent);
- accountability;
- the control of discretion;
- consistency;
- participation;
- efficiency;
- equity;
- equal treatment.

These principles can be collectively described as the requirements necessary for fairness, and are often referred to as the requirements of 'natural justice'. Sometimes they conflict with one another, and then the decision-maker must weigh up the various principles and make the best decision he or she can in the circumstances. Your understanding of professional ethics may help you at this point. We shall explore some of the guiding principles that exist when decisions under administrative law have to be made.

Natural justice

Natural justice embodies a set of principles that courts will apply. It is law because courts have consistently described it as governing their decisions, and therefore it forms part of the common law. It means that whatever the law is, citizens are entitled to have the law applied fairly, in accordance with law, and that the courts will uphold that right. These principles informed the work of the British lawyers who did most of the work drafting the European Convention on Human Rights after the Second World War. Many actions of the state have clearly defined avenues for challenging that action in a court: to contest care proceedings, for example.

The mechanism available for people who believe that they have not been treated fairly by the state and who have no right of appeal is to apply for judicial review. Judicial review is the process by which the courts oversee decisions made by public officials to ensure that they have been made fairly and lawfully. You will come across several cases of judicial review in the case studies we use at the beginning of each chapter and elsewhere in the book.

In general, judges will not substitute their decision for the public officials' decisions. The judges' task, as they see it, is not to make fair decisions, but to ensure that the state agents applied the principles of natural justice when making the decisions. What they will scrutinize, therefore, is the process of decision making. For example, a social worker may fail properly to assess whether someone is potentially eligible for community care services, perhaps because of personal antagonism. The person could seek a judicial review of the decision by stating that natural justice had been infringed since the law was not fairly applied. Facts which were relevant to the decision had not been considered. Facts which were not relevant were considered. The court could make such a ruling and overturn the decision of the local authority, or tell it to make a fresh decision, this time properly. The doctrine of natural justice means that the decision must be arrived at through the correct procedures and be reasonable in the light of facts that the decision-maker has.

The 'Wednesbury principles'

In establishing what is reasonable, judges will use what are often described by lawyers as 'principles', which were articulated by the judges sitting in a case called *Associated Provincial Picture Houses v Wednesbury Corporation* [1948] 1 KB 223. The corporation (local council) had the power to permit Sunday cinema opening and impose conditions. In this case it banned the cinema from allowing in children under 15. The cinema challenged the ban as unreasonable but lost. The judge, Lord Greene MR (Master of the Rolls, head of the Court of Appeal), set out the principle that a judge should only find unreasonableness if an administrative decision 'was so unreasonable that no reasonable authority could ever have come to it'. So, as long as the council was not acting 'ultra vires'—beyond its powers (which it was not)—what those conditions should be was a matter of its own judgement as long as they were not wholly unreasonable. The fact that you or I or even the judge might think letting children in to see the Sunday pictures would be perfectly reasonable or even *more* reasonable is irrelevant. This is the 'test of reasonableness'.

This test protects local authorities more on issues of policy than day-to-day decisions about individual social work cases—as the next section will show.

Proportionality

Decisions made by public authorities are constrained by the Human Rights Act 1998. One particular requirement is the need for decisions to be proportionate to the outcome which is sought. So, for instance, in *Re C and B (Children) (Care Order: Future Harm)* [2000] 2 FCR 614, the Court of Appeal allowed a mother's appeal against the making of a care order in respect of two of her children with a view to placement for adoption. Two older children had been taken into care on the basis of actual harm. The court accepted that there were reasons for concern about the younger children, one ten months and the other newborn, and that there was evidence to suggest there was a real possibility of future harm. However, there were no long-standing problems preventing the mother caring for her children. Intervention, which inevitably impacts on the European Convention right to respect for family life, had to be proportionate to the degree of risk, and a care order was not justified. Other options should have been looked at to help the mother, and the court decided a supervision order would be the proportionate response.

What do administrative law principles mean for a social worker making a decision?

These principles are not remote from you, the social worker. When you make a decision about a family or a vulnerable person, if your decision is to be lawful then it must follow these principles. You will ensure that you have followed the requirements of natural justice, you will have found out all the information that is relevant, you will have considered the relevant information carefully, and excluded from your considerations irrelevant matters. You will ensure that evidence which goes against the interests of, for example, the parents of the child about whom you are making a decision, has been put to the parents, and they have had an opportunity to consider it and respond. You will carefully document your decision-making process, so that if there is a dispute in the future you can demonstrate that your decision making was within the bounds of the law.

Law and devolution

In the introduction we talked about English law and the English legal system. Traditionally, the legal system for England and Wales has been described in this way. The National Assembly for Wales was set up in May 1999 with powers and functions determined by the Government of Wales Act 1998. The Government of Wales Act 2006 subsequently empowered the National Assembly for Wales to make its own legislation on devolved matters such as health, education, social services, and local government. Following a 'yes' vote in a referendum in 2011 there is no need for the National Assembly to get permission from Westminster before passing legislation known as Assembly Acts.

Further details of the powers given to the Assembly by various Acts of Parliament can be found on the Assembly website www.assemblywales.org. Inevitably, the National Assembly for Wales will have different priorities from the UK Parliament and be interested in different solutions to problems. There will be interesting opportunities to see how different projects proceed and develop best practice. The most up-to-date information on legislation relating to children in Wales can be found on www.childreninwales.org.uk. We will not describe provisions separately for England and Wales unless the laws do actually differ.

Our book does not cover Scotland, which has always had a separate legal system and separate law (despite sharing much law and legislative institutions).

Sources of law

Statute law

Social workers have 'statutory powers'. This means that their powers and their authority derive from statute—laws made in Parliament. This is not to say that the courts do not have a role. They interpret the meaning of statutes in particular factual situations and their decisions provide authoritative guidance for future decision-makers and courts. As time passes, the role of common law diminishes; more and more statutes are passed dealing with more and more areas of behaviour within society.

Primary legislation

Statutes—Acts of Parliament—start life as bills. These may be bills sponsored by government ministers, or private members' bills sponsored by backbench MPs. Most bills are government bills, but within the field of social care there have been some significant Acts that started life as private members' bills, for instance the Homeless Persons Act 1977 and the Disabled Persons (Services, Consultation and Representation) Act 1986.

Often the subject matter of a bill is discussed and consulted upon extensively before it gets to Parliament. The government may publish a Green Paper (originally with green covers) which will set out a number of proposals to change the law and ask for comments. Following this consultation, the government may set out its revised policy objectives in a White Paper. A relatively recent innovation is the draft bill procedure whereby the government publishes a bill in draft form, before it is introduced in Parliament as a formal bill. This enables consultation and pre-legislative scrutiny before it is issued formally. This procedure was used during the reforms to the law on adult social care. A draft bill, the Care and Support Bill, was published in July 2012, at the same time as the government's White Paper *Caring for our Future: Reforming Care and Support*. The government held a public consultation from July to October 2012. It attracted around 1,000 written responses through a variety of channels, including an online comments platform created for clause-by-clause comments. The government also held a number of engagement events with stakeholders, those who use social care services, and their carers. A summary of the responses was published in December 2012. Following consultation, a Joint Committee of Parliament was established to conduct pre-legislative scrutiny. Over three months, the Joint Committee received further written evidence and held ten oral sessions with a range of stakeholders. The Joint Committee's work concluded on 7 March 2013, and their final report was published on 19 March 2013. When the Care Bill was presented to Parliament on 19 May 2013, it reflected the government's responses to the consultation and the pre-legislative scrutiny. The presentation of a bill, generally by the minister responsible for it, marks the beginning of the normal parliamentary process. A bill may commence in either the House of Commons, or the House of Lords. The Care Bill started in the Lords and was presented by Lord Howe, the Parliamentary Under-Secretary of State for Health. There are a series of 'readings' when the bill is first presented in the Commons and the Lords and later debated, with time in between for scrutiny of the bill in committee. Eventually the bill reaches its final form when it is presented to the monarch for signature. Once it receives Royal Assent it becomes an Act of Parliament. Acts of Parliament are also described as primary legislation.

Even when the Act receives the Royal Assent there is often a long delay before particular sections are brought into effect, either on a date stated in the statute or by a Commencement Order issued by a minister under delegated powers (ie Parliament gives the minister the power to bring the Act into effect). If you would like to learn more about the legislative process, the Parliament website on www.parliament.uk contains user-friendly guidance. The various stages of the Care Bill are available on the Parliament website at http://services.parliament.uk/bills/2013-14/care.

Delegated legislation

Most Acts of Parliament contain only the essential principles of the new law. The details may be brought in later, usually by a minister or another body authorized by the Act to do so. This is delegated legislation or secondary legislation. It is generally done by issuing statutory instruments in the form of Regulations or Orders. It is not important to distinguish between these. For the delegated legislation to come into force, normally it must be 'laid before Parliament'. This requires a copy of the proposed delegated legislation to be placed (or laid) in the House of Commons and the House of Lords for a specified number of days. After that, the legislation comes into force. It may require a vote without a debate or, alternatively, it may come into effect by 'negative resolution'. This means that it will come into force unless sufficient MPs demand a vote be taken.

A good deal of the law that concerns social workers will be found in statutory instruments which can contain more of the practical details of how the law should be followed than is possible in primary legislation. Such statutory instruments can be updated more quickly than a new statute.

Guidance, directions, and intervention issued under statutory powers

We include this source of law (or authority, since we shall see that guidance is not law) under the section dealing with statutes, because in social work law the power of government to issue guidance or directions is created by statute.

Local authority social services functions are defined by the Local Authority Social Services Act 1970 (LASSA). We cover this in more detail in **chapter 2**. Under s. 7 these functions must be exercised under the general guidance of the Secretary of State. Where guidance is issued to local authorities under s. 7, it is not, in law, mandatory. Such guidance, nevertheless, must be followed unless there are justifiable reasons for not doing so. An explanation of the role of such guidance is to be found in the following quotation where Sedley J (the 'J' means a High Court judge: in this case Mr Justice Sedley) stated that local authorities have:

> to follow the path charted by the Secretary of State's guidance, with liberty to deviate from it where the local authority judges on admissible grounds that there is good reason to do so, but without freedom to take a substantially different course.
>
> (*R v Islington LBC, ex p Rixon* (1997))

It is also worth noting that although local authorities have to follow guidance, it cannot be guaranteed that by doing so they will be acting within the law. It remains the function of the court actually to decide what the legislation means. As the foreword to *An Introduction to the Children Act 1989* (Department of Health, 1989) says: 'The Government is not entitled to give an authoritative interpretation of the law and ultimately any interpretation is a matter for the courts.'

Examples of guidance issued under statutory powers

Although guidance can be linked to a particular Act (eg the Children Act 1989), some-times it can stand alone. One example is the *IRO Handbook: Statutory guidance for independent reviewing officers and local authorities on their functions in relation to case management and review for looked-after children 2010* which seeks to improve outcomes for looked-after children by providing guidance to independent reviewing officers about how they should discharge their distinct responsibilities to looked-after children. It can be found at www.education.gov.uk/publications/eOrderingDownload/DCSF-00184-2010.pdf.

Directions may be published in the form of circulars and other documents issued under s. 7B of LASSA. If a local authority does not follow a non-statutory direction, it is in breach of the law because s. 7B says it must be followed. The social worker should always check whether the document they are using is issued under s. 7B of LASSA. If it is, this is indicated clearly in the preface to the document.

In extreme circumstances, a Secretary of State (the chief minister of the main government departments) has powers to intervene to direct a local authority to take a particular course of action. This form of direction is what happened when the Secretary of State for Children, Schools and Families, Ed Balls, intervened to have Sharon Shoesmith, director of education and social services at Haringey Council, London, sacked following the high-profile death of 'Baby Peter' in 2007. In the event, Balls was later found by a judge to have overstepped the mark. Ms Shoesmith took the government to court alleging proper procedures were not followed in her sacking. The judicial review in 2011 found in her favour.

The Children Act 1989—an example of statute law and law derived from it

Later in the book we consider the effect of the Children Act 1989. The Act sets out in detail how the courts, local authorities, and others are to deal with the care and welfare of children. There are 108 sections in this particular Act and 15 schedules (additional material appended to the Act), and the bill which became the Act spent almost a year being debated in the House of Lords and the House of Commons. Despite all this, the Act could not come into force as soon as it was passed, and it has had to be amended many times since it was first enacted. Moreover, about 30 sets of regulations have been issued under the Act. Together with these go ten books of guidance. Merely looking at the Act will not give the full picture of what it is about. So detailed are the regulations and guidance that there is even a separate index published. We refer to these books of regulations and guidance throughout the relevant chapters. To help you to understand these books, the government has issued a book of guidance on *The Care of Children: Principles and Practice in Regulations and Guidance*. What the Act means in practice is also the subject of numerous reported court decisions (meaning reported in professional law reports), which will crop up throughout the first three parts of the book.

Finding statutes

You may need to read appropriate statutory provisions. Statutes are available in law libraries and on the internet, and are summarized and commented on in secondary sources (such as this book). It is important that you read the up-to-date version of any statute. This is not easy without the resources of a full law library or access to a commercial database. Our best advice is for you to talk to your legal department to find out what resources it has available for you to use. In a law library, a good source of up-to-date statute law can be the loose-leaf encyclopaedia. There is usually one for practitioners in major areas of law, and social workers should look out in particular for the online legal databases including up-to-date versions of statutes together with indicators of proposed changes—very useful in this fast-moving area of law.

Reading statutes

We think it is important that you feel confident enough to read some statutory materials for yourself and not rely solely on lawyers to do that for you. This book aims to provide you with a great deal of support in doing just that. If you find a particular word or phrase difficult, then ask your lawyer what he or she thinks it means. The chances are that it is genuinely a difficult word which could be interpreted in several different ways. Your opinion may be correct, or the lawyer's opinion may be better. Often we do not know what a word means in law until it has been interpreted by the courts. Once a court of record (one of the more important courts such as the Court of Appeal or Supreme Court) declares what a word or phrase means in a statute, that is in law what it means, unless and until a higher court explains why that was the wrong approach—either by considering the same case appealed from the lower court or a later case that involved similar facts and the same principles. In exceptional circumstances, a court of the same level considering a later similar case may also retrospectively declare a previous interpretation of the statutory phrase incorrect—in effect the court overrules itself. Normally, though, the earlier case remains the precedent that is followed. The courts use a variety of techniques to enable them to interpret statutes in a manner that is intended to be rational, objective, and consistent. These are the rules of statutory interpretation. Before we go on to discuss these, we provide some general guidance on reading a statute.

The Adoption and Children Act 2002 as an example

The date 2002 is the year that the Act received Royal Assent. It is not necessarily the year when the statute comes into force. Many statutes contain complex provisions which need to be prepared for. The delegated legislation is published after the Act.

In the case of a complex piece of legislation such as the Adoption and Children Act different parts of the Act will have different commencement dates.

The front cover of the statute has the Royal Coat of Arms, the name of the statute, and the words 'Chapter 38'—it is the 38th statute of this parliamentary session. You can ignore the chapter number. There is also a note to say that explanatory notes have been produced to assist in the understanding of this Act and are available separately. This is a relatively recent innovation. If an Act is one which you frequently use, the explanatory notes provide a really useful source of information about its provisions.

The contents of the statute

Turning the page you will see the contents of the statute. This particular Act is divided into three Parts and then each Part has a number of chapters. Part 1, adoption, is the largest part. It has seven chapters. Each chapter is subdivided. Chapter 2 is subdivided into sections on the adoption service, regulations, and supplemental provisions. In each of the subdivisions there are numbers. These relate to the section numbers of the Act. The contents page therefore provides you with a very useful navigation tool for the whole of the statute. If you are looking to find out how adoption orders are made under the legislation you can very quickly find out which are the relevant sections. A subdivision of Chapter 3 of Part 1 is headed 'The making of adoption orders', and we can see that the relevant section numbers are ss. 46–51.

Sections and subsections

If we look at one of those sections, say s. 47, we can see the typical layout for a section of an Act. The section has a heading, in this case 'Conditions for making adoption orders'. It is then divided into subsections which are numbered in brackets. If you want to refer to a particular subsection then you would say 'section forty-seven, subsection one'. In writing you would refer to s. 47(1). There may be further subdivisions indicated by letters and Roman numerals as here: s. 47(4)(a)(i). There is generally no need to refer to Parts or to Chapters when directing someone to a section of an Act.

Schedules

Not everything is contained in the body of the statute. Most Acts have schedules attached which contain further material, usually of a more detailed kind. The Adoption and Children Act 2002 has six schedules. They are listed after the contents of the Act. Schedules are set out slightly differently from the main body of the Act. If you turn to Schedule 1 you will see its title, 'Registration of Adoptions'. In small script to the right of the title there is a section number, s. 77(6). This is the section in the Act which gives legal effect to the schedule. The schedule is then set out in paragraphs and subparagraphs (rather than sections and subsections). If you wish to refer to a paragraph within a schedule then you refer to it as paragraph 1(2) of Schedule 1 to the Act. We say 'to' the Act rather than 'of' the Act because the schedule is attached to the Act.

Amendments

Frequently statutes contain provisions which amend the provisions of earlier statutes. The Adoption and Children Act 2002 is no exception. So, for instance, s. 113 of the Act provides:

> In section 9 of the 1989 Act (restrictions on making section 8 orders)—
> (a) in subsection (3)(c), for 'three years' there is substituted 'one year', and
> (b) subsection (4) is omitted.

What this means is that from the commencement date of this provision of the 2002 Act, that particular section of the Children Act 1989 has to be read in the new way. The earlier Act is nowadays reissued online in its amended, up-to-date, form but the printed version is not.

Acts can do more than amend particular sections. They can introduce whole new sections into other Acts. In the Adoption and Children Act 2002 new provisions are introduced to the Children Act 1989 to provide for special guardianship. The new sections are introduced by s. 115 of the Adoption and Children Act but they have become ss. 14A–14G of the Children Act 1989. You will always recognize sections of legislation which have been introduced by subsequent legislation because of the use of the capital letter.

Acts are also amended by subsequent legislation. You will not find these amendments in a hard copy of the Act, but they can easily be found on web versions and in loose-leaf encyclopedias. The Adoption and Children Act 2002 has been amended by the Children and Families Act 2014. For instance, that Act has added a new section—s. 3A—to the Adoption and Children Act 2002. The section concerns the recruitment, assessment, and approval of prospective adopters. A reference to another new section, s. 51A headed 'Post-adoption contact'—also inserted by the Children and Families Act 2014—is inserted into s. 1 of the Adoption and Children Act 2002.

Reading statutes—principles of statutory interpretation

Because the words of statutes are not necessarily clear and unambiguous judges have developed a series of so-called 'rules' to guide the courts. Traditionally, there are said to be three main 'rules':

- the 'literal rule', which says that the words in a statute are taken to have their literal meaning;
- the 'golden rule', which says that if the literal meaning produces an absurd result then you look at it in the overall context of the statute;
- the 'mischief rule' is applied when the first two rules do not help. This rule states that you interpret the meaning of the words in the light of what the problem or 'mischief' was that the statute was supposed to deal with.

For centuries no judge would deign to look at what ministers or parliamentarians may have said about the purpose of the Act under consideration. Now they may take such a purposive approach by looking at White Papers, statements to Parliament reported in Hansard, Law Commission reports, and any other documentation giving clues to the intention of the legislators. Individual judges may use any of the 'rules' or all of them, perhaps combining them into what is called a 'unified common approach'. This would say: use the literal meaning of the Act unless the words are unclear or a manifest absurdity would result; in which case look at the purpose of the Act—using official material to do so if necessary.

The Human Rights Act 1998 has an impact on statutory interpretation, in that it requires courts to interpret legislation in a way which is compatible with the European Convention on Human Rights (see **chapter 3**). Where it is not possible to interpret the legislation in this way, the courts may strike down delegated (secondary) legislation. If they find primary legislation to be incompatible they cannot strike it down, but they may make a declaration of incompatibility, which should prompt government action to change the law.

Reading statutes—powers and duties

Something else that you will need to check when you read statutes concerning social services is whether the statute provides you with a duty to act or a power to act. The distinction is relatively straightforward. Where a statute imposes a duty on a person or a body then they have to carry out that duty if the situation described in the statute occurs. There is no choice, however hard the carrying out of the duty may be. Lack of finance, for instance, is not an acceptable reason for not carrying out the duty. Where a statute gives a person or a body a power to do something, the person or the body may exercise that power but they are not obliged to do so.

The distinction is important for a number of reasons. First, it sets your priorities as a social worker. If Parliament has considered that carrying out a particular action is so significant that it should be a duty upon a social services department then it is a course of action which must be given priority. Second, it is significant when a person is unhappy with the behaviour of a statutory person or body. If there is a duty then in general the person will be able to take court action to enforce that duty. If there is only a power, then it is unlikely that there will be any legal redress—though, if the person can show that the way in which the decision to exercise or not exercise the power was made was unreasonable, that could be challenged by a judicial review.

It is important to read the scope of the duty in the statute carefully. The law has distinguished between general or target duties and personal or particular duties. General or target duties are expressed in broad terms, leaving the public authority with a wide measure of discretion over the steps to be taken to perform the duty owed to the relevant section of the public. Personal or particular duties are specific and precise and are owed to each individual member of a relevant section of the public. Target duties must be performed, notwithstanding their general nature, in accordance with the principles of public law and they can be enforced like powers through judicial review. However, the public authority has discretion on how it delivers services under the duty and individuals have no personal right of action. One particular general duty we will discuss in **chapter 6** is s. 17 of the Children Act 1989—the duty to safeguard and promote the welfare of children in need. The local authority must decide what services it thinks are appropriate to meet this duty. Personal duties provide no discretion to the public authority and are actionable (ie court proceedings can be taken) by the individual who can sue for breach of statutory duty.

Whatever you are doing as a social worker, you should be clear in your own mind whether you are acting under a personal duty, a general duty, or a power, and regulate your actions accordingly.

Case law

When we want to know what the law in a statute is, we first read the relevant part of that statute. As we explained earlier (**Reading statutes—powers and duties**, p 18), this is not always the whole solution. Often it is necessary for the courts to interpret what the words of the statute mean. Similarly, judges will interpret common law, where there is no statute, according to the circumstances of each case—and each new case becomes part of the common law. Whether we are concerned with statutory interpretation or the common law, to find out what the courts have declared the law to be we need to look at the law reports.

Reading and finding cases

Cases, like statutes, follow a standard format. They are referred to by their name (usually of the main people or organizations involved on each side) and a reference to a law report. You will notice that when we tell you about a case we provide the name of the case and a date. The full citation to the case is found in the table of cases at the beginning of the book. Take *F v Lambeth LBC, also known as F (Children: Care Planning), Re* as an example. If you want to find that case yourself you will first need to check the full reference. It is [2002] 2 FR 512, Fam Div.

The law reports

These are produced by private firms using specialist legal reporters. They are taken as accurate reflections of what went on in court and are referred to by judges when making their decisions since they contain legal precedents and the reasoning of judges in the earlier cases. They also contain references to previous related cases so the decisions on a particular issue of law can be tracked all the way back. Frequently used series of general law reports are:

> The Law Reports, currently issued in four series:
>> Appeal Cases (AC)
>> Chancery Division (Ch)
>> Queen's Bench (QB)
>> Family Division (Fam)
> The Weekly Law Reports (WLR)
> The All England Law Reports (abbreviated to All ER)
> Family Law Reports (FLR)

Summaries of recent cases can be found in *The Times* and the *Financial Times*, and in professional journals such as the *Solicitors Journal*, the *New Law Journal*, *Family Law*, and the *Law Society Gazette*.

Note that some citations use round brackets instead of square brackets around the date of the report. Round brackets indicate that it is the volume number, and not the date of the report, which is essential if you are to locate it on the shelves. The use of round and square brackets can be summarized as:

> [2010] Date is essential. The volumes are arranged on the shelves by year, and the volume number is used only to distinguish between different volumes published in the same year, for example [1999] 1 FLR 40.

> (1989) Date is not essential, but volume number is essential; that is, the arrangement on the shelves is by volume number, not by date, for example (1980) 70 Cr App R 193.

Most cases are now being published on the internet. A citation system which is more suitable for publication on the web has been introduced for all Supreme Court/House of Lords, Court of Appeal, and High Court (Administrative Division) judgments decided since 11 January 2001 and all High Court decisions since 14 January 2002. The citation should appear in front of the familiar citations set out above. The citation is media neutral, as page numbers are irrelevant on the internet.

The neutral forms of citation are shown in **Table 1.1**.

This system fits in with international practice and makes it easier to find cases electronically. Here is an example: *Re O (Supervision Order)* [2001] 1 FLR 923 is a Court of

TABLE 1.1 Forms of neutral citations

Supreme Court	[2010] UKSC 1, 2, 3 etc
House of Lords (functions taken over in October 2009 by the Supreme Court)	[2008] UKHL 1, 2, 3 etc
Court of Appeal (Civil Division)	[2005] EWCA Civ 1, 2, 3, etc
Court of Appeal (Criminal Division)	[2004] EWCA Crim 1, 2, 3, etc
Administrative Court	[2010] EWHC Admin 1, 2, 3, etc

Appeal decision published in the Family Law Reports. It should be cited as: [2001] EWCA Civ 16; [2001] 1 FLR 923. The '16' means that it was the sixteenth case heard in the Court of Appeal Civil Division in 2001. 'EW' stands for England and Wales. (The House of Lords had UK as a prefix because it was the highest court for the whole UK; it is now replaced by a Supreme Court, which is supreme in the UK apart from criminal matters in Scotland, which cannot be appealed to the UK Supreme Court.)

Note that the internet version of a case may have in apparently random places an asterisk and number that indicates the page of the case in the print version. These page references are used when quoting from the case.

Legal databases and non-subscription web sources

Cases are available from legal electronic databases. Lawyers subscribe to services such as Lexis@library and Westlaw and can search for and find cases and up-to-date versions of statutes relevant to the area of law they are researching extremely quickly. The databases may not offer all the cases you want but official transcripts produced by the courts are often available on the internet and are offered by the legal services too.

The best free website for accessing judgments (including tribunals such as the Asylum and Immigration Tribunal, and including European Court cases) is www.bailii.org. Reports of decisions of the House of Lords are also available on the Parliament website (www.publications.parliament.uk/pa/ld/ldjudgmt.htm); and those of the Supreme Court (which started in October 2009) on www.supremecourt.gov.uk.

Courts and tribunals

We are now moving from the law itself to look at the legal system which administers the law.

When a dispute cannot be resolved by agreement between the people involved, the legal system provides for decisions to be made at a judicial hearing. Sometimes there is a need for a judicial hearing even if there is total agreement between the persons involved; for example, if a couple agree to get divorced, they must get a decree of divorce at a judicial hearing. At some time, every social worker is going to have to attend some form of judicial hearing.

We use the term 'judicial hearing' since it is somewhat wider than just 'court'. For example, apart from courts there are tribunals dealing with mental health detentions which a social worker may be required to attend. From now on, where we use the term 'court', it is intended to include these other forms of judicial hearing. What we mean by the term 'court' in this chapter is 'court and tribunal hearings in England and Wales'.

The difference between criminal and civil courts

Criminal courts are required where the state prosecutes offences and courts impose penalties on those convicted. (In certain circumstances private individuals can take criminal proceedings themselves, but we will not cover these as they are unusual.) People can be convicted only where the evidence points to guilt 'beyond reasonable doubt'. This requirement, for almost a 100 per cent certainty, is known as the criminal standard of proof. The parties to proceedings are the prosecution and the accused or defendant.

Civil courts are used where people can gain remedies for injustices 'proved on the balance of probabilities'. This civil standard of proof means more likely than not, or more than 50 per cent likely. The remedies are normally financial, in the form of damages which compensate someone for loss, or restitutional, putting right the wrong complained of. The courts have a full range of orders that they can issue and the parties are obliged to follow, including orders that someone should do or not do a particular act. The parties to proceedings are described in most cases as the claimant (or plaintiff in cases before 1999), the person or organization asking for a court order, and the defendant, the person who is resisting the order. If a case is appealed to a higher court, the side that appeals is the appellant and the other side becomes the respondent. Social workers are more likely to come across cases where the parties are described as applicant and respondent. In tribunals, parties are called the applicant (rather than claimant) or the appellant (or in mental health cases, 'the patient'), and the government department whose decision is disputed is referred to as the respondent.

Sometimes the same facts can give rise to both a criminal and a civil case. If a person driving hits another car then the person may have committed a criminal offence, for example careless driving, and also be liable to be sued in civil law for damages. The civil case (known as the 'claim') for damages would be separate, unconnected with the careless driving charge. A person may be successfully sued for damages arising out of a road accident, without there being any proceedings for driving offences, or vice versa. Because of the different standard of proof, it is also possible for a case to be unsuccessful in the criminal courts but give rise to successful proceedings in the civil courts.

The court structure

Figure 1.1 gives an overview of the court system. It reflects the fact that courts are arranged in a hierarchical structure. A lower court must follow decisions of any court higher than itself in the judicial 'ladder'; there is also a system of appeals against the decision of one court from one level to another. Cases begun in the lower courts can, normally, work their way up to the highest court, by way of appeal. We will return to the question of appeals at a later stage.

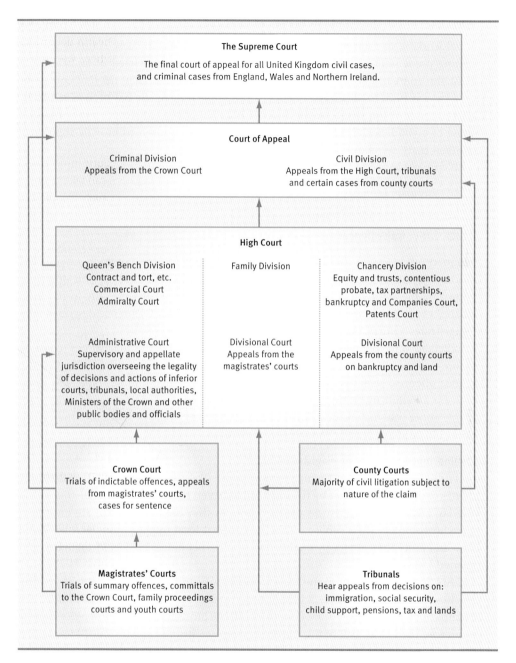

FIGURE 1.1   Overview of the court system

Source: **Figure 1.1** can be found here: www.judiciary.gov.uk/wp-content/uploads/JCO/Images/Layout/courts_structure.pdf.

What happens in the criminal courts?

Social workers, in their official capacity, will mostly appear in these courts when presenting pre-sentence reports on someone who has been convicted of an offence to assist the court in deciding upon appropriate punishment. They may, of course, be called as a witness to an alleged offence, for example if he or she has been assaulted by a service user or the service user's carer, or is able to give evidence in prosecution for abuse of a child. Social workers may also accompany children to provide support in criminal trials: see **chapter 10**.

All criminal cases start in the magistrates' court. There are three types:

   (a) summary offences;

   (b) indictable-only offences; and

   (c) either way offences.

Summary offences are the most numerous. Examples include common assault, less serious criminal damage, and taking a motor vehicle without consent (this offence is known by the acronym 'TWOC'). They can normally be dealt with only in the magistrates' court. Therefore, the court has the limited powers of sentence described later (**Magistrates' courts' powers of sentencing adults**, p 25).

Indictable-only offences are cases that are processed by the magistrates' court to ensure that they are ready for trial but cannot be tried or sentenced there. They are the serious offences, such as serious burglaries, serious assaults, murder, rape, and arson that, for an adult (over 18), can be dealt with only by the Crown Court. Those cases triable either way may be dealt with in the magistrates' court or sent up to the Crown Court if considered serious enough.

Criminal proceedings in the magistrates' court

All criminal cases begin in the magistrates' court. The vast majority (95 per cent) stay there. Cases are heard either by three lay (non-lawyer) magistrates or one district judge. The lay magistrates, or 'Justices of the Peace', as they are also known, are local people who volunteer their services. They lack formal legal qualifications, but are given legal and procedural advice by qualified clerks. District judges are legally qualified, and salaried.

Cases do not go straight to the Crown Court for historical and practical reasons. The practical reason is that where a person is accused of serious burglaries or murder, for example, it requires a great deal of time for both the prosecution and the defence lawyers to prepare their cases before the trial can take place in the Crown Court. Meanwhile, the question of what is going to happen to the accused person has to be dealt with. The magistrates will decide whether the accused person should be remanded into custody (meaning kept in prison) or be granted bail (which would be rare in serious cases, and those in which the accused might reoffend, abscond, or interfere with witnesses).

The youth court is part of the magistrates' court and is dealt with in **chapter 10**. Usually, an indictable-only offence is dealt with in the youth court if the accused is under 18—see **chapter 10**.

'Either way' offences are hybrid offences, because they can be dealt with either by the magistrates' court or by the Crown Court (before a judge and jury). An example of such an offence is theft. What may appear to be the theft of a small amount may be regarded by many as trivial, but for the defendant the consequences of being convicted of such an offence may be extremely serious. Therefore Parliament has decided that the person accused of such an offence can insist on the case being tried before a judge and jury in the Crown Court.

However, if the magistrates consider the case to be not too serious, they can offer the defendant a 'summary' trial. This has the advantage of being dealt with more quickly and sometimes, if the person pleads guilty, on the spot. In an 'either way' case the defendant or the court can insist on a Crown Court trial. A defendant's solicitor might consider that a trial before a jury may give the accused a better chance of being found not guilty; a magistrate or district judge might feel only a Crown Court can offer a punishment fitting the seriousness of the crime. If the magistrates or the defendant insist on a Crown Court trial, or if the case is indictable-only, the defence can require the magistrates' court to consider the written prosecution evidence before committing the case for trial, to see whether there is a case to answer (which is not difficult to prove and most solicitors do not spend time contesting this).

The different hats worn by the magistrates' court

The magistrates' court is divided into different parts. Youth courts are a specialist part of the magistrates' courts and deal with most juveniles accused of crime. For fuller details see **chapter 10**. The magistrates also have important civil functions. Until April 2014, all family proceedings commenced in the family proceedings court which was part of the magistrates' court system. However, the Children and Family Act 2014 abolished family proceedings courts. Instead, all family proceedings, including care proceedings, will take place within a unified family court which is outlined later (**The Family Court**, p 27).

Magistrates' courts' powers of sentencing adults

Magistrates have restricted powers in relation to the sentences that they can impose, including a maximum six months' imprisonment for any one offence committed by an adult. Many of the offences dealt with by the magistrates' court carry no power of imprisonment, and the heaviest penalty then can only be a fine or perhaps a community rehabilitation order. The courts are obliged by law to follow sentencing guidelines depending on the seriousness of the case, previous convictions, and whether a guilty plea was entered. If a person has committed more than one offence, each of which is an either way offence and each of which could have a six-month sentence imposed for it, then the total maximum sentence the magistrates could impose is 12 months' imprisonment (ie two six-month sentences to run consecutively). If they do not feel their powers of punishment are sufficient for either way offences, they can commit the offender to the Crown Court for potentially tougher sentencing. (The youth court does not have this power, although its maximum sentencing powers can be two years' custody. If a charge is particularly serious, the youth court may send the case to the Crown Court for trial—see **chapter 10**.)

Crown Court

By tradition there is deemed to be one Crown Court, which sits (ie is convened) in numerous cities around England and Wales, hence the use of capital letters. In reality they mostly sit daily in specific Crown Court buildings. Among them is the Old Bailey in London where the court is known as the Central Criminal Court. The Crown Court is where more serious criminal cases are heard before a judge and jury. Whereas the magistrates, in their court, decide on the facts of the case (deciding what happened on the basis of the evidence) and also decide the law (whether a law has been broken— after being advised by their clerk), in the Crown Court there is a separation of these functions. The judge, being a professional lawyer (barrister or, less often, solicitor), is the authority on the law. The jury, composed of randomly selected people on the electoral roll, decides the facts based on the evidence.

When sentencing an adult, the powers of sentence of the Crown Court are limited only by the lengths of sentence that are set out either in the statute governing the crime or by common law. The court's powers on sentencing a person under 18 are more limited—see **chapter 10**. The Crown Court can impose a maximum penalty of life imprisonment and almost unlimited financial penalties for some offences. The Crown Court hears some criminal appeals from the magistrates' court.

The civil courts

This section will look at the following courts:

(a) magistrates' courts;

(b) the County Court (this has capital letters because there is a single County Court, although hearings are heard in county court centres throughout England and Wales);

(c) High Court (this has capital letters because, again, there is one single High Court which sits in London but may sit in other places).

Civil functions cover such areas as:

(a) matrimonial cases;

(b) contact with children cases;

(c) child care cases;

(d) contract cases;

(e) personal injuries cases;

(f) administrative law cases.

You are most likely as a social worker to appear in these courts in family matters as:

(a) an applicant and/or witness in applications for an order under the Children Act 1989 or the Adoption and Children Act 2002 (details of the relevant law are dealt with in Part 3);

(b) a 'welfare officer' presenting a report to the court to assist it in deciding what, if any, type of order should be made.

Rules of court

The procedures of the courts are governed by rules of court. Those issued under the Children Act 1989 will be the ones the social worker will come across most often. They are a form of delegated legislation, as the powers to make these rules come from statute.

The Family Court

In England and Wales, the Family Court deals with most family proceedings including:

- divorce;
- dissolution of civil partnerships;
- child arrangements orders;
- care and supervision orders;
- adoption;
- non-molestation and occupation orders.

The Family Court is made up of High Court judges, circuit judges, recorders, district judges, magistrates, and legal advisers.

Social workers in the Family Court

The majority of the social worker's dealings with the courts will be in the Family Court. The Crime and Courts Act 2013 set up a single Family Court for England and Wales which replaces the three separate tiers of court that, in the past, dealt with family proceedings. It came into force on 22 April 2014 at the same time as provisions of the Children and Family Act 2014 designed to ensure a more effective and speedy system for dealing with cases involving children.

You may appear in the Family Court:

(a) on behalf of your authority when it is applying for a care or supervision order—your role is as an applicant and a witness;

(b) at the request of the court, where it appears during family proceedings that it may be appropriate for a care or supervision application to be made by the local authority (Children Act 1989, s. 37); or

(c) the most frequent, where the court requires a welfare report to assist it to decide what order should be made in family proceedings (Children Act 1989, s. 7).

We look at the work of the social worker in the Family Court more closely in **chapter 8**. We look at the range of tools—such as how to write a court report, how to give evidence, and to survive cross-examination—that social workers need to succeed in the Family Court in the Social Worker's Toolkit. The introduction of a single Family Court means that judges of all different levels will sit in the same building. This will mean that cases can be allocated to a judge of appropriate seniority quickly and it will reduce the delays in the old system caused by cases being transferred between different courts.

County Court divorce proceedings

The County Court is the court where most divorces are processed, and it follows that it is the court in which s. 8 Orders under the Children Act 1989 (see **chapter 5**) will be made ancillary to those divorce proceedings. Ancillary relief refers to the powers of the court to make orders related to divorce or other matrimonial proceedings. Section 7 of the Children Act gives the court, in any divorce proceedings, the power to ask either the local authority or the probation service to prepare a report in the course of divorce proceedings.

Civil hearings other than family matters

The magistrates' courts, the County Court, and the High Court exercise a civil jurisdiction other than in family matters. These cover such matters as contract disputes, alcohol licensing, claims for compensation arising from accidents, etc. The High Court hears applications for judicial review. Normally social workers will not deal with these cases in the course of their work. Perhaps the main distinction between these hearings and family hearings is that 'normal' civil hearings will take place in open court and can be openly reported in the press.

Appeal hearings

There are normally provisions for a party unhappy with a decision of a lower court to appeal to a higher court. A dissatisfied party may want to appeal because:

(a) they think the court got the facts of the case wrong;

(b) they think that the court got the law wrong;

(c) they think that the court in exercising its discretion in the case came to the wrong decision.

Most appeal hearings do not involve hearing the case again with the same witnesses. An exception is an appeal to the Crown Court against conviction in the magistrates' court. Normally the appeal court will look at the reasons the lower court gave for arriving at its decision. In some courts the reasons (the judgment) are available in writing. Having heard representations from the parties and having looked at the judgment, the appeal court will give its judgment. Accordingly, it will be difficult to succeed in an appeal on ground (a)—only in exceptional circumstances would a lower court be held to have got the facts wrong, since that court at least has heard the evidence directly.

Most decisions are on ground (b): that the lower court misstated or misunderstood the law. The clarification of the law is an important function of the appeal system. In the field of family matters it is ground (c) that presents the greatest difficulty. When dealing with such family proceedings there can rarely be only one correct decision. The question whether or not to grant a contact order or a residence order will always be a question of balancing a variety of conflicting demands. There will always be a certain amount of discretion as to whether or not an order should be made. The appeal courts, generally, will not interfere in such a case provided that the exercise of that discretion was not unreasonable. Thus an appeal court may say that it would have arrived at a different decision, but if the original decision was within the area of the lower court's discretion then it will not interfere. The case of MA, SA and HA set out in **Box 1.2** illustrates that different judges faced with the same facts may come to different views (just as Wilson and Hedley did), but also the reluctance of appeal courts to substitute their views for those of the judge hearing the original case who was presented with the evidence, the testimony of witnesses, and the cross-examination of those involved. All this is only available to appeal courts at second hand, in written submissions or a report of the original case. So, if the original judge has his or her law right, ground (b) for an appeal fails; and if the judge came to a judgment that is not unreasonable on the evidence before the court, ground (c) for an appeal fails. The judgment is then likely to stand since it is difficult to sustain an appeal on ground (a) that the judge got the facts wrong.

BOX 1.2 *MA, SA and HA (Children By Their Children's Guardian) v MA and HA and the City and Council of Swansea* [2009] EWCA Civ 853

The Pakistani parents of three children had been found to have physically and sexually abused another child, known as X, living with them. There was also a claim the child had been trafficked illegally from Pakistan. The three siblings were taken into care but a judge found that even though there had also been some physical abuse of one of the children, MA, there was no likelihood of significant harm coming to the three children if they were returned home. The parents were likely to act in a different way towards their own children than to X, who was no longer with them. The 'threshold criteria' between harm and significant harm (see the Children Act 1989, s. 31(2)) had not been crossed, so the judge, Hedley J, dismissed the care proceedings, saying 'society must be willing to tolerate very diverse standards of parenting, including the eccentric, the barely adequate and the inconsistent . . . It will mean that some children will experience disadvantage and harm, while others flourish in atmospheres of loving security and emotional stability.' The children should be returned to their parents.

The children's guardian (an official figure appointed to protect the interests of the children; see **chapter 5**) took the matter to the Court of Appeal claiming the judge's decision was irrational. The court refused to overturn the original judgment, with Ward LJ saying: 'Although [the father's] treatment of X was to be deplored, the judge had been best placed to decide on the primary facts and was plainly not wrong in declining to find that the threshold of significant harm had been crossed'. He added that it was a 'paradigm case where this court has to respect the findings and conclusions of an experienced judge and uphold his decision'. By 'paradigm case' he means one that fits the standard pattern of cases in which the original trial judge's view of the facts must be accepted.

In this case, however, one of the Court of Appeal judges, Wilson LJ, gave a minority dissenting judgment declaring that the facts before the original trial judge must have given rise to a likelihood that all three of the children were at significant risk of harm if returned to their parents.

If a court decides that there has been an error of law or failure to exercise discretion properly, it will either replace the decision with the correct decision or, if it cannot do this because the evidence must be looked at again, it will send the case back to a different judge or bench in the court below with instructions as to what matters need to be looked at again.

If you look at the diagram of the court structure (**Figure 1.1**) you will see that the two highest courts are the Court of Appeal (which has separate branches—criminal and civil) and the Supreme Court. The Supreme Court (formerly 'House of Lords', meaning the 'Judicial Committee of the House of Lords') is the court of final appeal. Even so, it must defer to decisions of the European Court of Justice (the European Union court) and must take account of the rulings of the European Court of Human Rights (the Council of Europe court). To give some understanding of the actual workings of the appeal system: the Court of Appeal will hear about 1,000 cases a year and the Supreme Court (assuming it continues to hear the same number as the old House of Lords) about 50 cases a year. So it will be a rare occasion when you have a case going to either of these courts.

The actual practicalities of appeals are beyond the scope of this book. If you do find yourself in a situation which you think should be the subject of an appeal, you should consult your lawyer immediately. You will need to know about appeal cases, however, because the appeal courts generate the reported cases which are vital to your understanding of the law as they tell you how the law should be understood. By definition, what an appeal court says is treated as correct, both on the facts of the particular case and in respect of the legal principles it sets out, unless a higher court declares it to have been wrong.

Tribunals

A great deal of dispute resolution within the English legal system is carried out by tribunals. Most disputes are between the citizen and the state, such as social security disputes; but they can also hear disputes between tenant and landlord, or employer and employee. Tribunal numbers have dramatically increased over the last 50 years. Currently there are over 80 types. Their purpose is to provide a quicker and less formal forum than the courts and to allow cases to be adjudicated on by judges sitting where appropriate with people with an expertise in the particular jurisdiction. For instance, psychiatrists sit on mental health cases and surveyors on property cases. Tribunals tend to be of particular importance to social work service users as their lives are likely to be more dependent on decisions made by state bodies, such as benefit decisions made by the Department for Work and Pensions.

Tribunals grew up in response to the need to settle particular disputes, and used to be managed by the same government department whose decisions were challenged. This is not now considered to be in accordance with the right to a fair determination, under Article 6 of the European Convention on Human Rights (ECHR). Tribunals now are managed within the HM Courts and Tribunals Service under the Ministry of Justice, and legal members are judges who must swear an oath to try cases without fear or favour, just like court judges. First Tier Tribunals (FTT) are divided in six chambers on the basis of their specialisms. So, for instance, the asylum support tribunal sits within the social entitlement chamber. Appeals from FTTs go the Upper Tribunal which is similarly divided into four chambers.

New jurisdictions for tribunals are created relatively frequently, partly in response to the increasing complexity of society and also stimulated by Article 6 of the ECHR which requires the existence of courts or tribunals to determine a person's civil rights. One example relevant to social work practice is the Care Standards Tribunal. This is an FTT within the health education and social care chamber. It considers appeals against a decision made by the Secretary of State to restrict or bar an individual from working with children or vulnerable adults and decisions to cancel, vary, or refuse registration of certain health, child care, and social care provision. Appeals from the Care Standards Tribunal go to the Administrative Appeals Chamber of the Upper Tribunal.

Inquiries

Here we are using the term 'inquiries' to refer to a whole range of investigations/hearings which take place outside the court system. Local authorities may initiate, participate in, or contribute to many types of inquiries. Some are more formal than others. They are a useful mechanism for dealing with complaints or investigating failure and may prove more helpful in finding out facts than the adversarial system used in the courts. We set out here some of those you may come across.

Inquiries ordered by a minister

These are the type of inquiry with which you are probably most familiar. They arise when a minister, acting under powers conferred upon him or her by statute, orders the local authority to conduct an inquiry. The Victoria Climbié Inquiry, which was set up by the Secretary of State for Health and the Secretary of State for the Home Department under the chairmanship of Lord Laming, is a typical example. Inquiries established by statute normally have power to order witness attendance and compel disclosure to the inquiry. The reports of ministerial inquiries are essential learning documents. We will refer to several of them throughout this book.

Inquiries established by the local authority

Local authorities are empowered to carry out inquiries by the Local Government Act 2000. These can cover a variety of different procedures depending upon the reason for the inquiry, and their remit will vary according to time and expense constraints, and whether criminal proceedings are pending. For instance, they can be chaired by an independent chair or by a member of the local authority, such as the chief executive. They can be public or private, though owing to the sensitive nature of many of these inquiries, they tend to be private. Clwyd Council carried out a series of inquiries into allegations of child abuse in its children's homes before the Waterhouse Inquiry ordered by Parliament (launched in 1996 and published in 2000). Clwyd had failed to publish its inquiry for fear of legal action by victims.

Inter-agency inquiries

These can be undertaken by one or more statutory bodies. They may involve local authorities, health authorities, police, or other interested parties. They may be ad hoc in nature or subject to standing procedures. The type of inter-agency inquiry which you are most likely to come across is the serious case review coordinated by the Local Safeguarding Children Board (LSCB). A serious case review is appropriate when a child has sustained a potentially life-threatening injury through abuse or neglect, serious sexual abuse, or sustained serious and permanent impairment of health or development through abuse or neglect, and the case gives rise to concerns about the way in which local professionals and services work together to safeguard and promote the welfare of children. Any professional may refer a case to the LSCB if it is believed that there are important lessons for inter-agency working to be learned from the case. In addition, the Secretary of State for Education has powers to demand an inquiry be held under the Inquiries Act 2005.

Ombudsman schemes

Public ombudsman schemes originated in Scandinavia and were imported into the UK in the 1960s. Ombudsman schemes are designed to provide a possible source of redress where private individuals believe they have suffered through the poor administration—maladministration—of a public body, such as a local authority. What the ombudsman looks at is not the failure of the public body to obey the law but its failure to implement the law in a competent way. Ombudsmen are not able to investigate complaints where legal proceedings are possible.

The Parliamentary Ombudsman

The first ombudsman created was the Parliamentary Commissioner for Administration, who deals with allegations of administrative failings by government departments. The public does not have direct access to the ombudsman. Complaints must go first of all to MPs. MPs are not obliged to refer the complaints they receive to the Parliamentary Ombudsman if they consider that they can deal with the matter themselves. This filter was introduced to preserve the primary responsibility of Parliament to call the administration to account.

The Local Government Ombudsman

The Local Government Ombudsman (technically called the Parliamentary Commissioner for Local Government) is the officer you are most likely to have dealings with. Typically, in any year there are 15,000 complaints to the Local Government Ombudsman, 6 per cent of which relate to social services (37 per cent, in contrast, relate to housing departments—mainly the administration of housing benefit). The objective of the Local Government Ombudsman is to provide, where appropriate, satisfactory redress for complainants and assist in the improvement of administration by local government. The Local Government Ombudsman has the power to issue general advice on good local administration.

A complainant must satisfy the ombudsman that all other procedures of internal complaint to the local authority have been tried and exhausted without giving the complainant redress. (While many complaints will be covered by the local authority complaints procedures, the ombudsman can investigate delays in hearing complaints or allegations that councils are trying to exclude people from using the complaints process.) The complainant has to approach the ombudsman through a local councillor. If the complainant cannot find a councillor willing to make the application, the complainant may approach the ombudsman direct. The ombudsman then has wide powers of investigation and the ability to look at files and compel people to give information.

More information is available on the Local Government Ombudsman's website www. lgo.org.uk. The site also contains reports of the Local Government Ombudsman's decisions and details on how to make a complaint.

Other Ombudsmen

There are several other examples of ombudsmen which may provide useful redress for your clients. The Health Service Commissioner investigates complaints about the failures of NHS hospitals or community health services and other NHS provision. Any member of the public may refer a complaint direct, though normally only if a full investigation within the NHS complaints system has been carried out first. More recently a range of specialist ombudsman has been created. For instance, the Housing Ombudsman Service deals with complaints against housing associations. An Office for Legal Complaints deals with complaints about lawyers, taking over from the Legal Services Ombudsman, now abolished.

Complaints

Complaints are an important driver for improvement in services. Complaints may be generally defined as expressions of dissatisfaction or disquiet that require a response. It is important not to define complaints too narrowly since this may prevent service users from having a legitimate outlet for their concerns.

Social services complaints procedure for adults

The procedure set up under the Local Authority Social Services and National Health Service Complaints (England) Regulations 2009 enables complaints about health or social care to be made under a single set of guidelines, whether it relates to health or social care. The guiding principles are that each local authority or health care provider must have a procedure which deals with complaints efficiently, courteously, thoroughly, in a timely manner, and which leads to the complainant being properly informed and any appropriate action being taken. The local authority must appoint a complaints manager. Complaints must be in writing and made within 12 months of the problem arising. The complaint may relate to a private carer or accommodation provider or to the authority itself. The local authority must publish an annual report of how it has dealt with complaints.

The Social Services Complaints Procedure (Wales) Regulations 2005 provide similar guidelines for complaints about both adult and children's services. There must be a publicized procedure, and a complaints officer. However, complaints can be made to any officer of the authority, and need not be in writing. A dissatisfied complainant can ask for a panel to be set up to consider the complaint and how it was dealt with. At the time of writing the Welsh government was considering responses to its consultation on the reform of these regulations.

We look at complaints about adult social care provision in greater detail in **chapter 14**.

The Children Act 1989 complaints procedure

The second procedure is that required by s. 26(3) of the Children Act 1989. Every local authority must establish a procedure for considering representations (complaints) about the exercise of its functions under Part III of the Act, made by or on behalf of any children looked after or in need—we explain these phrases fully in **chapter 5**. The requirements are set out in the Children Act 1989 Representations Procedure (England) Regulations 2006. Local authorities have to give complainants information about the representations procedure when they first make representations and they must also give information about advocacy services where relevant; that is, where the complainant is a looked-after child or a child in need and so is entitled to an advocate under s. 26A of the Act.

Important points to note about the complaints procedure are that it:

- imposes a one-year time limit on the making of representations so that local authorities and voluntary organizations do not have to consider representations that arise from incidents several years ago;

- imposes tight time scales for the handling of representations including a local resolution phase upfront so that issues may be resolved quickly and efficiently;

- requires the involvement of independent persons in the consideration of representations so that the process is fair and transparent for the complainant; and

- requires monitoring of the procedure and the outcome of each representation so that local authorities can learn and improve services as a result.

Figure 1.2 sets out the complaints procedure laid down by the Department for Children, Schools and Families for complaints relating to children's services.

Children's Commissioners

The Children's Commissioner for Wales is an independent body which has the role of ensuring that the rights of children and young people are upheld. It was set up following a recommendation in the report of the Waterhouse Tribunal which looked into the abuse of children in care in the former county council areas of Gwynedd and Clwyd (see **Inquiries established by the local authority**, p 31). The office of the Children's Commissioner for Wales was established under the Care Standards Act 2000. The Commissioner's functions include reviewing and monitoring the arrangements

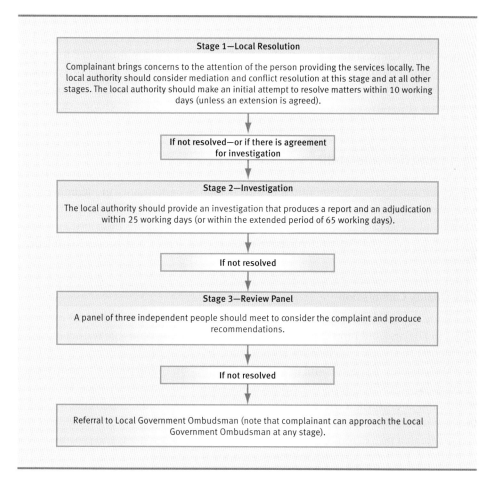

Stage 1—Local Resolution

Complainant brings concerns to the attention of the person providing the services locally. The local authority should consider mediation and conflict resolution at this stage and at all other stages. The local authority should make an initial attempt to resolve matters within 10 working days (unless an extension is agreed).

↓

If not resolved—or if there is agreement for investigation

↓

Stage 2—Investigation

The local authority should provide an investigation that produces a report and an adjudication within 25 working days (or within the extended period of 65 working days).

↓

If not resolved

↓

Stage 3—Review Panel

A panel of three independent people should meet to consider the complaint and produce recommendations.

↓

If not resolved

↓

Referral to Local Government Ombudsman (note that complainant can approach the Local Government Ombudsman at any stage).

FIGURE 1.2   The procedure for Children Act 1989 complaints

for complaints made by service providers, whistle-blowing (meaning 'protected disclosures' by staff reporting failings of their management or employer to someone outside the immediate organization such as to a lawyer, the police, or a politician and possibly to the media under certain circumstances), advocacy, the provision of advice and information, the power to examine particular cases, providing other assistance, and making reports. In 2001 the Children's Commissioner for Wales Act extended the Commissioner's role to all children. It also gave him or her the power to review proposed legislation and policy from the National Assembly for Wales considering the potential effect that it might have on children, and to make representations to the National Assembly for Wales about any matter that affects children. The website is www.childcom.org.uk.

The Children Act 2004 establishes the office of Children's Commissioner for England with the function of promoting and safeguarding the rights and interests of children in England. The website is www.childrenscommissioner.gov.uk. The Commissioner is required to have regard to the United Nations Convention on the Rights of the Child. The role is similar to the Children's Commissioner for Wales but does not include the power to review all proposed legislation to assess its impact upon children. Most significantly, the government has resisted any emphasis on individual children's rights.

Inspection and audit

The government says it is committed to improving the performance of public services. One particular mechanism by which it does this is via inspection and audit. In the health and social care system there are a number of organizations described as regulatory arm's-length bodies that hold services to account. These bodies operate independently of government.

Care Quality Commission

This body registers and monitors the care services of adult health and social care providers in England and protects the interests of people whose rights are restricted under the Mental Health Act. Its responsibilities were set out in the Health and Social Care Act 2008, broadly 'to protect and promote the health, safety and welfare of people who use health and social care services'. Provisions came into force in October 2010 when health and adult social care services in England became legally responsible for meeting new standards of quality and safety. The new system is described as looking at the actual care that people receive rather than simply looking at systems and processes. The intention is to ensure the person being cared for is consulted about their care and to promote their independence.

Where there is failure to register or to abide by legal requirements and conditions of registration in care provision, the Commission can use the enforcement powers listed in the Act. Improvement actions can be set for care providers but ultimately the Commission can use civil and criminal law to protect those being cared for or to punish care providers for causing harm or failing to meet requirements.

For full information on the work of the Commission, see its website www.cqc.org.uk.

Children's services and Ofsted

From April 2007 children's social care services have been regulated by the Office for Standards in Education, Children's Services and Skills—Ofsted.

Achieving public accountability

It is clear that there is a multitude of mechanisms to achieve public accountability. In **Table 1.2** we list them and provide a summary of the advantages and disadvantages they bring.

TABLE 1.2 A summary of the different forums for public accountability

Forum	Advantages	Disadvantages	Comment
The courts	Prestigious	Expensive and time-consuming	Very few cases that you are involved in will get reported in the law reports. Decisions which are reported tend to arise from very complex factual circumstances which you may feel have little relevance to your day-to-day practice
		Can be very alienating to people unfamiliar with its operations	Extensive expertise and specialist knowledge
Tribunals	Less formal hearings, with greater accessibility and speed	Different tribunals run on different procedural rules. Sometimes the informality can work to the disadvantage of the vulnerable person	You are likely to become increasingly familiar with tribunals because of the influence of the Human Rights Act
		Generally no funded legal help available	
Inquiries	Public inquiries are very influential on subsequent practice	Public inquiries are expensive and time consuming. Other inquiries may be held in private and provide very little public accountability	
Complaints	These provide a speedy informal system of addressing issues of concern to ordinary people	Children and vulnerable people may find it very difficult to complain	
Local Government Ombudsman		Limited compensation	
Children's Commissioner	Provides a service which children need since they find it difficult to complain or influence policy and the law	England's Commissioner has limited role	It will be interesting to see the extent of the added value the Children's Commissioner provides

Forum	Advantages	Disadvantages	Comment
	It will also provide a useful coordinating role		
Regulators	Can concentrate on improving the quality of services and respond to systemic problems	Do not respond to individual complaints although service users' views are taken into account	

EXERCISES

1 Explain the differences between courts and tribunals.

2 Accountability

A service user is dissatisfied with a decision you have made. Outline the various options open to her and indicate under what circumstances which option is likely to be most appropriate.

3 The Ombudsman

Find the Local Government Ombudsman's site on the web. Find the decisions on complaints about social services. What types of complaint are most common?

4 Reading statutes

Find the Care Standards Act 2000—on the internet or find a paper copy. Now answer the following questions:

(a) How many parts are there to the Act?

(b) What is the title of Part IX and how many chapters does it have?

(c) How many schedules are there to the Act?

(d) Find s. 11 of the Act. Does this impose criminal or civil liability on the person who fails to register?

(e) Find s. 16 of the Act. What is the legal status of regulations made under this section?

(f) Look at s. 23. What powers does the minister have? What statutory duties are imposed upon him?

(g) What section of the Act deals with the title 'social worker'? Write, in your own words, what it provides.

(h) How does the Act define 'vulnerable adults'?

(i) Has s. 81 of the Act come into force?

(j) Is your version of the Act up to date? How do you know?

6 Reading cases

Find *Gillick v West Norfolk and Wisbech Area Health Authority* [1985] UKHL 7 and answer the following questions:

(a) In which court was the case heard?

(b) Name the judges.

(c) When was the case heard? On what date was the judgment handed down?

(d) Who were the parties to the case?

(e) Set out briefly the legal history of the case.

(f) Is the case one of statutory interpretation, or is it about the common law?

(g) Was the decision of the court unanimous?

(h) Who were the barristers in the case? Who were the solicitors?

(i) Find Lord Scarman's judgment and copy it. If you have time, read it. It is a good decision to read as it has been extremely influential, as you will find out in **chapter 2**.

ONLINE RESOURCE CENTRE

For guidance on how to answer these exercises, visit the Online Resource Centre at: www.oxfordtextbooks.co.uk/orc/socialwork13e/.

WHERE DO WE GO FROM HERE?

This chapter makes it clear that you are operating in a legal arena and provides a very important foundation to your legal studies. The most important message to draw from this chapter is that the law determines what you do. Social workers must be able to account for their decisions. In addition, any correct answer that a social worker can give, when asked why he or she took a particular course of action, must include the statement 'I took the step because that was what appropriate social work practice demanded within the framework of the law'. Without the ability to say that, the professional social worker will have failed themselves and, more importantly, the service user. We now move to **chapter 2** where we look more closely at the regulation of the professional social worker.

ANNOTATED FURTHER READING

The legal system

If you would like to read more about the English and Welsh legal system there are any number of books available. Martin Partington's *Introduction to the English Legal System* (Oxford University Press) is concise, updated annually, and takes a critical as well as a descriptive approach.

Websites of (some of) the bodies mentioned in this chapter:

www.parliament.uk

www.assemblywales.org

www.justice.gov.uk

www.ombudsman.org.uk (covers Parliament and NHS)

www.lgo.org.uk (local government ombudsman)

www.childrenscommissioner.gov.uk (Children's Commissioner for England)

www.cqc.org.uk (Care Quality Commission)

2

The roles and responsibilities of the social worker

OVERVIEW AND OBJECTIVES

This chapter focuses on the roles and responsibilities of the social worker. In particular it looks at the role of the social worker as an ethical professional, a statutory creation, and an employee. It also considers the nature and extent of the redress that the law provides to those who are damaged in some way by the actions of social workers. The chapter concludes by providing some guidance on the thorny legal, ethical, and professional issue of consent.

CASE STUDY

A and another v Essex County Council (2003)

Mr A and Mrs B were married in 1985. Both had been married before and A had two children from his first marriage. They had no children together and, in 1990, applied to be approved as prospective adoptive parents. Their local authority, Essex, was the relevant adoption agency as defined under the Act then in force, the Adoption Act 1976. A and B were interviewed by a social worker and adoption adviser, employed by Essex, who recommended that they were suitable adoptive parents. In June 1991, A and B were approved by the adoption panel.

In June 1994 the adoption panel recommended two young children, a brother and sister, for adoption. The boy was born in 1990 and his sister in 1993. The children had had a very difficult start in life, witnessing and being at risk of physical and emotional abuse. By 1994 they were in the care of Essex. In October 1995 the adoption panel recommended linking A and B with the children. In February 1996 the children were formally placed with A and B, and finally on 1 May 1997, the court made adoption orders.

Following the adoption, the boy proved impossible to control, to such an extent that he had damaged A and B's home, health, and family life. The judge referred to evidence of the boy's behaviour as follows: 'B described his behaviour as "spiralling out of control". She has suffered black eyes, split lips, and bruises on various occasions and ended up in hospital as a result of being attacked by him while pregnant. He smashed their greenhouse with a spade, damaged their conservatory, poured gloss paint on the walls and carpets of the hall and their bedroom, and generally behaved violently including attacking other children. On one occasion at a party for the girls he attacked A's father and bit him, he attempted to attack the girls (his sisters), took a carving knife and threatened to kill A, and attempted to electrocute himself with bare wires from his bedside lamp which he had destroyed.' In October 1997 he was diagnosed as suffering from Attention Deficit Hyperactivity Disorder and is medicated with Ritalin. Since 1999 he had been in care appropriate to his special needs.

A and B wanted compensation—damages—from Essex. They alleged that Essex were negligent in particular in failing to inform A and B of the extent of the boy's difficulties of which it knew; had A and B been properly informed they would not have agreed to the placement. Essex denied negligence, in the sense of carelessness, but also denied that it owed A and B a duty of care and that it was responsible for the problem. Its argument was that a fair and sufficient amount of information was conveyed and it did not accept that A and B would have rejected the children in any event. The question before the court was whether Essex owed a common law duty of care to A and B when it was acting in a statutory context.

The judge in the High Court found that Essex had been negligent for failing to provide A and B with all the relevant information about the two children whom they were to adopt. This decision represented a considerable extension of the previous law on responsibility for decisions. However, he also found that Essex was only liable for injury, loss, and damage sustained between the time when the children were placed with A and B as prospective adopters and the date of the adoption orders. Both Essex and A and B appealed against the decision.

The Court of Appeal decision

The Court of Appeal, whilst still finding that Essex had some responsibility for the inadequate information that A and B received, came to a narrower view of Essex's responsibility. It asked a number of questions. One question was whether individual social workers and others can be held to account in their implementation of the adoption agency's policy and practice on disclosure of information. Other questions also arose. First, is there a duty of care in relation to the contents of the forms and reports which are made? Second, is there a duty of care in relation to the communication of the information which the agency has decided that the prospective adopters should have?

It answered the second question first. It saw no difficulty in a duty of care to communicate to the prospective adopters that information which the agency had decided that they should have. The first of the intermediate questions proved more difficult. Clearly the primary duty of social workers, doctors, and others who complete forms on behalf of an agency was to that agency. The reports were required by the agency so that it could fulfil its statutory obligations. Could the compilers of reports simultaneously owe duties towards the people who were the subject matter of those reports and towards the people who may read and rely upon them? For a number of reasons the court was reluctant to impose such a duty. The first reason it gave was that there was a statutory framework for adoption which was closely regulated 'with a view to ensuring best contemporary practice in this difficult and sensitive exercise in social engineering'. The second reason was that the agency owed its first duty to the child, who was the most likely to suffer lasting damage if things went wrong, who rarely had much choice in the matter, and was least likely to be able to protect his own interests, which may well conflict with those of the adults involved. It raised two further considerations. First, prospective adopters were proposing to be parents and like all parents had to be prepared for downs as well as ups. Second, prospective adopters had a trial period within which to get to know the child and decide that they could cope with the upheaval of adoption. For these reasons the court decided that it was not fair, just, and reasonable to impose upon professionals involved in compiling reports for adoption agencies a duty of care towards prospective adopters. It did not rule out a duty of care towards the child, but that was not the question before the court. The court further held that even if there were a duty of care, as long as the professional judgement made in the report was one which would be acceptable to a responsible body of opinion within that profession at that time then there would be no breach of duty. In this particular case it decided that the social worker was not in breach of her duty in compiling the form.

Another question the court answered was whether the agency had a duty of care in respect of the decision about what information should be passed on. The agency has to have a policy about this, but the court understood that it may be appropriate to depart from that policy in individual cases either in withholding information which would otherwise be given, or in divulging information over and above that contained in the various forms and reports disclosed. It therefore decided that there was in general no duty of care owed by an adoption agency or the staff whom it employed in deciding what information was to be conveyed to prospective adopters. Only if they took a decision which no reasonable agency could take could there be liability. However, once the agency had decided what information should be given, then there was a duty to take reasonable care to ensure that that information was both given and received.

The Court of Appeal therefore decided that the duty of care to the prospective adopters was more restricted than the judge in the High Court had held. A and B did not need to have all the relevant information; they should receive the information which a reasonable and competent agency would provide. However, once the agency decided on that information it had a duty of care in the provision of that information. The court was clear that Essex had breached that duty of care. Essex had not provided A and B with the information that it had decided they should be provided with. As a result they were liable for all of the harm that resulted from that failure, but only to the point of the adoption order. 'The adoption order changes everything for ever. From that point on the adopters became as much like birth parents as it is possible for them to be.' The court concluded with a thought-provoking statement of the limits of the law.

> Adoption is not a commercial transaction. It cannot be likened to the sale of goods or even the supply of services. Writing reports about a child is not like writing financial references and reports. The whole process is about doing the best one can for children who have not had the start in life which most of us take for granted. At times during the argument in this case it was easy to forget that [the children] are real people, every bit as real as the adults in the case . . . The long term calculation of gains and losses involved in this delicate piece of social engineering cannot be done on the cold computer programme of the law.

WHAT DOES THIS CASE TELL YOU ABOUT SOCIAL CARE LAW AND PRACTICE?

In each chapter from now on we start with real legal cases, designed to highlight the issues which that chapter will examine. The case study for this chapter received extensive media coverage. In a story headlined 'Couple sue over adopted "wild child"', the *Guardian* reported on 17 October 2002 that 'in the first claim for "wrongful adoption" a couple are suing Essex county council for negligence in failing to disclose reports indicating that the boy was "uncontrollable and vicious" and that his appalling behaviour would be "beyond the wildest imagination" of inexperienced adopters'. The case is of great significance for social workers. Do not be distracted by its notoriety or the technicalities of the law on adoption.

The judgment stresses social workers' professional responsibilities to the people who are affected by their decisions. It makes it clear that 'doing your best in difficult circumstances' is not always good enough. As you read through the case, ask yourself why the social workers did not tell the whole truth to A and B? Can you understand the pressures on them? Put yourself in the position of the prospective adopters—what pressures were upon them? Think about the children involved in this case—how have their lives been damaged by this? Do you agree with the barrister representing Essex who argued that the law must be careful not to impose burdens on social workers which get in the way of the interests of children and their statutory responsibilities? Or do you agree with the High Court judge when he said that the possibility of an award of damages should lead to an improvement in the practice of social work? What do you think the Court of Appeal meant when it did not rule out a duty of care to a child in these circumstances? What are the implications of the decision for your practice of social work? Does the case tell you anything about the extent of your professional responsibilities?

The case study illustrates how social service departments can be taken to court by those who are unhappy with the way social workers carried out their work. So one of the subjects we look at in this chapter is the accountability of the social worker through the courts.

The case also highlights some of the problems which social workers face: a hugely demanding role where there is pressure to achieve particular outcomes and where time to complete paperwork properly and consider the full implications of the course of action that you have embarked upon is in short supply.

■ The relevance of law to good social work practice

The relationship between law and social work is complex. Although social workers first emerged with the Charity Organisation Society in the 19th century, they are now largely the creation of government; government is therefore accountable to the public for their work and obliged to regulate their activities. Social workers are also professionals and are required to account for their actions and inactions to the government and the public within a framework of law which lays down their tasks, the scope of their work, their discretions, and their powers.

It is our task to emphasize the relevance and importance of law to social work practice. Law alone is not enough for good social work practice. But failure to practise according to the requirements of the law leaves you open to criticism. In 1998, the Social Service Inspectors at the Department of Health published a report called *Someone Else's Children* (Department of Health, 1998). This set out the results of a large-scale inspection of local authorities in England and Wales. It gave a dreadful picture of how the law is actually put into practice. It describes 'a catalogue of concerns about how important decisions are made and the arrangements to ensure that children are safe' (para. 1.3). Failure to understand and act within the legal framework let these children down. The law says that the interests of the child are important, or, where a court is concerned, 'paramount' (Children Act 1989, s. 1). It is the practitioner who carries this into effect.

Criticism of the law is valid and useful; but working outside the law is unacceptable. The rule of law requires the state—which you as a social worker represent—to use its formidable powers according to the law and in an accountable way. It is an illusion to think you can protect the interests of vulnerable people better outside the legal framework than within it. At the very least it will destroy your credibility in court and your chance of obtaining appropriate court orders; at its worst, there may be a disaster, and you will be the first in line for any criticism. That is not to say that values are not important to your work. It would be impossible for you to do your job without a strong set of values. Part of our purpose in this chapter is to demonstrate the link between value-driven, ethical practice, and legally informed practice.

We have already suggested that social workers are both social care professionals and creations of statute working within the law. In what follows we will identify the range of social work roles and responsibilities.

An ethical professional

One way of understanding what it means to be a social worker is through the Professional Capabilities Framework developed initially by the Social Work Reform Board and subsequently adopted by the College of Social Work. The framework identifies the following capabilities:

- *professionalism*—identify and behave as a professional social worker, committed to professional development;
- *values and ethics*—apply social work ethical principles and values to guide professional practice;
- *diversity*—recognize diversity and apply anti-discriminatory and anti-oppressive principles in practice;
- *rights, justice, and economic well-being*—advance human rights and promote social justice and economic well-being;
- *knowledge*—apply knowledge of social sciences, law, and social work practice theory;
- *critical reflection and analysis*—apply critical reflection and analysis to inform and provide a rationale for professional decision making;
- *intervention and skills*—use judgement and authority to intervene with individuals, families, and communities to promote independence, provide support, and prevent harm, neglect, and abuse;
- *contexts and organizations*—engage with, inform, and adapt to changing contexts that shape practice. Operate effectively within own organizational frameworks and

contribute to the development of services and organizations. Operate effectively within multi-agency and inter-professional settings;

- *professional leadership*—take responsibility for the professional learning and development of others through supervision, mentoring, assessing, research, teaching, leadership, and management.

Professionals have a particular type of relationship with the people who use their services because of the level of expertise and authority that being a professional implies. The law recognizes the particular nature of the relationship and imposes responsibilities to act with care, and also intervenes to ensure that the professional has the appropriate qualifications. In this section of the chapter we will look at both of these aspects of your professional identity but we will start with the most fundamental aspect of professional identity, integrity.

All professionals are bound by ethical codes and their actions are underpinned by agreed values. Before its demise, the General Social Care Council, which was responsible for registering social workers in England, published a Code of Practice for social care workers to which it expected all registered social workers to adhere. This established that a social worker must:

- Protect the rights and promote the interests of service users and carers;
- Strive to establish and maintain the trust and confidence of service users and carers;
- Promote the independence of service users while protecting them as far as possible from danger or harm;
- Respect the rights of service users whilst seeking to ensure that their behaviour does not harm themselves or other people;
- Uphold public trust and confidence in social care services; and
- Be accountable for the quality of their work and take responsibility for maintaining and improving their knowledge and skills.

The current regulator is the Health and Care Professions Council (HCPC) and it sets out ethical guidance for social work students (2012) at www.hpc-uk.org/assets/documents/ 10002C16Guidanceonconductandethicsforstudents. It has 13 points:

1 You must act in the best interests of service users.
2 You must respect the confidentiality of service users.
3 You must keep high standards of personal conduct.
4 You must provide (to us and any other relevant regulators) any important information about your conduct and competence.
5 You must limit your study or stop studying if your performance or judgement is affected by your health.
6 You must keep your professional knowledge and skills up to date.
7 You must act within the limits of your knowledge, skills, and experience and, if necessary, refer the matter to another practitioner.
8 You must communicate properly and effectively with service users and other practitioners.
9 You must get informed consent to provide care or services (as far as possible).
10 You must keep accurate records.
11 You must deal fairly and safely with the risks of infection.

12 You must behave with honesty and integrity.
13 You should make sure that your behaviour does not damage public confidence in your profession.

The British Association of Social Workers (BASW), after widespread consultation from a number of sources, also published a Code of Ethics for Social Workers. The latest Code was launched in January 2012 (see http://cdn.basw.co.uk/upload/basw_112315-7.pdf).

The summary of the values underpinning social work is expressed in the Code as follows:

Human dignity and worth

Respect for human dignity, and for individual and cultural diversity
Value for every human being, their beliefs, goals, preferences and needs
Respect for human rights and self determination
Partnership and empowerment with users of services and with carers
Ensuring protection for vulnerable people

Social justice

Promoting fair access to resources
Equal treatment without prejudice or discrimination
Reducing disadvantage and exclusion
Challenging the abuse of power

Service

Helping with personal and social needs
Enabling people to develop their potential
Contributing to the creation of a fairer society

Integrity

Honesty, reliability and confidentiality

Competence

Maintaining and expanding competence to provide a quality service

One particular aspect of your role as an ethical professional needs further consideration—your role as a champion of equality and diversity.

A champion of equality and diversity

The College of Social Work's Professional Capabilities Framework is clear that recognizing diversity and challenging discrimination are fundamental parts of the social work role. It states that:

> Social workers understand that diversity characterises and shapes human experience and is critical to the formation of identity. Diversity is multi-dimensional and includes race, disability, class, economic status, age, sexuality, gender and transgender, faith and belief. Social workers appreciate that, as a consequence of difference, a person's life experience may

include oppression, marginalisation and alienation as well as privilege, power and acclaim, and are able to challenge appropriately.

Chapter 16 of the Laming Report into the death of Victoria Climbié focuses on the role of race and diversity in the failure of social services and others to respond to Victoria's needs. As Laming points out, in para. 16.1 of the Report:

> Victoria was a black child who was murdered by her two black carers. Many of the profes-sionals with whom she came into contact during her life in this country were also black. Therefore, it is tempting to conclude that racism can have had no part to play in her case. But such a conclusion fails to recognise that racism finds expression in many ways other than in the direct application of prejudice.

The report emphasized that children from every background are entitled to the protec-tion of the law. Paragraph 16.10 states:

> The basic requirement that children are kept safe is universal and cuts across cultural boundaries. Every child living in this country is entitled to be given the protection of the law, regardless of his or her background. Cultural heritage is important to many people, but it cannot take precedence over standards of childcare embodied in law. Every organisation concerned with the welfare and protection of children should have mechanisms in place to ensure equal access to services of the same quality, and that each child, irrespective of colour or background, should be treated as an individual requiring appropriate care.

What we learn is that culturally aware ethical practice is not simple. The law also impacts upon your practice here.

We discuss the race relations legislation, including the duties it imposes on local authorities, as part of the legal framework for combating unlawful discrimination, in **chapter 3**. The law underpins this part of your professional role through equality leg-islation discussed there.

A competent professional

The next aspect of professional identity we must consider is competence. Professional competence is a key legal and ethical requirement. The College of Social Work's Professional Capabilities Framework states that:

> Social workers are members of an internationally recognised profession, a title protected in UK law. Social workers demonstrate professional commitment by taking responsibility for their conduct, practice and learning, with support through supervision. As representa-tives of the social work profession they safeguard its reputation and are accountable to the professional regulator.

The state translates this ethical requirement to a legal one by insisting on a rigorous qualification system. Under the Care Standards Act 2000 (CSA) a social worker falls within the general category of 'social care worker'. Section 55 of the CSA defines a social worker as someone who engages in social work (s. 55(2)(a))—the definition does not really help to define what social work is, but there is no doubt that if you act as, or call yourself, a social worker, you must be qualified and registered. In fact, it is a criminal offence for anyone else to use the title 'social worker' (s. 61).

You must be registered under s. 13B of the Health and Social Work Professions Order 2001 as amended by s. 215 of the Health and Social Care Act 2012 (in Wales the National Assembly). Not only social workers but, under s. 60 of the amended Health Act 1999, any of the following must register with the HCPC/Assembly:

(a) employment at a children's home, care home or residential family centre in England,

(b) management of a home or centre of a kind mentioned in paragraph (a),

(c) employment for the purposes of a domiciliary care agency, fostering agency, voluntary adoption agency or adoption support agency, in so far as the agency provides services to persons in England,

(d) management of an agency of a kind mentioned in paragraph (c),

(e) work for the purposes of the social services functions of a local authority whose area is in England,

(f) the provision in England of services similar to services which may or must be provided by a local authority in the exercise of its social services functions,

(g) the provision of personal care for persons in England,

(h) employment (in an undertaking other than an establishment or agency) which consists of or includes supplying, or providing services for the purpose of supplying, persons to provide personal care for persons in England,

(i) management of an undertaking of the kind mentioned in paragraph (h),

(j) employment in connection with the discharge of functions of the Secretary of State under section 80 of the Children Act 1989 (inspection of children's homes),

(k) employment as a member of staff of the Office for Standards in Education, Children's Services and Skills who inspects premises under—

(i) section 87 of the Children Act 1989 (welfare of children accommodated in independent schools and colleges),

(ii) section 31 of the Care Standards Act 2000 (inspections by persons authorised by registration authority), or

(iii) section 139 of the Education and Inspections Act 2006 (inspection by Chief Inspector),

(l) employment as a member of staff of the Care Quality Commission who, under Part 1 of the Health and Social Care Act 2008, inspects premises used for or in connection with the provision of social care (within the meaning of that Part),

(m) management of staff mentioned in paragraph (k) or (l),

(n) employment at a day centre in England,

(o) participation in a course approved by the Health and Care Professions Council (HCPC) under art. 15 of the Health and Social Work Professions Order 2001 for persons wishing to engage in the social work profession in England.

A qualified professional

The HCPC is responsible for the Standards of Education and Training in the professions it registers. The College of Social Work will also endorse social work training. At the time of writing the mechanisms for these processes were still being consulted on.

Both organizations will use the Professional Capabilities Framework as the basis for the standards of qualifying and post-qualifying social work training.

Under the Health and Social Care Act 2012 it is the statutory responsibility of the HCPC (or Welsh Assembly) to approve training courses on behalf of the Secretary of State and to recognize where appropriate foreign qualifications.

Professional responsibilities

The person you are responsible for used to be called your client. We used that term in early editions. That word was inaccurate in capturing the nature of your responsibilities, because the word 'client' somehow suggests a person who has chosen and instructed a professional. Nowadays the word is service user. The relationship is defined by the service, and there is no instruction by the service user. The service is made available by statute, so the social worker who provides it or arranges for it to be provided is not instructed, as a lawyer or accountant would be, by a client. Sometimes, as we shall see later in this chapter, it is provided without the service user consenting because they may be too young or otherwise incapacitated to do so.

You do not decide who is a service user. This is defined in the Local Authority Social Services Act 1970 (LASSA). We will come to that very important statutory list later in the chapter. The service user will either be a child in need, or an adult in need of some form of community care service.

In any case involving children, each individual child on your caseload is the service user, the person to whom you have statutory responsibilities. You need to build up an individual relationship with each child, distinct from the relationship you may have with the child's parents or guardians. The Report of the Inquiry into Victoria Climbié—the Laming Report (see **chapter 5**) was just one in the long series of reports which make it clear what happens when social workers lose sight of the core statutory responsibility to the child.

This point about service users is not just applicable to children. For example, if you are responsible for the well-being of an older person it is easy to overlook that that person is your service user and that his or her needs are the starting point for assessing what should be done. The pressures of the family can lead you to concentrate on what the family may want, which often may not be what the older person wants or what your statutory duty requires.

Responsibilities other than to service users

The dropping of the word 'client' is helpful. When that word was used, it was common to see the parent of a child as 'the client'. This is wrong. You do not have a client, and any responsibility is owed to the person who uses the services—which is not to minimize the vital importance of working with others, especially parents.

As the case study at the beginning of this chapter demonstrates, you do, of course, have responsibilities to others, such as prospective adopters, foster parents, and carers. You have duties to society at large, for instance in your responsibility to diminish offending by young people. These responsibilities may arise from your common law duty of care or from other statutory responsibilities, for instance those arising under the Carers (Recognition and Services) Act 1995 (C(RS)A)—see **chapter 13**. There will be legal consequences if you fail in your professional responsibilities to such people. Nonetheless, it is critical that your prime focus is the person to whom you have statutory responsibilities.

The nature of the responsibility to the service user

There is a conflict at the heart of the social work role. You have two clear relationships with the service user:

(a) an adviser/friend to the service user, or to those involved with the service user, such as their carers or parents. Such a role is often talked of as 'being an agent of social change'. That is to say, that you will be seeking to make life better for the service user. This is often the motivation behind the decision to become a social worker; and

(b) a statutory relationship in relation to the service user. This is more commonly referred to as being 'an agent of statutory control'. This is where you are sometimes required to use statutory powers to protect the service user.

This second function may well involve you in investigations of the conduct of a service user or of those who are close to that service user. The conflict is clear. A friend does not investigate you or monitor your behaviour. You may be required to make risk assessments of the future behaviour of the service user. A friend does not work out the likelihood of you behaving badly in the future. The tensions are even more apparent with the increased emphasis on partnership working with other agencies, such as the police—see **chapter 7**. Friends do not collude with others against our interests.

Is there a duty to act in the best interests of the service user?

Perhaps this gives us an insight into what went wrong in the case study at the beginning of this chapter. The children's social worker very much wanted the children to have this opportunity of a family life. She forgot that her statutory responsibilities were to act in the best interests of the children. Their best interests would have been served by full disclosure of the information about the difficulties of the boy to the prospective adopters. The social worker's wishes for the children overrode her professional judgement. However, best interests cannot override the legal rights of others. Even if the children's best interests had been served by achieving an adoption placement by concealing from the adopters the history of the children, the decision interfered with the legal duty of care to the adopters. You will come across the word 'paramount' when dealing with court cases such as care orders and contact orders concerning children. In those cases, s. 1 of the Children Act dictates that the court decision is driven by the interests of the child, which are paramount. What this means is that they override any other competing interests with which the court might have the power to interfere, not that they override the legal rights of all and sundry.

It is clear that your prime role has to be within the statutory framework that has created social workers. A social worker who fails to bear this in mind will ultimately fail him or herself and the service user. This does not mean that your role as friend and adviser is or should be diminished. Nevertheless you need to build up your relationship with the service user with your statutory role as your first consideration. This is to be honest with that person, which is the best basis for a relationship. The idea of honesty raises questions, however, about the extent to which information is for sharing. The issues are so complex that they require a full chapter to analyse—see **chapter 4**.

Duty of ethical practice in relation to the service user

The second domain in the College of Social Work's Professional Capabilities Framework concerns ethics and values. It says that:

> Social workers have an obligation to conduct themselves ethically and to engage in ethical decision-making, including through partnership with people who use their services. Social workers are knowledgeable about the value base of their profession, its ethical standards and relevant law.

Experienced social workers will be expected to:

- Demonstrate confident and critical application of professional ethical principles to decision-making and practice, supporting others to do so using a legal and human rights framework
- Model and support others to reflect on and manage the influence and impact of own values on professional practice
- Provide guidance and support to analyse, reflect on and work with ethical dilemmas
- Demonstrate confident application of an understanding of the benefits and limitations of partnership work, support others to do so, and promote service user and carer participation in developing service delivery. Promote and advance wherever possible individual's rights to autonomy and self-determination, providing support, guidance and challenge to others
- Demonstrate skills in the sensitive exploration of issues of privacy and information-sharing in complex or risky situations, offering support and guidance to colleagues in managing these dilemmas.

These are professional guidelines and will inform the assessment of social workers' capabilities throughout their professional career and must be respected.

Duty to respect autonomy of the service user

The ethical principle that every person has a right to self-determination and is entitled to their autonomy is set out clearly in the BASW Code of Ethics. In para. 2.1.2 of the Code, headed 'Respecting the right to self-determination', the following is set out:

> Social workers should respect, promote and support people's dignity and right to make their own choices and decisions, irrespective of their values and life choices, provided this does not threaten the rights, safety and legitimate interests of others.

These principles are also enshrined in law, through the requirement for consent and the duty of confidentiality. Actions taken without consent are unlawful, and in some circumstances criminal. We provide an overview of this difficult area of legal and ethical practice later in this chapter.

Professional accountability through the courts

Traditionally, local authorities have been protected by the courts from being sued for policy reasons—local authorities should be able to carry out the difficult task of child protection without the risk of being sued. For these reasons, the House of Lords, in *X (Minors) v Bedfordshire County Council* (1995), dismissed claims by children trying to sue for failures by local authorities. Recently, however, there has been a shift away from this absolute legal immunity. Local authorities can be sued for negligence as long as the three criteria for the imposition of a duty of care are present. The three criteria were explained by the House of Lords in *Caparo Industries plc v Dickman* (1990) as foreseeability of damage (to what extent was the loss or damage predictable), proximity of relationship (how close was the relationship between the person causing the damage and the victim), and the reasonableness or otherwise of imposing a duty. For social workers, the relationship with the service user is clearly sufficiently proximate, and the damage to the victim is generally predictable. The stumbling block in the past has been whether it was reasonable to impose a duty.

There has been a range of cases demonstrating that negligence by local authorities is now actionable. Among these are *S v Gloucestershire County Council* (2000), where the child was sexually abused by foster parents and *Barret v Enfield LBC* (1999), where a social worker was careless in implementing decisions made about a child in care. In *W and others v Essex County Council* (2000), the foster parents successfully sued where they had not been told by the social worker that the foster child had come into care for abusing his sister—a case similar to our case study in this chapter. These cases were distinguished from *X v Bedfordshire* on the basis that the facts in that case concerned the failure of the local authority to take children into care, which was a statutory responsibility which could not be ignored, and not the failure to carry out responsibilities in a particular way.

The House of Lords considered the extent of the duty of care of local authorities and the professionals it employs to carry out its statutory responsibilities in *Phelps v London Borough of Hillingdon* (2000). This case was the legal authority for the judge's decision in the case study at the beginning of this chapter. In *Phelps*, their Lordships make it clear that local authorities are liable for professional misjudgements by their staff; and where a duty of care arises between a professional and a particular child the professional can be sued if there is a breach of that duty.

You may be wondering about time limits for suing a local authority, given that a child who seeks to sue because social services are alleged not to have protected him or her probably will not be able to take action until adulthood. There is a normal three-year limitation period for personal (which includes psychological) injuries under the Limitation Act 1975, though time does not run until a person reaches adulthood. After that, time only starts to run when a person has actual knowledge of the injury caused, which may be years later in the case of suppressed memories of events in early childhood. Even after that, a court must exercise discretion: *A v Hoare* (2008).

Claims against social workers or agencies under the European Convention

We will be devoting half of the next chapter, **chapter 3**, to human rights questions, including the role of the European Court of Human Rights (ECtHR). For now, all you need to know is that individuals have the right to complain against the UK government at the ECtHR if they claim that their rights have been overridden within the UK. The judgment of the ECtHR in *Z and others v UK* (2001) (the name under which the *X v Bedfordshire County Council* case was taken to Europe) was that the English law on negligence was valid. However, the children's human rights had been breached and the law of negligence had not provided them with a way of getting a judgment in court; on that basis the court awarded the children substantial damages against the local authority. The authority's failure to remove the children from the home over a period of four and a half years, during which the children suffered emotional and physical abuse, meant that the authority had breached Article 3 of the Convention—'No one shall be subjected to torture or to inhuman or degrading treatment or punishment.' The failure of English law to allow the children to sue for breach of Article 3 was a breach of Article 13—'Everyone whose rights and freedoms as set forth in this Convention are violated shall have an effective remedy before a national authority notwithstanding that the violation has been committed by persons acting in an official capacity.'

What this means is that children can sue for breach of their Convention rights where there has been a failure to take appropriate preventive action, and can sue in negligence where local authorities have failed to act properly once the child is in care. However, it is only since the Human Rights Act 1998 that children can do so in English and Welsh courts. Of course there will be cases where the damage to children arose prior to the Human Rights Act. In such cases the only legal action available is to take the case direct to Strasbourg. *DP and JC v UK* (2003) and *E v UK* (2003) are examples of people claiming for breaches of their human rights inflicted on them decades previously.

This does not mean that social workers owe a duty of care to everyone who may be affected by their actions. The duty is only owed where, on the basis of the particular facts of a case, it is fair, just, and reasonable that such a duty should exist. This was made clear by the House of Lords in *JD v East Berkshire Community NHS Trust* [2005] UKHL 23. Here the parents sued health professionals for psychiatric harm caused by false allegations of child abuse committed by the parents against the children. The House of Lords decided that their complaint was non-actionable (they had no right to compensation). Health professionals responsible for investigating suspected child abuse did not owe the person suspected of having committed the abuse a duty if they carried out that investigation in good faith but carelessly. The court believed there were cogent public policy reasons for concluding that no common law duty of care should be owed to the parents, since the child's interests were paramount and in potential conflict with those of the parents. It would be inappropriate to have the important work of child protection hamstrung by the fear of litigation. In *Lawrence v Pembrokeshire*

County Council [2007] EWCA Civ 446 the appellant attempted to extend the ambit of negligence. She appealed against a decision striking out her claim in negligence against the local authority. It had placed L's children on the child protection register for about 14 months. The ombudsman upheld a number of complaints by L of maladministration by Pembrokeshire County Council and recommended that it should pay her compensation. L then issued proceedings in negligence against Pembrokeshire. L sought to challenge the reasoning of *JD v East Berkshire*, claiming that Article 8 called for an evolutionary change to the law of negligence where it overlapped with a parent's right to respect for family life. Her claim that the court should take a small incremental step beyond the East Berkshire decision was rejected. The Court of Appeal said that a 'small incremental step' was a step too far. The public interest in effective and fair investigation and the prevention of criminal behaviour had fashioned the common law to protect those suspected of it from malice or bad faith, but not from a well-intentioned but negligent mistake. There was a need to provide protection to those who had a duty to enforce the law in good faith from the imposition of a duty in negligence that could or might inhibit them in the effective fulfilment of that duty.

The social worker as statutory creation

Having considered what it means to be a professional social worker, we turn to the second identity of the social worker which we recognized at the beginning of the chapter, the social worker as a statutory creation.

Local Authority Social Services Act 1970

The principal Act imposing the social services function on local authorities (metropolitan boroughs and county authorities) is the Local Authority Social Services Act 1970 (LASSA). Social workers employed in local government, as we know them today, were effectively created by this Act. It is not an easy Act to understand. What it does is to establish the framework for local authority social work, and then refer you to all the other statutes that set out social work responsibilities (statutes dated both before and after 1970, since it is amended continuously). The modern social work professional role did not exist before this statute, and it is to this statute that you look to signpost your statutory powers and duties. Although there is plenty of room for good intentions, these do not define your role; the statute does. The statutes tell you who you have responsibilities towards, and to some extent define how those responsibilities shall be exercised.

Whatever the social services department does is supervised by the relevant Secretary of State. This is because s. 7 of LASSA provides:

> Local authorities shall, in the exercise of their social services functions, . . . act under the general guidance of the Secretary of State.

Section 7 also provides two other mechanisms to ensure that social services committees are accountable to their users and to the government. Section 7C provides for the

Secretary of State to set up inquiries into performance of functions and s. 7D provides for the Secretary of State to take over the running of the authority's functions.

You may remember that we discussed the complexity of devolution in **chapter 1**. Here is an example of the sort of differences which result. Section 7B which provided for complaints procedures was repealed *in England only* by the Health and Social Care (Community Health and Standards) Act 2003. Section 7B remains in force for Wales. While LASSA sets out the framework for the provision by the local authority of social care, it is not very specific about the particular way this is to be organized. For instance, it may or may not be of comfort to you to know that the only people within the social services department who actually warrant a specific mention in the Act are the directors of adult social services and directors of children's social services.

LASSA establishes the overall framework. Detailed specific duties, responsibilities, and powers are to be found in other relevant Acts such as the Children Act 1989, the Children Act 2004, or the Mental Health Act 1983. By and large, duties are placed by the legislation not on individual social workers but on the employing local authority. Children's guardians (formerly guardians *ad litem*) and Independent Reviewing Officers in child care work and approved mental health practitioners in mental health work, however, have duties imposed on them as individuals.

Further powers of the Secretary of State

Some of the specific legislative provisions which are listed in LASSA include the power for the Secretary of State to direct the local authority to take certain steps in relation to its social services function.

For example, under the Children Act 1989 there is a provision in s. 44(5) which deals with the exercising of parental responsibility once an emergency protection order has been granted. Paragraph (c) requires that the exercise of these powers 'shall comply with the requirements of any regulations made by the Secretary of State for the purposes of this subsection'. This subsection requires the Secretary of State to act by way of regulations, but in some cases the Secretary of State can act directly. For example, under s. 22, the general duty of the local authority to children can be overridden for the purposes of protecting members of the public from serious injury. By virtue of s. 22(7) the Secretary of State can tell the local authority what to do if there is a risk of serious injury. This may be applicable in the case of a child suspected of murder where the matter might become a case for public concern. The Secretary of State would have the politically useful power of being able to say 'I have directed the local authority to place the child in secure accommodation.' The Secretary of State must give any such direction in a rational and lawful manner. The former Director of Children's Services at Haringey Council successfully challenged the Secretary of State's direction to the local authority that she be sacked peremptorily for the failure to protect Baby Peter, [2011] EWCA Civ 642. The summary judgment says:

> We have allowed her appeal in relation to the Secretary of State's directions, having concluded that the Secretary of State did not afford Ms Shoesmith the opportunity to put her case. In short, she was denied the elementary fairness which the law requires . . . We rejected

a submission on behalf of the Secretary of State to the effect that the situation was too urgent to permit the adoption of a fairer procedure. Nor did we feel able to accept that the adoption of a fair procedure would inevitably have led to the same outcome.

The social worker as professional who complies with LASSA professional duties

In many ways this is the easiest identity to grasp. You are a professional social worker because of what you do. What you can (and the authority overall must) do is set out in the 1970 statute we mentioned above: LASSA. Schedule 1 sets out every statutory duty which a local authority must carry out. Although it does not specify that individual social workers carry out these duties, or even mention the social work profession, any local authority of necessity carries out these duties by employing social workers.

The 1970 legislation suffers from two major defects. First, it does not systematically organize and define social care services using any coherent framework or philosophy, or, in fact, any framework at all. It merely lists all the bits of all the existing statutes directing what local authorities do for children or for adults and states: this is what must be done. Second, as this list has been added to or amended over four decades, the collection of duties has become less and less coherent. The actual list covers enactments dating from 1933, which specify certain duties to assist children facing criminal proceedings. It sets out the most important sources of duties to adults which date back to 1948 and the beginnings of the welfare state. The 1989 legislation on children is, by comparison, recent. The list is constantly being tweaked, with duties frequently amended and occasionally added.

Box 2.1 gives a quick summary of some key areas of LASSA duties. Those duties which can be grouped under providing services to children in need, or protecting children, are considered in detail in Part 2 of this book. Those relating to adults are dealt with in Part 3. However, whilst these statutory functions are important, there is, as you are already becoming aware, far more law with which you have to be familiar.

The LASSA duties identify the service user, as well as providing the link to the statute which sets out in more detail how the needs for the service are to be assessed and provided. It would be nice, at this stage, to say that if a duty is not on this list, it does not exist. But there is a grey area where social service authorities have been given explicit duties without these creating a duty to provide a service to a service user. These mainly fall within the area of youth justice (**chapter 10**). It falls on social services to organize Youth Offending Teams, to send social workers to police stations when a child or vulnerable adult is being interviewed, to provide assistance to the court in deciding on sentence of children, and to assist in administering community sentences handed down by the courts. However, it is reasonably clear—though the link is not made explicit—that you can find a service user whose needs would otherwise fall into the LASSA list each time one of these responsibilities arises, either a child in need or a vulnerable adult.

BOX 2.1 Key statutory duties of the social worker

The Acts	Nature of the duties of local authority social services committees
Children and Young Persons Acts 1933 and 1963	Support for children involved in criminal prosecution
Children Act 1989	Support for children in need and to protect children at risk of significant harm
Adoption and Children Act 2002	Providing adoption services
National Assistance Act 1948	Providing care services in the community or residential care for those who cannot cope without such services
The Acts	Nature of the duties of local authority social services committees
Children Act 2004 (CA 2004)	Establishes a children's commissioner; reorganizes aspects of child protection work
Mental Capacity Act 2005	Appointment of independent advocates for patients
Children and Young Persons Act 2008	Strengthens the role of the Independent Reviewing Officer

The social worker as an employee with rights and duties

You have obligations, as does any employee, to do the best you can for your employer. This may produce conflicts arising in individual cases. As an employee you are legally required to follow the instructions of your employer. However, your employer has hired you because you are a professional, and the exercise of professional judgement is part—a major part—of your duties to the employer. We hope conflict occurs rarely, but it remains a real possibility.

In the event of irreconcilable conflict, you must do what the employer tells you to do, but this does not mean keeping quiet about your professional opinion. In fact, to express as your opinion a belief that you actually do not hold is itself a breach of your professional duty. If expressed in court it would be close to perjury (false testimony). It is, of course, rare that opinions differ in an irreconcilable way.

Accountability to your employer

Many social workers are concerned that they may be personally liable if they make mistakes. There is no doubt that if things go wrong you will have to explain your decisions. If you have taken reasonable care, kept your written records properly, and acted within an acceptable level of professional competence then you will be able to do this. If you do make a professional misjudgement there may be several consequences. First, the case may become the subject of an inquiry and you may be personally blamed in the report. Many feel that such an emphasis on individual social workers is unfair. The Laming Report on the death of Victoria Climbié made this point:

> It is not to the handful of hapless, if sometimes inexperienced, front line staff that I direct most criticism for the events leading up to Victoria's death. Whilst the standard of work done by those with direct contact with her was generally of very poor quality, the greatest failure rests with the managers and senior members of the authorities whose task it was to ensure that services for children like Victoria were properly financed, staffed, and able to deliver good quality support to children and families. (Para. 1.23)

Second, you are subject to the risk that you will be disciplined, and even dismissed, as a result of your mistake. The incompetent social worker will always take this risk. As Laming points out, the risk to you is almost always greater than the risk to senior managers.

Finally, as we saw earlier (**Professional accountability through the courts**, p 53), the person who suffers may be able to sue for compensation for the effects of your mistake. He or she is far more likely to sue the local authority than you, and even if you are sued you will be indemnified by your employer.

Confidentiality as an employee

We discuss in **chapter 4** the duty of confidentiality you have to service users and others. Social workers will also have duties of confidentiality which arise from their employment. If you breach a term of your contract then you may be disciplined, or even dismissed. Your trade union, professional association, or a lawyer experienced in employment law will have to advise you on procedure.

There may, however, be occasions when you would feel justified in breaching the requirement of confidentiality between you and your employer. For instance, a social worker may wish to disclose that the social services department is chronically understaffed or that a colleague is professionally incompetent. The BASW Code of Ethics may be of some assistance here. Paragraph 9 of the Ethical Practice Principles states:

> Social workers should be prepared to report bad practice using all available channels including complaints procedures and if necessary use public interest disclosure legislation and whistleblowing guidelines.

The responsibility is on the social worker to know the internal complaints procedures. Where these do not produce satisfactory results social workers should consult their trade union or professional association for advice. In the last resort, the Public Interest Disclosure Act 1998 may provide some assistance.

'Whistle-blowing' under the Public Interest Disclosure Act 1998 (as amended by the Enterprise and Regulatory Reform Act 2013)

The Public Interest Disclosure Act 1998 (PIDA) is designed to encourage people to raise genuine concerns about malpractice in the workplace by providing legal protection against dismissal or victimization. The motivation for the legislation is that workers are often aware of poor or dangerous work practices but are too scared to sound the alarm or do not know how to raise an issue. Examples of a reluctance to 'blow the whistle' can be found in social work inquiries. Since the implementation of the legislation, if a social worker makes a disclosure in good faith to a manager or an employer, he or she will be protected as a whistle-blower if he or she has a reasonable suspicion that the malpractice has occurred, is occurring, or is likely to occur. The Enterprise and Regulatory Reform Act 2013 (ERRA) amended the scope of the protection slightly by making it clear that any disclosure must be in the public interest. The Act also protects disclosures made in good faith to prescribed regulatory bodies where the whistle-blower reasonably believes that the information and any allegation in it are substantially true. Wider disclosures (eg to the police, the media, Members of Parliament (MPs), and non-prescribed regulators) are protected if, in addition to the test for regulatory disclosure, they are reasonable in all the circumstances and:

- they are not made for personal gain;
- the whistle-blower must have reasonably believed he or she would be victimized if he or she raised the matter internally or with a prescribed regulator; and
- reasonably believed a cover-up was likely and there was not a prescribed regulator, or had already raised the matter internally or with a prescribed regulator.

If the concern is exceptionally serious, a disclosure will be protected if it meets the test for regulatory disclosures and is not made for personal gain. The disclosure must also be reasonable, having particular regard to the identity of the person it was made to.

Where the whistle-blower is victimized in breach of the Act, he or she can bring a claim to an employment tribunal for compensation. The ERRA has amended the protection by enabling a tribunal to reduce any compensation awarded by 25 per cent if the disclosure was not made in good faith.

Your employer's responsibilities to you

Local authorities have responsibilities and duties towards you as their employee. The nature and volume of your work, with its associated risks of violence and abuse, place you under a great deal of stress. You have to balance individuals' needs with limited resources, and you are responsible for decisions which have significant implications for people's lives. In *Walker v Northumberland County Council (1995)*, where a social worker suffered a nervous breakdown as a result of stress, the court made it clear that all employers have a duty of care and a duty in contract to ensure that the employee is kept safe from psychiatric as well as physical harm. Local authorities which breach this duty may be liable to pay substantial compensation to social workers. In September 2001, headline news was made by a former social worker who received £140,000 damages in settlement of her claim against Worcestershire County Council for a stress-related illness developed through work. In *Gogey v Hertfordshire County Council (2001)*, a worker in a care home was suspended when concerns were raised about allegations of abuse made by a vulnerable child. The facts on which those concerns were raised were not clear. The court found that the local authority could suspend the worker only if it was 'reasonable and proper' to do so. So the law should protect you from excessive work pressure and being treated in an arbitrary manner. The Social Work Reform Board established a set of Standards for Employers and Supervision Framework following criticism explored in the Munro Report about social workers' excessive workloads. (The standards can be found at www.local.gov.uk/c/document_library/ get_file?uuid=8a333d13-8aa1-44d3-925a-a07682b07190&groupId=10180).

We now move to consider one important aspect of a social worker's relationship with service users—the need for consent or legal authority before taking action.

Lawful authority

Interference with another person's physical integrity, property, or affairs without their consent will be unlawful unless explicit legal authority is given. Examples of lawful authority in the absence of consent would be:

- a court order, for example a care or specific issue order under the Children Act 1989, a compulsory detention order under the Mental Health Act 1983, removal to residential accommodation under s. 47 of the National Assistance Act 1948, or a common law declaration of the lawfulness of carrying out medical treatment;

- an explicit police power, for example of arrest under the Police and Criminal Evidence Act 1984, a power to remove to a place of safety under the Mental Health Act 1983, or the Children Act 1989;

- powers to act for the benefit of an incapacitated person under the Mental Capacity Act 2005;

- power under s. 3(5) of the Children Act 1989 which provides that 'A person who (a) does not have parental responsibility for a particular child; but (b) has care of the child, may (subject to the provisions of this Act) do what is reasonable in all the circumstances of the case for the purpose of safeguarding or promoting the child's welfare';

- the power of the Department for Work and Pensions under social security legislation to appoint someone to apply for and receive benefits on another person's behalf, where this is in the interests of the claimant.

Alternatively, interference without consent would require implicit authority under previous court rulings, or explicit court authorization, for example:

- intervening as a matter of necessity to save life or prevent serious harm (permissible for medical treatment under the common law);

- other medical interventions including cessation of treatment and pain relief, for example if it is in the best interests of a terminally ill patient.

These two examples do not apply if the person has given advance directives or is presently able to give, or refuse, consent as to whether or not to be treated. If action is taken without consent or legal authority, the consequences could be criminal prosecution or civil liability for damages. Therefore in *Re B (Consent to Treatment: Capacity)* (2002) the Court of Appeal upheld the refusal of a woman with a deteriorating physical condition who made a deliberate choice to refuse artificial ventilation should her breathing deteriorate further. It was up to her to decide. The circumstances may not be so clear-cut. In *HE v A Hospital NHS Trust* (2003) the patient had given an advance directive that she did not wish to have a blood transfusion, but on admission to hospital it became clear that she was no longer a Jehovah's Witness and had not communicated any such desire prior to treatment. It was decided that she could be treated without consent as it was not proven that her wishes were, now, clearly opposed to such a transfusion.

▨ Social work ethics and consent

If there is no lawful authority enabling you to intervene then you must get consent for your actions. The ethical principle that every person has a right to self-determination and is entitled to their autonomy is set out clearly in the BASW Code of Ethics. In para. 2.12 of the Code, headed 'respecting the right to self determination', the Code sets out the following:

> Social workers should respect, promote and support people's dignity and right to make their own choices and decisions, irrespective of their values and life choices, provided this does not threaten the rights, safety and legitimate interests of others.

The principle is also enshrined in law, through the notion of consent. Actions taken without consent are unlawful, and in some circumstances criminal. They also breach the right to respect for private life under Article 8 of the Convention on Human Rights (see **chapter 3**).

We provide here a very brief outline of this difficult area of law. Most of the case law relates to health professionals, but the principles will be relevant to decisions which have to be made by social workers in relation to provision of services to children and adults. It is particularly important when you are asking a service user to consent to the sharing of confidential information.

Forms of consent

Consent may be express or implied. It is expressed when someone explicitly agrees to the action being taken. When a person signs a consent form in connection with the Data Protection Act they are consenting to the holding and using of personal information.

Implied consent is a more difficult concept. The person making the decision may from the circumstances deduce from a person's conduct their state of mind. An example is that when you participate in team sports you implicitly consent to the bodily contact, and risk of injury, that will almost inevitably arise. But if you are assaulted deliberately in the course of the game, you did not consent to that (unless the game is a form of fighting, such as boxing, where even severe injury will have been consented to).

Reliance on implicit consent, particularly to the sort of interventions in personal autonomy which arise in the course of social care, is probably not a wise course of action. Interestingly, following the cases involving retention of children's organs for many years for research purposes without explicit consent of the bereaved parents, guidance has been issued for hospitals, which must now obtain clear and detailed consent from families for post-mortem examinations of their relatives. Times have changed, and the assumption amongst the medical research profession that the parents would have given consent and did not need to be asked would now be seen as patronizing and plainly wrong. There have also been successful claims for psychiatric distress caused—for example, *AB and others v Leeds Teaching Hospital NHS Trust and another* (2004).

The nature of consent

Lawful consent has three qualities. First, the person must have the capacity or competence to consent; second, he or she must have sufficient information to enable them to give informed consent; and, third, consent must have been given voluntarily. Our main concern will be with the question of capacity.

What must be understood?

Clearly if the law requires a total understanding of all of the implications of the decision then few people are going to have legal capacity to consent. Before consenting to surgery a patient will not need to be provided with the research papers in which risk is analysed, and need not be capable of forming a useful judgement even if these were provided; but the patient is entitled to be informed of the nature and broad extent of risk of a particular type of complication, rather than being told merely not to worry. If the patient cannot understand at that general level, informed consent is not possible.

The Mental Capacity Act 2005 sets out to enable most people to make most decisions for themselves. Under s. 3(1) a person is able to make a decision for him or herself if able to manage the following:

(a) to *understand* the information relevant to the decision;

(b) to *retain* that information;

(c) to *use* or weigh that information as part of the process of making a decision; and

(d) to *communicate* his or her decision.

The level of understanding can vary according to the situation: a woman about to lose her child through refusing a clearly medically indicated caesarean, where her own and the child's lives are otherwise at great risk, was considered not really able to understand the decision she was making, and therefore her refusal of consent was not an informed refusal and could be overruled by a court: *Bolton Hospitals NHS Trust v O* (2002). The difference in this case and that of *Re B* (see **Lawful authority**, p 61) may have been the fact that the life of the unborn baby was also at risk. It is hard to see any evidence that the woman did not clearly understand and accept that she was risking her life and that of her baby, and the decision that she did not understand appears to have been a fig leaf to get round the implications of letting both of them die when this tragedy could be so easily avoided.

Actual understanding or ability to understand?

This is another difficult question which the law provides no clear answer to. It would be logical to require actual understanding, but then if the social worker or the doctor failed to provide sufficient information the person would be deprived of their capacity to consent. In *Gillick*—the leading case on the capacity of children to make informed decisions—the judges stated that what was important was that someone was capable of understanding the decision, and the gravity of the situation should be taken into account. In *Re L (Medical Treatment: Gillick Competency)* (1998) the court required actual understanding because of the consequences of a refusal of consent. Here the life of a 14-year-old girl was in danger as a result of serious and extensive burns. She was a practising Jehovah's Witness and refused to consent to the medical treatment as it might have required a blood transfusion. The court decided that what was required was actual understanding of the decision. The doctor had not explained to her the nature of the death she would endure if she did not undergo medical treatment. Because of that the court was able to decide that she did not have actual understanding of the decision and was therefore not competent to refuse the treatment. Her consent to receive the treatment, by contrast, would not have had such grave consequences and would probably have been sufficient, even against her parents' objections (though not had she been, say, aged 8, where a court order would have been necessary, if there was time to obtain it, to overcome her parents' refusal to consent on her behalf).

However, in the case of an adult, to override clear wishes is unusual. It can happen, for example, in the case of the woman in childbirth (**What must be understood?**, p 63), where the problem was temporary and urgent, and, in the opinion of the court, the woman could not at the time understand the consequences of what she was deciding. In *Malette v Shulman* (1991) a woman refused a blood transfusion and the court accepted this, and it inevitably led to her death. Interestingly, this same woman's refusal to consent before she turned 18 had been overruled and she had been treated under the court's consent, not her own.

Establishing competence to provide consent

We stated earlier that you need to start with the assumption that adults are competent. Legal authority for this comes, for example, from *Re T (Adult: Refusal of Treatment)* (1992). Section 8 of the Family Law Reform Act 1969 additionally provides that children aged between 16 and 18 are presumed competent. However, for both adults and 16–18-year-olds the presumption of competence is rebuttable. And the decision in the *Gillick* case means that the 1969 Act does not exclude under-16-year-olds from providing consent to their own treatment or, in principle, from refusing consent to treatment. An assessment of the child's competence is required in each case, and that assessment will vary according to the decision in question (as we discussed earlier when considering the gravity of a refusal of consent to a blood transfusion: **Actual under-standing or ability to understand?**, p 64).

Competence to refuse treatment

There are a number of extremely clear statements that a competent person has freedom of choice, 'whether the reasons for making that choice are rational, irrational, unknown or even non existent' per Lord Donaldson in *Re T*, cited in **Establishing competence to provide consent**, p 64. The principle was revisited by Dame Elizabeth Butler-Sloss in the well known case of *B* to which we referred in **Lawful authority**, p 61. Ms B, who had become completely paralysed following serious illness, sought declarations from the High Court that continued artificial ventilation against her wishes was unlawful. The judge was satisfied that Ms B was competent to make all relevant decisions and granted the declarations.

It should not be assumed that refusal of treatment is only possible where a person has no mental health problems. Each situation must be weighed up. In *Re C* (1993) a mental patient had gangrene, but refused treatment. The court decided, on the evidence, that he knew enough about the issues to refuse amputation and take the risk. As it happens, his leg recovered. Similarly in *Re W (Adult: Refusal of Medical Treatment)* (2002) a prisoner with severe psychosis wanted a transfer to a different hospital. To draw attention to his complaint, he cut his leg open repeatedly and forced foreign matter into the wound. He then refused treatment for the infection. The court refused an order to allow him to be treated. He clearly understood what he was doing and could not be treated against his will.

However, there are many situations with adults and children where competence to refuse treatment is found to be lacking. Competent children cannot, in general, withhold consent. In *Re R* (1991), the Court of Appeal held that although an anorexic 16-year-old girl could be said to be '*Gillick* competent', that fact did not prevent the court ordering that she be given drugs against her will. The court, in a much criticized decision, drew the distinction between the ability of the girl to give consent and her right to refuse consent. It said that while she could give valid consent, if she refused this did not mean that others such as parents or the court could not still impose consent on her behalf.

The court said:

> The failure or refusal of the 'Gillick competent' child is a very important factor in the doctor's decision whether or not to treat, but it does not prevent the necessary consent being obtained from another competent source.

Similarly, in *Re W (A Minor) (Consent to Medical Treatment)* (1993), the Court of Appeal again overrode the refusal of an anorexic to accept treatment. The notion of a competent child involves limited competence. The courts consider that the welfare of the child is not something to be decided solely by the child. The welfare of the child can be decided by others, particularly the court.

Refusal of consent also raises problems for adults—for example, the refusal to undergo a caesarean, which the court overruled (see **What must be understood?**, p 63). *NHS*

Trust v T (Adult Patient: Refusal of Medical Treatment) (2004) provides another example of particular interest because the patient had given a clear advance directive at a time when her mental competence was reasonably clear. She self-harmed to such an extent when in a state of temporary psychosis that she required frequent blood transfusions. Her advance directive stated that she knew the consequences of refusal, and she nevertheless did not consent to future transfusions. She believed her blood to be evil, though she acknowledged in her advance directive that this was a manifestation of her illness. She claimed in the directive that she had sufficient understanding of her situation and her illness at the time of making it to be able to refuse consent. Knowing the situation would arise again, the hospital which treated her applied in advance for court guidance. The judge used guidelines from an earlier case (*Re MB (Medical Treatment)* (1997)) which are helpful to repeat here:

1 Every person is presumed to have the capacity to consent to or to refuse medical treatment unless and until that presumption is rebutted.

2 A competent woman who has the capacity to decide may, for religious reasons, other reasons, for rational or irrational reasons or for no reason at all, choose not to have medical intervention, even though the consequence may be the death or serious handicap of the child she bears, or her own death. In that event the courts do not have the jurisdiction to declare medical intervention lawful and the question of her own best interests, objectively considered, does not arise.

3 Irrationality is here used to connote a decision which is so outrageous in its defiance of logic or of accepted moral standards that no sensible person who had applied his mind to the question to be decided it could have arrived at it . . . it might be otherwise if a decision is based on a misperception of reality (e.g. the blood is poisoned because it is red). Such a misperception will be more readily accepted to be a disorder of the mind. Although it might be thought that irrationality sits uneasily with competence to decide, panic, indecisiveness and irrationality in themselves do not as such amount to incompetence, but they may be symptoms or evidence of incompetence. The graver the consequences of the decision, the commensurately greater the level of competence is required to take the decision . . .

4 A person lacks capacity if some impairment or disturbance of mental functioning renders the person unable to make a decision whether to consent to or to refuse treatment. That inability to make a decision will occur when:
   (a) the patient is unable to comprehend and retain the information which is material to the decision, especially as to the likely consequences of having or not having the treatment in question;
   (b) the patient is unable to use the information and weigh it in the balance as part of the process of arriving at the decision. If, as Thorpe J observed in *Re C* [see earlier in this section], a compulsive disorder or phobia from which the patient suffers stifles belief in the information presented to her, then the decision may not be a true one. As Lord Cockburn CJ put it in *Banks v Goodfellow* (1870): '. . . one object may be so forced upon the attention of the invalid as to shut out all others that might require consideration'.

5 The 'temporary factors' mentioned by Lord Donaldson MR in *Re T* [**Establishing competence to provide consent**, p 64] (confusion, shock, fatigue, pain, or drugs) may completely erode capacity but those concerned must be satisfied that such factors are operating to such a degree that the ability to decide is absent.

6 Another such influence may be panic induced by fear. Again, careful scrutiny of the evidence is necessary because fear of an operation may be a rational reason for refusal to undergo it. Fear may also, however, paralyse the will and thus destroy the capacity to make a decision.

Balancing individual autonomy with welfare

When acting for children the position is clear. Section 1(1) of the Children Act provides that:

> When a court determines any question with respect to—
> (a) the upbringing of a child; or
> (b) the administration of a child's property or the application of any income arising from it, the child's welfare shall be the court's paramount consideration.

'Upbringing' under the Act will include decisions about social or health care where for any reason parents cannot make this decision themselves. These are dealt with under s. 8 and are further discussed in **chapters 8–11**.

In cases involving children, respect for autonomy involves not only that of the child, but also that of the parent. The tension between autonomy and welfare can be seen, taking a case involving children, in *South Glamorgan County Council v W and B* (1993). Here Douglas Browne J was faced with the problem of a young person who clearly was beyond parental control. She was aged 15. She had refused to do anything she was told. She had, in fact, barricaded herself in the front room of her father's house for 11 months. The local authority wanted an interim care order to have the child assessed. The difficulty was the provisions in s. 38(6) of the Children Act 1989 which deal with the court's powers to make orders for assessments to be carried out when making interim care orders (see **chapter 8**). This particular subsection has provision for informed consent by the young person, stating 'but if the child is of sufficient understanding to make an informed decision he may refuse to submit to the examination or other assessment'. The local authority and those acting for the girl put the view to the court that if she refused to submit to the assessment then there was little that anyone could do. The judge would not accept this and gave directions under the inherent power of the court (s. 100) for the authority to remove the child. In effect, he bypassed the provisions of the Act relating to informed consent. He did this without making the girl a ward of court. He said:

> In my judgment the court can in an appropriate case—and they will be rare cases—but in an appropriate case, when other remedies within the Children Act have been used and exhausted and found not to bring about the desired result, can resort to other remedies, and the particular remedy here is the remedy of providing authority, if it is needed, for the local authority to take all necessary steps to bring the child to the doctors so that she can be assessed and treated.

Re B (Wardship: Abortion) (1991) illustrates the range of issues which can arise when balancing autonomy with welfare. A 12-year-old girl was pregnant. She herself consented to abortion and was supported by her grandparents. Her mother refused. The local authority and several medical witnesses thought aborting the foetus would be in the girl's best interests, physically and emotionally. The mother's experts thought the opposite. The court had to decide, and decided in favour of a termination. The welfare rather than consent issues were uppermost, though what the child herself wanted influenced the assessment of what would also be in her best interests.

Legal representation of children

There have been a number of cases concerning the ability of children or young people to appoint guardians or solicitors to act on their behalf. In *Re S (A Minor)* (1993), the Court of Appeal held that a child of 11 could not remove the Official Solicitor as guardian. The court said:

> The 1989 [Children] Act enabled and required a judicious balance to be struck between two considerations. First was the principle, to be honoured and respected, that children were human beings in their own right with individual minds and wills, views and emotions, which should command attention. Second was the fact that a child was, after all, a child.

In *Re H (A Minor) (Care Proceedings: Child's Wishes)* (1993), the court said a 15-year-old did not have the right to address the court on his own behalf. This decision is implicitly supported by a more recent decision of the Court of Appeal in *Re W (Children)* (2008). The children clearly wanted to go with their mother to Sweden, but the judge hearing the application had refused to allow them to be taken out of the jurisdiction. Their mother's appeal was on the basis that the judge had refused to interview the children directly. The Court of Appeal thought this would not be a good course of action, though they did agree that the judge's decision itself was wrong. These were three *Gillick*-competent children who very clearly expressed to the court what they wanted, and it was wrong not to give their views considerably more weight.

In *Re N (Contact: Minor Seeking Leave to Defend and Removal of Guardian)* (2003), an 11-year-old child was refused leave to be a party in s. 8 contact proceedings (see **chapter 5** for an explanation of these) because the judge concluded he did not have sufficient understanding to participate in the proceedings. The judge could perceive no advantages in allowing a child of this age to be a full party to the proceedings, rather than participate through the court-appointed guardian.

These cases point to a view that, despite the apparent philosophy of legislation and statements supporting the right of children of understanding to participate in the decisions which concern them, and increasingly to make those decisions, the court retains the right to make the difficult decisions for itself, and, if it feels it must, to substitute its view for that of the child or young person. They appear to be particularly reluctant to allow a child to decide to participate in adversarial litigation. The *Gillick*-competent child is therefore only a competent person in a very limited sense.

Representation of adults

Family members may claim to speak for the adult, but there may be a conflict of interest. In straightforward litigation where there is no conflict—for example, a personal injuries claim following an accident—appointment of a litigation friend on behalf of an adult lacking capacity to conduct the proceedings is relatively straightforward. But where complex decisions have to be made about what is in the adult's own interests and whether he or she has capacity, a court will generally appoint the Official Solicitor to represent the adult's interests in the case.

Proxies

If people are not competent then decisions have to be made for them and others must act as proxies for them.

For children, those people are generally parents. Each parent or other person with parental responsibility is able to exercise the right to consent individually. However, there may be a duty to consult the other parent in relation to major decisions. In the absence of agreement between parents, the courts may impose a limitation on the power of one parent to take the decision: for example, a decision to change a child's surname will require the approval of the court if the parents cannot agree. In *Re J (Child's Religious Upbringing and Circumcision)* (1999) it was held that ritual circumcision did not fall within the power of one parent to consent to, where there was disagreement between the parents.

As you will see (in **chapter 8**) local authorities may acquire parental responsibility under Part IV of the Children Act. This enables them to consent to treatment etc on behalf of the children. Parents retain parental responsibility, but if a care order is made the local authority is allowed to restrict the exercise of that authority—see **chapter 8**.

The Children Act also provides for a further possible proxy. Section 3(5) provides:

A person who—
(a) does not have parental responsibility for a particular child; but
(b) has the care of the child,
may (subject to the provisions of this Act) do what is reasonable in all the circumstances of the case for the purpose of safeguarding or promoting the child's welfare.

Teachers or grandparents are able to make necessary decisions with the authority of this provision.

The court is also a decision-maker on behalf of children. The High Court has jurisdiction as part of its inherent jurisdiction, and family proceedings courts in respect of s. 8 orders. We consider the power of the courts to make 'specific issues' orders and 'prohibited steps' orders in **chapter 5**.

All proxies must make decisions consistent with the welfare, or best interests, of the child.

The Mental Capacity Act 2005

The Mental Capacity Act 2005 provides a comprehensive framework for assessing whether a person of 16 and over has capacity to make decisions, and making lawful an action to benefit the person who does not have capacity. The principles are very clearly stated in s. 1:

(2) A person must be assumed to have capacity unless it is established that he lacks capacity.
(3) A person is not to be treated as unable to make a decision unless all practicable steps to help him to do so have been taken without success.

(4) A person is not to be treated as unable to make a decision merely because he makes an unwise decision.

(5) An act done, or decision made, under this Act for or on behalf of a person who lacks capacity must be done, or made, in his best interests.

(6) Before the act is done, or the decision is made, regard must be had to whether the purpose for which it is needed can be as effectively achieved in a way that is less restrictive of the person's rights and freedom of action.

A 'person *lacks capacity* in relation to a matter if at the material time he is unable to make a decision for himself in relation to the matter because of an impairment of, or a disturbance in the functioning of, the mind or brain'. The problem can be temporary—the decision has to be made according to the issue that has arisen at a particular time.

The Act talks in terms of hypothetical figures D (the person intervening) and P (the person whose capacity is being considered). For our discussion, we limit it to social worker and service user, though please do not conclude that the Act is limited to this context. Anyone—benign relative, passerby, doctor, etc—is protected if they act on behalf of another person without consent under the terms of this Act.

The social worker who decides a service user lacks *capacity to make a decision* is protected if, at the time, and on the balance of probabilities (which means that something is more likely than not) the service user is 'unable to understand the information relevant to the decision, [or] to retain that information, [or] to use or weigh that information as part of the process of making the decision, or to communicate his decision (whether by talking, using sign language or any other means)'.

Actions taken must always be in the best interests of the service user. This is based on all the circumstances, but in particular 'whether it is likely that the person will at some time have capacity in relation to the matter in question, and if it appears likely that he will, when that is likely to be'. This means that there is no point acting now if there is a good chance the service user will have capacity for him or herself to take the necessary action later. Even though lacking capacity, the service user must, as far as possible, 'participate, or to improve his ability to participate, as fully as possible in any act done for him and any decision affecting him [in the light of] the person's past and present wishes and feelings [and] the beliefs and values that would be likely to influence his decision if he had capacity', and must consult if appropriate 'anyone named by the person as someone to be consulted on the matter . . . anyone engaged in caring for the person or interested in his welfare . . . any donee of a lasting power of attorney granted by the person' (we discuss these in **chapter 14**).

The result of going through this checklist is that if the social worker 'reasonably believes that what he does or decides is in the best interests of the person concerned' he or she is acting lawfully, so long as the actions which follow are neither negligent nor criminal, and are compliant with the terms of any advance directive (see **chapter 14**). The powers to act include physical restraint and payment out of the service user's available funds for goods and services. We strongly suggest taking legal advice in advance of taking such steps, unless physical restraint is needed in an emergency.

▓ Working with lawyers

Lawyers, like social workers, have a professional identity. They belong to a professional body—the Law Society or the Bar Council dependent upon whether they are solicitors or barristers—and are bound by a code of conduct. The code of conduct for solicitors, however, focuses on less complex dilemmas, such as not acting for people where you have a conflict of interest, and having to hold money that belongs to clients in a separate account from your own money. This is because lawyers have a more straightforward relationship with their clients than you have with the service user. If the lawyer and the client disagree on what is the best course of action then the client can sack the lawyer. The child or vulnerable adult who is your service user does not have that freedom.

Lawyers are originally not creations of statute; they are creatures of the market, though you will perhaps be reassured to know that the law now regulates them closely. There has always been a demand for lawyers to interpret the law and to argue for an interpretation which best suits the client who is paying them. This is not to say that the individual lawyer does not have ideals; indeed, the prime motivation for working in social welfare law is an idealistic one, since other areas of law pay far more. However, being a lawyer does not in itself require an idealistic vocation, perhaps in contrast with the social worker. If there is an overarching ideal it is perhaps best expressed as a commitment to the rule of law, which includes the right of all to have the best professional help to argue their case on an equal footing.

Lawyers also have different skills from social workers. Their skills lie in the interpretation of complex statutes and cases and in defending the interests of their clients through negotiation and advocacy.

However, it is probably at the quite different level of their view of the world that the essential difference between the social worker and the lawyer is seen most clearly. Social workers want what is best for the service user, which is not always the same as what the service user actually wants; lawyers are interested in achieving for the client what he or she wants, and the question of whether it should be what they want is wholly irrelevant. This is best illustrated by an incident involving one of our colleagues, a lawyer. When she was working at a law centre she was approached by a 16-year-old woman clutching the hand of a 35-year-old man. The young woman explained that she was in care and she wanted to marry her boyfriend. Our colleague explained the legal process of getting permission from the magistrates. Our colleague was then telephoned by the young woman's social worker, who was outraged at the advice. Marrying the boyfriend was not in the best interests of the young woman, in the opinion of the social worker, and therefore it was inappropriate to advise her how to go about it. Our colleague was perplexed; she considered she was only doing her job. The social worker was perplexed; the lawyer did not understand the best interests of the young woman. Our opinion is that both of these roles are important. When there are two conflicting sets of wants, the lawyer's role is to represent one, not both, sides. The lawyer does so within a framework which prevents any invention of evidence, any collusion in crime, or any attempt to mislead an opponent or a court. The lawyer should also help a client to reach an informed decision before acting on the client's instructions. So there is still a lot of professional responsibility and scope for some personal concern. But it does not go so far as telling the client she cannot do what she is legally entitled to do. The social worker in that situation should not have criticized the lawyers. She or he could and should have got advice from their own lawyer on what legal measures—if any—were available to protect this child's welfare.

 EXERCISES

1 Consider the following three perspectives on social work:

(a) The Department of Health gives the following guidance about the nature of social work on its careers website (http://webarchive.nationalarchives.gov.uk/20130107105354/http://www.dh.gov.uk/prod_consum_dh/groups/dh_digitalassets/@dh/@en/documents/digitalasset/dh_4127770.pdf):

> You form partnerships with people, helping them to assess and interpret the problems they face and supporting them in finding solutions.

> Sometimes you provide the service itself—you are advocate, guide, hand-holder, or critical friend. Other cases are complex and require carefully organised and communicated 'packages of care' that can include doctors, nurses, lawyers, police, court officials, probation workers among others. Whatever the situation, you need to know how the law works, what services are available and how to put them to best advantage on behalf of your client.

> You have certain legal powers and duties which are in place to protect people who cannot protect themselves, for example someone with a mental illness who is a danger to themselves or to others, or a child who is at risk of abuse.

(b) On the other hand, the Quality Assurance Agency, which specifies the standards which apply for social work degrees (see www.qaa.ac.uk/en/Publications/Documents/Subject-benchmark-statement-Social-work.pdf), acknowledges at para. 4.3 that:

> There are competing views in society at large on the nature of social work and on its place and purpose. Social work practice and education inevitably reflect these differing perspectives on the role of social work in relation to social justice, social care and social order.

(c) The British Association of Social Workers contains the following statement in its code of practice (para. 4.1.1):

Priority of service users' interest

Social workers will:

a Give priority to maintaining the best interests of service users, with due regard to the interests of others;

b In exceptional circumstances where the priority of the service users' interest is outweighed by the need to protect others or by legal requirements, make service users aware that their interests may be overridden;

c Seek to safeguard and promote the rights and interests of service users whenever possible;

d Endeavour to ensure service users' maximum participation in decisions about their lives when impairment or ill health require the social worker or another person to act on their behalf;

e Not reject service users or lose concern for their suffering, even when obliged to protect themselves or others against them or to acknowledge their inability to help them.

In the light of the duties set out in LASSA, which include intervention in people's lives, do you think your role is about justice, care, or social order? See the Online Resource Centre for our thoughts on this.

2 A neighbour reports the Lee family to social services because of fears for the welfare of the children. You are admitted to the home by Jasmine Lee and discover the following.

(a) Her daughter Susan Lee, aged 13, appears anorexic and seriously underweight. She also has an unrelated skin disorder. Her mother does not want her to receive treatment for either condition. Susan would like treatment for the skin disorder but does not accept that she suffers from anorexia.

(b) Mrs Lee's mother-in-law, Selina Lee, is aged 75 and speaks no English. Jasmine Lee indicates that her mother-in-law is suffering from serious mental health problems and asks you to take her to a specialist unit for assessment. Mr Lee says he does not want you to take his mother anywhere and he is quite capable of deciding what is best for her.

What are the principles involved in relation to issues of consent to treatment or assessment?

3 A decision of the Court of Protection (www.guardian.co.uk/society/2012/jun/15/anorexic-woman-fed-judge?newsfeed=true) to force-feed a 32-year-old woman with anorexia without her consent caused controversy. How is it possible to override lack of consent in such a case? Do you agree with the judge's decision?

4 Ms C, the parent of two children who were sexually abused by a neighbour's child, wants to sue the local authority. She claims that she is suffering from psychiatric illness which is the result of the local authority's failure to act upon her concerns about the safety of her children. When she reported her concerns about the possibilities of sexual abuse, the local authority did not believe her and asked the social worker allocated to the abuser's family to investigate her complaints. Will the courts allow her to pursue her claim?

 ONLINE RESOURCE CENTRE

For guidance on how to answer these exercises, visit the Online Resource Centre at www.oxfordtextbooks.co.uk/orc/socialwork13e/.

 WHERE DO WE GO FROM HERE?

This chapter builds upon **chapter 1**, which introduced you to the legal system. Here we have considered the relationship between the social worker and the law by identifying the multiple roles of the social worker and by demonstrating how the law, alongside ethics, determines each of those roles. We hope that this has provided an interesting introduction to your studies.

We may have given an impression that law and ideals are opposites. It is true that we have suggested that you should—indeed must—be guided by the powers and duties as laid down by law. If this might blunt your enthusiasm, we hope that **chapter 3** will show that law can be a vehicle for social change and the realization of ideals. We will be examining the Human Rights Act 1998 and follow this with an introduction to the legislation protecting people from inappropriate discrimination. These laws have changed, and are changing, the nature of our society. They require you, as a person working in a public authority, to respect individual rights including the right not to be discriminated against unlawfully.

 ANNOTATED FURTHER READING

Quality Assurance Agency, 'Social work' subject benchmark statement (2008) www.qaa.ac.uk/en/Publications/Documents/Subject-benchmark-statement-Social-work.pdf—a full analysis of the standards to be achieved in social work education.

Code of Ethics of the British Association of Social Workers, www.basw.co.uk—a comprehensive analysis of the standards of professional social work practice, including respect for human rights of service users, obligations to society, and issues concerning use of compulsory powers.

S. Nathanson, *What Lawyers Do—A Problem Solving Approach to Legal Practice* (Sweet & Maxwell, 1997)—if you want to look at the world through a lawyer's spectacles, this is readable and informative. Don't worry that it may be out of date; the core issues covered don't change.

J. Dickens, 'Risks and responsibilities—the role of the local authority lawyer in child care cases' (2004) *CFLQ* 16(1): 17. This article discusses key sticking points in the relationship between local authority lawyers and social workers. It suggests that awareness of each other's multiple and competing responsibilities will improve inter-professional relationships.

R. Bailey Harris and M. Harris, 'Local authorities and child protection—the mosaic of accountability' (2002) *CFLQ* 14(2): 117. This article, although now some years old, is particularly helpful in unravelling a difficult area of law. For a more recent analysis, see the 'Rights versus Duty' (2007) *New Law Journal* 157: 1002–3.

J. Morrell and R. Foster, *Local Authority Liability* (Jordan, 2009) has useful chapters covering liability for social service functions.

We recommend getting into the habit of looking at—and acquiring—the texts of the major pieces of legislation relevant to your area. All legislation likely to affect social workers is collected together in the loose-leaf *Encyclopedia of Social Services and Child Care Law* (published by Sweet & Maxwell and updated regularly), together with rules, regulations, circulars, and text. We use it a lot and recommend it to you too.

Human rights law

3

The Human Rights Act 1998 (HRA) and the Equality Act 2010 have created a framework which to some extent pervades all other law. Human rights legislation, particularly that derived from the European Convention on Human Rights (ECHR), applies to the government and its employees and to other 'emanations of the state' and their employees—including social services departments and hence social workers. This chapter comes early in the book because the principles we set out here underpin your practice as social workers. You may need to return to it as you become more familiar with the legal complexities of your work.

Look at this list of some of the main human rights enshrined in the ECHR. Consider how they might impact on your work, your relations with clients, and decision making as a social worker (some answers will be given later in the chapter):

- Article 2, right to life;
- Article 3, prohibition of torture and inhuman treatment;
- Article 5, right to liberty and security;
- Article 6, right to a fair trial or 'fair and public hearing within a reasonable time';
- Article 7, no punishment without law;
- Article 8, right to respect for private and family life;
- Article 9, freedom of thought, conscience, and religion;
- Article 10, freedom of expression;
- Article 13, right to an effective remedy 'notwithstanding that the violation has been committed by persons acting in an official capacity';
- Article 14, prohibition of discrimination in the application of human rights;
- Protocol 1 Article 1, protection of property and 'peaceful enjoyment of possessions'.

In some cases these rights are qualified rights; they come with a second part indicating that a breach may not be unlawful if it is prescribed by law and 'necessary in a democratic society in the interests of public safety, for the protection of public order, health or morals, or for the protection of the rights and freedoms of others'. So it might be necessary, for example, to restrain a person, contrary to the Article 5 right to freedom, for their own good or the safety of others. But such detention must be sanctioned by law and occur only after the legal procedures have been undertaken.

Article 13 has an important warning for social workers as for any state employee given authority over another person: you are not above the law simply because you have that authority. You must exercise it within the law even when you consider your decision to be for the good of the client or for the general good.

This means that you must know what powers you have in particular circumstances and should consider their use in the light of the human rights implications. It would be wise to record exactly how you arrived at a decision that might prove controversial, how you balanced necessity against rights. Courts will respect thought-out decisions and proper procedures and give due weight to fair decision making even in cases where breaches have occurred.

The first part of this chapter outlines how the HRA works, and indicates its impact on the work of a social worker. Some consideration is given to how the Conservative Party's policy of repealing the Act after the 2015 election might affect legal access to human rights. The second part of the chapter examines the protections provided by the Equality Act 2010. It is a little artificial to separate out human rights in general from equality law in particular, but that reflects the way the legislation is framed in England and Wales.

CASE STUDY

R (on the application of Johns) v Derby City Council (2011)

Mr and Mrs Johns were members of the Pentecostalist Church and believed that sexual relations other than those within marriage between one man and one woman were morally wrong. They applied to the local authority to be short-term foster carers. The local authority considered that Mr and Mrs Johns' views on same-sex relationships did not equate with the government's National Minimum Standards for Fostering Services, which required carers to value individuals equally and to promote diversity. The couple's application was considered by the local authority's fostering panel, which deferred a decision. The argument of the couple, who had fostered before, was that they should not be considered unsuitable to be foster carers solely because of their views. The local authority's response was that it could lawfully decide not to approve prospective foster carers who were unable to respect, value, and demonstrate positive attitudes towards homosexuality and same-sex relationships. Mr and Mrs Johns applied for a judicial review—a court's ruling on whether a public authority is acting lawfully. They argued that:

(1) the local authority's consideration of their Christian beliefs was an irrelevant consideration in the context of their application to become foster carers;

(2) the local authority's position constituted religious discrimination contrary to Article 9 of the ECHR;

(3) it was unreasonable for the majority of the population to be excluded from possible fostering because of their Christian beliefs.

The High Court refused to grant permission for judicial review.

(1) It held that the attitudes of potential foster carers to sexuality were relevant when considering an application for local authority approval. The *Statutory Guidance on Promoting the Health and Well-Being of Looked-After Children* issued under s. 10 of the Children Act 2004 (and under review in autumn 2014) provided that support in relation to the sexual health of looked-after children should be provided regardless of the children's sexual orientation and 'should not be affected by individual practitioners' personal views'. If children, whether they were known to be homosexual or not, were placed with carers who objected to or disapproved of homosexuality and same-sex relationships, there might be a conflict with the local authority's duty to safeguard and promote the welfare of looked-after children. There might also be a conflict with the National Minimum Standards and the 2009 Statutory Guidance. Religion, belief, and sexual orientation were protected characteristics under ss. 4, 10, and 12 of the Equality Act 2010. While there was no hierarchy of rights as between the protected rights concerning religion and sexual orientation, there might be a tension between equality provisions

concerning religious discrimination and those concerning sexual orientation. Where that was so, Standard 7 of the National Minimum Standards and the Statutory Guidance suggested that the equality provisions concerning sexual orientation should take precedence. Standard 7.1 said: 'The fostering service ensures that children and young people, and their families, are provided with foster care services which value diversity and promote equality.' (This wording has been removed from the latest 2011 version of the Standards: www.gov.uk/government/publications/fostering-services-national-minimum-standards.) The local authority was entitled to have regard to the extent to which prospective foster carers' beliefs might affect their behaviour and their treatment of a child being fostered by them. If it had failed to make a judgement on those matters it might have found itself in breach of its own guidance and of the National Minimum Standards and the Statutory Guidance.

(2) The local authority's rejection of Mr and Mrs Johns would not be less favourable than that afforded to other persons who, for reasons other than their religious views, expressed objection to, or disapproval of, homosexuality and same-sex relationships (in other words, they were being legitimately rejected for the effect their views might have, not because of their religion). Compliance with anti-discrimination legislation prohibiting sexual orientation discrimination and with the local authority's equal opportunities policies to the same effect would justify any indirect discrimination (ie apparently discriminating against a religion because of legitimate concerns about the views its adherents might hold). Article 9 of the Convention only provided a *qualified* (not absolute) right to manifest religious belief, and interferences with that right were found to be justified in employment and analogous areas, even where the members of a particular religious group would find it difficult in practice to comply. That would be particularly so where a person in whose care a child was placed wished to manifest a belief that was against the interests of the children. By applying for approval as foster parents, Mr and Mrs Johns had agreed to subject themselves to the National Minimum Standards.

(3) It could not be argued that an examination of the attitudes to homosexuality of a person who had applied to be a foster carer was '*Wednesbury* unreasonable' (meaning unreasonable according to the legal definition in the case of *Associated Provincial Picture Houses Ltd v Wednesbury Corporation* [1948] 1 KB 223: 'So outrageous in its defiance of logic or accepted moral standards that no sensible person who had applied his mind to the question to be decided could have arrived at it'.

WHAT DOES THIS CASE TELL YOU ABOUT SOCIAL WORK PRACTICE?

A reading of this case study demonstrates that human rights are not necessarily absolute and may be contradictory. If one person's right (eg to express religious views) might override another's right (eg to be brought up in a household sympathetic to his or her gender or sexuality issues), the law will probably require a balancing of respective claims. What you learn here is how the law might carry out the necessary balancing exercise. The claimants' religious views require respect and consideration, but they did not prevail because, on balance, they did not outweigh other considerations—including the National Minimum Standards and the Statutory Guidance. These require other values to be respected (those of diversity) and also the health (sexual and psychological) of any children who might be fostered with a couple.

This judgment was not uncontroversial (see the *Daily Mail*, 'Christian beliefs DO lose out to gay rights', 28 February 2011), and another message from this case is that the decisions of social workers about individual clients can be intensely political. Conservative voices objected to the undermining of Christianity implied by the judgment. Significantly perhaps, the Standard 7.1 wording of the Department for Education's National Minimum Standards on diversity no longer appears in the 2011 version. Instead, under the heading 'valuing diversity through individualised care' Standard 2.1 simply says: 'Children are provided with personalised care that meets their needs and promotes all aspects of their individual identity.' The word diversity is not mentioned anywhere else in the document. Additionally, all mention of the words equality, gender, religion, ethnic origin, language, culture, disability, and sexuality have been removed. (Note: the Welsh government, with devolved powers over social services, retained the old version of the Minimum Standards including the Standard 7 wording quoted in the court case.)

All this makes decision making for social workers in cases like *Johns* very difficult. Should you act according to the letter of the 2011 judgment and reject fosterers with strong religious views against homosexuality? Or can you assume that the new, less-specific wording would change a court's view, that a new context has been set by the government in order not to discourage religious people from fostering? The decision is all the harder given that a social worker cannot predict whether the issue would come up—whether any child will be gay and hence might at a future date have a grievance over his or her fostering. The important point, as noted in the introduction to this chapter, is that you must be able to prove that you considered the issues and came to a reasonable, proportionate, and balanced decision—following legal advice where necessary. Keeping records and following procedures is crucial.

Human rights law

By the end of this part of the chapter you will have some familiarity with:

- the origins of the ECHR;
- the extent of Convention rights;
- the legal mechanisms for enforcing human rights in England and Wales;
- the relevance of human rights for your practice as a social worker;
- some idea of how Conservative policy might change the situation.

The background to the European Convention on Human Rights 1950

The ECHR was framed in 1950 after the Second World War to prevent a repeat of the oppression of individual rights in the name of the state seen in Germany and other Fascist and Nazi countries in the 1930s. As Lord Justice Sedley put it in his lecture for the Legal Action Group in 2003:

> The Convention is a child of its time—the post-war years when the states of western Europe tried to set their faces both against the devastation of the recent past and against any new

form of totalitarianism. So the Convention says many important things about due process, personal integrity and free speech and ideas; but nothing directly about the most elementary of all human needs, a right to enough food and shelter to keep body and soul together.

(Lord Justice Sedley, Legal Action, December 2003, p 19)

British lawyers were actively involved in the drafting of the Convention, which was designed to give legal force within Europe to the principles set out in the United Nations Declaration of Human Rights of 1948. The UK signed the ECHR in 1951 and the Convention became binding upon its signatories in 1953. However, the UK for many years refused to incorporate the Convention into its domestic law. Enforcement of its provisions was via the European Court of Human Rights (ECtHR) in Strasbourg— an expensive, drawn-out process with minimal redress (including relatively small fines)—and not through the domestic courts.

The Human Rights Act 1998 was implemented on 2 October 2000. Its primary purpose is to enable individual Convention rights to be enforced through the UK courts, and to provide a legal check based on human rights principles on the activities of the government and public bodies. Parliament is, in effect, required to pass only 'Convention-compliant' legislation, meaning not at odds with the rights enshrined in the ECHR in the light of Strasbourg jurisprudence (ie as interpreted by cases that have been before judges at the ECtHR).

The HRA, crucially, allows courts to judge administrative actions not merely on the basis of English common law 'Wednesbury unreasonableness' but also on the more European legal principle of proportionality: what is the harm or 'mischief' that the government or public authority (including local social services) is seeking to deal with and is the method used proportionate to that harm? 'Wednesbury reasonable' means a decision 'no sensible person who had applied his mind to the question to be decided could have arrived at'—which allows the public authority or employee a fair range of decisions that some or even many people might think unreasonable. Indeed, a decision one way might be Wednesbury reasonable—but so might a completely opposite decision about exactly the same issue. The proportionality test is in many cases a stricter test than Wednesbury—giving authorities less leeway in their decision making. In effect, they must balance competing issues and make the best decision—not merely a reasonable one.

The HRA:

- requires judges in UK courts when interpreting new or already existing law to 'take account' of the ECHR and Strasbourg jurisprudence—s. 2(1);

- requires legislation to be interpreted in a way that is compatible with the Convention rights 'so far as it is possible to do so'—that is, 'expansively' but without stretching the meaning of words too far—s. 3(1);

- if it cannot do so, it allows the court to make a 'declaration of incompatibility'—a legal statement that a piece of UK primary legislation (that has passed through the full parliamentary procedure and been signed into law by the monarch) is at odds with Convention law—s. 4(2). The government should then change the law by passing new legislation through Parliament (using a Remedial Order that requires only limited parliamentary oversight rather than a new Act)—but how it changes the law is up to Parliament, not the judges.

Courts can quash secondary (delegated) legislation that it finds non-compliant. Secondary legislation includes statutory instruments (Orders in Council, Regulations, Rules, and Orders) containing amendments to statutes or details or updates added to them and also regulations issued by the government with minimal parliamentary input but under the authority of a piece of primary legislation. They can also be struck down by the courts if they are held to be ultra vires—beyond the powers Parliament intended when giving a minister the powers to issue such orders under the primary legislation (enabling Act).

Statutory guidance (which includes various codes of practice: see **chapter 1**) is another form of delegated legislation that may be quashed by courts. As HH Judge Anthony Thornton has noted: 'Statutory guidance is issued with statutory authority and it must therefore be complied with unless local circumstances indicate exceptional reasons to justify a departure from it in a specific case'—*R (RB & CD) v London Borough of Haringey* [2013] EWHC 416 (Admin). However, it may be challenged on human rights grounds—which raises the possibility that a practitioner is at liberty *not* to follow it if there is a human rights reason not to do so.

One compendium of guidance available to social workers is *Working Together to Safeguard Children*, issued by the government. Remarkably the 2013 edition makes no reference to the ECHR or the HRA—or, indeed, 'human rights' at all. The previous 2010 version made clear that the guidance was grounded in human rights, particularly Articles 6 (right to a fair hearing) and 8 (family and private life). It required those who chair child protection conferences to have 'knowledge of relevant legislation, including that relating to children's services and human rights'; and on data sharing it noted: 'No request should require a record holder to breach data protection principles, or other protections of confidential or personal information (for example, under the Human Rights Act) in a manner which cannot be justified'. Whether the new version is a precursor to a possible Conservative government's repeal of the HRA (see **The Conservative critique of human rights law**, p 96) or not, human rights should remain at the core of your thinking as a social worker.

Human rights controversies

Opinions differ about the appropriateness of a human rights culture at the beginning of the 21st century. In particular, Labour and Conservative-led governments have suggested that human rights cannot work in the context of the so-called war on terror. Indeed, the government has the right to derogate (which means withdraw) from certain human rights obligations such as the ban on imprisonment without trial to deal with serious threats to security. In addition, most rights are conditional and may be breached if there is sufficient reason to do so. The ban on torture and inhuman treatment, however, has no such qualification.

Former House of Lords (Supreme Court) judge Lord Steyn has noted:

> A constitutional democracy must protect fundamental rights. It is morally right that the state
> and all who act on its behalf in a broad functional sense, should respect the fundamental

rights of individuals. Without such a moral compass the state is bound to treat individual arbitrarily and unjustly.

(Lord Steyn, '2000–2005: Laying the Foundations of Human Rights Law in the United Kingdom' [2005] European Human Rights Law Review 4: 349)

Social workers may be confronted with just such dilemmas: necessity on the one hand (the urgent need to deal with a problem); and the danger of acting arbitrarily (without legal authority and without reasoned justification) on the other. Again, the emphasis must be on being able to set out your reasons for making your decision including understanding what powers you have and the discretion within those powers as well as the limitations they impose. This, after all, is best practice for the social work profession and following best practice will often be the best defence against human rights claims.

An example of the issues social services might face was the case of a social services department that put a camera in the bedroom of a couple with learning difficulties to assess whether they were fit to look after their baby (reported by the British Institute of Human Rights, 'The Human Rights Act—Changing Lives', 2008). Social services may place such parents in residential family centres and even use closed circuit television (CCTV) to help them to make a judgement. But can this include monitoring them while they are in bed together? The aim of the monitoring (the benefit of the baby) must be balanced against the clear breach of Article 8 privacy and family rights—surveillance of a couple in the most intimate circumstances. The council was eventually persuaded to turn off the bedroom camera when a friend of the couple cited the ECHR.

Such cases show that, although the human rights of suspected terrorists and prisoners tend to attract public attention (and controversy), the most significant impact of the HRA has been its effects on the ordinary lives of ordinary people—among them the clients of social workers. Perhaps one example will illustrate this. In *R (Bernard) v Enfield LBC* (2002), the High Court considered the application of Mrs Bernard, a severely disabled woman who lived with her family in inappropriate local authority accommodation. Social services assessed her needs and recommended special adaptations to the accommodation so that, for instance, she could access the toilet easily (she was doubly incontinent and hence frequently soiled herself) and gain a measure of privacy (six children lived in the small house and her bedroom was in fact the first-floor living room which was accessed directly through the front door and gave access to the stairs). The local authority failed to respond to the family's needs as assessed. The High Court found that the local authority had positive human rights obligations to enable the family to live as normal a life as possible and to secure Mrs Bernard's physical integrity and human dignity—meaning they had an obligation to act to achieve her rights under Article 8 of the ECHR ('everyone has the right to respect for his private and family life'). The lack of action by the local authority was a breach of Mrs Bernard's right under the Convention, though a claim under Article 3 ('no one shall be subjected to . . . inhuman or degrading treatment') was rejected despite the deplorable consequences of the local authority's inaction. Article 3 was conceived in terms of authoritarian states torturing or imposing other inhuman treatment. The judge in this case, Mr Justice Sullivan, did not wish to extend it to non-malevolent acts of a local authority: 'The claimants' suffering was due to the defendant's corporate neglect and not to a positive decision by the defendant that they should be subjected to such conditions.' However, it is not clear that a Strasbourg judge would necessarily come to the same conclusion when there is a clear responsibility and clear neglect.

Article 8 itself was originally conceived as seeking to curtail state interference with private family life but here and elsewhere it is interpreted more widely as a duty on the local authority 'to take positive measures to secure respect for private or family life' (Mr Justice Sullivan, the judge in the case). The local authority's actions 'condemned the claimants to living conditions which made it virtually impossible for them to have any meaningful private or family life for the purposes of [Article 8]'.

It should be noted that there was also a breach under s. 21(1)(a) of the National Assistance Act 1948, the duty to house those in need due to illness or disability. Often social workers may face legal action on the basis of specific legislation as well as under a wider human rights rubric.

The extent of human rights

In this part of the chapter we will consider some concepts that underpin the workings of the ECHR and discuss the contents of the Articles of the Convention. We start by considering who can take proceedings under the Act, and against whom.

Victims

Only victims of breaches of Convention rights (with their legal representatives) can bring proceedings under the HRA. So only the person who has been affected by an act or by the decision of (generally) a public authority, including the government, local authorities, the NHS, police, and any state body, can take action, in relation to that act or decision. This means that pressure groups cannot initiate legal proceedings, though they can help individual victims to pursue their case. Under the emerging doctrine of 'horizontality' there are opportunities for people to take action against private organizations too because the courts (which constitute a public body) must interpret laws to be in conformity with the ECHR since 'it is unlawful for a public authority to act in a way that is incompatible with a Convention right' (HRA, s. 6). Courts have, for example, imposed privacy obligations on the press by interpreting the common law principles of confidentiality in the light of Article 8 of the Convention. See, for example, *Campbell v Mirror Group Newspapers* [2004] 2 WLR 1232 in which the supermodel Naomi Campbell won a breach of privacy claim thanks to Article 8 even though in English law, for private individuals, there was 'no over-arching, all-embracing cause of action for invasion of privacy' (Lord Nicholls).

Public authorities

Generally a victim brings a case under the Act if the act or decision in question is one of a public authority. A public authority is a body carrying out a governmental or public function. Local authorities and their social services departments are public bodies. Other examples include schools, departments of central government such as

the Home Office, hospitals, and prisons. Private companies that exercise public functions, such as organizations that run private prisons which are also public authorities
under the Act. In the case of private residential homes, however, the government had
to pass legislation to ensure they complied with the Convention after the House of
Lords (Supreme Court) ruled in 2007 that they were not carrying out a public function.
(See *YL v Birmingham City Council* (2007) in **Box 3.1**.)

Some bodies have mixed public and private functions. Many housing associations,
for instance, carry out functions that courts may decide are public functions but other
functions would clearly be private functions. It is difficult to provide clear guidelines
on whether a housing association is or is not a public authority for the purposes of
HRA claims. In *Donaghue v Poplar Housing and Regeneration* (2002) the court decided
that because the housing association had a particularly close relationship with and
was performing very similar functions to a local authority, it was a public authority for
the purposes of human rights legislation. However, in *R (Heather) v Leonard Cheshire
Foundation* (2002), the charity, which provided residential care, was held not to be a
public authority. A decision in this area was made by the House of Lords in June 2007,
and concerned the scope of the HRA and the private provision of care. We set out the
detail in **Box 3.1**.

 BOX 3.1 *YL v Birmingham City Council* **(2007)**

An 84-year-old person with Alzheimer's lived in a private care home run by the care company
Southern Cross. She was facing eviction because of what was said to be the bad behaviour of
her family when they visited her. Medical opinion was that the person would be put at considerable risk if she were moved. Lawyers for the woman, known as YL to protect her privacy,
issued proceedings arguing that eviction would be a breach of YL's human rights regarding
respect for family life (Article 8—see **Summary of the Convention rights**, p 86). The House of
Lords decided by a 3–2 majority that the provision of care services by a private body did not
engage the provisions of the HRA, even in circumstances, as here, where a public body was
paying the fees of the service user after assessing that she was in need of care because of
her condition. This seems to contradict s 6(3) of the HRA, which says: 'In this section "public
authority" includes—. . . (b) any person certain of whose functions are functions of a public
nature'. However, the Act also says at s. 5: 'In relation to a particular act, a person is not a public authority by virtue only of subsection (3)(b) if the nature of the act is private'. Care homes
look after people paid for privately as well as those subsidized by the state.

Lord Scott explained: 'Southern Cross is a company carrying on a socially useful business
for profit. It is neither a charity nor a philanthropist. It enters into private law contracts with the
residents in its care homes and with the local authorities with whom it does business.' The
main contractual relationship was with the family of YL. The home was not 'publicly funded'
any more than any organization charging the government or local authorities fees for services,
and it had no special statutory powers. Since the ECHR applies to public bodies, not private, its
provisions did not apply to the care home.

This case highlights the limits of the HRA. Where a service is provided by a private organization, even though the provision is publicly funded, individual victims of bad treatment could not claim the protections of the ECHR. They are limited to their private law remedies, breach of contract for example. In 2008 the law was amended to deal with situations like YL's. The Health and Social Care Act 2008 says at s. 145(1): 'A person ("P") who provides accommodation, together with nursing or personal care, in a care home for an individual under arrangements made with P under the relevant statutory provisions is to be taken for the purposes of subsection (3)(b) of section 6 of the Human Rights Act 1998 (c. 42) (acts of public authorities) to be exercising a function of a public nature in doing so.'

The Care Act 2014 extends the HRA to all care homes whether or not privately run—even if a resident was placed by their family rather than a local authority. It also extends the HRA to care provided in a person's own home: 'personal care in a place where the adult [is] receiving the care'. We discuss the implications of this in Part 3.

Margin of appreciation

This is a technical term which has lost some clarity in its translation from French. What it means is that the ECtHR will allow domestic courts some space to make decisions which reflect their national domestic concerns, rather than impose its interpretation on the way the Articles should operate. This is particularly relevant when the courts have to weigh up competing priorities, for instance individual liberty and national security. Of course, the margin of appreciation can only go so far; the ECtHR does ensure some consistency in the interpretation of the Convention though it rejects the notion that it is a final appeal court, saying:

> The role of the Court is not one of final court of appeal or 'fourth instance'. Therefore, the main responsibility of ensuring the rights provided in the Convention rests with the Member States, and the role of the Strasbourg organs is limited to ensure whether the relevant authorities have remained within their limits.

('The Margin of Appreciation', Council of Europe)

Lord Hope has described the situation thus: 'By conceding a margin of appreciation to each national system, the court [ECtHR] has recognised that the Convention, as a living system, does not need to be applied uniformly by all states but may vary in its application according to local needs and conditions'—*R v DPP, ex p Kebilene* (2000).

Rights can be absolute, limited, or qualified

Rights are formulated in different ways under the Convention. Some rights are so fundamental that they are absolute. These rights include the right to protection from torture, inhuman and degrading treatment, and the prohibition on slavery. Others, such as the right to liberty, are limited under explicit and finite circumstances that are set out in the Convention itself. Finally, certain rights are qualified which means that interference with these rights is permissible only if the interference is:

- prescribed by law;
- done with a permissible aim set out in the Convention; and

- necessary in a democratic society, which means that it must fulfil a pressing social
  need, pursue a legitimate aim, and be proportionate to the aims being pursued.

Proportionality is a particularly important requirement. Interference with rights is not
justified if the means used to achieve a legitimate outcome are disproportionate.

Examples of qualified rights are the right to respect for private and family life and the
right to freedom of expression. We can illustrate what we mean by qualified right by
looking at the wording of Article 8 which sets out the right to respect for private and
family life.

Paragraph 1 describes the right:

> Everyone has the right to respect for his private and family life, his home and his
> correspondence.

Paragraph 2 sets out its limits:

> There shall be no interference by a public authority with the exercise of this right except
> such as is in accordance with the law and is necessary in a democratic society in the inter-
> ests of national security, public safety or the economic well being of the country, for the
> prevention of disorder or crime, for the protection of health or morals or for the protection
> of the rights and freedoms of others.

This leaves considerable discretion to the judges. They must exercise the discretion in
the light of previous decisions of the Strasbourg Court and the body of human rights
case law built up in this country.

Summary of the Convention rights

The full text of the Convention rights, which are included within the HRA, can be
accessed directly via www.legislation.gov.uk/ukpga/1998/42/contents. We provide you
with relevant extracts where it is important within later chapters. The key rights are summarized in the following paragraphs, with recent examples to illustrate their working.

Article 2 establishes a right to life. This could be relevant to a social services department which failed, for example, to protect a child who is killed by an abusive parent,
or if there is a failure to properly investigate any such death.

Example: *Re OT* (2009). A baby had developed serious complications shortly after birth.
By the age of nine months the brain stem had atrophied and breathing was sustained
only by a ventilator. He could not suck or swallow so feeding was via a gastric tube.
The hospital sought an emergency order that they could cease providing care, saying
it was not in the baby's own interests to receive it. The parents opposed the application, both on the basis of the child's right to life, and the fact that their own right to
a fair trial under Article 6 (see later in this section) meant this should not proceed as
an emergency application. The High Court noted that the right to life under Article
2 was not absolute and to prolong it in breach of the baby's best interests was wrong.
Withdrawal of treatment was lawful with a court order, and the parents' involvement
in these proceedings gave them a fair hearing.

Example: *Anna Savage v South Essex Partnership NHS Foundation Trust & MIND* (2007). The claimant's mother, a known suicide risk, absconded from detention in a hospital and killed herself. It was held that the patient's right to life meant that she was entitled to be looked after in a way that would not have allowed her to abscond. Her right was breached because 'a duty to take steps to prevent a particular patient from committing suicide arises if the authorities know or ought to know that there is a real and immediate risk of her doing so'. The state and its organs have a positive obligation to protect life.

Example: *R (on the application of Verna Wilson) v Coventry City Council* [2008] EWHC 2300 (Admin). The closure of a care home may engage the right to life, particularly where the resident is old and in a state of advanced dementia. HH Judge Pelling QC said that 'it was accepted before me that Article 2 is capable of applying to a council considering the closing of a care home. Article 2 imposes a positive obligation to take appropriate steps to safeguard the lives of relevant persons.' But here medical evidence as to whether moving a resident may increase mortality was found to be inconclusive. The council was aware of the potential risk and took measures to examine it, considering a fair summary on the medical literature regarding the risks. The judge noted that 'as a matter of law, the local authority is obliged to undertake individual assessments before deciding to move individual residents' and the council did so. The claimant had to prove 'the authorities did not do all that could reasonably be expected of them to avoid a real and immediate risk to life of which they have or ought to have knowledge'. This was not established.

Article 3 is the right not to be subjected to torture or inhuman or degrading treatment, and could be relevant to social workers' duties to protect children and perhaps vulnerable adults from abuse or, in extreme cases, failure of the state to provide economic support. As noted, this is an absolute right and cannot be violated under any circumstances. The issue therefore becomes: is the conduct complained of sufficiently serious to constitute torture or inhuman or degrading treatment? Lawyers describe this as reaching the necessary threshold to engage the Article. We have seen already in *R (Bernard) v Enfield LBC* (2002) that the judge was unwilling to consider non-malevolent treatment as falling within the definition even though the outcome was degrading for the complainant. Severity of the treatment is also an issue. In *A v UK* (1998) the ECtHR stated that: 'ill-treatment must attain a minimum level of severity if it is to fall within the scope of Article 3. The assessment of this minimum is relative: it depends on all the circumstances of the case, such as the nature and context of the treatment, its duration, its physical and mental effects and, in some instances, the sex, age and state of health of the victim.'

Example: *R (on the application of A & B) v East Sussex County Council* [2003] EWHC 167 (Admin). A and B were young sisters who suffered learning disabilities and impaired mobility requiring assistance by their carers for many simple movements such as getting out of bed. Their mother and stepfather and the council differed about how far this assistance should be given by manual handling or by use of equipment—preferred by East Sussex (ESCC). The court considered the 'legality of what is said to be ESCC's policy of not permitting care staff to lift A and B manually'. The claim was that the ban on manual handling 'improperly failed to take into account the needs of the disabled people involved' but also that it amounted to degrading treatment.

The council cited a requirement in s. 2(1) of the Health and Safety at Work Act 1974 'to ensure, so far as is reasonably practicable, the health, safety and welfare at work of all his employees'. Mr Justice Munby saw Article 3 engaged in safeguarding (with Article 8) the right to respect for physical and mental integrity, particularly for vulnerable persons. Munby considered the case law pointed to an increasingly strict application of Article 3 (ie shifting against public bodies) as the protection of human rights improves. 'Changes in social standards demand better provision for the disabled if their human dignity is not to be impaired.' So he suggested: 'Article 3 might well be engaged, for example, in circumstances where the consequences of failing to lift A or B manually might result in them remaining sitting in bodily waste or on the lavatory for hours, unable to be moved.'

A council must decide its policy on manual handling but guided by the law. 'A lifting policy is most unlikely to be lawful which either on its face [ie in its wording] or in its application imposes a blanket proscription of all manual lifting' or allows it only in exceptional circumstances such as where other means are impossible or a life is in danger. So it would be wrong, for example, to restrict the number of times the sisters could go out shopping, swimming, or horse-riding because manual handling was required, perhaps because the hoist was not working.

This is a crucial point in human rights law: very often a blanket policy decision, however reasonable it may seem, is the wrong decision because a balancing exercise has not been done (the health and safety issue balanced against the dignity and rights of the disabled person) and a disproportionate answer has been arrived at (a blanket ban that goes too far to achieve its end, such as health and safety). Again human rights principles are also good social work practice principles: a proportionate response to the problem after balancing the competing issues. Munby pointed out that the court cannot write the manual handling policy but can guide its principles: 'Plainly, in a case such as this, there is a margin of appreciation and the court must afford some degree of deference to ESCC's assessments.'

Munby's view about the probable increased intensity with which Article 3 is imposed on public bodies seems to be at odds with Sullivan J in *R (Bernard) v Enfield*. Munby said 'thoughtless, uncaring and uncharitable actions can be quite as damaging and distressing to the victim as the vicious, wilful or malicious'. He seeks to extend the concept of 'torture' or degrading treatment into the ordinary and day to day; Sullivan is unwilling to do so unless there is a malevolent act. Often judges differ in their approaches and UK case law has tended to follow Sullivan rather than Munby. Dignity, or 'physical and psychological integrity', is held to be protected by the qualified rights of Article 8 (family life) rather than the unqualified rights of Article 3 (torture, etc). While this allows more leeway for public authorities, it does not allow them to avoid making the balancing considerations and the duty to act proportionately. This must be reflected in their policies.

Article 5 provides a right to liberty and security. This means that a person can be detained only following a proper, lawful procedure, and must have a speedy right to challenge any detention. This Article has led to a change in the procedures for detaining people who lack mental capacity which we will discuss further in **chapter 14**.

Example: *Dorset County Council v EH* [2009] EWHC 784 (Fam). EH was living in her own home, but at 84 and with diagnosed Alzheimer's, was also largely out of touch with the real world. She did not seem to have capacity to consent to going into a care home and did not wish to be moved. The Court of Protection declared, and the High Court confirmed, that the best interests test applied—but there was conflict about what her best interests were. The Official Solicitor (who acts on behalf of those lacking capacity) argued that moving her to a home would deny her autonomy; but to stay at home put her at risk of cold, malnutrition, and fire. The courts found on balance that it was lawful to move her to and detain her in a particular care home (in other words, deprive her of liberty as an exception to Article 5), but because the evidence suggested she could be managed without physical restraint, powers of physical restraint were not included.

Example: *P v Cheshire West and Chester Council* and *P&Q v Surrey County Council* [2014] UKSC 19. A person without capacity to give consent may be placed in a residential home without her permission albeit probably in her best interests and albeit that the living arrangements may be 'benevolent', as Lady Hale called them in this case. This Supreme Court case established that in effect and in law such a placing is deprivation of liberty and hence falls within Article 5. But, of course, this does not make it unlawful—as long as it is justified and 'in accordance with a procedure prescribed by law'. It may seem odd to declare residential homes or fostering to be a form of prison, at least for those residents incapable of giving consent to be there, but the practical result is that the resident gains certain rights beyond a simple assessment of best interests. As Lady Hale said: 'the deprivation has to be authorised, either by a court or by the procedures known as the deprivation of liberty safeguards [DoLS], set out in the Mental Capacity Act 2005'. DoLS are examined in **chapter 14**. Basically they require a local authority to examine whether deprivation of liberty is in the best interests of the individual, whether it is proportionate, and whether there is a reasonable alternative. In the *Surrey County Council* case sisters with learning disabilities were removed from their home to protect them from sex abuse. (Their mother and stepfather were later convicted of sex attacks on their half-sister.) One child (MIG, who had less serious learning difficulties) was successfully fostered and the other (MEG) placed in an NHS residential facility. When they reached 16 and 17 their case came before the Court of Protection (which has jurisdiction over people aged 16 or over, whereas a family court cannot make a care order once a child has reached 17: Children Act 1989, s. 31(3)). In 2010 Mr Justice Parker decided their living arrangements were in their best interests and did not amount to a deprivation of liberty.

Hale, however, pointed to the Strasbourg judgment in *Austin v UK* (2012) 55 EHRR 14 where it was said that an underlying public interest motive 'has no bearing on the question whether that person has been deprived of his liberty . . . The same is true where the object is to protect, treat or care in some way for the person taken into confinement, unless that person has validly consented to what would otherwise be a deprivation of liberty'. Although Strasbourg had not considered cases where the individual was placed without objecting 'in a small group or domestic setting which is as close as possible to "normal" home life', Hale said: 'We should not let the comparative benevolence of the living arrangements with which we are concerned blind us to their essential character if indeed that constitutes a deprivation of liberty.' Deprivation of liberty is one issue; justification is a separate one that then has to be considered. Benevolent and justified deprivation of liberty, without consent, remains deprivation of liberty. The person concerned 'was under continuous supervision and control and was not free to leave'. The issue then becomes: is it legal deprivation of liberty?

In the case of MEG 'the staff did exercise control over every aspect of her life. She would not be allowed out without supervision, or to see people whom they did not wish her to see, or to do things which they did not wish her to do'. For MIG 'her foster mother and others responsible for her care exercised complete control over every aspect of her life.' The deprivation is ultimately the responsibility of the state (even with a foster parent) so Article 5 is engaged. The proper safeguards (the DoLS regime) should be in place in order to render that deprivation of liberty lawful. Furthermore, periodic independent checks should be made to ensure the arrangements made for them remain in their best interests.

This case is important for social workers since it provides a means of analysing a situation that goes beyond saying: this is in their best interests; it must be right. If, instead, you use a two-step process, looking first at the potential breach in ECHR provisions (here Article 5 on liberty) and then how that breach can be rendered lawful, you will, all being well, avoid what would be an arbitrary decision (in the sense of lacking legal authority), albeit intended to be benevolent.

Example: *London Borough of Hillingdon v Steven Neary and others* [2011] EWHC 1377 (COP). The Steven Neary case shows how far things can go wrong if social workers fail to get the balance right between an urgent necessity and an individual's human rights. This is examined in detail in **chapter 14** on DoLS. In brief, Steven had been held 'in his own interests' in a support unit against his own and his father's wishes for a year.

Hillingdon had issued Deprivation of Liberty authorizations to its Adult Social Services Department, designed under the Mental Capacity Act 2005 to bring deprivation of liberty within the law, in particular Article 5 of the ECHR. However, the Court of Protection found the local authority had breached Article 5 and Article 8 (right to family life). The following principles (looked at in more detail in **chapter 14**) can be taken from the case:

- your assessment of best interests is not enough to deprive someone of their liberty;
- a case should be approached on the presumption that liberty is better than deprivation of liberty;

- this presumption may be rebutted by good evidence with independent, objective oversight of that evidence;

- the authorizing body must approach the matter objectively, itself preferring liberty over deprivation of liberty rather than rubber-stamping a decision of social workers;

- effective review must be built in and this must take on board the individual's desires and those of the family or another interested party;

- an Independent Mental Capacity Advocate must be appointed at the appropriate time to represent the individual;

- if disagreement remains, the local authority cannot leave it to the individual or interested parties to take the matter to court; it must be proactive to ensure Article 5(4) rights of a speedy hearing.

Article 6, right to a fair hearing, refers to the requirement for civil rights to be fairly determined, and criminal trials to contain full safeguards. The basic right is to a fair and public hearing within a reasonable time by an independent and impartial tribunal established by law. The way you conduct case conferences and make decisions about use of your statutory powers, particularly in relation to children, can also be challenged under this Article. In other words, it does not just apply to formal legal hearings in tribunals and courts but constitutes a right to a fair hearing whenever an issue arises that might have a legal effect.

Example: *C (Children)* [2009] EWCA Civ 959. A divorced mother had formed a relationship with a man against whom she also made a number of allegations of violence and emotional abuse, including of her young children, and who had a conviction for assaulting a previous partner. As part of the plans agreed following an interim care order, the children would continue to live with her and there would be no contact with this former partner. After a tip-off, social workers visited unannounced, to find the partner and another man (following an initial denial by the mother) in a caravan, and the children responding violently to social workers. They removed the children. They had statutory powers, because of the interim care order, but the mother alleged a proper considered decision was required under Article 6. The court agreed that it was, but the greater the emergency, the less the formality required. In this situation, a proper evaluation had taken place on the spot, the mother had—even under extreme emotional pressure—put her viewpoint forward. Additionally, the matter came to court the next morning for further directions and was under court review thereafter before a full interim care hearing a few weeks later.

Article 8 provides a right to respect for family life and private life; any interference with this right must be lawful, necessary, and proportionate. Much of social work with children involves the use of compulsory powers, or the possibility of their use if other support fails. If the interference is carried out within the legal framework the first test for interference—lawfulness—is satisfied. It is unlikely that you will fall foul of the second test—was the interference necessary?—because the Children Act, which is where most of your powers reside, requires a court to be satisfied that the interference was in the interests of a child. But there are some actions taken within other legal frameworks which also interfere with privacy or family life—for example, placing a child on an 'at-risk' register. These actions are lawful, but because they are not sanctioned by a court, your department and those who participate in the decision making must be satisfied that, on balance, the action was necessary and the procedure for making the decision fair under Article 6. Article 8 is probably the most important Article you will encounter.

Example: *C (Children)*, in the example for Article 6, involved consideration of Article 8. Removal of the children was in interference with the right to respect for the family life of the mother, but it was lawful (the children were subject to an interim care order) and proportionate.

Example: *Bury MBC v D* [2009] EWHC 446 (Fam). The court hearing took place as the mother was in labour. The local authority wanted a declaration that it would not be a breach of the mother's human rights to take immediate steps to remove the child as soon as it was born. (No order could be obtained in advance of the birth, because the Children Act does not cover unborn children.) They had not told the mother about their plans to do so. Her first child had already been made the subject of a care order. The mother held the view that if she could not be with her children, they would be better off dead. The local authority thought that if they discussed their intentions with her before the birth it would lead her to self-harm or to harm the child as soon as it was born.

Such secretive planning to remove a child once born engaged the right to respect for family life, and would normally not be justified, but the judge was satisfied that in the circumstances the secrecy was proportionate and justified.

Example: *Louisa Watts v UK* [2010] ECHR 793 (Strasbourg). Mrs Watts, aged 106, claimed her removal from a home that was to be closed breached Articles 2, 3, 6, 8, and 14 (on discrimination). On Article 8 her claim was 'the move represented an unjustified interference with her private and family life'. The court found Article 8 engaged, but there was no suggestion that the move was not sanctioned by law; it was in pursuit of a legitimate aim (councils might be criticized for *not* closing dilapidated homes); and the interference with family or private life was proportionate to that aim. It was noted that Wolverhampton City Council had consulted with Mrs Watts before moving her. It was willing to place her with friends at a nearby home. The council did not overstep the 'margin of appreciation' allowed to signatories to the Convention in terms of pursuing social and economic policies. Her claim under the other Articles was also rejected.

Article 14 prohibits discrimination in the enjoyment of Convention rights. The grounds for discrimination are very broad; the Article forbids discrimination on any ground such as sex, race, colour, language, religion, political or other opinion, national or social origin, association with a national minority, property, birth, or other status.

There is one important limit; it can only be invoked when there has been a breach of another Article of the Convention. In effect, it piggybacks on the other Articles of the Convention. It means, for instance, that it is illegal to discriminate against looked-after children in respect of any of their Convention rights.

The legal mechanisms for enforcing human rights

Human rights claims may be attached to any other proceedings a claimant is bringing against a public authority. The time limit for the claim is the same as for the substantive cause of action. For example, if someone brings a personal injuries claim with additional arguments on human rights grounds, the limit is two years.

Generally, though, when someone has been the victim of a breach of their Convention rights, the appropriate legal action will be judicial review of the public body's action by the High Court. Judicial reviews should be started as soon as possible after the action complained of or after no more than three months. However, a specific human rights claim under s. 7(5) of the HRA may be taken within one year of the action complained of. Courts have discretion to extend these periods. When the court considers the human rights issue raised, it will review the law to see if the public authority had any choice about the action it took. It will try to interpret the legislative basis of the public authority's action to see if it can be interpreted in a way that is compatible with Convention rights. If the legislation can be interpreted compatibly and the public authority is found to have acted in breach then the court can remedy that breach using its usual powers.

We summarize the impact of the HRA on the law in **Box 3.2**.

 BOX 3.2 Overview of the Human Rights Act 1998

How HRA impacts on:	Obligations created by the HRA	Comment
Interpretation of statutes by courts	Judgments must 'take account of' Strasbourg judgments and opinions where relevant—HRA, s. 2(1). Words in statutes should be given a meaning compatible with Convention rights 'so far as it is possible to do so'—s. 3(1)	If statute conflicts with ECHR, statute prevails—s. 3(2)(b). A court may declare statute incompatible—s. 4(2). The incompatible law remains valid and continues to operate until remedied by Parliament—s. 4(6)
Interpretation of case law and delegated legislation by courts	ECHR rights prevail over common law (non-statute case law) and delegated/ secondary legislation (rules made by government departments or public authorities)	All existing common law principles and all secondary legislation open to challenge as not human rights compliant

How HRA impacts on:	Obligations created by the HRA	Comment
Obligations of public authorities	Public authorities (including social service departments) must act at all times in ways which comply with the Convention rights—s. 6(1)	A public authority can be taken to court by a victim who alleges its actions are not compatible with Convention rights—s. 7(1)
Decisions of the European Court of Human Rights	Human rights law in England and Wales requires ECtHR case law to be taken into account when applying Convention law—s. 2(1)	Principles derived from cases involving human rights complaints in other countries are also relevant to challenges against the UK

The relevance of human rights for your work as a social worker

Box 3.3 provides an extract from guidance published by the government to health and social care professionals. What does this mean in practice? Circular LAC (2000)17 was issued to guide local authorities when the Human Rights Act came into force in 2000:

> Social Service Departments should actively develop good practice in a manner suited to the new human rights culture, linking as appropriate the equality and race relations agenda.

This is, perhaps unavoidably, a rather bland statement. What it highlights is that human rights compliant practice is not defensive but requires a proactive approach. We aim to highlight the relevance of human rights in the context of your legal practice as a social worker throughout the chapters which follow. The Ministry of Justice has useful information—see www.justice.gov.uk. One particularly useful publication is its handbook on human rights for public authorities *Human rights: human lives*: www.justice.gov.uk/downloads/human-rights/human-rights-handbook-for-public-authorities.pdf. We reproduce the flow chart on human right-compliant decision making in **Figure 3.1**.

Good professional practice

Human rights and professional practice share an ethical basis of concern with citizens' (including service users') autonomy, privacy, and dignity. Even before the vocabulary of human rights was developed, good practice in the delivery of personal care recognized needs for privacy and dignity, and also recognized the tensions between these requirements and the need sometimes to protect vulnerable service users or the public from harm. Therefore much of what is required for human rights compliance is already a prerequisite for ethical practice.

We have set out in **Box 3.3** two straightforward hypothetical scenarios where good social work practice reinforces service users' human rights.

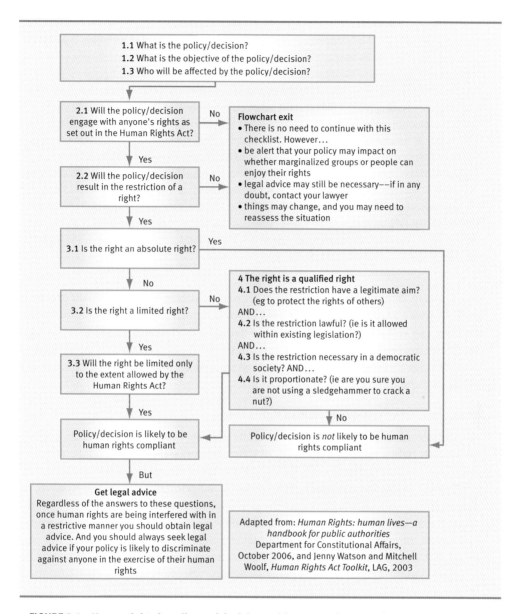

FIGURE 3.1   Human rights in policy and decision making—some key questions
Source: Department of Health.

BOX 3.3   Examples of good practice

Samantha and Ben, who both live in a group home for people with learning disabilities, start a sexual relationship. Samantha's social worker talks to her independently about this decision and about the risks. Ben's community nurse has a similar conversation with him. The practitioners ensure as far as possible that both have consented to the relationship, and see their role as supportive rather than preventative.

Here the practitioners have worked with the service users to try to ensure that their best interests are considered but that also the service users have autonomy and a private life.

Carla, who lives in a supported housing project since leaving care, has put her health at risk by eating an excessive amount of cakes and biscuits. The staff in the project decide that, as they owe her a duty of care, they should restrict her spending money so that she cannot binge on sweet things. Carla has capacity to make decisions, it is just that the staff think that what she is doing is not right for her. Carla's social worker explains to the project staff that they cannot restrict her money. Carla's Article 8 rights mean that she has a right to her money and to make decisions about how it should be spent. However, it is appropriate for the project staff to tell Carla of their concerns and to give her advice. It is also sensible to record this advice in writing.

Age Concern, along with a number of other organizations, has produced an excellent leaflet *Behind Closed Doors: Using the toilet in private* which provides useful information on best practice for the preservation of human rights and dignity in the use of toilets. While the material applies to hospital settings, we think it can usefully be applied to other settings and you may find the suggested approaches helpful. See www.bgs.org.uk/Publications/dignity/BehindClosedDoors.pdf.

The Conservative critique of human rights law

The Conservative critique of human rights law suggests that the balance has swung too far towards rights, impeding the work of state agencies acting for the public good. In particular, the fear is that human rights and the ECHR are an attack on parliamentary sovereignty. While courts cannot strike down or substantially change the wording of Acts of Parliament, it is argued that the powers they have may stray too far into revising the meaning of those Acts—which should instead be established by a democratic Parliament, not unelected and unaccountable judges. Judges themselves are not unaware of this problem. For example, in a case on how far the Rent Act of 1977 should be interpreted in the light of the HRA (whether 'spouse' should be interpreted as including same-sex couples), Lord Nicholls noted:

> Parliament . . . cannot have intended that in the discharge of this extended interpretative function [of s. 3 of the HRA] the courts should adopt a meaning inconsistent with a fundamental feature of legislation. That would be to cross the constitutional boundary that section 3 seeks to demarcate and preserve. Parliament has retained the right to enact legislation in terms which are not Convention-compliant.

> (*Ghaidan v. Godin-Mendoza (FC)*, para. 33)

Not all judges agree, suggesting Parliament cannot pass non-compliant laws. However, laws can be passed that come within a margin of appreciation—adapted to the specific needs and traditions of the individual nation-state.

Conservative proposals in part are intended to reassert parliamentary sovereignty—the right to pass non-compliant legislation if it wishes—and are in part to offer a more distinctly *British* set of human rights. Many, as it happens, are exactly the same as in the ECHR (largely drafted by British lawyers and based on British values, after all). However, the proposals put rights in the context of a rather un-British and illiberal notion of 'duties'—that rights are a privilege of citizenship and can be lost by individuals exhibiting illegal or even immoral conduct.

A private member's bill (an individual Member of Parliament's piece of legislation brought before Parliament) by Charlie Elphicke, the Human Rights Act 1998 (Repeal and Substitution) Bill was a first draft of a Conservative human rights bill promised for the 2015 general election. It expunged the ECHR's Article 13 from a 'British Bill of Rights'—a provision, as noted earlier, crucial to how social workers (as well as other state agents) do their job. Article 13 states in full: 'Everyone whose rights and freedoms as set forth in this Convention are violated shall have an effective remedy before a national authority notwithstanding that the violation has been committed by persons acting in an official capacity.' This means that state agents are not above the law. The fact that you are 'acting in an official capacity' does not mean you may act arbitrarily. You have to seek the legal authority for your action and do the balancing act set out earlier—take account of conflicting rights, both individual and public interest—and come to a reasonable and proportionate conclusion. At the time of writing it is not known whether the Conservatives will indeed abolish the Article 13 principle.

The Elphicke version of human rights also would have allowed breaches of the law by public authorities if 'the act was reasonable with regard to all the circumstances, including a reasonable understanding of primary or subordinate legislation applying to the public authority concerned' (s. 9). This suggests that a breach of the law following a 'reasonable' misunderstanding of it might lead to a human rights claim being rejected. This seems to be a quite new—and absurd—principle in law. It brings in uncertainty where law strives for certainty—and to that extent it is rather unhelpful to public authorities, including social workers. It is to be hoped that Elphicke's s. 9 does not make it into the actual legislation.

The Conservative idea that human rights might be contingent on the claimant's moral standing is also unhelpful—and one would think anathema to the way social workers think and work. Elphicke's bill said courts 'determining a question which has arisen in connection with a UK right shall take into account all the facts and circumstances of the case, including the conduct of the person seeking to assert the UK right' (s. 2). It lists some of the conduct that may be taken into account: obeying the law; rendering civil or military service; protecting children; 'upholding basic public order', implying an obligation to intervene to stop public order offences; seeking to support oneself 'without recourse to a public authority' (ie benefits); and helping people, particularly the elderly.

The implication that members of a public authority, including social workers, might be allowed to make a moral judgement about the person in front of them before needing to extend human rights to him or her seems bizarre and throws up yet more uncertainty.

If the Conservatives do, indeed, pursue these proposals, including repealing the HRA, they have said that they will not exit the ECHR. This means its principles will still be broadly applicable albeit available to claimants only via a long and expensive process of taking their cases to the ECtHR in Strasbourg. For social workers, then, it would seem safest to continue to take the ECHR rights into account, to balance necessity and an assessment of the public good against the rights of the individual, to come to a reasonable and proportionate decision—to follow procedure and continue to give potential complainants a right to be heard.

Equality law

By the end of this part of the chapter you will:

- have been introduced to the Equality Act 2010;
- understand the basic requirements of the law preventing direct and indirect discrimination on the grounds of race, sex, sexual orientation, age and disability discrimination, marriage or civil partnership, religious belief, and gender reassignment;
- understand the duty on public authorities to promote racial and disability equality.

The division between human rights law and equality law is not rigid. One example will illustrate this: *Young v UK* [2007] All ER (D) 49. It involved a prisoner with cerebral palsy who had to use a wheelchair and had some impairment to cognitive function. She had little voluntary control of urine. She was in prison following breach of requirements of a probation order. She failed to supply a urine sample for a mandatory drug test, and at a disciplinary hearing 14 days were added to her sentence. She complained that in the hearing her disability was not taken into account. It was held that in the determination of her rights (alleged non-compliance with lawful order) she had not had a fair trial, under Article 6 of the Convention. The reason she had not had a fair trial was because her disability was not taken into account.

What do we mean by equality?

What good practice and law mean by equality is complex. All citizens are not equal in what they need. A child with a learning disability needs more care and educational support than other children. An old person may need services which a young person does not. A child has less autonomy than an adult and his or her decisions may have to be overridden. A pregnant woman may need to be protected from particular workplace demands. A blind person may need to be exempted from rules banning animals. All of these examples are of people who, at a particular time, need particular forms of unequal treatment for a particular, identified, justifiable purpose. That unequal treatment should be restricted to achieving that purpose—so that they can live as equally respected members of society. These are relevant differences that can justify, indeed demand, discrimination to place them in the same position as other people when it comes to leading fulfilled lives.

By contrast, many differences between people have no relevance to how they should be treated. Sex, faith, skin colour, sexual orientation, or age, for example, should have no relevance in deciding who gets a job, what they are paid, where they live, what services they are entitled to, etc. The same applies for disability, once any appropriate adjustments are put in place to enable access, communication, etc. Those differences should play no part when weighing, for example, who is the best candidate for a post or who is eligible for a vacant property. If such differences might become relevant, for example in dictating working hours, they should be respected, so that, for instance, religious observances can take place.

The law has gradually been developed to reflect these principles. It also reflects what is sometimes called positive discrimination. Positive discrimination occurs where an imbalance in the workforce can be addressed by favouring an under-represented group for additional training. This is wholly different from appointing people to jobs for which other people are better qualified, just to correct an imbalance: that form of positive discrimination is not permitted under equality laws in England and Wales.

The Equality and Human Rights Commission

Under the Equality Act 2006 the Equality and Human Rights Commission (EHRC) was created out of the merger of the Equal Opportunities Commission, the Commission for Racial Equality, and the Disability Rights Commission. It started work in October 2007. It promotes equality and tackles discrimination in relation to race, gender, gender reassignment, disability, sexual orientation, religion or belief, age, and human rights. It is able to help people to pursue court cases including against the government. It does important work in researching and publicizing systemic breaches of human rights and equality law. One relevant example is its formal inquiry into the actions of public authorities to eliminate disability-related harassment and its causes. The website of the EHRC is www.equalityhumanrights.com. Its establishment was the first stage in producing a single and coherent framework for the promotion of equality in the UK. An even more significant step was the introduction of the Equality Act 2010.

The Equality Act 2010

The Equality Act came into force on 1 October 2010. It provides a legal framework to protect individuals from discriminatory and unfair treatment. It brings together more than 116 separate pieces of legislation into one Act and at the same time simplifies, and strengthens, the law.

The main pieces of legislation that have been merged into the Equality Act are:

- the Equal Pay Act 1970;
- the Sex Discrimination Act 1975;
- the Race Relations Act 1976;
- the Disability Discrimination Act 1995;
- the Employment Equality (Religion or Belief) Regulations 2003;
- the Employment Equality (Sexual Orientation) Regulations 2003;
- the Employment Equality (Age) Regulations 2006;
- the Equality Act 2006, Part 2;
- the Equality Act (Sexual Orientation) Regulations 2007.

In brief, the Equality Act works by: (a) prohibiting certain types of conduct towards individuals who have certain characteristics protected by the legislation; (b) requiring public bodies to consider how their policies, programmes, and service delivery will affect people with the protected characteristics; and (c) in limited circumstances enabling positive action to support inclusion of individuals with protected characteristics.

Protected characteristics

The protected characteristics are set out in s. 4 of the Equality Act. They are:

- age;
- disability;
- gender reassignment;
- marriage and civil partnership;
- pregnancy and maternity;
- race;
- religion or belief;
- sex;
- sexual orientation.

The protected characteristics are defined within the statute. We have set out the statutory definitions of disability, race, and religion and belief in **Box 3.4**.

 BOX 3.4 Definitions of some of the protected characteristics in the Equality Act 2010

s. 6 Disability

(1) A person (P) has a disability if—
    (a) P has a physical or mental impairment, and
    (b) the impairment has a substantial and long-term adverse effect on P's ability to carry out normal day-to-day activities.

s. 9 Race

(1) Race includes—
    (a) colour;
    (b) nationality;
    (c) ethnic or national origins.

s. 10 Religion or belief

(1) Religion means any religion and a reference to religion includes a reference to a lack of religion.

(2) Belief means any religious or philosophical belief and a reference to belief includes a reference to a lack of belief.

Prohibited conduct

The Equality Act prohibits direct discrimination (including because of a combination of two relevant protected characteristics), discrimination arising from disability, indirect discrimination, harassment and victimization, and failure to make reasonable adjustments for a disability. What is meant by these terms is set out in the following sections.

Direct discrimination

Direct discrimination occurs when someone is treated less favourably than someone else in similar circumstances on the grounds of their gender/marital status/race/disability/age. A couple of examples will illustrate this.

Example: racially offensive graffiti appears on a tenant's property. The tenant complains to the landlord, but nothing is done to remove it. If the landlord normally takes prompt action to deal with complaints about other types of anti-social behaviour, the tenant could successfully argue that the landlord has not provided housing management services on a fair and equal basis and has directly discriminated against her.

Example: a social services department refuses to employ a qualified social worker because she is deaf. Her skills, experience, and abilities were appropriate to the job but had not been considered because the employer had assumed that a deaf person could not do the job.

Discrimination arising from a disability

Such discrimination occurs when a person (A) discriminates against a disabled person by treating them less favourably because of something arising in consequence of B's disability, and A cannot show that the treatment is a proportionate means of achieving a legitimate aim. Discrimination arising from a disability is not unlawful if A shows that A did not know, and could not reasonably have been expected to know, that B had the disability.

Indirect discrimination

This occurs when a condition or requirement is applied equally to everyone but in practice the proportion of one race or gender or person of a particular religion, etc who can comply is considerably smaller than other groups and an employee is unable to comply because of, for example, their race or gender and the employer cannot show that the condition or requirement is objectively justifiable.

Note that it is lawful to discriminate indirectly if the condition or requirement imposed is objectively justifiable.

Example: a firm restricts recruitment to recent graduates—fewer older people would be able to meet this requirement and if the employer could not justify the requirement, then it would be unlawful.

Failure to make reasonable adjustments for a disability

Employers and service providers are required to make reasonable adjustments to the physical environment so that disabled people are not substantially disadvantaged. A successful claim would require that the employer knows, or should have known, that the person concerned had a disability.

Example: a social work student is dyslexic. She has informed her university of her disability. She has a specialist report from the university learning support unit stating that she needs additional time in examinations. Her law tutor refuses to extend the length of the examination for her. She is thus placed at a substantial disadvantage to her colleagues who do not have a disability.

Victimization

A person is victimized if she is treated detrimentally because she has made a complaint or allegation or has given evidence against someone else in relation to a complaint of discrimination.

Example: a local authority employee gives evidence at an internal grievance hearing concerning a colleague who believes that he has been refused promotion on grounds of his visual impairment. Within weeks of giving evidence, the witness is moved to another post where she considers she will not get sufficiently demanding work to enable her to apply for promotion.

Harassment

Harassment occurs when someone is subjected to harassment by their employer or by someone for whom the employer is responsible on the basis of their sex/race/disability/age.

Example: a social worker complains to her manager that a particular family of service users subjects her to racial abuse. Her manager says that this is one of those things that are part of a social work career and does nothing about it.

Example: a woman has a partner who is significantly younger than her and this is the basis of repeated comments and jokes from colleagues. This could be unlawful if she finds it humiliating or offensive, and the employer does not address the problem.

Disability discrimination

As we said earlier (**The Equality Act 2010**, p 99), the Equality Act is largely a consolidation and re-enactment of previous laws on discrimination. However, there are some significant changes, particularly in the field of disability discrimination. The definition of disability has been extended under the Equality Act 2010. A person has a disability if he or she has a physical or mental impairment that has a substantial and long-term adverse effect on that person's ability to carry out normal day-to-day activities. For the purposes of the Equality Act 2010, 'substantial' means more than minor or trivial; 'long-term' means that the effect of the impairment has lasted or is likely to last for at least 12 months; and 'normal day-to-day activities' include everyday things like eating, washing, walking, and going shopping. **Box 3.5** provides a summary explanation of the difference between the provisions in the Disability Discrimination Act 1995 and the Equality Act 2010.

BOX 3.5 Key differences between the Disability Discrimination Act 1995 and the Equality Act 2010

The Disability Discrimination Act 1995 provided protection for disabled people from direct discrimination in employment and related areas only. The Equality Act 2010 protects disabled people against direct discrimination in a broader range of areas including the supply of goods, facilities, and services

The Equality Act 2010 introduced improved protection from discrimination that occurs because of something connected with a person's disability. This form of discrimination can be justified if it can be shown to be a proportionate means of achieving a legitimate aim.

The Equality Act 2010 introduced the principle of indirect discrimination for disability. Indirect discrimination occurs when something applies in the same way to everybody but has an effect which particularly disadvantages, for example, disabled people. Indirect discrimination may be justified if it can be shown to be a proportionate means of achieving a legitimate aim.

The Equality Act 2010 applies one trigger point at which there is a duty to make reasonable adjustments for disabled people. This trigger point is where a disabled person would be at a substantial disadvantage compared to non-disabled people if the adjustment was not made.

The Equality Act 2010 extends protection from harassment that is related to disability beyond work.

The Equality Act 2010 provides protection from direct disability discrimination and harassment where this is based on a person's association with a disabled person, or on a false perception that the person is disabled.

The Equality Act 2010 contains a provision which limits the type of inquiries that a recruiting employer can make about disability and health when recruiting new staff. This provision will help to prevent disabled candidates from being unfairly screened out at an early stage of the recruitment process.

The Equality Act 2010 provides protection against indirect discrimination on the grounds of disability. This is a change from the previous position and is a useful extension of the law. **Box 3.6** provides an example of indirect discrimination.

 BOX 3.6 Examples of indirect discrimination (taken from the leaflet provided by the Government Equalities Office)

Because of your disability, you might need to take more leave from work than people you work with. Your employer must not treat you unfavourably because you are off work, as long as it knows that you have a disability. However, your employer may be able to justify anything it does, and if its action can be justified then it will not be against the law.

Your employer brings in a new shift pattern which means that everyone has to work fewer days, but longer days. You have a disability that means you are exhausted after two long days of working. So the new shift pattern puts you and other people who have the same disability as you at a disadvantage. Your employer will have indirectly discriminated against you if it cannot justify the new shift pattern.

Positive action

Section 158 of the Equality Act allows positive action enabling or encouraging people with a protected characteristic to overcome or minimize that disadvantage, meeting those needs, or enabling or encouraging people with the protected characteristic to participate in that activity. Any action must be proportionate. The proportionality of action will depend, among other things, on the seriousness of the relevant disadvantage, the extremity of need or under-representation, and the availability of other means of countering them. Positive discrimination remains illegal. Section 158(3) allows regulations to be made to specify actions, or descriptions of actions, that are not permitted as positive actions in order to provide greater legal certainty about what action is proportionate in particular circumstances.

Positive action in recruitment and promotion can be used where an employer reasonably thinks that people with a protected characteristic are under-represented. The profiles of the workforce and/or making inquiries of other comparable employers in the area or sector as a whole may provide information which would enable an employer to take action. However, positive action under section 158 does not allow 'anything that is prohibited by or under an enactment other than this Act'. Positive action therefore cannot include positive discrimination, such as taking on more women when there are men more qualified for a job or instituting quotas for the numbers of those with protected characteristics employed in defiance of the qualifications of those who come forward.

Section 159 provides for much more specific action in connection with promotion or recruitment. It permits (but does not require) an employer to take a protected characteristic into consideration when deciding whom to recruit or promote, where people having the protected characteristic are at a disadvantage or are under-represented—this can be done only where the candidates are as qualified as each other and is sometimes called the 'tie-break rule'. The question of whether one person is as qualified as another is not limited to formal qualifications, but includes the criteria the employer uses to establish who is best for the job so could include matters such as suitability, competence, and professional performance. The section does not allow employers to have a policy or practice of automatically treating people who share a protected characteristic more favourably than those who do not have it. Rather, each case must be considered on its merits. Any action taken must be a proportionate means of addressing such disadvantage or under-representation.

Duties on public authorities

One of the most significant legal advances in combating inequality in recent years has been the move towards imposing a positive duty upon public bodies to take action to eliminate discrimination and advance equality of opportunity. The pre-existing equality duties in connection with gender, race, and disability have now been consolidated and extended. The duty known as the public sector equality duty is set out in s. 149 of the Equality Act 2010 (**Box 3.7** sets out the most important provisions) which came into force on 5 April 2011. What the general equality duty requires is for relevant organizations to consider how they could positively contribute to the advancement of equality and good relations. It requires equality considerations to be built into the design of policies and the delivery of services, including internal policies, and for these issues to be kept under review.

 BOX 3.7 Public sector equality duty—s.149 of the Equality Act 2010

(1) A public authority must, in the exercise of its functions, have due regard to the need to—
  (a) eliminate discrimination, harassment, victimisation and any other conduct that is prohibited by or under this Act;
  (b) advance equality of opportunity between persons who share a relevant protected characteristic and persons who do not share it;
  (c) foster good relations between persons who share a relevant protected characteristic and persons who do not share it.

(2) A person who is not a public authority but who exercises public functions must, in the exercise of those functions, have due regard to the matters mentioned in subsection (1).

(3) Having due regard to the need to advance equality of opportunity between persons who share a relevant protected characteristic and persons who do not share it involves having due regard, in particular, to the need to—
  (a) remove or minimise disadvantages suffered by persons who share a relevant protected characteristic that are connected to that characteristic;
  (b) take steps to meet the needs of persons who share a relevant protected characteristic that are different from the needs of persons who do not share it;
  (c) encourage persons who share a relevant protected characteristic to participate in public life or in any other activity in which participation by such persons is disproportionately low.

(4) The steps involved in meeting the needs of disabled persons that are different from the needs of persons who are not disabled include, in particular, steps to take account of disabled persons' disabilities.

The general duty in s. 149 of the Equality Act 2010 is supplemented by specific duties set out in regulations. The specific duties, which impose obligations to publish information and set equality objectives, differ in England, Scotland, and Wales. The EHRC has published guidance on complying with the equality duties, an extract from which is set out in **Box 3.8**. The full guidance is available from the EHRC website, www.equalityhumanrights. com/advice-and-guidance/public-sector-equality-duty/introduction-to-the-equality-duty.

 BOX 3.8 The essential guide to the public sector equality duty—The Equality and Human Rights Commission

Part 3 What the law requires

The general equality duty is not prescriptive about the approach a public authority should take in order to comply with their legal obligations. The specific duties are limited to requirements about publishing equality information and objectives.

Case law on the previous equality duties is still relevant to the public sector equality duty. The follow-ing principles, drawn from case law, explain that in order to properly have due regard to the general equality duty aims, each public authority should ensure that:

- Those who exercise its functions must be aware of the general equality duty's requirements. Compliance with the general equality duty involves a conscious approach and state of mind. General regard to the issue of equality is not enough to comply.

- The general equality duty is complied with before and at the time a particular policy is under consideration, as well as at the time a decision is taken. A public authority subject to the general equality duty cannot satisfy the general equality duty by justifying a decision after it has been taken.

- It consciously thinks about the need to do the things set out in the general equality duty as an integral part of the decision-making process. Having due regard is not a matter of box ticking. The duty must be exercised in substance, with rigour and with an open mind in such a way that it influences the final decision.

- It has sufficient information. A body subject to the to the general equality duty will need to consider whether it has sufficient information about the effects of the policy, or the way a function is being carried out, on the aims set out in the general equality duty.

- It takes responsibility for complying with the general equality duty in relation to all its functions to which the general equality duty applies. Responsibility for the general equality duty cannot be delegated to external organisations that are carrying out functions on its behalf.

- It consciously thinks about the need to do the things set out in the general equality duty, not only when a policy is developed and decided upon, but when it is being implemented. The general equality duty is a continuing one, so public authorities may need to review policies or decisions in light of the general equality duty, for example if the make-up of service users changes.

- Although a body subject to the general equality duty is not legally required to keep records of its consideration of the aims of the general equality duty in making decisions, it is good practice to do so and it encourages transparency. If a body is challenged it will be difficult to demonstrate that it has had due regard to the aims of the general equality duty if records are not kept.

There have been some significant cases in relation to the public sector equality duty regarding to the provision of adult social care services. These are considered in **chapter 13**. We set out in the following sections, in our examples from equality cases, one recent case, *Blake and others v London Borough of Waltham Forest* [2014] EWHC 1027 (Admin) which provides a useful demonstration of the operation of the duty.

Some examples from equality cases

Note: these mostly predate the 2010 Act but the principles are the same in the older legislation.

Azmi v Kirklees MBC (2007)

Ms Azmi was employed as a bilingual support worker at a school in Kirklees. She was a devout Muslim and wore a veil which covered her head and face when in the presence of adult males. Her request to wear a veil when teaching with male teachers was refused by the council's education department on the ground that obscuring the face and mouth impeded effective communication with the pupils. She was instructed to be unveiled at all times in the classroom but could continue to wear her veil in communal areas. Ms Azmi refused to remove her veil and was suspended for disobeying an instruction. She made a claim to an employment tribunal that she had been discriminated against directly and indirectly on the ground of her religion. The tribunal dismissed the claims. The veil ban was held to be indirectly discriminatory because a denial of work to veiled women disproportionately affected Muslim women. However, it was lawful as a proportionate means of achieving a legitimate aim—that children receive maximum benefit from their education. An Employment Appeal Tribunal agreed.

Derbyshire and others v St Helens MBC (Equal Opportunities Commission and others intervening) (2007)

The applicants were some of the 510 female catering staff employed by the council in its school meals service who brought equal pay claims against the council. The majority of the claims were agreed, but 36 did not accept the settlement, pursued their claims, and won compensation. But two months before the hearing of the claims the council wrote letters to all the catering staff, including the applicants, pointing out that a successful claim was likely to lead to the cost of school meals rising to such an extent that the council would have to consider ceasing to provide them except to those entitled to receive them by law, with a consequent reduction in the school meals service and loss of jobs. The applicants complained to the employment tribunal of victimization, contrary to the Sex Discrimination Act 1975, alleging that the letters had caused them anxiety and distress and had amounted to an attempt to induce them to abandon their claims. The House of Lords (Supreme Court) considered the question: 'did the Council . . . discriminate against the appellants . . . because . . . the appellants had brought proceedings against the Council under the Equal Pay Act 1970?' The Lords decided that the employment tribunal had been entitled to take the view that the council had gone further than was reasonable in protecting its interests in the equal pay litigation. What the council had done was 'effectively a threat', as Lord Neuberger put it, as a result of the women taking a discrimination claim.

R (on the application of Lunt) v Liverpool City Council (2009)

The council favoured the 'London Taxi' for the city, and believed it to be suitable for all wheelchair users. The claimant needed a longer wheelchair than most, and could only ride in the London Taxi sideways, without restraints, and therefore illegally. The council had refused a licence application from an applicant who proposed a different taxi vehicle adapted to take such a longer wheelchair. The Divisional Court held the council to be in breach of its duty under the Disability Discrimination Act 1995 to take all reasonable steps to develop policies allowing access to services by disabled people.

Islington LBC v Ladele (2009)

Lillian Ladele was a registrar of births, marriages, and deaths. She held strong convictions based on her Christian faith that, she felt, prevented her from being personally involved in registering civil partnerships. The council's published policies were to promote equality of opportunity regardless of sexual orientation, and it did not agree that she could avoid this part of her duties. She applied to the employment tribunal on the basis that the requirement to conduct partnership registration was a form of direct discrimination on grounds of faith. The council said this was not discrimination: all registrars were asked to carry out identical duties. The Employment Appeal Tribunal agreed, finding that the appellant had been disciplined for failure to carry out her job, not because of her faith. In 2010 the Supreme Court refused her permission to appeal.

Hampton v Lord Chancellor (2008)

It was unlawful to force recorders (part-time judges in the County Court and Crown Court) to retire at 65. The stated justification, to create career opportunities for younger people was, on the facts, not needed as there was significant turnover every year.

Blake and others v London Borough of Waltham Forest [2014] EWHC 1027 (Admin)

The council had terminated the licence for a mobile soup kitchen run by Christian Kitchen on one of its car parks. There were claims that the kitchen was a focus for anti-social behaviour. The council decision engages the public sector equality duty (PSED) in s. 149(1) of the Equality Act: 'A public authority must, in the exercise of its functions, have due regard to the need to—(a) eliminate discrimination, harassment, victimisation and any other conduct that is prohibited by or under this Act; (b) advance equality of opportunity between persons who share a relevant protected characteristic and persons who do not share it; (c) foster good relations between persons who share a relevant protected characteristic and persons who do not share it.'

This duty applied even though it was not a council-run or funded soup kitchen. The claimants said that the council should have considered the likely impact of its decision on vulnerable, disabled, and elderly users of the soup kitchen. An alternative site in a lay-by a bus-ride away was not considered suitable for those reasons. The judge considered that the risk to the elderly and disabled 'was not addressed in any of the impact assessments set out in the Equality Analysis, nor are mitigating steps addressed to this risk'. A balancing exercise could not have been done without assessing that risk.

Some principles relating to the PSED were set out, based on case law:

- the duty applies to the exercise of all public authority functions even where the relevant decision relates to a public authority's private law arrangements such as the termination of a private contract or licence;

- the question whether a decision-maker has had due regard is a question of substance, not form or box-ticking. The duty must be performed with rigour and an open mind;

- the duty must be fulfilled before and at the time a particular policy is being considered, and not afterwards;

- there must be an analysis of the material 'with the specific statutory consideration in mind';

- in a case where large numbers of vulnerable people very many of whom fall within one or more of the protected groups, the due regard necessary is very high;

- in considering the impact, the authority must assess the risk and extent of any adverse impact and the ways in which such risk may be eliminated;

- the PSED may involve a duty of inquiry. If the relevant material is not available, there will be a duty to acquire it and this will mean some consultation with appropriate groups is necessary;

- 'The concept of due regard requires the court to ensure that there has been a proper and conscientious focus on the statutory criteria, but if that is done, the court cannot interfere with the decision simply because it would have given greater weight to the equality implications of the decision than did the decision-maker'— *Hurley & Moore v Secretary of State for BIS* (2012), per Elias LJ. The principles of '*Wednesbury* reasonableness' would apply;

- a sense of proportionality and reality is required. If a fair reading of the equality analysis makes clear that the decision-maker considered and conscientiously applied his or her mind to the relevant equality impact or impacts of the proposed decision, the court will not micromanage such decisions.

So the decision-maker must make a proper investigation, not a box-ticking exercise, and show that the results of that investigation are given due weight when the decision is made. Mrs Justice Simler said that 'the decision-maker should be clear precisely what the equality implications are when he puts them in the balance, and that these equality implications should be given due consideration side by side with all the other pressing circumstances relevant to the decision.' If that can be shown, a court will not simply replace its decision with that of the decision-maker on the ground nor require some greater weight to be given to equality implications as long as the decision-maker took a (*Wednesbury*) reasonable view of this. Waltham Forest's analysis was contradictory and made assumptions with no evidence or attempt to establish the accuracy of its assertions; the Equality Analysis 'fails to accord with reality or common sense'. The decision was quashed as unlawful.

Enforcement in race and sex discrimination cases

The victim of discrimination has two direct avenues of complaint, apart from enlisting the help of the EHRC. If discrimination is alleged at work, including unfair dismissal, he or she can bring a case in an employment tribunal; there must be no delay, as the

time limit for starting the case is normally three months from the date of the last discriminatory act or dismissal. A tribunal can declare the rights of the individual, can
order compensation to be paid (which can include a sum for distress to feelings, even
if there is no other financial loss), and can order the employer to take specified steps to
prevent further discrimination against this employee, failure to do so leading to a possible further award of compensation.

If the discrimination takes place outside the employment field (eg refusal to serve
someone in a restaurant or to consider them for a partnership), the case is brought
in the County Court. Proceedings have to be started within six months of the last act
complained of, or eight months where the alleged discrimination was to do with education. The court can order damages to be paid, including compensation for distress to
feelings, and an injunction requiring the discriminator to do or stop doing certain acts
(eg ordering a landlord to cease harassing a tenant).

 EXERCISES

What effect does the law have in each of the situations set out in the bullet points?

1 The Jones family comprises Mr Jones, who is Welsh; Mrs Jones who is English, but of African
   racial background. They have adopted Gemma, who was born in China. They have two children,
   Matthew, age 12, who has attention deficit hyperactivity disorder, and Christine, age 6, who
   is confined to a wheelchair. Mr Jones has HIV. Mrs Jones has a severe facial disfigurement following a road accident.

   • Mrs Jones, who has a science doctorate and a high-profile research and publication record,
      is refused several posts for which she meets all of the essential criteria. The University of
      Anytown told her that they might have trouble with the Home Office getting her a work per-
      mit. Science Labs plc told her that with her family problems she was unlikely to be commit-
      ted to the work. Newtown College said the students would find her disfigurement difficult to
      handle.

   • Gemma needs special English-language tuition but the school says it is not allowed to
      spend more money on her than on other children.

   • Mr Jones is continuously taunted at work with offensive comments about his multi-racial
      family. The employer treats this as a joke, and up to now Mr Jones has tried to pretend that
      he does not mind.

   • Mr Jones wants a clerical job. He is 45, and he has been told by the local authority that he is
      too old. He spent much of his twenties and thirties at home bringing up his first family, from
      whom he is separated, and his new family. He is told by Admin R Us that they do not want
      anyone around with HIV as it will put off the other staff.

   • Mrs Jones takes Christine to the Gateside Cinema, which is situated in an old building
      recently modernized. They are refused admission because Christine's wheelchair 'will cre-
      ate a safety hazard for other customers'.

   • Social Housing Ltd, the family's landlord, has written to say that Matthew's loud behaviour
      is anti-social and the family will have to leave.

2 You are a social worker for Careborough MBC. Your statutory service user is Maggie, a 14-year-old who has been sleeping rough and, you believe, taking drugs. You have been accommodating Maggie with her mother Jane's agreement. Because of Maggie's frequent absconding, you are considering secure accommodation. Jane has formed a relationship with John and wants Maggie to come home and the family to make a fresh start. Maggie's father Will wants Maggie to remain in local authority accommodation. You are about to set up a case conference. Maggie's headteacher does not want to participate if Will or Jane are present. Will wants to see copies of a psychologist's report which recommends that it would be disastrous for Maggie to return home or have contact with Will. John's former wife has phoned you to say she thinks John has sexually abused her daughter. Jane is deaf and can only communicate if a signer is present.

 • What are the human rights law considerations you should be aware of before the case conference takes place?

3 Paragraph 2.5 of the Department of Health publication *Human Rights in Healthcare—A Framework for Local Action* (last published 2008 and now withdrawn) contains a table which considers some Articles of the ECHR and their implications for health-care decisions. We reproduce an extract from this table in **Figure 3.2**. Decide which Articles of the ECHR are most significant for your practice as a social worker, then decide which aspects of social work practice might raise possible compliance issues. Finally, illustrate your considerations with a specific example, as the Department of Health have done.

HUMAN RIGHT	SOME RELEVANT ISSUES IN HEALTHCARE	AN EXAMPLE...
The right not to be tortured or treated in an inhuman or degrading way – Inhuman treatment means treatment causing severe mental or physical harm – Degrading treatment means treatment that is grossly humiliating and undignified Inhuman or degrading treatment does not have to be deliberate	• Physical or mental abuse • Unchanged sheets • Leaving trays of food without helping patients to eat, when they are too frail to feed themselves • Excessive force used to restrain patients • Washing or dressing without regard to dignity • Staff not being protected from violent or abusive patients	A man with learning disabilities was living in a residential care home. He was regularly tied to a bed or his wheelchair for 16 hours at a time, to prevent him from hitting his head and face. This kind of situation could breach the right not to be treated in an inhuman or degrading way.

FIGURE 3.2   Articles of the ECHR and their implications for health-care decisions
Source: Department of Health.

HUMAN RIGHT	SOME RELEVANT ISSUES IN HEALTHCARE	AN EXAMPLE…
The right to liberty The right to liberty is not a right to be free to do whatever you want. The right to liberty is a right not to be locked in a cell or a room, or have any other extreme restriction placed on movement. The right to liberty is a limited right. It can be limited in a number of specific circumstances, for example the lawful detention of someone who has mental health issues.	• Informal detention of patients who do not have the capacity to decide whether they would like to be admitted into hospital e.g. learning disabled or older patients • Delays in reviewing whether mental health patients who are detained under the Mental Health Act should still be detained • Excessive restraint of patients e.g. tying them to their beds or chairs for long periods	A large number of patients throughout the UK who do not have capacity to make their own decisions are informally admitted into hospital. This kind of admission has been ruled to breach the right to liberty, as there are no clear rules about who decides that someone should be detained, and for what reasons. The government is currently exploring ways of protecting people who are admitted informally in this way, to make sure that their right to liberty is not breached.
The right to a fair trial The right to a fair trial contains a number of principles that need to be considered at *some stage* during the decision making process. The person whose rights will be affected has the right to: – an independent and impartial tribunal; – be present at some stage during the decision making process; – a reasonable opportunity to present their case before the decision is made; – an adversarial hearing; – disclosure of all relevant documents; – have their hearing take place within a reasonable time; and – be given reasons to enable them to understand the decision that has been made.	• Staff disciplinary proceedings • Compensation claims • Independence of Tribunals e.g. the Mental Health Review Tribunal	Ensure that there is a robust and fair process for removing a doctor or dentist from the Performers List.

FIGURE 3.2 (Continued)

ONLINE RESOURCE CENTRE

For guidance on how to answer these exercises, visit the Online Resource Centre at: www.oxfordtextbooks.co.uk/orc/socialwork13e/.

WHERE DO WE GO FROM HERE?

The duty to respect the dignity and the rights of all the people you work with, including those service users or their families in whose lives you are required to intervene, will become a fundamental aspect of your work. It must underpin your understanding of your legal powers. In this chapter we have provided an introductory framework only. We will make reference to human rights and equality law in greater detail throughout the book and we will draw your attention to some significant cases. We have explained how one of your roles is to balance competing rights. The next chapter considers another important area where you must balance competing interests where human rights come into play: it concerns the obligations to and restrictions on sharing information.

ANNOTATED FURTHER READING

The body set up in place of the race, gender, and disability rights commissions is the Equality and Human Rights Commission, which is charged with advising on and enforcing good practice in all aspects of human rights and discrimination, including types of discrimination not covered by the previous bodies. See www.equalityhumanrights.com.

Human rights

Liberty is the leading organization monitoring the effectiveness of the HRA and bringing test cases. It has a range of useful information at www.liberty-human-rights.org.uk.

The Department of Health has ceased to maintain a website on 'Managing Your Organisation: Human Rights', which included useful case studies with reference to actual court decisions on the impact of the HRA on areas of work which will be relevant to social workers and health professionals. You may still find it on the government's online archive.

The government operates a more general human rights website. This is hosted at the time of writing by the Ministry of Justice. The current website address is www.justice.gov.uk/human-rights. It is particularly useful for the free publications it offers and the list of web links it provides.

The United Nations has all of the international charters on human rights and discrimination issues at www.un.org/en/rights.

Useful guidance to the HRA include the following:

British Institute of Human Rights: *Your Human Rights Guides* (2006) (available from www.bihr. org.uk).

Ministry of Justice: *Human Rights, Human Lives: a handbook for public authorities* (October 2006), www.justice.gov.uk/downloads/human-rights/human-rights-handbook-for-public-authorities.pdf.

J. Watson and M. Woolf, *Human Rights Act Toolkit* (2nd edn, Legal Action Group, 2008).

N. Kang-Riou, *Confronting the Human Rights Act 1998: Contemporary Themes and Perspectives* (Routledge 2012).

K. Starmer, *European Human Rights Law: The Human Rights Act 1998 and the European Convention on Human Rights* (2nd edn, Legal Action Group, 2010).

J. Wadham, H. Mountfield, and A. Edmundson, *Blackstone's Guide to the Human Rights Act 1998* (6th edn, Oxford University Press, 2011).

The value of the United Nations Convention on the Rights of the Child is considered by U. Kilkelly and L. Lundy, 'Children's rights in action: using the UN Convention on the Rights of the Child as an auditing tool' (2006) *CFLQ* 18(3): 331.

The Equality Act 2010

J. Wadham, D. *Ruebain*, A. Robinson, and S. Uppal, *Blackstone's Guide to the Equality Act 2010* (2nd edn, Oxford University Press, 2012).

B. Hepple, *Equality: The New Legal Framework* (Hart, 2011).

Information sharing 4

 OVERVIEW AND OBJECTIVES

This chapter is designed to help you to understand the principles involved when you make decisions about whether or not to disclose information belonging to or concerning the service user. We start with the government guidance on information sharing and explain the relevant provisions of the Human Rights Act 1998 (HRA), the common law of confidentiality, and the Data Protection Act 1998. These provide you with your basic tools for lawful practice in this area. We go on to consider particular circumstances which demonstrate the balancing acts that you must undertake when you are deciding whether or not to disclose information. Finally, we look at the interaction of the various legal frameworks and explain the decision-making process which underpins lawful information sharing.

CASE STUDY

BBC v Rochdale MBC [2005] EWHC 2862 (Fam)

Rochdale Council applied for an injunction (a ban issued by a court) to prevent the BBC from publishing the names of two social workers who had given evidence in wardship proceedings. The children concerned had been returned to the care of their families after allegations of satanic abuse were rejected. Injunctions were made following the hearing to prevent disclosure of the identities of the children. The social workers had also been granted anonymity to prevent identification of the children. Several years later, the BBC intended to broadcast a documentary examining the criticisms made by the judge. It reached an agreement with the former wards—by now adults—who agreed to the use of materials protected by the injunction. The outstanding issue was whether the social workers could be identified in the documentary. Their argument, and that of the council, was that social workers work in a confidential environment which should be protected by anonymity unless there had been dishonesty or bad faith. Under Article 8 of the European Convention on Human Right (ECHR) (respect for private and family life: see previous chapter) maintenance of their anonymity was proportionate and being identified by the BBC would have a seriously detrimental impact on their families and their professional standing. The BBC argued that the social workers had failed to establish a pressing need to restrict the public interest in freedom of expression under Article 10 of the ECHR.

The application to uphold the injunction was refused. As a matter of general principle, there was nothing to prevent the identification of a witness who gave evidence in a case, including a witness in proceedings concerning the welfare of children. The court should conduct a balancing exercise between the competing rights, considering the proportionality of any interference with each right independently. What mattered here was the interface between Articles 8 and 10. The local authority had not established a pressing need for the injunction, and restraint would be a disproportionate interference with the BBC's Article 10 rights. While publication of the social workers' identities would interfere with their Article 8 rights to respect for private life, that interference was in pursuit of a legitimate aim, namely informed and open discussion of public interest issues relating to the earlier proceedings and to family proceedings generally. It would be proportionate. The Article 10 rights of the BBC and the former wards, and the public interest in enabling public scrutiny of court proceedings and family justice, should prevail over the Article 8 rights of the social workers.

WHAT DOES THIS CASE TELL YOU ABOUT SOCIAL WORK PRACTICE?

The problem faced by the courts in this case was balancing the right of social workers' privacy with the right of the press to scrutinize the workings of the civil justice system. The decision involves a complex balancing exercise, which in this particular situation the court resolved in favour of the media and the former wards of court. Notice how the court used human rights principles in reaching its decision; also how proportionality is crucial to the resolution of the conflict in rights.

You may remember from **chapter 1** that injunctions are equitable remedies. They are awarded at the discretion of the court. Using discretion means that each case has to be decided on its own facts—there is no one answer to the difficult questions posed when it comes to information sharing.

A more recent case, *Bristol City Council v C and others* [2012] EWHC 3748 (Fam), has also asserted the Article 10 rights of the media where there is a public interest in care proceedings. A child, A, was removed from her father's care and fostered after an interim care order issued at family court proceedings. The local authority received information that a member of the foster household had accessed indecent images of children and another may have grabbed A by the throat. Police and social workers visited the house, computers were removed, and A was taken to another foster home. The following day the male foster carer was found dead having apparently killed himself. The father of A approached the *Sun* newspaper to do a story based on his concerns about social services' handling of the case.

A court order banned media reports that could identify the child, foster carers, the local authority, or the social workers involved. Most care proceedings are held in private and while accredited members of the press may attend, what they can report is restricted by s. 12 of the Administration of Justice Act 1960, which, broadly, treats reports involving minors as contempt of court. However, this Act must now be seen in the light of Article 10 freedom of expression rights of the press balanced against Article 8 privacy rights—here for the girl and her family (albeit that the father wanted the *Sun* to publish material about the case) and the foster family. Mr Justice Baker concluded that the reporting restrictions barring the naming of the social workers and local authority should be lifted; the names of the two families should remain unpublished but the fact of the apparent suicide should be published on the basis that that information would not lead to identification of A or his daughter. Baker also allowed the word 'strangling' to be used in relation to the assault on the girl given similar wording was used by social services in reports on the case. In effect, the judgment suggests that there was potentially a public interest in how a particular social services department and particular social workers dealt with a case and hence the suicide following the indecent images claim and the seriousness of the assault were important elements of the *Sun*'s potential article. So 'there is a clear public interest in facilitating an open discussion of the issues relating to child protection and fostering that arise in this case. In all the circumstances, I find no evidence of any pressing social need for a restricting exercise of the right to freedom of expression on that issue'. The principle of non-identification (hence Article 8 privacy) was preserved and balanced against Article 10 freedom of expression—for the father to make his complaint about social services known publicly and for the *Sun* to publish it.

▉ Introduction

Information sharing is essential for the protection of vulnerable people and crucial to the integrated system of child protection which has been put in place by the Children Act 2004 as well as systems for safeguarding adults. There is a danger that social workers and those advising them interpret the law in a way that prevents them using information effectively. The potential legal barriers to information sharing received careful scrutiny within the Laming Report, published in January 2003, into the death of Victoria Climbié, which we discussed in **chapter 2**. Paragraph 17.115 states:

> The evidence put to the Inquiry was that unless a child is deemed to be in need of protection, information cannot be shared between agencies without staff running the risk that their actions are unlawful. This either deters information sharing, or artificially elevates concern about the need for protection—each of which is not compatible with serving well the needs of children and families.

On the other hand, social workers may be using information given in the expectation of confidentiality, and individuals are entitled to have their privacy respected. Moreover, the state in its various guises holds a great deal of information about us all. If there is no check on its use there is potential for oppression.

Government has an interest in ensuring that the information it holds is seen to be used only for legitimate and proportionate purposes. It would be all too easy for individuals to lose their trust in the state if it is believed to have abused its powers. The government has provided user-friendly practitioners' guides on information sharing which are designed to help you to solve these dilemmas. These are:

- *Information Sharing: Guidance for Practitioners and Managers*;
- *Information Sharing: Further Guidance on Legal Issues*; and
- *How to identify which rules apply when sharing information.*

These are very helpful and we discuss them in **Information Sharing: Guidance for Practitioners and Managers**, p 119. You should download them from www.gov.uk/government/publications/information-sharing-for-practitioners-and-managers.

We start, however, by reminding you of your ethical and legal responsibilities and considering why confidentiality is so important.

The Code of Ethics

The British Association of Social Workers (BASW) Code of Ethics is a key tool in helping you with the difficult conflicts that can arise in the relationships between professionals and their service users. Paragraph 10 of the Code sets out the ethical position on confidentiality and disclosure. We have set this out for you in **Box 4.1**.

You will see as you go through this chapter that the ethical principles are reflected in both the common law and the statutory framework. Confidentiality is the starting point, both legally and ethically. This is because social work, like many of the caring professions, is based upon the concept of respecting individual autonomy. Social workers obtain private information about individuals as a result of their privileged position in society. Unwarranted disclosure of that information is a breach of an individual's personal integrity. A relationship of confidentiality between a service user and the social worker promotes trust in social workers and allows people to discuss their problems knowing that the information will not be disclosed. Without this assurance, people may be unwilling to seek help.

Of course, there are circumstances when a social worker owes a greater duty to the community than to the individual who has disclosed information. The social worker may be obliged, or may have the discretion, to breach any obligation of confidence they owe to an individual. The difficulty is recognizing when those circumstances arise. Behaving ethically and legally in problematic circumstances and ensuring that an individual service user is appropriately protected involves difficult dilemmas.

BOX 4.1 Paragraph 10 of the BASW Code of Ethics

Maintaining confidentiality

Social workers should respect the principles of confidentiality that apply to their relationships and ensure that confidential information is only divulged with the consent of the person using social work services or the informant. Exceptions to this may only be justified on the basis of a greater ethical requirement such as evidence of serious risk or the preservation of life. Social workers need to explain the nature of that confidentiality to people with whom they work and any circumstances where confidentiality must be waived should be made explicit. Social workers should identify dilemmas about confidentiality and seek support to address these issues.

Information Sharing: Guidance for Practitioners and Managers

This practitioners' guidance was published by the government in 2008 to help social workers to develop good practice in information sharing. It sets out clearly when and how information can be shared legally and professionally, in order to achieve improved outcomes for service users. At the heart of the guidance are seven questions which must be answered in order to inform legal and ethical information sharing. These questions are set out in **Box 4.2**.

BOX 4.2 Seven key questions for information sharing

3.1 If you are asked, or wish, to share information, you must use your professional judgement to decide whether to share or not and what information it is appropriate to share, unless there is a statutory duty or a court order to share.

3.2 To inform your decision making this section sets out further information in the form of seven key questions about information sharing:

1. Is there a clear and legitimate purpose for you or your agency to share the information?

2. Does the information enable a living person to be identified?

3. Is the information confidential?

4. If the information is confidential, do you have consent to share?

5. If consent is refused, or there are good reasons not to seek consent to share confidential information, is there a sufficient public interest to share the information?

6. If the decision is to share, are you sharing information appropriately and securely?

7. Have you properly recorded your information sharing decision?

In order to answer these questions you need an understanding of the HRA, the common law of confidentiality, and the Data Protection Act. We discuss each of these in turn.

The Human Rights Act 1998

We have already described (in **chapter 3**) the significance and the impact of the HRA for social work practice. Every decision you make must comply with the Act. We set out the European Convention Articles which are of particular relevance to decisions about confidentiality in **Box 4.3**. We have emphasized the words that are important for this chapter in bold. The case study also demonstrated the importance of human rights in this context.

BOX 4.3 Extracts from key Articles

Article 6—Right to a fair trial

(1) In the determination of his civil rights and obligations or of any criminal charge against him, everyone is entitled to a fair and public hearing within a reasonable time by an independent and impartial tribunal established by law. **Judgment shall be pronounced publicly** but the press and public may be excluded from all or part of the trial in the interests of morals, public order or national security in a democratic society, where the interests of juveniles or the protection of the private life of the parties so require, or to the extent strictly necessary in the opinion of the court in special circumstances where publicity would prejudice the interests of justice.

(3) Everyone charged with a criminal offence has the following minimum rights:

(a) to be informed promptly, in a language which he understands and in detail, of the nature and cause of the accusation against him;

. . .

(b) to examine or have examined witnesses against him and to obtain the attendance and examination of witnesses on his behalf under the same conditions as witnesses against him;

. . .

Article 8—Right to respect for private and family life

Everyone has the right **to respect for his private and family life**, his home and his correspondence.

There shall be no interference by a public authority with the exercise of this right except such as is in accordance with the law and is necessary in a democratic society in the interests of national security, public safety or the economic well being of the country, for the prevention of disorder or crime, for the protection of health or morals, or for the protection of the rights and freedoms of others.

Article 10—Freedom of expression

Everyone has the right to freedom of expression. This right shall include freedom to hold opinions and to receive and impart information and ideas without interference by public authority and regardless of frontiers. This article shall not prevent States from requiring the licensing of broadcasting, television or cinema enterprises.

The exercise of these freedoms, since it carries with it duties and responsibilities, may be subject to such formalities, conditions, restrictions or penalties as are prescribed by law and are necessary in a democratic society, in the interests of national security, territorial integrity or public safety, for the prevention of disorder or crime, for the protection of health or morals, for the protection of the reputation or rights of others, for preventing the disclosure of information received in confidence, or for maintaining the authority and impartiality of the judiciary.

Human rights and privacy

It is important at this stage to consider the distinction between privacy and confidentiality. Traditionally, there has been no right to privacy recognized in English law, as distinct from the legal protections given to confidential information. However, the European Court of Human Rights (ECtHR) is increasingly stressing the legal significance of privacy as the three cases set out in **Box 4.4** indicate.

 BOX 4.4 The increasing importance of privacy

Peck v UK (2003)

On the evening of 20 August 1995, at a time when he was suffering from depression, Mr Peck walked alone down Brentwood High Street, with a kitchen knife in his hand, and attempted suicide by cutting his wrists. He was unaware that he had been filmed by a closed circuit television (CCTV) camera installed by Brentwood Borough Council.

The CCTV footage did not show the applicant cutting his wrists; the operator was solely alerted to an individual in possession of a knife. The police were notified and arrived at the scene, where they took the knife, gave the applicant medical assistance, and brought him to the police station, where he was detained under the Mental Health Act 1983. He was treated by a doctor and released without charge.

The council sought to publicize the value of CCTV and used the incident to demonstrate how CCTV had ensured prompt action was taken to protect Mr Peck's life. Footage of the incident was used in the local paper and in a national television programme. Mr Peck was identifiable from this footage.

The court observed that, following the disclosure of the CCTV footage, the applicant's actions were seen to an extent which far exceeded any exposure to a passerby or to security observation and to a degree surpassing that which the applicant could possibly have foreseen. The disclosure by the council of the relevant footage therefore constituted a serious interference with the applicant's right to respect for his private life.

Perry v UK (2003)

Mr Perry was arrested in connection with a series of armed robberies. When he refused to take part in an identity parade, he was covertly videotaped in a police station and as a result identified by two witnesses. Mr Perry was subsequently convicted.

The ECtHR ruled that Mr Perry's right to respect for private life under Article 8 of the ECHR was breached. The covert videotaping had gone beyond the normal use of their station camera and was not in accordance with the law on identification procedures laid out in the code of practice. The police had not informed Mr Perry or his solicitor that the tape was being made or obtained his consent, and had not informed him of his rights in that respect.

Mosley v News Group Newspapers [2008] EWHC 1777 (QB)

In this well-publicized case Mr Mosley, a prominent figure in Formula 1 racing, and son of Oswald Mosley, the 1930s fascist leader, was covertly filmed taking part in paid-for consensual sadomasochistic sex, leading to sensationalized news and web publications. He did not deny the activity, though he did deny the suggestion that participants were wearing Nazi uniforms. He claimed that his right to confidence and to respect for private life was breached, and argued that there was no corresponding public interest in broadcasting his private sexual activities.

Eady J started from the premise, set out in many Strasbourg decisions, that a person's sex life is a private matter, and covert filming is generally an intrusion. Whether it could be justified as a proportionate interference depended on other factors. Here there was no criminal offence being committed; whether the activities were depraved or not did not create a public interest in knowing about them; Mr Mosley's public persona did not require the public to know about his private life. He had not put any aspect of his private life, or his opinions about sexual conduct, into the public domain. The public interest in responsible journalism did not outweigh the right to respect for private life, and this was not responsible journalism.

These developments are very much in line with your ethical responsibilities set out in the BASW Code of Ethics and you should be aware that there is likely to be an increasing emphasis on privacy in the courts. However, rights are not absolute and the state has responsibilities to protect its citizens lives. Often, keeping vulnerable people safe requires that private information is disclosed. The starting point for decisions to disclose is the common law duty of confidentiality.

The common law duty of confidentiality

The common law provides individuals with a cause of action (a right to sue) for damages if there is a breach of the legal duty of confidentiality. We discussed what we mean by common law in **chapter 1**. The branch of common law that we are concerned with here is tort. A person (or organization) can sue in tort if they claim a breach of some duty: for example, a duty to take appropriate care (eg as a driver), a duty to respect persons or property, or in this case a duty to keep information confidential. In a case involving confidentiality a court can interfere, either by making an award of damages or by making an order, known as an injunction, prohibiting the disclosure of the relevant information. Note that the duty of confidentiality extends to children and adults who lack capacity, and even to the dead.

Breach of confidence is a tort that can apply to the collection, use, or disclosure of personal information. But not all information is protected by the law of tort. There are three basic requirements.

The information must actually be confidential. If someone consents to information which they provide being shared then it is no longer confidential. Paragraph 3.8 of the practitioners' guidance puts it like this:

> Confidence is only breached where the sharing of confidential information is not authorised by the person who provided it or to whom it relates. If the information was provided on the understanding that it would be shared with a limited range of people or for limited purposes, then sharing in accordance with that understanding will not be a breach of confidence. Similarly, there will not be a breach of confidence where there is explicit consent to the sharing.

Further, the courts will generally not protect information that is in the public domain or readily available from another source. The 'Spycatcher' case (*Attorney General v Observer Newspaper and others* (1989)) involved a former spy whose book revealing secrets gained in the course of his employment had been published in the US and Australia. The House of Lords refused an injunction as there was nothing left to protect: nevertheless, they were clear that there had been a breach of confidentiality between employer and employee.

However, courts may act to limit further disclosure, even if the information is already in the public domain. Moreover, the cases that we discussed earlier about the increasing importance of privacy indicate that the public/private divide is not clear-cut. Mr Peck's suicide attempt was in a public place, but he did not anticipate that it would be televised to nine million viewers, and he had the right to be protected from that dissemination.

So the information should have a degree of sensitivity and value which gives it the quality of confidentiality. Furthermore, it must have been communicated in circumstances giving rise to an obligation of confidence. If you guaranteed that you would not disclose the information, that guarantee would give rise to the obligation. However, the obligation can also be implied from the relationship between the person who communicated the information and the recipient. Mr Mosley, in the sadomasochism case, was entitled to expect confidentiality from his fellow participants, and bringing in a secret camera was a breach of that expectation. If there is a professional relationship such as exists between a lawyer and their client or a social worker and service user then information divulged is likely to give rise to the obligation of confidence. The obligation will extend to information you learn indirectly, for instance from a relative of a service user, because the information was received in your professional capacity.

Third, there must have been an unauthorized use of the information. If a service user gives you permission to divulge particular information then the tort cannot arise. However, the service user could give you permission to disclose information only in certain circumstances or to certain people. Communication of the information in breach of those requirements would give rise to the tort. Moreover, the service user must have capacity to consent to the disclosure.

However, confidentiality is not an absolute right. Having 'just cause or excuse' or acting in the public interest are defences to an action for breach of confidence. You can breach a duty of confidentiality to prevent serious crime. Paragraph 3.10 of the practitioners' guide explains:

> A public interest can arise in a wide range of circumstances, for example, to protect children or other people from harm, to promote the welfare of children or to prevent crime and disorder. There are also public interests, which in some circumstances may weigh against sharing, including the public interest in maintaining public confidence in the confidentiality of certain services.

Government departments and local authorities owe duties of confidentiality in the same way that individuals do. As there may be uncertainty about when it will be in the public interest to disclose information, legislation is sometimes used to provide clarity. Sometimes the legislation prevents the disclosure of information by imposing specific obligations of confidence, for instance in the Abortion Act 1967. Sometimes there is an obligation to inform a statutory authority. For instance, in the case of specific diseases there is an obligation to inform the NHS. Courts too can order the provision of information. The guidance explains (at para. 3.8) that:

> these situations are relatively unusual and where they apply you should know or be told about them. In such situations, you must share the information, even if it is confidential and consent has not been given, unless in the case of a court order, your organisation is prepared to challenge it and is likely to seek legal advice.

Consent

Information about service users can be shared if you get consent. Depending on the circumstances you may need the consent of the person who provided the information in confidence, and the consent of the person to whom the information relates. We explained some of the complexities of consent in **chapter 2**. Remember the person giving consent must understand the consequences of giving consent. Also, although consent may be implied, it is far better to get explicit consent to any sharing of information. Get the consent in writing and keep it on file. The best time to explain how you will handle confidential information is at the beginning of your relationship with the service user.

So where are we up to?

What you have learned so far from consideration of your ethical responsibilities, the HRA, and the common law duty of confidentiality is that whilst the starting point is that information is confidential, there may be a range of circumstances which justify disclosure. Your role is to balance the competing interests, bearing in mind the need for proportionality. The practitioners' guide says, at para. 3.10:

> The key factor in deciding whether or not to share confidential information is proportionality, i.e. whether the proposed sharing is a proportionate response to the need to protect the public interest in question. In making the decision you must weigh up what might happen if the information is shared against what might happen if it is not, and make a decision based on a reasonable judgement.

In **Box 4.5** and **Box 4.6** we set out in summary the balancing exercise which you must undertake.

BOX 4.5 The basic duty to protect confidences

Confidences should be kept because	But, bear in mind . . .
Privacy is protected both legally and ethically—Article 8 of the ECHR, the common law, statute such as the Data Protection Act, etc, and the social work code of ethics	This is only a starting point and in exceptional cases both legally and ethically disclosure will be necessary. Note that human rights jurisprudence requires that disclosure must be necessary and proportionate
Litigation privilege protects communications with lawyers	The cases show that it is strong but not immutable and the privilege is limited to the litigants
Children require privacy	Not in serious criminal cases, or in cases of anti-social behaviour
Public interest immunity	It is in the public interest that certain facts, such as the identity of police informers, are kept confidential. Note, however, that human rights jurisprudence limits the extent of public interest immunity

BOX 4.6 Reasons to disclose information

Disclosure is required because . . .	But, bear in mind . . .
Child protection and partnership working requires information to be shared	There is no presumption of disclosure; each case must be considered on its own merits
Allegation should be spelled out—Article 6 of the ECHR	Article 6 has great weight, but must be weighed against the public interest

Disclosure is required because . . .	But, bear in mind . . .
Secrecy damages trust	Personal information should be kept private, and disclosed only as far as necessary
Open media—Article 10 of the ECHR	Sources will have to be protected but can be disclosed if it is in the overriding public interest
Other reasons—particularly relating to the abuse of children by professionals and others	But only where there is evidence of a pressing need; disclosure must be limited to what is necessary

The Data Protection Act 1998

The third legal element of information sharing identified by the practitioners' guidance is the Data Protection Act 1998. Information held by social services departments is governed by the requirements of the Data Protection Act 1998. The Act requires data controllers who process personal information to comply with a range of data protection principles.

Data controllers are people, including organizations, who decide how and why personal data are processed. 'Personal data' refers to information relating to an identified or identifiable living individual which is processed automatically (including information processed on a computer) or recorded manually as part of a filing system or part of an accessible record. This will include records such as social services files. Processing covers anything done in relation to such data, including collecting it, holding it, disclosing it, and destroying it. The eight data protection principles are key to understanding the Act. We have set them out in **Box 4.7**. You will notice how similar they are to the ethical principles we set out at the beginning of this chapter:

> the detection or prevention of crime, or the protection of members of the public against dishonesty malpractice or incompetence or enabling confidential counselling, or enabling research.

 BOX 4.7 The data protection principles

Data protection principles	Comment
Fairly and lawfully processed	Lawfully refers to the requirements found in the common law of confidentiality, administrative law (the processing must not be ultra vires, ie outside the authority of the organization or contrary to statutory provisions) and conforming with the provision of Article 8 of the ECHR
Processed for limited purposes	Information is held for a purpose. You should be clear what that purpose is and the information should only be used for that purpose

Data protection principles	Comment
Adequate, relevant, and not excessive	Only necessary information should be held
Accurate	You have a responsibility to ensure that the information is accurate and you should have systems in place for checking the accuracy, for instance confirming details with your service user
Not kept longer than necessary	Once the reason for holding the information is past then the information should be destroyed. There should be a system in place for checking regularly the continuing relevance of information held
Processed in accordance with the data subject's rights	These are set out in Schedules 2 and 3 to the Act, discussed in Conditions for processing data
Secure	Non-authorized people should not be able to get access to the information. You should be clear who has authority to access information and who does not
Not transferred to countries without adequate protection	Information should not automatically be sent to other countries when the service user moves abroad. The new country may not have similar standards of protection of information

Conditions for processing data

Data Protection Principle One goes on to state that personal data shall not be processed (which includes disclosure) unless: '(a) at least one of the conditions in Schedule 2 is met, and (b) in the case of sensitive personal data, at least one of the conditions in Schedule 3 is also met'. Sensitive personal data are concerned with ethnic origin, political or religious beliefs, trade union membership, physical or mental health, sexual life, and criminal offences. Conditions of most relevance to social services departments within both Schedule 2 and Schedule 3 are the need to protect the vital interests of the subject and for the exercise by a government department of functions of a public nature exercised in the public interest by any person. Schedule 3 includes an additional relevant condition—where there is a substantial public interest in crime prevention, policy, and regulatory functions.

Principle One also requires that data subjects—individuals—must be told the identity of the data controllers and the purposes for which their data are to be processed. Individuals should also be made aware of any additional purposes for which their data may be used.

Therefore disclosure can be made for many purposes without obtaining consent and in compliance with the Act as long as the information in question was obtained fairly and no breach of the common law was involved.

Access to personal information

The Data Protection Act 1998 provides a right of access to personal information held by *public authorities* and *private bodies*, regardless of the form in which it is held. One important practical implication is that social workers must be aware that individuals are entitled to request a copy of information held about them and that the local authority has an obligation to ensure that information relating to individuals is structured in such a way that specific information relating to an individual is readily accessible. Not all information need be disclosed; the right is subject to exemptions. **Box 4.8** summarizes the position.

To obtain access the individual must write to the data controller, stating that they are applying under s. 7 of the Data Protection Act 1998 for access to any personal data about themselves. The data must be disclosed unless it is exempt information, which we summarize in **Box 4.9**. Note that there is an important additional exemption which relates to social work records which we discuss in **Access to social work and NHS records**, p 129.

 BOX 4.8 Access to information

An individual can see information held about them:

- by anyone on computers (or in other forms where data can be processed automatically);
- in health, social work, housing, and school records held on paper. This applies to all information, not just that in 'structured' files;
- in all structured files held by any organization, including government departments, local authorities, the police, employers, and private companies. The right applies regardless of when the files or filing system was created;
- Under the Freedom of Information Act 2000, 'unstructured' information (not accessible by computer or in manual records, including material that relates to an individual but is not specifically about him or her) held by any public authority is accessible (with cost restrictions) under the Data Protection Act Section 9A.

All these rights are subject to a variety of exemptions, which allow certain information to be withheld.

'Structured' files are collections of files or papers organized in a way that makes it easy to find information about a particular individual.

 BOX 4.9 Exempt information under the Data Protection Act 1998

Personal information about someone else—this will not normally be released without that person's consent. However, the Data Protection Act does allow such information to be disclosed *without consent* if this is reasonable in all the circumstances. If the information can be disclosed in a way that does not identify the individual—for example, by deleting the name or other identifying features—then the individual is entitled to it.

Information that would identify someone who has supplied information—only identifiable *individuals*, not organizations, are protected. The exemption does not protect the identity of a health professional, social worker, or teacher who has provided information which is recorded on the health, social work, or educational record.

Law enforcement—personal data held for the purpose of preventing or detecting crime, apprehending or prosecuting offenders, or assessing and collecting any tax or duty is exempt if disclosure would prejudice one of those purposes.

National security—information can be withheld on national security grounds.

References are generally exempt. There is no right to obtain a confidential reference from the person or body *which gave it*. But you would be entitled to see a reference *held by the person to whom it was supplied*, except where this would identify the *individual* who gave it.

Information about the course of negotiations between the data controller and the individual are exempt, if disclosure would prejudice those negotiations. General opinions and intentions are not exempt.

Examination marks and examiners' comments are exempt for a short period. An individual is entitled to see these 40 days after the examination results have been announced or five months after the request has been received, whichever is shorter.

Adoption records and reports are exempt.

Access to social work and NHS records

A service user is entitled under the Data Protection Act 1998 to see all information held by a local authority social services department, including 'unstructured' information. However, there is an important additional safeguard preventing disclosure of certain information. Information can be withheld if disclosure would be likely to cause serious harm to the service user or to any other person's physical or mental health. This includes the physical or mental health of a health or social care professional. In a mental health tribunal, the presumption is that patients should have access to the material in their own records, but information can be withheld under the Tribunal Procedure (First Tier Tribunal) (Health Education and Social Welfare) Rules 2008 which would be likely to cause serious harm to the patient or another individual.

An individual is entitled to see only their own records. If the child is too young to consent, the parent can apply on the child's behalf. Any information that a child has provided in the expectation that it would not be shown to the parents is exempt.

The result of these exemptions means that a parent who is accused of child abuse is unlikely to be given access to the child's records, or to information provided by the child but recorded on the parent's file. However, the parent should still be able to see other information recorded about him or herself such as the notes of an interview or home visit, as long as disclosure would not expose the child to risk or prejudice law enforcement; if the evidence is to be used in court, the right to full disclosure would prevail.

A family member caring for a mentally handicapped adult who cannot give informed consent to their application has no explicit right of access to that person's file, unless they are acting under a power of attorney (ie an authorization to make decisions on behalf of an individual) or an order of the Court of Protection.

Remember that information about someone else recorded on a service user's file and anything that would identify an individual who has provided information about a service user will normally be exempt unless disclosure is reasonable in the circumstances.

The Freedom of Information Act 2000

The Data Protection Act 1998 gives individuals the right to access information about themselves. The Freedom of Information Act 2000 extends this right to include non-personal information.

The Freedom of Information Act 2000 provides statutory rights for those requesting information. Under the Act any member of the public can apply for access to information held by a range of public authorities, including local authorities. There are exemptions.

First, information such as that relating to investigations and proceedings conducted by public authorities, court records, and trade secrets is covered by what are called category-based exemptions.

Second, information is exempt if it satisfies a prejudice test (ie is likely to harm someone's interests), for example where disclosure would or would be likely to prejudice the interests of the UK abroad or the prevention or detection of crime.

However, the public authority must consider whether the information must be released in the public interest, on a case-by-case basis.

The Information Commissioner and Information Tribunal

The Information Commissioner and an Information Tribunal oversee and enforce both the Freedom of Information Act 2000 and the Data Protection Act 1998. Each statute is concerned with responsible handling of personal information and therefore having one office overseeing the implementation of the legislation should ensure the coherent development of the law.

Particular examples

Bear in mind that the decision to disclose information requires more rigorous analysis than the maintenance of confidentiality. Public interest, the general justification for disclosure, is a slippery concept. This is particularly so for social workers whose role ranges from caring for the individual, through broader statutory responsibilities to protect the vulnerable, and beyond, to the investigation of harmful, often criminal, activities. Social workers are also required to work in partnership with a number of state agencies, including the police. The courts demonstrate an increasingly sophisticated understanding of the professional role of the social worker and provide some case-specific examples of appropriate and responsible information handling. Further, in this chapter we consider some common situations when confidentiality is a particular issue.

Disclosure of confidential material to the police

Many agencies hold their records under an express or implied undertaking to hold them in confidence. Police investigating crime can obtain warrants to search the records of agencies such as social services and, subject to judicial discretion, will be able to use the material in criminal prosecutions, notwithstanding the confidential nature of the contents. But while powers exist to force disclosure under a court order, those holding information must still start from an assumption of confidentiality, as para. 28 of circular *Personal Social Services: Confidentiality of Personal Information*, DoH Circular LAC (88)17 (now archived) indicates (emphasis added):

> The disclosure of personal information [to the police] may *exceptionally* be justified if it can help to prevent, detect or prosecute a serious crime . . . Before such a disclosure is made at least the following conditions must be satisfied:
> the crime must be sufficiently serious for the public interest to prevail. A record should be kept of when information is disclosed for this purpose;
> it must be established that, without the disclosure, the task of preventing or detecting the crime would be seriously prejudiced or delayed;
> satisfactory undertakings must be obtained that the personal information disclosed will not be used for any other purpose and will be destroyed if the person is not prosecuted, or is discharged or acquitted; request from a police officer of suitably senior rank, e.g. superintendent or above.

Paragraph 30 continues:

> In addition, evidence may come to the attention of staff which may justify disclosure on their own initiative to the police so as to protect another individual. The most common example of this is in cases of child abuse.

Legislation provides for some very specific circumstances when information must be disclosed to the police if they ask for it, for instance under the Prevention of Terrorism Act 1989, the Misuse of Drugs Act 1971, and the Police and Criminal Evidence Act 1984. If the particular provisions under these statutes apply then social workers have no choice but to disclose confidential information. We do not have space to detail these provisions, and advise you to take legal advice as soon as a request to provide information is received. However, the more challenging scenario is where legislation gives only a power to disclose information. Section 115(1) of the Crime and Disorder Act 1998 provides:

> Any person who, apart from this subsection, would not have power to disclose information—
> (a)   to a relevant authority; or
> (b)   to a person acting on behalf of such an authority,
> shall have power to do so in any case where the disclosure is necessary or expedient for the purposes of any provision of this Act.

This is a broad provision which impacts upon social services as members of Crime and Disorder Reduction Partnerships alongside the police and other local authority departments. This provision is not unique. For instance, s. 17 of the Anti-terrorism, Crime and Security Act 2001 extends the existing disclosure powers of public authorities contained in 66 Acts where disclosure would assist (amongst other things) criminal investigations, criminal proceedings, the initiation or bringing to an end of any such investigation or proceedings, or facilitating a determination of whether any such investigation or proceedings should be initiated or brought to an end.

Decisions to disclose

When should social services choose to use these extensive powers to disclose information? Disclosure is allowed only if it conforms with the public interest exception to the common law duty and the proportionality and necessity requirements of the Human Rights Act. Disclosure may exceptionally be justified if it can help to prevent, detect, or prosecute a serious crime. However, the nature of the relationship between local authorities and the police has changed dramatically since 1988. Emerging partnerships mean that social services are likely to feel greater responsibilities to work with the police. Society has also become more risk-averse. What in the past may have been exceptional may become more routine to eliminate risks to children through criminal or anti-social activities.

The Regulation of Investigatory Powers Act 2000

Social workers do much more than provide support for families. They also investigate abuse. It may be that social services acquire information other than through direct information gathering. Local authorities, as public authorities, are able to engage in covert surveillance such as entry to or interference with property, following suspects, and use of informers. There are legal controls on these activities. Covert information gathering is governed by the Regulation of Investigatory Powers Act 2000. The Act aims to ensure that the use of powers to investigate individuals through surveillance or to intercept telecommunication complies with the HRA, in particular Article 8. (It also implemented Article 5 of EU Directive 97/66/EC, now Directive 2002/58/EC, which to some extent provides a European framework for handling such information and surveillance.) Public authorities have only the surveillance powers conferred by the Act, and if they exceed these powers they will be acting unlawfully. Surveillance operations to obtain evidence require prior authorization from a designated person. Local authorities can designate assistant chief officers and officers responsible for the management of investigations. A written record must be kept and include the reasons for granting the authorization and its terms. Necessity and proportionality are the bases for granting authorization. Proportionality is tested against the object to be achieved by carrying out the surveillance in question. The Act establishes a Surveillance Tribunal which oversees the Act and considers allegations that public authorities have infringed human rights by surveillance activities.

If a local authority fails to get activities authorized, then the evidence produced will be tainted if used in any court proceedings, as it will have been obtained in breach of s. 6 of the HRA ('It is unlawful for a public authority to act in a way which is incompatible with a Convention right'). Any prosecution using the evidence will be vulnerable to arguments that evidence acquired in breach of Convention rights should be excluded under s. 78(1) of the Police and Criminal Evidence Act 1984 (a court 'may refuse to allow evidence on which the prosecution proposes to rely to be given if it appears to the court that . . . the admission of the evidence would have such an adverse effect on the fairness of the proceedings that the court ought not to admit it'). Decisions to use these powers are likely to be taken at the highest level, but any social worker exceptionally involved in any covert activity should be fully briefed on what is and is not permissible.

Adoption and confidentiality

The difficulties and fragilities of adoption seem to pose particular challenges. Two ombudsman decisions indicate the dilemmas which can face social services. In Report 97/A/3857, Mrs W complained about the way a council placed two children with her and her husband with a view to adoption. One aspect of the complaint was the lack of information about the children's behavioural problems. The ombudsman accepted that social workers had to make difficult decisions about what they could disclose without improperly breaching confidentiality. Some of the information Mrs W asked for could not be disclosed, but the ombudsman said that the council did not tell her and her husband things which would not have entailed an improper breach of confidence and which they reasonably needed to know, such as information about the children's health and history of abuse. The ombudsman concluded that as it became clear to the prospective adopters that they had not been told enough about the children, they became increasingly anxious about what they did not know. That prolonged anxiety was an important element of the injustice caused by the way the council acted.

Inappropriate disclosure

The second case demonstrates that openness must be appropriate. Report 97/C/3985 concerned the induction process between the complainant and child she hoped to adopt, which was terminated without good reason, without proper notice, and without adequate explanation. One particular aspect of the complaint was that the council had allowed the child's foster parents full access to the complainant's adoption form. The ombudsman commented:

> Whilst it may be perfectly proper for a foster carer, who has an in depth knowledge and understanding of a child, to play some part in the selection process of a suitable adoptive parent, I can see no justification nor statutory basis for extending this to providing the foster carer with detailed personal and confidential information about the prospective adoptive parent. It appears to me to be totally inappropriate and unprofessional for such confidential information to be made available to anyone other than the most essential personnel.

The council's action exposed the complainant to unnecessary and unwarranted intrusion into her private affairs.

Perpetrators of abuse

Professionals who abuse

Professionals who abuse their own children are unlikely to be able to protect themselves from the disclosure of the information to their professional bodies. In *A County Council v W (Disclosure)* [1997] 1 FLR 574 disclosure of the care proceedings to the General Medical Council where the father involved was a doctor was allowed on the basis that disciplinary proceedings would possibly protect other children. In *Re L (Care Proceedings: Disclosure to Third Party)* [2000] 1 FLR 913 the mother, a paediatric nurse suffering mental and emotional problems, had caused her child significant emotional harm which resulted in an interim care order. The court gave leave to disclose the judgment and the medical reports to the UK Central Council for Nursing. The rights of the mother and child had to be balanced against the public interest in demanding protection from nurses who were or who were potentially unfit to practise. In *London Borough of Brent v SK and HK (A Minor)* [2007] 2 FLR 914 Brent applied to court for permission to disclose evidence from care proceedings, which arose from an assault by a mother upon her child, to the mother's employers, a residential home for the elderly. The judge gave permission for limited and confidential disclosure. The case is also useful because it reviews the existing case law in this area.

Other perpetrators

Even where perpetrators do not have professional responsibilities disclosure may be ordered. In *R v Chief Constable of North Wales, ex p AB* [1997] EWHC Admin 667 a married couple released from prison after serving long sentences for serious sexual offences against a number of children rented a caravan on a caravan site as their home. The police informed the site owner of the convictions, and as a result the site owner required the couple to leave. They then sought a judicial review of the police decision to disclose the convictions. The Court of Appeal confirmed the Divisional Court's dismissal of the application. It was compatible with Article 8 because there was a pressing need for the police to disclose material already in the public domain to a caravan site owner, when the material related to paedophiles on the site who were a considerable risk to children and vulnerable adults who might come onto the site during the holidays.

What was critical here was the real evidence of a pressing need for disclosure. Without such evidence the authorities are much more vulnerable, as the following case demonstrates. In *R v Local Authority in the Midlands, ex p LM* [2000] 1 FLR 612 the applicant, who owned a bus company, had his contract to transport school children terminated. This was because of social services and police concerns arising from an allegation against him of indecent assault on his daughter seven years previously, along with a further allegation against him of sexual abuse three years before that. He wished to take up a new contract for school bus services and therefore asked for assurances from the police and social services that such allegations would not be further disclosed. The authorities refused to give those assurances and he sought judicial review of the refusals. The court held that it was not compatible with Article 8 for the police to disclose stale and unproven allegations of sexual abuse to a county council which employed the applicant to provide school transport because there was no 'pressing need' for disclosure.

Information governance

The law relating to confidential information illustrates the difficult and conflicting demands upon professionals striving to carry out their responsibilities. In the context of health services, the Caldicott review of personally identifiable information in 1997 recommended that 'guardians' of personal information be created to safeguard and govern the uses made of confidential information within NHS organizations. The review advocated a managerial approach, based upon a framework of quality standards for the management of confidentiality and access to personal information. The Caldicott approach has been extended by the government to councils with social services responsibilities which were required to appoint a Caldicott guardian by 1 April 2002. Full details are set out in LAC (2002)2. Caldicott guardians must audit existing systems, procedures, and organizational capabilities relating to confidentiality and security. The 18 audit areas require consideration of a range of prerequisites for responsible information handling, for example examining the level of information provided to service users about the proposed uses of information, the extent of confidentiality requirements in staff contracts, the extent of information-sharing protocols, and the extent of confidentiality and security training. The results of audits should inform subsequent performance reviews of social services departments. Whilst there is a great deal of value in the approach, it reflects its origins in the context of health care as it does not indicate how the greater policing responsibilities of social services should be incorporated into the framework.

The Care Act 2014 and information sharing

Safeguarding adults boards (SABs) (see **chapter 14**) are local groups set up to facilitate joint working on protecting any vulnerable adult with needs for care and support or experiencing or at risk of abuse or neglect. The new Act has put these on a statutory basis with Schedule 2 requiring that they include representatives from the local authority and NHS clinical commissioning group and the chief officer of police. Others with care or support functions may be represented such as providers of housing and organizations or individuals to be specified in later regulations. As is the case with local safeguarding children boards, there is now a duty on relevant organizations to supply SABs with information on request. The request must be made 'for the purpose of enabling or assisting the SAB to exercise its functions'; it must be made 'to a person whose functions or activities the SAB considers to be such that the person is likely to have information relevant to the exercise of a function by the SAB'; and the information must relate to: (a) the person to whom the request is made; (b) a function or activity of that person; or (c) a person in respect of whom that person exercises a function or engages in an activity.

The provision may be to deal with worries that bureaucratic interpretation of the Data Protection Act is standing in the way of perfectly sensible information sharing for legitimate purposes. As such, a rather wide and somewhat ill-defined power has been created to demand information from anyone who has 'functions or engage in activities such that the SAB considers it likely to have information relevant to a function of the SAB'. Explanatory notes list family members of the adult, carers, GP, someone who has done voluntary work with the individual, or a church minister with knowledge of the family or the individual. The information may be used by the SAB or other person to whom it is supplied 'only for the purpose of enabling or assisting the SAB to exercise its functions'. The Act applies no sanctions against misuse of the information, which may be a worry, particularly given the wide range of non-professional people the government intends to be involved in SABs—who could include members of the family of a vulnerable adult. The rules on confidentiality certainly apply to all such information, as outlined earlier, as does the Data Protection Act once the SAB has gained the information. But presumably so too does the Article 10 right of freedom of expression. What if a SAB member received a controversial report as part of his or her SAB duties and felt it should be given wider publicity? Could family members on a SAB talk to their lawyers about what went on at its meetings? Or does the 'only to exercise its functions' provision act in effect to sterilize that information, putting it beyond use even as evidence in a court of law? At this stage we cannot really know.

Data sharing—a summary

You are very likely to be involved in data sharing; perhaps you will receive a request for confidential data you hold, or perhaps you will be involved in a data-sharing partnership.

The government's information-sharing guidance provides a summary of the principles underpinning good practice.

- You should explain to children, young people, and families at the outset, openly and honestly, what and how information will, or could, be shared and why, and seek their agreement. The exception to this is where to do so would put that child, young person, or others at increased risk of significant harm or an adult at risk of serious harm, or if it would undermine the prevention, detection, or prosecution of a serious crime including where seeking consent might lead to interference with any potential investigation.

- You must always consider the safety and welfare of a child or young person when making decisions on whether to share information about them. Where there is concern that the child may be suffering or is at risk of suffering significant harm, the child's safety and welfare must be the overriding consideration.

- You should, where possible, respect the wishes of children, young people, or families who do not consent to share confidential information. You may still share information, if in your judgement on the facts of the case, there is sufficient need to override that lack of consent.

- You should seek advice where you are in doubt, especially where your doubt relates to a concern about possible significant harm to a child or serious harm to others.

- You should ensure that the information you share is accurate and up to date, necessary for the purpose for which you are sharing it, shared only with those people who need to see it, and shared securely.

- You should always record the reasons for your decision—whether it is to share information or not.

The guidance also summarizes in a diagram the legal questions which need to be answered in deciding whether to disclose information. The diagram is provided in **Figure 4.1.**

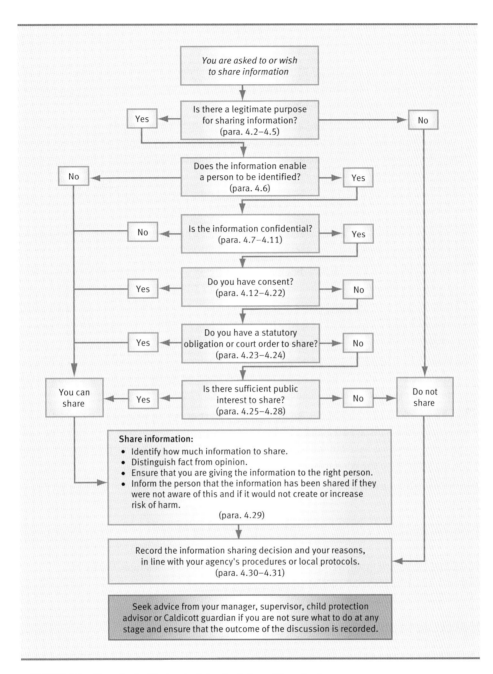

FIGURE 4.1 Flowchart of key principles for information sharing

Source: Department for Education and Skills.

EXERCISES

1 Why is confidentiality important? When do you think confidentiality should be breached? Does your thinking accord with the legal position? The ethical position? Are there ever circumstances when your ethical obligation is to breach a confidence?

2 In the following circumstances what issues are raised about human rights, your professional responsibilities, and confidentiality? How would you suggest they should be resolved? Do not forget to consider the Human Rights Act 1998 and the Data Protection Act 1998 in preparing your response.

   (a) The Housing Department of a local authority asks the Social Services Department for any information it has about anti-social behaviour by a particular family.

   (b) An anonymous caller rings social services because she has seen evidence of physical abuse of a child. The local authority asks the family's health visitor for information.

   (c) You, a child-care professional, tell the headteacher of a secondary school about your concerns for a particular child. The headteacher tells the child's form teacher.

   (d) You suspect Mr X of sexual abuse of his grandchildren. Mr X has found himself accommodation with a housing association which is housing him in a block of flats which also accommodates families. You want to tell the housing association of your concerns.

   (e) When you were visiting a family you overheard a telephone conversation which indicated that one of the adult children of the family was involved in criminal activities. You want to tell the police but your team leader says that the issue is not serious enough.

3 You have serious concerns about Fred who you suspect of having physically and emotionally abused his two sons aged 12 and 14. You have recorded these concerns on both of the children's files. Fred has asked to see his file. He has obtained signed consents from his sons. What are his rights to do so? What information will he be allowed to see?

4 Why do you think there are specific provisions for information sharing within the Care Act 2014?

ONLINE RESOURCE CENTRE

For guidance on how to answer these exercises, visit the Online Resource Centre at www.oxfordtextbooks.co.uk/orc/socialwork13e/.

WHERE DO WE GO FROM HERE?

Our overview of the common law duty of confidentiality and its interface with the HRA and information legislation illustrates the complexity of the area. Clearly, a balance needs to be reached between the necessity to protect children and other vulnerable people and the right to privacy. The law is moving towards greater sharing of information, provided the decision to share is one that is proportionate and necessary. On the other hand, we also see that public opinion is strongly in favour of privacy and resists state intrusion. It is this tension which causes legal uncertainty. We can understand and sympathize with the confusion and bewilderment the law creates for many social care professionals who are at the sharp end of this dilemma. The law does not necessarily make your decision making any easier—but it should help to clarify the issues you must consider.

This chapter concludes the first part of the book. You are now armed with the necessary tools to enable you to understand the more specific legal responsibilities we consider in Part 2 (relating to children) and Part 3 (relating to vulnerable adults).

 ANNOTATED FURTHER READING

Confidentiality

R. S Taylor, '*Re S (A Child) (Identification: Restrictions on Publication)* and *A Local Authority v W*: children's privacy and press freedom in criminal cases' (2006) *CFLQ* 18 (2): 269. This commentary considers the decisions in two difficult cases which raised the question of whether the courts can and should restrain publication of the identity of defendants in criminal trials in order to protect the welfare of their children. The cases reveal the ways in which the courts seek to reconcile press freedom and the privacy of the vulnerable.

T. Keyser and C. Dainty, *The Information Governance Toolkit: Data Protection, Caldicott, Confidentiality* (Radcliff Publishing, 2004). It is difficult to find anything specifically aimed at social work, but this is a good overview aimed at health care professionals and the issues are the same for social workers.

Information sharing

C. Cobley, '"Working Together?"—admissions of abuse in child protection proceedings and criminal prosecutions' (2004) *CFLQ* 16 (2): 175. This article considers the way in which information is exchanged between the child protection and criminal justice systems. It suggests that tensions between the two systems increase as cases progress.

'Public Sector Data Sharing: Guidance on the Law', www.justice.gov.uk/downloads/information-access-rights/data-sharing/annex-h-data-sharing.pdf.

Part 2

Responsibilities towards children

Part 2 Responsibilities towards children

The state has for many years taken on the role of looking after children when families cannot adequately meet their needs. On behalf of the state, this is a large part of what social workers do. Child protection and child welfare issues are far more prominent in social work than adult protection issues, and involve significantly greater use of the courts, so as a result this part of the book is considerably longer than Part 3.

This part of the book considers the range of statutory duties the social worker has towards children. The Children Act 1989 provides the legal framework for these responsibilities. The need to provide services for, or protect, children can often be triggered by family breakdown, so private family law needs to be considered as well.

Chapter 5 considers Part I of the Children Act 1989, which sets out the overarching principles of the law relating to children. We explain the critical importance of the welfare principle and the other principles which are set out in the legislation. The chapter also sets out how social services departments should work with other agencies which have a role in safeguarding children. Those agencies can be statutory, such as the police and health authorities, or voluntary. Working with these agencies ensures that the most effective outcomes for children are achieved. This chapter then explains the government's legislative response in the Children Act 2004 including *Working Together to Safeguard Children* before going on to consider inter-agency working.

Chapter 6 explains the responsibilities that local authorities have towards children in need, 'looked-after' children and care leavers. The chapter also considers the extensive amendments made to the Children Act 1989 by the Children and Young Persons Act 2008.

The next three chapters are concerned with the processes which are triggered when social workers take action to protect children. **Chapter 7** describes the local authority responsibilities to investigate cases where there are concerns about the welfare of children and to assess the needs of children. Investigations may be required by the court, or as a result of an agency or a member of the public expressing concerns about a child. It is vital for social workers to respond appropriately.

Chapter 8 sets out the law relating to applications for court orders. There are a variety of court orders available to the local authority, ranging from orders which provide for the long-term care of the child to short-term orders which enable the local authority to respond to emergency situations. Different considerations apply in each of these orders, reflecting the extent to which they interfere with the integrity of the family, the duration of the order, and the nature of the circumstances in which the application is made.

Chapter 9 moves on from the initial investigative role of local authorities to consider the role of local authorities in providing long-term security for children. Long-term plans need to be formulated as soon as possible, so as to avoid children 'drifting' in care, with local authorities failing to address their specific needs. This can involve consideration of adoption, and we explore the Adoption and Children Act 2002, which sought to modernize and increase the use of adoption. The Act also includes provision for special guardianship orders, which enable children to have long-term security in circumstances where there are good reasons for not permanently severing their links with their birth family.

Chapter 10 goes in a different direction. It explains how the criminal justice system deals with children when they are accused of crime. What is interesting is that the philosophy of the criminal justice system is quite different from that of the Children Act, despite the fact that in each arena we are concerned with the needs of children.

The principles of children's law

5

OVERVIEW AND OBJECTIVES

The aim of this chapter is to look at the overall structure and philosophy of the Children Act 1989 and at some common definitions in relation to children and the law. It also describes the Safeguarding and Inter-Agency System created to protect children. We consider in some detail the agencies which share your statutory responsibilities towards children and other vulnerable people and explain their roles. We also briefly consider the range of problems which vulnerable people may face and describe a range of voluntary sector agencies which provide advice and assistance to those families. In subsequent chapters we look at the more detailed provisions of the Children Act 1989. You will find it useful to have your own full copy of the statute via www.legislation.gov.uk/ukpga/1989/41/contents. These chapters provide an introduction to the Children Act.

In this chapter we shall look at:

(a) the overall structure of the Children Act 1989;

(b) the philosophy behind the Children Act 1989;

(c) some relevant concepts;

(d) principles applicable to court proceedings under the Children Act 1989;

(e) the role of children's guardians and Cafcass;

(f) how your role complements the roles of other professionals concerned with vulnerable people including an outline of the Children Act 2004 which provides the legislative framework for improving service provision for children.

CASE STUDY

R (G) v Nottingham City Council (2008)

Facts (taken from the judgment of Munby J)

G was born on 31 May 1989, so she is 18 years old. She has had a sad and troubled life. She has been in the care of Nottingham City Council. She has a history of alcohol and drug abuse. She has self-harmed. She is a very vulnerable young adult. In 2007 she became pregnant. The baby was due to be born on 3 February 2008. Unexpectedly ... the mother went into labour. She gave birth in the small hours of Wednesday at about 2 a.m. Her son was born seemingly healthy and well. At about 4 a.m. her son was removed from her and placed in a different room in the hospital.

Application

An immediate application was made for mother and child to be reunited. The local authority produced two documents which explained the basis upon which the child had been removed. Munby explains,

> The first was the minutes of an inter-agency child protection conference which had taken place on 18 December 2007. The minutes record the conference recommendation, inter alia, that the local authority 'apply for an Interim Care Order once the child is born [and] organise a care placement for when the child is born'. They recite that 'the birth plan for the baby is to remain in hospital until he is taken into foster care', further noting that 'the baby must not be removed from the ward by [G] ... if necessary an Emergency Protection Order should be sought if the Interim Care Order is not in place'.

The minutes further record the recommendation that what was described as 'details of the agreed birth plan' be sent to all hospitals in the region.

  The other document was the 'Birth Plan' prepared for the medical staff at the hospital by Nottingham City NHS Primary Care Trust. Referring to the child protection meeting that had been held on 18 December 2007, the Birth Plan said that 'Baby is to be placed in foster care.' In relation to delivery in hospital it said 'please discuss with [G] at delivery if she wishes to see or hold baby.' It continued:

> Baby will be removed at birth and there will be no contact without supervision. . . . The baby will not ... be left in her sole care. ... Further contact with baby on the ward will be supervised by Social Services.

There was no reference in that document to obtaining any emergency protection order or interim care order. So the need for one or other of those steps to be taken if the child was to be removed from G was not brought to the attention of the midwives and other medical staff to whom the document was addressed.

Decision

The application was granted. There was no legal authority for separating mother and child. The judgment is worth reading for the clarity with which it explains the legal principles. The relevant paragraphs are set out below.

15. The law is perfectly clear but perhaps requires re-emphasis. Whatever the impression a casual reader might gain from reading some newspaper reports, no local authority and no social worker has any power to remove a child from its parent or, without the agreement of the parent, to take a child into care, unless they have first obtained an order from a family court authorising that step: either an emergency protection order in accordance with section 44 of the Children Act 1989 or an interim care order in accordance with section 38 of the Act or perhaps, in an exceptional case (and subject to section 100 of the Act), a wardship order made by a judge of the Family Division of the High Court.

16. Section 46 of the Children Act 1989 permits a police constable to remove a child where he has reasonable cause to believe that the child would otherwise be likely to suffer significant harm, and that power can be exercised without prior judicial authority. But the powers conferred on the police by section 46 are not given to either local authorities or social workers.

17. Local authorities and social workers have no power to remove children from their parents unless they have first obtained judicial sanction for what they are proposing to do. Only a court can make a care order. Only if a court has authorised that step, whether by making an emergency protection order or by making a care order or an interim care order or in some other way, can a local authority or a social worker remove a child from a parent. And the same goes, of course, for a hospital and its medical staff.

18. As I said during the course of the hearing, no baby, no child, can be removed simply 'as the result of a decision taken by officials in some room.'

19. This is all elementary. It is well known to all family lawyers. And it is, or ought to be, well known to all social workers. That is why, as the media accurately reported, I made the comment during the course of the hearing that 'The professionals involved in this case should have known better.' I went on to point out, however, that the midwives and doctors in a delivery room in the small hours could not have been expected to understand this. No doubt they acted as they did in accordance with the 'Birth Plan' that had been given to them by their superiors.

Munby J did make two points of clarification in his judgment. The first relates to the situation where a child is at risk of immediate harm.

21. In the first place, a social worker or a nurse is of course entitled to intervene if that is necessary to protect a baby from immediate violence at the hands of a parent. That is not, however, because they have any special power or privilege entitling them to intervene. It is merely an application of the wider principle that anyone who happens to be present is entitled, whether by restraining the assailant or by removing the defenceless victim from his assailant's reach, to intervene in order to prevent an actual or threatened criminal assault taking place before his very eyes.

The second point relates to s. 3(5) of the Children Act 1989, which provides that:

A person who—

    (a)   does not have parental responsibility for a particular child; but

    (b)   has care of the child,

may (subject to the provisions of this Act) do what is reasonable in all the circumstances of the case for the purpose of safeguarding or promoting the child's welfare.

What Munby says about the operation of that section is helpful.

> 24. Now section 3(5) could not avail the local authority, because it did not have the 'care' of G's son. But there might be circumstances in which a hospital could rely upon section 3(5) as justifying action taken in relation to a child in its medical care, despite the absence of parental consent and the absence of any court order.
>
> 25. For instance, medical intervention might be required in order to preserve the child's life or to protect a child from irreversible harm in circumstances of such urgency that there is not even time to make an urgent telephone application to a judge. In such a situation of emergency a doctor can act without parental or judicial consent and, if parents are acting unreasonably or contrary to the child's best interests, even despite a parental refusal of consent: see Grubb, *Principles of Medical Law*, ed 2, para 4.21.
>
> 26. Doctors, midwives and nurses do not have to stand idly by waiting for a court order if, for example, a premature baby desperately needs to be put in a special unit or placed on a ventilator. They are of course entitled to separate the child from the mother if medical necessity dictates, and even if she objects. Law, medical ethics and common sense march hand in hand.

WHAT DOES THIS CASE TELL YOU ABOUT SOCIAL WORK PRACTICE?

Munby J's decision provides a valuable opportunity to re-emphasize one of the most important principles of the Children Act 1989. The state can only interfere in the lives of its citizens if it has legal authority to do so. That has to be your starting point. The fact that the local authority was about to make an urgent application to the family proceedings court for an interim care order or an emergency protection order was not relevant to the legality of separating the mother and child prior to any order being made by the court.

Nonetheless, you will probably be interested in the outcome of the subsequent proceedings. Munby delivered his judgment on the morning of Friday 1 February 2008. The day before the local authority had made an application to the family proceedings court in Nottingham for an interim care order in respect of G. That application was transferred by the family proceedings court to the Nottingham County Court. On 1 February the judge in the County court made an interim care order.

The overall structure of the Children Act 1989

The Act has over 100 sections and 15 schedules. It is a very large piece of legislation. It is divided into Parts. The Parts group together different sections under headings. We reproduce, in **Box 5.1**, an outline of the Parts in the Children Act and the main chapters in this book in which we consider those Parts. We do not have the space to examine every Part in great depth. We concentrate on those Parts the 'field' social worker will have to be familiar with.

BOX 5.1 The Parts of the Children Act 1989

Part number	Title	Chapter number and comment
Part I	Introductory	**Chapter 5** Outlines key principles underpinning the legislation
Part II	Orders with respect to Children in Family Proceedings	**Chapter 5** This deals with the private law proceedings Key section is s. 8
Part III	Local Authority Support for Children and Families	**Chapter 5** Children in need Key section is s. 17 Concerned with public law proceedings
Part IV	Care and Supervision	**Chapter 8** Deals with care orders and supervision orders concerned with public law proceedings
Part V	Protection of Children	**Chapter 6** Sets out the key s. 47 local authority duty to investigate **Chapter 8** Provides for emergency protection orders and other short-term measures to protect children concerned with public law proceedings
Part VI	Community Homes	Essentially regulatory
Part VII	Voluntary Homes and Voluntary Organizations	These Parts, set below and to the left, whilst important, fall outside the scope of this textbook
Part VIII	Registered Children's Homes	
Part IX	Private Arrangements for Fostering Children	
Part X	Child Minding and Day Care for Young Children	
Part XA	Child Minding and Day Care for Children in England and Wales (inserted by the Care Standards Act 2000)	
Part XI	Secretary of State's Supervisory Functions and Responsibilities	
Part XII	Miscellaneous and General	

The philosophy of the Act

Guidance and regulation

You are advised to read this chapter in conjunction with the Children Act 1989 statutory guidance. Five volumes can be found at www.gov.uk/government/publications/children-act-1989-court-orders--2.

A word of clarification and warning: these excellent books contain guidance which has to be considered by all local authorities, as they are issued under s. 7 of the Local Authority (Social Services) Act 1970 (LASSA) (see **chapter 1**). They are not the final statement of the law. They reflect the government's view of what it hopes the words of the Act say. Therefore, while you should read them, do not take them to be the final, definitive statement of the law.

It is the courts that finally decide what the law means and, whilst helped by guidance, the social worker has to consult with his or her lawyers for the best interpretation.

The underlying philosophy

It may be easier to understand the philosophy of the Children Act 1989 if you have some knowledge of the complex and perhaps contradictory forces which led to its implementation. One major impetus was the need to address a number of child abuse scandals. These ranged from reports of social service failure, for instance in *A Child in Trust—The Report of the Panel of Enquiry into the Circumstances Surrounding the Death of Jasmine Beckford* (Louis Blom-Cooper, London Borough of Brent, 1985), *Whose Child?*—Report on the death of Tyra Henry (London Borough of Lambeth, 1987), and *A Child in Mind*—Report on the death of Kimberley Carlile (London Borough of Greenwich, 1987), to reports of overzealous social work, for instance in the *Report of the Inquiry into Child Abuse in Cleveland 1987*. Another impetus was the need to provide a legal statement of the increasing importance of children's rights. These had been articulated in the courts as a result of the *Gillick* judgment (see **chapter 2**) and in international commitments, such as the United Nations Convention on the Rights of the Child 1989.

Finally, the Act provided a reaffirmation of the belief that the best place to bring up children is usually within their family. This is clearly stated in the published guidance.

> A key principle of the 1989 Act is that children are best looked after within their families, with their parents playing a full part in their lives, unless compulsory intervention in family life is necessary.
>
> (*The Children Act 1989 Guidance and Regulations, Volume 2: Care Planning, Placement and Case Review*, para. 1.4)

Thus, the philosophy is that the child should be brought up with the child's family, and the local authority should be providing support to that end. This needs to be both understood and, more importantly, accepted by all those who carry out statutory work under the Children Act 1989.

In addition to this concept is the belief that the state, in the shape of the local author-ity, should not, normally, take control of a child's life unless some strict statutory cri-teria are met. These criteria—described as the threshold criteria—are the grounds for care and supervision orders contained in s. 31 of the Act—see **chapter 6**.

■ Some relevant concepts

The welfare of the child is paramount

There are three different welfare duties in the Act. These are set out in **Box 5.2**.

The Children Act 1989 requires the welfare of the child to be the paramount consid-eration only when the court is making a decision under its powers under the Act. Even then, if the Act lays down other statutory considerations, the welfare of the child is not paramount.

It is only when a court is dealing with a case that affects a child directly that that child's welfare is paramount. So, when the House of Lords was considering what should happen to a young baby born to a 16-year-old mother in care, it had to put the welfare of the baby as being paramount above that of the baby's mother (even though the mother was under 16 and, as such, a child). This was because the court was dealing with an appli-cation concerning the baby—not the mother (*Birmingham City Council v H (No 3)* (1994)).

BOX 5.2 The welfare duties in the Act

- A court making a decision as to the upbringing of a child must have the welfare of the child as the paramount consideration (s. 1(1)). This is unless there are statutory requirements that apply different criteria. (For example, the court can never make a care order if the sig-nificant harm test is not satisfied. This is true even if the welfare of the child would be best served by the care order.)

- A local authority must safeguard and promote the welfare of a child, in its area, who is in need (s. 17).

- A person who has the care of a child but not parental responsibility can do what is rea-sonable in all the circumstances for the purpose of safeguarding or promoting the child's welfare (s. 3(5)).

The welfare concept might be better expressed if it were stated that the Children Act requires everybody to safeguard and promote the welfare of children as far as is pos-sible, because that is the primary and universal duty.

Human rights and the welfare of the child

Article 8 of the European Convention on Human Rights specifically relates to respect for family life, which could potentially conflict with the welfare of the child unless the court is satisfied that interference by a public authority is warranted. Local authority and social work decision making will need to justify any interference in family life (see **chapter 8**). Decisions will need to be proportionate (see *Re C and B (Children) (Care Order: Future Harm)* (2000) and in general **chapter 3**). Overall, however, lawyers' views are that the requirement that the welfare of the child be the court's paramount consideration is consistent with Convention case law and within the margin of appreciation (allowance for local circumstances) permitted to national authorities under Article 8, and is therefore compatible with that Article.

Respect for the child

This is a concept that is difficult to define but which pervades all the questions of how the law looks at the child. There are two particular aspects. First, the child, and not the parents, for instance, is the focus of your decision making and, second, you should take account of the wishes and feelings of the child in your decision making. It would be wrong however, to consider the child's welfare as something which does not involve the parents. A famous British psychiatrist, D. W. Winnicott, argued, as long ago as 1953, that 'there is no such thing as a baby' (*Collected Papers: Through Paediatrics to Psycho-Analysis*, Tavistock Publishing), meaning that without a parent, an infant does not exist. Empirical evidence from modern-day neuroscience would tend to agree. No matter how poor, neglectful, or abusive parenting is, the child should always be seen in relationship with the parent. Respect for a child includes respect for the child's relationships.

The child is your primary responsibility

In dealing with children you need to recognize that the law regards the child as your primary responsibility. You cannot escape the comment made on behalf of the British Association of Social Workers to the Jasmine Beckford inquiry, which fully endorsed:

> [the] clear and unequivocal view that in any child abuse case the primary client for the social worker is the child. The many conflicts are easier to resolve if social workers always bear in mind who is the primary client.

The wishes of the child

Conflict is inevitable between parent and child at some stage of the child's development. Part of the growing process is the assertion of the child's independence. When the state becomes involved in the essentially private area of family life, the real difficulty is for the state to ascertain when that independence should be allowed to become a reality. Clearly, a six-month-old baby cannot be independent, and if the parents fail the child then the state must step in and either assume parental responsibility or ensure someone else takes it up. But what is to be said for a 12-year-old child or a 16-year-old young person? If their parents fail, what consideration has to be given to the wishes of the child or young person?

For a statutory recognition of this concept we need to look at s. 22 of the Children Act 1989 which we set out in **Box 5.3**.

BOX 5.3 The wishes of the child—s. 22 of the Children Act 1989

(4) Before making any decisions with respect to the child whom they are looking after, or proposing to look after, a local authority shall, so far as is reasonably practicable, ascertain the wishes and feelings of—

   (a) the child;

   (b) his parents;

   (c) any person who is not a parent of his but who has parental responsibility for him; and

   (d) any other person whose feelings the authority consider to be relevant, regarding the matter to be decided.

(5) In making any such decision a local authority shall give due consideration—

   (a) having regard to his age and understanding, to such wishes and feelings of the child as they have been able to ascertain;

   (b) to such wishes and feelings of any person mentioned in subsection (4)(b) to (d) as they have been able to ascertain; and

   (c) to the child's religious persuasion, racial origin and cultural and linguistic background.

The child is mentioned before the parents or any other person in this section. This suggests that the child's wishes are to be the first consideration. This applies whether or not the child is subject to a court order. It should also be borne in mind that if any matter concerning the child is taken to court, then the court will apply the welfare principle, placing the child's welfare as paramount; that is, coming before and overriding anyone else's welfare or convenience.

Respect for the child's autonomy

The statutory responsibilities are expanded by the decisions of the courts, notably the *Gillick* case discussed in **Informed consent**, p 157 and more fully in **chapter 2**. In dealing with any children, you have to ensure that an appropriate level of respect is given to the child as an individual who is entitled to separate consideration in his or her own right. As the Cleveland Report put it, 'the child is a person not an object of concern'. As a result of the respect principle, you will find courts and local authorities are required, throughout the Act, to take into account the wishes and feelings of the child. (This does not necessarily mean carrying out those wishes.) Respect for the child does not mean the child has absolute right above all other.

Partnership with parents under the Children Act 1989

Whilst partnership with parents is not a legal requirement under the Children Act, guidance makes it clear that a local authority is required to work, as far as possible, in partnership with children and their families. For instance:

parents should be encouraged to exercise their responsibility for their child's welfare in a constructive way and that where compulsory intervention in the family is necessary it should, where possible, support rather than undermine the parental role. The 1989 Act places a strong emphasis on the local authority working in partnership with parents when undertaking their statutory functions.

(*The Children Act 1989 Guidance and Regulations, Volume 2: Care Planning, Placement and Case Review,* para. 1.6)

The principle is reflected in the statute in a number of ways set out in **Box 5.4**.

There are a number of ways in which the state can and does promote the involvement of parents to participate in Children Act 1989 proceedings. Parents with parental responsibility are automatically parties to the proceedings and parents without parental responsibility have the right to be notified of public law proceedings. Parents are entitled to public funding in most public law proceedings without any means test, and in dealing with social services, parents of looked-after children have a right to be consulted, a right to have their views taken into account and a right to participate in case conferences. The courts have also insisted on fair procedures, particularly since the advent of the Human Rights Act 1998 (see *Re L (Care Assessment Fair Trial)* (2002) and *Re J (Care; Assessment; Fair Trial)* [2006] EWCA Civ 545). In addition, the new 2014 Public Law Outline, Practice Direction 12A—Care, Supervision and Other Part 4 Proceedings: Guide to Case Management, establishes a pre-proceedings checklist which should include a range of assessments conducted on the family and in specific instances a Letter Before Proceedings and a pre-proceedings meeting. As noted in **chapter 2**, a Letter Before Proceedings indicates to parents the concerns held by the authority about their care of the child and what they and the authority will do to protect that child. This letter and the assessments conducted on the family rather suggest that local authorities should exhaust voluntary means to help parents and their children by seeking to work collaboratively with them before instigating proceedings.

 BOX 5.4 Partnership with parents under the Children Act 1989

(a) accommodation of children looked after should be provided as a consumer-led service (s. 22);

(b) that accommodation should be near the children's parents;

(c) contact with parents is presumed if a child is in care (s. 34), and during emergency protection (s. 44) or police protection (s. 46);

(d) care orders do not remove parental responsibilities (s. 2(6));

(e) abolition of care by stealth, that is, that the placing of a child or young person into local authority accommodation cannot lead, of itself, to that child or young person becoming subject to any form of statutory control; and

(f) the duty of the local authority to consult parents when they accommodate a child (s. 20) or provide services (s. 17).

Limits on partnership

It is important to note that the concept of partnership with parents and families does not remove the overriding duty of the local authority to safeguard and promote the welfare of the child. Allowing partnership to become paramount is both misapplying the law and bad practice. The death of Peter Connelly in 2008 has highlighted the difficulties inherent in a partnership first approach.

Social workers must have the professional skills to recognize when partnership with parents is failing to protect a child. At that point, it must necessarily cease to be the underpinning strategy of child protection work. This is put clearly in *Statutory guidance on court orders and pre-proceedings: For local authorities* (Department for Education, 2014):

> Where concerns do arise and are identified by a local authority, the local authority is under a duty to act.

Parental responsibility

The concept of continuing parental responsibility is critical to the Act. Married parents, unmarried mothers, and, since 1 December 2003, when the relevant section of the Adoption and Children Act 2002 was implemented, unmarried fathers who are registered on the birth certificate gain parental responsibility automatically; unmarried fathers who are not registered on the birth certificate or whose child was born before December 2003 have to apply to court to acquire parental responsibility. Parental responsibility is defined—as far as it can be defined—in s. 3 of the Act set out in **Box 5.5**.

 BOX 5.5 The meaning of parental responsibility—s. 3(1)

(1) In this Act 'parental responsibility' means all the rights, duties, powers, responsibilities and authority which by law a parent of a child has in relation to the child and his property.

Parents derive their authority from their commitment to bringing up their children, and not from anything else.

Once acquired, parental responsibility continues. The only way in which parental responsibility can be terminated is via an adoption order: see **chapter 9**. However, the extent of parental responsibility can vary. It is at its most extensive when exercised by parents and guardians. It is less extensive when it is given to non-parents in child arrangements orders (see **chapter 6**) and when given to local authorities as a result of a care order. It is most limited in scope when the child is the subject of an emergency protection order and parental responsibility is given to the applicant for the order (see **chapter 8**).

▧ Informed consent

The principle of 'informed consent' permeates the Act. As a general rule, anyone (including a local authority) with parental responsibility can give a valid consent to the treatment of a child. (There are important limitations on the local authority's power when it has parental responsibility by virtue of an emergency protection order—see **chapter 8**.) However, there are limits on the powers of those with parental responsibility. First, irreversible medical treatment for non-therapeutic purposes (such as sterilization) should take place only with the leave of the court. Second, the age and understanding of the child are significant. The older and more mature a child becomes, the less the parent is entitled, as a matter of right, to know about and manage the child's affairs. The child does not have to wait for the age of majority (18) to be able to decide matters in his or her own right; that informed choice can be made at an earlier age. This statement of the law is based upon the decision of the House of Lords in *Gillick v West Norfolk and Wisbech Area Health Authority* (1986). The case concerned the question whether or not a parent was entitled to be informed that a child under the age of 16 was going to be given contraception. The notion of the *Gillick*-competent child is built into the statute. There are several examples of statutory provisions along the lines of 'but if the child is of sufficient understanding to make an informed decision he may refuse to submit to the examination'. We discussed consent and capacity in **chapter 2**.

Limits on autonomy

Our discussion on the legal competence of children in **chapter 2** indicated that there are a number of difficulties in treating the *Gillick*-competent child as capable of having informed consent. Court decisions do not completely support the notion of autonomy for children, yet the statutory statements within the Act are clear. The social worker must follow the requirements of the Act. However, in some extreme circumstances there may be the need to seek court approval to override the wishes of children if you consider that their decision is not in their own best interests.

Refusal to consent

One difficulty that is raised by the idea of informed consent is 'what happens if the child refuses to consent?' Much will depend on the matter for which consent is refused and whether the child is deemed to be *Gillick* competent. It would be prudent to engage with a *Gillick*-competent young person's reasons for refusing treatment since it would be an exception to give treatment in such circumstances against their will. However, the courts have overruled young people's refusal to treatment (*see Re R (A Minor) (Wardship: Consent to Medical Treatment)* 1992 1 FLR 190, *Re W (A Minor) (Medical Treatment: Court's Jurisdiction)* [1993] 1 FLR 1, and *Re M (Medical Treatment: Consent)* [1999] 2 FLR 1097).

The position of parents

The court also has powers to override the decisions of parents to refuse medical treatment for their children. In *Re A (Children) (Conjoined Twins: Surgical Separation)* (2000), the Court of Appeal sanctioned the separation of conjoined twins against the wishes of the parents, even though the result would be the death of the weaker twin. The court in these circumstances makes its decision based on the best interests of the child and not on the reasonableness of the parents' refusal of consent.

Diminishment of court proceedings

This applies only in the public law area of the Act. Its provisions are to be found tucked away in Schedule 2, Part I, para. 7, which we set out in **Box 5.6**.

This provision imposes a duty on local authorities, and in carrying out your responsibilities you should be looking for ways in which to give effect to it.

BOX 5.6 The diminishment of court proceedings

Every local authority shall take reasonable steps designed—

(a) to reduce the need to bring—

    (i)   proceedings for care or supervision orders with respect to the children within their area;

    (ii) criminal proceedings against such children;

    (iii) any family or other proceedings with respect to such children which might lead to them being placed in the authority's care; or

    (iv) proceedings under the inherent jurisdiction of the High Court with respect to children;

(b) to encourage children within their area not to commit criminal offences;

(c) to avoid the need for children within their area to be placed in secure accommodation.

Principles applicable to court proceedings under the Children Act

There are three main principles that guide courts under this Act, all of which are found in s. 1 of the Act. They are:

(a) the welfare principle (s. 1(1));

(b) the non-delay principle (s. 1(2)); and

(c) the 'no order' principle (s. 1(5)).

The welfare principle

When a court (but only a court) considers any matter concerning the welfare of the child, the court shall treat the child's welfare as its paramount consideration. This means that although the Act tries to balance the rights of the child and the rights of the parents, finally the court must do what the court sees as being best for the child. That is the function of the court, to arrive at a hard decision with which not all the parties may agree.

Not all court decisions

The welfare principle in s. 1 does not apply to all decisions by the court. Within the Act there are sections that have specific statutory requirements for the court to consider. If the Act gives such requirements, the court must follow these. It cannot apply only the s. 1 paramount welfare principle. For example, s. 10(9) deals with applying for leave to make an application for an order by a private individual. There are specific grounds for the court to consider (*Re A and W* (1992)). Where an application is made to place a child in secure accommodation under s. 25, again, specific statutory criteria apply (*Re M (A Minor) (Secure Accommodation Order)* (1995)). The court (per Butler Sloss LJ) said in that case:

> This duty cast upon the local authority to safeguard and promote the welfare of the child is not the same duty cast upon the court by section 1 to place welfare as the paramount consideration. Other considerations can and frequently do affect the local authority's approach.

So, even if a court is dealing with a specific case involving children under the Children Act, the welfare principle may not be paramount. It cannot override statutory time limits, such as the length of time an emergency protection order may last. It will not allow the court to go behind established principles of law. In *Re M (A Minor) (Appeal) (No 2)* (1994), the guardian *ad litem* sought to introduce evidence before the Court of Appeal of the effect on the child of being told that the child would have to return home to the mother. The child became hysterical and distressed. The court would not allow the evidence to be introduced. Yet another example is the case of *Nottinghamshire County Council v P* (1993).

The non-delay principle

The court 'shall have regard to the general principle that any delay in determining the question is likely to prejudice the welfare of the child' (s. 1(2)). The 'question' here means the question on upbringing the court is deciding. In addition to the emphasis in the Children Act 1989, decisions of the European Court of Human Rights (ECtHR) in connection with Article 6 emphasize the need for appropriate speed in decision making. The Children and Families Act 2014 introduces a statutory time limit of 26 weeks to complete care or supervision proceedings.

Avoiding delay

In any proceedings involving children, both in private law and public law, there are sections which provide that the court shall:

(a) draw up a timetable with a view to determining the question without delay; and

(b) give such directions as it considers appropriate for the purpose of ensuring, as far as is reasonably practicable, that that timetable is adhered to.

These provisions are to be found for private law in s. 11 and for public law in s. 32. The rules, under the Children Act, require the holding of a directions hearing (rule 14) for the court to make arrangements for preparing the case and hearing it. The first item to be addressed is the timetable for the proceedings. The non-delay principle will be applied. The Children and Families Act 2014 amends s. 32 so that when a court draws up a timetable for proceedings, it must in particular have regard to—

    (a) the impact which the timetable would have on the welfare of the child to whom the application relates; and

    (b) the impact which the timetable would have on the conduct of the proceedings.

In addition, when appointing experts a court must consider amongst other things the impact which giving permission to admit expert evidence would be likely to have on the timetable for, and duration and conduct of, the proceedings. The Public Law Outline 2014—an agreed procedure for the handling of public law Children Act cases— replaces previous protocols. We discuss the Public Law Outline in **chapter 8**.

The 'no order' principle

The court should not make an order unless it considers 'that doing so would be better for the child than making no order at all' (s. 1(5)). It is important to realize that the 'no order' principle is a principle for the court, not for social workers.

    The first *Annual Report on the Children Act* (Cm 2144) showed a considerable drop in the number of court proceedings taken under the Children Act compared with similar provisions under the former law.

    Since that first report was published, there have been interesting fluctuations in the number of applications for orders to the court. In recent years there has been an upturn in applications, in response perhaps to the deaths of children known to social services including Peter Connelly, Daniel Pelka, and Hamzah Khan, although the picture does fluctuate.

- Between April 2013 and March 2014 Cafcass received a total of 10,595 applications.

- This figure is 5 per cent lower when compared to the same period in the previous year, when 11,110 applications were received.

- New applications for all months except April, June, and October 2013 were lower compared to the same months in the previous financial year.

- Demand peaked during a few months. For example, new applications received in the months of April, May, September, and October 2013 were the highest ever recorded by Cafcass in those individual months.

April 2012–March 2013:

- During 2012–13, Cafcass received 11,110 new applications. This figure was 8 per cent higher when compared to the previous financial year.

- The 1,006 applications received in February 2013 were the highest ever recorded for a single month.

However, the general point about the misunderstanding of the 'no order' principle remains true. The duty of the social worker is to promote and safeguard the welfare of children who are in need. Therefore, the 'no order' principle should not in any way inhibit the social worker from taking statutory steps, including going to court, to carry out this duty. It is not the function of the social worker to second-guess the court and say, 'Well, the court may apply the no order principle and therefore I will not take any action.' Only when it is clear that it is a hopeless case should you consider not going to court because of the 'no order' principle.

In *T (A Child) (Care Order)* (2009) the Court of Appeal clearly restated the principle that it is the responsibility of the court and not the parties to the case to decide upon the appropriate order under the Children Act. The duty to treat the welfare of the child as the paramount consideration required the court to undertake the appropriate judicial investigation. In this case, all parties supported the care plan prepared by the local authority in which the child who had suffered non-accidental injuries would be returned to his parents' care under a supervision order which included provisions for monitoring the child. The judge, however, considered that the child remained at risk and imposed a care order. Whilst the Court of Appeal considered that the judge was acting perfectly properly in substituting the court's judgment for that of the local authority, it overturned the imposition of the care order. It considered that there were no strong and cogent reasons to force upon the authority a more draconian order than that which had been requested. In those circumstances, the care order would be varied to a 12-month supervision order.

In addition to these three main principles we find others, as set out in the following sections.

No compulsory intervention by the state without an application

This is a reflection of the philosophy of the Act and is applicable to both private and public law elements of the statute. The first point to be made here is that you cannot remove a child from its family without going to court. *R (G) v Nottingham City Council*, which we discussed at the beginning of this chapter, makes this absolutely clear. Second, the court cannot intervene to protect a child it perceives to be at risk without there being an application by the local authority or authorized person.

A salutary case to read is *Nottinghamshire County Council v P* (1993). In this case the local authority applied for an order under s. 8 of the Children Act that a self-confessed child abuser stepfather vacate the household and that the children should have no contact except under supervision. The court held that, since the effect of the order was in fact to make a residence and contact order, it could not make that order.

Local authorities are specifically excluded from applying for such orders (s. 9(2)), now referred to child arrangements orders. As the authority wished to ensure that the children were not put at risk by seeing their father unsupervised, they would have been better to apply for a care order. This is the view that the High Court judge and the Court of Appeal took. As the report of the judgment states:

> the route chosen by the council was wholly inappropriate. In cases where children were found to be at risk of suffering significant harm within s. 47 a clear duty arose on the part of the local authorities to protect them. . . . The council persistently and obstinately refused to undertake what was the appropriate course of action and thereby deprived the judge of the ability to make a constructive order. . . . The position was one which it was hoped would not recur.

Here the Court of Appeal found itself totally frustrated by being unable to make the order asked for. The local authority was seeking to obtain the effect of a care order by the back door. This is clearly contrary to the concept that the only basis on which statutory control can be obtained is by an application which satisfies the significant harm test.

The welfare checklist

This is found in s. 1(3) of the Children Act 1989. It is applicable to all court proceedings in both private and public law, except court proceedings under Part V (the emergency protection of children). It consists of a uniform checklist to which the courts need to have regard when they are faced with a dispute concerning any child. It is applicable whether the dispute is between individuals, or a local authority is applying for an order. Section 1(3) is set out in **Box 5.7**.

BOX 5.7 The welfare checklist—s. 1(3)

A court shall have regard in particular to—

(a) the ascertainable wishes and feelings of the child concerned (considered in the light of his age and understanding);

(b) his physical, emotional and educational needs;

(c) the likely effect on him of any change in his circumstances;

(d) his age, sex, background and any characteristics of his which the court considers relevant;

(e) any harm which he has suffered or is at risk of suffering;

(f) how capable each of his parents, and any other person in relation to whom the court considers the question to be relevant, is of meeting his needs;

(g) the range of powers available to the court under the Children Act in the proceedings in question.

Each point in the checklist is considered separately. There is no priority in the order in which the points appear. If you are seeking an order from the court, you must give careful attention to the checklist in your presentation of evidence and within your report. Also, expect in any disputed case to be cross-examined under each heading.

'Mix and match'

This is a useful expression derived from the Department of Health publication, *An Introduction to the Children Act*, where it states:

> [a] full menu of orders is also available to a court hearing a local authority application for a care or other order in respect of a child. Thus a court might, for example, order that a child

live with a suitable relative or friend rather than make a care order in favour of the local authority. Or it may mix and match by, for example, ordering that a child live with a non abusing parent and making a supervision order at the same time.

The best order in the circumstances

What this means is that the court should always seek to choose the best order for the child, and that choice is not limited to the orders that the parties have applied for. But the court cannot make a care or supervision order unless it has been applied for. How this works in practice can be seen in the case of *C v Solihull MBC* (1993). A 12-month-old child had suffered a non-accidental injury. The magistrates' court refused to grant a local authority application for a care order but returned the child subject to a supervision order with no conditions attached. On appeal, the High Court made a residence order which no one had applied for, with conditions attached, and an interim supervision order.

Family proceedings

Most proceedings in any area of family law are defined as 'family proceedings'. Inclusion in this category means that, if they have any family proceedings before them, the courts are free—in fact obliged—to apply the 'mix and match' principle, and make the best order for the child, not necessarily the one applied for, and quite possibly where no one has applied for an order under the Act.

The list of family proceedings is given in s. 8(3) and (4) of the Children Act 1989 as amended. We have reproduced this in **Box 5.8**. In **Box 5.9** we remind you of the orders that can be made in the context of family proceedings.

BOX 5.8 Family proceedings for the purposes of the Children Act

(a) High Court proceedings relating to children under the residual powers of wardship;

(b) Parts I, II, and IV of the Children Act 1989;

(c) Matrimonial Causes Act 1973;

(d) Schedules 5 and 6 to the Civil Partnership Act 2004;

(e) Domestic Violence and Matrimonial Proceedings Act 1976;

(f) Adoption and Children Act 2002;

(g) Domestic Proceedings and Magistrates' Courts Act 1978;

(h) Matrimonial Homes Act 1983;

(i) Matrimonial and Family Proceedings Act 1984;

(j) Family Law Act 1996;

(k) ss. 11 and 12 of the Crime and Disorder Act 1998.

BOX 5.9 Children Act orders in private disputes about the child

Section 8 covers disputes about the upbringing or treatment of a child. Orders can be made in favour of any person, not just the applicant and not just a parent; a grandparent, step-parent, unmarried father, friend, or even a sibling, for example. Courts must make the appropriate s. 8 order, regardless of which one was applied for. Anyone can apply, including a public authority; for example (a) instead of seeking care, social services can apply for an order that a child lives with a relative; or for example (b) a hospital can apply for an order that a child receives a blood transfusion against parental wishes.

A child arrangements order is an order regulating arrangements relating to with whom a child should live, spend time, or have other types of contact, or when they should do so. The 'other types of contact' a child arrangements order may provide for could include indirect contact such as a telephone call by the parent.

Specific issue order s. 8: where a person with parental responsibility normally makes (shares) decisions about a child (eg schooling, medical treatment) and there is dispute, any person (not just a parent, eg a local authority or another relative) can ask the court to make the decision about that specific issue. Specific issue orders have been used to determine religious issues (eg circumcision of boys), name changes, and consent to abortion.

Prohibited steps order s. 8: mirrors the specific issue order. The court order prevents parental responsibility being exercised in relation to a specified action, for example taking a child abroad or carrying out a non-therapeutic medical procedure.

What else can the court order when considering s. 8 applications? If a s. 8 application comes before a court, the court can make any other order under s. 8. As a s. 8 application is a family proceeding, a court could also make a Family Assistance Order or order a s. 37 report from the local authority, which could then lead to care proceedings. In an extreme case an interim care order could be made.

Section 8 orders in public law proceedings: if it is in the best interests of the child, a court can (indeed must) make a s. 8 order instead of the care or supervision order which the local authority has applied for.

Section 5 order: where the child has no parent or guardian, the court can appoint a guardian who will have parental responsibilities.

Not family proceedings

It is important to remember that proceedings under Part V of the Act (protection of children) are not family proceedings. So there can be no 'mix and match', only an emergency protection order, or a child assessment order, or no order at all.

Family assistance orders

In any family proceedings the court can, under s. 16 of the Children Act 1989, make a family assistance order, where the court is satisfied that there are exceptional circumstances and the people named in the order agree. Only the court can make the order; it cannot be applied for by a party. When a family assistance order is made the officer named in the order is to advise, assist, and (where appropriate) befriend the person named in the order.

This order is intended to be a short-term order; it can last for only a maximum of six months. It is to help the family over the difficulties that have led to the court appearance.

In *Re C (Family Assistance Order)* (1996), when the local authority said that it did not have the resources to implement the order, the court held that it had no power to force the authority to do so. Nor would the court compel a local authority under a family assistance order to accompany a child to visit that child's father in prison (*S v P (Contact Application: Family Assistance Order)* (1997)). Practice Direction 12M which came into force in October 2007 states that:

> Before making a family assistance order the court must have obtained the opinion of the appropriate officer (LA [local authority] or Cafcass) about whether it would be in the best interests of the child in question for a family assistance order to be made and, if so, how the family assistance order could operate and for what period.

It further stated that:

> Before making a family assistance order the court must give any person whom it proposes be named in the order an opportunity to comment upon any opinion given by the appropriate officer.

The role of children's guardians

The role of the guardian is one, historically, that has been long known to the court. Out of the context of child care, the guardian—also known as the child's 'next friend'—acted on behalf of children in court actions such as a claim for damages arising from an accident.

Maria Colwell

Guardians were introduced into the statutory framework of child-care law following the report of the Maria Colwell Inquiry published in 1974. In that case Maria was killed by her stepfather, having been returned from the care of the local authority following the revocation of the care order with the consent of the local authority. It was felt that the tragedy could have been avoided if Maria had been separately represented in the proceedings. A person acting solely on behalf of Maria could have argued that it was not in Maria's best interest for the care order to be revoked.

The Children Act 1989 contains the duty for courts to appoint guardians *ad litem* 'unless it is satisfied that it is not necessary' to safeguard the child's interests (s. 41(1)). Following the creation of Cafcass (see **Children and Family Court Advisory and Support Service**, p 166) the term 'children's guardian' is used instead of 'guardian *ad litem*' (Family Proceedings (Amendment) Rules 2001). The guardian then has to appoint a solicitor for the child (Family Proceedings Rules 1991). The rules permit the older child who is *Gillick* competent and who is in conflict with the recommendations of the children's guardian, to instruct their solicitor directly.

The functions of the guardian

Rules of court set out the functions of the guardian. The way in which the guardian works is by a process of investigation involving interviewing the local authority personnel, the child, the parents, relatives, and any other persons the guardian considers relevant. The guardian then prepares a report stating what the guardian considers to be in the best interest of the child's welfare. This report must be made available to all parties to the proceedings in advance of the final hearing.

Resources

In tandem with the lawyer acting for the child, the system ensures that the child's interests are protected and his or her rights respected and upheld by the court. Since the commencement of the Children Act 1989, you can expect guardians to be involved in proceedings concerning children, even at the stage of the application for an emergency protection order. The practical difficulty in the past was one of resources, there not being sufficient suitably qualified people to act as guardians. In some parts of the country, this shortage delayed proceedings.

Inspection of records

The guardians have the advantage of s. 42 of the Children Act 1989, which provides that a guardian has the power to inspect any local authority or NSPCC records relating to the child who is the subject of the court proceedings. In addition, in *Re R (Care Proceedings: Disclosure)* (2000), the court held that the guardian had a right to see a report compiled by the Area Child Protection Committee on the child's half-sibling who had been killed by the child's father. Having inspected those records, the guardian may take copies, and those copies shall be admissible as evidence both in the guardian's report and, if the guardian gives oral evidence, during the proceedings.

Your approach to the handling of any case must be carried out in the full knowledge that an officer of the court, the children's guardian, is possibly going to have the chance both to look at and produce in court all the records that you have made. More important, that person may be able to draw the court's attention to the fact that although you claim to have done a particular thing, there exists no record of this fact in your case notes. Accurately and comprehensively record all your actions and decisions as soon as possible after the events. Cafcass appoints the individual officer, who might be a Cafcass employee or a self-employed contractor. Note that the Cafcass appointee should be invited to all formal meetings relating to the child. This includes statutory reviews of children who are accommodated or looked after, child protection conferences, and relevant Adoption Panel meetings.

Children and Family Court Advisory and Support Service

The Children and Family Court Advisory and Support Service (Cafcass) was created by ss 11–17 of and Schedule 2 to the Criminal Justice and Court Services Act 2000. It is designed to carry out the functions set out in s. 12 of that Act, that is, to:

(a) safeguard and promote the welfare of children;

(b) give advice to any court about any application made to it in any family proceedings;

(c) make provision for the children to be represented in such proceedings; and

(d) provide information, advice, and other support for children and their families.

Cafcass—a non-departmental public body—came into operation on 2 April 2001. It unites the Family Court Welfare Service (FCWO) (which advises the courts in private law cases), the Children's Guardian Service and Reporting Officers Service, and the Children's Division of the Official Solicitor's Department.

▓ Private family law

We use the word 'private' to indicate that any recourse to law is initiated by individuals, not by the state. But family problems may well trigger an intervention by the state to provide services to children or to protect them. What we provide here is a brief glimpse of the various forms in which adults can come together in a relationship, and the legal provisions which can apply to them and to any children if that relationship falls apart.

Marriage, civil partnership, and other couple relationships

Since March 2014 following the Royal Assent of the Marriage (Same Sex Couples) Act 2013, marriage is for two people of the same or different gender; civil partnership is a formal commitment for people of the same gender (Civil Partnership Act 2004). In either case, the gender need not be the birth gender assigned (Gender Recognition Act 2004). In most respects marriage and civil partnerships have the same legal consequences for the parties. In the following discussion, therefore, we use the word 'marriage' to cover both types of state-recognized partnership.

You should be aware that in different cultures different norms and different legal structures will exist. What is set out here is what is recognized in England and Wales.

A valid marriage cannot be polygamous, though a potentially polygamous marriage, if there is in fact only one spouse, does not present problems.

The law defines who has or lacks capacity to marry—for example, there is a minimum age of 16, there are prohibited relationships such as marriage between siblings—and certain positive requirements such as where it can be celebrated, and the need for genuine consent. A marriage is not valid if one of the parties is already married. This is the case even if that party obtained a divorce abroad which was recognized abroad, if that divorce was not also recognized in the UK. Foreign divorces are in general recognized in the UK, but some are not: for example, where the divorce involves a couple, one of whom is settled in the UK, and the divorce procedure is a 'bare talaq' (pronouncement of divorce by the man, with no involvement of the civil authorities).

Foreign marriages are also generally recognized in the UK, so couples who married abroad before settling in the UK can use courts here to obtain a divorce, and any orders open to the courts to deal with property and money. There are, however, exceptions to this principle. For example, in *Westminster City Council v C* (2008) an autistic child had a severe impairment of mental function, as well as a diagnosis of autistic spectrum disorder. He had no capacity to marry. However, he took part in a marriage ceremony in

Bangladesh (his participation was by telephone from the UK, but that in itself is not an obstacle to recognition); under Bangladeshi law the marriage was valid, and such a marriage would normally call for recognition in the UK. The court, however, refused to recognize it for UK purposes as a valid marriage; the young man was a UK resident and needed protection, at least within the UK, from a marriage to which he could not consent.

Marriage is in principle an equal relationship. (This was not always the case. Until 1892 married women could not own their own property; and as late as the 1990s marital rape was not a crime.) So a spouse or civil partner has no control over the other spouse's freedom of movement, over their ownership of property, or over their right to do what they please as an individual. Marriage does, however, create preferential status in relation to inheritance (which is tax-free between spouses), next of kin status (eg being consulted where a person lacks capacity to consent to medical treatment—see **chapter 8**), acting as the nearest relative to a mental patient (see **chapter 15**), and on death the right to receive part of the occupational payment paid to the late spouse/partner. Marriage confers a right of occupation of the marital home, whichever party is the owner or tenant; this right can be registered in the Land Registry if the property is owned by the other spouse, as a way to prevent it being sold off. The right to occupation on the basis of marriage ends on divorce, though it continues if there is another basis to remain there (ownership, tenancy, or court order).

Marital status confers the right to go to court to seek financial maintenance from the other spouse/partner, which is not available for cohabitees or for people in other close relationships, such as friends or siblings living together.

A marriage ends on death, of course, but can also be terminated by choice. A party petitions the court, and has to show a recognized ground (living apart for at least two years, adultery, or unreasonable behaviour are the most common grounds in cases of married parties). Divorce or dissolution proceedings are almost never defended—what is the point?—so despite them being dealt with in court, it is in reality a bureaucratic procedure.

Where the courts do get involved is in dealing with disputes over children, property, and money—but courts can do that whether or not the parties are married. The difference is that without marriage, the courts are limited to dealing with disputes over children and disputes as to who owns what; they cannot make adjustments to ownership and they cannot award maintenance, except for the support of children.

It is widely, but wrongly, believed that there is also a legal status called common law marriage. It is true that people living together without being married, or in a civil partnership, are sometimes treated as a couple in law; this is when the state assesses their entitlement to social security as a couple. The result of being assessed as a couple is almost invariably a reduction of entitlement compared with what the claimant might get if not living with a partner.

Neither marriage, civil partnership, cohabitation, nor any other arrangement can compel people to live together. Housing and money problems, however, may lead to the same result, which is why those helping families need to know who to turn to for advice on escaping domestic violence, applying for housing, or seeking social security benefits. We will look at these topics in **Roles and responsibilities**, p 184.

Parental responsibility

Where more than one person has parental responsibility they must agree on decisions about the child's care and upbringing, and, if unable to agree, the court decides that issue. A court can under s. 8 of the Children Act 1989 (see **Private disputes involving children—s. 8 orders**, p 169) limit the way either a mother or a father exercises their parental responsibility, and can (s. 31—see **chapter 8**) make a care order, which then gives the local authority the upper hand, allowing it to determine the extent to which the parents may exercise their parental responsibilities.

Step-parents do not have parental responsibilities unless a court orders it. Where there is no person with parental responsibility a court can appoint a guardian—Children Act, s. 5.

Any person who does not have parental responsibility (eg a teacher or a babysitter) can take necessary action to safeguard the interests of a child who is in their actual care—Children Act, s. 3.

Private disputes involving children—s. 8 orders

Although we have drawn a distinction between public and private disputes concerning children, you should know from the outset that a local authority can be asked at any time in the course of private proceedings to provide a report to the court to help it to decide what is in the interests of the child, and a court can order an investigation by the local authority on whether child protection proceedings should be commenced (Children Act, s. 37).

You should also be aware that a court can make private law-type orders while hearing a public law case: for example, in the course of care proceedings they might make a child arrangements order detailing that the child should live with a grandparent or directing to whom a child should have contact. The boundaries between public and private law are blurred—they will be crossed whenever the interests of the child require it.

We will briefly look at the three types of s. 8 order a court can make. The following can apply for a s. 8 order:

- a parent;
- a guardian;
- a step-parent who has treated the child as a member of the family;
- a person who lived with the child for at least three years (if they apply within three months);
- the child, if he or she has sufficient understanding to do so;
- anyone else, with the court's leave.

In deciding whether to make an order, s. 1 says that 'the child's welfare shall be the court's paramount consideration'. So, even though s. 8 orders are matters of private law, the private needs and desires of family members come second to the public interest in making an order for the benefit of the child. The court must take into account the child's wishes, needs, the likely effect of any change in circumstances, age, sex, and background;

whether the child has suffered harm or is at risk; and who is best able to meet his or her needs. The courts should also presume, unless the contrary is shown, that involvement of a parent in the life of the child concerned will further the child's welfare (Children and Families Act 2014, s. 11(2A)). The court does not have to make any order if no order at all is thought to be in the best interests of the child (s. 1(5)). Or the court can make a different order from the one requested. Before making its decision, the court can also call for a report from Cafcass or the social services department (see **chapter 9**). It may call for the child to be separately represented by Cafcass. It may, as we noted earlier in this section, decide that the local authority should investigate with a view to care proceedings.

Section 8 allows the court to settle almost any dispute about the future arrangements for a child, but it does not touch on financial questions. A s. 8 order can be made in favour of any person the court thinks appropriate, after hearing all the evidence, not just the applicant and not just a parent; for example, a grandparent, step-parent, an unmarried father, or even a sibling. Let us look at the range of orders available.

Section 8 child arrangements order

A child arrangements order is an order regulating arrangements relating to with whom a child should live, spend time, or have other types of contact, or when they should do so. The right to contact is that of the child and the interests of the child are the court's paramount consideration. An order can provide that a person who the child is not living with shall have contact with the child. The court can lay down the exact nature and extent of the contact; for example, overnight stays, supervised visits, use of a contact centre, telephone contact, or in a difficult case, perhaps where a parent has been violent, just an annual birthday card.

Each case must be decided on its own facts, but some presumptions apply. For example, there is a presumption that children should have an ongoing relationship with both parents after family separation, where that is safe and in the child's best interests. In making decisions on contested s. 8 orders, a court should presume that a child's welfare will be furthered by the involvement of each of the child's parents in his or her life, unless it can be shown that such involvement would not in fact further the child's welfare. Involvement means any kind of direct or indirect involvement but not any particular division of the child's time. Interestingly at the time of writing, this section of the Children and Families Act 2014 is yet to commence. You are advised to check online for Commencement Orders for the Act when reading this section.

If a child of sufficient understanding, or *Gillick* competence (see **chapter 2**), does not want contact there is no point in imposing it: *Re S (Contact: Children's Views)* (2002).

Supported contact may be facilitated by the National Association of Child Contact Centres (www.naccc.org.uk/).

A child arrangements order will also settle the arrangements as to with whom the child is to live. The arrangements stipulated in the order concerning where a child shall live will specify who will have parental responsibility for the child while it is in effect.

A child arrangements order can be made in favour of more than one person, even specifying exactly how the child's time will be split, if this serves the child's interests. The case study at the start of the chapter provides an example.

Section 8 specific issue order

This order ensures that, where there is disagreement, major decisions are brought before the court. It can be used in cases such as *Re B* (1991), where the court authorized a 12-year-old girl to have an abortion, overriding her mother's wishes. It has been used to authorize vaccination, where the mother feared the triple vaccine for MMR but the father wanted the child vaccinated: *B (Child)* (2003). The court accepted expert evidence that the treatment was in the child's best interests.

A common example of a specific issue order is to obtain a change to a child's surname where one parent objects. The courts, applying s. 1 of the Children Act, generally consider the interests of the child are harmed by such a change. But not always: in *Re S (A Child) (Change of Name: Cultural Factors)* (2001), the father was Sikh and the child had a Sikh name. She lived with her mother, a Bangladeshi. The court ordered that she be known by a Bangladeshi name so as not to stand out in her community, but that she should keep her Sikh name in her own best long-term interests. The Court of Appeal, in *Re G* [2012] EWCA Civ 1233, set out how a judge should decide in cases where there is a disagreement. In this case an ultra-orthodox father disagreed with the children's mother that the children should be educated in a new co-educational school where there were greater educational opportunities than in a traditional Talmudic school. The Appeal Court said:

> In the conditions of current society there are, as it seems to me, three answers to this question. First, we must recognise that equality of opportunity is a fundamental value of our society: equality as between different communities, social groupings and creeds, and equality as between men and women, boys and girls. Second, we foster, encourage and facilitate aspiration: both aspiration as a virtue in itself and, to the extent that it is practical and reasonable, the child's own aspirations. Far too many lives in our community are blighted, even today, by lack of aspiration. Third, our objective must be to bring the child to adulthood in such a way that the child is best equipped both to decide what kind of life they want to lead—what kind of person they want to be—and to give effect so far as practicable to their aspirations. Put shortly, our objective must be to maximise the child's opportunities in every sphere of life as they enter adulthood. And the corollary of this, where the decision has been devolved to a 'judicial parent', is that the judge must be cautious about approving a regime which may have the effect of foreclosing or unduly limiting the child's ability to make such decisions in future.

Section 8 prohibited steps order

This order prevents parental responsibility being exercised in relation to a specified matter. This could, for example, prevent a child being taken abroad or living with a certain individual. In *Re J (A Minor) (Prohibited Steps Order: Circumcision)* (1999), the court granted an order prohibiting a boy's circumcision. It was not in this child's interests to proceed unless both parents wanted it.

New arrangements for private law disputes

The Children and Families Act 2014 sets out new procedures for the way the law deals with private disputes between parents. The Act requires a potential applicant to attend a family mediation, information and assessment meeting (MIAM) to find out about and consider mediation before being able to apply for certain types of court order. The National Family Mediation organization provides information about MIAMs. See www. nfm.org.uk/index.php/family-mediation/mediation-information-meeting-miam.

Changing the Safeguarding and Inter-Agency System

The Children Act 2004 was defined by the then Labour Government as 'the first step in a long-term programme of change'. It created the legislative spine for developing more effective and accessible services focused around the needs of children, young people, and their families. It described the principal purposes of the legislation as putting the improvement of children's well-being at the heart of government policies by creating:

- clear, shared outcomes embedded in legislation;
- an independent champion for the views and interests of children;
- robust partnership arrangements;
- improved local arrangements for child protection;
- clearer accountability for children's services;
- a new integrated inspection framework;
- a legislative basis for better sharing of information.

Ten years on those objectives have been subject to considerable challenge, not least because child deaths have continued to occur and different political objectives have been established which involve less bureaucracy, smaller government, and potentially further involvement of the private sector in the running of services. The Every Child Matters (ECM) policy and the five outcomes for children—stay safe, be healthy, enjoy and achieve, make a positive contribution, and achieve economic well-being—have been largely ignored. The ECM outcomes would not need a 'massive bureaucratic super-structure to police it' (Michael Gove's evidence to the Education Select Committee, 27 July 2010). Gove went on to say that he had no problem with ECM as a list but that it should be policed in a hands-off way and signalled that the way to realize the outcomes was for children to achieve well in schools. The ECM website was removed and critically the five outcomes no longer form part of Ofsted's framework for the inspection of local authority arrangements for the protection of children. No announcements have been made to date about potential changes to the Children Act 2004 although some sections have not been implemented (see **The key provisions of the Children Act 2004**, p 176). Additionally, the multi-disciplinary statutory guidance, *Working Together to Safeguard Children*, has been updated. The new *Working Together to Safeguard Children* was published in March 2013 and is substantially shorter than the previous version (390 pages) in line with proposals made in the Munro Review of Child Protection (2012). It replaces *Working Together to Safeguard Children* (2010), the *Framework for the Assessment of Children in Need and their Families* (2000), and *Statutory guidance on making arrangements to safeguard and promote the welfare of children under section 11 of the Children Act 2004* (2007).

The non-statutory sections have been cut out and the statutory sections shortened.

■ The Munro Review of Child Protection

Professor Eileen Munro was invited by Michael Gove, the Secretary of State for Education to review the child protection system in England on 10 June 2010. She published three reports with the final one, in May 2011, making a series of 15 recommendations. These are set out below followed by a commentary on their implementation so far.

Recommendation 1: The government should revise both the statutory guidance, *Working Together to Safeguard Children* and *The Framework for the Assessment of Children in Need and their Families* and their associated policies to:

- distinguish the rules that are essential for effective working together, from guidance that informs professional judgment;
- set out the key principles underpinning the guidance;
- remove the distinction between initial and core assessments and the associated time-scales in respect of these assessments, replacing them with the decisions that are required to be made by qualified social workers when developing an understanding of children's needs and making and implementing a plan to safeguard and promote their welfare;
- require local attention is given to:
  - timeliness in the identification of children's needs and provision of help;
  - the quality of the assessment to inform next steps to safeguard and promote children's welfare; and
  - the effectiveness of the help provided;
- give local areas the responsibility to draw on research and theoretical models to inform local practice; and
- remove constraints to local innovation and professional judgment that are created by prescribing or endorsing particular approaches, for example, nationally designed assessment forms, national performance indicators associated with assessment or nationally prescribed approaches to IT systems.

Recommendation 2: The inspection framework should examine the effectiveness of the contributions of all local services, including health, education, police, probation and the justice system to the protection of children.

Recommendation 3: The new inspection framework should examine the child's journey from needing to receiving help, explore how the rights, wishes, feelings and experiences of children and young people inform and shape the provision of services, and look at the effectiveness of the help provided to children, young people and their families.

Recommendation 4: Local authorities and their partners should use a combination of nationally collected and locally published performance information to help benchmark performance, facilitate improvement and promote accountability. It is crucial that performance information is not treated as an unambiguous measure of good or bad performance as performance indicators tend to be.

Recommendation 5: The existing statutory requirements for each Local Safeguarding Children Board (LSCB) to produce and publish an annual report for the Children's Trust Board should be amended, to require its submission instead to the Chief Executive and Leader of the Council, and, subject to the passage of legislation, to the local Police and Crime Commissioner and the Chair of the health and wellbeing board.

Recommendation 6: The statutory guidance, *Working Together to Safeguard Children*, should be amended to state that when monitoring and evaluating local arrangements, LSCBs should, taking account of local need, include an assessment of the effectiveness of the help being provided to children and families (including the effectiveness and value for money of early help services, including early years provision), and the effectiveness of multi-agency training to safeguard and promote the welfare of children and young people.

Recommendation 7: Local authorities should give due consideration to protecting the discrete roles and responsibilities of a Director of Children's Services and Lead Member for Children's Services before allocating any additional functions to individuals occupying such roles. The importance, as envisaged in the Children Act 2004, of appointing individuals to positions where they have specific responsibilities for children's services should not be undermined. The Government should amend the statutory guidance issued in relation to such roles and establish the principle that, given the importance of individuals in senior positions being responsible for children's services, it should not be considered appropriate to give additional functions (that do not relate to children's services) to Directors of Children's Services and Lead Members for Children's Services unless exceptional circumstances arise.

Recommendation 8: The Government should work collaboratively with the Royal College of Paediatrics and Child Health, the Royal College of General Practitioners, local authorities and others to research the impact of health reorganisation on effective partnership arrangements and the ability to provide effective help for children who are suffering, or likely to suffer, significant harm.

Recommendation 9: The Government should require LSCBs to use systems methodology when undertaking Serious Case Reviews (SCRs) and, over the coming year, work with the sector to develop national resources to:

- provide accredited, skilled and independent reviewers to jointly work with LSCBs on each SCR;
- promote the development of a variety of systems-based methodologies to learn from practice;
- initiate the development of a typology of the problems that contribute to adverse outcomes to facilitate national learning; and
- disseminate learning nationally to improve practice and inform the work of the Chief Social Worker.

In the meantime, Ofsted's evalution [*sic*] of SCRs should end.

Recommendation 10: The Government should place a duty on local authorities and statutory partners to secure the sufficient provision of local early help services for children, young people and families. The arrangements setting out how they will do this should:

- specify the range of professional help available to local children, young people and families, through statutory, voluntary and community services, against the local profile of need set out in the local Joint Strategic Needs Analysis (JSNA);
- specify how they will identify children who are suffering or who are likely to suffer significant harm, including the availability of social work expertise to all professionals working with children, young people and families who are not being supported by children's social care services and specify the training available locally to support professionals working at the frontline of universal services;

- set out the local resourcing of the early help services for children, young people and families; and, most importantly
- lead to the identification of the early help that is needed by a particular child and their family, and to the provision of an 'early help offer' where their needs do not meet the criteria for receiving children's social care services.

Recommendation 11: The Social Work Reform Board's Professional Capabilities Framework should incorporate capabilities necessary for child and family social work. This framework should explicitly inform social work qualification training, postgraduate professional development and performance appraisal.

Recommendation 12: Employers and higher education institutions (HEIs) should work together so that social work students are prepared for the challenges of child protection work. In particular, the review considers that HEIs and employing agencies should work together so that:

- practice placements are of the highest quality and—in time—only in designated Approved Practice Settings;
- employers are able to apply for special 'teaching organisation' status, awarded by the College of Social Work;
- the merits of 'student units', which are headed up by a senior social worker are considered; and
- placements are of sufficiently high quality, and both employers and HEIs consider if their relationship is working well.

Recommendation 13: Local authorities and their partners should start an ongoing process to review and redesign the ways in which child and family social work is delivered, drawing on evidence of effectiveness of helping methods where appropriate and supporting practice that can implement evidence based ways of working with children and families.

Recommendation 14: Local authorities should designate a Principal Child and Family Social Worker, who is a senior manager with lead responsibility for practice in the local authority and who is still actively involved in frontline practice and who can report the views and experiences of the front line to all levels of management.

Recommendation 15: A Chief Social Worker should be created in Government, whose duties should include advising the Government on social work practice and informing the Secretary of State's annual report to Parliament on the working of the Children Act 1989.

Munro's recommendations have not led to immediate changes in the structure of child protection agencies as was the case following Lord Laming's report into the death of Victoria Climbié. That report ultimately paved the way for the Children Act 2004 and the splitting of social services departments into children's and adults' services which has led to criticism from some commentators. Munro's recommendations, which have been accepted by the government, provide a more subtle approach to influencing how services are organized to protect children. In the introduction to her first report, Munro says:

The problem is that previous reforms have not led to the expected improvements in frontline practice. Moreover, there is a substantial body of evidence indicating that past reforms are creating new, unforeseen complications. It is therefore important to think carefully before producing more recommendations for change.

(E. Munro, *The Munro Review of Child Protection*: Part One: A Systems Analysis (Department for Education, 2010))

A year on, Munro further comments in *The Munro Review of Child Protection: Progress Report: Moving Towards a Child-Centred System* (Department for Education, 2012) that 'progress is moving in the right direction but that it needs to move faster'. Perhaps this was inevitable since her recommendations, shown earlier in this section, were not designed to change the law, certainly not substantially, nor were they designed to change the structure of the agencies involved in child protection. She was, however, interested in changing expectations about what could be achieved in the protection of children and in the provision of early help for them. She was also concerned to change the way social work is practised through influencing everyday decisions and behaviour. It is probably still too early to tell whether the plans set out by Munro have been fully implemented and whether they are having the desired effect. High-profile inquiries into the deaths of children have continued with similar responses from the media. Local authorities all now have an early help strategy funded by grants from government. But the real test is whether social work practice has improved. Little evidence of this is currently available.

The key provisions of the Children Act 2004

The duty to cooperate to improve well-being

The Act is designed to create a holistic approach to children's services. Service providers must cooperate in order to improve children's well-being. Section 10 of the Act, which is set out in **Box 5.10**, creates the statutory framework for this to happen. It requires local cooperation between local authorities, key partner agencies ('relevant partners'), and other relevant bodies ('other bodies or persons'), including the voluntary and community sectors, in order to improve the well-being of children in the area. 'Well-being' is defined in terms of five outcomes for children. The legislation describes these as:

(a) physical and mental health and emotional well-being;

(b) protection from harm and neglect;

(c) education, training and recreation;

(d) the contribution made by them to society;

(e) social and economic well-being.

The duty to make the arrangements to improve well-being is placed on the local authority and a duty to cooperate with the local authority is placed on the relevant partners. As well as underpinning wide cooperation arrangements, these duties and powers are also designed to provide the statutory context within which agencies will be encouraged to integrate commissioning and delivery of children's services, under-pinned by pooled budgeting arrangements. As you read the section, notice the recognition of the range of bodies which are responsible for children's well-being, the extensive delegation of responsibilities, and the role of the local authority as the 'enabler' of effective provision. Notice also the specific mention of the importance of parents within the section.

The Children and Young Persons Act 2008 places a complementary duty upon the Secretary of State to promote the well-being of children and young people—this is discussed in **chapter 6**.

BOX 5.10 Section 10 of the Children Act 2004—cooperation to improve well-being

(1) Each local authority in England must make arrangements to promote co-operation between—
 (a) the authority;
 (b) each of the authority's relevant partners; and
 (c) such other persons or bodies as the authority consider appropriate, being persons or bodies of any nature who exercise functions or are engaged in activities in relation to children in the authority's area.

(2) The arrangements are to be made with a view to improving the well-being of children in the authority's area so far as relating to—
 (a) physical and mental health and emotional well-being;
 (b) protection from harm and neglect;
 (c) education, training and recreation;
 (d) the contribution made by them to society;
 (e) social and economic well-being.

(3) In making arrangements under this section a [local authority] in England must have regard to the importance of parents and other persons caring for children in improving the well-being of children.

(4) For the purposes of this section each of the following is a relevant partner of a local authority in England—
 (a) where the authority is a county council for an area for which there is also a district council, the district council;
 (b) the local policing body and the chief officer of police for a police area any part of which falls within the area of the local authority;
 (c) a local probation board for an area any part of which falls within the area of the authority;
 (ca) the Secretary of State in relation to his functions under sections 2 and 3 of the Offender Management Act 2007, so far as they are exercisable in relation to England;
 (cb) any provider of probation services that is required by arrangements under section 3(2) of the Offender Management Act 2007 to act as a relevant partner of the authority;
 (d) a youth offending team for an area any part of which falls within the area of the authority;
 (e) a Strategic Health Authority and Primary Care Trust for an area any part of which falls within the area of the authority;

> (f) a person providing services in pursuance of section 68 of the Education and Skills Act 2008 in any part of the area of the authority;
>
> (fa) the governing body of a maintained school that is maintained by the authority;
>
> (fb) the proprietor of a school approved by the Secretary of State under section 342 of the Education Act 1996 and situated in the authority's area;
>
> (fc) the proprietor of a city technology college, city college for the technology of the arts or Academy situated in the authority's area;
>
> (fd) the governing body of an institution within the further education sector the main site of which is situated in the authority's area;
>
> (fe) the Secretary of State, in relation to the Secretary of State's functions under section 2 of the Employment and Training Act 1973.
>
> (5) The relevant partners of a local authority in England must co-operate with the authority in the making of arrangements under this section.

Children and Young People's Plans (CYPP)

Children's services authorities are no longer required by s. 17 of the Act to prepare and publish a strategic plan which will explain how they intend to carry out their responsibilities towards children and young people. The regulations requiring such plans were revoked in October 2010. Local partnership can produce plans if they see fit but there is no requirement to do so or to do so in a particular format.

Safeguarding children

Section 8 of the 2004 Act imposes a duty on specified agencies (set out in **Box 5.11**) to make arrangements to ensure that their functions are discharged having regard to the need to safeguard and promote the welfare of children.

The aim of the duty (set out in **Box 5.12**) is to complement the general cooperation duty in the specific area of children's safeguards by:

- ensuring that agencies give appropriate priority to their responsibilities towards the children in their care or with whom they come into contact;
- encouraging agencies to share early concerns about safety and welfare of children and to ensure preventative action before a crisis develops.

Safeguarding and promoting the welfare of children is not statutorily defined in primary legislation but *Working Together* defines it as:

- protecting children from maltreatment;
- preventing impairment of children's health or development;
- ensuring that children grow up in circumstances consistent with the provision of safe and effective care; and
- taking action to enable all children to have the best outcomes.

It is somewhat distinct from the notion of child protection, which is key to the Children Act 1989 which we discuss in the following chapters. Child protection is linked to legally based state intervention and referred to by the first two bullet points above; safeguarding is a means of ensuring that children receive the support they need for their well-being.

The statutory duty requires agencies actively to consider the need to safeguard children and promote their welfare in the course of carrying out their normal functions. The duty requires agencies that come into contact with children to recognize that their needs are different from adults.

 BOX 5.11 Specified agencies in s. 11 of the Children Act 2004

(a) a local authority in England;

(b) a district council which is not such an authority;

(c) a Strategic Health Authority;

(d) a Special Health Authority, so far as exercising functions in relation to England, designated by order made by the Secretary of State for the purposes of this section;

(e) a Primary Care Trust;

(f) an NHS trust all or most of whose hospitals, establishments and facilities are situated in England;

(g) an NHS foundation trust;

(h) the local policing body and chief officer of police for a police area in England;

(i) the British Transport Police Authority, so far as exercising functions in relation to England;

(j) a local probation board for an area in England;

(ja) the Secretary of State in relation to his functions under sections 2 and 3 of the Offender Management Act 2007, so far as they are exercisable in relation to England;

(k) a youth offending team for an area in England;

(l) the governor of a prison or secure training centre in England (or, in the case of a contracted out prison or secure training centre, its director);

(m) any person to the extent that he is providing services in pursuance of section 74 of the Education and Skills Act 2008.

 BOX 5.12 The duty to make arrangements to safeguard and promote welfare—
s. 11(2) of the Children Act 2004

Each person and body to whom this section applies must make arrangements for ensuring that—

(a) their functions are discharged having regard to the need to safeguard and promote the welfare of children; and

(b) any services provided by another person pursuant to arrangements made by the person or body in the discharge of their functions are provided having regard to that need.

Local Safeguarding Children Boards

The Children Act 2004 provides that children's services authorities in England and Wales must establish Local Safeguarding Children Boards (LSCB) to ensure that the necessary local arrangements are in place for coordinating the work of the key agencies in safeguarding children.

Section 13 of the Act, which we summarize in **Box 5.13**, sets out membership of the Board.

 BOX 5.13 Representatives on Local Safeguarding Children Boards—s. 13 of the Children Act 2004

The following bodies/persons must be represented on the Board:

- the children's services authority which establishes the Board;
- district councils in local government areas which have them;
- the chief officer of police;
- the Community Rehabilitation Company;
- the Youth Offending Team;
- the NHS Commissioning Board and clinical commissioning groups;
- NHS Trusts and NHS Foundation Trusts all or most of whose hospitals, establishments, and facilities are situated in the local authority area;
- Cafcass;
- the governor or director of any secure training centre in the area of the authority; and
- the governor or director of any prison in the area of the authority which ordinarily detains children.

The Apprenticeships, Skills, Children and Learning Act 2009 amended ss. 13 and 14 of the Children Act 2004 and provided that the local authority must take reasonable steps to ensure that the LSCB includes two lay members representing the local community.

Section 13(4) of the Children Act 2004, as amended, provides that the local authority must take reasonable steps to ensure that the LSCB includes representatives of relevant persons and bodies of such descriptions as may be prescribed. Regulation 3A of the LSCB Regulations prescribes the following persons and bodies:

- the governing body of a maintained school;
- the proprietor of a non-maintained special school;
- the proprietor of a city technology college, a city college for the technology of the arts, or an Academy; and
- the governing body of a further education institution the main site of which is situated in the authority's area.

Section 10(7) sets out the crucial duty to cooperate—see **Box 5.14**.

BOX 5.14 The duty to cooperate—s. 13(7) of the Children Act 2004

In the establishment of a Local Safeguarding Children Board under this section—

(a) the authority establishing it must cooperate with each of their Board partners; and

(b) each Board partner must cooperate with the authority.

Section 14 sets out the objectives of the Local Safeguarding Boards—see **Box 5.15**.

BOX 5.15 The objective of Local Safeguarding Children Boards—s. 14 of the Children Act 2004

The objective of a Local Safeguarding Children Board established under section 13 is—

(a) to co-ordinate what is done by each person or body represented on the Board . . . for the purposes of safeguarding and promoting the welfare of children in the area of the authority by which it is established; and

(b) to ensure the effectiveness of what is done by each such person or body for those purposes.

The LSCB is the key statutory mechanism for ensuring that the relevant organizations in each local area will cooperate effectively to safeguard and promote the welfare of children in that locality. The core functions are set out in regulations—the Local Safeguarding Children Boards Regulations 2006. Details of the role and operation of LSCB are set out in Chapter 3 of the new *Working Together*. Following the Munro Review of Child Protection, the government amended the guidance to require the LSCB to report annually to the local authority chief executive and lead member for children's services.

You can get a flavour of the work of LSCBs by looking at the website of the pan-London LSCB: www.londonscb.gov.uk/.

The Board may also include representatives of other relevant persons or bodies as the children's services authority which established it considers appropriate following consultation with the Board.

One of the most important tasks of the LSCB is to carry out Serious Case Reviews. These are carried out when a child has died or been seriously injured or harmed and abuse is known or suspected to have been a factor. New guidance on serious case reviews is contained in Chapter 4 of *Working Together*.

Local authority administration

Local authorities that are children's services authorities—that is, county level or unitary authorities—have a number of specific duties to organize and plan services and to safeguard and promote the welfare of children. The Children Act 2004 required all children's services authorities in England to appoint a director of children's services and to designate a lead member for children's services prior to 1 January 2008.

The functions of the director of children's services include (s. 18(2)):

- local authority education functions (other than those relating to adults);
- social services functions for children;
- functions in relation to young people leaving care;
- functions under ss. 10–12 and 17 of the Children Act 2004;
- any function delegated to the authority by an NHS body relating to children;
- any other function prescribed by regulations.

In addition, directors of children's services will take responsibility for local cooperation arrangements in relation to children's services. Two or more local authorities may
appoint a director of children's services jointly.

The lead member for children's services is designed to ensure political leadership
and accountability for the performance of children's services. Updated statutory guidance was published in April 2013 detailing the responsibilities of these roles. It is
available at www.gov.uk/government/uploads/system/uploads/attachment_data/file/
271429/directors_of_child_services_-_stat_guidance.pdf.

Children's Trusts

Children's Trusts are not provided for in the Children Act 2004. However, they were the
vehicle which the Labour Government designed to provide a framework for organizations to work together in a local partnership where this assists them to commission
and, where relevant, directly provide services for children, in particular those children
with a combination of health, educational, and social care needs. In other words, they
are a vehicle to achieve the reforms provided for by the Children Act 2004.

From 31 October 2010 the *Statutory Guidance on Children's Trusts* was withdrawn
which resulted in the following:

- there are no guidelines setting out how often the Board should meet and operate;
- there is no prescription on the name of the Board or that it should have a clear
  and separate identity within the wider cooperation arrangements. For example, it
  would be possible for the Board to be a subset of another board in the local area;
- there is no need for a separate representative for each relevant partner. The local
  authority and the other relevant partners can agree that one person or body can
  represent others. For example, the director of children's services, if agreed, can
  represent schools and Jobcentre Plus.

▨ Responsibilities on agencies

In this section of the chapter we discuss the ways in which agencies must take joint
responsibility for outcomes for children. *Working Together to Safeguard Children*, the
details of which we set out earlier, explains that safeguarding children is a shared
responsibility.

Crime and child protection

Safeguarding Children also includes within the definition of safeguarding the responsibilities of agencies, particularly the police and probation services in respect of potentially dangerous persons who present a risk of harm to the public, including children.
Since the mid-1990s, there has been a range of developments in criminal justice legislation aimed at protecting children and other vulnerable people. They include the
legislation set out in **Box 5.16**.

 BOX 5.16 Recent developments in criminal legislation

Legislation	Requirement
Sex Offenders Act 1997	Requires specified sex offenders to register with the police. The Association of Chief Police Offices has assessed compliance with the requirements by sex offenders as 97 per cent
Crime and Disorder Act 1998	Introduced Sex Offenders Orders which give the police powers to monitor the activities of people subject to the orders
Protection of Children Act 1999	Requires the disclosure of criminal backgrounds of those with access to children
Criminal Justice and Courts Services Act 2000	Requires police and probation services to set up joint arrangements known as Multi-Agency Public Protection Arrangements (MAPPA) for the assessment and management of offenders at high risk of causing serious harm
Sexual Offences Act 2003	A major overhaul in the sexual offences framework including the extension of the abuse of position of trust offences set out in the Sexual Offences (Amendment) Act 2000. This Act also introduced:
	Sexual Offences Prevention Orders which can impose prohibitions on sex offenders who pose a risk of serious sexual harm
	Risk of Sexual Harm Orders, restricting those who have not committed sex offences but are at risk of doing so
	Foreign Travel Orders banning travel abroad
Violent Crime Reduction Act 2006	Enables the police to enter and search when visiting homes of registered sex offenders, for the purpose of assessing risk
Safeguarding Vulnerable Groups Act 2006	Creates a new vetting and barring scheme for all those working with children and vulnerable adults. All those working with children will be required to be centrally vetted, and employers will need to check their status in the scheme which went live in October 2009. For further details see **chapter 14**

Roles and responsibilities

The following discussion of roles and responsibilities draws heavily on *Working Together to Safeguard Children* (2013). The guidance makes clear that all organizations which work with children have certain responsibilities. These are set out in Chapter 2, para. 4:

- a clear line of accountability for the commissioning and/or provision of services designed to safeguard and promote the welfare of children;
- a senior board level lead to take leadership responsibility for the organisation's safeguarding arrangements;
- a culture of listening to children and taking account of their wishes and feelings, both in individual decisions and the development of services;
- arrangements which set out clearly the processes for sharing information, with other professionals and with the Local Safeguarding Children Board (LSCB);
- a designated professional lead (or, for health provider organisations, named professionals) for safeguarding. Their role is to support other professionals in their agencies to recognise the needs of children, including rescue from possible abuse or neglect. Designated professional roles should always be explicitly defined in job descriptions. Professionals should be given sufficient time, funding, supervision and support to fulfil their child welfare and safeguarding responsibilities effectively;
- safe recruitment practices for individuals whom the organisation will permit to work regularly with children, including policies on when to obtain a criminal record check;
- appropriate supervision and support for staff, including undertaking safeguarding training:
  - employers are responsible for ensuring that their staff are competent to carry out their responsibilities for safeguarding and promoting the welfare of children and creating an environment where staff feel able to raise concerns and feel supported in their safeguarding role;
  - staff should be given a mandatory induction, which includes familiarisation with child protection responsibilities and procedures to be followed if anyone has any concerns about a child's safety or welfare; and
  - all professionals should have regular reviews of their own practice to ensure they improve over time.
- clear policies in line with those from the LSCB for dealing with allegations against people who work with children. An allegation may relate to a person who works with children who has:
  - behaved in a way that has harmed a child, or may have harmed a child;
  - possibly committed a criminal offence against or related to a child; or
  - behaved towards a child or children in a way that indicates they may pose a risk of harm to children.

In addition:

- county level and unitary local authorities should have a Local Authority Designated Officer (LADO) to be involved in the management and oversight of individual cases. The LADO should provide advice and guidance to employers and voluntary organisations, liaising with the police and other agencies and monitoring the progress of cases to ensure that they are dealt with as quickly as possible, consistent with a thorough and fair process;

- any allegation should be reported immediately to a senior manager within the organisation. The LADO should also be informed within one working day of all allegations that come to an employer's attention or that are made directly to the police; and

- if an organisation removes an individual (paid worker or unpaid volunteer) from work such as looking after children (or would have, had the person not left first) because the person poses a risk of harm to children, the organisation must make a referral to the Disclosure and Barring Service. It is an offence to fail to make a referral without good reason.

Duties to cooperate

The Children Act 1989 places two specific duties on agencies to cooperate in the interests of vulnerable children. The first of these is s. 27 of the Children Act 1989 set out in **Box 5.17**.

 BOX 5.17 Agencies' responsibilities under s. 27 of the Children Act 1989

Section 27 provides that a local authority may request help from:

- any local authority;

- any local housing authority;

- any Local Health Board, Special Health Authority, Primary Care Trust, NHS Trust or NHS Foundation Trust; and

- any person authorized by the Secretary of State in exercising the local authority's functions under Part 3 of the Act.

Part III of the Children Act 1989, which we discuss in **chapter 6**, places a duty on local authorities to provide support and services for children in need, including children looked after by the local authority and those in secure accommodation. The authority whose help is requested in these circumstances has a duty to comply with the request, provided it is compatible with its other duties and functions.

The second duty is in s. 47 of the Children Act 1989 set out in **Box 5.18**. We discuss s. 47 of the Children Act 1989 fully in **chapter 7**.

 BOX 5.18 Agencies' duties under s. 47 of the Children Act 1989

Section 47 places a duty on:

- any local authority;

- any housing authority;

- any Local Health Board, Special Health Authority, Primary Care Trust, NHS Trust or NHS Foundation Trust; and

- any person authorized by the Secretary of State to help a local authority with its inquiries in cases where there is reasonable cause to suspect that a child is suffering or is likely to suffer, significant harm.

The responsibilities of other agencies

Working Together outlines the main roles and responsibilities of statutory agencies, professionals, the voluntary sector, and the wider community in relation to child protection.

Education services

Schools and colleges, whether state or independent, have a critical role in the protection of children. Schools are often the place where abuse is first noticed. Schools do not have a direct investigative responsibility in child protection work, but schools and colleges should assist social services departments by referring concerns and providing information for s. 47 child protection inquiries. Further new guidance for schools and colleges was published in April 2014 and can be found at www. gov.uk/government/uploads/system/uploads/attachment_data/file/300309/KCSIE_gdnce_FINAL.pdf.

All educational settings should contribute to safeguarding and promoting children's welfare in the following ways.

- All school and college staff have a responsibility to provide a safe environment in which children can learn.

- All school and college staff have a responsibility to identify children who may be in need of extra help or who are suffering, or are likely to suffer, significant harm. All staff then have a responsibility to take appropriate action, working with other services as needed.

- In addition to working with the designated safeguarding lead, staff members should be aware that they may be asked to support social workers to take decisions about individual children.

Health services

Individual health professionals such as GPs, midwives, health visitors, and school nurses are extremely well placed to contribute to child protection. Hospital staff, particularly those working in accident and emergency departments, should be fully aware of child protection procedures. Mental health practitioners, particularly those working with child and adolescent mental health services, can provide evidence of child abuse or neglect. All staff working in health care settings—including those who predominantly treat adults—should receive training to ensure they attain the competences appropriate to their role and follow the relevant professional guidance.

Strategic leadership should be provided by health authorities and clinical commissioning groups. *Working Together* highlights statutory responsibilities placed on health services.

> **The NHS Commissioning Board** will be responsible for ensuring that the health commissioning system as a whole is working effectively to safeguard and promote the welfare of children. It will also be accountable for the services it directly commissions. The Commissioning Board should also ensure that there are effective mechanisms for Local

Safeguarding Children Boards (LSCBs) and health and wellbeing boards to raise concerns about the engagement and leadership of the local NHS.

Clinical commissioning groups (CCGs) will be the major commissioners of local health services. The CCG should employ, or have in place a contractual agreement to secure the expertise of, designated professionals, i.e. designated doctors and nurses for safeguarding children and for looked after children (and designated paediatricians for unexpected deaths in childhood). Designated professionals are a vital source of advice to the CCG, the local authority and the LSCB, and advice and support for other health professionals.

All providers of NHS funded health services including NHS Trusts, NHS Foundation Trusts and public, voluntary sector, independent sector and social enterprises should identify a named doctor and a named nurse (and a named midwife if the organisation provides maternity services) for safeguarding. In the case of NHS Direct, ambulance trusts and independent providers, this should be a named professional. GP practices should have a lead and deputy lead for safeguarding, who should work closely with named GPs. Named professionals have a key role in promoting good professional practice within their organisation, providing advice and expertise for fellow professionals, and ensuring safeguarding training is in place. They should work closely with their organisation's safeguarding lead, designated professionals and the LSCB.

Health professionals and organizations have a key role to play in actively promoting the health and well-being of children. Section 11 of the Children Act 2004 places a duty on Trusts to make arrangements to ensure that, in discharging their functions, they have regard to the need to safeguard and promote the welfare of children.

Day care services

Day care services including family centres, early years centres, nurseries, childminders, playgroups, and holiday and out-of-school schemes play an important role in the lives of large numbers of children. *Working Together* says:

> Early Years providers must ensure that:
>
> - staff complete safeguarding training that enables them to recognise signs of potential abuse and neglect; and
> - they have a practitioner who is designated to take lead responsibility for safeguarding children within each early years setting and who should liaise with local statutory children's services agencies as appropriate. This lead should also complete child protection training.

The Police Service

The Police Service has a commitment under the Children Act 1989 to protect children from abuse. *Working Together* says:

> Offences committed against children can be particularly sensitive, and usually require the police to work with other organisations, such as children's social care, in the conduct of any criminal investigation.
>
> All police officers, and other police employees such as Police Community Support Officers, are well placed to identify early when a child's welfare is at risk and when a child

may need protection from harm. Children have the right to the full protection offered by the criminal law. In addition to identifying when a child may be a victim of a crime, police officers should be aware of the effect of other incidents which might pose safeguarding risks to children and where officers should pay particular attention. For example, an officer attending a domestic abuse incident should be aware of the effect of such behaviour on any children in the household. Children who are encountered as offenders, or alleged offenders, are entitled to the same safeguards and protection as any other child and due regard should be given to their welfare at all times.

The police can hold important information about children who may be suffering, or likely to suffer, significant harm, as well as those who cause such harm. They should always share this information with other organisations where this is necessary to protect children. Similarly, they can expect other organisations to share information to enable the police to carry out their duties. Offences committed against children can be particularly sensitive and usually require the police to work with other organisations such as local authority children's social care. All police forces should have officers trained in child abuse investigation.

The police have emergency powers under section 46 of the Children Act 1989 to enter premises and remove a child to ensure their immediate protection. This power can be used if the police have reasonable cause to believe a child is suffering or is likely to suffer significant harm. Police emergency powers can help in emergency situations but should be used only when necessary. Wherever possible, the decision to remove a child from a parent or carer should be made by a court.

Adult Social Care Services

Local authorities provide services to adults who are responsible for children who may be in need. These services are subject to the section 11 duties . . .

When staff are providing services to adults they should ask whether there are children in the family and consider whether the children need help or protection from harm. Children may be at greater risk of harm or be in need of additional help in families where the adults have mental health problems, misuse substances or alcohol, are in a violent relationship or have complex needs or have learning difficulties.

Housing authorities

Housing and homelessness services in local authorities and others at the front line such as environmental health organisations are subject to the section 11 duties.

Professionals working in these services may become aware of conditions that could have an adverse impact on children. Under Part 1 of the Housing Act 2004, authorities must take account of the impact of health and safety hazards in housing on vulnerable occupants, including children, when deciding on the action to be taken by landlords to improve conditions. Housing authorities also have an important role to play in safeguarding vulnerable young people, including young people who are pregnant or leaving care.

National Offender Management Service

Probation services

Community Rehabilitation Companies are primarily responsible for providing reports for courts and working with adult offenders both in the community and in the transition from custody to community to reduce their reoffending. They are, therefore, well placed to identify offenders who pose a risk of harm to children as well as children who may be at heightened risk of involvement in (or exposure to) criminal or anti-social behaviour and of other poor outcomes due to the offending behaviour of their parent/carer(s).

Where an adult offender is assessed as presenting a risk of serious harm to children, the offender manager should develop a risk management plan and supervision plan that contains a specific objective to manage and reduce the risk of harm to children.

The Prison Service

The Prison Service has a responsibility to identify prisoners who pose a risk of harm to children. Where an individual has been identified as presenting a risk of harm to children, the relevant prison establishment:

- should inform the local authority children's social care services of the offender's reception to prison and subsequent transfers and of the release address of the offender;

- should notify the relevant Probation Trust in the case of offenders who have been sentenced to 12 months or more. The police should also be notified of the release address; and

- may prevent or restrict a prisoner's contact with children. Decisions on the level of contact, if any, should be based on a multi-agency risk assessment. The assessment should draw on relevant information held by police, probation, prison, and local authority children's social care.

Youth Justice Service

Youth Offending Teams (YOTs) are multi-agency teams responsible for the supervision of children and young people subject to pre-court interventions and statutory court disposals. They are therefore well placed to identify children known to relevant organizations as being most at risk of offending and to undertake work to prevent them offending. YOTs should have a lead officer responsible for ensuring safeguarding is at the forefront of their business.

Under s. 38 of the Crime and Disorder Act 1998, local authorities must, within the delivery of youth justice services, ensure the 'provision of persons to act as appropriate adults to safeguard the interests of children and young persons detained or questioned by police officers'.

The work of YOTs is discussed further in **chapter 10**.

UK Visa and Immigration

Section 55 of the Borders, Citizenship and Immigration Act 2009 places responsibility upon the Secretary of State to ensure that immigration, asylum, nationality, and customs functions are discharged having regard to the need to safeguard and promote the welfare of children in the UK.

Cafcass

The Children and Family Court Advisory and Support Service (Cafcass) was established in April 2001 as a non-departmental government body. Note that the National Assembly for Wales carries out the functions of Cafcass for children who are ordinarily resident in Wales.

The principal functions of Cafcass are set out in the Criminal Justice and Court Services Act 2000. These are in respect of family proceedings in which the welfare of children is or may be in question to:

- safeguard and promote the welfare of children;
- give advice to any court about an application made to it in such proceedings;
- make provision for children to be represented in such proceedings;
- provide information, advice, and other support for children and families.

Cafcass is represented on LSCBs.

The Crown Prosecution Service

The Crown Prosecution Service (CPS) advises the police on possible prosecutions and takes over prosecutions begun by the police. It is responsible for the preparation of cases for court and for their presentation at court. It works in partnership with the police, the courts, and other agencies throughout the criminal justice system. The role of the CPS is to prosecute cases firmly, fairly, and effectively, when there is sufficient evidence to provide a realistic prospect of conviction and when it is in the public interest to do so.

There are three principles which underpin the approach of the CPS to allegations of child abuse—expedition, sensitivity, and fairness.

▨ Advice and assistance to the service user

The service user is likely to be facing a number of problems. You have a range of statutory duties towards the service user, but he or she may need independent advice on a range of matters which fall outside your expertise, or even where the advice is needed to challenge your department's actions. **Table 5.1** sets out a number of agencies which may be able to provide advice and assistance to vulnerable people. A more complete list is available on Liberty's website at www.yourrights.org.uk/get-advice. Whenever you recommend an advice centre you should ensure that it offers a satisfactory standard of advice.

High Street lawyers

There are a huge number of solicitors' firms available. You are unlikely to find a solicitor with the expertise the service user requires in every firm. The Law Society runs a panel of specialist child-care solicitors. These are solicitors who have undertaken specialist training and have expertise in public child-care cases. Their names can be found from the Law Society website, www.lawsociety.org.uk/.

TABLE 5.1 Advice agencies

Name of organization	Brief description of services	Contact
Citizens Advice Bureaux (CAB)	Free impartial advice by both volunteers and professional advisers in local bureaux throughout the country. Details of local citizens advice bureaux are available from the umbrella organization, Citizens Advice. The website also provides a useful advice guide	www.citizensadvice. org.uk/
Law Centres	Law Centres provide free and independent professional legal services to people who live and work within their catchment areas. Law Centres tend to specialize in immigration, employment law, social security, mental health, housing, and community care issues. Information on Law Centres is available from their umbrella organization, the Law Centres Federation	www.lawcentres.org.uk/
Shelter	Shelter is a national organization which campaigns for homeless and inadequately housed people. It runs a number of Housing Advice Centres, a telephone advice line, and a website. You can access these services via the website	www.shelter.org.uk/
DIAL	DIAL is a national organization for a network of 140 local disability information and advice services run by and for disabled people. The website contains useful resources for disabled people and carers including how to find a local DIAL, fact sheets, and links to other organizations	www.scope.org.uk/ support/disabled-people/ local-advice
Independent Advice Centres	There are a very large number of independent advice centres. Information about these advice centres is available from the Federation of Independent Advice Centres	telephone: 020 7489 1800

EXERCISES

1 Read the whole of this chapter carefully and construct a checklist for yourself of the issues you will need to consider before recommending that your department makes a court application in respect of an individual child.

2 Locate and read one of the articles listed in Annotated further reading. Summarize the article in 100–150 words.

3 Try to construct a time line of events leading up to the Children Act 1989 and then onwards to the present. Include the UK's international commitments. You will find a helpful start on the Guardian Society website.

4 What is the relationship between the Children Act 1989 and the Children Act 2004? Do you understand the difference between 'safeguarding children' as a concept, and child protection?

5 Do you think that working in partnership with parents undermines the professional skills of social workers? Is there a need for greater intervention in family life in order to protect children?

6 You are investigating an anonymous phone call which expresses concern about a particular family. The caller tells you that there is a young baby and three other children under 10 in the family. Which agencies are likely to have information about the family? What is their role in protecting children? Can you ask for assistance from them?

7 A child has been assaulted by her father. What agencies are likely to become involved as a result of the assault? What duties do they have to help with investigations into the incident?

ONLINE RESOURCE CENTRE

For guidance on how to answer these exercises, visit the Online Resource Centre at www.oxfordtextbooks.co.uk/orc/socialwork13e/.

WHERE DO WE GO FROM HERE?

In this chapter we have considered a number of aspects of Part I of the Children Act 1989, in particular its philosophy, structure, overarching principles, and the principles which guide decision making by the courts. This chapter serves as an introduction to the remaining chapters about your responsibilities to children. However, it is more than an introduction. If you understand the purposes and the principles upon which the Act is based, you are going to be in a far better position to understand your role within the Act. In addition, this chapter is to help you to understand where social services fits into the organizational framework which exists to support and protect children. It has also suggested that you should be aware of other specialist advice organizations which may help your service user. You should not see your work with service users as separate from the poverty, poor housing, and vulnerability to crime and anti-social behaviour that affect their everyday lives. If you can do something to help, even if it is only pointing them in the right direction, you will have achieved something positive for them.

Chapter 6 considers Part III of the Act, local authority responsibilities to children in need.

ANNOTATED FURTHER READING

The welfare principle

J. Eekelaar, 'Beyond the welfare principle' (2002) *CFLR* 14(3): 237—a stimulating article which argues that the very ease of the welfare test encourages an unwillingness to pay proper attention to all the interests that are at stake in decision making.

E. Jackson, 'Conception and irrelevance of the welfare principle' (2002) *Modern Law Review* 65(2): 176. This article looks at the use of the welfare principle in decisions about fertility treatment.

S. Jivraj and D. Herman '"It is difficult for a white judge to understand": orientalism, racialisation, and Christianity in English child welfare cases' (2009) *CFLQ* 21(3): 283. This article analyses particular cases to discover how judges understand non-Christianness when applying the welfare principles.

The best interests of the child

M. Woolf, 'Coming of age?—The principle of "the best interests of the child"' (2003) 2 *EHRLR* 205. This article contrasts the approaches of the ECtHR and the English courts in decisions about the best interests of the child.

The involvement of both parents

F. Kaganas, 'A presumption that involving both parents is best: deciphering law's messages' (2013) *CFLQ* 25(3): 270. This article suggests that the provision in the Children and Families Act which requires courts to consider the involvement of both parents is part of a 'moral crusade' to uphold the importance of particular notions of the father and his role in the family.

Safeguarding or child protection

N. Parton, 'Child protection and safeguarding in England: changing and competing conceptions of risk and their implications for social work' (2010) *British Journal of Social Work* 41(5): 854. This articles presents a lively debate about the rights and wrongs of safeguarding and child protection.

Children's rights

There is a host of information available on children's rights. A useful introduction to the issues can be found in C. Booth, 'In search of children's rights', Editorial (2003) *Journal of Local Government Law*.

You can access a variety of websites giving you access to the text of the UN Convention on the Rights of the Child, for instance www.unicef.org/crc or the vibrant and punchy website of the Children's Rights Alliance for England www.crae.org.uk.

The Howard League for Penal Reform

You may be interested in the other work on behalf of children in custody undertaken by the Howard League for Penal Reform, which took the case against the government that formed the case study featured in this chapter. They have produced reports on girls in prison, the use of anti-social behaviour orders against children, and deaths of children in custody. Their website www.howardleague.org/ provides a range of useful information.

Reform of care proceedings

Family Justice Review, Final Report (Justice Department, 2011) is a wide-ranging review of the law relating to both public and private law proceedings.

Safeguarding System

The Munro Review of Child Protection includes three primary reports plus a progress report. These and other helpful material can be found at www.education.gov.uk/munroreview.

The Laming Report on the Victoria Climbié Inquiry is available on http://webarchive. nationalarchives.gov.uk/20130401151715/http://www.education.gov.uk/publications/ eOrderingDownload/CM-5730PDF.pdf. It is a report which repays careful reading.

Local authority support for children and families

6

OVERVIEW AND OBJECTIVES

As you read this chapter, consider the extent of the services that social services departments can offer to children in need and the way in which those services underpin the philosophy of the Children Act 1989. Also consider the limited resources available to authorities, particularly deprived urban authorities. What impact does this have on the successful operation of the Children Act 1989? What risks does it pose to the new emphasis on 'safeguarding' children? By the end of the chapter you should know the range of powers and duties available to social services departments to assist children 'in need'.

CASE STUDY

R (on the application of G) v Barnet LBC; R (on the application of W) v Lambeth LBC; R (on the application of A) v Lambeth LBC (2003)

Facts

These three cases were heard together by the House of Lords. They concern the lack of residential accommodation suitable for the children if they were to remain within the family unit without the risk of significant harm to their welfare. The children were children in need of adequate housing.

G was a person from abroad who was a Dutch national of Somali origin. Her son was born in 1999. G left the Netherlands because of social ostracism due to her child's illegitimacy and she came to the UK to look for the child's father. She was refused income support and housing because she did not satisfy the habitual residence test. She then sought assistance from Barnet Council as the local social services authority. The council assessed the child's needs as best served by the return of both mother and child to the Netherlands where they would be immediately entitled to accommodation and other benefits. G applied for judicial review of the decision. It was common ground that she was suitable to look after her son and that it was not in his best interests to be removed from her care. It was also common ground that if the mother refused to return to the Netherlands, the council intended to place the child with foster parents and to provide no accommodation for the mother. The judge granted her application, the local authority appealed, and the Court of Appeal allowed its appeal.

W, the mother of two children born in 1987 and 1998, was evicted from her home in February 2001. She was found by the local housing authority (Lambeth) to be intentionally homeless because there were substantial arrears of rent. She applied immediately to the local social services authority (also Lambeth) for assistance in securing private sector housing for herself and her two children as a family unit, but that authority declined to help her. She was able to find temporary accommodation with a niece between August 2001 and January 2002. She said that no other member of her family was able to help her to house her family.

At her solicitors' request, Lambeth social services carried out assessments of the needs of her children in January 2002. The assessing officer found nothing exceptional and said that the council's social services department did not provide accommodation for the families of children in need. They would place the children with extended family members as a short-term measure whilst W sought alternative accommodation. But if the need arose, the authority would make provision for the children alone. Her application for judicial review of the refusal of the local social services authority to provide assistance with accommodation was dismissed. The Court of Appeal dismissed her appeal.

In A's appeal, two of her three children were in need because they were disabled. Assessments of the needs of A's children under the Children Act 1989 indicated that the family needed to be rehoused. A sought an order compelling the local social services authority to find and provide suitable accommodation which provided for the children's assessed needs. The High Court and the Court of Appeal held that the court had no power to intervene to make such an order.

In all three cases the parents argued that the effect of s. 17 of the Children Act 1989 was that, once there had been an assessment of the needs of an individual child in need, there was a specific duty on the local social services authority to provide services to meet the child's assessed needs, and that it followed that, if the identified need was the provision of residential accommodation, the child had an absolute right to that accommodation. In G's and W's appeal the parents contend that the effect of s. 23 of the 1989 Act, which requires a local social services authority looking after a child to make arrangements to enable him or her to live with a parent or with relatives or friends, was to put the authority under a duty to make arrangements to enable the child to live with his or her parent.

Held

The House of Lords decided (by a majority) that s. 17 of the Children Act 1989 set out duties of a general nature only which were not intended to be enforceable as such by individuals. The 'general duty' was owed to all the children who were in need within the area of the local social services authority and not to each child in need individually. It provided the broad aims which the local social services authority was to bear in mind when it was performing the 'other duties' set out in Part III of the 1989 Act and the 'specific duties' set out in Part I of Schedule 2 to the 1989 Act as to which it had a discretion as to how it should meet the needs of each individual child in need. Although the services which the local social services authority provided could include the provision of accommodation, the provision of residential accommodation to rehouse a child in need so that he could live with his family was not the principal or primary purpose of the legislation. Housing was the function of the local housing authority.

Section 23 of the Act did not impose an obligation on a local social services authority to provide accommodation for the parent or other persons. Section 23 was concerned with the way a local social services authority was to discharge its obligation to provide accommodation for a child whom it was looking after. It required the local social services authority to make arrangements to allow the child to live with a parent or other specified person unless that would not be reasonably practicable or consistent with his welfare. The provision assumed the parent of the child already had accommodation which the child could live in with his parent. It was concerned with placement, not housing. Accordingly, the appeals were dismissed.

WHAT DO THESE CASES TELL YOU ABOUT SOCIAL WORK PRACTICE?

The House of Lords decided that the duty under s. 17 of the Children Act to an individual child is very limited. The duty is:

- a general duty and not a targeted, specific duty owed to an individual child;
- intended to be for the benefit of all the children in need in the local social services authority's area in general;
- discharged by providing a range and level of services appropriate to meet the various needs of children in its area.

Even assessment of a particular child's individual needs does not transform the general duty to a specific duty owed to the child as an individual.

So, although social services departments are able to provide accommodation under s. 17, this is not the principal purpose of the legislation. In other words, while a homeless child is very likely to be a child in need and should be accommodated by social services, this does not impose a duty upon the local authority to provide accommodation for the child's family as well. The decision demonstrates the desperate plight of some families who for one reason or another are excluded from welfare provision. It is clear that social services departments are inevitably constrained in the support they can give to children in need because of limited resources.

Introduction

Part III of the Children Act contains a range of duties which are imposed upon local authorities. These duties are summarized in **Box 6.1**.

These duties have been amplified by three important pieces of legislation, the Children (Leaving Care) Act 2000, the Care Standards Act 2000, and the Children and Young Persons Act 2008. This latter Act in particular substantially amends the provisions of Part III of the Children Act.

 BOX 6.1 The duties contained in Part III of the Children Act

Section	Description
17	The general preventive duty to 'children in need'
17A and 17B	Direct payments or vouchers for services to those with parental responsibility for disabled children, to disabled people with parental responsibility, or to disabled children aged 16 and 17
18(1), (3)	Day care for some under fives who are 'children in need'
20	Provision of accommodation for some 'children in need'
22, 22C, 22F, 23, and 24(1)	Duties to children and young persons looked after by the local authority
23ZA and 23ZB	Duties to ensure visits to and contact with looked-after children and young people
23A, 23B, 23C, 23D, 23E, and 24	Duties to some people who have been in care. Persons qualifying for advice and assistance
25	Secure accommodation
25A, 25B and 26	Independent review and complaints
Schedule 2, Part 1	Provision of services in the community
Schedule 2, Part 2	Children looked after by local authorities
Schedule 2, Part 3	Contributions towards the maintenance of children looked after by local authorities

This chapter will consider:

- the general duty in s. 17 of the Children Act to safeguard and promote the welfare of children within their area who are in need;
- the range of services which may be provided for children in need;

- local authority responsibilities to 'looked-after' and accommodated children;
- duties to people who have been in care;
- complaints/representation and planning/review procedures.

It will also note the provision of secure accommodation by local authorities, the particular problems facing 'looked-after' children, and the role of the voluntary sector in supporting vulnerable families.

The renewed emphasis on improving outcomes for children in need and looked-after children should be understood in the context of the *Safeguarding Children* programme that we discussed in **chapter 5**. The Children and Young Persons Act 2008 imposed a general duty upon the Secretary of State to promote the well-being of children. The meaning of 'well-being' in that Act is set out in s. 10 of the Children Act 2004. In the 2008 Act there is a particular emphasis on the role of the Secretary of State in improving the well-being of care leavers. The statutory duty is designed to complement the role of the local authorities set out in Part III of the Children Act.

The scope of Part III of the Children Act

Part III is extensive and affects every area of service provision under the Children Act 1989. It ranges from providing for very basic 'one-off' support to ensuring that young people who have left care still have support available to them.

The provision of local authority support

Local authority support, designed to safeguard and promote the welfare of the child in need, and enabling the child to be brought up with his or her family, is a cornerstone of the Children Act 1989. The local authority works in partnership with the child and the child's parents. The aim is to provide positive support to avoid the need, as far as possible, for the local authority to have to seek statutory control.

The promotion of welfare

The welfare principle imposed upon the courts requires them to treat the child's welfare as the paramount consideration. For local authorities the requirement is distinct: they must safeguard and promote the welfare of children within their area who are in need. To discharge this duty the local authority has to carry out a balancing act. There will always be a conflict between what it may want to do for an individual child and what it can do, given its resources and the demands of other children whose welfare it has to safeguard and promote. This was the problem that social services departments faced in the case study at the beginning of the chapter.

Section 17

Section 17(1) of the Children Act sets out the general preventive duty which local authorities owe to 'children in need' in their area. We reproduce s. 17(1) in **Box 6.2**.

BOX 6.2 Section 17(1)—the general duty on local authorities

(1) It shall be the general duty of every local authority (in addition to the other duties imposed on them by this Part)—

(a) to safeguard and promote the welfare of children within their area who are in need; and

(b) so far as is consistent with that duty, to promote the upbringing of such children by their families by providing a range and level of services appropriate to those children's needs.

'Children in need'

The local authority's duty to safeguard and promote the welfare of a child extends only to those children who are 'in need'. Being in need is therefore a necessity if a child is going to benefit from the general duty.

Who are 'children in need'?

The latest Children in Need census indicates that there were 378,600 children in need at 31 March 2013 in England, which was a rate of 332.2 per 10,000 children. This overall rate hides a huge range across different local authorities. The rate in Wokingham was 154.4 children in need per 10,000 children, whereas the rate in Middlesbrough was 785.3 children in need per 10,000 children.

Abuse and neglect are the biggest single reason for services and account for 47.3 per cent of all children served.

For a definition of a child in need we have to look at s. 17(10) which we set out in **Box 6.3**.

 BOX 6.3 Children in need—s. 17(10) and (11)

(10) For the purposes of this Part a child shall be taken to be in need if—

(a) he is unlikely to achieve or maintain, or to have the opportunity of achieving or maintaining, a reasonable standard of health or development without the provision for him of services by a local authority under this Part;

(b) his health or development is likely to be significantly impaired, or further impaired, without the provision for him of such services; or

(c) he is disabled, and 'family', in relation to such a child, includes any person who has parental responsibility for the child and any other person with whom he has been living.

(11) For the purposes of this Part, a child is disabled if he is blind, deaf or dumb or suffers from mental disorder of any kind or is substantially and permanently handicapped by illness, injury or congenital deformity or such other disability as may be prescribed; and in this Part—

'development' means physical, intellectual, emotional, social or behavioural development; and 'health' means physical or mental health.

The majority of children and young people with whom the local authority is going to come into contact will fall within the definition of 'children in need'. The definition is broad to emphasize the preventive element of the local authority's role. There are three different elements of the definition:

(a) reasonable standard of health or development;

(b) significant impairment of health or development;

(c) disability.

The local authority must consider the provision of services for those who fall within any of the headings. It is the local authority that makes the decision as to whether or not a particular child is in need (*Re J (Specific Issue Order: Leave to Apply)* (1995)). In a more recent Supreme Court judgment, Lady Hale commented:

> where the issue is not, what order should the court make, but what service should the local authority provide, it is entirely reasonable to assume that Parliament intended such evaluative questions to be determined by the public authority, subject to the control of the courts on the ordinary principles of judicial review. Within the limits of fair process and 'Wednesbury reasonableness' there are no clear cut right or wrong answers.

> (*A v London Borough of Croydon; M v London Borough of Lambeth* [2009] UKSC 8, para. 26)

Families with no recourse to public funds

An infamous case for local authorities involved a family who had no recourse to public funds but did have an outstanding application for leave to remain. The Court of Appeal found in the family's favour. Dyson, LJ indicated the way forward when he said:

> The first question that Birmingham should have considered was whether the claimant and her family were destitute. If they were satisfied that they were destitute, it follows ... that, upon learning that the claimant had made an application for indefinite leave to remain on grounds which expressly or implicitly raised article 8 of the Convention, they should then have considered whether the application was abusive or hopeless. If they considered that the application was not abusive or hopeless, they should not have refused assistance pending the determination of the application.

> (*Clue v Birmingham City Council* [2010] EWCA Civ 460)

More recently in *KA v Essex County Council* [2013] EWHC 43 (Admin), a Nigerian mother and her children were resident unlawfully in the UK and had had three applications for leave to remain turned down. They were living with a relative but had to leave. The local authority eventually supported the family with accommodation but following two assessments—a needs assessment of the children and a human rights assessment—the authority decided that the children would not be in need if they returned to Nigeria. In this instance, the mother refused to leave voluntarily but the authority withdrew its support. This left the family with no right of appeal since removal directions had not been forthcoming. The Deputy High Court Judge, Robin Purchas QC concluded:

Where on the facts of the case it is demonstrated that a person has a substantive convention claim, for example to a family or private life in this country, that would found an appeal against removal directions if made, a decision that effectively deprived the person of that protection would in my judgment be in breach of his convention procedural right.

In my judgment, the proper approach on the facts of this case, should have been to provide support as far as necessary to preserve the procedural right to protection of the Claimant's and her family's article 8 rights unless the Defendant concluded that it was in effect obviously hopeless or abusive.

'Looked after'

This term is not actually defined specifically in the Children Act 1989. To become 'looked after', the child first has to be in need. In addition, to be looked after the child has either to be the subject of a care order or be supplied with accommodation by the local authority. This is explained in s. 22 set out in **Box 6.4**. The 'looked-after' child has access to the range of services the local authority provides for children in need. It is important to note that once a child is looked after the child becomes subject to the Care Planning, Placement and Case Review (England) Regulations 2010. You are advised to also consider the *Children Act 1989 Guidance and Regulations, Volume 2: Care Planning, Placement and Case Review*. We discuss this and the responsibilities of local authorities to accommodated children more fully later in the chapter (**Local authority accommodation**, p 211). Looked-after children may be in more serious need than children in need living with their families.

 BOX 6.4 The general duty of the local authority in relation to children looked after by it

(1) In this Act, any reference to a child who is looked after by a local authority is a reference to a child who is—

   (a) in their care; or

   (b) provided with accommodation by the authority in the exercise of any functions (in particular those under this Act) which are social services functions within the meaning of the Local Authority Social Services Act 1970 apart from functions under sections 17, 23B and 24B.

(2) In subsection (1) 'accommodation' means accommodation which is provided for a continuous period of more than 24 hours.

(3) It shall be the duty of a local authority looking after any child—

   (a) to safeguard and promote his welfare; and

   (b) to make such use of services available for children cared for by their own parents as appears to the authority reasonable in his case.

(3A) The duty of a local authority under subsection (3)(a) to safeguard and promote the welfare of a child looked after by them includes in particular a duty to promote the child's educational achievement.

Section 34 of the Children and Families Act 2014 also places a duty on the local authority to allow contact.

(1) Where a child is in the care of a local authority, the authority shall (subject to the provisions of this section **and their duty under section 22(3)(a)** [ie to safeguard and promote a care under their care's welfare]) allow the child reasonable contact with—

   (a) his parents;

   (b) any guardian or special guardian of his;

 (ba) any person who by virtue of section 4A has parental responsibility for him;

   (c) where there was a residence order in force with respect to the child immediately before the care order was made, the person in whose favour the order was made; and

   (d) where, immediately before the care order was made, a person had care of the child by virtue of an order made in the exercise of the High Court's inherent jurisdiction with respect to children, that person.

Note: 'care' in subsection (1) means the local authority has a court order for that particular child.

Services for a child in need

Once it is established that a child is in need, the local authority has the power to provide the appropriate services. Section 17(4A) (inserted by the Children Act 2004) requires the local authority to ascertain and take appropriate account of the child's wishes regarding the provision of services.

Services may be supplied direct to the child or to other members of the child's family (s. 17(3)). 'Family' is defined broadly (in s. 17(10)) so that it encompasses any family grouping you are likely to encounter. It is acceptable to target the services on someone other than the child, provided that this is done with the aim of promoting and safeguarding the welfare of the particular child in need. So if a mother was finding it difficult to cope with a child because she also had the responsibility of looking after an elderly parent, it would be possible to use the budget for the provision of services to children under s. 17 to provide the elderly parent with day-care facilities, so as to enable the child's mother better to look after the child. A direct link needs to be made with the care of the children, however. In *MK v London Borough of Barking and Dagenham* [2013] EWHC 3486 (Admin) a claimant, who was an adult niece of the mother of two children, claimed that she should receive services under s. 17 since not to do so made her homeless and destitute, whilst she was appealing against removal directions as an overstayer. The local authority refused and the High Court agreed, arguing that her presence was not essential to the welfare of the children.

Cash help

The services can, if necessary, be provided by means of cash assistance, as s. 17(6)–(9) of the Children Act 1989 set out in **Box 6.5** shows.

> **BOX 6.5** Assistance in kind or in cash
>
> (6) The services provided by a local authority in the exercise of functions conferred on this by this section may include providing accommodation and giving assistance in kind or, in exceptional circumstances, in cash.
>
> (7) Assistance may be unconditional or subject to conditions as to the repayment of the assistance or of its value (in whole or in part).
>
> (8) Before giving any assistance or imposing any conditions, a local authority shall have regard to the means of the child concerned and of each of his parents.
>
> (9) No person shall be liable to make any repayment of assistance or of its value at any time when he is in receipt of income support under Part VII of the Social Security Contributions and Benefits Act 1992 of any element of child tax credit other than the family element, of working tax credit of an income-based jobseeker's allowance or of an income-related employment and support allowance.

These important powers mean that if the need can be met by cash then there is nothing to stop the local authority giving cash. The local authority is entitled to take into account the resources of the child and the family before providing assistance. The majority of people who receive cash are likely to be in receipt of family credit or income support and therefore will not have to repay the money received.

Accommodation

Section 17 powers include the provision of accommodation—this power was made explicit by the insertion of a new phrase into subsection (6) of s. 17 which came into effect in November 2002. Guidance on the provision of accommodation is provided by the Department of Health LAC (2003) 13. It is important to stress that s. 17(6) provides the local authority with the *power* to provide accommodation and not a *duty* to do so. However, local authorities should be wary of sidestepping their responsibilities. In *G v London Borough of Southwark*, henceforth known as the Southwark judgment, the local authority suggested that G's needs could be met under the Housing Act 1996. The authority tried to suggest that he required *help with accommodation* rather than the *provision of accommodation*. Baroness Hale's lead opinion in this judgment was more than clear:

> Under the Homelessness (Priority Need for Accommodation) (England) Order 2002 (SI 2002/2051), article 3, however, children aged 16 and 17 were expressly included in the list. So there was now a real possibility that they might be owed duties under the homelessness legislation. But two groups of children are excluded from those in priority need under article 3: those to whom a children's authority owe a duty under section 20 and 'relevant' children who have previously been looked after by a local authority (see para 6). As was said in the *Hammersmith and Fulham* case (*R (M) v Hammersmith and Fulham London Borough Council* [2008] UKHL 14), at para 31:

'Such a young person has needs over and above the simple need for a roof over her head and these can better be met by social services. Unless the problem is relatively short-term, she will then become an eligible child, and social services accommodation will also bring with it the additional responsibilities to help and support her in the transition to independent adult living. It was not intended that social services should be able to avoid those responsibilities by looking to the housing authority to accommodate the child.'

Direct payments

Sections 17A and 17B of the Act allow local authorities to make direct payments to persons with parental responsibility for a disabled child or provide vouchers instead of services which would otherwise have been provided for them by the local authorities. This increases the flexibility, for instance, in making arrangements for a carer's short-term break.

Specific duties

In addition to the general duty in s. 17 of the Children Act 1989, Part I of Schedule 2 to the Act contains a number of specific duties to provide services for the families of children in need. Part I of Schedule 2 is set out in **Box 6.6**.

BOX 6.6 The Children Act 1989, Schedule 2

1. *Identification of children in need and provision of information*
   (1) Every local authority shall take reasonable steps to identify the extent to which there are children in need within their area.
   (2) Every local authority shall—
      (a) publish information—
         (i) about services provided by them under sections 17, 18, 20, 23B to D, 24A and B and
         (ii) where they consider it appropriate, about the provision by others (including, in particular, voluntary organisations) of services which the authority has power to provide under those sections; and
      (b) take such steps as are reasonably practicable to ensure that those who might benefit from the services receive the information relevant to them.

2. *Maintenance of a register of disabled children*
   (1) Every local authority shall open and maintain a register of disabled children within their area.
   (2) The register may be kept by means of a computer.

3. *Assessment of children's needs*

   Where it appears to a local authority that a child within their area is in need, the authority may assess his needs for the purposes of this Act at the same time as any assessment of his needs is made under—

    (a) the Chronically Sick and Disabled Persons Act 1970;

    (b) the Education Act 1981;

    (c) the Disabled Persons (Services, Consultation and Representation) Act 1986; or

    (d) any other enactment.

4. *Prevention of neglect and abuse*

  (1) Every local authority shall take reasonable steps, through the provision of services under Part 3 of this Act, to prevent children within their area suffering ill treatment or neglect.

  (2) Where a local authority believes that a child who is at any time within their area—

    (a) is likely to suffer harm; but

    (b) lives or proposes to live in the area of another local authority they shall inform that other local authority.

  (3) When informing that other local authority they shall specify—

    (a) the harm that they believe he is likely to suffer; and

    (b) (if they can) where the child lives or proposes to live.

5. *Provision of accommodation [to the suspected abuser] in order to protect child*

  (1) Where—

    (a) it appears to a local authority that a child who is living on particular premises is suffering, or is likely to suffer, ill treatment at the hands of another person who is living on those premises; and

    (b) that other person proposes to move from the premises; the authority may assist that other person to obtain alternative accommodation.

  (2) Assistance given under this paragraph may be in cash.

6. *Provision for 'disabled' children*

  (1) Every local authority shall provide services designed—

    (a) to minimise the effect on disabled children within their area of their disabilities; and

    (b) to give such children the opportunity to lead lives which are as normal as possible;

    (c) to assist individuals who provide care for such children to do so, or to do so more effectively, by giving them breaks from caring.

  (2) The duty imposed by sub-paragraph (1)(c) shall be performed in accordance with regulations made by the appropriate national authority.

7. *Provision to reduce need for care proceedings etc.* [This paragraph was considered in the previous chapter as the diminishment of court proceedings principle.]

8. *Provision for children living with their families*

Every local authority shall make such provision as they consider appropriate for the following services to be available with respect to children in need within their area while they are living with their families—

    (a) advice, guidance and counselling;

    (b) occupational, social, cultural or recreational activities;

    (c) home help (which may include laundry facilities);

    (d) facilities for, or assistance with, travelling to and from home for the purpose of taking advantage of any other service provided under this Act or of any similar service;

    (e) assistance to enable the child concerned and his family to have a holiday.

9. *Family centres*
   (1) Every local authority shall provide such family centres as they consider appropriate in relation to children within their area.
   (2) 'Family centre' means a centre at which any of the persons mentioned in subparagraph (3) may—
      (a) attend for occupational, social, cultural or recreational activities;
      (b) attend for advice, guidance or counselling; or
      (c) be provided with accommodation while he is receiving advice, guidance or counselling.
   (3) The persons are:
      (a) a child;
      (b) his parents;
      (c) any person who is not a parent of his but who has parental responsibility for him;
      (d) any other person who is looking after him.

10. *Maintenance of the family home*

   Every local authority shall take such steps as are reasonably practicable, where any child within their area who is in need and whom they are not looking after is living apart from his family—
      (a) to enable him to live with his family; or
      (b) to promote contact between him and his family,
      (c) if, in their opinion, it is necessary to do so in order to safeguard or promote his welfare.

11. *Duty to consider racial groups to which children in need belong*

   Every local authority shall, in making any arrangements—
      (a) for the provision of day care within their area; or
      (b) designed to encourage persons to act as local authority foster parents, have regard to the different racial groups to which children within their area who are in need belong.

Publicity

Paragraph 1 of the schedule requires the local authority to give publicity to services that the Act requires it to provide and also to services provided by voluntary groups.

The information must be published and steps taken to ensure that it reaches the people who need it.

Prevention of neglect and abuse

Paragraph 4 focuses on the prevention of abuse and neglect. The appearance of the words 'reasonable steps' diminishes somewhat the duty set out in para. 4. The steps that may be taken are to prevent 'ill treatment or neglect'. This is a lower standard than the 'significant harm' test in s. 31 of the Act and therefore enables help to be given at an earlier stage. Neglect is not defined in the Act and therefore has to be given its normal meaning. Ill-treatment includes sexual abuse and forms of ill treatment which are not physical: Children Act 1989, s. 31(9).

Accommodation of abusers away from the family home

Paragraph 5 gives a power to the children's services department to help a suspected abuser to find accommodation and pay for it. The limit in the power is that there can be no compulsion applied to the man (statistically it is usually the man). This power is in addition to the power of a court to exclude a suspected abuser when making either an emergency protection order or an interim care order.

Breaks from caring for disabled children

Section 25 of the Children and Young Persons Act 2008 amends para. 6 of Schedule 2 to the 1989 Act (provision for disabled children) to impose a duty on local authorities to provide, as part of the range of services they provide for families, breaks from caring to assist parents and others who provide care for disabled children to continue to do so, or to do so more effectively. The intention is that breaks should not only be provided to those struggling to care for disabled children but also to those for whom a break from their caring responsibilities will improve the quality of the care they provide. Local authorities must provide such services in accordance with regulations made by the appropriate national authority. See Chapter 6 of the *Children Act 1989 Guidance and Regulations, Volume 2: Care Planning, Placement and Case Review*. **Box 6.7** sets out the current regulations.

 BOX 6.7 The Breaks for Carers of Disabled Children Regulations 2011

Duty to make provision

3. In performing their duty under paragraph 6(1)(c) of Schedule 2 to the 1989 Act, a local authority must—
    (a) have regard to the needs of those carers who would be unable to continue to provide care unless breaks from caring were given to them; and
    (b) have regard to the needs of those carers who would be able to provide care for their disabled child more effectively if breaks from caring were given to them to allow them to—
        (i) undertake education, training or any regular leisure activity,
        (ii) meet the needs of other children in the family more effectively, or
        (iii) carry out day to day tasks which they must perform in order to run their household.

Types of services which must be provided

4.—
    (1) In performing their duty under paragraph 6(1)(c) of Schedule 2 to the 1989 Act, a local authority must provide, so far as is reasonably practicable, a range of services which is sufficient to assist carers to continue to provide care or to do so more effectively.

(2) In particular, the local authority must provide, as appropriate, a range of—
    (a) day-time care in the homes of disabled children or elsewhere,
    (b) overnight care in the homes of disabled children or elsewhere,
    (c) educational or leisure activities for disabled children outside their homes, and
    (d) services available to assist carers in the evenings, at weekends and during the school holidays.

Short breaks services statement

5.—

(1) A local authority must, by 1st October 2011, prepare a statement for carers in their area (a 'short breaks services statement') setting out details of—
    (a) the range of services provided in accordance with regulation 4,
    (b) any criteria by which eligibility for those services will be assessed, and
    (c) how the range of services is designed to meet the needs of carers in their area.
(2) The local authority must publish their short breaks services statement, including by placing a copy of the statement on their website.
(3) The local authority must keep their short breaks services statement under review and, where appropriate, revise the statement.
(4) In preparing and revising their statement, the local authority must have regard to the views of carers in their area.

Support for children living with their families

Paragraph 8 requires the local authority, in accordance with the philosophy of the Children Act 1989, to support the child who is living with his or her family. The schedule provides a wide range of provisions that the local authority should consider.

Family centres

Paragraph 9 clearly states that the assistance of a family centre can be given to someone other than a particular child. This, again, is on the basis that the overall aim must be to safeguard and promote the welfare of a particular child.

Again we see the philosophy spelt out, requiring the local authority to take steps to enable children they are not looking after to live with or to have contact with their families.

Housing

The responsibility upon the local authority implies the need to ensure that the family is kept together, although clearly it cannot take on an open-ended commitment to pay the rent and arrears. Ultimately, it may be that the authority might have to seek care orders to house the children. This is because the statutory duty is to the individual children rather than to the family as a whole.

Diversity

This is a requirement for the local authority to take account of race and ethnicity in the provision of day care and recruiting foster parents. Where a local authority is 'looking after' a child, there is a requirement before making any decisions in respect of that child to give due consideration to the child's religious persuasion, racial origin, and cultural and linguistic background (Children Act 1989, s. 22(5)(c)). **Box 6.6** sets out the relevant provisions of Schedule 2.

Other sources of support

Voluntary sector organizations

The Act recognizes, in s. 17(5) set out in **Box 6.8**, that the voluntary sector has a critical role in providing services for children in need.

There are hundreds of voluntary sector projects working to support children and their families in a multiplicity of settings. **Table 6.1** contains some information on some of the national voluntary sector organizations which help families in need. You should get to know your own local organizations, and what help they can offer.

BOX 6.8 The role of the voluntary sector—s. 17(5)

Every local authority—

(a) shall facilitate the provision by others (including in particular voluntary organisations) of services which it is a function of the authority to provide by virtue of this section, or section 18, 20, 22A to 22C, 23B to 23D, 24A or 24B; and

(b) may make such arrangements as they see fit for any person to act on their behalf in the provision of any such services.

Local authority accommodation

Accommodation

The local authority may consider that the only way to safeguard and promote the welfare of a child is through the provision of accommodation. Accommodation is defined in s. 22(2) of the 1989 Act as meaning accommodation which is provided for a continuous period of more than 24 hours.

The status of accommodated children

If a local authority is providing accommodation for a child, the local authority is 'looking after' the child. 'Looked-after' children are defined in s. 22(1) of the Children Act

TABLE 6.1 Some national voluntary sector organizations

Organization	Information	Contact
Barnado's (UK)	Runs nearly 300 projects with children affected by poverty, homelessness, disability, bereavement, and abuse	www.barnados.org.uk
The Children's Society (UK)	Works to help vulnerable children and young people	www.childrenssociety.org.uk
Family Fund Trust	Provides grants and information relating to the care of severely disabled children	www.familyfund.org.uk
Gingerbread	Enables lone parents to meet others who are bringing up children alone. The website offers information on welfare benefits	www.gingerbread.org.uk
National Children's Bureau	Works with policy-makers and professionals of all sectors to share good practice in creating child-centred services	www.ncb.org.uk
NCH Action for Children (UK)	Runs over 320 projects to help vulnerable children and their families. It tackles issues relating to families in need, social exclusion, and special needs	www.nchafc.org.uk
Young Minds	Aims to promote the mental health of children and young people through a parents' information service, training and consultancy, advocacy, and publications	www.youngminds.org.uk

1989 which is set out in **Box 6.9**. The section makes it clear that 'looking after' covers both children subject to court orders and those who are not. The provision of accommodation does not in itself mean that the child is in 'care', it does not affect the parental responsibilities of any person, or give the local authority parental responsibility. It is only if the local authority has a court order that it has any control over the child. A child subject to a care order will automatically be looked after by an authority and provided with accommodation.

BOX 6.9 Looked-after children—s. 22(1) of the Children Act 1989

In this Act, any reference to a child who is looked after by a local authority is a reference to a child who is—

(a) in their care; or

(b) provided with accommodation by the authority in the exercise of any functions (in particular those under this Act) which are social services functions with the meaning of the Local Authority Social Services Act 1970 apart from functions under sections 17, 23B and 24B.

The exclusion of accommodation provided under ss. 17, 23B, and 24B from the definition of looked-after children removes such children from the obligations placed upon local authorities under the Children Act 1989 (**Box 6.10**) and the Children (Leaving Care) Act 2000 (see **Box 6.15**).

BOX 6.10 The duty of local authorities towards looked-after children—s. 22(3)–(5) of the Children Act 1989

(3) It shall be the duty of a local authority looking after any child—
  (a) to safeguard and promote his welfare; and
  (b) to make such use of services available for children cared for by their own parents as appears to the authority reasonable in his case.

(3A) The duty of a local authority under subsection (3)(a) to safeguard and promote the welfare of a child looked after by them includes in particular a duty to promote the child's educational achievement.

(4) Before making any decision with respect to a child whom they are looking after, or proposing to look after, a local authority shall, so far as is reasonably practicable, ascertain the wishes and feelings of—
  (a) the child;
  (b) his parents;
  (c) any person who is not a parent of his but who has parental responsibility for him; and
  (d) any other person whose wishes and feelings the authority consider to be relevant, regarding the matter to be decided.

(5) In making any such decision a local authority shall give due consideration—
  (a) having regard to his age and understanding, to such wishes and feelings of the child as they have been able to ascertain;
  (b) to such wishes and feelings of any person mentioned in subsection (4)(b) to (d) as they have been able to ascertain; and
  (c) to the child's religious persuasion, racial origin and cultural and linguistic background.

The local authority duty towards looked-after children

This duty is provided for in s. 22(3)–(5) of the Children Act 1989 which we have set out for you in **Box 6.10**. Notice the responsibilities upon local authorities to take into account the wishes of the child, his or her parents, and other people who are important to the child. The authority is also obliged to take into account the child's religious and cultural needs.

The power to provide accommodation

The local authority also has power to provide accommodation for a child even though there is someone who is willing and able to provide accommodation, if the local authority considers that the provision of accommodation would promote the child's welfare (s. 20(4)). This power may well be used to protect a child by removing the child from the unsatisfactory home setting. However, the provision of accommodation for a child under the age of 16 under this section is subject to parental consent (s. 20(7)). Without that consent no accommodation can be provided. If a child has been provided with accommodation and parental cooperation is withdrawn then, if you are seeking to protect the child, you should consider applying for an emergency protection order or care order.

A service for families

Section 20 makes it quite clear that the provision of accommodation without a care order is only provided on a 'service' basis. This is spelled out in s. 20(7) and (8) set out in **Box 6.11**.

 BOX 6.11 Section 20(7) and (8)

(7) A local authority may not provide accommodation under this section for any child if any person who—
  (a) has parental responsibility for him;
  (b) is willing and able to—
    (i)   provide accommodation for him; or
    (ii) arrange for accommodation to be provided for him,

objects.

(8) Any person who has parental responsibility for a child may at any time remove the child from accommodation provided by or on behalf of the local authority under this section.

Removal of a child from accommodation

The 'at any time' in s. 20(8) means that no notice need be given to the authority. This is in contrast to the previous law where, after a six-month period in local authority accommodation, notice of the removal of the child had to be given. If you are supplying accommodation to a particular child and you are notified of the possibility of the child's removal by the child's parents, and you consider this to be against the welfare of the child, then you should consider whether there are grounds for an emergency protection order. The grounds are discussed in **chapter 8**. If a child is subject to a court order in favour of the local authority, a parent has no right to remove the child from the accommodation without the local authority's consent.

A young person in accommodation

A young person of 16 or over is in control of whether or not he or she receives or stays in accommodation. This is because of s. 20(11):

> (11)   Subsections (7) and (8) [power of parents to refuse accommodation and to remove the child] do not apply where a child who has reached the age of sixteen agrees to being provided with accommodation under this section.

Accordingly, the parents may disagree about the future of the young person but the choice is always that of the young person.

Disputes between parents

If one parent has a child arrangements order regulating where a child should live, the other parent cannot remove the child from accommodation without first successfully applying to the court for a residence order in their favour. If neither parent has a child arrangements order and both parents have parental responsibility, then either parent could remove the child, as stated in s. 20(8). This could mean that one parent places the child into accommodation and the other parent removes the child from that accommodation. This would be a good example of where the parent who wants the child to stay in the accommodation should apply to the court for a prohibited steps order under s. 8. Remember that s. 8 orders, other than a child arrangements order, cannot be made where the child is subject to a care order.

No child arrangements orders

Where there is no child arrangements order settling where a child should live, then there can be management difficulties. If during the breakdown of a marriage the mother were to place a child under the age of 16 into local authority-provided accommodation, what is to stop the father removing the child? The simple answer is nothing. The Act is quite clear that if a parent objects to the provision of accommodation, or seeks, at any time, to remove the child, then the local authority cannot prevent it.

The only guidance in this situation is to look to s. 3(5) of the Children Act 1989 which states that a person without parental responsibility but who has care of the child may, subject to the Act, do what is reasonable in all the circumstances of the case for the purpose of safeguarding or promoting the welfare of the child. The local authority is covered by this section, not having parental responsibility, and it has to do all it can to safeguard and promote the welfare of the child. Unfortunately, this does not give clear guidance as to what to do when the drunken father turns up at 2 am. It cannot be promoting the welfare of the child to allow the child to go with the father, and yet the statute says you should. What will be required here are negotiating skills. If these fail, then an application for an emergency protection order would have to be made, or a request should be made to the police to take the child into police protection (see **chapter 8**).

The supply of accommodation

The Children and Young People Act 2008 has substantially revised the system for provision of accommodation for children and young people. Section 8 of the Children and Young People Act 2008 replaces s. 23 of the Children Act with new ss. 22A–22F. We will consider the planning and review obligations in **chapter 9**.

Section 22A re-enacts the duty on local authorities to provide accommodation for children who are in their care, and s. 22B re-enacts the duty to maintain all looked-after children other than providing for their accommodation. The duties and powers of local authorities to provide accommodation for children under ss. 20 and 21 of the 1989 Act (ie those who are 'voluntarily accommodated' or accommodated for their own protection or by virtue of an order made in criminal proceedings) are unaffected by the changes.

Section 22C outlines the ways in which the local authority must perform its accommodation functions.

Placements with parents and others with parental responsibility

The local authority must make arrangements for a child they are looking after to live with their parents; any other person who has parental responsibility for the child; or, in the case of a child who is the subject of a care order (ie who is 'in care'), a person with whom a child lived under a child arrangements order immediately before the care order was made. This duty applies only where it is consistent with the child's welfare to do so and reasonably practicable. If the local authority is unable to place a child with a person specified in subsection (3), the local authority must place the child in the most appropriate placement available—s. 22C(5).

Placements

'Placement' is defined in s. 22C(6). This may include, for example, supporting young people to live independently in rented accommodation, residential employment, or in supported lodgings/hostels. When a local authority is deciding upon the most appropriate placement for a child, it must have regard to the other provisions of Part III of the 1989 Act—s. 22C(7). This includes the duty to safeguard and promote the welfare of the child (subsection (3)(a)) and the duty in particular to promote the child's educational achievement (subsection (3A)); the duty to ascertain the wishes and feelings of the child, his parents, and other relevant persons before making a decision with respect to the child they are looking after (subsection (4)); and the duty to give those wishes and feelings and the child's religious persuasion, racial origin, and cultural and religious background due consideration (subsection (5)).

The local authority must give preference to a placement with a relative, friend, or other person connected with the child over the other placement options.

Impact of placement

The local authority must, so far as is reasonably practicable in all the circumstances of the child's case, ensure that the placement:

- allows the child to live near their home;
- does not disrupt the child's education or training;

- if the child has a sibling who is also being looked after by the local authority, enables the child and that sibling to live together; and

- if the child is disabled, is suitable to the child's particular needs.

In general, local authorities are required to ensure that placements are within their own area.

Foster parents

A child in care or being looked after on a voluntary basis can, under s. 22C, be provided with accommodation by being placed with foster parents. Foster parents are suitable people selected by the local authority to provide accommodation and maintenance for a child being looked after. The selection and registration of foster parents are subject to detailed guidance, *Assessment and approval of foster carers: Amendments to the Children Act 1989 Guidance and Regulations*. Section 22C allows the local authority to pay any person with whom it has placed a child, but the local authority can recover all or part of the costs from the parents unless the parents are in receipt of particular benefits.

Foster parents who wish to challenge the process by which they are approved by local authorities are supported by an independent review mechanism. The details of the independent review mechanism are set out in regulations.

Services to accommodated children

Section 19 of the Children and Young Persons Act 2008 inserts a new para. 8A into Schedule 2 to the Children Act. This is set out in **Box 6.12**. This ensures that accommodated children receive the same range of services as other children in need and promotes contact between accommodated children and their families.

 BOX 6.12 Section 8A Provision for accommodated children

(1) Every local authority shall make provision for such services as they consider appropriate to be available with respect to accommodated children.

(2) 'Accommodated children' are those children in respect of whose accommodation the local authority have been notified under section 85 or 86.

(3) The services shall be provided with a view to promoting contact between each accommodated child and that child's family.

(4) The services may, in particular, include—
   (a) advice, guidance and counselling;
   (b) services necessary to enable the child to visit, or to be visited by, members of the family;
   (c) assistance to enable the child and members of the family to have a holiday together.

(5) Nothing in this paragraph affects the duty imposed by paragraph 10.

Concern with the poor educational outcomes of looked-after children has led to another innovation. Section 20 of the Children and Young Persons Act 2008 requires schools to designate a member of staff to take responsibility for the educational attainment of looked-after children attending the school.

Responsibilities to care leavers

The local authority is acting as parent to the children it accommodates. One role of parenting is to prepare children for independence. Another is to provide continuing support after the child has left home. Research into the life chances of young people living in and leaving local authority care indicated that local authorities in general fail in these two roles. The Children (Leaving Care) Act 2000 attempts to address these failings. The explanatory notes to the Act state that its main purpose is to:

> help young people who have been looked after by a local authority move from care into living independently in as stable a fashion as possible.

To understand the amendments and new duties it introduces into the Children Act, it is necessary to explain some key definitions. We have set these out in **Box 6.13**.

 BOX 6.13 Definitions used in the Children (Leaving Care) Act 2000

(a) Eligible children—those children in care aged 16 and 17 who have been looked after for 13 weeks or more.

(b) Relevant children—those young people aged 16 and 17 who meet the criteria for eligible children but who leave care. The Regulations exclude certain groups, such as children who return home permanently and children who receive respite care.

(c) Former relevant children—those who before reaching the age of 18 were either eligible or relevant children.

(d) The responsible local authority—the local authority who last looked after an eligible or relevant young person.

Duties to care leavers

The Children (Leaving Care) Act introduced new paras 19A, 19B, and 19C into Part 2 of Schedule 2 to the Children Act 1989. Part 2 of Schedule 2 imposes duties on local authorities in connection with those children it looks after. The new paragraphs ensure that some responsibilities continue after the child leaves care. Paragraph 19A imposes a duty on local authorities which is set out in **Box 6.14**.

BOX 6.14 Preparation for ceasing to be looked after

(19A) It is the duty of the local authority looking after a child to advise, assist, and befriend him with a view to promoting his welfare when they have ceased to look after him.

Subparagraph (4) of para. 19B requires that a local authority carry out an assessment of the needs of each eligible child for the advice, assistance, and support that would be appropriate for the local authority to provide. They will then prepare a pathway plan, which is defined in s. 23E. The pathway plan should take over from the care plan. The plan is to be reviewed regularly (s. 19B(5)).

Relevant and former relevant children

The amended s. 22 of the Act and the new ss. 23A–23C impose duties on the local authority towards children and young people formerly looked after by them. Section 22 is amended so that local authorities can provide accommodation to a child who has left care, without the fact of their doing so classifying him or her as still being 'looked after'. Section 23B, set out in **Box 6.15**, contains the duties of the responsible local authority towards relevant children. Section 23C provides for similar duties towards former relevant children. This has been amended to include a duty to pay a contribution towards the costs of higher education of former relevant children.

BOX 6.15 The duties towards relevant children—s. 23B

(1) It is the duty of each local authority to take reasonable steps to keep in touch with a relevant child for whom they are the responsible authority, whether he is within their area or not.

(2) It is the duty of each local authority to appoint a personal adviser for each relevant child (if they have not already done so under paragraph 19C of Schedule 2).

(3) It is the duty of each local authority, in relation to any relevant child who does not already have a pathway plan prepared for the purposes of paragraph 19B of Schedule 2—

    (a) to carry out an assessment of his needs with a view to determining what advice, assistance and support it would be appropriate for them to provide him under this Part; and

    (b) to prepare a pathway plan for him.

Sections 23D and 23E set out the details of personal advisers and pathway plans. Section 24 defines those qualifying for advice and assistance. The definition includes care leavers as a whole as well as children and young people leaving accommodation provided by certain other providers.

Section 24(4) establishes a duty on a local authority to keep in touch as it thinks appropriate with any child whom it has looked after. Section 24B(5) obliges authorities to provide, or enable the young person to pay for, suitable vacation accommodation should it be needed, if they are in full-time higher education or further education. These provisions are amplified by the Care Leavers (England) Regulations 2010 which came into force on 1 April 2011. You are advised to read the revised volume of *Guidance and Regulations to the Children Act 1989, Vol 3: Planning Transition to Adulthood for Care Leavers*, which can be downloaded from www.gov.uk/government/uploads/system/uploads/attachment_data/file/312530/Planning_Transition_to_Adulthood_for_Care_Leavers.pdf.

Assistance to pursue education and training

The Children and Young Persons Act 2008 inserts a new s. 23CA into the Children Act. This extends the duties of local authorities to appoint a personal adviser to include a former relevant child who informs the local authority who previously looked after him or her that he or she is pursuing or intends to pursue a programme of education or training but to whom the local authority would otherwise owe no duty under s. 23C because the young person is over 21 years of age and has completed (or abandoned) the programme set out in his or her original pathway plan.

As long as the young person is under 25, the local authority must also carry out an assessment of needs, prepare a pathway plan, and provide such assistance as the person's educational and training needs require.

Regulatory framework

The whole field of 'looking after' is dominated by regulations that have been issued under the Children Act 1989:

- *Children Act 1989 Guidance and Regulations, Volume 4: Fostering Services* (1991);
- *Children Act 1989 Guidance and Regulations, Volume 2: Care Planning, Placement and Case Review*;
- *Family and Friends Care: Statutory Guidance for Local Authorities*;
- *Temporary approval of prospective adopters as foster carers: Statutory guidance for local authorities, directors of children's services (DCSs) and social workers* (May 2013);
- *Children Act 1989 Guidance and Regulations, Volume 3: Planning Transition to Adulthood for Care Leavers*;
- *Children Act 1989 Guidance and Regulations, Volume 5: Children's Homes Statutory guidance for local authorities* (October 2013);
- *Looked-after children: contact with siblings. Update to 'The Children Act 1989 guidance and regulations, Vol 2: Care Planning, Placement and Case Review'* (February 2014);

- *IRO Handbook: Statutory guidance for independent reviewing officers and local authorities on their functions in relation to case management and review for looked-after children.*

Children Act 1989 Guidance and Regulations, Volume 4: Fostering Services and *Children Act 1989 Guidance and Regulations, Volume 2: Care Planning, Placement and Case Review* are essential reading for all social workers working with children in the public care system. The regulations set down procedures, specify dates, forms, the types and nature of review, and time limits. They govern who should be consulted about steps to be taken by a local authority concerning a child, and so on. In this chapter, we have the space only to give outline coverage of this large area, and you must read the guidance stated above.

Quality of services and accountability for provision are important. Services are regularly inspected and reports made to Parliament. The Education and Inspections Act 2006 transferred responsibilities for the inspection of children's services from a variety of inspectorates to the Office for Standards in Education, Children's Services and Skills—known as Ofsted. More information on inspection and audit is provided in **chapter 1**.

Promoting family links

One finding of research into children who have been looked after by local authorities in the past was the concept of the child being 'lost in care'. This arose when a child may have been provided with accommodation (placed in voluntary care under the old law) at some time of crisis within the family. The child being out of the family may have defused that particular crisis, but the reception of the child took place without any forward planning and the child just went on to 'hold' in the accommodation. The parents, relieved of the pressures, were often not encouraged to keep up contact and time passed, so that links were lost. Further crises with other families meant that the original child was not given attention and eventually the child became 'lost' in care.

The Children Act 1989 addresses this problem in a number of ways. It treats all children regardless of the route by which they came to be looked after by a local authority in the same way. We start with s. 23(6) and (7), which seeks to promote this contact between child and parent. These subsections are set out in **Box 6.16**.

 BOX 6.16 The promotion of contact with the family

(6) Subject to any regulations made by the Secretary of State for the purposes of this sub-section, any local authority looking after a child shall make arrangements to enable him to live with—

(a) a person falling within subsection (4) [that is a parent]; or

(b) a relative, friend or other person connected with him, unless that would not be reasonably practicable or consistent with his welfare.

> (7) Where a local authority provide accommodation for a child whom they are looking after, they shall, subject to the provisions of this Part and so far as is reasonably practicable and consistent with his welfare, secure that—
> (a) the accommodation is near his home; and
> (b) where the authority are also providing accommodation for a sibling of his, they are accommodated together.

The regulations set out the requirement for a written plan before any placement is made. All the people involved in the plan, including the child (as far as is consistent with age and understanding), should be consulted about it. The plan must include the proposals for contact. Volume 2 of the Guidance and Regulations sets out, at para. 2.44, the suggested contents of such a plan.

Schedule 2

There are comprehensive powers contained in Schedule 2 (see **Box 6.6**) to assist the maintaining of links with the child's family. By way of an example: one allegation that may be made against a social worker is that, having provided a child with accommodation, he or she then places the child with a foster parent remote from the child's parents. To visit the child, the parents may have to get two buses and a train, and find this difficult. As a consequence, the visits to the child drop off, and this is then used as an argument for saying that the parents do not really care for the child. The parents would say: 'This, of course, was what the authority was trying to prove all along. Indeed, this was the very reason why the child was placed with these particular foster parents.' Often the truth is closer to the fact that the harassed placement officer had only those foster parents available on the day the child had to be supplied with accommodation. Using the powers in Schedule 2, para. 16 should remove this argument. It provides that if the authority believes that visits could not be made without undue financial hardship, then the authority is permitted to make payments to any parent, or indeed any relative, friend, or person connected with the child. These payments can cover not only the cost of travel but subsistence and other expenses that may be involved. The payments need not be subject to a requirement for repayment, and indeed cannot be subject to that condition if the parents are in receipt of benefits.

In addition, new provision set out in the Care Planning, Placement and Case Review (England) Regulations 2010 requires that a nominated officer in the local authority must first approve a child's placement out of the local authority area. In doing so, before approving a decision under para. (1), the nominated officer must be satisfied that:

- the child's wishes and feelings have been ascertained and given due consideration;
- the placement is the most appropriate placement available for the child and consistent with his or her care plan;
- the child's relatives have been consulted, where appropriate;

- the area authority have been notified; and
- the independent reviewing officer has been consulted.

A child subject to a court order

All that we have said previously about the treatment of a child being looked after will be applicable to a child under a care order (see **Box 6.10**). We discuss care orders in **chapter 9**. However, there are some aspects of care orders which are relevant to our current discussion.

Links with families when children are subject to care orders

It is important to note that the statutory duty to consider placing the child with the child's family applies even if the child is subject to a care order. See the comments of the Court of Appeal in *Re T (A Minor) (Care or Supervision Order)* (1994). Put another way, the making of a care order does not require the local authority to remove the child from the child's home. This is often misunderstood, as in *Re A (Supervision Order: Extension)* (1995). This was resisted by the mother and at that time by the local authority in the mistaken belief that they would not be able to leave the child with her mother if a care order was made.

If such a placement is made, it must be done in accordance with Part 4, paras 15–20 of the Care Planning, Placement and Case Review (England) Regulations 2010.

Placement of the child with parents whilst in care

If it is intended to place a child in care with a parent of the child, s. 23(5) will permit this only if it is done in accordance with the Care Planning, Placement and Case Review (England) Regulations 2010. The purpose of these regulations is to ensure that when the decision is made to place at home a child who is the subject of a court order without the order being discharged, control and supervision is exercised over that procedure.

Before deciding to return the child, the 'respect for the child' principle dictates that the child's wishes be ascertained. The local authority must also obtain the written comments of all those agencies involved in the welfare and protection of this child, including the relevant health authority, the education authority, and the police, and must notify the people it has consulted, in writing, of the decision taken.

The regulations also provide a framework for the practical social work that will be needed to prepare the child and parent for the child's return. There has to be a written agreement with the parent recording the objective and plan of the placement, the arrangements for supervision, details of health, and educational arrangements. The agreement must record the fact that the child can be removed if the authority considers that the child's welfare is no longer being promoted. Whilst the agreement need not be signed, signing it may nonetheless be good practice.

On the return home, the register, which has to be kept of such returned children, must record the fact of the return and further record the regular visits of the social worker to the child that have to be undertaken. The first has to take place within one week and the visits then have to take place at intervals of six weeks at the most.

Having placed a child in care with the parents, the authority must not allow the situation to drift. It must review the placement within the first three months and then at six-month intervals. The reviews are to see whether the purpose of the placement is being met. If the placement is successful, the authority should consider whether to seek to discharge the care order. These reviews must be recorded in writing, as must the regular visits.

Contact

Under s. 34, where a child is under a care order there is a presumption that the child will have reasonable contact with his or her parents. Before the making of any care order, the authority shall inform the court of the plans it intends to make for contact between individuals and the child (s. 34(11)). The court can then define the extent of the contact that should take place. The presumption also applies whenever the local authority accommodates the child under an emergency protection order or a child assessment order.

At the stage of making a care order, the court has power under s. 34 to make what is in effect an interim contact order, with specific provision for a further hearing with a view to making provision for contact at the subsequent hearing (*Re B (A Minor) (Care Order: Review)* (1993)).

Contact decisions

At the same time as a care order is made, or following a later application by either the local authority or the child, or the child's parents or others who had a residence order, the court may decide the amount of contact (s. 34(2), (3)). The court may instead make an order authorizing the local authority to refuse contact between the child and his or her parents (s. 34(4)). Section 34—with the rest of the Children Act—was written to ensure compliance with the European Convention. This judicial scrutiny of contact is necessary to satisfy the Human Rights Act 1998, and means that decisions to terminate parental contact are very likely to comply with Articles 6 and 8 of the Convention.

Local authority restriction of contact

There is also a general power given to the local authority in respect of contact under s. 34(6). If the authority believes that it would not promote the welfare of the child to allow contact, then it may refuse contact, but only as a matter of urgency and then only for a period of up to seven days. During that period it would have to make an application to the court for an order. The use of the word 'urgency' implies that the situation which has arisen must have occurred within the recent past, this power not being available to solve long-standing difficulties. The Children and Families Act 2014 amends the Children Act 1989 to make it clear that the local authority's duty to allow reasonable contact between a child in the care of the local authority and his or her parents and other relevant people (any guardian or special guardian, any person who by virtue of s. 4A has parental responsibility for him or her, where there was a child arrangements order in force with respect to the child immediately before the care order was made, the person in whose favour the order was made, and where, immediately before the care order was made, a person had care of the child by virtue of an order made in the exercise of the High Court's inherent jurisdiction with respect to children) is subject to the local authority's duty to safeguard and promote the welfare of looked-after children under s. 22(3)(a) of the Children Act 1989. If allowing contact with any of those persons would not safeguard and promote the welfare of the child, the local authority should not allow the contact. It follows equally that preventing contact between a child and his or her parents should only be considered where a parent is likely to harm the child.

Variation or discharge

The parent can apply to the court to vary or discharge the order under s. 34(9). The child concerned may also use both s. 34(4) to stop a parent seeing him or her, and s. 34(6) to vary such an order.

Regulations concerning contact with looked-after children

Section 8 of the Care Planning, Placement and Case Review (England) Regulations 2010 covers contact between a child in care and the child's parents and others. The regulations are applicable to all children looked after by the local authority.

Reviewing the local authority plans for a child subject to a care order by contact application

Unless there has been an order to refuse contact under s. 34(4), or an order preventing a person from applying without leave of the court for contact under s. 91(14), the parents may apply to the court to consider the contact arrangements (s. 34(3)). If an application has been made and the application has been refused, then the parents must wait six months before applying again for contact unless they obtain the leave of the court (s. 91(17)).

Challenges to the local authority plans for the child in care can be made during the regular reviews. Importantly, the decision in *Re B (Minors) (Care: Local Authority's Plans)* (1993) has indicated that the Court of Appeal views s. 34 as another possible way of challenge. In this case it was argued that the discretion of the local authority with a care order could not be challenged and the court could not look at the local authority's long-term plans. The court would not accept this and said:

> If, however, a court was not able to intervene, it would make a nonsense of the paramountcy of the welfare of the child, which is the bedrock of the Act, and would subordinate it to the administrative decision of the local authority in a situation where the court is seized of the contact issue. That cannot be right.

This means that whilst the local authority has a wide discretion in caring for the child, this discretion can be reviewed by the courts when looking at the contact issue.

Independent visitor

A step that can be taken when links with the child's family have failed is the appointment of an independent visitor (ss. 23ZA and 23ZB). The role of the visitor is to visit, befriend, and advise the child. In doing this, the authority must apply the 'respect for the child principle' and the child has the right of informed consent to object to the initial appointment and to the continuation of the appointment. The revised provisions for independent visitors (inserted into the Children Act by the Children and Young Persons Act 2008) extends the group of looked-after children for whom an independent person must be appointed to visit, befriend, and advise the child to include all those for whom an appointment would be in their interests. The purpose of an independent visitor is to:

- promote the child's developmental, social, emotional, educational, religious, and cultural needs;
- encourage the child to exercise his or her rights and to participate in decisions which will affect him or her;
- support the care plan for the child and his or her carers; and
- aim, as far as possible, to complement the activities of carers.

Reviews of children being looked after

One extremely important responsibility that local authorities have to looked-after children is the requirement to review regularly the position of and plans for each looked-after child (Children Act 1989, s. 26). Each authority is required to appoint an independent review officer (s. 25A) who must participate in and chair the review, monitor the performance of the local authority, and where appropriate refer a case to Cafcass (s. 25B).

The nature and format of the reviews are set down in the *Children Act 1989 Guidance and Regulations, Volume 2: Care Planning, Placement and Case Review* (2010). The regulations stipulate that the independent reviewing officer (IRO) should be independent of the matter in hand, and be a registered and experienced social worker. Reviews must keep any s. 31A plan (see **Section 31A plans**, p 227) for the child under review and if there is no plan for the future care of the child one must be prepared. Reviews are to be held within four weeks of the initial placement, again not more than three months after that first review, and subsequently every six months. A review must also be carried out before the specified times if the IRO so directs. There are stipulations as to who should be consulted before a review, who should attend, and the matters for consideration. If cases are referred to Cafcass by the IRO, it may be appropriate to start court proceedings against the local authority seeking an order requiring it to put right its failings in relation to the care plan. The options for court action are judicial review proceedings, a compensation claim, or a freestanding Human Rights Act 1998 application. Few cases have been referred to Cafcass by an

IRO since 2004, when the first regulations for care planning were established. The government responded to this by increasing the powers of the IRO in new regulations in 2010 ('**Looked after**', p 203). The statutory duties of the IRO (Children Act 1989, s. 35B(1)) are to:

- monitor the performance by the local authority of their functions in relation to the child's case;

- participate in any review of the child's case;

- ensure that any ascertained wishes and feelings of the child concerning the case are given due consideration by the appropriate authority; and

- perform any other function which is prescribed in regulations.

The primary task of the IRO is to ensure that the care plan for the child fully reflects the child's current needs and that the actions set out in the plan are consistent with the local authority's legal responsibilities towards the child. As corporate parents, each local authority should act for the children they look after as a responsible and conscientious parent would act.

The primary purpose is one given to the individual IRO not the authority for which he or she works. This is one of the very few instances where social workers have a duty accorded to them personally rather than as an officer of the local authority. The IRO can and has been cited in judicial review proceedings. In *A and S v Lancashire County Council* [2012] EWHC 1689 (Fam) two brothers applied for declarations under Articles 8, 6, and 3 of the Human Rights Act 1998. The defendants to the claim were Lancashire County Council and the IRO. The boys had been freed for adoption in 2001 and had moved from foster placement to foster placement, 77 times and 96 times respectively. It was plain that the boys were unlikely to be adopted and yet the freeing order had not been revoked thus preventing the boys from contact with the birth families. The IRO was found to have made no substantial challenge to the local authority's practice in respect of the boys. In effect, he had failed to execute the primary purpose of the role. He had a caseload of three times the recommended limit and had no access to training or independent legal advice.

Paragraph 2.13 of the IRO Handbook suggests that as part of the monitoring function, the IRO also has a duty to monitor the performance of the local authority's function as a corporate parent and to identify any areas of poor practice. This should include identifying patterns of concern emerging not just around individual children but also more generally in relation to the collective experience of its looked-after children of the services they receive. Where IROs identify more general concerns around the quality of the authority's services to its looked-after children, the IRO should immediately alert senior managers about these. Equally important, the IRO should recognize and report on good practice.

Section 31A plans

Section 31A of the Children Act 1989 provides that 'No care order may be made with respect to a child until the court has considered a section 31A plan.' Therefore every child who is subject to a care order subsequent to the implementation of the section will have the benefit of a care plan which has been scrutinized by the courts. However, the Children and Families Act 2014 now requires the courts only to consider the 'permanence provision' in the plan, that is, the court is to consider whether the local authority care plan is for the child to live with a parent or any member or friend of the child's family, or whether the child is to be adopted or placed in other long-term care. The s. 31A plans will continue to be scrutinized by IROs.

The requirements of s. 31A care plans are set out in **Box 6.17**.

 BOX 6.17 Care orders: care plans—s. 31A of the Children Act

(1) Where an application is made on which a care order might be made with respect to a child, the appropriate local authority must, within such time as the court may direct, prepare a plan (a 'care plan') for the future care of the child.

(2) While the application is pending, the authority must keep any care plan prepared by them under review and, if they are of the opinion some change is required, revise the plan, or make a new plan, accordingly.

(3) A care plan must give any prescribed information and do so in the prescribed manner.

(4) For the purposes of this section, the appropriate local authority, in relation to a child in respect of whom a care order might be made, is the local authority proposed to be designated in the order.

(5) In section 31(3A) and this section, references to a care order do not include an interim care order.

(6) A plan prepared, or treated as prepared, under this section is referred to in this Act as a 'section 31A plan'.

The restriction on the liberty of a child being looked after

It is important for social workers to understand that the only basis on which the liberty of a child or young person accommodated by the local authority may be restricted is in accordance with s. 25 of the Children Act 1989 (unless the child is remanded from a criminal court—see **chapter 10**).

The restriction of liberty

The restriction of liberty does not only mean locking a door. Anything that goes beyond the bounds of ordinary domestic security will probably be a restriction of liberty. The failure to understand or accept this was the cause of the 'pin down' affair in Staffordshire. All social workers involved in caring for children and young persons should read the report on this experience (Allan Levy QC and Barbara Kahan, *The Pindown Experience and the Protection of Children* (Staffordshire County Council, 1991)).

What is secure accommodation?

Secure accommodation is accommodation that restricts the liberty of a child (s. 25). Detailed regulations have been issued under this section (written in the light of 'pin down') in respect of the type of accommodation and who may be placed in it. See the *Children Act 1989 Guidance and Regulations, Volume 5: Children's Homes* and the Children (Secure Accommodation) Regulations 1991.

Section 25 of the Children Act 1989

Section 25 prescribes that the restriction of liberty and the use of secure accommodation are available in strictly limited circumstances. A child may not be placed in secure accommodation unless:

(a) it appears that the child has a history of absconding; and

(b) is likely to abscond from any other type of accommodation; and

(c) if the child absconds, he or she is likely to suffer significant harm; or

(d) if the child is kept in any other type of accommodation, the child is likely to injure him or herself or other people.

Under the section, a child or young person whom a local authority is looking after may be placed in secure accommodation by a local authority only for a limited period of time; up to 72 hours in any period of 21 days.

It is not necessary for the child to be the subject of a care order before he or she can be placed in secure accommodation. But if the parent objects and there is no care order, in that situation the child must not be placed in secure accommodation.

Court application

If the authority wishes to keep the child in secure accommodation for a longer period than that prescribed by the regulations, then it must make an application for an authority from a court. A court can grant such an authority only if it is satisfied that the criteria of a history of absconding, etc, set out in the previous section are fulfilled. In doing this, the court does not apply the welfare principle (*Re M (A Minor) (Secure Accommodation Order)* (1995)).

Legal representation

What is important from the social worker's point of view is the fact that the court cannot grant an authority unless the child is legally represented. Section 99 states that where an application for a secure accommodation order is being made, the child/ young person must be granted the necessary funding. Notice of the proceedings must be served on all relevant parties. A children's guardian should be appointed. Secure accommodation orders involve a serious deprivation of liberty, and therefore procedural safeguards are extremely important.

Cases

In the light of this, the decisions in *A Metropolitan Borough Council v DB* (1997) and *Re C (A Minor) (Medical Treatment: Courts' Jurisdiction)* (1997) are worrying.

In the first case, the court said that a maternity ward was secure accommodation and ordered that the 17-year-old be detained there. The young woman was a crack cocaine addict, who lived in squalor, and had received no antenatal care until very shortly before the birth of her child. Two days prior to the birth, she was admitted to hospital suffering from pre-eclamptic fits brought on by high blood pressure. She then discharged herself from hospital. The local authority obtained an emergency protection order and sought permission to detain her in the maternity ward. The court granted permission, saying that it was the restriction of liberty that made a particular place into secure accommodation.

In the second case, the local authority was granted authority to detain an anorexic young woman without reference to s. 25 under the court's inherent powers contained in s. 100.

There was a greater respect for the procedural safeguards in the next case. In *LM v Essex County Council* (1999), Holman J expressed the view that once the criteria justifying a secure accommodation order ceased to be made out, the local authority should no longer keep the child in such accommodation. He also held that the court had no power to discharge or set aside such an order. If a local authority declined to release a child once it appreciated that the basis for the order was no longer present, a writ of habeas corpus would be appropriate. If the local authority failed to conclude that the grounds for the order no longer existed, the appropriate procedure might be judicial review.

The European Convention

The question arises whether secure accommodation orders made under s. 25 comply with Article 5 of the European Convention on Human Rights. Article 5(1) lists a finite set of circumstances in which persons may be deprived of their liberty, one of which is educational supervision. Despite the fact that the Children Act criteria make no reference to such supervision, the Court of Appeal in *Re K (Secure Accommodation Order: Right to Liberty)* (2001), rejected the argument that s. 25 was incompatible with the Convention, as the local authority has a duty to provide education for all those aged under 16. The court did, however, leave open the question of whether the words 'for the purposes of educational supervision' covered the facts of a particular case.

Seeking to place a child into secure accommodation will always cause the social worker the greatest of difficulties, both personally and professionally. It is difficult in such situations to see how to square your duty to the child with your wider duty to society.

Representations from children and others

Someone Else's Children considered complaints procedures and reported that:

> young people we met had little confidence in the complaints process and felt that their concerns were not heard:
> 'You never get believed but have to believe everything told to you. They never tell you what people say about you, but what I say has to be written down.'

Young people told us that, when they were better informed about the process, their confidence in it increased.

(Para. 4.30)

It is one of the core principles of the UN Convention on the Rights of the Child that children's views and wishes should be at the forefront of the decision-making process. The Children Act 1989 enacts this principle.

Representations

We discussed the regulations which require local authorities to consider representations (complaints) about the exercise of its functions under Part III of the Act, made by or on behalf of any children looked after or in need in **chapter 1**. At this point we simply remind you about the significance of enabling and responding to complaints from children.

EXERCISES

1   Sheila contacts the children's services department because she has concerns about her 14-year-old daughter, Claire. Claire has been refusing to go to school because she believes that her mother needs her to help at home. Sheila, a single mother, has 2-year-old twins and she cares for her elderly mother at home. What help can you offer the family?

2   Fred contacts the children's services department. He wants you to assess the needs of his three children, all aged under 10, because he is about to be evicted by his housing association for non-payment of rent and the local housing department has found him intentionally homeless. On a brief consideration of the facts, you believe that Fred's children are not vulnerable. Is there any help your department can offer Fred?

3   Jameel has been living with foster parents for two years, since he was 13. He was placed there following his mother's remarriage to a man who has in the past been violent towards Jameel. Jameel's mother has now left her husband and would like Jameel to return to her care. Jameel does not want to return. What advice can you offer?

4   If Jameel's wishes are ignored and he is returned home, can he make a complaint? If he can, explain the procedure to him and the help that is available to him.

ONLINE RESOURCE CENTRE

For guidance on how to answer these exercises, visit the Online Resource Centre at www.oxfordtextbooks.co.uk/orc/socialwork13e/.

WHERE DO WE GO FROM HERE?

Part III of the Children Act is a wide-ranging Part of the Act which contains a range of powers and duties necessary to ensure the welfare of children in need. Many children can be supported in their own families, and the Act contains a range of provisions to ensure that, where appropriate, children can remain with their families. Inevitably, some families will fail to support their children. Part III of the Act sets out the responsibilities of local authorities to those children that they are required to look after, including preparing children and young people for the time when they leave care. However, outcomes for 'looked-after' children are very poor and the government has set itself demanding targets to improve those outcomes. Part III straddles the two concerns of the Act, supporting families and caring properly for those children who require protection either through accommodation or through court orders. **Chapter 7** considers how social workers investigate concerns about children, and plan for the appropriate provision of services and, where necessary, for court applications.

 ANNOTATED FURTHER READING

More extensive information on Part III of the Children Act can be found in specialist texts on the Children Act 1989 such as:

R. White, P. Carr, and N. Lowe, *The Children Act in Practice* (4th edn, Butterworths, 2008).

Advice for young people in care is provided by:

Coram Voice—a national organization offering advice, help, and advocacy to young people and care leavers, www.coramvoice.org.uk.

The limitations of s. 17 are made clear in a case commentary in:

'R (LM and MM) v LB Lambeth—the provision of services for disabled children' (2007) *CFLQ* 19(4): 496.

Children in need and housing

D. Cowan (2004) CFLQ 16(3): 331. In a case commentary on the House of Lords case *R (G) v Barnet LBC*, discussed at the beginning of the chapter, Cowan considers Lambeth's policy, which survived the House of Lords' ruling, of offering accommodation only to children in need, without their family. He argues that these decisions make the general duty in s. 17(1) irrelevant; in addition, paradoxically, housing legislation gives greater protection to households with children than the Children Act 1989.

Investigation and case planning

7

OVERVIEW AND OBJECTIVES

This chapter focuses on the process of investigation and case planning. Our purpose is to ensure that you understand how to use the guidance and procedures and when to use your professional judgement, all informed by the law. Equally important is your role on planning for children. As you read this chapter think about the steps involved from the initial expression of concern about a child to effective protection of the child and finally through to a satisfactory long-term outcome. Achieving the latter depends upon a number of stages: investigation, assessment, and planning and using court orders where necessary. You should not think of these as separate stages but overlapping. In particular, planning for the future of the child concerned is a critical stage which should begin as soon as possible.

 CASE STUDY

R (on the application of A) v Enfield LBC (2008)

The parents of T applied for judicial review of a decision by the London Borough of Enfield to place T, their son, on the child protection register by reason of neglect. The decision to place T on the child protection register was taken at a child protection conference in 2006. T, who had been born in 2003 weighing 3.1 kg, was seriously underweight compared with similar children of his age. The conference noted that the parents had failed to attend numerous appointments in connection with T's progress. It considered that it was incomprehensible that the parents could not appreciate how dangerously underweight T had become. The parents argued that (1) on the evidence, no rational authority could have concluded that the case was one of neglect; rather, the parents had sought medical help and the local authority had overreacted because of the severity of T's condition; (2) the proceedings had been unfair, as insufficient account had been taken of the parents' views at the conference; moreover, the conference had approached the matter in the wrong way by failing to consider whether the parents posed any prospective risk of neglect so that T was at continuing risk of significant harm.

The parents' application for judicial review was refused. In the first place, the judge pointed out that recourse to judicial review should be rare in the field of child protection, Second, although one of the reports before the conference recorded that the parents loved their children, and because of that no doubt felt a genuine grievance at the finding of neglect, the issue to be decided was not whether T was in fact neglected, but whether there was a rational basis for the local authority's decision to place him on the child protection register. The material before the conference was sufficient to justify its decision. It went considerably beyond evidence of severe malnutrition and nutritional rickets and it could reasonably be taken to point at least in part to parental responsibility for T's condition. There had been failures to keep appointments, and it was open to the conference to conclude that the deterioration in T's health was caused by the parents' failure to seek medical attention and that T was at continuing risk of significant harm. That decision reflected the unanimous view of all the professionals present at the conference. In response to the parents' second argument, their views had been properly taken into consideration at the conference and there was a proper evidential basis for the decision reached. The conference had asked itself the correct question, namely whether

T was at continuing risk of significant harm, and its approach could not be faulted. The final observation of the judge was *obiter*—that is, it did not form part of the reasoning for the decision. He stated that the complaints procedure should have been followed by the parents as it would have provided an alternative remedy to proceedings for judicial review. A decision in the parents' favour as a result of making a complaint might not have resulted in the quashing of the original registration, but it could have resulted in their vindication.

> **WHAT DOES THIS CASE TELL US ABOUT SOCIAL WORK PRACTICE?**
>
> This case provides a useful overview of the framework of decision making. By s. 47 of the Children Act 1989, a local authority has a duty to investigate when it has reasonable cause to suspect that a child in its area is suffering, or likely to suffer, significant harm. There is no dispute that this duty was engaged in the case of T. The local authority followed the guidance in *Working Together to Safeguard Children*. The guidelines define neglect, which was the cause of concern in this case. The social workers followed the procedures laid down in the guidance. A child protection conference was called at which the relevant question, 'Is the child at continuing risk of significant harm?', was considered. The child protection conference was chaired by an independent chair and the parents were involved. The case arose because the parents thought that the outcome was unfair; they loved their children and they felt that they were being blamed for T's condition. The fact that statutory guidance and proper procedures were followed and rational decisions substantiated by evidence protected the social workers from the legal challenge. Just one point of clarification—the case refers to the child protection register. That mechanism for protecting children was replaced in April 2008 with a requirement that the child is made the subject of a *child protection plan* (CP plan).

Introduction

This chapter will look at three critical stages of child protection which follow from an initial expression of concern. In appropriate cases, these stages will be crucial to successful court proceedings by a local authority. We shall consider:

- the investigation of child protection concerns;
- the bureaucratic structures designed to protect children; and
- case planning including preparation for possible court proceedings.

Initial referral and assessment

The first step in the whole process of child protection is the initial referral. The protection of children is dependent upon everyone who works with children or is in contact with them being able to recognize indicators that a child's welfare or safety may be at risk. Many cases will not need to go beyond the initial referral. **Box 7.1** shows the most recent (June 2011) statistical data available showing referrals and outcomes. It is interesting to note that in the year ending 31 March 2011, only 18 per cent of referrals led to a s. 47 inquiry, and an even smaller number (8.6 per cent) of referrals led to a child protection conference. It is also interesting to note that during the same year 49,000 children became the subject of a CP plan but 45,000 plans were ended. This suggests that in any one year there is a great deal of activity occurring in local authorities with children starting and ending CP plans.

BOX 7.1 Child protection referral data

- There were 593,500 referrals to children's social care services in the year ending 31 March 2013. This is the lowest level since 2009–10.
- There were 441,500 initial assessments completed in the year ending 31 March 2013.
- The number of initial assessments completed in the year as a percentage of all referrals in the year was 74.4 per cent.
- There were 232,700 core assessments completed in the year ending 31 March 2013, an increase of 5.4 per cent on the previous year.

The number of children subject to a s. 47 inquiry which started in the 2012–13 year was 127,100. Of these, 52,700 (47.5 per cent) were subject to a CP plan.

Children who were the subject of a child protection plan

- At 31 March 2013, there were 43,100 children who were the subject of a CP plan.
- In the year ending 31 March 2013, 52,700 children became the subject of a CP plan. Of these, 7,850 (14.9 per cent) became the subject of a plan for the second or subsequent time.
- 52,100 CP plans came to an end in the year. 2,700 (5.2 per cent) of these children had been the subject of a plan for two years or more.

Assessment

Hitherto, the assessment of children referred to children's services departments was set out in the *Framework for the Assessment of Children in Need and their Families* (TSO, 2000). This document, issued under s. 7 of the Local Authority (Social Services) Act 1970 (LASSA), together with its associated volume of Practice Guidance, Scales and Questionnaires and forms, prescribed how assessments of children in need should be carried out. Assessments would be divided into initial and core assessments and timescales were applied of seven days for the former and a further 35 days for the latter. These timescales together with an inspection scheme which placed significant weight on adherence to the timescales were overwhelmingly instrumental in encouraging local authorities to structure social work services with referral and advice teams at the front end followed by child in need/protection teams and looked-after children teams. Children and families could therefore expect a change of social worker as they progressed through the service, contrary to the importance of maintaining continuity.

The Munro Review of Child Protection recommended that the government look again at the emphasis on slavish adherence to timescales in assessments. In the *Progress Report: Moving towards a Child Centred System*, Munro says:

> The fixed timescale for assessments ... has for many become the overriding concern so that an assessment is concluded because the deadline has been reached not because the worker thinks they have acquired a good enough understanding of the child's needs to make a sound decision about what to do.

(Para. 2.7)

The Final Report of the Munro Review recommends that both the *Framework for the Assessment of Children in Need and their Families* and *Working Together to Safeguard Children* should be revised (see **chapter 5** for further details). Consultation documents on both of these were published in June 2012 together with a third document concerning Serious Case Reviews. The final *Working Together to Safeguard Children* was published in March 2013 bringing together the multi-agency guidance, a revised assessment framework, and procedures in the case of child deaths. **Box 7.2** shows key passages from *Working Together* concerning the assessment of children in need.

 BOX 7.2 *Working Together To Safeguard Children* (2013)—assessing need

The Purpose of an Assessment

27. Whatever legislation the child is assessed under, the purpose of the assessment is always:

- to gather important information about a child and family;
- to analyse their needs and/or the nature and level of any risk and harm being suffered by the child;
- to decide whether the child is a child in need (section 17) and/or is suffering or likely to suffer significant harm (section 47); and
- to provide support to address those needs to improve the child's outcomes to make them safe.

28. Assessment should be a dynamic process, which analyses and responds to the changing nature and level of need and/or risk faced by the child. A good assessment will monitor and record the impact of any services delivered to the child and family and review the help being delivered. Whilst services may be delivered to a parent or carer, the assessment should be focused on the needs of the child and on the impact any services are having on the child.

The principles and parameters of a good assessment

32. High quality assessments:

- are child centred. Where there is a conflict of interest, decisions should be made in the child's best interests;
- are rooted in child development and informed by evidence;
- are focused on action and outcomes for children;

- are holistic in approach, addressing the child's needs within their family and wider community;

- ensure equality of opportunity;

- involve children and families;

- build on strengths as well as identifying difficulties;

- are integrated in approach;

- are a continuing process not an event;

- lead to action, including the provision and review of services; and

- are transparent and open to challenge.

Timeliness

54. The timeliness of an assessment is a critical element of the quality of that assessment and the outcomes for the child. The speed with which an assessment is carried out after a child's case has been referred into local authority children's social care should be determined by the needs of the individual child and the nature and level of any risk of harm faced by the child. This will require judgements to be made by the social worker in discussion with their manager on each individual case.

55. Within one working day of a referral being received, a local authority social worker should make a decision about the type of response that is required and acknowledge receipt to the referrer.

56. For children who are in need of immediate protection, action must be taken by the social worker, or the police or NSPCC if removal is required, as soon as possible after the referral has been made to local authority children's social care (sections 44 and 46 of the Children Act 1989).

57. The maximum timeframe for the assessment to conclude, such that it is possible to reach a decision on next steps, should be no longer than 45 working days from the point of referral. If, in discussion with a child and their family and other professionals, an assessment exceeds 45 working days the social worker should record the reasons for exceeding the time limit.

58. Whatever the timescale for assessment, where particular needs are identified at any stage of the assessment, social workers should not wait until the assessment reaches a conclusion before commissioning services to support the child and their family. In some cases the needs of the child will mean that a quick assessment will be required.

59. The assessment of neglect cases can be difficult. Neglect can fluctuate both in level and duration. A child's welfare can, for example, improve following input from services or a change in circumstances and review, but then deteriorate once support is removed. Professionals should be wary of being too optimistic. Timely and decisive action is critical to ensure that children are not left in neglectful homes.

60. It is the responsibility of the social worker to make clear to children and families how the assessment will be carried out and when they can expect a decision on next steps.

61. To facilitate the shift to an assessment process which brings continuity and consistency for children and families, there will no longer be a requirement to conduct separate initial and core assessments. Local authorities should determine their local assessment processes through a local protocol.

The Guidance retains the use of the dimensions associated with child developmental needs, parenting capacity, and family and environmental factors. For instance, if a court was considering an application for a divorce and became concerned about the welfare of the children, it could ask the local authority to undertake a s. 37 investigation.

The next steps

The result of the assessment may be that no further action needs to be taken. It may be that the child is a 'child in need' and the family will benefit from additional support and practical help in promoting the child's health and development. **Chapter 6** sets out the responsibilities of the local authority to children in need. It may be that there are concerns sufficient to prompt a s. 47 inquiry—we discuss this in **The objective of local authority inquiries under s. 47**, p 243. It may be that there is a need for a parallel police investigation. It may be that the child's life is at risk, or that there is a likelihood of serious immediate harm. In that case, the children's services department must act quickly to secure the immediate safety of the child. Legal advice should be obtained as soon as possible. Full details of the emergency protection order and the other available court orders are set out in **chapter 8**. Details of the power to exclude perpetrators of violence or other abuse from the family home are set out in **chapter 6**. The s. 47 inquiries should proceed in parallel with seeking protection via the courts if appropriate. Whatever decision is made, it should be endorsed at managerial level and recorded in writing with the reasons. The family, the person who originally expressed concern, and other professionals and services involved in the assessment should be told what action has been taken, consistent with respecting the confidentiality of the child and family.

Referral from the courts

The vast majority of referrals are going to be from social care and health professionals and others who have contact with children. In the course of any family proceedings not involving a local authority, a court may have legitimate reasons to be concerned about the care of children. If that is the case, the court has the power under s. 37 of the Children Act 1989 to give directions to a local authority to investigate and consider whether care proceedings should be brought.

The powers of the court under s. 37

Section 37 is set out in **Box 7.3**. This is a comprehensive section that has wide implications for the local authority. It gives the residual power to the court to require the state, via the local authority, to consider intervention in the affairs of a family. The court can exercise the power in any family proceedings and the use of these powers can lead to a supervision order, or indeed a care order.

 BOX 7.3 Section 37 investigations

(1) Where, in any family proceedings (i.e. other than care proceedings) in which a question arises with respect to the welfare of any child, it appears to the court that it may be appropriate for a care or supervision order to be made with respect to him, the court may direct the appropriate authority to undertake an investigation of the child's circumstances.

(2) Where the court gives a direction under this section the local authority concerned shall, when undertaking the investigation, consider whether they should—

    (a) apply for a care order or for a supervision order with respect to the child;

    (b) provide services or assistance for the child or his family; or

    (c) take any other action with respect to the child.

(3) Where a local authority undertake an investigation under this section, and decide not to apply for a care order or supervision order with respect to the child concerned, they shall inform the court of—

    (a) their reasons for so deciding;

    (b) any service or assistance which they have provided, or intend to provide, for the child and his family; and

    (c) any other action which they have taken or propose to take, with respect to the child.

(4) The information shall be given to the court before the end of the period of eight weeks beginning with the date of the direction, unless the court otherwise directs.

(5) The local authority named in a direction under subsection (1) must be—

    (a) the authority in whose area the child is ordinarily resident; or

    (b) where the child is not ordinarily resident in the area of a local authority, the authority within whose area any circumstances arose in consequence of which the direction is being given.

(6) If, on the conclusion of any investigation or review under this section, the authority decide not to apply for a care order or supervision order with respect to the child—

    (a) they shall consider whether it would be appropriate to review the case at a later date; and

    (b) if they decide that it would be, they shall determine the date on which the review is to begin.

Explanations of inaction are required

Even if a care or supervision application is not made, the local authority is still required to explain its actions, the reasons for non-action, and its plans for the future. If the court makes a direction under s. 37, it can appoint a guardian to act on behalf of the child.

The local authority decides

Although it is possible to envisage circumstances in which the local authority and guardian may disagree over the course of action, it remains solely the choice of the local authority whether or not to apply for an order. Even if the court prefers the views of the guardian, it cannot compel the local authority to make an application for a care order.

Interim care or supervision orders pending s. 37 investigations

There are provisions in s. 38 of the Children Act 1989 for making interim orders during the s. 37 investigations. **Box 7.4** sets out the court's power.

This section is a partial exception to the principle that no care or supervision order may be made without an application being made to the court. Under s. 37 of the 1989 Act, no application need be before the court for it to have the power to make an interim care or supervision order. However, before a full care or supervision order can be made it is necessary for a local authority actually to make an application, so the principle is essentially intact.

If the court has ordered a s. 37 investigation and is thinking of making an interim care or supervision order, it must be certain, first, that the normal test for an interim order is satisfied. Section 38(2) is set out in **Box 7.5**.

The words 'reasonable grounds for believing' mean that the grounds do not have to be 'proved' before an interim order can be made, but merely that there have to be some grounds for believing that a full order may be made. The making of an interim order does not presuppose that a full order will be made. You will find more information about interim care orders in **chapter 8**.

BOX 7.4 The power to make interim orders—s. 38

(1) Where—
   (a) in any proceedings on an application for a care order or supervision order, the proceedings are adjourned; or
   (b) the court gives a direction under section 37(1), the court may make an interim care order or an interim supervision order with respect to the child concerned.

BOX 7.5 There must be reasonable grounds for an interim order—s. 38(2)

A court shall not make an interim care order or interim supervision order under this section unless it is satisfied that there are reasonable grounds for believing that the circumstances with respect to the child are as mentioned in section 31(2) [ie the grounds for a care order—the likelihood of significant harm, the child beyond parental control].

Section 8 child arrangements orders during or after s. 37 investigation

An alternative course open to the court would be to make a s. 8 child arrangements order. It has the power in any family proceedings to make a s. 8 order, even though it has not disposed of the main proceedings (s. 11(3)).

Time limits

One of the practical difficulties is the requirement that the investigation under s. 37 of the Children Act 1989 be completed within a period of eight weeks, unless 'the court otherwise directs'. The resource implications for s. 37 are immense, and in the absence of greatly increased resources the court may need to 'otherwise direct' in many cases.

You can imagine that s. 37 can cause tension between the courts and the local authority. The court's priorities are imposed upon the local authority. An example of this occurred in *Lambeth LBC v TK* (2008). The facts were as follows: T had arrived in the UK from Uganda on a visa which K, a British citizen of Ugandan ethnicity, had arranged for his 14-year-old daughter (X). K thought that T was his 19-year-old daughter and refused to accommodate her. T maintained that she was X and sought help from the local authority, who provided her with accommodation as if she were a child. A DNA test later revealed that K was not T's father. During family proceedings the High Court had ordered the local authority to file a report under s. 37 of the Children Act 1989 as to T's current and future circumstances. The local authority filed a report which concluded that T was not a child and that it was not obliged to provide accommodation for her. The local authority argued that it had complied with the direction under s. 37 and since T was not a child, the local authority's obligations under s. 37 were at an end. The local authority submitted that the only proper forum for T to challenge its decision as to her age was by way of judicial review. The Court of Appeal rejected this argument. Lambeth had not opposed the s. 37 direction and there could be no appeal against an unopposed direction. Section 37 set three threshold requirements for the exercise of its power, namely: there was a child, there were family proceedings, and a question had arisen with respect to the child's welfare. The reference in s. 37 was to a child, not to any person whom the local authority considered to be a child. A local authority was entitled to submit to the court that one or none of those thresholds existed. However, it was for the court to determine whether the threshold requirements set by statute for the exercise of judicial power were satisfied. The local authority had not yet made a substantive report in response to the court's direction under s. 37. Instead they had made a preliminary report to the effect that the requirement that T be a child was not satisfied. It was for the court which made the direction to determine whether T was a child and whether the direction made by the court should be discharged or maintained in order to extract from the local authority a report both upon the past, present, and optimum future circumstances of T and upon the local authority's assessment of whether in such circumstances they should discharge any of the functions identified in s. 37(2). *E v X LBC* (2005) approved. Local authorities could not be the arbiters of whether courts had jurisdiction to make directions to them. The court was entitled to direct that a fact-finding hearing take place to determine T's identity and whether she was a child.

■ The local authority's duty to investigate (s. 47)

Prompting the duty to investigate

If the initial assessment or the result of inquiries following referral from the court indicate that there is *reasonable cause to suspect that a child is suffering or is likely to suffer significant harm then the local authority is placed under a statutory duty to investigate*. The duty also arises if a child is the subject of an emergency protection order, is in police protection, or has contravened a ban imposed by a curfew notice under the Crime and Disorder Act 1998. The meanings of significant harm, police protection, and emergency protection order are discussed in **chapter 8**. There has been inserted, in the case of a breach of a child curfew order only, a requirement for the inquiries to be commenced as soon as practicable and, in any event, within 48 hours of the authority receiving the information.

Section 47 makes it clear that the main responsibility for the protection under the Act falls on local authorities. Section 47(1) is set out in **Box 7.6**.

BOX 7.6 The local authority's duty to investigate—s. 47

(1) Where a local authority—
    (a) are informed that a child who lives, or is found, in their area—
        (i)   is the subject of an emergency protection order; or
        (ii) is in police protection; or
        (iii) has contravened a ban imposed by a curfew notice within the meaning of Chapter I of Part I of the Crime and Disorder Act 1998;

or

    (b) have reasonable cause to suspect that a child who lives, or is found, in their area is suffering or is likely to suffer significant harm,

the authority shall make, or cause to be made, such enquiries as they consider to be necessary to enable them to decide whether they should take any action to safeguard or protect the child's welfare.

In the case of a child falling within para. (a)(iii), the inquiries shall be commenced as soon as practicable and, in any event, within 48 hours of the authority receiving the information.

Low-level threshold

Note that the local authority has an overall duty to make inquiries as soon as it has 'reasonable cause to suspect' the possibility of significant harm. This is a relatively low-level threshold for triggering action, and is lower than the threshold for justifying interim care or supervision orders, or emergency protection orders. These, by contrast with the s. 47 inquiries, involve a compulsory intervention in the lives of both child and family (see **chapter 9**) and therefore require a different balance to be drawn between the concerns of the state to protect children and the rights of individuals.

The objective of local authority inquiries under s. 47

Working Together to Safeguard Children makes it clear that the objective of the local authority is to decide whether and what type of action is required to safeguard and promote the welfare of the child who is suspected of suffering or likely to be suffering significant harm. It goes on to say:

> Under the Children Act 1989, local authorities are required to provide services for children in need for the purposes of safeguarding and promoting their welfare. Local Authorities undertake assessments of the needs of individual children to determine what services to provide and action to take.

'Any action'

The 'any action' referred to in s. 47(1)(b) may constitute applying for a court order or providing any form of support under Part III of the Children Act—see **chapter 5**. Providing access to a wide range of support services to help children in need is likely to be the outcome in most cases.

Despite this emphasis, s. 47(3) goes on to state that the inquiries should in particular be directed towards establishing whether the local authority should make any application to court.

Statutory requirements

In making its inquiries, the local authority is required actually to see the child unless it is satisfied that it has sufficient information (s. 47(4)). *Working Together to Safeguard Children* guidance also stresses that assessments:

> must be informed by the views of the child as well as the family. Children should, wherever possible, be seen alone and local authority children's social care has a duty to ascertain the child's wishes and feelings regarding the provision of services to be delivered.

If in making the inquiries the local authority finds matters concerned with the child's education, it is required to consult the relevant education authority (s. 47(5)).

Where the local authority does try to carry out this statutory duty and is refused access to the child or is denied information as to the child's whereabouts, the authority is required to apply for an emergency protection order, a child assessment order, a care order, or a supervision order unless satisfied that the child's welfare can be satisfactorily safeguarded without doing so (s. 47(6)). These court orders are explained in **chapter 8**. The requirement to make an application to court if access is refused, again, is a statutory duty, albeit that there is a narrow area of discretion.

Next steps

Once the local authority has concluded its inquiries under s. 47, it has to consider what is to be done. Even a decision not to make a court application prompts a positive duty—to consider whether it is appropriate to review the case at a later date. Subsection (8) sets out the overriding statutory duty on the local authority if it concludes that action is necessary. It must take action—'so far as it is both within their power and reasonably practicable for them to do so'. If the local authority concludes as a result of its inquiries that the child needs some form of support, it must supply that support. If it fails to do so then its decision may be liable to judicial review. If the local authority believes that court proceedings are required, the local authority must take proceedings. **Box 7.7** sets out s. 47(7) and (8).

BOX 7.7 The duty to take action—s. 47(7)–(8)

(7) If, on the conclusion of any enquiries or review made under this section, the authority decide not to apply for an emergency protection order, a child assessment order, a care order or a supervision order they shall—

    (a) consider whether it would be appropriate to review the case at a later date; and

    (b) if they decide that it would be, determine the date on which that review is to begin.

(8) Where, as a result of complying with this section, a local authority conclude that they should take action to safeguard or promote the child's welfare they shall take that action (so far as it is both within their power and reasonably practicable for them to do so).

Recording of decisions

Whatever the outcome of the s. 47 inquiries, decisions should be recorded, and parents (together with professionals and agencies who have been significantly involved) should receive a copy of the record.

Cooperation from other agencies

The local authority may require assistance from other bodies and authorities. This duty, in s. 47(9), (10), and (11) is set out in **Box 7.8**. We considered the relationship between other agencies and local authorities in **chapter 5**.

BOX 7.8 The duty on other agencies—s. 47

(9) Where a local authority are conducting enquiries under this section, it shall be the duty of any person mentioned in subsection (11) to assist them with those enquiries (in particular by providing relevant information and advice) if called upon by the authority to do so.

(10) Subsection (9) does not oblige any person to assist a local authority where doing so would be unreasonable in all the circumstances of the case.

The nature of the duty

The local authority must do all within its power to safeguard or promote the welfare of a child brought to its attention as being at possible risk, in partnership with other agencies if appropriate. The aim of the legislation has been to avoid the local authority being put in a situation of saying 'we would like to do this but we do not have the legal power'.

This is merely emphasizing the concept of 'diminishment of court proceedings' discussed in **chapter 6** which, in turn, is a reflection of the overall philosophy of the current law relating to children. This is that the local authority shall do all that is within its power to safeguard children and should apply for court orders only as a final and last resort, but always bearing in mind that it should apply for a court order if that is necessary.

The inquiry process

Section 47 inquiries need to be carried out effectively and skilfully. *Working Together to Safeguard Children* no longer prescribes how assessments should be carried out.

Instead, emphasis is placed on describing the principles of assessment including an emphasis to focus on the needs and views of the child, clear decision-making analysis which is focused on outcomes, and timeliness. Some of the key responsibilities of professionals are described in **Box 7.9**.

 BOX 7.9 Professional responsibilities during s. 47 inquiries

Social workers and managers should:

- lead the assessment in accordance with this guidance;
- carry out inquiries in a way that minimizes distress for the child and family;
- see the child who is the subject of concern to ascertain their wishes and feelings; assess their understanding of their situation; assess their relationships and circumstances more broadly;
- interview parents and/or caregivers and determine the wider social and environmental factors that might impact on them and their child;
- systematically gather information about the child's and family's history;
- analyse the findings of the assessment and evidence about what interventions are likely to be most effective with other relevant professionals to determine the child's needs and the level of risk of harm faced by the child to inform what help should be provided and act to provide that help; and
- follow the guidance set out in *Achieving Best Evidence in Criminal Proceedings: Guidance on interviewing victims and witnesses, and guidance on using special measures*, where a decision has been made to undertake a joint interview of the child as part of any criminal investigation.

The police should:

- help other agencies understand the reasons for concerns about the child's safety and welfare;
- decide whether or not police investigations reveal grounds for instigating criminal proceedings;
- make available to other professionals any evidence gathered to inform discussions about the child's welfare; and
- follow the guidance set out in *Achieving Best Evidence in Criminal Proceedings: Guidance on interviewing victims and witnesses, and guidance on using special measures*, where a decision has been made to undertake a joint interview of the child as part of the criminal investigations.

Health professionals should:

- undertake appropriate medical tests, examinations, or observations to determine how the child's health or development may be being impaired;
- provide any of a range of specialist assessments. For example, physiotherapists, occupational therapists, speech and language therapists, and child psychologists may be involved in specific assessments relating to the child's developmental progress. The lead health practitioner

(probably a consultant pediatrician, or possibly the child's GP) may need to request and coordinate these assessments; and

• ensure appropriate treatment and follow up health concerns.

All involved professionals should:

• contribute to the assessment as required, providing information about the child and family;

• consider whether a joint inquiry/investigation team may need to speak to a child victim without the knowledge of the parent or caregiver.

The structures designed to protect children

The mechanisms for child protection in summary

The structure for protection of children following initial referral consists of:

• Local Safeguarding Children Boards (see *Working Together*);
• the child protection conference;
• the CP plan.

In this chapter we discuss the short-term arrangements for the protection of children. In **chapter 9** we look at long-term planning.

The Local Safeguarding Children Boards (LSCBs)

The core objects of LSCBs are set out in s. 14(1) of the Children Act 2004. We have set these out in **Box 7.10**.

BOX 7.10 The core objectives of LSCBs

• To coordinate what is done by each person or body represented on the Board for the purposes of safeguarding and promoting the welfare of children in the area of the authority.
• To ensure the effectiveness of what is done by each such person or body for that purpose.

Membership of LSCBs

The LSCB should draw its members from the local authority and its Board partners which are the statutory organizations required to cooperate with the local authority in the establishment and operation of the LSCB and have shared responsibility for the effective discharge of its functions. We have set those partners out in **Box 7.11**. *Working Together* sets out other members, including the chair (**Box 7.12**).

BOX 7.11 Board partners—s. 13(3) of the Children Act 2004

LSCBs should include representatives of the local authority and its Board partners. Board partners which must be included in the LSCB are as follows:

(a) where the authority is a county council for an area for which there is also a district council, the district council;

(b) the chief officer of police for a police area any part of which falls within the area of the authority;

(c) a local probation board for an area any part of which falls within the area of the authority;

(ca) the Secretary of State in relation to his functions under sections 2 and 3 of the Offender Management Act 2007, so far as they are exercisable in relation to England;

(cb) any provider of probation services that is required by arrangements under section 3(2) of the Offender Management Act 2007 to act as a Board partner of the authority;

(d) a youth offending team for an area any part of which falls within the area of the authority;

(e) the NHS Commissioning Board and clinical commissioning groups;

(f) an NHS trust and an NHS foundation trust all or most of whose hospitals, establishments and facilities are situated in the area of the authority;

(g) a person providing services in pursuance of section 68 of the Education and Skills Act 2008 in any part of the area of the authority;

(h) the Children and Family Court Advisory and Support Service;

(i) the governor of any secure training centre in the area of the authority (or, in the case of a contracted out secure training centre, its director);

(j) the governor of any prison in the area of the authority which ordinarily detains children (or, in the case of a contracted out prison, its director).

(5) A Local Safeguarding Children Board established under this section may also include representatives of such other relevant persons or bodies as the authority by which it is established consider, after consulting their Board partners, should be represented on it.

(5A) A local authority in England must take reasonable steps to ensure that the Local Safeguarding Children Board established by them also includes two persons who appear to the authority to be representative of persons living in the authority's area.

BOX 7.12 LSCB chair and other members

12. In order to provide effective scrutiny, the LSCB should be independent. It should not be subordinate to, nor subsumed within, other local structures.

13. Every LSCB should have an independent chair who can hold all agencies to account.

14. It is the responsibility of the Chief Executive (Head of Paid Service) to appoint or remove the LSCB chair with the agreement of a panel including LSCB partners and lay members. The Chief Executive, drawing on other LSCB partners and, where appropriate, the Lead Member will hold the Chair to account for the effective working of the LSCB.

15. The LSCB Chair should work closely with all LSCB partners and particularly with the Director of Children's Services. The Director of Children's Services has the responsibility within the local

authority, under section 18 of the Children Act 2004, for improving outcomes for children, local authority children's social care functions and local cooperation arrangements for children's services.

16. The Chair must publish an annual report on the effectiveness of child safeguarding and promoting the welfare of children in the local area. The annual report should be published in relation to the preceding financial year and should fit with local agencies' planning, commissioning and budget cycles. The report should be submitted to the Chief Executive, Leader of the Council, the local police and crime commissioner and the Chair of the health and wellbeing board.

17. The report should provide a rigorous and transparent assessment of the performance and effectiveness of local services. It should identify areas of weakness, the causes of those weaknesses and the action being taken to address them as well as other proposals for action. The report should include lessons from reviews undertaken within the reporting period.

18. The report should also list the contributions made to the LSCB by partner agencies and details of what the LSCB has spent, including on Child Death Reviews, Serious Case Reviews and other specific expenditure such as learning events or training. All LSCB member organisations have an obligation to provide LSCBs with reliable resources (including finance) that enable the LSCB to be strong and effective. Members should share the financial responsibility for the LSCB in such a way that a disproportionate burden does not fall on a small number of partner agencies.

Statutory functions

Working Together (set out in **Box 7.13**) describes the statutory functions of LSCBs.

BOX 7.13 The statutory functions of LSCBs

1 developing policies and procedures for safeguarding and promoting the welfare of children in the area of

(a) the authority, including policies and procedures in relation to:

(i) the action to be taken where there are concerns about a child's safety or welfare, including thresholds for intervention;

(ii) training of persons who work with children or in services affecting the safety and welfare of children;

(iii) recruitment and supervision of persons who work with children;

(iv) investigation of allegations concerning persons who work with children;

(v) safety and welfare of children who are privately fostered;

(vi) cooperation with neighbouring children's services authorities and their Board partners;

(b) communicating to persons and bodies in the area of the authority the need to safeguard and promote the welfare of children, raising their awareness of how this can best be done and encouraging them to do so;

(c) monitoring and evaluating the effectiveness of what is done by the authority and their Board partners individually and collectively to safeguard and promote the welfare of children and advising them on ways to improve;

(d) participating in the planning of services for children in the area of the authority; and

(e) undertaking reviews of serious cases and advising the authority and their Board partners on lessons to be learned.

Functions in connection with child deaths and other serious cases

In June 2012, the government published new draft guidance on dealing with child deaths and other serious cases. This was in response to the recommendations in the Munro Review of Child Protection (see **chapter 5**).

> **Recommendation 9:** The Government should require LSCBs to use systems methodology when undertaking Serious Case Reviews (SCRs) and, over the coming year, work with the sector to develop national resources to:
>
> - provide accredited, skilled and independent reviewers to jointly work with LSCBs on each SCR;
> - promote the development of a variety of systems-based methodologies to learn from practice;
> - initiate the development of a typology of the problems that contribute to adverse outcomes to facilitate national learning; and
> - disseminate learning nationally to improve practice and inform the work of the Chief Social Worker. In the meantime, Ofsted's evalution of SCRs should end.

Working Together sets out the revised processes LSCBs have to carry out in relation to continuous learning and in particular Serious Case Reviews (**Box 7.14**).

 BOX 7.14 Revised processes of LSCBs in relation to continuous learning and Serious Case Reviews

3. Local Safeguarding Children Boards (LSCBs) should maintain a local learning and improvement framework which is shared across local organisations who work with children and families. This framework should enable organisations to be clear about their responsibilities, to learn from experience and improve services as a result.

4. Each local framework should support the work of the LSCB and their partners so that:
   - reviews are conducted regularly, not only on cases which meet statutory criteria, but also on other cases which can provide useful insights into the way organisations are working together to safeguard and protect the welfare of children;
   - reviews look at what happened in a case, and why, and what action will be taken to learn from the review findings;
   - action results in lasting improvements to services which safeguard and promote the welfare of children and help protect them from harm; and
   - there is transparency about the issues arising from individual cases and the actions which organisations are taking in response to them, including sharing the final reports of Serious Case Reviews (SCRs) with the public.

It is debatable whether LSCBs have been effective in improving child protection services. Most include large memberships and frequent attendance at meetings is not always guaranteed. Practitioners working with front-line services are oblivious to the workings of LSCBs and rarely recognize their impact. The bureaucratic mandate to work collaboratively is perhaps insufficient.

Initial child protection conference

Purpose

The purpose of the initial child protection conference is set out in *Working Together*—see **Box 7.15**.

 BOX 7.15 Purpose of child protection conference

To bring together and analyse, in an inter-agency setting, all relevant information and plan how best to safeguard and promote the welfare of the child. It is the responsibility of the conference to make recommendations on how agencies work together to safeguard the child in future. Conference tasks include:

- appointing a lead statutory body (either local authority children's social care or NSPCC) and a lead social worker, who should be a qualified, experienced social worker and an employee of the lead statutory body;

- identifying membership of the core group of professionals and family members who will develop and implement the child protection plan;

- establishing timescales for meetings of the core group, production of a child protection plan and for child protection review meetings; and

- agreeing an outline child protection plan, with clear actions and timescales, including a clear sense of how much improvement is needed, by when, so that success can be judged clearly.

Attendance and timing

Working Together suggests that the social worker and their manager have specific functions at the initial conference. This is set out in **Box 7.16**.

 BOX 7.16 Functions of social worker and their manager at the initial conference

The social worker and their manager should:

- convene, attend and present information about the reason for the conference, their understanding of the child's needs, parental capacity and family and environmental context and evidence of how the child has been abused or neglected and its impact on their health and development;

- analyse the information to enable informed decisions about what action is necessary to safeguard and promote the welfare of the child who is the subject of the conference;

- share the conference information with the child and family beforehand (where appropriate);

- prepare a report for the conference on the child and family which sets out and analyses what is known about the child and family and the local authority's recommendation; and

- record conference decisions and recommendations and ensure action follows.

Working Together places a requirement on LSCBs to define the criteria for which other professionals should attend and when specialist opinions should be sought. In addition, LSCBs are also required to determine the timing of conferences based on the nature and seriousness of the harm to the child and the time required to obtain relevant information about the child and family.

Action and decisions for the conference

The conference is expected to determine the following:

- **either** the child can be shown to have suffered ill-treatment or impairment of health or development as a result of physical, emotional, or sexual abuse or neglect, and professional judgement is that further ill-treatment or impairment is likely;

- **or** professional judgement, substantiated by findings of inquiries on this individual case or by research evidence, is that the child is likely to suffer ill-treatment or the impairment of health or development as a result of physical, emotional, or sexual abuse or neglect.

The child protection plan

Working Together sets out the actions and responsibilities following an initial conference (see **Box 7.17**).

BOX 7.17 Actions and responsibilities following the Initial Plan

Responsibilities of local authority children's social care

- designate a social worker to be the lead professional as they carry statutory responsibility for the child's welfare;

- consider the evidence and decide what legal action to take if any, where a child has suffered, or is likely to suffer, significant harm; and

- define the local protocol for timeliness of circulating plans after the child protection conference.

Responsibilities of the lead social worker and their manager

- be the lead professional for inter-agency work with the child and family, co-ordinating the contribution of family members and professionals into putting the child protection plan into effect;

- develop the outline child protection plan into a more detailed inter-agency plan and circulate to relevant professionals (and family where appropriate);

- undertake direct work with the child and family in accordance with the child protection plan, taking into account the child's wishes and feelings and the views of the parents in so far as they are consistent with the child's welfare;

- complete the child's and family's in-depth assessment, securing contributions from core group members and others as necessary;

- explain the plan to the child in a manner which is in accordance with their age and understanding and agree the plan with the child;

- coordinate reviews of progress against the planned outcomes set out in the plan,

- updating as required. The first review should be held within 3 months of the initial conference and further reviews at intervals of no more than 6 months for as long as the child remains subject of a child protection plan;

- record decisions and actions agreed at core group meetings as well as the written views of those who were not able to attend, and follow up those actions to ensure they take place. The child protection plan should be updated as necessary; and lead core group activity.

To support joint working, responsibilities of the core group

- meet within 10 working days from the initial child protection conference if the child is the subject of a child protection plan;

- develop the outline child protection plan, based on assessment findings, and set out what needs to change, by how much, and by when in order for the child to be safe and have their needs met;

- decide what steps need to be taken, and by whom, to complete the in-depth assessment to inform decisions about the child's safety and welfare; and

- implement the child protection plan and take joint responsibility for carrying out the agreed tasks, monitoring progress and outcomes, and refining the plan as needed.

EXERCISE

Consider the following evolving scenario and then answer the questions arising.

Mary, the 6-year-old child of Tom and Ann, was found at school with a series of dark bruises on her back. She was examined by a paediatrician who said that they were the result of being hit and that there were some additional fingertip bruises on her arm. Mary said her dad had hit her. When questioned, Tom denies hitting Mary. Ann, whilst not saying what happened, talks about Tom's drinking and problems in the marriage. There are financial difficulties and the family want to be rehoused. There is a new baby, Peter, who is three months old. Ann appears to be finding coping a strain. Your initial conclusion (which may only be an instinctive feeling) is that the current pressures faced by the family are responsible for the situation in which Tom takes out his frustrations by hitting Mary.

1 What further inquiries would you make?

2 What, if any, statutory duties arise?

You discuss the case with colleagues, there is a child protection case conference.

3 Who would you expect to be present at the case conference?

4 What questions need to be decided at the initial case conference?

The case conference decides to make Mary the subject of a CP plan. You are the lead professional.

5 How would you explain that decision to Tom and Ann?

6 Who would you expect to be in your core group?

7 What action needs to be taken to record your decisions?

ONLINE RESOURCE CENTRE

For guidance on how to answer this exercise, visit the Online Resource Centre at
www.oxfordtextbooks.co.uk/orc/socialwork13e/.

WHERE DO WE GO FROM HERE?

You have read in this chapter an account of the structures which have been set up to respond to
concerns about children. They rely on effective cooperation and clear understanding of roles. You
also know something of the process of responding to concerns about particular children, and
the need to move from investigation of possible abuse to starting the planning process which is
necessary for the future welfare of a child. The investigation and planning process prepares the
social worker for a potential court application. However, the social worker also needs to consider
the long-term future of children. **Chapter 8** focuses on preparing for court.

We return to planning for the long-term security of the child in **chapter 9**.

ANNOTATED FURTHER READING

Planning

J. Hann and M. Owen, 'The implementation of care plans and its relationship to children's
welfare' (2003) CFLQ 15(1): 71. An interesting piece of research into what constitutes a good
or bad care plan.

Official guidance on planning and reporting

A critical commentary on the case study at the beginning is provided by N. Mole, a leading
human rights lawyer, in 'Re W & B, RE W (Care Plans) and Re S (Minors) (Care Order:
Implementation of Care Plan) Re W (Minors) (Care Order: Adequacy of Care Plan). A note
on the judgment from the perspective of the European Convention for Protection of Human
Rights and Fundamental Freedoms' (2002) *CFLQ* 14(4): 447.

Investigating child abuse

B. Corby, 'Towards a new means of inquiry into child abuse cases' (2004) *Journal of Social
Welfare Law* 25(3): 229. This article suggests there should be a more realistic approach to child
protection cases.

A new challenging text on child protection as published in 2014 examining whether services
reinforce deprivation in families subject to child protection inquiries or ameliorate them is
B. Featherstone, S. White, and K. Morris, *Re-Imagining Child Protection: Towards Humane Social
Work with Families* (Policy Press, 2014).

Applying to court

8

OVERVIEW AND OBJECTIVES

This chapter is concerned with Parts IV and V of the Children Act 1989. Part IV deals with care and supervision. Part V is concerned with child protection. These Parts of the Act contain the compulsory orders which require in general an application to a court. The exception to this requirement is the power of the police to remove a child to a place of safety under s. 46 of the Act. It is the courts which ensure that local authority action is legitimate. Legitimacy requires that the statutory provisions are observed and that the protections provided by the Human Rights Act are maintained. A key concept that justifies compulsory intervention in family life and which underpins both Part IV and Part V of the Act is *significant harm*, which we will discuss at length in this chapter. We summarize the range of orders available under the Children Act 1989. We will then describe the longer term orders available under Part IV of the Act—care orders and supervision orders—before turning to the short-term orders contained in Part V. As we set out the requirements and effects of each order, compare and contrast these. Which orders are easier to obtain? What impact does the order have on the parent(s)' parental responsibility? What constraints are there on the powers of the local authority? Why is s. 46 an exception to the general requirement of supervision by the courts?

Court orders cannot, of course, be obtained without proper preparation by those applying for them. Thorough preparation is necessary in order to minimize delay and to maximize the effectiveness of the courts in dealing with inevitably complex cases.

The Review of the Family Justice System conducted by David Norgrove reported in 2011 and set the basis for the Children and Families Act 2014. The government was concerned to address the problem of delay in care proceedings which could last for as long as 18 months. A revised Public Law Outline was produced placing renewed emphasis on timescales through better case management. We begin this chapter by considering what local authorities need to do before applying to court.

All statutory references in this chapter are to the Children Act 1989, unless otherwise stated.

CASE STUDY

A (Children) v A (2009), Court of Appeal

Facts

M, S, and H, aged 4 years, 20 months, and four months respectively, had been placed in the care of the local authority following an allegation that their parents (P) had physically and sexually abused another child (X) who was living in the family home. During a fact-finding hearing, the judge found that P's treatment of X had been shocking and that M and S had been exposed to it. Findings of physical abuse against M were also made.

Issues

The issue before the judge was whether the evidence established to the satisfaction of the court on the balance of probabilities that the threshold set by s. 31 of the Children Act 1989 had been crossed. However, the judge concluded that in relation to M, S, and H, the threshold under s. 31(2) of the Children Act 1989 had not been crossed. The judge reached that conclusion on the basis of findings that (a) neither M nor S had suffered significant emotional harm as a result of their exposure to P's treatment of X; (b) the emotional harm suffered by M as a result of her physical abuse could not be described as significant; (c) it was not likely that M and S would suffer more harm through exposure to P's ill-treatment of X because X had been removed from the family home; (d) there was a real distinction in the way that P chose to treat their own children from the way they treated X and so there was no basis for finding a likelihood of significant harm in relation to them. The children's guardian appealed on behalf of M, S, and H. What the Court of Appeal had to decide was whether the judge, having decided that M had suffered some harm, was plainly wrong in concluding that she had not suffered significant harm. The court also had to determine whether the judge had erred in concluding that there was no likelihood of significant harm in relation to each or all of the children.

Decision

The appeal by the children's guardian was dismissed for two reasons:

(1) Given the underlying philosophy of the 1989 Act, the harm must be significant enough to justify the intervention by the state. It must be significant enough to enable the court to make a care order or a supervision order if the welfare of the child demanded it. In the instant case, the judge was fully entitled to conclude that the harm suffered by M was not significant.

(2) The judge had asked himself whether, on the proven facts, there was a real possibility of the children suffering or being likely to suffer significant harm in the future. Although P's treatment of X was truly shocking, the judge had not erred in concluding that it did not necessarily follow that P's biological children would suffer in the same or similar way. There had been good evidence before the judge that P's biological children were treated differently. Although P's treatment of X was to be deplored, the judge had been best placed to decide on the primary facts and was plainly not wrong in declining to find that the threshold of significant harm had been crossed.

One judge dissented—Lord Justice Wilson. He considered that the conduct of the parents towards X was so grossly abnormal as to show a capacity for cruelty towards children which, surely, gives rise to a real possibility that it would also be directed towards their own children. Nonetheless, the majority dismissed the appeal.

WHAT DOES THIS CASE TELL US ABOUT SOCIAL WORK PRACTICE?

The case demonstrates how important it is to appreciate the meaning of the words of the statute. Unless the children were suffering or were likely to suffer 'significant' harm, the necessary threshold for the making of a care order was not crossed. On the other hand, the dissent shows that the assessment of when harm is significant enough to justify intervention is likely to vary from judge to judge. Variations in judging the threshold for significant harm also affects the hundreds and thousands of decisions that social workers, managers, and lawyers face every week in local authorities.

We will return to the words used in s. 31 of the Children Act later in this chapter. At this point what we want you to do as you work through the chapter is to notice how the legislation and the case law attempt to strike a balance between the need to protect children and the rights of individuals to a family life. The legislation sets out checks and balances on the responsibilities of the state. The courts supervise state intervention, ensuring that it provides appropriate protection for children, but preventing intervention which oversteps the boundaries set by Parliament. Having a thorough knowledge of significant harm is an essential prerequisite for any social worker working in the field of child protection.

Preparing for court proceedings

Review of the family justice system

David Norgrove was asked by Gordon Brown's Labour government to form a committee to review the family justice system. The committee began its work in March 2010 and provided a final report in November 2011. The government recognized the strain the system was working under and in its response to the Family Justice Review, it commented:

> Case volumes have increased in recent years and are still increasing. The number of children involved in public law applications was 10% higher in the last 12 months than the preceding 12 months. Similarly it was 10% higher in 2010 than in 2006. Care and supervision cases are taking longer—applications take an average of 55 weeks. There are around 20,000 children currently waiting for a decision in public law, compared to some 11,000 at the end of 2008. The Family Justice Review estimated that the total cost of public law cases in 2009–10 was over £1bn.

Similar strains were identified for children in private law proceedings. Following this review, the Family Justice Board was established in March 2012 to drive forward changes identified in the Family Justice Review. The remit of the Board was to:

> provide the leadership and direction necessary to implement … ambitious plans for change. … The Board's overall aim is to drive significant improvements in the performance of the family justice system where performance is defined in terms of how effective (and efficient) the system is in supporting the delivery of the best possible outcomes for children who come into contact with it.

The Board's terms of reference were:

i)   reducing delay in public law cases and making progress against the proposed 26-week time limit for care cases;
ii) resolving private law cases out of court where appropriate;
iii) building greater cross-agency coherence; and
iv) tackling variations in local performance.

In the first annual report, the Board (www.gov.uk/government/uploads/system/uploads/attachment_data/file/226854/family-justice-board-annual-report-2012-13.pdf) demonstrated that the average duration of s. 31 cases reduced from 53.9 weeks from January–March 2012 to 42.2 weeks from January–March 2013. At the time of writing it is early days in terms of sustaining this kind of reduction in the time taken to conclude care proceedings.

The proposed 26-week time limit for care proceedings will no doubt focus the minds of those in the court process. But just what impact it will have set against the court's other duties to safeguard children and respect family life remains to be seen.

The government also accepted another recommendation of the Family Justice Review to make the distinction between the role of the courts and local authorities in children's care plans clear. Lord Phillips and Lady Hale, Supreme Court justices, commented in their submission to the Family Justice Review:

> If parental rights and responsibilities are to be changed or rearranged, article 6(1) of the ECHR [European Convention on Human Rights] requires that the decision be made by a court after a fair hearing. A fair process is also required by article 8 where the state interferes with the right to respect for family life. But the court's current close involvement with the formulation of the care plan in care proceedings goes beyond what was originally envisaged when the Children Act was passed and probably beyond what is required by the ECHR. Article 8 requires that the courts have some control over the contact between parents and children in care and also over the decision to sever contact with the birth family. But it does not require that the courts have control over how the child is looked after in care. Courts cannot look after children or conjure up the resources with which to do so.

The Family Justice Review concluded:

- Courts must continue to play a central role in public law in England and Wales.
- Courts should refocus on the core issues of whether the child is to live with parents, other family or friends, or be removed to the care of the local authority.
- When determining whether a care order is in a child's best interests the court will not normally need to scrutinise the full detail of a local authority care plan for a child. Instead the court should consider only the core or essential components of a child's plan. We propose that these are:
  - planned return of the child to their family;
  - a plan to place (or explore placing) a child with family or friends;
  - alternative care arrangements; and
  - contact with birth family to the extent of deciding whether that should be regular, limited or none.

The Children and Families Act 2014 amends s. 31 so that courts are required to consider the permanence provisions for the child concerned only insofar as this addresses whether the child should:

(a) live with any parent of the child's or with any other member of, or any friend of, the child's family;

(b) be adopted

(c) or remain in permanent fostering.

This new provision will require the continued promotion of the enhanced role of the local authority independent reviewing officer in scrutinizing care plans and ensuring that they address the needs of the child. Indeed, the Government Response to the Family Justice Review has suggested that ongoing work to provide greater confidence in the scrutiny role of the independent reviewing officers (IROs) in England will be particularly important.

Revised guidance—*Volume 1: Court Orders and Pre-Proceedings*

The introductory remarks in this revised guidance summarizes it aims and objectives:

> The Children and Families Act 2014 implements the Government's reforms in response to the Family Justice Review. These legislative changes are accompanied by a simplification of the court system with the majority of family cases heard by a Single Family Court. In private law, reforms make clear that, where safe and appropriate, a child should have the opportunity to benefit from the involvement of both parents. In public law new legislation addresses unjustified and potentially damaging delays in court proceedings.

The provision of early help for children and families is the bedrock of the reforms first muted in the Munro Review of Child Protection (see **chapter 5**). Local authorities and other agencies are urged to recognize that:

> Providing early help is more effective in promoting the welfare of children than reacting later. Local authorities will need to work with other agencies, as appropriate, to put processes in place for the effective assessment of the needs of individual children who may benefit from early help services and to ensure that support is provided.

What matters is that children's needs are met and this is clearly better done earlier than later. However, sometimes problems in families are more deep-seated and require more intensive intervention. In these instances, local authorities are likely to be called upon to undertake more detailed assessments and this is certainly the case if professionals are worried that a child is or is likely to be significantly harmed. Engaging parents and children is nearly always essential when undertaking assessments in these circumstances and this is likely to increase the validity and reliability of reports. In turn, when social work reports are well written and based on carefully collected evidence, and which include all of the relevant historical information, decision making is improved. When these reports are used in care proceedings, courts are less likely to require expert evidence. The hope is that the duration of proceedings will reduce. Family Group Conferences are a way to promote understanding amongst wider family members of the seriousness of cases where significant harm is likely or has occurred, prompting action to protect children or relatives to come forward to provide alternative care. Once again, early intervention from wider family members can help to reduce delay in care proceedings.

Legal Planning Meeting

When the local authority is concerned that the threshold described in s. 31(2) has been met it is likely to consult with legal advisers at a Legal Planning Meeting. The *Statutory Guidance on Court Orders and Pre-Proceedings* states that the Legal Planning Meeting should:

[decide] in principle about whether the threshold criteria have been met. The local author-ity should then decide, based on a robust analysis of the level of assessed risk, whether it is in the best interests of the child to provide a further period of support for the family with the aim of avoiding proceedings, or whether proceedings should be initiated immediately. The meeting should also identify any evidence gaps, clarify whether additional assessments will be required, and consider what would be a suitable draft care plan for the child.

When a decision has been made to apply to the court under s. 31, the local authority should issue one of two letters to the parents and anyone else with parental responsibil-ity. The Letter Before Proceedings states that proceedings are being contemplated and the Letter of Issue states that proceedings are being initiated. Templates for these letters can be found in the statutory guidance but you are advised to explore the templates available locally.

The social work documents which should accompany an application are:

- Social Work Chronology;

- Social Work Statement and Genogram;

- the current assessments relating to the child and/or the family and friends of the child to which the Social Work Statement refers and on which the local authority relies;

- care plan.

In preparedness for proceedings under s. 31 it is vital that these documents are complete. **Box 8.1** sets out the headings under which the social work statement should be organized.

 BOX 8.1 The Social Work Statement should contain

Summary

(a) The order sought;

(b) Succinct summary of reasons with reference as appropriate to the Welfare Checklist;

Family

(c) Family members and relationships especially the primary carers and significant adults/other children;

(d) Genogram;

Threshold

(e) Precipitating events;

(f) Background circumstances—
    (i) summary of children's services involvement cross-referenced to the chronology;
    (ii) previous court orders and emergency steps;
    (iii) previous assessments;

(g) Summary of significant harm and or likelihood of significant harm which the LA will seek to establish by evidence or concession;

Parenting capability

(h) Assessment of child's needs;

(i) Assessment of parental capability to meet needs;

(j) Analysis of why there is a gap between parental capability and the child's needs;

(k) Assessment of other significant adults who may be carers;

Child impact

(l) Wishes and feelings of the child(ren);

(m) Timetable for the child;

(n) Delay and timetable for the proceedings;

Permanence and contact

(o) Parallel planning;

(p) Realistic placement options by reference to a welfare and proportionality analysis;

(q) Contact framework;

Case Management

(r) Evidence and assessments necessary and outstanding;

(s) Any information about any person's litigation capacity, mental health issues, disabilities or vulnerabilities that is relevant to their capability to participate in the proceedings; and

(t) Case management proposals.

The full range of orders and powers available under Parts IV and V of the Act is set out in summary tabular form in **Box 8.2**.

 BOX 8.2 The range of orders and powers in Parts IV and V

Order/Power	Section	Comment
Care order	s. 33	A long-term order which commits the child to the care of the local authority. It provides extensive powers to local authorities but requires evidence which demonstrates to the court that a child is suffering, or likely to suffer, significant harm and that the harm or likelihood of harm is attributable to a lack of adequate parental care or control
Supervision order	s. 35	An order which places the child under the supervision of a social worker or probation officer. The grounds upon which an order can be made are identical to the care order
Interim care/ supervision order	s. 38	Orders made pending a full hearing of the application for a care order. An initial interim order cannot last longer than eight weeks

Order/Power	Section	Comment
		Subsequent interim orders cannot last longer than four weeks
Emergency protection order	s. 44	A short-term order which either removes the child on a short-term basis, or allows the child to be kept in a place of safety or requires an alleged abuser to leave the family home. The grounds for the emergency protection order are much easier to prove but successful applicants gain limited powers
Child assessment order	s. 43	A short-term order (maximum seven days) which provides for the compulsory assessment of the child's state of health and development
Removal and accommodation of children by police	s. 46	No court order is necessary for the police to implement this power which enables the police to remove a child or to keep a child in a safe place
Child recovery order	s. 49	Enables the return of the child to a 'responsible person'

The flowchart of pre-proceedings work issued as part of the statutory guidance is detailed in **Figure 8.1**.

Care plans for court

Since the implementation of s. 31A of the Children Act 1989, when any application is made upon which a care order might be made, the local authority must, within such time as the court may direct, prepare and submit to the court a s. 31A care plan which will set out basic information for the court including details about the management of the child's case and long-term planning for the child. This should have been carefully scrutinized by the authority and conform with the guidance set out in the *Children Act 1989 Guidance and Regulations, Volume 2: Care Planning, Placement and Case Review*. This states that the care plan should include:

- the information about the long-term plan for the child, including timescales (the permanence plan);
- the arrangements to meet the child's needs in line with the child's developmental needs domain of the Assessment Framework, including arrangements for contact:
  - arrangements for contact with a brother or sister who is also looked after but not placed with the child;
  - details of any court orders made under s. 8 or s. 34; and
  - arrangements for promoting and maintaining contact with a parent and anyone else with parental responsibility;
- details of the placement plan and why the placement was chosen, unless the child is in care and not provided with accommodation by the responsible authority;
- the name of the child's IRO;

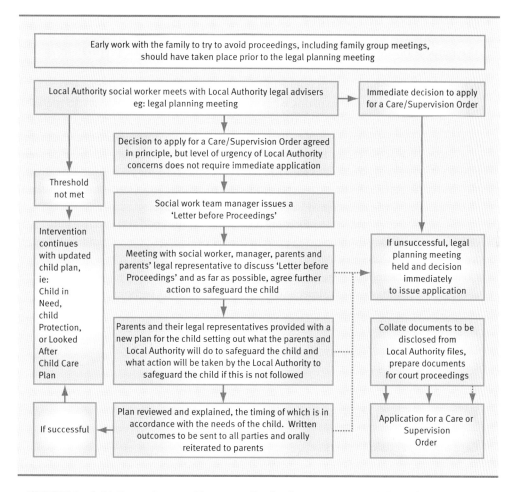

FIGURE 8.1   Guidelines prior to making an application for a care or supervision order
Source: Department for Education, April 2014.

- details of the health plan and personal education plan (PEP);
- the wishes and feelings of relevant people about the arrangements for the child; and
- the wishes and feelings of these people about any proposed changes to the care plan;
- in drawing up a care plan, the responsible authority should have a contingency plan in the event that the care plan is not achievable.

It is the permanence plan that the court is most likely to scrutinize, although the paramountcy principle means that the court is not prevented from a more detailed analysis of the care plan if it considers it is in the child's best interests. Courts are less likely to carry out this detailed analysis when local authorities are able to demonstrate that they have carried out rigorous assessments.

The Public Law Outline

The purpose of the Public Law Outline is to ensure improved case preparation, active case management by judges, and the early identification of the key issues requiring determination by the courts in public law applications under the Children Act.

The Public Law Outline explains what judges must do in order actively to manage cases to ensure most effective outcomes for children. This is very much nuts and bolts procedural stuff and may seem a million miles away from your role as a social worker. Nevertheless, it is necessary for you to comply if you wish to make the most of your applications to the court and to gain the respect of the court for your professionalism.

There is a useful overview of what is required by the Public Law Outline in Appendix A to the guidance, which is copied in **Figure 8.2** and **Table 8.1**.

Although careful attention to procedure is crucial to ensure good and effective outcomes of court proceedings, it should never prevent the proper airing of the substantive issues in a case. Judges received a salutary reminder of this when, in *P and P (Children)* (2009) the Court of Appeal slapped down the refusal of a judge, in a case management conference, to allow the local authority to instruct a second expert paediatrics pathologist on the ground that this would cause excessive delay. In its opinion, the judge acted prematurely. Until the judge knew what the expert would say, he could not make an informed decision about the value of the report. Moreover, the judge should respect the expertise of the local authority in determining what evidence it considers necessary to substantiate its application.

Long-term orders for the protection of children

Care and supervision orders

These orders provide for the long-term welfare of the child. They require identical grounds to be proved to the court. The difference between the two orders concerns control over the child involved.

A care order gives the local authority the power to protect a child through acquisition of parental responsibility. That may involve removing the child, but equally it can and does permit the child to be left at home. A supervision order puts the child under the supervision of a social worker or probation officer. If the court makes a supervision order, the child will not normally be removed from home, although there are powers to direct the child to live at a specified address for a limited period. Supervision orders are less intrusive, and if the balance between a care order and a supervision order is equal, the court should adopt the least interventionist and most proportionate approach.

Intervention must be proportionate

This was made clear by the Court of Appeal in *Re O (Supervision Order)* (2001). The Court of Appeal considered the relationship between a care order and a supervision order in the light of the need for intervention to be proportionate to the risk to the child, as required by the Human Rights Act 1998. In the particular case, the risk was felt by the court to be at the low end of the scale, and that provided the parents cooperated

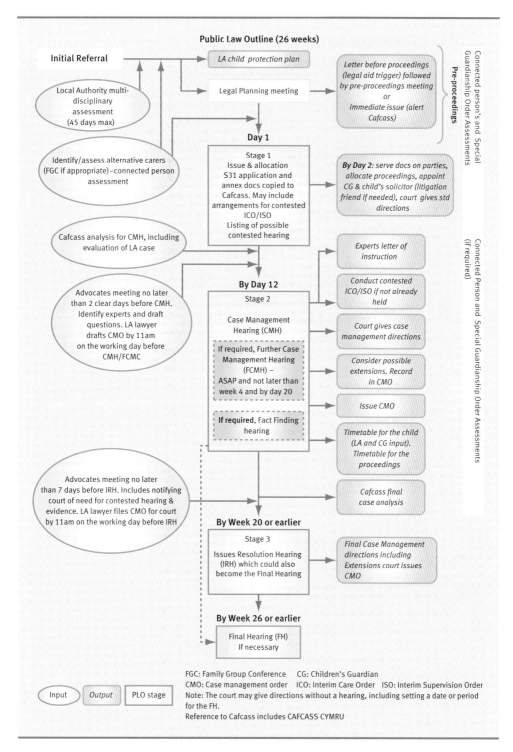

FIGURE 8.2 Court proceedings—Public Law Outline

Source: Department of Education, April 2014.

TABLE 8.1 Court proceedings—Public Law Outline

STAGE 1 ISSUE AND ALLOCATION

DAY 1 AND DAY 2 (see interpretation section)

On Day 1 (Day of issue):

- The LA files the Application Form and Annex Documents and sends copies to Cafcass/CAFCASS CYMRU
- The LA notifies the court of the need for an urgent preliminary case management hearing or an urgent contested ICO hearing where this is known or expected
- Court officer issues application

Within a day of issue (Day 2):

- Court considers jurisdiction in a case with an international element
- Court considers initial allocation to specified level of judge, in accordance with the Allocation Rules and any President's Guidance on the distribution of business
- LA serves the Application Form, Annex Documents and evidential Checklist Documents on the parties together with the notice of date and time of CMH and any urgent hearing
- Court gives standard directions on Issue and Allocation including:
  - Checking compliance with Pre-Proceedings Checklist including service of any missing Annex Documents
  - Appointing Children's Guardian (to be allocated by Cafcass/CAFCASS CYMRU)
  - Appointing solicitor for the child only if necessary
  - Appointing (if the person to be appointed consents) a litigation friend for any protected party or any non subject child who is a party, including the as where appropriate
  - Identifying whether a request has been made or should be made to a Central Authority or other competent authority in a foreign state or a consular authority in England and Wales in a case with an international element
  - Filing and service of a LA Case Summary
  - Filing and service of a Case Analysis by the Children's Guardian
  - Filing and Serving the Parents' Response
  - Sending a request for disclosure to, e.g., the police or health service body
  - Filing and serving an application for permission relating to experts under Part 25 on a date prior to the advocates meeting for the CMH
  - Directing the solicitor for the child to arrange an advocates' meeting no later than 2 business days before the CMH
  - Listing the CMH
- Court considers any request for an urgent preliminary case management hearing or an urgent contested ICO hearing and where necessary lists the hearing and gives additional directions.
- Court officer sends copy Notice of Hearing of the CMH and any urgent hearing by email to Cafcass/CAFCASS CYMRU.

STAGE 2—CASE MANAGEMENT HEARING

ADVOCATES' MEETING (including any litigants in person)

No later than 2 business days before CMH (or FCMH if it is necessary)

- Consider information on the Application Form and Annex documents, the LA Case Summary, and the Case Analysis
- Identify the parties' positions to be recited in the draft Case Management Order
- Identify the parties' positions about jurisdiction, in particular arising out of any international element
- If necessary, identify proposed experts and draft questions in accordance with Part 25 and the Experts Practice Directions
- Identify any disclosure that in the advocates' views is necessary
- Immediately notify the court of the need for a contested ICO hearing and any issue about allocation
- LA advocate to file a draft Case Management Order in prescribed form with court by 11a.m. on the business day before the CMH and/or FCMH

CASE MANAGEMENT HEARING

CMH: Not before day 12 and not later than day 18

A FCMH is to be held only if necessary, it is to be listed as soon as possible and in any event no later than day 25

- Court gives detailed case management directions, including:
  - Considering jurisdiction in a case with an international element;
  - Confirming allocation
  - Drawing up the timetable for the child and the timetable for the proceedings and considering if an extension is necessary
  - Identifying additional parties, intervenors and representation (including confirming that Cafcass/CAFCASS CYMRU have allocated a Children's Guardian and that a litigation friend is appointed for any protected party or non subject child)
  - Giving directions for the determination of any disputed issue about litigation capacity
  - Identifying the key issues
  - Identifying the evidence necessary to enable the court to resolve the key issues
  - Deciding whether there is a real issue about threshold to be resolved
  - Determining any application made under Part 25 and otherwise ensuring compliance with Part 25 where it is necessary for expert(s) to be instructed
  - Identifying any necessary disclosure and if appropriate giving directions
  - Giving directions for any concurrent or proposed placement order proceedings
  - Ensuring compliance with the court's directions
  - If a FCMH is necessary, directing an advocates' meeting and Case Analysis if required
  - Directing filing of any threshold agreement, final evidence and Care Plan and responses to those documents for the IRH
  - Directing a Case Analysis for the IRH
  - Directing an advocates' meeting for the IRH
  - Listing (any FCMH) IRH, Final Hearing (including early Final Hearing) as appropriate
  - Giving directions for special measures and/or interpreters and intermediaries
  - Issuing the Case Management Order

STAGE 3 – ISSUES RESOLUTION HEARING

ADVOCATES' MEETING (including any litigants in person)	IRH
No later than 7 business days before the IRH	As directed by the court, in accordance with the timetable for the proceedings

• Review evidence and the positions of the parties
• Identify the advocates' views of–
  – the remaining key issues and how the issues may be resolved or narrowed at the IRH including by the making of final orders
  – the further evidence which is required to be heard to enable the key issues to be resolved or narrowed at the IRH
  – the evidence that is relevant and the witnesses that are required at the final hearing
  – the need for a contested hearing and/or time for oral evidence to be given at the IRH
• LA advocate to–
  – notify the court immediately of the outcome of the discussion at the meeting
  – file a draft Case Management Order with the court by 11 a.m. on the business day before the IRH
	• Court identifies the key issue(s) (if any) to be determined and the extent to which those issues can be resolved or narrowed at the IRH
	• Court considers whether the IRH can be used as a final hearing
	• Court resolves or narrows the issues by hearing evidence
	• Court identifies the evidence to be heard on the issues which remain to be resolved at the final hearing
	• Court gives final case management directions including:
	  – Any extension of the timetable for the proceedings which is necessary
	  – Filing of the threshold agreement or a statement of facts/issues remaining to be determined
	  – Filing of:
	    ○ Final evidence and Care Plan
	    ○ Case Analysis for Final Hearing (if required)
	    ○ Witness templates
	    ○ Skeleton arguments
	  – Judicial reading list/reading time, including time estimate and an estimate for judgment writing time
	  – Ensuring Compliance with PD27A (the Bundles Practice Direction)
	  – Listing the Final Hearing
	• Court issues Case Management Order

Source: Department of Education, April 2014.

and the local authority delivered the necessary range of services to protect the child, a supervision order (rather than the care order requested by the local authority) was appropriate. The court indicated that previous case law was not necessarily helpful on this distinction, as each case has to be decided on its own facts and the requirements of the Human Rights Act 1998 must be considered.

Care orders

A care order should be applied for only when the principle of the diminishment of the need for court proceedings has been tried or considered and been found to be unsuccessful or inapplicable. Both the revised guidance and the Public Law Outline emphasize this.

Applications

Section 31(1) of the 1989 Act determines who may apply for a care order: **Box 8.3** sets this out. You will see that a distinction is made between the application, which can be made by any local authority or the NSPCC, and the actual care order which is made to a *designated* authority. The purpose of this is to ensure that the local authority close to the children concerned has the long-term responsibility for managing and implementing the care plan. The designated local authority is defined in s. 31(8) of the Children Act 1989 as the local authority where the child is ordinarily resident or, where the child does not reside in the area of a local authority, the authority within whose area any circumstances arose in consequence of which the order is made.

 BOX 8.3 Section 31(1) of the Children Act

(1) On the application of any local authority or authorised person [only the NSPCC is authorized], the court may make an order—
   (a) placing the child with respect to whom the application is made in the care of a designated local authority; or
   (b) putting the child under the supervision of a designated local authority or a probation officer.

The grounds for a care order

The grounds, known as the 'threshold criteria', are contained in s. 31(2) set out in **Box 8.4**. They set out the minimum criteria necessary before the court can consider compulsory intervention in family life. The court will proceed to apply the welfare principles contained in s. 1 only if it is satisfied that the threshold criteria apply.

 BOX 8.4 The grounds for a care order—s. 31(2)

(2) A court may only make a care order or supervision order if it is satisfied—
   (a) that the child concerned is suffering, or is likely to suffer, significant harm; and
   (b) that the harm, or likelihood of harm, is attributable to—
      (i) the care given to the child, or likely to be given to him if the order were not made, not being what it would be reasonable to expect a parent to give to him; or
      (ii) the child's being beyond parental control.

Two questions require answering

You will notice that the section requires that the court answers two distinct questions. When considering an application for a care or supervision order, a court must:

(a) be satisfied that the grounds in s. 31 (the threshold criteria) are met; and

(b) decide whether, by applying the grounds in s. 1, to make an order and what order to make.

Whilst there are two steps that the courts must take, these are not distinct but inter-linked. This was made clear by Baroness Hale in *Re B (Children) (Care Proceedings: Standard of Proof)* (2008) which we will discuss further (see **Re B (Children) (Care Proceedings: Standard of Proof)** (2008), p 278). The observation she made about the decision-making process is set out in **Box 8.5.**

BOX 8.5 Baroness Hale's observations in *Re B (Children) (Care Proceedings: Standard of Proof)*

74 Care proceedings are not a two stage process. The court does have two questions to ask. Has the threshold been crossed? If so, what will be best for the child? But there are many cases in which a court has two or more questions to ask in the course of a single hearing. The same factual issues are often relevant to each question. Or some factual disputes may be relevant to the threshold while others are relevant to the welfare checklist: it may be clear, for example, that a child has suffered an injury while in the care of the mother, but whether the father or stepfather has a drink problem and has been beating the mother up is extremely relevant to the long term welfare of the child.

75 The purpose of splitting the hearing is not to split the two questions which the court must answer. It is to separate out those factual issues which are capable of swift resolution so that the welfare professionals have a firm foundation of fact upon which to base their assessments of family relationships and parenting ability.

The threshold criteria in detail

Understanding the threshold criteria is a prerequisite for effective social work with children. Later we examine exactly what is required by s. 31 of the Children Act.

Present or future harm

Notice that care orders are obtained either on the basis that the child is currently suffering significant harm or on the basis of the likelihood that the child will suffer significant harm in the future.

When does the child have to have suffered significant harm?

The temporal qualities of the suffering need careful attention. Whilst past harm cannot be the basis of a care order, the necessity for present suffering for the purposes of the section has caused some difficulty because the child is unlikely to be suffering at the time of the hearing. In *Northampton County Council v S* (1992), the court considered at what time the significance of the harm should be considered. In this case the mother had two children, a girl born in 1986 and a boy born in 1989. The children had different fathers. Following a non-accidental injury, the children were taken into voluntary care under the old law. The Children Act then came into force. The local authority applied for a care order. The father of the boy sought a residence order that the boy only was to live with the boy's grandmother. The magistrates granted the care order. The father appealed to the High Court. The High Court had to consider the meaning of 'suffering significant harm'. What is the effect of the present tense? It held that the phrase referred to the period immediately before the action commenced. Ewbank J said:

> That means the court has to consider the position immediately before the emergency protection order, if there was one or an interim care order, if that was the initiation of protection, or, as in this case, when the child went into voluntary care. In my judgment, the family proceedings court was quite entitled to consider the position when the children were with the mother prior to going into care and was correct in doing so.

The meaning of 'likely'

Care orders can be made on the basis of the likelihood of future significant harm. As we shall show later, predictions of what is likely to happen in the future are made on the basis of what has happened in the past.

Harm

Harm is defined in s. 31. The relevant subsections (9) and (10) are set out in **Box 8.6**.

 BOX 8.6 The meaning of harm—s. 31(9) and (10)

(9) In this section—
  'harm' means ill treatment or the impairment of health or development;
  'development' means physical, intellectual, emotional, social or behavioural development;
  'health' means physical or mental health; and
  'ill treatment' includes sexual abuse and forms of treatment that are not physical including for example impairment suffered from seeing or hearing the ill treatment of another.

(10) Where the question of whether harm suffered by a child is significant turns on the child's health or development, his health shall be compared with that which could reasonably be expected of a similar child.

The cause of the harm

The harm that a child suffers or is likely to suffer must emanate from a failure of parenting. However, there is no expectation that the care which has to be provided for a child is at the standard of a perfect parent. What is required is reasonable parenting.

The reasonable parent

The presence or likelihood of significant harm has to be attributable to the fact that the care given or likely to be given to the child (as appropriate) is not what a parent would reasonably be expected to give to the child. Therefore, you have to look at the child in his or her context (home, surroundings, locale, etc) and ask what a reasonable parent in that situation would be expected to do. So, for instance, a reasonable parent in most, but not all, circumstances would ensure that a child attends school or takes prescribed medicine.

Being beyond parental control

'Being beyond parental control' in s. 31(1)(b)(ii) is largely a self-explanatory matter of fact for the court to decide. An example of the use of this concept can be found in *South Glamorgan County Council v W and B* (1993), and also in *M v Birmingham City Council* (1994).

Significant harm

Harm is not sufficient for the purposes of the threshold criteria. The key phrase within s. 31(2) is *significant harm*. Whether harm is significant is a matter for the court to decide as a question of fact. In *Re A (Children) (Care Proceedings: Threshold Criteria)* (2009), the case we considered at the beginning of the chapter, the Court of Appeal made it clear that Article 8 of the European Convention on Human Rights informs the meaning of 'significant' in the phrase 'significant harm' and serves to emphasize that there has to be a relevant and sufficient reason for crossing the threshold. However, Lord Wilson, in *Re B* [2013] UKSC 33, contends that the Court of Appeal added an inappropriate layer of complexity in suggesting that Article 8 informs the meaning of the word 'significant'. Lord Wilson says at para. 29:

> No interference (with the right to family life) occurs when a judge concludes that the threshold is crossed. The interference occurs only if, at the welfare stage, the judge proceeds to make a care or supervision order; and it is the order which must therefore not fall foul of article 8.

Lord Wilson went on the argue that the court should avoid explaining the meaning of the word 'significant'. To do so he said would merely be a gloss.

The statute provides little help in making decisions about when harm is significant. Section 31(10) (see **Box 8.6**) requires that the significance of the harm is measured via comparison with a similar child. This may be a difficult comparison to achieve when children come from a huge variety of cultural and social backgrounds. Social workers must be careful not to impose particular norms of development. In *Re O* (1992) the judge made these comments about the meaning of 'similar child' in the context of whether non-attendance at school caused significant harm:

> In my judgment, in the context of this type of case, 'similar child' means a child of equivalent intellectual and social development, who has gone to school, and not merely an average child who may or may not be at school. In fact, what one has to ask oneself is whether this child suffered significant harm by not going to school. The answer, in my judgment, as in the magistrates; judgment is obvious.

Dictionary definitions indicate that 'significant' encompasses something more than the question of the magnitude of the harm. A broken arm, for instance, may not be 'significant' if it was suffered following a fall from playground equipment, but may be if it was suffered during a period when the child was left alone in the house or following a push from a parent. The use of a dictionary definition was endorsed in *Humberside County Council v B* (1993), hence 'considerable, noteworthy or important' would describe significant. These terms rather imply that 'significant' harm is harm which is excessive, prominent, or critical to the child. Critical in this context is perhaps associated with damage to the child's developmental progress. But where does this leave you the social worker? You have to decide along with your colleagues whether the harm done to a child is significant or not and this judgement can be very difficult and not without controversy (see the case at the beginning of this chapter). The World Health Organization provides a definition of child maltreatment as:

> all forms of physical and/or emotional ill-treatment, sexual abuse, neglect or negligent treatment or commercial or other exploitation, resulting in actual or potential harm to the child's health, survival, development or dignity in the context of a relationship of responsibility, trust or power.
>
> (A. Butchart et al, *Preventing Child Maltreatment: A Guide to Taking Action and Generating Evidence* (WHO and ISPCAN, 2006))

In this definition the stress is on the 'relationship of responsibility, trust or power'. The government defines abuse and neglect as 'forms of maltreatment of a child. Someone may abuse or neglect a child by inflicting harm, or by failing to act to prevent harm or which in itself harms a child' (*Working Together to Safeguard Children*, 2013).

The categories of abuse are shown in **Box 8.7**, but these definitions are not without their inherent problems. The definition of physical abuse is merely a list of what might be classed as physical abuse and the definition of emotional abuse simply mentions the word 'maltreatment' so as to cause adverse effects on the child, which could mean many things. The definition of neglect is largely about the physical neglect of a child. What is not mentioned is emotional neglect which might be thought to involve inadequate parents who are simply not able to provide 'good enough' parenting despite their best endeavours. They are not 'abusive' but nonetheless their inadequacies lead to lasting damage to a child's developmental progress. Such parents probably make up the bulk of parents whose children come before the courts in care proceedings and yet the 'official' definitions give them little mention.

 BOX 8.7 Categories of abuse and neglect

Physical abuse	A form of abuse which may involve hitting, shaking, throwing, poisoning, burning or scalding, drowning, suffocating or otherwise causing physical harm to a child. Physical harm may also be caused when a parent or carer fabricates the symptoms of, or deliberately induces, illness in a child

Emotional abuse	The persistent emotional maltreatment of a child such as to cause severe and persistent adverse effects on the child's emotional development. It may involve conveying to a child that they are worthless or unloved, inadequate, or valued only insofar as they meet the needs of another person. It may include not giving the child opportunities to express their views, deliberately silencing them or 'making fun' of what they say or how they communicate. It may feature age or developmentally inappropriate expectations being imposed on children. These may include interactions that are beyond a child's developmental capability, as well as overprotection and limitation of exploration and learning, or preventing the child participating in normal social interaction. It may involve seeing or hearing the ill-treatment of another. It may involve serious bullying (including cyber bullying), causing children frequently to feel frightened or in danger, or the exploitation or corruption of children. Some level of emotional abuse is involved in all types of maltreatment of a child, though it may occur alone
Sexual abuse	Involves forcing or enticing a child or young person to take part in sexual activities, not necessarily involving a high level of violence, whether or not the child is aware of what is happening. The activities may involve physical contact, including assault by penetration (eg rape or oral sex) or non-penetrative acts such as masturbation, kissing, rubbing and touching outside clothing. They may also include non-contact activities, such as involving children in looking at, or in the production of, sexual images, watching sexual activities, encouraging children to behave in sexually inappropriate ways, or grooming a child in preparation for abuse (including via the internet). Sexual abuse is not solely perpetrated by adult males. Women can also commit acts of sexual abuse, as can other children
Neglect	The persistent failure to meet a child's basic physical and/or psychological needs, likely to result in the serious impairment of the child's health or development. Neglect may occur during pregnancy as a result of maternal substance abuse. Once a child is born, neglect may involve a parent or carer failing to: • provide adequate food, clothing, and shelter (including exclusion from home or abandonment); • protect a child from physical and emotional harm or danger; • ensure adequate supervision (including the use of inadequate caregivers); or • ensure access to appropriate medical care or treatment. It may also include neglect of, or unresponsiveness to, a child's basic emotional needs

Other examples of thinking about emotional neglect might help you to decide whether a child has suffered significant harm. First, from Salford LSCB Neglect Strategy:

> Neglect may be defined as occurring when the child's needs are not consistently at the centre of the carer's thoughts, feelings and actions such that this has an impact on the child's healthy development and this is known to be reflected within 'a video over the life of the child' rather than a snapshot of their experience.
>
> (Salford LSCB Neglect Strategy)

This definition focuses on the way the parent or carer cares for the child where the emphasis is on the parental cognitive and affective states. The second definition has emerged from neuropsychiatry. Bruce Perry describes neglect as the 'absence of critical organising experiences at key times during development' (B. Perry, 'Childhood experience and the expression of genetic potential: what childhood neglect tells us about nature and nurture' (2004) 3 *Brain and Mind* 79).

Emotional neglect and, indeed, emotional abuse 'impedes emotional development … it retards the process through which a child acquires the ability to feel and express different emotions appropriately, and eventually, to regulate and control them' (K. O'Hagan, *Identifying Emotional and Psychological Abuse* (Open University Press, 2006)).

Lady Hale in her judgment in the case mentioned earlier in this section (*Re B* [2013] UKSC 33) sets out five criteria which she hoped courts would find useful in determining whether the threshold criteria had been met. By extension, you may also find these criteria helpful when you are considering whether a child has suffered significant harm:

(1) The court's task is not to improve on nature or even to secure that every child has a happy and fulfilled life, but to be satisfied that the statutory threshold has been crossed.

(2) When deciding whether the threshold is crossed the court should identify, as precisely as possible, the nature of the harm which the child is suffering or is likely to suffer. This is particularly important where the child has not yet suffered any, or any significant, harm and where the harm which is feared is the impairment of intellectual, emotional, social or behavioural development.

(3) Significant harm is harm which is 'considerable, noteworthy or important.' The court should identify why and in what respects the harm is significant. Again, this may be particularly important where the harm in question is the impairment of intellectual, emotional, social or behavioural development which has not yet happened.

(4) The harm has to be attributable to a lack, or likely lack, of reasonable parental care, not simply to the characters and personalities of both the child and her parents. So once again, the court should identify the respects in which parental care is falling, or is likely to fall, short of what it would be reasonable to expect.

(5) Finally, where harm has not yet been suffered, the court must consider the degree of likelihood that it will be suffered in the future. This will entail considering the degree of likelihood that the parents' future behaviour will amount to a lack of reasonable parental care. It will also entail considering the relationship between the significance of the harmed feared and the likelihood that it will occur. Simply to state that there is a 'risk' is not enough. The court has to be satisfied, by relevant and sufficient evidence, that the harm is likely.

The meaning of the word 'likely'

In 2008 the House of Lords in *Re B (Children) (Care Proceedings: Standard of Proof)*, clarified the law in respect of the meaning of 'likely'. This is an important and helpful case.

Re B (Children) (Care Proceedings: Standard of Proof) (2008)

The facts were as follows: the husband and wife lived in the family home with their two children, N, a girl aged 9, and A, a boy aged 6, and with the wife's two children from a previous marriage, R, a girl aged 16 and S, a boy of 17. The husband left the family home and applied for residence orders in respect of N and A. Instead, the district judge made interim care orders in respect of R as well as N and A, on the basis of a plan to remove them from the wife and place them with the husband at his parents' home. Whilst they were being removed from the wife's home, R alleged that the husband had sexually abused her and had also physically assaulted both her and S. The husband denied the allegations. R was initially placed with foster carers and then returned to the wife. N and A were initially placed with the husband's parents and were subsequently moved to foster carers. The care proceedings were transferred to the High Court and a fact-finding hearing took place to ascertain whether the threshold criteria under s. 31(2) of the Children Act were satisfied.

The legal problem

The judge had found working out what had happened in the family difficult. He could not decide that it was 'more likely than not' that R was telling the truth in making the allegations, nor could he find that it 'was more likely than not' that the husband was telling the truth when denying the allegations. The judge decided that the sexual abuse allegations could not form any part of the findings which would be required to demonstrate whether or not the threshold criteria were met. He ordered that the basis for the instruction of expert witnesses and the basis for the final welfare hearing would be that R had not been sexually abused by the husband. The judge also recused (released) himself from the case. The children's guardian appealed. The Court of Appeal dismissed the appeal on the ground that it was bound by the House of Lords' authority to do so. The children's guardian appealed to the House of Lords.

Judgment

What the House of Lords decided was:

(a) The purpose of the threshold conditions were to protect children and their parents from unjustified intervention by the state.

(b) The court first had to be satisfied that the alleged significant harm to a child or likelihood of such harm existed and, if so satisfied, then to decide what outcome would be best for the child.

(c) Care proceedings are of a civil nature, intended not to punish or deter but to protect a child from harm.

(d) As the consequences of a wrong decision are equally serious either way, the standard of proof applicable in finding the facts necessary to establish the threshold criteria was the simple balance of probabilities, irrespective of the seriousness of the allegations or of the consequences.

(e) Care proceedings are not a two-stage process and the same factual issues were often relevant to questions as to whether the criteria had been crossed and if so what was best for the child. Therefore the same judge should hear both elements of the case.

Baroness Hale's judgment

Baroness Hale provides some clear answers to the questions which arise when trying to grapple with the concept of significant harm.

How is a court to be satisfied that a child is likely to suffer significant harm?

> This is a prediction from existing facts, often from a multitude of such facts, about what has happened in the past, about the characters and personalities of the people involved, about the things which they have said and done, and so on.

Do those facts have to be proved in the usual way?

Hale drew on previous authorities but also clarified them to answer this question in the affirmative.

> I … announce loud and clear that the standard of proof in finding the facts necessary to establish the threshold under section 31(2) or the welfare considerations in section 1 of the 1989 Act is the simple balance of probabilities, neither more nor less.

Does the seriousness of the allegation make a difference to the standard of proof?

> Neither the seriousness of the allegation nor the seriousness of the consequences should make any difference to the standard of proof to be applied in determining the facts. The inherent probabilities are simply something to be taken into account, where relevant, in deciding where truth lies.

Does it make a difference if it is impossible to determine who is responsible for the harm that a child has suffered?

No—the balance of probabilities applies in exactly the same way. What Hale said was:

> The court cannot shut its eyes to the undoubted harm which has been suffered simply because it does not know who was responsible.

Any confusion about the conduct of a case when there is uncertainty about which carer has perpetrated abuse, was clarified in a subsequent case, *Re D (Children)* (2009). Here the Court of Appeal was concerned that judges might consider that the effect of *Re B* was that they were required to identify the perpetrator of the significant harm. It observed:

> Nothing in *Re B*, in our judgment, requires the court to identify an individual as the perpetrator of non-accidental injuries to a child, simply because the standard of proof for such an identification is the balance of probabilities. If such an identification is not possible, because, for example, a judge remains genuinely uncertain at the end of a fact finding hearing, and cannot find on the balance of probabilities that A rather than B caused the injuries to the child, but that neither A nor B can be excluded as a perpetrator—it is the duty of the judge to state that as his or her conclusion.

What is the distinction between the role of the local authorities and the role of the courts?

> To allow the courts to make decisions about the allocation of parental responsibility for children on the basis of unproven allegations and unsubstantiated suspicions would be to deny them their essential role in protecting both children and their families from the intervention of the state, however well intentioned that intervention may be. It is to confuse the role of the local authority, in assessing and managing risk, in planning for the child, and deciding what action to initiate, with the role of the court in deciding where the truth lies and what the legal consequences should be. I do not underestimate the difficulty of deciding where the truth lies but that is what the courts are for.

In summary, then, the standard of proof is the balance of probabilities and neither the character of the abuse nor the difficulty in identifying perpetrators makes any difference to this. Interestingly, Baroness Hale commented on this case again in an academic journal as follows:

> In *Re B*, the House of Lords discarded the mantra once and for all. Inherent probabilities are not to be equated with the seriousness of the allegation. It may be unlikely that the animal you see while out walking in Regent's Park is a lion rather than a dog. But if you are in the zoo next door to the lion's enclosure and there is a great big hole in the fence, it is not unlikely at all. It may be unlikely that anyone would swing a tiny child by the arm and slam him into the wall. But when there is incontrovertible evidence that this is what happened, it is not unlikely at all.
>
> (B. Hale, 'The Children Act 1989 in the highest courts' (2006) 5(2) *Journal of Children's Services* 17)

The effect of a care order

Section 33—set out in **Box 8.8**—describes the effect of a care order. It gives the local authority parental responsibility; it makes the local authority the child's parent—with all the implications that are contained in that phrase.

 BOX 8.8 The effect of a care order–s. 33

(1) Where a care order is made with respect to a child it shall be the duty of a local authority designated by the order to receive the child into their care and to keep him in their care while the order remains in force.

(2) Where—
    (a) A care order has been made with respect to a child on the application of an authorised person [ie the NSPCC]; but
    (b) the local authority designated by the order was not informed that the person proposed to make the application (there is a requirement for the local authority to be informed of applications),
    the child may be kept in the care of that person until received into the care of the local authority.

(3) While a care order is in force with respect to a child, the local authority designated by the order shall—

(a) have parental responsibility for the child; and

(b) have the power (subject to the following provisions of this section) to determine the extent to which a parent or guardian of the child may meet his parental responsibility for him.

(4) The authority may not exercise the power in subsection (3)(b) unless they are satisfied that it is necessary to do so in order to safeguard or promote the child's welfare.

(5) Nothing in subsection (3)(b) shall prevent a parent or guardian of the child who has care of him from doing what is reasonable in all the circumstances of the case for the purpose of safeguarding or promoting his welfare.

Parental responsibility under a care order

Sharing parental responsibility

The mere fact of making a care order and giving parental responsibility to the local authority does not remove parental responsibility from the parents (s. 2(5) and (6)). What happens is that the principal responsibility rests with the local authority. Section 33(3)(b) echoes the philosophy of the Act. It seeks to encourage the local authority to consider how it can share the care of the child with the child's parent, albeit that this is a power and not a duty on the local authority.

The welfare of the child

Section 33(4) provides that although the local authority may share the care of the child with the parent, it may not exercise this power unless it is necessary to do so in order to safeguard or promote the child's welfare.

Limits on the local authority's parental responsibility

Section 33(6), (7), (8), and (9) imposes limitations on the power of the local authority in possession of a care order in respect of the child. We set out a summary of those in **Box 8.9**.

BOX 8.9 Limiting the local authority's parental responsibility

Whilst a care order is in force the local authority may not:

(a) cause the child to be brought up in a different religious persuasion (this can present problems in the choice of foster parents);

(b) cause the child to be adopted without a court order;

(c) appoint a guardian for the child (that is a testamentary guardian for when the parents die); or

(d) cause the child to be known by a different surname (again this needs to be watched with foster parents); or

(e) allow the child to be removed from the UK without the leave of the court (except for periods of less than four weeks).

Planning

In making applications to court it has always been necessary for the local authority to present its plans for contact (s. 34(11)) and its proposals for the future care of the child if a care order is made (*Manchester City Council v F* (1993)). This responsibility is made explicit as a result of the insertion of a new subsection (3A) into s. 31. This provides that 'no care order may be made with respect to a child until the court has considered a section 31A plan' (see **Care plans for court**, p 264).

Once a care order is made the local authority has the task of deciding how to look after the child.

In care—but at home

The local authority's duty once a care order is made is still that contained in s. 17; that is, to safeguard and promote the child's welfare and, as far as is consistent with that duty, to encourage the child to be with his or her family. A care order adds to this a power, if necessary, to remove the child. Regulations still apply when a child is placed at home, see the *Children Act 1989 Guidance and Regulations, Volume 2: Care Planning, Placement and Case Review* (**chapter 3**).

Discharge of care orders

The procedure for the discharge of care orders is identical to that for supervision orders. Section 39 provides the powers for the variation and discharge of both care and supervision orders. Applications can be made by the authority, the child, or the parent. In the case of a supervision order, the child may be living with a person who does not have parental responsibility, for example a relative. In that case that person may apply for the supervision order to be discharged.

The welfare principle

There are no particular requirements for a court to consider when deciding an application to have a care or supervision order discharged except to do what is best for the welfare of the child (the welfare principle). The court does have the power, when an application is made to discharge a care order, to substitute a supervision order. In those particular circumstances, under s. 39(5), the court does not have to apply the significant harm test in s. 31 which would otherwise apply when considering a supervision order.

Unsuccessful applications

If an application to discharge a care or supervision order, or to have contact with a child in care, has been unsuccessful, then a further application may not be made for a period of six months (s. 91(15)). But there are provisions for the court to grant leave to make an application within the six-month period.

Rehabilitation

In attempting to rehabilitate a child, the local authority does not have available any particular court order. The choice is either a care order or a supervision order, or no order at all. The court does not have the power to make an order requiring either the local authority or the parents to undertake a rehabilitation plan. This is a situation in which the absence of the availability of wardship for local authorities is a real loss. The problem is that the court cannot impose restrictions or conditions on a full care order. (See *Kent County Council v C* (1992).)

Discharge of care order by a child arrangements order

There is an alternative way to have a care order discharged and that is by an application for a s. 8 child arrangements order. Under s. 91(1), the making of a child arrangements order *with respect to the living arrangements* discharges any care order. Applications for a child arrangements order are made under s. 10(4) and (5). For the purposes of seeking to discharge a care order by this means, the following people could apply:

(a) the mother or father;

(b) any person with whom the child has lived for a period totalling at least three years out of the last five, ending at the latest three months ago;

(c) any person who has the consent of the local authority. A foster parent will come within this category unless the child has lived with the foster parent for a period of three years or the foster parent is a relative of the child. Then they can apply without consent. (A relative is defined in s. 105 as a grandparent, brother, sister, uncle, aunt, or step-parent.)

Applications with leave

In addition to these people, the court has power under s. 10(9) to grant leave to any person, except a foster parent, to apply for a s. 8 order. In considering whether to grant leave the court has to have regard to a number of points:

(a) what form of order is sought;

(b) the connection with the child;

(c) the risk that the application would disrupt the child so as to harm the child; and

(d) where the child is looked after by the local authority, what plans the authority has for the child and the wishes and feelings of the child's (actual) parents.

Whilst a hearing for leave ought to be shorter than the full hearing, experience does not always bear this out. In an extreme case an authority may be faced with a number of persons seeking leave to apply for a child arrangements order with respect to the living arrangements with the consequent pressures on staff dealing with a series of legal proceedings. Of course, the granting of leave does not mean that the child arrangements order itself will be granted. That is decided at a full hearing on the basis of what is in the child's best interest. The decision in *Re B (Minors) (Contact)* (1994) said that a court could refuse leave without a full hearing, if it was clear that leave should be refused. Therefore, if an application had just been refused by the Court of Appeal and the same parent applied in the magistrates' court for leave for a contact order, the court could refuse.

Supervision orders

Identical grounds

The grounds for making a supervision order are exactly the same as those for a care order. They are set out in s. 31(2) (ie the likelihood of significant harm or the child being beyond parental control). Indeed, all the provisions of s. 31 are applicable to the making of a supervision order. Therefore the questions of the meaning of 'significant harm' etc, which we discussed when looking at care orders, are just as applicable.

Choosing supervision orders

A supervision order is an alternative to a care order. In the Act there is no guidance on when a supervision order, rather than a care order, should be made. The decision is going to be the decision of the court, although the court will listen to the representations of all the parties, which can include a children's guardian, before coming to that decision. The order is made to either a local authority or a probation officer.

The Act creates three distinct supervision orders—the one made in the course of civil proceedings which we are considering here, the education supervision order which we look at later (**Education supervision orders (s. 36)**, p 286), and one made in criminal proceedings which we consider in **chapter 10**.

The value of a supervision order

An interesting case which considered the need for a supervision order is *Re K (Supervision Orders)* (1999). Here the local authority and the mother agreed that the threshold criteria in s. 31 were satisfied. They also agreed that a supervision order would be the appropriate way to safeguard the interests of the children. However, the children's guardian thought that the obligations of the local authority to safeguard the interests of the children under s. 17, as children 'in need', were sufficient to deal with their welfare. The judge found that as a concession had been made by the mother which appropriately reflected the gravity of the case, there was no need for a full investigation by the courts. He made it clear that a guardian should not lightly propose a contentious hearing. While accepting that the least intrusive order possible should be made, the supervision order imposed duties on the mother as well as on the local authority, which would be useful if the mother did not continue to cooperate, and that in practice the result of the supervision order would be to secure the allocation of a social worker and therefore greater protection for the children.

The effect of a supervision order

Section 35 of the Children Act sets out the effect of a supervision order. Its provisions are set out in **Box 8.10**.

BOX 8.10 The effect of a supervision order—s. 35

(1) While a supervision order is in force it shall be the duty of the supervisor—
  (a) to advise, assist and befriend the supervised child;
  (b) to take such steps as are reasonably necessary to give effect to the order; and
  (c) where—
    (i) the order is not wholly complied with; or
    (ii) the supervisor considers that the order may no longer be necessary, to consider whether or not to apply to the court for its variation or discharge.

There are no definitions of the terms 'advise', 'assist', or 'befriend' to give any guidance. The order need not specify a particular person in respect of a local authority. Note that a probation officer can be a supervisor only with the agreement of the probation authority and where the probation officer is already dealing or has dealt with another member of the child's household (Sch. 3, para. 9). This means that the majority of supervision orders will be made in favour of the local authority. Schedule 3 to the Act gives more detailed guidance on what a supervision order means.

The responsible person

The first paragraph of Schedule 3 introduces the idea of the 'responsible person' who is either a parent or someone with whom the child is living who consents to the role. This 'responsible person' can have duties imposed upon them in addition to any requirements that are imposed on the supervised child.

Requirements

The court, under a supervision order, can require the supervised person to obey certain directions given by the supervisor. Amongst these are that the supervised child:

  (a) be required to live at a specified address for a specified period;
  (b) present themselves to a specified person at a specified time and place; and
  (c) participate in specified activities.

In addition, the responsible person can be required to:

  (a) take all reasonable steps to ensure that the supervised child complies with directions given by the supervisor or contained in the order;
  (b) keep the supervisor informed of the supervised child's address; and
  (c) attend at a specified place to take part in any specified activities.

The supervision order can require the supervised child to submit to a medical or psychiatric examination, or to submit to such examinations as are required by the supervisor. This requirement is subject to the informed consent of the child, if the child has sufficient understanding. It is also possible for the court to require specified medical or psychiatric treatment but, if psychiatric, the court must have first heard the evidence of a Mental Health Act-approved doctor. The order can also require the child to keep the supervisor informed of his or her address.

Time limits

There are time limits on the supervision order. Any particular supervision order may not last, initially, for more than a period of one year, but the supervisor can apply to the court to have it extended for up to three years from the date on which the order was first made. The significant harm test need not be satisfied.

Can you replace a supervision order with a care order?

The answer is 'no'. The 'no order without an application' principle means there has to be a fresh application by the local authority. In making any new application the threshold criteria must be satisfied afresh. So in *Re A (Supervision Order: Extension)* (1995), the local authority obtained a 12-month supervision order in respect of an 11-year-old child. Before the expiry of the 12-month period, the local authority applied for an extension of the order. The guardian *ad litem* recommended that a care order be made in place of a supervision order. The Court of Appeal held that on an application for an extension of a supervision order, the court could make only a further supervision order and could not make a care order.

Discharge of a supervision order

This is dealt with in s. 39. We discuss the procedure, which is identical to that of the discharge of a care order earlier in the chapter (**Discharge of care orders**, p 282).

Education supervision orders (s. 36)

If a local education authority (which in most areas is the same authority as the social services department) can satisfy the magistrates' court that a particular child is both of compulsory school age and not being properly educated (s. 36(3)), the court may make an education supervision order. Section 36(4) defines a child as being properly educated only if the child is receiving efficient full-time education suitable to age, ability, and aptitude and any special educational needs that the child may have. An application for an order cannot be made if the child is in the care of the local authority, and the education department must consult with the social services department before the application is made. The order is designed to ensure that children do not go into care merely for school non-attendance.

The effect of an education supervision order

Under Schedule 3, Part III, there are detailed provisions as to the effect of the education supervision order. In essence, the supervisor has to advise, assist, and befriend the child and give directions to the child to ensure that the child is properly educated. **Chapter 3** of volume 7 of *Guidance and Regulations* considers the order in detail.

The directions might include directions for the child and parents to attend meetings to discuss the child's education or for the child to see an educational psychologist. Under the provisions there is the need to consult with the parents and child before the directions are made. If parents persistently fail to comply with directions that are reasonably given they may be fined, on conviction, in the magistrates' court. There is no penalty for the child.

Time limits

The education supervision order lasts for 12 months or until the child is no longer of compulsory school age (whichever is the shorter). It can be extended for up to three years.

Appeals

There is a particular provision for appeals in s. 40. The aim is to allow the court to decide what will happen to a child where an application for an order is dismissed and there is to be an appeal. This is a safety net provision. No application will be made without an investigation by the local authority or authorized person, and it therefore follows that there should have been reasonable grounds for concern. The safety net that is provided gives the court the power to make an order of the type originally sought, pending the hearing of the appeal.

The requirement that needs to be satisfied is that there must have been an interim order made at an earlier stage in the proceedings. This means that at an earlier stage a court believed that there were reasonable grounds for believing that a final order might be made.

The order made pending appeal is not an interim order since the dismissal of the application is an end to the proceedings as far as the lower court is concerned. The length of time that the order will last is strictly limited to the 'appeal period', which means that the order will last only until the hearing of the appeal. There are provisions for the appeal court to extend the period until it is practicable for it to hear the appeal. In *Re O* (1992), the court held that the magistrates had no power to stay (suspend) such an order pending an appeal.

As we have indicated earlier, if you are involved in a case where your application is dismissed, you should immediately seek the advice of your agency lawyer.

A flow chart setting out the key questions for determining the outcomes of an application for a care or supervision order is set out in **Figure 8.3**.

Interim care and supervision orders

Interim care or supervision orders are usually made when the full hearing cannot take place. Section 38(1) of the Children Act, set out in **Box 8.11**, provides the power for the court to make an interim care or supervision order. To make an interim order:

(a) the court must have reasonable grounds for believing there are grounds for the full care order;

(b) the making of the interim order does not mean that there will be a full order; and

(c) the court must act judicially in making an order.

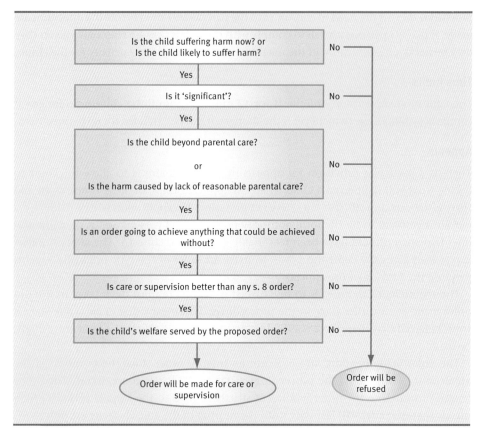

FIGURE 8.3 Getting a care order/supervision order

 BOX 8.11 Interim care or supervision orders—s. 38

(1) Where—
  (a) in any proceedings on an application for a care order or supervision order, the proceedings are adjourned; or
  (b) the court gives a direction under section 37(1),

  the court may make an interim care order or an interim supervision order with respect to the child concerned.

Hearings are not always necessary

This does not mean that there will always have to be a hearing with evidence being given. Inevitably, after the first interim order is made, within the constraints of the timetable provisions listed in the following section, there are occasions on which everybody is agreed that for one reason or another a further interim order will need to be made—the medical report is not available, there is no available court time, etc. In this case, the court could make an interim order without hearing evidence but merely hearing representations from the applicant, as happened in *Devon County Council v S* (1992).

The timetable

Section 38(4) sets out a timetable for the granting of interim care or supervision orders. It is not reproduced verbatim here since it is unnecessarily complex and unclear. What it appears to say is set out in **Box 8.12**.

 BOX 8.12 Timetabling interim care and supervision orders

(a) An initial interim order may not last more than eight weeks;

(b) if the initial interim order has been made for a period of less than eight weeks then any subsequent orders may be made for a period or periods that will not exceed that eight-week period starting on the date on which the initial order was made;

(c) if any interim orders are made after that initial eight-week period, then those further interim orders may not exceed a four-week period, although they may be made for periods less than four weeks; and

(d) any number of interim orders could be made subject to the non-delay principle.

This approach was approved in *Gateshead MBC v N* (1993).

Directions

When making an interim order, the court has the power to give directions as follows (s. 38(6)):

> Where the court makes an interim care order, or interim supervision order, it may give such directions (if any) as it considers appropriate with regard to the medical or psychiatric examination or other assessment of the child; but if the child is of sufficient understanding to make an informed decision he may refuse to submit to the examination or other assessment.

Section 38(7) specifies what directions may be given. This subsection is an exact reproduction of s. 44(8) and (9) relating to emergency protection orders which is discussed later.

Medical examinations

If you are going to have any medical examination, investigation, or any other type of assessment carried out, you must obtain the leave of the court.

Assessments during interim care orders

In *Re C (A Minor) (Interim Care Order: Residential Assessment)* (1996), a four-month-old child was admitted to hospital suffering from non-accidental injuries. The child's parents, aged 16 and 17, were not able to give a satisfactory explanation of the injuries. An emergency protection order was made, and then an interim care order under s. 38 of the Children Act 1989. The social workers decided that an in-depth assessment of the child and the parents together needed to be undertaken as soon as possible at a residential unit. However, their managers refused to agree to, or pay for, the residential assessment and decided to apply for a care order so that the child could be placed in a permanent alternative placement with a view to adoption.

At first instance, the judge held that she had jurisdiction under s. 38(6) to order a residential assessment. Having weighed the cost (estimated at £18,000 to £24,000) against the recommendations from the professionals involved, she decided to exercise her discretion by ordering the local authority to carry out the residential assessment.

The House of Lords held that s. 38(6) and (7) conferred jurisdiction on the court to order or prohibit any assessment which involved the participation of the child, and was to provide the court with the material to enable it to reach a proper decision at the final hearing. In exercising its discretion, the court would have to take into account the cost of the proposed assessment and the fact of local authorities' lack of resources. In this case, their Lordships ordered the assessment. The care plan here indicated that the local authority was going to place the child for adoption. To allow the local authority to decide what evidence was to go before the court at the final hearing would allow the local authority by administrative decision to pre-empt the court's judicial decision. However, not all parents can expect a residential assessment as a right. In *Re S* [2011] EWCA Civ 812, Black LJ rejected the submission that:

> parents should be given every reasonable opportunity of presenting a positive case … There is no right for a parent facing permanent removal of a child to have the assessment of their choice; rather, the relevant question is always whether the assessment in question would assist the judge in reaching the right conclusion at a final hearing.

Reducing delay

The final provision relating to interim orders is s. 38(10):

> Where a court makes an order under or by virtue of this section [an interim order] it shall, in determining the period for which the order is to be in force, consider whether any party who was, or might have been, opposed to the making of an order was in a position to argue his case against the order in full.

This is designed to cope with a situation where a parent has not had the opportunity to instruct lawyers to act on their behalf at the time of the interim hearing. The court should then consider making an interim order for just sufficient time to enable a lawyer to be properly instructed. This is another reflection of the Act's aim to try to reduce the delays that can be present in such cases. Section 14 of the Children and Families Act 2014 amends s. 32(1) of the Act to impose a strict timetable for care proceedings that they should be concluded in 26 weeks. In addition, s. 13 of the Children and Families Act lays out the conditions on which expert evidence can be submitted to the court. Subsection (7) says that in deciding whether permission should be granted for expert evidence the court shall consider:

(a) any impact which giving permission would be likely to have on the welfare of the children concerned, including in the case of permission as mentioned in subsection (3) any impact which any examination or other assessment would be likely to have on the welfare of the child who would be examined or otherwise assessed,

(b) the issues to which the expert evidence would relate,

(c) the questions which the court would require the expert to answer,

(d) what other expert evidence is available (whether obtained before or after the start of proceedings),

(e) whether evidence could be given by another person on the matters on which the expert would give evidence,

(f) the impact which giving permission would be likely to have on the timetable for, and duration and conduct of, the proceedings,

(g) the cost of the expert evidence, and

(h) any matters prescribed by Family Procedure Rules.

The Family Justice Review was concerned about the growth in the use of experts in care proceedings and the effect this was having on the duration of those proceedings. Reducing delay is important but so too is the need for the consideration of cases to be carried out justly. These matters were explored in a recent case in which the President of the Family Division was giving the judgment. Sir James Munby said in *Re S (A Child)* [2014] EWHC B44 (Fam):

> Section 32(1)(a)(ii) does not describe some mere aspiration or target, nor does it prescribe an average. It defines … a mandatory limit which applies to all cases. It follows that there will be many cases that can, and therefore should, be concluded well within the 26 week limit. I repeat what I said in my first 'View from the President's Chambers: The process of reform', [2013] Fam Law 548: 'My message is clear and uncompromising: this deadline can be met, it must be met, it will be met. And remember, 26 weeks is a deadline, not a target; it is a maximum, not an average or a mean. So many cases will need to be finished in less than 26 weeks.'

This requirement places an onerous duty on case management judges particularly in respect of the directions they give for expert evidence. The President, however, in *Re B-S* [2013] EWCA Civ 1146 (which is also considered in **chapter 9**), indicated that:

> If, despite all, the court does not have the kind of evidence we have identified, and is therefore not properly equipped to decide these issues, then an adjournment must be directed, even if this takes the case over 26 weeks. Where the proposal before the court is for non-consensual adoption, the issues are too grave, the stakes for all are too high, for the outcome to be determined by rigorous adherence to an inflexible timetable and justice thereby potentially denied.

Power to exclude alleged abuser while the interim order is in force

The Family Law Act 1996 amended the Children Act to include a new s. 38A—a power in interim care orders to require an alleged abuser to leave the house in which the child is living. The court would have to be satisfied of the following:

(a) that there is reasonable cause to believe that if a person is excluded from a dwelling house in which the child lives, the child will cease to suffer or cease to be likely to suffer significant harm; and

(b) another person living in the same house, whether or not a parent, is able and willing to give to the child the care which it would be reasonable to expect a parent to give; and

(c) that person consents to the inclusion of the exclusion requirement.

There are also powers of arrest available, subject to certain requirements. The difficulty with this power is that it does require the consent of the person who is to care for the child. This would normally be the mother. In the absence of her consent, it is not possible to compel the alleged abuser to leave. While this power is a welcome addition to the interim order, the requirement of consent may mean that it is not used as much as could be expected. There is an identical power in relation to the emergency protection order which we discuss later.

A fail-safe provision

Section 38(3) requires that the court makes an interim supervision order when making a residence order in certain circumstances. We set out s. 38(3) in **Box 8.13**.

BOX 8.13 Section 38(3)

Where, in any proceedings on an application for a care order or supervision order, a court makes a residence order with respect to the child concerned, it shall also make an interim supervision order with respect to him unless satisfied that his welfare will be satisfactorily safeguarded without an interim order being made.

The court would need to be satisfied that the access was being unreasonably refused by the parent. The local authority would have to show that access was required as a matter of urgency. An application on these grounds may be simpler to obtain than one where you have to satisfy the court that the child is actually suffering significant harm.

This section covers the situation where the court, instead of making an interim care order, decides to make a s. 8 residence order, say to a grandparent. As a 'fail safe', the court is required to make an interim supervision order. An example of this in practice is *C v Solihull MBC* (1993), which we discussed in **chapter 5**. It needs to be stressed again that the making of any particular interim order does not mean that type of order will be made as a final order.

Short-term orders to protect children

We will now discuss the orders and the police power set out in Part V of the Act. These provisions are all short term. The most important of these is the emergency protection order.

The emergency protection order—a summary

An emergency protection order is a short-term order that either:

(a) removes the child on a short-term basis; or

(b) allows the child to be kept in a place of safety (eg a hospital); or

(c) requires the alleged abuser to leave the family home (see **Power to exclude alleged abuser**, p 295).

An emergency protection order is not an end in itself. It is a critical step in the local authority's investigation under s. 47 which will lead to the local authority either being satisfied about the child's welfare or to care proceedings.

Emergency protection orders are provided for within s. 44 of the Children Act. Section 44(1) is set out in **Box 8.14**.

BOX 8.14 The emergency protection of children—s. 44(1)

(1) Where any person ('the applicant') applies to the court for an order to be made under this section with respect to a child, the court may make the order if, but only if it is satisfied that—

  (a) there is reasonable cause to believe that the child is likely to suffer significant harm if

    (i) he is not removed to accommodation provided by or on behalf of the applicant; or

    (ii) he does not remain in the place in which he is then being accommodated;

  (b) in the case of an application made by a local authority—

    (i) enquiries are being made with respect to the child under section 47(1)(b); and

    (ii) those enquires are being frustrated by access to the child being unreasonably refused to a person authorized to seek access and that the applicant has reasonable cause to believe that access to the child is required as a matter of urgency; or

  (c) in the case of an application made by an authorized person—

    (i) the applicant has reasonable cause to suspect that a child is suffering or is likely to suffer, significant harm;

    (ii) the applicant is making enquires with respect to the child's welfare; and

    (iii) those enquires are being frustrated by access to the child being unreasonably refused to a person authorized to seek access and the applicant has reasonable cause to believe that access to the child is required as a matter of urgency.

The key features of an emergency protection order

Duration

The emergency protection order may be granted for a period of up to an initial eight days, extendable, once only, for a period of up to a further seven days—s. 45. These are the maximum periods allowed. It may well be that the court will decide that the order should last for a shorter period.

The different forms of emergency protection order

There are two forms the applications can take:

The 'any person basis' under s. 44(1)(a)

The 'any person' includes a social worker. The court, on the application of any person, may grant an order if a version of the significant harm test is satisfied. Where any person applies for it, the court may grant an emergency protection order only if the court is satisfied that there is reasonable cause to believe that the child is likely to suffer significant harm unless removed to accommodation provided by the applicant or unless allowed to remain in present accommodation.

'Likely to suffer significant harm'

This application is designed to cover situations where, for instance, a social worker is notified of a child with severe injuries and believes that the child should be removed from home for the protection of the child. The ground is that the child is likely to suffer significant harm. There will have to be evidence that there is a possibility that the harm which has already been inflicted will be repeated—so a 'one-off' incident cannot be a ground for granting an emergency protection order under this subsection.

Alternatively, the 'any person' emergency protection order envisages the situation where a child has been admitted to hospital and the parents are threatening to remove the child, and the court believes the removal would be likely to cause the child significant harm. It would also be possible to make an application where a child is being looked after by a local authority in accommodation and the parents are again threatening to remove the child.

The obstruction of investigation basis under s. 44(1)(b)

Here, if the investigations of a local authority or the NSPCC are obstructed then the court may grant an emergency protection order without being satisfied on the significant harm test—but, like the child assessment order (see **Child assessment orders**, p 303), the applicant has to be satisfied there is a risk of significant harm.

Part of continuing investigation

An application under s. 44(1)(b) is to be made by the local authority only as part of a continuing investigation under s. 47 of the Children Act. That is the investigation the authority or NSPCC has to carry out when it has reasonable cause to suspect that a child is suffering or is likely to suffer significant harm.

Parents

An order may be granted in the absence of the parents (ie without notice of the hearing), but as with the child assessment order there are provisions for the parents to seek to have the order discharged under s. 45(8). At that stage it would be possible for the parents to state that access will be granted and, if the statement is believed by the court, for the basis of the local authority application to be totally undermined.

Common elements between these different forms of emergency protection orders

Even though the court may be satisfied that the grounds for an emergency protection order exist, it still need not grant one, for it has to apply the 'welfare' principle and the 'non-intervention' principle which are contained in s. 1 of the Children Act. This means that it has to be satisfied that the order is in the best interests of the child and necessary for its protection. It does not have to consider the welfare checklist in s. 1.

Safeguards

The various safeguards point to the need for the social worker to be adequately prepared before seeking an emergency protection order. Adequate preparation means that you will need to have answers ready for all the points that the court requires: the grounds (harm or obstruction of your investigation), the welfare of the child, and the need to intervene.

The operation of an emergency protection order

An emergency protection order does not give the applicant unfettered powers. **Box 8.15** sets out the relevant subsections of s. 44. Not to produce the child—showing the child to you—is a criminal offence (s. 44(15)). If you have such an order and ask for the child to be produced and he or she is not produced, you must draw the person's attention to the explanatory notes attached to the order and warn them that failure so to do will render them liable to criminal proceedings. If the child is produced then you may take him or her to, and/or keep him or her in, accommodation.

BOX 8.15 The operation of an emergency protection order—s. 44

(4) While an order under this section ('an emergency protection order') is in force it—
  (a) operates as a direction to any person who is in a position to do so to comply with any request to produce the child to the applicant;
  (b) authorizes—
    (i) the removal of the child at any time to accommodation provided by or on behalf of the applicant and his being kept there; or
    (ii) the prevention of the child's removal from any hospital or other place in which he was being accommodated immediately before the making of this order; and
  (c) gives the applicant parental responsibility for the child.

(5) Where an emergency protection order is in force with respect to a child the applicants—
  (a) shall only exercise the power given by virtue of subsection (4)(b) in order to safeguard the welfare of the child;
  (b) shall take, and shall only take, such action in meeting his parental responsibility for the child as is reasonably required to safeguard or promise the welfare of the child (having regard in particular to the duration of the order); and
  (c) shall comply with the requirements of any regulation made by the Secretary of State for the purpose of this subsection.

Power to exclude alleged abuser

The Family Law Act 1996 amended the Children Act to include s. 44A—which provides a power in an emergency protection order to require an alleged abuser to leave the house in which the child is living. There are also powers of arrest available, subject to certain requirements. **Box 8.16** sets out what needs to be demonstrated to the court.

BOX 8.16 Factors necessary for an exclusion requirement

(a) That there is reasonable cause to believe that if a person is excluded from a dwelling house in which the child lives, the child will cease to suffer or cease to be likely to suffer significant harm; and

(b) another person living in the same house, whether or not a parent, is able and willing to give to the child the care which it would be reasonable to expect a parent to give;

(c) that person consents to the inclusion of the exclusion requirement;

(d) the contact which is, or is not, to be allowed between the child and any named person;

(e) the medical or psychiatric examination or other assessment of the child.

The question of medical examinations is further dealt with in s. 44(7) and (8), which provide:

(a) that a child may give informed consent to any medical examination;

(b) that the court may order that there should be no medical or psychiatric examination, or that such an examination shall take place only if further permission is obtained from the court.

Consent

The difficulty with the exclusion power is that it requires the consent of the person who is to care for the child. This is normally the mother. In the absence of her consent it is not possible to compel the alleged abuser to leave. Note that an identical power to exclude an alleged abuser exists in relation to interim care orders (see **Power to exclude alleged abuser while the interim order is in force**, p 291).

Guidance on the exclusion requirement

In *Re W (Exclusion: Statement of Evidence)* (2000), the judge set out guidance on the relevant procedure. While it is not necessary for the local authority to make a specific application, there does need to be a separate statement of evidence supporting the case for an exclusion requirement. The consent can be given orally in court or in writing. If it is in writing, it should clearly state that the person giving consent understands the provision.

Limited power of removal under an emergency protection order

The power to remove the child is to be used only when necessary to safeguard the welfare of the child. This means that if you have obtained an order and then go to the house and find the child is safe, you are not permitted to remove the child.

It is easy to imagine an extreme case where this might be applied: you receive an anonymous telephone call stating that it sounds as if a child is being beaten in a certain house. You go to the house, knock on the door, get no answer but hear the sounds of a child sobbing and screaming. You knock next door and are told that there is a child in the house and that 'they are an odd lot'. You go to court and are granted an emergency protection order under s. 44(1)(b) (on the ground that you are investigating and your investigation is being obstructed). You go to the house with the emergency protection order, a surprised parent opens the door holding a cheerful, smiling toddler with no visible signs of injury. The parent readily agrees to you examining the child undressed and there are no signs of injury. When asked about the noise of crying, the parent says that they were listening to a play on the radio, about a child-beating case, which may explain the sounds, and they had the radio up very loud and therefore your knocks were not heard. Clearly s. 44(5)(a) applies and you would have no grounds for the removal of the child, despite holding the emergency protection order.

Assistance of other professionals

Most cases are not like this and the particular subsection may prove challenging. The only sensible advice is to err on the side of caution and not be afraid to remove the child if in doubt. To assist you in making the decision as to whether removal is necessary, you may want to have the assistance of some other professional person when you go to the house. In these circumstances, you may ask the court to make a direction under s. 45(12), which states that the court may direct that the applicant may be accompanied by a doctor, nurse, or health visitor, if the applicant so chooses.

Parental responsibility under an emergency protection order

The local authority, or whoever was the applicant, will also gain parental responsibility, but this does not mean that the parent of the child loses parental responsibility. The exercise of parental responsibility under an emergency protection order in accordance with s. 44(5) means that only steps that are reasonably required during the order (which will be eight, or at the very most 15, days) may be taken by the person with temporary parental responsibility. This does not mean that a child may, for instance, have their school permanently changed; only temporary educational provision can be made. It does not mean that a child may be allowed to undergo a cosmetic surgery operation, but it would allow for an emergency operation.

Contact

There is a general presumption that the parent will have reasonable contact with the child whilst an emergency protection order is in force, unless a direction under s. 44(6) is made.

Medical examinations

Medical examinations are allowed only for purposes that promote or safeguard the welfare of the child. This means that any examinations required for the purpose of preparing your case prior to applying for a care order would not be permitted unless you have the additional power contained in s. 44(6).

This subsection sets out the directions that the court can make at the time of granting the order. The court may decline to make any directions under this subsection.

The need for directions

If you are seeking an emergency protection order and you or your agency feel that there may be the need for some form of medical examination, then you should, at the time of the application, seek a direction from the court. If it is not sought at the time of the initial application and it is decided that such an examination ought to be carried out then a direction should be sought under the provisions of s. 44(9).

Religious objections to treatment

The position of children of Jehovah's Witnesses and parents with similar religious objections to treatment needs particular mention. The use of emergency protection orders would not provide the degree of parental responsibility to override the parents' objections to treatment. In *Re R (A Minor) (Blood Transfusion)* (1993), Booth J stated that the use of an emergency protection order in such cases was not appropriate. Either the inherent jurisdiction of the High Court should be used, or the local authority should apply under s. 8 to a High Court judge.

Variation

Section 44(9) deals with applications to vary—change—the order whilst it is still in force. If directions have been made about contact with parents or other people, or medical examinations, then an application can be made to alter these.

Limits on the emergency protection order

Returning the child before the emergency protection order expires

The Act contains various provisions to mitigate the disruption caused to the child and family. Section 44(10) requires that although an emergency protection order may have been granted, the child should be kept away from 'home' only as long as necessary, and if it is safe the child should be returned 'home'. These provisions are set out in **Box 8.17**.

 BOX 8.17 Section 44(10)

Where an emergency protection order is in force with respect to a child and—

(a) the applicant has exercised the power given by subsection (4)(b)(i) [removed a child] but it appears to him that it is safe for the child to be returned; or

(b) the applicant has exercised the power given by subsection (4)(b)(ii) [prevented the child from being removed from accommodation] but it appears to him safe for the child to be allowed to be removed from the place in question, he shall return the child or (as the case may be) allow him to be removed.

In the case of a child needing an emergency operation, once the operation has taken place then the child should be 'returned' (albeit that the child may stay in hospital). The duty to return in s. 44(11) is an important example of the necessary checks and balances built into the legislation. The state has a power to intervene in children's lives where it is necessary to protect them, but that power must not be excessive. You can return the child to a different person—not the parent or the person caring for the child at the time of the emergency protection order—only with the court's permission (s. 48(11)).

The emergency protection order continues

The return of a child under this subsection does not bring the emergency protection order to an end. Section 44(12) states that if, having returned the child at any time whilst the order is still in force, it appears to the applicant that the child should again be removed, then that can be done. This is without the need for a fresh application. So suppose the parent of the child who had the emergency operation tried to remove the child against medical advice, the current emergency protection order would give the power to stop this.

Applications to discharge an emergency protection order

The next 'check' on the emergency protection order is the right of the parent to challenge the order—s. 45. There was a limit on this power set out in s. 9—it was not available for the first 72 hours of an emergency protection order. However, this restriction has been repealed by the Children and Young Persons Act 2008 following a decision of the Northern Ireland High Court in 2007 that such a restriction was contrary to Article 8 and Article 6 of the European Convention. Courts can now hear applications for discharge from the time that the emergency protection order is made.

The discharge provisions are not available for a parent who was present at the hearing of the application for the emergency protection order (ie was given the chance to put their side of the case to the court). Similarly, there is no right to have an order discharged after that order has been extended. This is because the relevant court rules require that an extension application take place only after notice has been given to all parties. So, again, the parents will have had their chance to put their side of the case. The application to discharge the order can be made by the child (through his or her guardian) or the child's parents.

No appeals

The Act allows for any particular emergency protection order only to be discharged, not to be appealed against.

Section 45(10) provides:

> No appeal may be made against the making of, or refusal to make, an emergency protection order or against any direction given by the court in connection with such an order.

This point was clearly made in *Hounslow LBC v A* (1993) and *Re P (Emergency Protection Order)* (1996).

This would not exclude an application for judicial review if the circumstances were appropriate. However, the case study at the beginning of this chapter indicates that the basis for an application for judicial review is very limited. There is a need to ensure that the expertise of the Family Proceedings Court is appropriately applied. If the emergency protection order was made by the High Court, there can be no judicial review of that decision.

Additional powers to protect children

Disclosure of information

Section 48 of the Children Act 1989 gives additional powers. For instance, you may not know the whereabouts of the child in need of emergency protection. The court may include a provision in the emergency protection order requiring a person who may have information about the child's whereabouts to disclose that information (s. 48(1)). The order may also authorize an applicant to enter premises and search for the child, although this section in any event requires that the parents or whoever is in control of the premises cooperate. If you are prevented from entering premises or gaining access to the child, or it appears to the court that you may be, the court can issue a warrant authorizing the police to assist the entry and search.

Other children

You may believe that there are other children on the premises who also ought to be the subject of an emergency protection order. If so, you may seek an order authorizing a search for them. If the child (or children) is found and you are satisfied that the grounds for an emergency protection order exist, the order authorizing the search has effect as if it were an emergency protection order. This is useful when you are not able to identify all the children in the family, or, for instance, where there is evidence of the existence of a paedophile ring but the number and identities of the children involved are unknown.

Recovery orders

Lastly, the Act gives you powers through the mechanism of recovery orders (s. 50) in respect of a child in care, or the subject of an emergency protection order, or in police protection, where the child has unlawfully been taken away, has run away, or is staying away from the 'responsible person'. A responsible person is anyone who has the care of the child by virtue of a care order or an emergency protection order. The order operates as a direction to produce the child, or to disclose his or her whereabouts, and authorizes the police to enter named premises and search for the child, using reasonable force if necessary.

Practical considerations for emergency protection orders

Record keeping

Meticulous records must be kept by the social worker involved so that there is evidence of the investigation, which is one branch of the grounds for an emergency protection order, together with the details of any obstruction by the parents.

Before taking action

Always stop to think clearly about why you want an emergency protection order and what you are going to do with it. Always try and consult with a colleague, even if your particular management guidelines allow you to take such steps without consultation.

Refusal of an emergency protection order

If an emergency protection order is refused then, in principle, there does not appear to be any bar to making another application. This is particularly true if further information becomes available concerning the likelihood of potential harm to the child.

Identification

Under s. 44(3) of the Children Act a person seeking access to a child for an investigation must produce some duly authenticated document stating that they are authorized to seek access. All local authority social workers are such authorized persons. Failure by you to produce such proof, if asked for, is just the sort of point that a lawyer acting for a parent would love to have as an opening question in cross-examination. The mere failure to have identification does not on its own prevent you obtaining the order, but it makes you look less professional to the court. In addition, the explanatory notes that are part of the statutory form of the emergency protection order have a box telling the parent to ask anyone who tries to carry out the order for evidence of their identity.

Out-of-hours applications

The magistrates' courts' rules allow a single justice (magistrate) to hear an application for an emergency protection order. If the hearing is to be made without notice, leave of the clerk to the justices has to be obtained.

Time limits

There is a long list of tasks for the social worker to complete in the short period of time that the emergency protection order lasts. Fifteen, let alone eight, days is a very short period of time, especially when lawyers and courts are involved. Given the chance for parties to seek a discharge of the order and to seek contact with the child, the entire time between the granting and expiration of the order could be occupied with court hearings instead of carrying out the intended assessment.

To set this in some context, we reproduce in **Box 8.18** a list of possible tasks following an emergency protection order. (This, slightly modified, is taken from J. Bridge, S. Bridge, and S. Luke, *Blackstone's Guide to the Children Act 1989* (Blackstone Press, 1990).)

 BOX 8.18 Tasks that may be necessary during the emergency protection order

(a) Arrange for accommodation for the child.

(b) Place the child with foster parents or in an institution, and explain to the child what is happening and give sufficient information to those who will be caring for the child to do so appropriately.

(c) Explain to the parents why their child has been removed from them, and discuss concerns and allegations with them.

(d) Spend further time with the child, to be satisfied that the child's welfare is being met, and also ask the child about any concerns or allegations.

(e) Take the child for medical examination and/or treatment, and obtain the doctor's diagnosis, having obtained leave of the court, if required.

(f) Make decisions about who the child should be allowed to have contact with (from those listed in s. 47(11)).

(g) Arrange for such contact to take place.

(h) Instruct the authority's solicitor in time for extension hearings. Consider making application for directions governing contact or medical examination. Instruct the local authority solicitor to commence appropriate proceedings, and provide sufficient information for the solicitor to do so.

(i) Discuss the case with a children's guardian if one has been appointed.

(j) Convene a child protection conference, ensuring a sufficient number of those involved with the family attend.

(k) Keep under review whether it is safe to return the child home.

(l) Decide, with senior social work staff, whether action needs to be taken to promote or safeguard the child's welfare.

(m) Attend court in respect of an application for an interim care order.

Summary of the key features of the emergency protection order

In **Box 8.19**, we provide a summary of the key features of the emergency protection order.

BOX 8.19 Key features of the emergency protection order

Feature	Provision	Section	Note
Grounds	Child likely to suffer significant harm or cannot be seen where child is at risk of suffering significant harm	s. 44(1)	See the full discussion of significant harm earlier in this chapter
	Must apply the welfare principle and the non-intervention principle but not the welfare checklist		
Duration	8 days—possible extension for additional 7 days	s. 45(3), (5)	Could be for a shorter period
Application	Any person can apply	This includes the police	
Discharge	Certain persons may be able to apply for discharge of the emergency protection order	s. 45(8), (9)	Cannot apply during extension of emergency protection order

Feature	Provision	Section	Note
Parental responsibility	Grants very limited parental responsibility to the local authority. The parent of the child does not lose parental responsibility	s. 44(4)	This is a critical check on the scope of the emergency protection order
Directions	Court has the power to order contact, medical, and/or psychiatric reports, assessment, etc	s. 44(6)	The child's informed consent is required

Child assessment orders

Section 43 of the Children Act allows the local authority to obtain a child assessment order. This provides for the compulsory assessment of the child's state of health and development, by removing the child from the home if necessary. **Box 8.20** sets out the relevant provisions of s. 43.

BOX 8.20 The child assessment order—s. 43

(1) On the application of a local authority ... for an order under this section, the court may make the order if, but only if, it is satisfied that—
   (a) the applicant has reasonable cause to suspect that the child is suffering, or is likely to suffer, significant harm;
   (b) an assessment of the state of the child's health or development or of the way in which he has been treated, is required to enable the applicant to determine whether or not the child is suffering, or is likely to suffer, significant harm; and
   (c) it is unlikely that such an assessment will be made, or be satisfactory, in the absence of an order under this section.

(2) ...

(3) A court may treat an application under this section as an application for an emergency protection order.

(4) No court shall make a child assessment order if it is satisfied—
   (a) that there are grounds for making an emergency protection order with respect to the child; and
   (b) that it ought to make such an order rather than a child assessment order.

The necessity of the order

To obtain an order you need to show to the court not that, objectively speaking, the child is at risk, but that you have reasonable cause to believe the child is at risk. Then you must show that an assessment of health and development is required actually to find out whether the child is suffering or is likely to suffer significant harm. Having satisfied the court of this, you then have to show that you could not make a satisfactory assessment without the order.

Is an emergency protection order more appropriate?

Whenever there is a child at risk, the question whether or not the child would be safe if left in his or her home will be uppermost in most people's minds. That is why this section states that the court shall not make a child assessment order if it thinks that the child should be removed from the home. This would be done by means of an emergency protection order. If there are no grounds for making an emergency protection order then the court may grant the application for the child assessment order. This 'fail safe' measure may explain why the courts are reluctant to grant a child assessment order, preferring to grant an emergency protection order.

Planning for an assessment

Just as the child assessment order is not intended to be dealt with on a 'without notice' basis, neither does the assessment have to begin on the day the order is made. Section 43(5) specifies that the date on which the order may begin can be set by the court. This enables a plan for an assessment to be made, in advance, to begin at some future date.

Speed

The order may last for only seven days. It is difficult to make an adequate form of assessment within that timescale. Clearly, all that the assessment in a child assessment order is capable of achieving is to show whether other court orders should or should not be applied for.

If an order is granted then its purpose will be to allow this limited type of assessment to be carried out. To this end, the order may include directions for the child to be produced for medical or psychiatric examination. Such examinations are subject to the informed consent of the child.

Removal for assessment only

The order does allow the child to be compulsorily removed from the home, but only for the purposes of the assessment, and, if that occurs, there are provisions for reasonable contact by the child with parents or other persons. These are contained in s. 43(9) and (10) which is set out in **Box 8.21**.

 BOX 8.21 Limited removal from home under the child assessment order—s. 43(9) and (10)

(9) The child may only be kept away from home—

    (a) in accordance with directions specified in the order;

    (b) if it is necessary for the purposes of assessment; and

    (c) for such period as may be specified in the order.

(10) Where the child is to be kept away from home, the order shall contain such directions as the court thinks fit with regard to the contact that he must be allowed to have with other persons while away from home.

Therefore, the child may be removed only if the court order says so. This would be where it was necessary for the child to attend for a short residential assessment. The order is not designed to protect the child by removal from the home—that is the function of the emergency protection order.

Parents must know of the application

An application for a child assessment order cannot be made on a 'without notice' basis. It must be made when the parents have been told of the hearing and have the chance to be represented there.

Variation and discharge of a child assessment order

It may be that the order having been made, the arrangements for the assessment cannot be carried out on the set date. The court can vary or even discharge the order if required.

Removal by the police to accommodation

Police powers

The police are given powers under s. 46 of the Children Act to take children into police protection. The powers apply to children whom the police find and contain no provisions enabling the police to search for a child. They can be used for runaways or for abandoned children, or where the police come across children with drunk parents or living in unhygienic conditions.

A Home Office Circular, *The Duties and Powers of the police under the Children Act 1989* (Home Office Circular 017/2008), provides guidance to the police about when and how they should use police protection powers under the Children Act 1989.

No court order necessary

The police are not equipped to deal with children at risk, and therefore the police are required to arrange to place the children in suitable accommodation. They also have the power to ensure that a child remains in suitable accommodation such as a hospital (s. 46(1)(a) and (b)). Neither of these powers (to remove a child or to keep a child in a safe place) requires a court order. The police therefore have powers which a social worker does not.

Duties to notify

As soon as the police have taken a child into their protection they have to notify the relevant local authority, notify the child, if appropriate, of what steps are to be taken, take steps to discover the wishes of the child concerned, move the child to suitable accommodation, and inform the designated officer of the fact that a child has been taken into police protection (s. 46(3)).

The 'designated officer' within the police is the liaison point between the local authority and the police in these cases, and every social worker should be aware of who this person is—every police force is required to appoint one.

The police also have to inform the child's parent of the fact that the child has been taken into police custody. The police do not obtain parental responsibility for the child by taking the child into police custody but must do what is reasonable to safeguard or promote the child's welfare (s. 46(9)).

The relationship with emergency protection orders

If the police think that an emergency protection order should be sought then they have to apply for it. They can do this whether or not the local authority is aware of the application or, more importantly, whether or not the local authority agrees with the making of such an application (s. 46(7) and (8)). If a child is in police protection that triggers the duty for a local authority to carry out an investigation under s. 47.

Time limits and contact

No child may be kept in police protection for more than 72 hours, and during that time the police must allow both the child's parent and anybody having a contact order under s. 8 to have reasonable contact with the child (s. 46(10)).

However, if the child in police protection has been placed in local authority accommodation then it is for the local authority to arrange contact (s. 46(11)). Therefore, for the best of reasons, whenever the police take a child into their protection, they will wish to accommodate the child with the local authority as soon as possible. Either the police or, more probably, the local authority can apply for an emergency protection order if appropriate.

The relationship between the police and social services

The question whether the social worker should use their own powers under the Act or turn to the police will be a decision that will greatly depend on the circumstances of the particular case and the extent and nature of the cooperation and liaison between the local police and the social services department.

In an extreme case, if you believe that a child is in serious physical danger, you can ask a police officer to exercise their powers under s. 17 of the Police and Criminal Evidence Act 1984 to enter any premises and to search for and remove the child. No court order is required. The police may also arrest without warrant any person who has committed any offence where the arrest is necessary to protect a child from that person (Police and Criminal Evidence Act 1984, s. 25). The police also have powers under the Crime and Disorder Act 1998 to remove truants either to home, or to a place of safety.

EXERCISES

1 What needs to be done by the local authority prior to making an application to court? What is the value of this pre-proceedings work?

2 Work through the various court orders in this chapter and produce a grid of their main features, such as duration, directions, discharge, etc.

3 In the following scenarios, consider what order you may be seeking and why:

   (a) Jon has been found wandering in the street by the police. He is bruised and crying. He is about 3 years old.

   (b) Tim is 11 years old. The headteacher of his school has contacted you with the following informa-tion. He is underweight and dressed in cast-off clothes. He is the youngest child of a family of seven. He has been absent from school on numerous occasions during the last year. When you consult your records you find that two of the older children in the family have had short periods subject to a care order. There is a note on the file suggesting that Tim's mother finds it difficult to cope. You have talked to Tim, who seems depressed and tells you he is unhappy at home.

   (c) Lizzie has serious drug-addiction problems. She has tried to stop her drug abuse but fre-quently relapses. Her children, who are aged 5 and 9, are neglected. You suspect that in the long term the children would progress better with a foster placement.

4 Sarah is the subject of an emergency protection order. What are your responsibilities to Sarah and her parents during the period of the order?

5 Paula's child, Ian, is subject to a care order and has been placed with a foster family for the last six years. Ian has told Paula that he is unhappy in his placement. Paula would like to apply for the discharge of the care order. How does she go about this?

ONLINE RESOURCE CENTRE

For guidance on how to answer these exercises, visit Online Resource Centre at:
www.oxfordtextbooks.co.uk/orc/socialwork13e/.

WHERE DO WE GO FROM HERE?

This chapter has explained the range of court orders for which your department may apply to pro-tect children. These orders must not be seen separately from the need to plan appropriately for children which we discussed in **chapter 6**. One way of planning for children is to consider their needs for permanence. **Chapter 9**, on adoption and special guardianship, sets out the legal frame-work for finding children new families on a permanent basis.

ANNOTATED FURTHER READING

Further guidance on the range of orders is provided by specialized texts, such as R. White (ed), *Clarke Hall and Morrison on Children* (Butterworths, 2000). This loose-leaf encyclopaedia is authoritative and up to date.

The Family Justice Review

K. Holt and N. Kelly, 'Rhetoric and reality surrounding care proceedings: family justice under strain' (2012) *Journal of Social Welfare and Family Law* 34(3): 155. This article explores the issues surrounding the boundary of decision making between the courts and the local authority following the publication of the Family Justice Review.

The work of the courts

C. Mullins, 'At work with the principal family judges' [2003] *Law Society's Gazette* 28.

J. Masson, 'Fair trials in children protection' (2006) *Journal of Social Welfare and Family Law* 28(1): 15.

Threshold criteria

There has been a wave of commentary on the *Re B* case which you will find helpful.

T. Booth, W. Booth, and D. McConnell, 'Parents with hearing difficulties, care proceedings & the family courts: threshold decisions and the moral matrix' (2004) *CFLQ* 16(4): 409. This article investigates how social sciences and the courts handle child protection cases involving parents with learning difficulties, and explores the factors that are weighed in the balance when decisions are made in the best interests of the children from such families.

Similar commentary has emerged in the *A (Children) v A* (2009) Court of Appeal case which appears at the beginning of this chapter and makes for interesting reading.

H. Keating, '*Re MA*: the significance of harm' (2011) *CFLQ* 23(1): 115.

Police protection

J. Masson, 'Police protection—protecting whom?' (2002) *Journal of Social Welfare and Family Law* 24(3): 72. An overview and critique of the use of police protection under s. 46 of the Children Act 1989.

Historical overview

J. Masson, 'From Curtis to Waterhouse: state care and child protection in the UK 1945–2000' in S. Katz, J. Eekelaar, and M. Macken(eds), *Cross-Currents: Family Law and Policy in the United States and England* (Oxford University Press, 2000).

J. Eekelaar, 'Then and now—family law's direction of travel' (2013) *Journal of Social Welfare and Family Law* 35(4): 415. This article explores similarities and differences between cases from the 1960s and those of the present day to examine the direction of travel in family law.

Long-term planning for children

9

OVERVIEW AND OBJECTIVES

By the end of this chapter you should be familiar with the legal framework for domestic adoption discussed in this case and set out in the Adoption and Children Act 2002. You will also learn about the alternative to adoption—special guardianship. The chapter, however, starts by considering the responsibilities upon children's social care to start planning for the long-term future of children who become their responsibility from the time that any emergency problems are resolved. Long-term planning emerges from the investigative and immediate planning responsibilities that we considered in **chapter 8**.

CASE STUDY

F (A Child) (Placement Order) (2008), Court of Appeal

The father (F) of a daughter (J) appealed against a decision of the judge that the court had no jurisdiction to grant him leave to make an application to revoke a placement order made in respect of
his daughter. F had had a casual relationship with J's mother, and had not initially been aware that
he was J's father. DNA tests later established F's paternity after J had been placed in the care of the
first respondent local authority. F subsequently learned that plans for J's adoption were well advanced. In fact, J had already been matched for placement. F sought information as to J's progress
towards adoption and the authority informed him that she had not been placed but had been to a
matching panel the previous day. F filed an application under s. 24 of the Adoption and Children
Act 2002 for leave to revoke the placement order. Due to staff shortages, the County Court did not
process F's application for nearly two weeks, when notices of a hearing were sent to the parties. In
the meantime, however, and despite F's emerging challenge, the local authority's decision-maker
ratified the matching panel's decision. At the hearing, the local authority submitted that the terms
of s. 24(2)(b) of the Act removed the court's jurisdiction to grant F leave to make the application
as J had already been placed for adoption. The judge upheld that submission. F contended that
it was open to the court, in reliance on s. 3 of the Human Rights Act 1998 in giving effect to his
rights both to a fair hearing and to family life under the European Convention on Human Rights
to interpret s. 24(5) of the Act so that the words 'an application for the revocation of a placement
order has been made' could include the application for leave to make the application.

The Court of Appeal dismissed F's application. The words of s. 24 of the Adoption and
Children Act 2002 were clear, unambiguous, and capable of only one meaning. The words 'an
application for the revocation of a placement order' in s. 24(5)(a) meant just that: they did not
mean and could not be read as also meaning 'an application for leave to apply for the revocation of a placement order'. Further, s. 24 of the 2002 Act, properly applied and implemented,
was compliant with the 1998 Act and the Convention. The fact that the 2002 Act had permitted
the travesty of good practice which had occurred in the instant case was not a reason for declaring it incompatible with F's human rights or for construing s. 24(5) as F had contended.
There was also a need for good practice to supplement the 2002 Act. The conduct of the local
authority in the instant case had been disgraceful and was an example of the worst kind of
sharp practice. Good practice demanded that what should have happened in the instant case
was, first, that F should have invited the local authority to give an undertaking not to take any
steps to place J with prospective adopters pending the hearing of his s. 24 application. Next,
the local authority should have explained that its plans were at an advanced stage and about
to be implemented. It could then itself have applied to the court, on short notice, for leave to
place J for adoption under s. 24(5). Either way, there would have been a hearing on the merits.
Local authorities and adoption agencies had to understand that it was the court which was in
control and which had been given the responsibility for making those decisions by Parliament.

Certain paragraphs from the judgment provide salutary reminders of the need for good
practice when dealing with parents.

> 78 I find it very dispiriting, some 16 and a half years after the implementation of the Children
> Act 1989 and some time after the implementation of the 2002 Act, that this court is still hav-
> ing to remind local authorities of the basic principles underlying the legislation. This is by no
> means the first time that this court has been critical of the conduct of a local authority although,

speaking for myself, the behaviour of the agency in the instant case is about the worst I have ever encountered in a career now spanning nearly 40 years.

79 The first point about which the social workers and the agency's lawyers in the instant case need to be reminded is that when dealing with parents, however inadequate or abusive, they are dealing with human beings who have both feelings and rights. I do not propose to identify any of the individual social workers in the present case by name. In my judgment, the failings demonstrated in this case are in principle failings of management. The social workers in question appear, in my judgment, not only to have been inadequately managed; they do not appear to have been properly trained. Worse than that, they do not appear to see the need for good management. It is, I think, the arrogance of the agency's behaviour in this case which is its most shocking aspect.

80 In saying this, I am prepared to work on the premise that all the members of the agency genuinely believed that what they were doing was in the best interests of the child. I am equally prepared to assume, contrary to the father's case, that his proposed application to revoke the placement order is hopeless, and would stand no prospect of success. In my judgment, however, these two factors, as I have already indicated, do not make matters any better—if anything, they make them worse. Any system can cope with compliant recipients or recipients who take no action and do not stand up for their rights. Social workers should be trained to deal with and treat properly those who are often irrational and offensive, although neither accusation can be levelled at the father or his solicitors in this case.

81 I also wish to make it clear that the suggestions which I make in this judgment as representing good practice are, in my view, very basic. Nothing I am going to propose will make excessive or unreasonable demands on hard pressed and inadequately funded agencies: nothing which follows expects the social workers in question to behave in anything other than a simple, straightforward and appropriate fashion.

[The judgment then revisits the facts of the case.]

97 In my judgment, one of two things should have happened. Firstly, although this is not intended as a criticism, the letter from the father's solicitors dated 17 January should have contained an additional paragraph along the following lines:—

'We invite you to give an undertaking that you will take no steps to place (*the child*) with prospective adopters pending the hearing of our client's application. If that undertaking is not received by 10.00 am on 18 January, we shall apply without notice in the first instance to the county court for an order in those terms.'

98 At the hearing of this appeal, we had some debate about the jurisdiction of the court to grant such an injunction. This is not a subject on which I, like Wilson LJ, whose judgment I have also read in draft, entertain any doubts. I am satisfied that the county court has such jurisdiction and would, moreover, have exercised it as a temporary, holding measure, until both sides could be before the court. The judge would either then have given directions for a swift hearing, or resolved the matter summarily. But even if there had been a summary adjudication against the father, he would have been heard.

99 What should have happened in the alternative is; (1) that the agency should have replied promptly to the letter of 17 January; and (2) that it should have explained that its plans were at an advanced stage of preparation and, indeed, about to be implemented. It could then itself have applied to the court, on short notice, for leave to place the child for adoption under section 24(5) of the 2002 Act.

100 Either way, there would have been a hearing on the merits. It might have been very short. Mr. Cobb realistically accepted that the judge would have had a very broad discretion to deal

with the matter summarily if necessary—see Re B to which reference was made earlier in this judgment. If the case had gone against him, the father would have lost. But he would have been heard. The court would have made the decision, and justice would have both been done and been seen to be done.

101 Local authorities and adoption agencies must understand that it is the court which is in control, and which has been given by Parliament the responsibility for making these decisions. The courts are not a rubber stamp for local authority/agency actions, however, reprehensible.

102 In paragraph 14 of his judgment in the Warwickshire case, Wilson LJ emphasised the need for good practice to supplement the 2002 Act. I wholeheartedly agree with him. I hope that this judgment makes crystal clear not only what that good practice should be in relation to section 24(5) of the 2002 Act but *why* good practice is so important. It is for this reason that I propose widespread dissemination of our judgments in this case. Any local authority falling below the standards of good practice, and indulging in the shoddy behaviour demonstrated by the East Sussex County Council in the instant case can expect not only severe judicial displeasure, and applications for judicial review: it is also likely that any repetition of the disgraceful behaviour identified in this case will be visited by orders for costs.

103 With all these reservations, I would, nonetheless, and with reluctance, dismiss this appeal. To the father I would only say that he has done a public service by exposing the local authority's disgraceful conduct to the public gaze, and I hope that this is some small consolation to him for the fact that, as the law stands, he had to fail in this court.

WHAT DOES THIS CASE TELL US ABOUT SOCIAL WORK PRACTICE?

The judges in the Court of Appeal wanted this decision to be disseminated as widely as possible. What it emphasizes is the need for good practice as well as compliance with the letter of the law. It also reminds local authorities that birth parents deserve to be treated with dignity and respect.

Perhaps we can have some sympathy for the local authority. It was acting in the best interests of the child and trying to provide her with long-term security as quickly as possible. Although it behaved disgracefully towards the father, it is also important to prioritize planning for the long-term future of children. Adoption is one possible outcome for children who become the subject of child protection.

Introduction

Local authorities should plan for the long-term future of all the children they look after. The Waterhouse Report, *Lost in Care—The Report of the Tribunal of Inquiry into the Abuse of Children in Care in the Former County Council Areas of Gwynedd and Clwyd since 1974* (to be found on the web at http://tna.europarchive.org/20040216040105/http://www.doh.gov.uk/lostincare/20102a.htm) points out the 'lamentable' effects of failing to do so. *There is now a legal obligation to consider permanence at the four-month statutory review* of looked-after children which we discuss later. When you consider permanent resolutions you will inevitably find that there are some children who will never be in a position to return to their parents or any other family member. In those circumstances, the authority, to safeguard and promote the child's welfare, must look for an alternative permanent substitute family, unless there are compelling reasons not to do so.

If you have come to the conclusion that a permanent substitute family is the appropriate course of action then you are likely to be considering adoption. However, there may be particular reasons why adoption is not appropriate for children; for instance, older children may be unhappy about severing legal links with their birth families. For this reason the Adoption and Children Act 2002 introduced the legal status of special guardianship orders which allow for a form of long-term placement with legal safeguards.

A note of caution: whilst we give you an overview of the law, for full details you need a specialized text, and if you are involved in the adoption process you must consult specialist social workers and your agency lawyer.

Long-term planning

Good care plans should be prepared for all children looked after by the local authority.

There is extensive advice available. Chapter 2 of the *Children Act 989 Guidance and Regulations, Volume 2: Care Planning, Placement and Case Review*, provides information about the planning process for children's placements. The guidance identifies four stages: assessment, planning, intervention, and review (see paras 2.18–2.34). This volume gives excellent suggestions and a checklist of whom to involve in the planning process and how to carry it out. Paragraph 2.44 sets out the key elements of a care plan, which we mentioned in **chapter 8** in respect of plans for care proceeding and which we have reproduced in **Table 9.1**. Long-term planning should start as early as possible.

TABLE 9.1 Key elements of care plans

- the information about the long term plan for the child, including timescales (the permanence plan) **[regulation 5(a)]**;
- the arrangements to meet the child's needs **[regulation 5(b)(i) to (vii)]** in line with the child's developmental needs domain of the Assessment Framework, including arrangements for contact:
  - arrangements for contact with a brother or sister who is also looked after but not placed with the child;
  - details of any court orders made under section 8 or section 34; and
  - arrangements for promoting and maintaining contact with a parent and anyone else with parental responsibility **[regulation 5(b)(v) and paragraph 3, Schedule 1]**;
- details of the placement plan and why the placement was chosen, unless the child is in care and not provided with accommodation by the responsible authority;
- the name of the child's IRO;
- details of the health plan and personal education plan (PEP);
- the wishes and feelings of relevant people about the arrangements for the child; and
- the wishes and feelings of these people about any proposed changes to the care plan.

Working Together to Safeguard Children (2013) includes a flow chart which illustrates the process which follow the initial child protection conference. We have copied this diagram for you at **Figure 9.1**. The process contains certain safeguards against 'drift' which we now discuss.

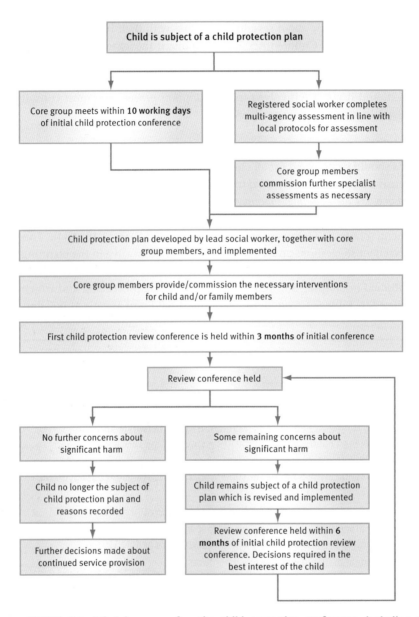

FIGURE 9.1 What happens after the child protection conference, including the review process?

Source: HM Government, March 2013.

The child protection review conference

Child protection review conferences should take place within three months of the initial child protection conference and then at six-monthly intervals whilst the child is the subject of a child protection plan. The purpose of the child protection review conference is set out in **Box 9.1** including the responsibilities of local authority children's social care and how joint working is enabled.

 BOX 9.1 *Working Together to Safeguard Children*

The purposes of the child protection review are to:

- Review whether the child is continuing to suffer, or is likely to suffer, significant harm, and review developmental progress against child protection plan outcomes.
- Consider whether the child protection plan should continue or should be changed.

Responsibilities of local authority children's social care:

- Attend and lead organisation of the conference.
- Determine when the review conference should be held within three months of the initial conference and thereafter at maximum intervals of six months.
- Provide information to enable informed decisions about what action is necessary to safeguard and promote the welfare of the child who is the subject of the child protection plan, and about the effectiveness and impact of action taken so far.
- Share the conference information with the child and family beforehand (where appropriate).
- Record conference outcomes.
- Decide whether to initiate family court proceedings (all the children in the household should be considered, even if concerns are only expressed about one child) if the child is considered to be suffering significant harm.

Other professionals should:

- Attend, when invited, and provide details of their involvement with the child and family; and produce reports for the child protection review. This information will provide an overview of work undertaken by family members and professionals, and evaluate the impact on the child's welfare against the planned outcomes set out in the child protection plan.

The core group has a collective responsibility, which is laid out in *Working Together*, to:

- meet within ten working days from the initial child protection conference if the child is the subject of a child protection plan;
- develop the outline child protection plan, based on assessment findings, and set out what needs to change, by how much, and by when in order for the child to be safe and have their needs met;

- decide what steps need to be taken, and by whom, to complete the in-depth assessment to inform decisions about the child's safety and welfare; and

- implement the child protection plan and take joint responsibility for carrying out the agreed tasks, monitoring progress and outcomes and refining the plan as needed.

As the social worker you are likely to be the person who has the key responsibility for organizing the core group, ensuring its work is carried out, and for reporting back to the child protection review conference.

One important function of the child protection review conference is to consider explicitly whether the child continues to be at risk of significant harm. If not, then the child should no longer be the subject of a child protection plan. **Box 9.2** explains the decision-making process.

 BOX 9.2 Discontinuing the child protection plan

A child should no longer be the subject of a child protection plan if:

- it is judged that the child is no longer continuing to, or be likely to, suffer significant harm and therefore require safeguarding by means of a child protection plan;

- the child and family have moved permanently to another local authority area. In such cases, the receiving local authority should convene a child protection conference within 15 working days of being notified of the move, only after which event may discontinuing the child protection plan take place in respect of the original local authority's child protection plan; or

- the child has reached 18 years of age (to end the child protection plan, the local authority should have a review around the child's birthday and this should be planned in advance), has died, or has permanently left the UK.

Looked-after children

There are specific regulatory requirements upon local authorities to review looked-after children's care plans. These are set out in the *Children Act 1989 Guidance and Regulations, Volume 2: Care Planning, Placement and Case Review*. The regulations make provision for the minimum frequency of the review and the matters that must be discussed. The role of the independent reviewing officer (IRO) is set out in the *IRO Handbook: Statutory guidance for independent reviewing officers and local authorities on their functions in relation to case management and review for looked after children* (2010). The primary task of the IRO is to 'ensure that the care plan for the child fully reflects the child's current needs and that the actions set out in the plan are consistent with the local authority's legal responsibilities towards the child' (para. 2.10). The IRO will normally chair the review meeting. Their responsibilities, set out in s. 2B(1) of the Children and Young Persons Act 2008, are to:

(a) monitor the performance by the local authority of their functions in relation to the child's case;

(b) participate, in accordance with regulations made by the appropriate national authority, in any review of the child's case;

(c) ensure that any ascertained wishes and feelings of the child concerning the case are given due consideration by the local authority;

(d) perform any other function which is prescribed in regulations made by the appropriate national authority.

The first duty provides the IRO with considerable power to require the local authority to address the needs of the child at all times and not just at review meetings. The local authority must ultimately cooperate with the IRO. In practice, the execution of the role has not been a great success. The government is continuing to monitor the performance of the IRO and may well introduce further regulations or even pass the role to a separate body outside the control of the local authority. The National Children's Bureau (NCB) has carried out research into the effectiveness of the IRO service (see www.ncb.org.uk/media/1124381/ncb_the_role_of_independent_reviewing_officers_in_england_-_final2.pdf).

Coordinating the reviewing processes

As you have seen, there are two different types of review process applicable to looked-after children. The care planning regulations indicates that 'where a looked after child remains the subject of a child protection plan it is expected that there will be a single planning and reviewing process, led by the IRO, which meets the requirements of both the 2010 Regulations and guidance and *Working Together to Safeguard Children*'. If IROs are used to chair the child protection review conference, the authority must ensure that their independence is not compromised. Their role is to ensure that the interests of the child are protected, which may be different from protecting the interests of the authority.

Considering the possibility of adoption may form part of planning for permanence. The rest of this chapter considers the law on adoption.

Adoption

The law on adoption is set out in the Adoption and Children Act 2002. The Act and the explanatory notes to the Act are available on the Legislation.co.uk website at www.legislation.gov.uk/ukpga/2002/38/contents. Note that amendments to the Act are not made to the internet version. The explanatory notes are extremely helpful in understanding the purpose of the statutory provisions.

The Adoption and Children Act 2002

In brief, the Adoption and Children Act 2002:

- aligns the principles of adoption law with the principles underpinning the Children Act where relevant to do so;
- improves and extends the regulation of adoption and adoption support services;

- sets out and modernizes the legal basis for the process of adoption;
- provides for both disclosure of and protection of information about adopted people and their birth relatives;
- regulates inter-country adoptions;
- regulates the advertising of children for adoption and payments in connection with adoption;
- provides the legal underpinning for an Adoption and Children Act Register;
- attempts to reduce delay in the adoption process.

Human rights and adoption

The Adoption and Children Act 2002 addresses several human rights-based concerns about adoption. In particular, it clarifies the role of the unmarried father and sets up a system that allows adopted people access to information about their past. Independent reviews are available for crucial decisions about selection of prospective adopters and where access to information is denied by the state.

However, it is inevitable that the adoption process will raise Human Rights Act considerations for adoption agencies as the case used at the beginning of the chapter demonstrated. First, any decision to remove a child from its birth parents must be proportionate and necessary in a democratic society. Second, the views of the birth parents must always be taken into account, and if the matter goes to court they must be able to argue their case properly.

P, C and S v UK (2002) provides an excellent example of the way that precipitate action by the local authority can lead to a breach of the birth parents' and the child's human rights. The facts were as follows: P was convicted in the US in 1995 of deliberately administering laxatives to her young son and thus endangering his health. She was diagnosed as suffering from Munchausen's syndrome, which led her to induce illness in her child and exaggerate her own medical history. In 1996, P moved to the UK and married C. Before the birth of their child, S, the local authorities expressed concern about P's conviction in the US and sought to initiate care proceedings in relation to the unborn child. Upon birth, S was removed from P and C and freed for adoption—a procedure now abolished under the 2002 Act. Despite initial legal representation, P conducted her own legal case. The judge ordered S to be removed from P and C's care. His decision was based upon P's treatment of her previous child. Subsequent appeals were dismissed. P, C, and S applied to the European Court of Human Rights alleging that the adoption process had violated their rights under Article 6(1) (right to a fair trial), Article 8 (right to respect for family life), and Article 12 (right to marry and found a family) of the European Convention. The Court held that there had been a violation of Articles 6(1) and 8 both as regards the removal of S at birth and as regards the subsequent care and adoption procedures. It also held that there were no separate issues arising under Article 12. The Court pointed out that the key principle of Article 6 was fairness. In the light of the human rights principles of effective access to court and fairness, the complexity of the case, the importance of what was at stake, and the highly emotive nature of the subject matter, the Court concluded that P must receive the assistance of a lawyer. As regards Article 8, the Court made it clear that there must be extraordinarily compelling reasons before a baby can be physically removed from its mother, against her will, immediately after birth as a consequence of a procedure in which neither she nor her partner has been involved. In the particular circumstances of the case, the Court concluded that the draconian step of removing S from her mother shortly after birth was not supported by relevant and sufficient reasons and that it cannot be regarded as having been necessary in a democratic society for the purpose of safeguarding S.

Of course, concern for the birth family's rights will often be outweighed by the urgency of the need to protect the child. You may feel that this case is yet another instance where social workers are condemned for taking action, but would also have been condemned for failing to act.

More recently, the Court of Appeal in *Re B-S* [2013] EWCA Civ 1146 dismissed an appeal by a mother under s. 47(5) for leave to oppose the making of adoption orders in relation to her two children. The judgment has wider ranging implications for practice in respect of adoption and human rights. The facts of the case are set out below.

> The mother has two children, the elder born in November 2007 and the younger in September 2008. In February 2011 they were removed from the mother's care. In October 2011 they were made the subject of care and placement orders, the court dispensing with the mother's consent in accordance with section 52(1)(b) of the 2002 Act. Contact between the mother and the children ceased in December 2011. The children were placed with prospective adopters in April 2012. An application for adoption followed in 2013. It was listed before Parker J on 7 May 2013. The mother applied under section 47(5) of the Act for leave to oppose the adoption. The basis of her application was that there had been what MacFarlane LJ described as 'an astonishing change of circumstances' since the making of the care and placement orders. Parker J gave a full judgment explaining why she refused the mother's application and then proceeded to make adoption orders. Parker J refused the mother permission to appeal.

> The mother filed an appellant's notice on 23 May 2013 setting out seven grounds of appeal and seeking a new trial. McFarlane LJ explained in some detail why he was giving permission to appeal on all except one of the grounds relied on. He was concerned that the full court should have the opportunity of considering the then very recent decision of the Supreme Court in *In re B (A Child) (Care Proceedings: Threshold Criteria)* [2013] UKSC 33 [see **chapter 8**].

The change of circumstances which the mother was relying on in her appeal was considered by the Court of Appeal and eventually dismissed but not before the court provided detailed analysis of the law in respect of adoption. *Adoption is to be considered a last resort when nothing else will do, not merely being a good idea but where the child's circumstances require the making of an adoption order.* The judgment quotes a Strasbourg case, *YC v UK* (2012) 55 EHRR 967:

> Family ties may only be severed in very exceptional circumstances and . . . everything must be done to preserve personal relations and, where appropriate, to 'rebuild' the family. It is not enough to show that a child could be placed in a more beneficial environment for his upbringing.

(Para. 134)

The Court of Appeal judgment also stressed the need for local authorities and others to provide proper evidence so that all of the options can be considered by the court. An analysis of the arguments for and against each option is necessary, echoing the views of the President of the Family Division when he said: 'I want to send out a clear message: local authority materials can be much shorter than hitherto, and they should be more focused on analysis than on history and narrative' ('The process of reform: the revised PLO and the local authority' [2013] Fam Law 680).

Adoption

Timescales

We have already made it clear that social workers should treat as urgent the need to provide for the long-term security of a child. The statutory guidance on the Adoption and Children Act 2002 sets out the timescales for decisions about adoption. The relevant paragraphs are set out in **Box 9.3**.

 BOX 9.3 Timescales

Adoption Statutory Guidance (July 2014)

1.1 Unnecessary delays in the adoption process may have an adverse effect on the child's development and welfare and may reduce their chances of being adopted. The child's need for a permanent home must be addressed and a permanence plan should be made as early as possible; well before and no later than the second statutory review (four months after the child becomes looked after) (see *Children Act 1989 Guidance and Regulations: Volume 2: Care Planning, Placement and Case Review*). The adoption scorecards expect that children for whom adoption is the plan will be placed with their prospective adoptive family, on average, within 14 months of entering care by 2016.

The child's welfare

Decisions about adoption must be shaped by the legal requirements set out in the Adoption and Children Act 2002. Section 1 is the linchpin of the Act. It sets out the overarching principles upon which decisions made either by courts or by adoption agencies relating to the adoption of children should be based. The principles dovetail with the principles of the Children Act 1989. The child's welfare is placed at the centre of decision making (s. 1):

> (2) The paramount consideration of the court or adoption agency must be the child's welfare, throughout his life.

Note, however, that in s. 1(1) of the Children Act, it is court decisions only, and not those of social services or other agencies, which must be guided by the paramount consideration of the welfare of the child. There remains, therefore, a contrast between the welfare principle in adoption and in other proceedings in respect of children.

The statute then sets out a checklist of matters which a court or an adoption agency must consider. This welfare checklist is very similar to the checklist within the Children Act. It does not provide an exhaustive statement of what needs to be taken into account, nor is it written in order of priority. However, you should notice that decision-makers must bear in mind that the decision is one which affects the rest of the child's life—and the long-lasting impact of adoption decisions must be reflected in their decision-making process. We have set the checklist out in **Box 9.4**. Note that the requirement for local authorities and adoption agencies to give due consideration to the child's religious persuasion, racial origin, and cultural and linguistic background has been repealed by the Children and Families Act 2014. These factors are no longer prefaced as being more important than other factors but are factors which will be taken into account by s. 1(2)–(4).

The importance of s. 1 of the Act cannot be overemphasized. All decisions relating to adoption are to be based upon it.

 BOX 9.4 The Adoption and Children Act checklist—s. 1

(2) The paramount consideration of the court or adoption agency must be the child's welfare, throughout his life.

(3) The court or adoption agency must at all times bear in mind that, in general, any delay in coming to the decision is likely to prejudice the child's welfare.

(4) The court or adoption agency must have regard to the following matters (among others)—
  (a) the child's ascertainable wishes and feelings regarding the decision (considered in the light of the child's age and understanding),
  (b) the child's particular needs,
  (c) the likely effect on the child (throughout his life) of having ceased to be a member of the original family and become an adopted person,
  (d) the child's age, sex, background and any of the child's characteristics which the court considers relevant,
  (e) any harm (within the meaning of the Children Act 1989) which the child has suffered or is at risk of suffering,
  (f) the relationship which the child has with relatives, and with any other person in relation to whom the court or agency considers the relationship to be relevant, including—
    (i) the likelihood of any such relationship continuing and the value to the child of its doing so,
    (ii) the ability and willingness of any of the child's relatives, or of any such person, to provide the child with a secure environment in which the child can develop, and otherwise to meet the child's needs,
    (iii) the wishes and feelings of any of the child's relatives, or of any such person, regarding the child.

References to a relative include the child's mother and father.

Placement for adoption

There are two stages to the adoption process. The first is placement for adoption. Placement allows adoption agencies to plan effectively for any subsequent adoption. In most circumstances this will not require court intervention. Placement can either be actual placement with the prospective adopters or it can act as an authority to place with prospective adopters once these have been identified.

Placement of children by adoption agencies for adoption is covered by ss. 18–29 of the Act. The placement provisions replace the freeing provisions of the Adoption Act 1976. An adoption agency may place a child for adoption only with the consent of the parent or guardian under s. 19, or under a court placement order under s. 21. The consent of both birth parents is necessary to avoid court proceedings. Babies under six weeks old cannot be placed for adoption.

The purpose of the placement provisions is set out in the explanatory notes to the Act:

> The intention is to ensure key decisions are taken earlier in the adoption process than at present, with court involvement where necessary. This is intended to provide greater certainty and stability for children by dealing with consent to placement for adoption before they have been placed (at present this issue is often not addressed until the final adoption order hearing); to minimize the uncertainty for prospective adopters, who under the current system possibly face a contested court hearing at the adoption order stage; and to reduce the extent to which birth families are faced with a 'fait accompli' at the final adoption hearing (as they may be under the current system, where their child has not been freed for adoption but has been placed with an adoptive family for some time before the application or an adoption order is made).

Section 18(1) provides that an adoption agency (except in the case of a child who is less than six weeks old) may place a child for adoption with prospective adopters or, where it has already placed a child with any persons, leave the child with them as prospective adopters only if it does so with consent under s. 19 or under a placement order. Section 18(2) makes it clear that an adoption agency may place a child for adoption with prospective adopters only if the agency is satisfied that the child ought to be placed for adoption. So there are two placement routes, one with parental consent and the other by court order.

Placement with consent

Section 19 provides the mechanism by which children may be placed for adoption with parental consent and without a court order. Parents or guardians may consent either to the child being placed for adoption with prospective adopters identified in the consent, or being placed for adoption with any prospective adopters who may be chosen by the agency. Consent can be withdrawn at any point before an application for the final adoption order is made. As we explain later, if care proceedings have already been launched under the Children Act, s. 19 consent is not possible. Instead, the local authority which is proposing an adoption must apply under s. 22(2) for a placement order—see the following section. Section 20 provides that parents or guardians may consent at the same time or subsequently to the making of a future adoption order

Placement by court order

If parents do not consent then a court order is necessary. Section 21 provides that place-ment orders, court orders authorizing local authorities to place children for adoption with prospective adopters, may be made only if (s. 21(2)):

(a)   the child is subject to a care order;

(b)   the court is satisfied that the conditions for a care order are met; or

(c)   the child has no parent or guardian.

The placement order can be made only if either the parent or guardian has consented to the placement or the court is satisfied that the parent's or guardian's consent should be dispensed with.

In determining whether the conditions are met, a clear link is made with the Children Act 1989. The Adoption and Children Act explanatory notes explain:

> The same threshold for compulsory intervention in family life is to apply where a local authority seeks authority to place a child for adoption without parental consent as applies where an authority seeks to take a child into care under a care order. In placement order cases, where the court is satisfied that the 'significant harm' threshold is met, it will then consider whether a placement order should be made.

That decision will be made using the s. 1 welfare criteria.

Section 22 sets out the circumstances when the local authority must apply for a placement order. We have set these out in **Box 9.5**.

BOX 9.5 Section 22(1)

(a)   the child is placed for adoption by them or is being provided with accommodation by them,

(b)   no adoption agency is authorised to place the child for adoption,

(c)   the child has no parent or guardian or the authority consider that the conditions in section 31(2) of the 1989 Act are met, and

(d)   the authority are satisfied that the child ought to be placed for adoption.

What happens if the child's future is already being considered by the courts? Subsection (2) provides that, if an application has been made the outcome of which may be a care order, or the child is subject to a care order, and the parents have not consented to the placement for adoption, the authority must, if satisfied that the child ought to be placed for adoption, apply for a placement order. However, if the child is subject to a care order and the parents are prepared to consent, the authority can choose whether to apply for a placement order or to place with parental consent under s. 19.

Fostering for Adoption

The Children and Families Act 2014 amends s. 22C of the Children Act so that when a local authority is considering placing a child for adoption but does not yet have the court's permission to do so, it has a duty to consider placing the child in a Fostering for Adoption placement. The foster parents in these placements are also approved as prospective adopters. The local authority must first have considered placing the child with relatives, friends, or other connected persons and have ruled them out as not being the most appropriate potential carers for the child.

Parental consent to placement and adoption

Either the birth parents must consent to the placement or the court must decide that consent can be dispensed with. Consent, and when it can be dispensed with, are obviously critical to the placement and, indeed, the whole adoption process. The following discussion about consent in relation to placement orders is equally relevant to adoption orders, which we discuss later in this chapter.

Section 52 sets out the necessity for consent, the circumstances in which the court can dispense with consent, and the meaning of consent. We have set out the key subsections for you in full in **Box 9.6**.

BOX 9.6 Consent—s. 52

(1) The court cannot dispense with the consent of any parent or guardian of a child to the child being placed for adoption or to the making of an adoption order in respect of the child unless the court is satisfied that—

   (a) the parent or guardian cannot be found or is incapable of giving consent, or

   (b) the welfare of the child requires the consent to be dispensed with.

(2) . . .

(3) Any consent given by the mother to the making of an adoption order is ineffective if it is given less than six weeks after the child's birth.

(4) The withdrawal of any consent to the placement of a child for adoption, or of any consent given under section 20, is ineffective if it is given after an application for an adoption order is made.

(5) 'Consent' means consent given unconditionally and with full understanding of what is involved; but a person may consent to adoption without knowing the identity of the persons in whose favour the order will be made.

Dispensing with consent

In the light of s. 52, it is apparent that consent can be dispensed with only in limited circumstances. The decision of the court will be based upon the criteria in s. 1 of the Act. Each case will be based upon its own facts. Careful judgements will have to be made about the best possible future for the child.

Parental responsibility

The impact of placement for adoption on parental responsibility is set out in s. 25. If a child is placed for adoption under s. 19 or an adoption agency is authorized to place a child for adoption under s. 19 or a placement order is in force in respect of a child, then parental responsibility for the child is given to the agency. While the child is placed with prospective adopters, then parental responsibility is given to them. The agency may restrict the exercise of parental responsibility of any parent or guardian, or of prospective adopters, in the same way as they can under a care order (see previous chapter).

Contact while the child is placed

Section 26 empowers the court to make orders for contact with the child placed for adoption or authorized to be placed. Applications for such contact may be made by the child or the agency, a parent, guardian, or relative and any person who previously had contact under the Children Act 1989. Applications may also be made by a person who was caring for a baby under six weeks old and had the benefit of a residence order or child arrangements order settling the living arrangements of the child immediately before the adoption agency was authorized to place the child for adoption or placed the child for adoption. Applications may, in the rare cases where this occurs, be made by someone who had the care of a child prior to wardship. Finally, any person may apply who has obtained the court's leave to make the application.

Courts may on their own initiative make contact orders under s. 26. It may, for instance, become apparent during the court proceedings that the child gains great benefit from contact with a particular person.

Contact orders under s. 26 may be varied or revoked by the court on application by the child, the agency, or a person named in the order. If there are urgent short-term problems with contact, for instance where a child has become extremely upset following a visit and the social worker thinks that a cooling-off period is required, then, despite the existence of the contact order, s. 27(2) enables the agency to stop contact for up to seven days in order to safeguard or promote the child's welfare. Clearly, where there are longer term concerns then agencies should make proper application to the court for variation or revocation.

Legal implications

Sections 28 and 29 set out the legal relationship between placement, adoption, and other orders. Once a child is placed for adoption or authorized to be placed then the parent or guardian may not apply for child arrangements orders unless an application for an adoption order has been made and the parent or guardian has obtained the court's leave. Likewise, once an application is made for an adoption order, a guardian of the child may not apply for a special guardianship order without the court's leave. We discuss special guardianship later in the chapter (**Special guardianship orders**, p 335). These provisions operate to restrict the availability of court proceedings and prevent unnecessary disruption to the placement process.

Children placed for adoption, authorized to be placed, or subject to a placement order cannot be given new surnames or removed from the UK without the leave of the court or the consent of each parent or guardian. Removal for a holiday of less than one month by prospective adopters does not require permission of the court or the parents or guardians.

There are additional legal implications of placement orders. When a placement order is in force it supersedes any care order, any supervision order, and any s. 8 orders. Nor can prohibited steps orders, child arrangements orders, specific issues orders, supervision orders, or child assessment orders be made in respect of the child—s. 29(3). There is an exception in respect of child arrangements orders. These can be applied for where an application for an adoption order has been made in respect of the child and the applying parent or guardian has the court's leave under s. 47 of the Act, or other applicants given leave by the court under s. 29—see earlier in this section. Similarly, special guardianship orders may be made in respect of a child when an application has been made for an adoption order only when the person applying has the leave of the court. This allows for applications which compete with the adoption but only with the leave of the court.

Modifying the 'looked-after' status under the Children Act 1989

The Adoption and Children Act extends the 'looked-after' status under s. 22 of the Children Act 1989 (see **chapter 6**) to children authorized to be placed for adoption, which ensures that the local authority retains clear legal responsibilities for the welfare of the child. However, it would be inappropriate if all of the requirements of the 'looked-after' status applied to children authorized to be placed for adoption. For instance, it may not always be necessary to consult the child's parent before making decisions in respect of that child. Regulations modify the operation of s. 22 of the Children Act 1989 in these circumstances.

Removal and recovery

Removal means taking a child away from where he or she has been placed. Section 30 sets out extensive general restrictions on the removal of children involved in the placement process. No one can remove children who have been placed for adoption with prospective adopters except the adoption agency; no one, unless they have the leave of the court, may remove children accommodated by the local authority while a placement order is under consideration by the court; and no one can remove a child from accommodation provided by an adoption agency once the agency is authorized to place the child for adoption under s. 19 (this also applies where consent has been given and then withdrawn). In these circumstances, only the agency may remove the child. Any person who removes a child in contravention of the section commits an offence.

There are, however, some circumstances where the removal of a child is allowed. First, where the child is arrested and, second, in particular circumstances set out in ss. 31 and 32. These sections cover the situation where the child is not subject to a care order. If the child either has been placed for adoption or is being provided with accommodation by an adoption agency prior to being placed, and any parent or guardian withdraws consent to placement and requests that the child is returned to him or her, then the agency must return the child within seven days if the child has not been placed or within 14 days if the child has been placed. Prospective adopters who do not return the child to the agency commit an offence. If the agency wishes to prevent the removal then it must apply for a placement order. If a placement order is refused and the parent or guardian wishes the child to be returned to him or her then the court which refused the placement order will determine when the child is returned.

Where a placement order is in force or has been revoked but the child remains with the prospective adopters or remains accommodated by the local authority then no one other than the local authority may remove the child except in accordance with any order made by the court. If prospective adopters wish to return a child placed for adoption, or the adoption agency decides that the child should not remain with the prospective adopters, then the child should be returned within seven days of the decision and the parents or guardian of the child should be informed by the agency.

Sections 36–40 apply to a child who is the subject of an application for an adoption order and:

- where notice of intention to adopt has been given; or
- there has been an application for leave to apply for an adoption order; and
- where the child has not been placed in its current home by an adoption agency.

There is a limit on who can remove children in these circumstances. Generally, only someone who has the leave of the court, someone with parental responsibility, or the local authority may remove the child.

Recovery

Section 41 provides for recovery orders. Where it appears to the court that a child has been or may be removed in contravention of the provisions of the Act, then s. 41(2) permits the court to:

(a)   direct any person who is in a position to do so to produce the child on request to any person mentioned in subsection (4);

(b)   authorize the removal of the child by any person mentioned in that subsection;

(c)   require any person who has information as to the child's whereabouts to disclose that information on request to any constable or officer of the court;

(d)   authorize a constable to enter any premises specified in the order and search for the child, using reasonable force if necessary.

Key features of placement

We summarize the key features of placement in **Box 9.7**.

 BOX 9.7 A summary of the key features of placement

Feature	Section	Comment
Parental consent required	s. 19 and s. 20	• consent can be withdrawn at any time • consent may at the same time or subsequently be given for adoption • prospective adopters do not need to have been identified
Placement order necessary if no consent	s. 21	• child must be subject to a care order, or the conditions for care order made out, or the child has no parent or guardian

Feature	Section	Comment
Parental responsibility	s. 25	• with the adoption agency • with prospective adopters once placed • with birth parents • agency may restrict birth parents', guardians', or prospective adopters' parental responsibility
Contact	s. 26	• contact under Children Act 1989 ceases to have effect • contact may be ordered by the court with anyone following application from a wide range of persons and anyone with the leave of the court
Lack of consent	s. 52	• either parent cannot be found, or is incapable of giving consent or the welfare of the child requires consent to be dispensed with
Quality of consent	s. 52	• consent must be unconditional and given with full understanding • all decisions are underpinned by s. 1 criteria

Adoption orders

Preliminaries to adoption

Section 42 of the Act requires that the child must live with the adopter(s) before the application to adopt is made. The time periods depend upon the identity of the applicant or applicants and who has placed the child for adoption. We have set the time periods out in **Box 9.8**.

 BOX 9.8 Time periods prior to application

Placed by/applicant	Time period
Placed by adoption agency	Ten weeks preceding application
Applicant a parent	Ten weeks preceding application
Applicant or one of applicants is partner of parent	Six months
Applicant(s) local authority foster parents	One year
Any other applicant	Not less than three years out of the period of five years preceding application The three-year period does not need to have been continuous

---

The section also requires that the court is satisfied that the adoption agency or the local authority has had sufficient opportunities to see the child with the applicant or applicants together in the home environment.

Reporting requirements

Section 43 sets out the reporting requirements imposed on an adoption agency:

> The agency must—
> submit to the court a report on the suitability of the applicants and on any other matters relevant to the operation of section 1, and
> assist the court in any manner the court directs.

Notice of intention to adopt

Where proposed adopters wish to adopt a child who is not placed for adoption with them by an adoption agency, s. 44 requires them to give notice of intention to adopt to their local authority. They can give this notice as much as two years before applying, or as little as three months. The local authority must then investigate and report to the court on the suitability of the proposed adopters and other matters relevant to s. 1 of the Act.

Regulations provide the detail of the matters to be taken into account in the investigation and report. Section 45(2) provides:

> In particular, the regulations may make provision for the purpose of securing that, in determining the suitability of a couple to adopt a child, proper regard is had to the need for stability and permanence in their relationship.

This is designed to ensure that all couples who wish to adopt jointly, whether married or unmarried, demonstrate the strength of their relationship. Individual people can, of course, adopt. We will discuss the different requirements for individual people and couples who wish to adopt later.

Adoption orders

The adoption order is the court order which gives effect to the adoption. Section 46 of the Act gives parental responsibility for a child to the adopters or adopter. The order extinguishes any other person's parental responsibility and any order under the Children Act 1989, the Children (Northern Ireland) Order 1995, and the Children (Scotland) Act 1995. It also extinguishes any obligation to make payments for the maintenance of the child after the making of the adoption order, whether that obligation arises under an agreement or a court order. Section 46(6) provides that:

> Before making an adoption order, the court must consider whether there should be arrangements for allowing any person contact with the child; and for that purpose the court must consider any existing or proposed arrangements and obtain any views of the parties to the proceedings.

Section 47 is a key section of the Act. It sets out the three conditions, one of which must be met before the court may make an adoption order. The first condition is in s. 47(2) in **Box 9.9**. The first condition will be appropriate where, for instance, the child is being adopted by a parent and step-parent.

BOX 9.9 The first condition

In the case of each parent or guardian of the child the court must be satisfied that—

(a) the parent or guardian now consents to the making of the adoption order,

(b) the parent or guardian consented at the time of the placement order under s. 20 (and has not withdrawn the consent) and does not oppose the making of the adoption order, or

(c) parent's or guardian's consent should be dispensed with.

The second condition is set out in **Box 9.10**. The second condition will be appropriate where the adoption follows a placement by an adoption agency.

BOX 9.10 The second condition

(a) the child has been placed for adoption by an adoption agency with the prospective adopters in whose favour the order is proposed to be made,

(b) either—

(i) the child was placed for adoption with the consent of each parent or guardian and the consent of the mother was given when the child was at least six weeks old, or

(ii) the child was placed for adoption under a placement order, and

(c) no parent or guardian opposes the making of the adoption order.

Parents or guardians may not oppose the making of adoption orders under either the first or second condition unless they have the leave of the court. The court can only give leave if it is satisfied that there has been a change in circumstances since the consent of the parent or guardian was given or when the placement order was made—s. 47(7).

The third condition is that the child is free for adoption under s. 18 of the Adoption (Scotland) Act 1978 or under article 17(1) or 18(1) of the Adoption (Northern Ireland) Order 1987.

Adoption orders may be made even if the child to be adopted is already an adopted child—s. 46(5). However, adoption orders may not be made in relation to someone who is or has been married (s. 47(8)) or who is 19 or older (s. 47(9)). An application for adoption can be made only if the person to be adopted is at the time of the application under 18—s. 49(4). Applications for adoption may be made by a couple or one person.

Adoption by a couple—s. 50

If the application is made by a couple then at least one of them must be domiciled in a part of the British Islands and both must have been habitually resident for one year prior to the making of the application. Domiciled means that their settled home is in the British Islands. Both should be over 21 unless one is the birth parent of the child to be adopted and is over 18, in which case the other must be over 21. The definition of 'couple' is set out in s. 144(4) of the Act:

A couple means—

(a) a married couple, or

(b) two people (whether of different sexes or the same sex) living as partners in an enduring family relationship . . .

Therefore unmarried heterosexuals and gay and lesbian couples are able to adopt as couples as long as they can demonstrate an enduring family relationship. Allowing couples who are not married to adopt widens the pool of potential adoptive parents and therefore supports the aim of increasing the number of children who are adopted. Of course no couple, however stable their relationship, is automatically entitled to adopt. It will be up to the adoption agencies and ultimately the courts to decide upon each individual couple's suitability.

Adoption by a single person—s. 51

Single people who are 21 and over and not married and are domiciled in a part of the British Islands may adopt. One member of a couple who is 21 or over may adopt if the court is satisfied that the person is the partner of a parent of the person to be adopted.

Someone who is married may adopt as a single person if the court is satisfied that:

(a) the person's spouse cannot be found;

(b) the spouses have separated and are living apart, and the separation is likely to be permanent; or

(c) the persons spouse is by reason of ill health, whether physical or mental, incapable of making an application for an adoption order.

Parental consent

Parental consent or a court decision that parental consent should be dispensed with is critical to the adoption process. The discussion on the meaning of consent and the circumstances when it can be dispensed with in the context of placement for adoption is equally relevant here.

Key features of the legal process of adoption

We set out the key features of the legal process of adoption in **Box 9.11**.

BOX 9.11 The key features of the adoption process

Feature	Section	Comment and details
The child must live with adopters prior to application	s. 42	• parent of child—ten weeks • placed by agency—ten weeks • placement order—ten weeks

Feature	Section	Comment and details
		• partner of parent—six months
		• foster parent—one year
		• anyone else, total of three out of last five years
Proposed adopters of child not placed by agency must give notice of intention to adopt to local authority	s. 44	• to be given not more than two years or less than three months before application is made
Local authority to prepare reports for court	ss. 44 and 45	• regulations to provide detailed requirements but include: – suitability of applicant(s) – stability and permanence of couple's relationship – s. 1 matters
Adoption orders	ss. 46, 47, and 48	• gives parental responsibility to adopters • extinguishes previous parental responsibility • one of three conditions in s. 47 must be complied with, the most important being consent of parents, or court satisfied consent should be dispensed with
Potential applicants	ss. 49, 50, and 51	• couples • single people • domiciled in British Islands • habitually resident for one year or more • aged 21+ (unless one of a couple and the birth parent in which case must be 18+)
Lack of consent	s. 52	• either parent cannot be found, or is incapable of giving consent or the welfare of the child requires consent to be dispensed with
Quality of consent	s. 52	• consent must be unconditional and given with full understanding • decisions underpinned by s. 1 criteria

The status of adopted children

Section 67 sets out the status of adopted children. We have reproduced this in **Box 9.12**.

The section has effect from the date of the adoption. You may recall that s. 51(2) is about adoptions by one of a couple where the partner is the birth parent of the child.

> **BOX 9.12** An adopted person is to be treated in law as if born as the child of the adopters or adopter
>
> (1) An adopted person is the legitimate child of the adopters or adopter and, if adopted by—
>   (a) a couple, or
>   (b) one of a couple under section 51(2) is to be treated as the child of the relationship of the couple in question.
>
> (2) An adopted person—
>   (a) if adopted by one of a couple under section 51(2), is to be treated in law as not being the child of any person other than the adopted and other one of the couple, and
>   (b) in any other case, is to be treated in law, subject to subsection (4), as not being the child of any person other than the adopters or adopter;
>
> but this subsection does not affect any reference in this Act to a person's natural parent or to any other natural relationship.

Information about a person's adoption

The Act attempts to achieve a balance between information being properly recorded and maintained and available to an adopted person and ensuring that private information is properly controlled. It also sets up a 'gateway' for access to information about adopted persons. The provisions apply only to adoptions which take place after the Act has been implemented.

Adoption registers

The Act provides the statutory basis for three adoption registers. The first two registers provide the infrastructure for the maintenance of key information about adoption. The first is the Adopted Children Register originally set up under the Children Act 1989 which the Registrar General must continue to maintain—s. 77. Entries are made in the Adopted Children Register following adoption orders, or following registrable foreign adoptions (Sch. 1 to the Act—not covered in this chapter). The Registrar General must make traceable the connection between any entry in the registers of live births or other records which has been marked 'Adopted' and any corresponding entry in the Adopted Children Register—s. 79.

The second register which must be kept is the Adoption Contact Register. The register contains information about adopted people who wish to make contact with their birth relatives and birth relatives who wish to make contact with adopted people—see s. 80.

A third adoption register, the Adoption and Children Act Register, is provided for in another Part of the Act. This must contain (s. 125(1)):

(a) prescribed information about children who are suitable for adoption and prospective adopters who are suitable to adopt a child;
(b) prescribed information about persons included in the register in pursuance of paragraph (a) in respect of things occurring after their inclusion.

This provision puts onto a statutory basis the Adoption and Children Act Register for England and Wales which was launched in August 2001. Further information about the operation of the register can be found on the adoption register website, www. Adoptionregister.org.uk. This site also lists a range of other useful websites.

Prescribed information

Protected information

Some prescribed information will be protected information. Protected information is information which allows the adopted person or any other person connected with the adoption to be identified—see s. 57. Any information held by an adoption agency which the agency has obtained from the Registrar General and any other information which would enable the adopted person to obtain a certified copy of the record of his or her birth, or information about an entry relating to the adopted person in the Adoption Contact Register, is identifying information.

Section 57 restricts the circumstances in which an adoption agency may disclose prescribed information to anyone other than the adopted person except where there has been an agreement to which the adoption agency is a party. Section 58 provides for the disclosure of information which is not protected by an adoption agency where it is necessary for its functions. Such disclosures will be governed by regulations. The explanatory notes suggest, 'This could, for example, be background information about the child's progress to be disclosed to his birth family without disclosing his new identity or his whereabouts'.

Adopted adults' rights to information

Section 60 sets out the rights of an adopted adult (someone over 18) to any information from the adoption agency which enables him or her to obtain his or her birth certificate (unless the adoption agency successfully applies to the High Court for an order preventing this) and any information disclosed to the adopters by the agency. In this way, the adoptive adult is able to access some part of the story of the adoption.

Procedure for disclosure

Not all applications for disclosure of protected information will succeed—see ss. 60 and 61. An agency is not required to proceed with an application unless it considers it appropriate to do so. In making a decision, the agency must consider the welfare of the adopted person, the views of the person to whom the information relates, and all the other circumstances of the case including matters which will be prescribed by regulation. Where the information relates to a child, there are additional requirements to consider the views of any parent or guardian of the child and the views of the child, if appropriate to do so having regard to the child's age and understanding and to all the other circumstances of the case. If the child is an adopted child, the child's welfare must be the paramount consideration of the adoption agency in processing the request, and in the case of any other child, the agency must have particular regard to the child's welfare.

Special guardianship orders

There are some children for whom adoption is not appropriate but who cannot return to their birth parents and could benefit from the permanence provided by a legally secure family placement. The explanatory notes to the Act explain:

> For example some older children (who may, for instance, be being looked after in long term foster placements) do not wish to be adopted and have their legal relationship with their parents severed, but could benefit from greater security and permanence. Adoption may also not be the best option for some children being cared for on a permanent basis by members of their wider family. Some ethnic minority communities have religious or cultural difficulties with adoption in the form provided for in the law of England and Wales.

Special guardianship is not, however, a replacement for adoption. In *AJ (A Child) (Adoption Order or Special Guardianship Order)* (2007), the Court of Appeal made clear that each case had to be decided on what was in the best interests of the particular child on the particular facts of the case. In particular, adoption provides carers with assurance that a placement will not be disturbed. Special guardianship cannot do this.

Section 115 of the Act amends the Children Act 1989 to insert provisions, ss. 14A–14G, which create special guardianship. Statutory references in this section of this chapter are therefore references to the Children Act 1989 as amended.

The special guardianship order, as the explanatory notes set out, is intended 'to provide the child with the stability he needs', and therefore 'the special guardian has clear responsibility for all the day to day decisions about caring for the child or young person and for taking decisions about his upbringing'.

Section 14A sets out the basic legal requirements which we reproduce in **Box 9.13**.

BOX 9.13 Special guardianship

(1) A 'special guardianship order' is an order appointing one or more individuals to be a child's 'special guardian' (or 'special guardians')

(2) A special guardian—
    (a) must be aged eighteen or over; and
    (b) must not be a parent of the child in question.

Special guardianship orders may be made following an application from someone who is entitled to make an application or from someone who has the leave of the court to make the application. The people who are entitled to apply for a special guardianship order with respect to a child are set out in s. 14A(5): see **Box 9.14**.

BOX 9.14 Those entitled to apply

(a) any guardian of the child;

(b) any individual in whose favour a residence order is in force with respect to the child;

(c) any individual listed in subsection (5)(b) or (c) of section 10 (as read with subsection (10) of that section);

(d) a local authority foster parent with whom the child has lived for a period of at least one year immediately preceding the application.

Subsection (6) provides for circumstances where the court may make a special guardianship order. Its provisions are set out in **Box 9.15** with respect to a child in any family proceedings in which a question arises with respect to the welfare of the child if:

(a) an application for the order has been made by an individual who falls within subsection (3)(a) or (b); or

(b) the court considers that a special guardianship order should be made even though no such application has been made.

BOX 9.15 Other circumstances when a court may make a special guardianship order

The court may also make a special guardianship order with respect to a child in any family proceedings in which a question arises with respect to the welfare of the child if—

(a) an application for the order has been made by an individual who falls within subsection (3)(a) or (b); or

(b) the court considers that a special guardianship order should be made even though no such application has been made.

No individual may make an application unless they give written notice of their intention to do so, either to the local authority which is looking after the child in question or otherwise to the local authority in whose area the individual is ordinarily resident.

Subsection (8) provides that on receipt of such a notice, the local authority must investigate the matter and prepare a report for the court dealing with:

(a) the suitability of the applicant to be a special guardian;

(b) such matters (if any) as may be prescribed by the Secretary of State; and

(c) any other matter which the local authority consider to be relevant.

The court may itself ask a local authority to conduct such an investigation and report on the results. The court may only make a special guardianship order if it has received a report from the local authority.

Section 14B sets out other matters to be considered when a special guardianship order is made. We have set this out in **Box 9.16**.

BOX 9.16 Additional matters to be considered

(1) Before making a special guardianship order, the court must consider whether, if the order were made—

    (a) a contact order should also be made with respect to the child, and

    (b) any section 8 order in force with respect to the child should be varied or discharged.

(2) On making a special guardianship order, the court may also—

    (a) give leave for the child to be known by a new surname;

    (b) grant the leave required by section 14C(3)(b) either generally or for specified purposes.

Section 14C(3)(b) prevents the removal of the child from the UK, without either the written consent of every person who has parental responsibility for the child or the leave of the court. However, the special guardian can remove the child for a period of up to three months.

The effect of a special guardianship order is set out in s. 14C—see **Box 9.17**.

BOX 9.17 The effect of special guardianship

Whilst the order is in force then—

(a) a special guardian appointed by the order has parental responsibility for the child in respect of whom it is made; and

(b) subject to any other order in force with respect to the child under this Act, a special guardian is entitled to exercise parental responsibility to the exclusion of any other person with parental responsibility for the child (apart from another special guardian).

Special guardianship orders may be varied or discharged following an application by someone listed in s. 14(D)(1), set out in **Box 9.18**.

BOX 9.18 Variation and discharge can be applied for by

(a) the special guardian (or any of them, if there are more than one);

(b) any parent or guardian of the child concerned;

(c) any individual in whose favour a residence order is in force with respect to the child;

(d) any individual not falling within any of paragraphs (a) to (c) who has, or immediately before the making of the special guardianship order had, parental responsibility for the child;

(e) the child himself; or

(f) a local authority designated in a care order with respect to the child.

The court may also of its own motion vary or discharge a special guardianship order if it considers that it should be varied or discharged during the course of any family proceedings. Anyone listed in paras (b) to (e) of s. 14D will require leave of the court before they can apply for variation or discharge. In all applications for leave other than that of the child, leave will be granted only if there has been a significant change in circumstances since the making of the special guardianship order.

Special guardianship is therefore distinct from adoption. The distinctions lie in the ability to vary or discharge the order and in the continuation of the legal link, although diluted, with the birth parents. As the explanatory notes to the Act put it 'unlike adoption, there is the possibility of discharge or variation of the order, and the child's legal relationship with his birth parents is not severed. They remain legally the child's parents, though their ability to exercise their parental responsibility is limited'.

Section 14F sets out the responsibilities of local authorities to make provision for special guardianship support services, which include counselling, advice and information, and financial support. Following a request for support services, the local authority may carry out an assessment of that person's needs for support, and must do so if the regulations prescribe. If the assessment leads to a decision by the local authority that a person has needs for support services then it may decide to provide them, and if it does it must prepare a plan of provision and keep the plan under review. Regulations will provide the detailed requirements of the assessment, planning, and review procedures. Finally, s. 14G provides that local authorities must establish a procedure for considering representations including complaints about the discharge of responsibilities to provide support services.

Key features of special guardianship orders

We summarize the key features of special guardianship orders in **Box 9.19**.

BOX 9.19 Special guardianship orders

Feature	Section of the Children Act	Comment and details
Special guardians	s. 14A(2)	Must be over 18 Must not be a parent of the child
Applications	s. 14A(3) and (5)	Guardians Individuals with residence orders Local authority foster parents Others with leave Can be appointed on court's own motion
Notice of intention of application	s. 14A(7) and (8)	Must be made Notice initiates investigation and report

Feature	Section of the Children Act	Comment and details
Parental responsibility	s. 14C	Special guardian gains parental responsibility Birth parents retain residual parental responsibility
Variation and discharge	s. 14D	Applications may be made as of right or with leave Child can apply with leave Court may make of own motion
Entitlement to support from local authority	s. 14F	Counselling, advice and information, etc

EXERCISES

Sonia has three children, Anita who is 12, Ben who is 6, and Caitlin who is 2. Sonia suffers from chronic alcoholism. Unfortunately, her sober intervals are becoming increasingly rare. She had a serious relapse about 18 months ago. The children were found on their own in Sonia's flat and it appeared that she had been gone for some days. Care orders were obtained on all three children. Anita is now settled with her grandmother. Ben and Caitlin are living with foster parents. You have been allocated this case and you would like to achieve some permanence for the children. Sonia has recently reluctantly begun to accept that she is unlikely to be able to care for her children again. The three children are very close to each other, and Anita is particularly close to Caitlin as she was her primary carer for large parts of her babyhood. Anita is very happy living with her grandmother. She has made it quite clear that she does not want to end her relationship with her mother. Ben and Caitlin are settled with the foster parents who have expressed a wish to adopt them. Caitlin in particular is very attached to them. The foster parents are white and in their mid-forties. Ben and Caitlin are mixed race.

What suggestions would you make to provide for the children? Why? What further information would you need? Assuming you decide that adoption may be appropriate, explain the procedure to Sonia. What contact provisions would you recommend?

ONLINE RESOURCE CENTRE

For guidance on how to answer these exercises, visit the Online Resource Centre at: www.oxfordtextbooks.co.uk/orc/socialwork13e/.

WHERE DO WE GO FROM HERE?

This chapter has been concerned with local authority responsibilities to plan for the long-term future of the children who are in their care. The next chapters have a quite different focus—they are concerned with children who get caught up in the criminal justice system and the complex responsibilities that arise in these circumstances.

 ANNOTATED FURTHER READING

The policy background to the Adoption and Children Act 2002

You may find it useful to read the proposals for adoption reform published by Sir Martin Narey who was appointed by the Secretary of State for Education to examine the need for reform of the adoption system. His report was published in *The Times* as the Narey Report on Adoption and can be found at www.mnarey.co.uk/publications.php.

You will also find useful information on the website of the British Association for Adoption and Fostering at www.baaf.org.uk.

Reform in context

D. Kirton, 'Kinship by design' in England: reconfiguring adoption from Blair to the coalition' (2013) *Child and Family Social Work* 18 (1): 97. This article analyses recent efforts to reform adoption in England, arguing that they represent an attempt to curtail the powers of adoption professionals and their established practices of assessing and responding to risk.

Contact

C. Smith and J. Logan, 'Adoptive parenthood as a "legal fiction"—its consequences for direct post adoption contact' (2002) *CFLQ* 14(3): 281.

Further details on the Adoption and Children Act 2002

N. Allen, Making *Sense of the New Adoption Law—A Guide for Social and Welfare Services* (Wiley, 2007).

F. Smith, et al., *Adoption Now: Law, Regulations, Guidance and Standards* (BAAF, 2013).

Both these books are aimed at the social worker wanting to understand the law.

Youth justice

10

OVERVIEW AND OBJECTIVES

There seems to be an ever-hardening rhetoric about crime and young people. Theresa May, the Home Secretary, writes in the forward to *Putting Victims First: More Effective Responses to Anti-Social Behaviour* (Cm 8367, 2012):

> We will introduce faster and more effective powers to stop the dangerous and yobbish behaviour of those who make victims' lives a misery. We will replace 19 complex existing powers with six simple new ones. The powers will include a new court order available on conviction that will stop the behaviour of the most destructive individuals and will address the underlying causes of that behaviour – addressing one of the main failings of the ASBO. There will be a new civil injunction that agencies can use immediately to protect victims and communities; simpler powers to close premises that are a magnet for trouble; and a more effective police power to stop anti-social behaviour in public places. We will also help speed up the eviction of anti-social tenants to stop 'nightmare neighbours' who ruin the lives of those around them.

But punishment has never been part of the statutory role of a social worker. The welfare of the child and the reduction of crime are, as we see shortly, the main statutory principles. Working with children suspected or convicted of crime means working with them when they are highly vulnerable, in order to help get them through the process with minimum damage and in a way that reduces future criminality.

In this chapter we will look at your statutory responsibilities, then we will work chronologically through the criminal process, focusing on those parts where a social worker is most likely to be involved: the police station interview; decisions to prosecute and alternative outcomes; youth courts and their sentencing powers; and consideration of how children can end up being sent for trial and sentence in adult courts. We will consider how social services can be involved in accommodating the child during the trial process, and we will look at helping the court make fair sentencing decisions.

Social workers can be involved when vulnerable adults are suspected of crime, particularly those with a mental disorder, in the police station, and we will flag up those responsibilities too.

 CASE STUDY

***V v UK* (1999) Case 24888/94 (also *T v UK* (1999) Case 24724/94), European Court of Human Rights**

Two boys, aged 10 and 11 at the time, were convicted in the Crown Court for abducting and murdering a 2-year-old boy, James Bulger. It was a highly publicized case. They were vilified in the press before, during, and after the trial.

V did not appeal against conviction but brought proceedings which eventually came before the European Court of Human Rights (ECtHR). He complained of a breach of Article 3 (the right not to suffer inhuman and degrading treatment), Article 6 (right to a fair trial), and Article 14 (he claimed, as a 10-year-old, he had been discriminated against; if he had been 9 years old, he would not have been tried since he would have been below the age of criminal responsibility). He complained that indefinite detention ('at Her Majesty's pleasure', the sentence instead of life imprisonment for those under 18) breached his right to liberty (Article 5). Finally, he complained that the Home Secretary's personal decision to increase the 'tariff' (the time he would actually spend in custody) was made by a politician and not an independent body (breach of the Article 6 requirement for a fair determination of his rights).

The ECtHR ruled that the welfare of the child, even one accused of a horrific crime, must be a guiding factor in all decisions within the criminal justice process. The right to understand and participate in his trial was the right of the child, not of his lawyers. He should have been personally able to follow and understand. The procedure of the case in an adult court was deemed 'incomprehensible and intimidating' to the boys, and they had been unable to discuss the case with their lawyers because they were suffering post-traumatic shock after having killed James.

Sentence should be determined impartially, by a court, not by a politician. However, the claim that V had been subjected to inhuman or degrading treatment was rejected. The Court ruled that the age of criminal responsibility in each state had to start at some arbitrary age, so he had not been discriminated against because of his age.

It noted:

> Special measures were taken in view of the applicant's young age and to promote his understanding of the proceedings: for example he had the trial procedure explained to him and was taken to see the courtroom in advance, and the hearing times were shortened so as not to tire the defendants excessively. Nonetheless, the formality and ritual of the Crown Court must at times have seemed incomprehensible and intimidating to a child of 11.

WHAT DOES THIS CASE TELL YOU ABOUT SOCIAL WORK PRACTICE?

What this case tells you is really straightforward. The investigation and trials of children accused of crime—however ghastly—affect real children whose welfare must be taken into account as a matter of law.

Statutory responsibilities of social workers

Box 10.1 highlights the main social work statutory responsibilities.

BOX 10.1 Statutory duties involving social workers in the justice system

Duties of an overarching nature	Legislation
Protection of welfare of children in criminal proceedings	Children and Young Persons Act 1933, Part III and Children and Young Persons Act 1969, Part I
Social services department must produce an annual youth justice plan	Crime and Disorder Act 1998, s. 40
Children in trouble trigger the social services duty to investigate and if necessary act to protect the child	Children Act 1989, s. 47
Children in need to be provided with support and in particular to be kept out of criminal justice system	Children Act 1989, s. 17 and Sch. 2

Duties of an overarching nature	Legislation
Local authority must provide support for child awaiting trial or sentence	Crime and Disorder Act 1998, s. 38
Vulnerable adults to be provided with support services	National Assistance Act 1948, s. 29
Social workers may be involved when a court sentences a person with a mental disorder	Mental Health Act 1983, s. 37
Every local authority must carry out all of its work in a way designed to reduce crime and disorder	Crime and Disorder Act 1998, s. 17
Services listed in Crime and Disorder Act 1998 s. 39 which social services authorities must ensure Youth Offending Teams can carry out; and additional statutory material relating to such services	
(a) appropriate adults to be available when the police interview juveniles	Police and Criminal Evidence Act 1984 Code of Practice
(b) rehabilitation following a police warning (to be abolished and replaced with youth caution: LAPSO 2012)	Children Act, s. 17; Crime and Disorder Act 1998, s. 65
(c) support for children awaiting trial or sentence	Children and Young Persons Act 1933, ss. 34 and 34A; CYPA 1969, s. 5(8)
(d) accommodation for children who are denied bail	Children and Young Persons Act 1969, s. 23; Children Act 1989, s. 20
(e) making reports to the court	Children and Young Persons Act 1969, s. 9
(f) persons to act as responsible officers where a court has made a parenting order	Crime and Disorder Act 1998, s. 8
(g) supervision of community sentences including Youth Rehabilitation Order (YRO)	Criminal Justice and Immigration Act 2008, s. 1
(h) supervision of children who are released from custody	Powers of Criminal Courts (Sentencing) Act 2000, ss 102–7
(i) arranging for convicted juveniles to go into secure accommodation if sentenced to a detention and training order and supervision during period served in the community	Powers of Criminal Courts (Sentencing) Act 2000, ss 102–7

Children's age in the justice system

Almost every European country sets the age of criminal responsibility higher than 10 (in Scotland it is 12), but in the case study we saw that the ECtHR did not find prosecuting a 10-year-old was in itself a breach of human rights. So at the age of 10 a child can be charged with, tried, and convicted of a criminal offence, and in a range of courts including the Crown Court.

But a child under 10 cannot, in English law, commit a crime, and therefore cannot be prosecuted (Children and Young Persons Act 1933, s. 50). Below that age, conduct which would otherwise be criminal must be dealt with informally by the police and/ or social services (a telling-off and a word with the parents) or through statutory proce- dures. One might be an application for a child safety order which could put the child under the supervision of a Youth Offending Team (YOT) set up by local authorities and made up of social workers liaising with other local authority workers, police, and pro- bation officers (see **Youth Offending Teams—liaison with police and other agencies**, p 347 and **chapter 8**); or a local curfew order could be issued; or care, supervision, or emergency protection orders (**chapter 8**). The behaviour of the child could be evidence of significant harm under s. 31 of the Children Act 1989.

Under 18-year-olds in most of the legislation are designated children (aged 10 to 13) or young persons (aged 14 to 17). Age is relevant to how children are treated in the justice system, but it is not as simple as applying safeguards to all children under 18.

- Defendants under 18 are called juveniles (but the old juvenile courts are now called youth courts, part of the magistrates' court system with specially trained magistrates).
- Children under 17 are considered vulnerable when being questioned by police.
- Children under 18 refused bail (ie not freed pending the case coming to court) should generally be accommodated by social services.
- Available sentences vary according to the age of the convicted child (and in some circumstances according to their sex).
- Secure children's homes run by local authorities take child offenders who are 10 to 14, those who have been in care, and those with mental health problems.
- Older children may be sent to secure training centres which offer education and training and are run by private companies.
- Young offender institutions, run by the Prison Service or private firms, can take those from 15 to 21, though social workers will not be involved after age 18.

Youth justice philosophy—tough on crime or concern for a vulnerable child?

Section 44 of the Children and Young Persons Act 1933 (CYPA 1933) makes the *welfare of the juvenile* the number one priority in the criminal justice system, as does the 1989 United Nations Convention on the Rights of the Child (UNCRC, to which the UK is a signatory). From 1933 to 1998 that core principle was taken for granted as the starting point for social workers, magistrates, police, and everyone else. But more recently the 'tough on crime' political mood led to s. 37 of the Crime and Disorder Act 1998 (CDA):

> It shall be the principal aim of the youth justice system to *prevent offending* by children and young persons. [Emphasis added]

Tied to this, under s. 17(1) of the CDA the local authority must:

> exercise its various functions with due regard to the likely effect of the exercise of those functions on, and the need to do all that it reasonably can to prevent, crime and disorder in its area.

The wording covers not just social services functions—housing services, for example, must also be managed for crime reduction. Indeed, every local authority (at district, borough, or county level, not just those with social service functions) must have a youth justice plan (CDA, ss. 6 and 40) setting out their strategy and targets for reducing crime and disorder.

Government policy on naming young offenders is an example of the conflict between protecting young offenders and the new punitive agenda. Court cases involving adults can be freely reported. Since the 1933 Act, the principle for young offenders was generally to separate them from the adult justice system, maintain their anonymity, and hope that they could enter adulthood without the stigma of youthful offending and without having been drawn into the adult criminal world (including in prison). The absolute anonymity provision in youth courts was originally contained in s. 49 of the 1933 Act. If they were tried in an adult court, as the Bulger killers were, the anonymity assumption would not apply but the judge could use his or her discretion to ban identification (s. 39).

The issue was considered in *McKerry v Teesdale and Wear Valley Justices* [2001] Crim LR 594 in which a 15-year-old, who was guilty of taking a car, appealed against a court's action in allowing a newspaper reporter to address the court on dispensing with reporting restrictions and the resultant lifting of the restrictions regarding his name (though not address). His argument was that 'naming and shaming' should not be used as punishment and the reporter had no right to address the court on the matter. The order lifting anonymity was upheld, however, the test being, according to an amendment to the 1933 Act (s. 49(4A) inserted by the Crime (Sentences) Act 1997, s. 45) whether the court is 'satisfied it is in the public interest to do so'. On the one hand, there were the child's privacy rights (Article 8 of the European Convention on Human Rights and Article 40 of the UNCRC guaranteeing the right of a child defendant 'to have his or her privacy fully respected at all stages of the proceedings'). On the other, these had to be balanced against freedom of expression rights (Article 10). However, Lord Bingham (then Lord Chief Justice) said:

> It is in my judgment plain that power to dispense with anonymity, as permitted in certain circumstances . . . must be exercised with very great care, caution and circumspection. It would be wholly wrong for any court to dispense with a juvenile's *prima facie* right to anonymity as an additional punishment.

It is not clear that government (of either hue) sees matters that way. For example, anti-social behaviour orders (ASBOs) are made in open civil court without anonymity (unless imposed by the court) and they may also be published by the authorities after assessing the need to do so and the vulnerability of the young person involved. The Serious Organised Crime and Police Act 2005 included a provision—s. 141(2)(a)—abolishing s. 49 anonymity for those sent to youth courts for breaching ASBOs (treated as a criminal offence) unless the court imposed an anonymity order.

The anomalous, even contradictory, position in which local authorities are put as a result of the move against anonymity is illustrated by the case of *Medway Council v BBC* [2001] All ER (D) 243. The local authority obtained ASBOs on eight children from the magistrates' court. The authority's motivation, the court noted in the case, had been in part to make an example of these problem children. But these problem children were also troubled children; indeed, they soon came to be recognized as children in need under s. 17 of the Children Act and children at risk of significant harm under s. 47. The same council now had to view the children from its Children Act perspective. It applied for a care order for one of the children. Given its responsibilities to the child's welfare it now needed to restrict, not encourage, publicity. Any information revealed in the care proceedings themselves was protected (Children Act 1989, s. 97(2)), but the council additionally sought an injunction to prevent the broadcast of an interview with the child's mother about the ASBO. The Family Division refused an injunction: the publicity related to proceedings over which it had no control, and (to paraphrase) it was too late to lock the stable door.

In other criminal cases prosecutors are now encouraged to ask for the anonymity of young people to be lifted after conviction. In the past it was generally only local papers that felt they had an interest in making such applications. The Crown Prosecution Service (CPS) has issued guidelines about 'circumstances where it will be appropriate for the prosecutor to make representations that there is a strong public interest in favour of lifting restrictions' (*Guidance on Imposing and Lifting Reporting Restrictions in Cases Involving Youths who are Convicted*). These include where there has been significant public disorder (the guidance was issued after the 2011 riots in England), 'where the public will rightly need to be satisfied that offenders have been brought to justice and there is a need to deter others'; serious offences 'which have undermined the public's confidence in the safety of their communities'; and hate crimes 'which can have a corrosive impact on the confidence of communities'. Previous guidance had said anonymity should be lifted when the offences were 'persistent, serious, affected a large number of people and where identifying the offender might prevent further offences'.

The new CPS guidance (2011) cites *McKerry*, saying: 'The public interest criterion will rarely be satisfied and it is wholly wrong to exercise the power as an additional punishment or for "naming and shaming".' However, it is clear that the perceptions of the public are now given a high priority and it is difficult to see how 'naming' can in reality be separated from 'shaming'. The argument must always be put, however, that the effect on each individual child's welfare interests must be assessed before a decision is made to name them.

As a social worker, you additionally have duties under s. 17 of and Schedule 2 to the Children Act 1989 which require you to promote the welfare of children and keep them out of the criminal courts (see **chapter 6**).

The Court of Appeal has considered the purpose of the youth justice system in *R v Shoban Butt* (2009) and made clear that while adults could be sentenced on a punitive basis (ie to reflect society's abhorrence of an offence), this was not the purpose of sentencing a juvenile. The sentence should be no longer than was required to deter crime.

▨ Youth Offending Teams—liaison with police and other agencies

The CDA created a Youth Justice Board (YJB) to sets standards and coordinate all parts of youth justice work, and to advise the government on policy.

The YJB is concerned with the funding of local YOTs, your most likely point of contact with the youth justice process, also set up under the CDA in 1998. There are 158 YOTs in England and Wales. Social services departments are at the heart of the YOT. Under s. 38 of the CDA, the social services department must secure all necessary youth justice services—listed in **Box 10.1**. It does this, under s. 39, by setting up YOTs for its area, or jointly with another area. The cooperation of police, probation, health, and education authorities is required by statute. The functions of the YOT in **Box 10.1** must be secured by the social services department, but need not necessarily be provided directly by it. Curiously, none of these appears in the Local Authority Social Services Act 1970 as a statutory duty (see **chapter 2**).

You are likely to work with the police at four levels: to work with children in general or a particular child to steer them away from criminality (a long-term process involving self-esteem, protection, education, housing, etc); to attend a police station when a child has been brought in as a suspect; to advise the police on welfare issues when they and the CPS are deciding whether to charge a child; and, if there is a conviction, to advise a court on sentence, consistent with the welfare of the child, most likely to cut future offending.

In an individual case police are likely to consult social services before making any but the most obvious decisions. Even if they do not consult you, the police must notify social services if they decide to prosecute a child (CYPA 1969, ss. 5 and 34).

The social worker in the police station

A suspect may have been arrested and taken to the police station, or bailed by the arresting officer with a requirement to attend at a future date. Or the child may attend 'voluntarily'—that is, without compulsion but having been told to.

What goes on when a suspect is held in the police station is governed by the Police and Criminal Evidence Act 1984 (PACE), and the PACE codes made by the Home Office. The important code is Code C on Detention, Treatment and Questioning, last updated in 2014. Code C can be consulted in every police station and at www.gov.uk/government/uploads/system/uploads/attachment_data/file/311276/PaceCodeC2014.pdf (Annex L details the regulations for searching transgender people).

The code recognizes two groups as being vulnerable in the police station. The first is 'juveniles', children under 17 (although much of the provision in Code C also applies to 17-year-olds, in particular the requirements for an appropriate adult, see Code C, para. 1.5A which follows a High Court judgment ([2013] EWHC 982 (Admin)) indicating the incompatibility of 17-year-olds being treated as adults with the UNCRC). The other is suspects who are mentally vulnerable (Code C, Part 11). Under Code C, para. 1.5, if the police have any suspicion, or are told in good faith, that a person is a juvenile, they must act accordingly unless they have reliable evidence to the contrary. An 'appropriate adult' (usually parent or guardian) should be called to assist the suspect; no questioning should normally take place until an appropriate adult has arrived.

Where a parent cannot or will not come, or is deemed not to be suitable, a social worker will frequently be asked to be the appropriate adult.

Identifying the appropriate adult

Code C contains several references to the appropriate adult: see **Box 10.2**.

BOX 10.2 Extract from Code C, para. 1.7, defining who is an appropriate adult, with emphasis added to show where social workers can be involved

(a) in the case of a juvenile:

   (i) the parent, guardian or, if the juvenile is in local authority or voluntary organisation care, or is otherwise being looked after under the Children Act 1989, *a person representing that authority* or organisation;

   (ii) *a social worker of a local authority;*

   (iii) failing these, some other responsible adult aged 18 or over who is not a police officer or employed by the police.

(b) in the case of a person who is mentally disordered or mentally vulnerable:

   (i) a relative, *guardian*, or other person responsible for their care or custody;

   (ii) *someone experienced in dealing with mentally disordered or mentally vulnerable people* but who is not a police officer or employed by the police;

   (iii) failing these, *some other responsible adult aged 18 or over who is not a police officer or employed by the police.*

Note: someone experienced or trained in the person's care is to be preferred unless the individual wants a relative rather than a qualified stranger.

Where the police detain a juvenile or a person mentally disordered or mentally vulnerable, para. 3.15 of Code C requires them to identify who they think is the appropriate adult and to inform the appropriate adult as soon as practicable of the grounds for detention, and where the suspect is being detained. They will then request the appropriate adult to come to the police station. This is not least because if they interview the suspect without an appropriate adult, any evidence obtained is likely to be seen as unreliable or unfair under ss. 76 and 78 of PACE, and therefore not available if there is a trial (see **Exclusion at trial of evidence obtained in police questioning**, p 356).

However, in exceptional cases, Code C, para. 11.18 allows the police to interview a juvenile or mentally disordered adult without an appropriate adult. This must be authorized by a superintendent or more senior officer who must certify that delay will (not might) lead to immediate risk of harm to anyone, tip-offs to other suspects, or interference with evidence, and that proceeding without the appropriate adult will not harm the suspect mentally or physically. The Code warns that the evidence obtained may be unreliable (and, consequently, as we see later, may be unusable):

> 11C Although juveniles or people who are mentally disordered or otherwise mentally vulnerable are often capable of providing reliable evidence, they may, without knowing or wishing to do so, be particularly prone in certain circumstances to provide information that may be unreliable, misleading or self-incriminating.

Special care should always be taken when questioning such a person, and the appropriate adult should be involved if there is any doubt about a person's age, mental state or capacity. Because of the risk of unreliable evidence it is also important to obtain corroboration of any facts admitted whenever possible.

As well as enlisting an appropriate adult before interviewing, the police must attempt to inform the person responsible for the child's welfare (usually a parent or guardian) of the arrest and detention of any juvenile (CYPA 1933, s. 34(2)); if the juvenile is under supervision they must inform the supervisor, and, if in local authority care or accommodation, the local authority.

A social services department must have appropriate adults available, but there is no statutory duty for one to be sent or for the police to approach a social worker rather than a parent. Clearly, where a juvenile is in your care, a social worker from that authority is the appropriate adult. But in other situations it may be better for a parent or other relative to attend. It will depend on your knowledge of the circumstances. For example, in *DPP v Blake* (1989), Norfolk Social Services had a policy of never sending a social worker if a parent was available. In this case the father of a detained 16-year-old girl was available, but the girl had no real relationship with him. She asked for her social worker. During the police interview the father played no part and his daughter ignored him. She eventually confessed and, based on this confession, was tried and convicted. The Court of Appeal held that the confession should not have been admitted into evidence; it was unreliable because the appropriate adult had not provided any assistance to the juvenile. In *R v Jefferson* (1994), the appropriate adult, the father, actually helped the police to interrogate the suspect, often contradicting the boy's account. This is not what is expected of the appropriate adult. The confession should not have been used, but because of other evidence the boy's conviction for riot and violent disorder was allowed to stand.

Home Office Study No 174 of 1997 found that for juveniles the appropriate adult is a social worker in 23 per cent of cases, and generally does a better job than parents, relatives, or other adults. The social worker is calmer, more supportive, and understands the task. But an individual social worker to whom the juvenile has previously admitted the offence is not the appropriate adult—another social worker will be required (Code 1C). In that case, of course, your reason for not attending in person should not be given to the police (see **chapter 4** for guidance on confidentiality).

An appropriate adult has only one task, that of assisting the detainee, and must never double as an interpreter (*R v West London Youth Court, ex p J* (2000)).

The Home Office research study found that the appropriate adult in cases of mental disorder is a social worker in 60 per cent of cases.

Attending as an appropriate adult

It is important to get to the police station as soon as possible, to minimize the period of detention. Once you arrive, you should obtain basic details from the custody officer or suspect's solicitor—suspected offence, time of arrest, and what the police are intending to do, in particular.

Your role is described in the following sections. Your objective is not that of helping the police. Resist the police advice along the lines 'Between you and me, if you could persuade him to tell us what happened, he'll be out of here much quicker . . .'

The detainee is entitled to consult you privately at any time (Code C, para. 3.18). Make sure that your discussion is entirely in private: conversations overheard can be used in evidence at trial (*R v Ali* (1991)). If a solicitor has been called, he or she may wish to hold the first interview without you being present. This is because the solicitor's duty of confidentiality is virtually absolute, whereas something said in front of a social worker could, exceptionally, be ordered to be revealed in court. (We say '*virtually absolute*' in the light of the case of *Re McE* (2009), where the House of Lords accepted that police can in law eavesdrop even on solicitor–client interviews in circumstances set out in the Regulation of Investigatory Powers Act 2000.)

Police powers of detention

The only lawful purpose of detention is for the police to obtain evidence to make a decision whether to charge or not—not to obtain evidence to use at trial. They should charge or release as soon as possible, which means as soon as they have enough evidence to decide (s. 37 and Code C, para. 16).

Home Office Circular 60/2003 states that a child should not be detained for more than 24 hours unless the offence is a serious arrestable offence and bail is considered inappropriate. As well as the obvious serious crimes of rape, possessing firearms, or grievous bodily harm (GBH), any arrestable offence can be serious if the consequences are serious, such as causing death or serious injury, or substantial financial gain or loss. Code C says that detention of a juvenile or mentally disordered suspect beyond 24 hours will involve consideration of:

  (a) special vulnerability;
  (b) the legal obligation to provide an opportunity for representations to be made prior to a
       decision about extending detention;
  (c) the need to consult and consider the views of any appropriate adult; and
  (d) any alternatives to police custody.

The police cannot in any event detain beyond 36 hours after arrival at the police station (PACE, s. 41). But a magistrates' court can renew the period for a further 36 hours, and again up to a final total of 96 hours (s. 43). (In a terrorism case detention can be extended even longer: currently 28 days.)

Decisions concerning detention and charge are made by an officer called the custody officer (ss. 37 and 38), who must be independent of the investigation. Any complaints or problems should be addressed to the custody officer. One of the first things the appropriate adult should ask the custody officer is whether the suspect has in fact been detained. If the suspect is not detained, they are a 'volunteer' and they are free to leave. Of course, once they say they wish to leave this may trigger an arrest; but at least at that point the time clock for maximum periods of detention has started to run.

Right to legal advice

Section 58 of PACE and Code C give detainees and volunteers a right to legal advice in person or on the telephone, in private, at any time, day or night, before they are questioned and during police interview. This legal advice is paid for by the Legal Aid Agency and is not means-tested. The detainee can nominate an adviser, or ask for the duty solicitor (or representative).

A detainee who declines legal advice must sign the custody record to confirm this decision. However, it is possible to 'just sign the custody record here, and again, here, please' without realizing the importance of the right which has been declined. Home Office research in 1997 (Study 155, *PACE Ten Years On*) showed that only 41 per cent of juveniles requested legal advice. Even this is higher than the adult rate, thanks to social workers routinely insisting on calling a lawyer.

The s. 58 right to advice never stops, and the appropriate adult can call a legal adviser even if the suspect declined to do so. But it is the decision of the suspect whether to actually see the solicitor or not (Code C, para. 6.5A).

If a solicitor is called, the advice on law should be left to him or her. Nevertheless, it will help you to communicate between solicitor and detainee if you know what is going on.

Right to have someone informed of the detention

A detainee is entitled on request to have the police notify a person who is likely to have an interest in their welfare (s. 56 of the Act, para. 5.1 of the Code—the notification condition). If the police cannot contact the person chosen, they must try at least two further people chosen by the suspect. The police should normally allow the detainee to speak to the person by telephone.

Informing the suspect of PACE rights

On arrival, the suspect must be told of these rights, and the right to consult the Code. When the appropriate adult arrives, the suspect should be told this again, in the adult's presence. Suspects are entitled to written notice of their rights under the Code, which must be available in a range of languages and in audio (Code, Notes for Guidance to s. 3).

Denial of PACE rights

Refusal or delay in the right to legal advice and to have someone notified requires the authority of a superintendent or higher ranking officer, and can only occur where the offence is a serious arrestable offence (discussed in **Attending as an appropriate adult**, p 350). The officer must be satisfied that the exercise of the right *will* (not may) lead to harm to others, interference with evidence, or a tip-off of other suspects, or hinder the recovery of property (PACE, s. 58, and Annex B to Code C). But as refusal necessarily requires the police to believe that the adviser intends to commit a criminal offence, this is most unlikely.

After 36 hours in the police station, no delay in the right to advice can be authorized.

Once an adviser has been requested, there must be no further questioning until he or she arrives, unless the superintendent believes that delay will lead to immediate risk of harm to persons or serious damage to property, or will unreasonably delay the investigation, or unless the suspect and the appropriate adult both consent (it is hard to think of circumstances where this is appropriate).

We stated earlier that the purpose of detention is to decide whether or not to charge. That decision is taken by the custody officer. This officer must formally review the detention after 6 hours, and then every 9 hours, to confirm whether detention is required or consider the decision could be made now.

Once charged, the accused person should, normally, be released on bail, which we discuss shortly. If a decision is made not to charge, the suspect must be released. If the police realize that they need more time and more information before they can decide whether to charge, the suspect may be bailed to report to the police station on a later date.

Drug testing children in the police station

Section 63B of PACE enables urine or non-intimate samples to be taken, in approved police stations, to test detainees for Class A drugs. For those aged at least 14 but below 18 it can be done only if they have been charged with a 'trigger offence' (eg theft, burglary, robbery, and others set out in Sch. 6 to the Criminal Justice and Court Services Act 2000) or charged with an offence that an officer of at least the rank of inspector believes was linked to drug taking. The notification condition must also have been met, as outlined in **Right to have someone informed of the detention**, p 352. The suspect must be informed that refusal to give a sample without good cause may result in prosecution. Detainees should be told or reminded that they have a right to get legal advice before the sample is taken (Code C), and the sample must be taken in the presence of the appropriate adult where the suspect is below the age of 18.

Conditions of detention

As soon as someone is detained (but not helping as a 'volunteer') at the police station, a custody record must be opened, to record all events, decisions, and reviews, as well as listing the property of the detainee. Code C gives the detainee and the appropriate adult a right to inspect the record. You will particularly be looking to see reasons for any refusal of the right to legal advice, either by the detainee or by the police. If any complaints are made they must be noted in the record—this includes complaints by the appropriate adult.

Code C sets out how detainees must be treated. Requirements include adequate heating and lighting, temperature, toilet facilities, and sufficient meals, taking account of special dietary requirements. A juvenile should not be kept in a cell unless no other suitable accommodation or supervision is available; the reason must be entered in the custody record. If you suspect treatment may be improper, check s. 8 of Code C (you must be allowed to see a copy) and if appropriate make your complaint, which has to be recorded.

Under s. 9 of Code C, a police surgeon must be called if there is any indication of physical illness or mental disorder, injury, or other apparent need, or upon request by the detainee. If the police surgeon is unavailable, another GP must be called or the detainee taken to hospital. It is therefore vital that you check if the detainee has a medical problem or needs medication, and inform the custody officer.

Under s. 5, the police should allow the detainee to receive visits (but may refuse if short-staffed). A social worker can assist in this by contacting family or friends of a detainee. (Be careful, of course, not to inadvertently pass on messages that may help to dispose of evidence or enable another suspect to avoid arrest.)

Any interview should not proceed while the suspect is unfit through drink or drugs—if you think this applies, you need to insist on a delay. If necessary, insist on a delay and ask for a doctor.

When the interview starts, the first thing that happens is that a tape recorder, with two tapes, is switched on and the parties present identify themselves. One tape is used as a working copy and the other is sealed in front of the parties as a secure copy. The suspect will later be provided, via the solicitor, with a transcript, and can ask for the tape as well. A suspect must be cautioned or re-cautioned before any questioning starts.

If, before the interview, the suspect has made any statement that may be important if the case goes to court, or alternatively failed to answer any significant question which a court could take into account, the police must put it to him or her at the start of the formal interview (Code C, para. 11.4).

There should be a break at least every 2 hours and at usual mealtimes. There must normally be a break of 8 continuous hours every 24 hours, usually at night time. Inducements to confess should not be offered, although if a suspect asks what course the police will take if he or she divulges certain information ('If I tell you, will I be out of here quicker?') the police are allowed to answer.

Code D, the Code of Practice for the Identification of Persons by Police Officers, like the other codes, is available at the police station for consultation, and covers fingerprinting and identification procedures. The detainee, or you on his or her behalf, should exercise the right to legal advice before consenting. If the police insist on proceeding before the solicitor arrives, ensure that the reasons are given and recorded, and stay with the detainee to observe what happens and also to reduce the risk of an informal interview taking place.

Fingerprints and DNA samples may be taken after arrest or charge for a recordable offence (all but the most minor offences such as breach of the peace). The appropriate adult cannot give consent to fingerprints or DNA samples on behalf of a juvenile. Consent in the case of a child—aged 10 to 14—is the consent of parents alone; in the case of a young adult—aged 14 to 17—of the parents and the juvenile.

Police can only authorize taking samples if they believe they will confirm or disprove the suspect's involvement in the offence. Intimate samples can only be taken by a medical practitioner with written consent. A refusal without good reason may be used as evidence of guilt in a court case. Non-intimate samples (hair that is not pubic hair, a swab from the skin or mouth but not any other orifice, and a sample from a nail or under a nail) can be taken by use of reasonable force if consent is not forthcoming and an officer of the rank of inspector or above authorizes it. Photographs may be taken without consent if consent is not forthcoming.

The detainee has the right to refuse an identification parade, but should be aware that alternative methods of identification—direct confrontation or identification by photographs—are more likely to lead to a positive identification.

The role of the appropriate adult at the police station

Where the appropriate adult is present at an interview, they shall be informed that they are not expected to act simply as an *observer*, and that the purposes of their presence are, first, to *advise* the person being questioned and to observe whether or not the interview is being conducted properly and fairly, and secondly, to *facilitate communication* with the person being interviewed. [Emphasis added]

(Code C, para. 11.17)

As an observer, your presence should ensure that correct procedures are followed, and you should formally complain if they are not, insisting your concerns are noted in the custody record: evidence of breach of procedures could lead to evidence from questioning being excluded, which the police do not want. See **Exclusion at trial of evidence obtained in police questioning**, p 356, for more detail on how courts decide whether to exclude this evidence.

As an adviser you are not being requested to advise on the law: that is for the legal adviser. The Code is not clear on what advice it is for you to give, but if it is not legal, it will be everything else: how to cope with the ordeal, in particular.

Your third task is to help the suspect communicate with the lawyer and with the police. This means you need to understand what advice is being, or should be, given. So we need to look at some of the legal issues which can arise in the police station or as a result of what happens there.

There is also an important role as an advocate of the detainee's rights and interests. If, for example, a senior officer wishes to delay the right to see a solicitor, to continue to detain for questioning, or to refuse bail after charge, the police ought to listen to your views before deciding. It means interrupting if the questioning is oppressive (eg repetition of questions already dealt with) or incomprehensible (eg asking an over-complex question). If the interview is extremely oppressive, you will need to consider whether to state your concerns and then leave. Advocacy includes insisting on breaks for refreshment.

Legal issues during police questioning

The right to remain silent under interrogation is an ancient feature of the common law as well as a human right under Article 6, which states:

> Everyone charged with a criminal offence shall be presumed innocent until proved guilty in accordance with the law.

However, the Criminal Justice and Public Order Act 1994 (ss. 31–38) permits a court, and in particular a jury, to draw adverse conclusions from silence. So there is a risk in failing to answer questions, and this must be explained to the suspect. The wording of the obligatory police caution (Code C, para. 10) is quite complex:

> You do not have to say anything. But it may harm your defence if you do not mention when questioned something which you later rely on in court. Anything you do say may be given in evidence.

The legal adviser will have to explain the consequences of not answering questions before questioning starts. Adverse inferences can be drawn, even if he or she stayed silent on the advice of a solicitor (*R v Daniel* (1998)) and even where the detainee was of low intelligence (*R v Friend* (1997): a 14-year-old with an IQ of 63).

A lawyer might nevertheless advise a detainee not to answer questions, for example where the police have failed to outline the allegations which have to be answered. Failure to provide this information is in fact a breach of Article 6(1) (right to a fair trial); the case of *Edwards v UK* (1992) establishes that a right to disclosure of the prosecution case applies at all stages of the criminal process. The lawyer, of course, must be the person giving advice to the suspect on the issue of whether or not to answer questions.

If the police interview a suspect who has requested an adviser but before one is available, no inferences can be drawn from silence. So a simpler caution is then used:

> You do not have to say anything, but anything you do say may be given in evidence.

Exclusion at trial of evidence obtained in police questioning

When a confession is part of the prosecution case, it is up to the prosecution to prove that there was no oppression and there were no other circumstances in play at the time which might cause it to be unreliable (PACE, s. 76).

To decide whether the circumstances at interview amounted to oppression, or led to unreliability, the court holds a 'trial within a trial'. Prosecution and defence present evidence of how the confession was obtained (in the Crown Court the jury is sent out). On rare occasions, an appropriate adult may be called as a witness in this mini-trial. Just in case, you should always go to the police station with paper, pens, and an accurate watch. You should record the time, to the minute, of every stage of the procedure—arrival, talking to the custody officer, waiting to see the detainee, length of interview, etc—and the names, rank, and numbers of the people you deal with. If the police see you noting these details, they should respect your professional approach, and may resist the temptation to do anything in breach of the code. If you are called as a witness you can refresh your memory from these notes.

Courts also look at confessions in the light of s. 78 of PACE which requires a court to exclude evidence if to admit it would be unfair. An example would be tricking the suspect by lying about having found fingerprint evidence against the detainee.

Taking Code C, ss. 58, 76, and 78 of PACE, and Article 6 into account, courts tend to exclude confessions obtained in a non-urgent case in the absence of an appropriate adult (*R v Delaney* (1989)).

The police may have talked to the suspect about the offence 'informally' before you or the lawyer are allowed to see him or her, and obtained damaging evidence. You obviously cannot prevent this. But if at the same time you have a record that you were waiting in the foyer and available, it is possible that any evidence obtained will be ruled inadmissible (*R v Franklin* (1994)). If you are kept waiting unnecessarily, make a complaint to the custody officer, so that it is registered in the custody record. Code C (para. 11.1) forbids this type of informal questioning, except where there is a risk to property or people, or the likelihood of evidence being tampered with.

Charges, youth cautions, or no action

At some point during the detention of the juvenile, the police must make a decision. The options are to charge and prosecute, to give a youth caution (under the Legal Aid, Sentencing and Punishment of Offenders Act 2012 (LASPO) s. 135, which abolishes the old reprimand and warning system in the CDA 1998), or to take no further action. With a juvenile the decision may take time, in which case police bail should be granted until the decision is made.

A decision to charge must be approved by the CPS, which will wish to be sure that adequate evidence is there for a conviction, and that prosecution is in the public interest. But as well as consulting the CPS, if the suspect is a juvenile the police should consult with the YOT. They can only avoid this if it is obvious that there should be a charge because of the seriousness of the offence, or the case is so trivial that no charge is appropriate. In between these clear-cut cases, liaison with appropriate agencies is normal before a decision is made; but the decision is still that of the police and CPS. Guidance on whether to prosecute in the public interest is found in the Code for Crown Prosecutors (www.cps.gov.uk/publications/code_for_crown_prosecutors/codetest.html). The Code states in relation to young suspects:

> The criminal justice system treats children and young people differently from adults and significant weight must be attached to the age of the suspect if they are a child or young person under 18. The best interests and welfare of the child or young person must be considered including whether a prosecution is likely to have an adverse impact on his or her future prospects that is disproportionate to the seriousness of the offending. Prosecutors must have regard to the principal aim of the youth justice system which is to prevent offending by children and young people. Prosecutors must also have regard to the obligations arising under the United Nations 1989 Convention on the Rights of the Child.

> As a starting point, the younger the suspect, the less likely it is that a prosecution is required.

> However, there may be circumstances which mean that notwithstanding the fact that the suspect is under 18, a prosecution is in the public interest. These include where the offence committed is serious, where the suspect's past record suggests that there are no suitable alternatives to prosecution, or where the absence of an admission means that out-of-court disposals which might have addressed the offending behaviour are not available.

In principle, the High Court, on judicial review, can quash a decision to prosecute if it is demonstrably not in the public interest to prosecute. But it is very unlikely an application will succeed. For example, in *R (on the application of S) v DPP* (2006) a boy of 15 was charged with rape of a 12-year-old girl. She could not give consent to intercourse in view of her age, though on the evidence the sex was consensual. The court refused to stop the prosecution as the defendant, while young, was still three years older than the victim.

Reprimands, warnings, and youth cautions

The system of reprimands and warnings was formerly governed by ss. 65 and 66 of the CDA 1998. These sections have been removed by LASPO and replaced with sections on youth cautions (new ss. 66ZA and 66ZB). Reprimands/warnings last for two years so you may still come across them—but they will be treated retrospectively as if they were youth cautions.

Reprimands used to be issued for a first offence if it was not too serious; a warning was the next step for a person who had previously been reprimanded, or for a first more serious offence. The new youth cautions can cover both these situations; they may be more flexibly issued, not necessarily for first offences.

New s. 66ZA(1) says:

> A constable may give a child or young person ('Y') a caution under this section (a 'youth caution') if—
>
> (a) the constable decides that there is sufficient evidence to charge Y with an offence,
>
> (b) Y admits to the constable that Y committed the offence, and
>
> (c) the constable does not consider that Y should be prosecuted or given a youth conditional caution in respect of the offence.

The Secretary of State has published guidance on the appropriate circumstances for youth cautions (see www.justice.gov.uk/downloads/oocd/youth-cautions-guidance-police-yots-oocd.pdf). For children under 17 years of age they have to be given in the presence of the appropriate adult. That child's admission must be genuine and not obtained by inducement or pressure (*R v Commissioner of Police of the Metropolis, ex p Thompson* (1997)). It must be unambiguous (*R (on the application of M) v (1) Leicestershire Constabulary (2) Crown Prosecution Service* (2009), where a juvenile admitted unsolicited sexual activity with a girl but nothing amounting to attempted rape. He should not have been given a warning.)

The guidance on the old warnings and reprimands made clear that they should not be administered where the evidence against the juvenile is weak. If the police do not consider on the evidence they have that a conviction is more likely than an acquittal, the case should simply be dropped. In *DPP v Ara* (2001) the police wanted to issue an old-style caution to A (which predated reprimands and warnings), but refused to tell his solicitor what evidence they had, and the solicitor could not advise A whether to accept the caution. So the police charged A instead. The magistrates dismissed the charge as an abuse of process. Evidence, including a taped interview not made available to the solicitor by police, showed that there was a good case against the suspect. If the solicitor had been given that evidence he would have advised accepting the caution—the case would therefore not have come to court. The High Court agreed with this logic and upheld the magistrates' decision. The same principle applies now: police must reveal their evidence so a suspect can, on advice, decide whether to accept the youth caution.

Under s. 66ZB of LASPO:

> (1) If a constable gives a youth caution to a person, the constable must as soon as practicable refer the person to a youth offending team.
>
> (2) . . . on a referral of a person under subsection (1), the youth offending team—
>
> (a) must assess the person, and
>
> (b) unless they consider it inappropriate to do so, must arrange for the person to participate in a rehabilitation programme.

While a youth caution is not a criminal conviction, for example for job applications, if a person is later found guilty of an offence, it may be taken into account for sentencing. Under the old system, if someone was convicted of an offence within two years of a warning, the court would not consider a discharge but moved to a more serious sentence. A warning in relation to a sexual offence resulted in the offender being placed on the register of sex offenders. The same is likely to apply to youth cautions.

Legal advice and representation in criminal cases

Help from a solicitor out of public funds is governed by the Access to Justice Act 1999, modified by the Legal Aid, Sentencing and Punishment of Offenders Act 2012. In the police station, as we have seen under s. 58 of PACE, any suspect can insist on seeing a solicitor. The scheme is known as the police station duty solicitor scheme. A move to means test this service through the 2012 Act was withdrawn by the government under intense political pressure.

A similar scheme operates at court for an accused person who is brought directly to court following police detention or police bail. The court duty solicitor can deal with bail applications, ask for an adjournment, and make a plea in mitigation if there is an immediate guilty plea and no adjournments for reports.

For representation and advice beyond this, a specialist criminal solicitor has to be sought. This will normally be a solicitor working in a private firm. Legal aid for representation in criminal proceedings of under 16s, or under 18s without independent income, is free.

Waiting for the final hearing—bail or custody

Police bail after charge

If a juvenile is charged, he or she should normally be released on bail. Police are not required to liaise with social services on bail decisions, though it is likely they will do so.

Police, like courts, can make bail conditional—for example, requiring that the accused live at a certain address or does not approach a witness. Another person can be asked to stand surety, which means that person is liable to pay a penalty if the accused absconds. A court can also impose bail conditions which have nothing to do with preventing offending or with securing attendance at court, and under s. 3(6)(ca) of the Bail Act 1976 (as amended in 2003) can impose conditions 'for his own protection or, if he is a child or young person, for his own welfare or in his own interests'.

A breach of police bail is a criminal offence. It also makes it less likely that the court will grant bail when an application is made.

Refusal of police bail

The police can refuse bail only on grounds set out in s. 38 of PACE:

(a)   the custody officer is not satisfied of the identity or address of the person charged;

(b)   the custody officer believes that the person will not answer bail, will interfere with evidence or witnesses, cause injury to themselves or others, or damage to property;

(c)   the custody officer believes that it is necessary for the person's own protection; or

(d)   granting bail would not be in a juvenile's own interests.

Section 38 does not offer guidance on what the interests of the juvenile are in this situation; but on refusal of bail the juvenile must be transferred to local authority accommodation, and it will be this transfer pending trial that the police may see as being in the juvenile's interests.

If a suspect is charged and bail is refused, he or she must be brought before a court at the earliest practicable time. Until that point, s. 38(6) of PACE requires the custody officer to make arrangements for the juvenile to be taken into local authority accommodation. The subsection makes it lawful for the local authority to detain the juvenile in secure accommodation (but there is no obligation to do so). It will be up to the authority to transport the juvenile to court.

Under s. 38(6), following a refusal of bail, the custody officer can refuse to transfer the detained juvenile to local authority accommodation on one of two grounds.

(a)   If the juvenile is 15 or older, the custody officer considers that the juvenile is a danger to the public and that the local authority lacks adequate secure accommodation.
(b)   It is not practical to make the arrangements for a transfer. This should be exceptional, for example social services are on strike or the roads are blocked by snow.

The custody officer must give a certificate to this effect and may then detain the juvenile in the same way as an adult until the first court appearance; that is, in the police station (but not in a cell if this can be avoided).

Court bail

Courts which adjourn before they have completely disposed of a case can either release the accused unconditionally or on bail or in custody.

The grounds in s. 4 of the Bail Act 1976 for a court to refuse bail are almost identical to those for police bail under PACE (see **Refusal of police bail**, p 359). Breach of court bail or bail conditions is a criminal offence and will make further bail applications more difficult.

Court remand into custody

If bail is refused and the child is at least 12 and below 18 years of age, the remand will normally be to local authority accommodation (formerly under CYPA 1969, s. 23; now under LASPO, ss. 91 and 92).

The court designates a local authority (LASPO, s. 92(3)) which is (a) in the case of a child who is being looked after by a local authority, that authority or (b) the local authority in whose area it appears to the court that the child habitually resides or the offence or one of the offences was committed.

The court can impose conditions on the child and hence under s. 93(3) of LASPO on the local authority (a) to secure compliance with any conditions imposed on the child or (b) requirements stipulating that the child must not be placed with a named person (eg the parent or someone involved in the alleged offence).

Among conditions may be electronic tagging of a child aged 12 or over who is alleged to have committed one of certain serious imprisonable offence and where the YOT has told the court electronic monitoring would be suitable for the child (LASPO, s. 94; s. 95 for those where the offence gives rise to extradition proceedings).

In the case of serious offences, the child may be remanded to youth detention accommodation to protect the public or prevent any further imprisonable offence (LASPO, s. 98); or if, additionally, the child has a history of absconding or there is a history of the child committing imprisonable offences or there is a high likelihood of him or her receiving a custodial sentence (LASPO, s. 99). Sections 100 and 101 have similar conditions for cases involving the possibility of extradition.

Serious offences are defined as a violent or sexual offence, or an offence punishable in the case of an adult with imprisonment for a term of 14 years or more.

In the case of remand into youth detention, a local authority will be designated for various responsibilities (including potentially the cost of youth detention) and consulted about the detention. The child will have 'looked-after child status'; that is, 'is to be treated as a child who is looked after by the designated authority' (LASPO, s. 104(1)—in local authority care or accommodated by the authority under the Children Act 1989, s. 22(1)). The *Children Act 1989 Guidance and Regulations, Volume 2: Care Planning, Placement and Case Review* will regulate these placements. (See chapter 8 of the guidance.)

It is for the authority to decide how to accommodate the juvenile. The considerations are the same as for any child it is looking after (see **chapter 6**).

Remand to hospital

A court can remand any person accused of a criminal offence who may be mentally disordered to a hospital for the purpose of obtaining a medical report, or for treatment: Mental Health Acts, ss. 35 and 36.

Allocation of the juvenile to youth court, magistrates' court, or Crown Court for trial and sentence

Most cases involving a juvenile are dealt with in the youth court. The exceptions arise where the alleged offence is serious, or where an adult is a co-accused. **Box 10.3** explains these exceptions. Where a child becomes an adult during the course of the proceedings he or she can be sent to the adult court for trial or sentence (Crime and Disorder Act 1998, s. 47). If the youth court decides not to do so, it must sentence him or her as if still under 18 (CYPA 1969, s. 29: *A v DPP* (2002), where an 18-year-old was sentenced to a detention and training order, a sentence not available for adult offenders).

 BOX 10.3 Use of adult courts for juvenile cases

Case factually connected to an adult defendant (CYPA 1933, s. 16; CYPA 1969, s. 18; Magistrates' Courts Act 1980, s. 24):

- magistrates *must* try juvenile with adult if adult is to be tried by magistrates and juvenile and adult are jointly charged with same offence;
- may send juvenile to youth court for separate trial if adult pleading guilty and juvenile pleading not guilty, or charges are factually connected but not joint;
- Crown Court committal for adult: magistrates *must* separate juvenile from adult if in interest of justice—for example, wide difference in ages; evidential issues not closely connected.

Murder and grave crimes (Powers of Criminal Courts (Sentencing) Act 2000 (PCCSA), ss. 90 and 91); grave crime means:

- could attract 14-year prison sentence if committed by adult;
- indecent assault;
- death by dangerous driving, careless driving while under the influence of alcohol or drugs, or firearms offence and accused is at least 14.

More than two years custody likely to be the sentence (Magistrates' Courts Act 1980, s. 24):

- youth court must commit case to Crown Court for trial if powers of punishment of youth court (maximum two years' custody) would be insufficient. The decision must be made before conviction.

Case involves a child witness (CDA 1998, s. 51B).

In *R v Ghafoor* (2002) the Court of Appeal reminded sentencing courts that it is a breach of human rights to impose a harsher penalty on an offender than could have been applied at the date the offence was committed. In this case an 18-year-old convicted of riot had been sentenced to four and a half years in a young offender institution; but he was only 17 at the time of the offence and the maximum for a 17-year-old was 24 months' detention and training.

Supporting a child appearing before the criminal court

Box 10.4 indicates ways in which the child's vulnerability must, by statute, be taken account of.

 BOX 10.4 Statutes or child rules recognizing defendants are vulnerable

Court shall to have regard welfare of child	CYPA 1933, s. 44
Local authority to be notified of proceedings	CYPA 1969, s. 5
Explain the charge and proceedings in language child will understand	Magistrates Courts (Children and Young Persons) Rules 1992 ('Rules') ss 6 and 17
Child may be required to withdraw if hearing evidence would be damaging	Rules, s. 19
Parent or guardian (local authority if in care) may be present (normally must if juvenile under 16)	CYPA 1933 s. 34
Local authority must provide support for child awaiting trial or sentence	Crime and Disorder Act 1998 s. 38
No one not involved in case or press to be present in the youth court	CYPA 1933 s. 47

Press reports not to identify child in criminal cases unless court permits (does not apply to ASBOS or, in all likelihood, to the new Crime Prevention Injunctions unless imposed by a court)	CYPA 1933 ss 39 and 49
No child to be tried in adult court unless murder or other very serious ('grave') crime alleged or adult is co-accused	CYPA 1933 s. 46; Magistrates Courts Act 1980 s. 24

Where the trial takes place in the Crown Court the Lord Chief Justice has published guidelines for measures to reduce formality and stress, such as regular breaks, removal of wigs, access to social workers and guardians, etc: [2013] EWCA Crim 1631. These guidelines are the result of the criticism voiced by the ECtHR in relation to the trial arrangements in the James Bulger murder trial, where the young boys on trial had been intimidated by the formality (see the case study at the beginning of the chapter).

We do not have space to describe the trial process. Some of this was discussed in **chapter 1**. Your role will be supporting the child through this process rather than participating. The guidance in **Box 10.5** is an extract from *Youth Court Cases—Defence Good Practice*, which was prepared by the Law Society for lawyers using the youth court. It is no longer published on the Law Society website but remains useful to social workers as well as defence lawyers when children are on trial.

BOX 10.5 **Extract from Law Society Guidance for Lawyers,** *Youth Court Cases—Defence Good Practice*

[E]xplain the layout of the court and the roles of all those present. This need not take long as few are allowed to be present and if this is a pre-trial hearing should usually consist of:

- the client, who in most courts, wherever possible, sits next to his or her legal representative—if not, the client sits in the 'front row' before the bench;
- the parent, guardian or appropriate adult who sits behind;
- the YOT court officer who sits usually behind a table at right angles to the bench, to the right of the prosecutor;
- the bench of three lay magistrates, or single district judge who sits at the 'top' of the room opposite all other seating places;
- the court clerk who sits next to or sometimes in front of the bench; and
- the prosecutor who sits to the left of the defence.

The Youth Court 2001—The Changing Culture of the Youth Court—Good Practice Guide (March 2001) suggests that parents should be seated next to their dependent children, and that justices should be moved from a raised bench to sit at or near the same level as defendants. However, the *Guide* recognizes that existing architecture in courts around the country may restrict what can be achieved, though all courts should aim for a more approachable court layout.

The layout of courts vary and you should not be embarrassed to ask the usher where the personnel all sit. Some courts have a picture of the layout of the court in the waiting area outside the court. If there is any other person in court and you don't know their identity, then ask the usher.

You should explain the procedure you expect at the hearing to the client but warn them that sometimes other issues come up and the procedure may change. Prepare the client for what their involvement might be. For example, where you are trying to persuade the bench to adopt a community disposal, some benches routinely ask the defendant's advocate if they can address the client directly, and in some cases permission is not sought at all. Technically you can decline permission or intervene but this approach may not always assist the client's best interests. Unless there is good reason such as mental health problems or communication problems, you should prepare the client for this possibility. All magistrates sitting in the Youth Court receive 'engagement' training and you may find that your clients are increasingly expected to engage with the court.

If questions are put to the client and parents you should be invited to make representations on what has been said. Before considering sentence, if the defendant has pleaded guilty or been found guilty, the chairman is likely to try to talk to the defendant and parents/guardians, focusing on the offending behaviour and how to change it. Adverse inferences should not be drawn by the failure or the inability of the defendant to reply.

The informality of the Youth Court is generally observed but within limits. You should also advise the client about the impact of their body language and physical attitude—it won't help your client if he or she is slouching, chewing, or apparently ignoring the proceedings, even if their attitude is clearly a result of fear or bravado. In the atmosphere of the court a youth may behave in a disruptive manner, including in the public area, to impress other youths in the vicinity. You should advise such a client that excessive disruptive behaviour may lead to exclusion from the court building and will not make a good impression with the court.

Drug testing after conviction

A court can order a sample to be taken from anyone if it is contemplating a community or suspended sentence. This must be done in the presence of the appropriate adult if the child is under 17. The results can be used to help to decide the appropriate sentence. This may include a drug rehabilitation requirement under s. 209 of the Criminal Justice Act 2003 (CJA) if 'the offender is dependent on, or has a propensity to misuse, drugs' and would be amenable to treatment. Similarly, under s. 212 an alcohol treatment requirement may be imposed.

Section 76 of LASPO also introduces an alcohol abstinence and monitoring requirement (inserting a new s. 212A into the CJA 2003) if alcohol was an element in the offence of which the individual was convicted. The new requirement (not in force at the time of writing) was to be introduced by order of the Secretary of State with an initial pilot scheme. The implication seems to be to move away from seeing alcohol abuse as an illness that can be treated but rather as bad behaviour that can be deterred. LASPO also lifts the six-month limit on the drug rehabilitation and alcohol treatment laid down in the CJA, leaving the court to set an appropriate time.

Sentencing of juveniles

You are likely to be involved in the sentencing process because you will be required to prepare a pre-sentence report for the court. You will need to know which court is dealing with sentencing and what its powers are.

The CJA states at s. 142A that the principal aim of the youth justice system is to prevent offending and reoffending as under s. 37(1) of the CDA. Courts must have regard for the welfare of offenders as under s. 44 of the CYPA 1933. The purpose of sentencing juveniles is:

- punishment;
- reform and rehabilitation;
- protection of the public; and
- reparation by offenders to persons affected by their offences.

The sentencing powers of courts are largely found in the PCCSA with amendments in the CJA and LASPO. In what follows, section numbers are references to the PCCSA. Central to the government's approach when amending this Act in 2003 was the creation of a Sentencing Guidelines Council. Courts must refer to the Council's guidelines and must justify any departure from these. Guidelines are available on http://sentencingcouncil.judiciary.gov.uk/sentencing-guidelines.htm. Your pre-sentence report must take account of relevant guidelines. An important example is the guideline on offence seriousness which requires the young age of an offender to be taken into account where it affects responsibility for the offence.

When sentencing juveniles, the courts must take account of s. 44 of the CYPA 1933:

> Every court in dealing with a child or young person who is brought before it, either as an offender or otherwise, shall have regard to the welfare of the child or young person, and shall in a proper case take steps for removing him from undesirable surroundings, and for securing that proper provision is made for his education and training.

This does not mean the child's welfare is paramount, for the court has a statutory duty—as do social workers as part of the youth justice system—'to prevent offending by children and young persons' (CDA, s. 37). But welfare must be a factor in deciding on the appropriateness of a sentence, and gives you some leverage if you wish to suggest outcomes which will benefit the child as well as punish. The Court of Appeal frequently notes that juveniles should receive shorter custodial sentences than adults, and that reform of the young offender is the best way of protecting society. When we look at community sentences, you will see that a community sentence must not only be appropriate to the seriousness of the offence, but also to reforming the offender.

When sentencing a juvenile offender, a court must not impose a greater penalty than it could have imposed on an adult. An example of this is *P v Leeds Youth Court* (2006). The conviction was for criminal damage valued at under £5,000. The magistrates could not send an adult to prison for more than three months, so a youth court sentence of four months' detention and training order was quashed. The Divisional Court pointed out that youth is a mitigating and not an aggravating factor.

Sentencing powers of the adult magistrates' court

These powers are strictly limited. This court can sentence a juvenile only where it has already dealt with the juvenile together with a connected adult (**Box 10.3**). It only has power to fine or discharge the juvenile, or require parents to enter a recognizance. If it wishes to impose a custodial or community sentence following a conviction, it must send the case to the youth court (s. 8).

Sentencing powers of the youth court

This court's maximum power is to impose a two-year detention and training order.

Sentencing powers of the Crown Court

The Crown Court may be dealing with a juvenile offender not because the offence is serious, but because it also tried a linked adult. In this case it should not in principle sentence a juvenile but remit the case to the youth court. However, the judge can declare him or herself satisfied that it would be undesirable to do so (s. 8) and in practice the judge will do this, rather than delay a sentencing decision by sending the case to a youth court. This also enables the sentences of the adult and the juvenile to be considered together by the court which has heard all the evidence.

If the youth court has sent the case to the Crown Court for trial (see **Box 10.3**), this would have been because its maximum sentencing power of a two-year detention and training order was considered insufficient, or because it was a charge of murder. Under ss. 90–92, the Crown Court then has the power to order detention of the juvenile for a period up to the maximum period that could have been imposed on an adult. So a juvenile can be detained 'during Her Majesty's pleasure' for crimes which carry a life sentence. (However, the court must set a target date for eligibility for release. Failure to do so leaves this decision in the hands of the Home Secretary rather than an independent body, and was a breach of the human rights of the juveniles who murdered James Bulger: see *T v UK* (2000); *Practice Statement (Juveniles: Murder Tariff)* (2000); *Re Thompson and Venables (Tariff Recommendation)* (2000).)

Sentencing procedure

A court cannot lawfully impose custody if there is no pre-sentence report (CJA, Part 12). The Magistrates' Courts (Children and Young Persons) Rules 1992 require the court to have evidence on the child's circumstances before sentencing, though lack of a report does not invalidate a non-custodial sentence.

How to approach writing such a report is discussed in the **Appendix**, 'The Social Worker's Toolkit', p 539. The report writer will be a social worker for any convicted child under 14, but after that age the local authority can by agreement leave this to probation officers.

You can quite reasonably be asked for your report before conviction, if it is known that the child will admit the offence. In any event s. 9 of the CYPA 1969 requires you to start making investigations and preparing the information as soon as the young person is charged, and not to wait until conviction. There is no reason to expect the juvenile to cooperate with the preparation of a pre-sentence report if he or she intends to deny the charge. The preparation of the report may well make the child think their guilt has been pre-judged. So if you have not been able to prepare the report by the time of conviction, the case will need to be adjourned; as with all adjournments, the child may be released on bail, remanded to the accommodation of the local authority, or remanded in custody.

Your report will be in writing. You do not have to be in court to give it, but a representative of your department must be there. The court, or the defence, may wish you to be present to explain and justify what has been put in the report. You are reporting to the court as an officer of the court. The child is not your client and it is not your job to push for a lenient, or indeed any particular, outcome. Your task is to advise on the individual needs and circumstances of the juvenile, something which cannot be done by the court without your help.

Seriousness and sentencing

Courts, unless sentencing for murder when there is only one sentence of life imprisonment, exercise discretion in sentencing decisions. They cannot exceed the maximum penalty, and they must take into account Court of Appeal and Sentencing Council guidelines. They are likely also to take into account the Magistrates' Court Guidelines. All of these can be accessed from the Sentencing Council's website at http://sentencingcouncil.judiciary.gov.uk/.

The starting point is how serious this offence is, and the guideline punishment appropriate to that seriousness. The Magistrates' Association guidelines can be used as an example, as it is quite specific on the range of offences and does not just talk about principles. The Association sets an 'entry point' for each offence, then looks at aspects of the offence that are 'aggravating' or 'mitigating'. For example, the defendant has been convicted of taking a vehicle without the owner's consent (TWOC) under s. 12 of the Theft Act 1968, where the statutory maximum punishment is six months' custody (more if it is 'aggravated vehicle-taking'—a different offence). The guidelines suggest that a community penalty is a starting point. Factors listed in the guidelines pushing the seriousness upwards could be, for example, driving while disqualified, offending while on bail, driving badly, or premeditation. Mitigating factors could be, for example, that no damage was caused, the owner left the keys in the car, or the driving was not itself bad. The sentencing court then looks at any case law guidance, which may be in relation to the offence itself or general. For example, in *Attorney General's Reference (Nos 54, 55, and 56 of 2004)* (2004), three juveniles had approached the 14-year-old victim at night and took his bicycle; knocked him to the ground; punched and kicked him about the face and head; threatened to kill him; broke his arm; and threw him into a canal. The Court of Appeal agreed with the Attorney General that community punishment and rehabilitation orders were too lenient, even though each defendant had personal mitigation in their background, and three years' custody should be imposed. Another example of guidance from the Court of Appeal is *R v Howells* (1998), which raised the important question: seriousness in whose eyes? The old test used to be 'What would right-thinking people regard as serious?' This was dismissed as useless—the judges admitted they simply had no evidence, only their own opinions. Instead the Lord Chief Justice said the sentencing courts must look at specific issues: Was the offence spontaneous or premeditated? Was the victim physically or mentally injured? Was there an admission of guilt? Did the offender have a previous record?

The CJA gives statutory guidance on some aspects of seriousness. Under s. 153, racial aggravation explicitly increases seriousness. Pleading guilty—the sooner the better—reduces seriousness under s. 152. The Act additionally requires seriousness to be calculated with reference to culpability, and any harm caused which was intended or foreseeable; it says that seriousness is aggravated by each previous offence on the offender's record, particularly recent offences. It is also aggravated if an offence was committed while the offender was already on bail and if it involves racial or religious aggravation, or hostility towards gay or disabled persons. Section 73 of the Serious Organised Crime and Police Act 2005 requires courts to take account of cooperation with the authorities as reducing seriousness.

Each penalty that a court is thinking of imposing—whether custody, a community penalty, or a particular level of fine—should be imposed only if the court considers the offence to be so serious that only that level of sentencing is appropriate. But under s. 166 of the CJA the court must take into account any mitigating factors, and not decide the sentence just on seriousness. Mitigating factors may include, for example, remorse or the effect that the punishment will have on the offender and/or other people.

There is, therefore, much for the probation officer or social worker to say in a pre-sentence report. A good record, or a bad record with redeeming features, can be used to mitigate the sentence—to reduce it below the sentence the court would think of imposing if seriousness alone were taken into account.

Box 10.6 shows a simplified step-by-step approach to deciding on sentence which mirrors the court's decision-making process.

BOX 10.6 Choosing the right sentence

(a) Does the court have a choice, or is the sentence fixed by law?

(b) How serious is the offence? (Consider issues such as violence; effect on the victim; amount of gain or loss; planning; breach of trust; racial aggravation.)

(c) Is it so serious that only custody is appropriate?

(d) If not, is it so serious that only a community sentence involving restrictions on liberty is appropriate? Is such a sentence appropriate for this offender?

(e) If not, is another community sentence appropriate, or a fine?

(f) If not, a discharge should be ordered, unless a warning or a reprimand was given within the last two years (youth caution if LASPO is in force).

Custody where court has no discretion

The penalty for murder is fixed, even for a juvenile (see **Seriousness and sentencing,** p 367).

The CJA creates the concept of the *dangerous offender*, who also must be sentenced to custody for life. This applies under s. 226 if the offender:

• is under 18;

• has committed a violent or sexual offence;

- will pose a significant danger to the public;
- the offence is a grave offence.

Section 124 of LASPO creates extended sentences for certain violent or sexual offences where there is considered to be serious risk to the public. (This amends the CJA with a new s. 226B.)

The minimum penalty for a number of other offences is fixed, unless there are exceptional circumstances, if the offender has a previous record of such offending. See ss. 109–115 of the PCCSA where, for example, domestic burglary committed for a third time attracts at least three years' imprisonment. These minimum sentences do not apply to offenders aged under 18. However, juvenile offences will be taken into account if the person is later convicted before the adult court.

Custody where court has discretion

Children in custody are also children in need under s. 17 of the Children Act: *R (on behalf of the Howard League) v Secretary of State for the Home Department* (2002). The local authority must continue to assess and meet the needs of children whom the courts have locked up in the prison system, insofar as a prison sentence allows.

The minimum period for custody for a juvenile is four months and it cannot be suspended. There is no corresponding minimum for an adult of 21 or over. Is this unfair on the juvenile? The idea is that courts are deterred from the idea of a short, sharp shock; the thinking is that custody is wrong unless the offence is serious enough to merit longer periods.

Nevertheless, custody is required in certain circumstances. There are then two regimes for locking up children.

(a) *Custody for murder or grave crimes* (PCCSA, ss. 90–92, see **Sentencing powers of the Crown Court**, p 366). The Crown Court sentences the juvenile to be detained for a defined term or 'during Her Majesty's pleasure', and the place of detention is left to the Home Secretary to determine. It can include detention in local authority accommodation (CYPA 1969, s. 30). While the offender is under 21, prison is not used; the offender is held in a young offenders' institution.

(b) *A detention and training order*. This comprises a custodial part, which is served in a young offenders' institution or at a secure training centre (STC), and a training part, which is served in the community.

In either case, before a custodial sentence can be imposed on a juvenile, the following statutory criteria must be met:

- the juvenile must be represented (or has refused to apply for legal aid, or it was withdrawn as a result of his or her behaviour); and
- the offence meets one of the following tests:
  - (i) it was so serious, on its own or taking into account one or more associated offences, that neither a fine alone nor a community sentence can be justified for the offence; or
  - (ii) is a violent or sexual offence and *only* custody will adequately protect the public from *serious* harm (injury or death); or

(iii) the juvenile refuses to accept the requirements of a proposed community order; or

(iv) the offender fails to comply with an order under s. 161(2) of the CJA to undergo pre-sentence drug testing;

- the court has obtained a pre-sentence report (CJA, s. 156).

Even if the court decides that custody is justified, it is still entitled to consider whether what is known about the offender mitigates the sentence in favour of something non-custodial. Under s. 166 of the CJA it must always take into account any mental disorder before considering a custodial sentence, even if the offence is otherwise sufficiently serious for custody.

It may help you, if you are called on to prepare a pre-sentence report where custody is likely, to recall that the statutory purpose of the criminal justice system (see **Sentencing of juveniles**, p 365) is the prevention of offending. A pre-sentence report can contain very important information about the likely effect on this offender's future risk of offending, of custody versus community or other sentences. The actual imposed custodial sentence should be no longer than is necessary to reflect the seriousness of the offence or the need to protect the public from violence: CJA, s. 153. However, we referred earlier to sentencing 'dangerous offenders' to custody for life for 'grave' crimes where the juvenile has committed a sexual or violent offence and there is significant danger to the public (new s. 226B of the CJA, amended by LASPO, s. 124). Grave crimes were defined in **Box 10.3**. If the conditions are otherwise met, but it is not a grave crime as defined, the court has the power not only to impose the appropriate custodial sentence, but to add a period on licence of up to five years (for a violent offender) and eight years (for a sexual offender). This means he or she can be recalled to custody for breach of licence conditions, or continue to be detained if the Parole Board consider that he or she continues to present an unacceptable risk to the public. The licence still runs after the juvenile becomes an adult.

If a young offender is still serving a period of detention at the age of 21, he or she is transferred to a prison sentence for the remainder of the custodial term (s. 99).

Custody under a detention and training order

These custodial sentences are governed by ss. 102–107 of the PCCSA. The seriousness and statutory custody criteria must be satisfied. For offenders below the age of 15, the courts also have to find that the child is a 'persistent' offender. Courts will, it seems, define 'persistent' for themselves. See *R v C (A Juvenile) (Persistent Offender)* (2000), where C was convicted of burglary and aggravated vehicle-taking, committed while on bail for an earlier burglary. This was enough to make his offending persistent, even though he had no convictions.

The maximum term is two years. The actual term has to be one of the following: four months; six months; eight months; ten months; 12 months; 18 months; or 24 months. Half of the term is served in custody undergoing training, with some reduction for good behaviour. The detention is served in an STC, a young offenders' institution, or in local authority secure accommodation.

After release, the offender is supervised for the remaining period by a social worker, probation officer, or YOT member. The offender must comply with the requirements of the supervisor. Breach can be reported to the court, which has the power to fine or to order detention for up to three further months. Commission of an imprisonable offence during the period can put the offender back into custody for some or all of the remaining supervision period, with additional custody for the new offence. (New provisions have been added by s. 80 of LASPO.)

The referral order under ss. 16–32 of the PCCSA

A court *must* make a referral to the youth offender panel following conviction for any offence if the following conditions apply:

- the offender is under 18, pleads guilty to all the offences, and has no previous convictions;
- the court decides that custody is not appropriate but something greater than an absolute discharge is required. (LASPO, s. 79(1) allows conditional discharge as a further option.)

A court *may* make a referral where such an offender has pleaded guilty to at least one of the offences of which he or she was eventually convicted.

The essence of the order is that the court passes the responsibility to a panel nominated by the local YOT. A new panel is constituted for each offender. Together with that panel the offender works out a contract of behaviour for between three and 12 months (the period is predetermined by the court). The consequence of not agreeing a contract is that the offender will be sent back to court for sentencing.

You need to understand and apply the concept of restorative justice to work with referral orders—this is beyond the scope of our book but the government maintains a restorative justice website (www.justice.gov.uk/youth-justice/working-with-victims/restorative-justice).

A parenting order can be made at the same time as a referral order. These require a parent to attend counselling sessions.

Principles of community sentencing

An offender must consent to a community sentence. But refusal is not advisable, as this is a ground for triggering custody and enables the court to bypass the seriousness requirement.

A key feature of the community sentence is that it is a punishment. To count as punishment, the offence must be serious enough to warrant the particular type of community order chosen. Seriousness as a concept has already been discussed in terms of custodial sentences, but s. 148 of the CJA repeats similar seriousness criteria for deciding if a community sentence, including a Youth Rehabilitation Order (YRO: see **Available community sentences for juvenile offenders**, p 372), is appropriate.

(1)   A court must not pass a community sentence on an offender unless it is of the opinion that the offence, or the combination of the offence and one or more offences associated with it, was serious enough to warrant such a sentence.

(2)   Where a court passes a community sentence—

   (a)   the particular requirement or requirements forming part of the community order or YRO must be such as, in the opinion of the court, is, or taken together are, the most suitable for the offender, and

(b) the restrictions on liberty imposed by the order must be such as in the opinion of the court are commensurate with the seriousness of the offence, or the combination of the offence and one or more offences associated with it.

(3) Where a court passes a community sentence which consists of or includes one or more youth community orders—

(a) the particular order or orders forming part of the sentence must be such as, in the opinion of the court, is, or taken together are, the most suitable for the offender, and

(b) the restrictions on liberty imposed by the order or orders must be such as in the opinion of the court are commensurate with the seriousness of the offence, or the combination of the offence and one or more offences associated with it.

Under s. 151 of the CJA a juvenile offender of 16 or over with three previous convictions and fines can be given a community order or YRO even if the seriousness criteria are otherwise not met.

Available community sentences for juvenile offenders

The Criminal Justice and Immigration Act 2008 introduced the YRO in an attempt to combine a number of juvenile community sentences into a single generic sentence with various requirements that may be attached to it. They are listed in **Box 10.7** and include curfews, residence in a particular local authority area or particular residence, exclusion from a particular area, mental health treatment, drug testing and treatment, electronic monitoring, intensive supervision or fostering, unpaid work, or education (see Criminal Justice and Immigration Act 2008, s. 1). The rules on seriousness in ss. 147–8 of the CJA apply: any restriction of liberty must be proportionate to the offence. So with intensive supervision and surveillance (ISS) or intensive fostering the offence must be an imprisonable one and custody would otherwise be warranted. Those under 15 must be persistent offenders. Custody may be an option for breach of a YRO only if it could have applied to the original offence or there is 'wilful and persistent' non-compliance and ISS or intensive fostering have been tried.

  BOX 10.7 Requirements that may be attached to a Youth Rehabilitation Order

The court can impose a community order lasting up to three years (unless a shorter period is specified) containing one or more of the following requirements, supervised by probation officers not YOT members:

- Activity Requirement;
- Curfew Requirement (up to 16 hours a day for up to 12 months as amended by LASPO);
- Exclusion Requirement;
- Local Authority Residence Requirement;
- Education Requirement;

- Mental Health Treatment Requirement;
- Unpaid Work Requirement (16/17 years);
- Drug Testing Requirement;
- Intoxicating Substance Misuse Requirement;
- Supervision Requirement;
- Electronic Monitoring Requirement;
- Prohibited Activity Requirement;
- Drug Treatment Requirement;
- Residence Requirement;
- Programme Requirement;
- Attendance Centre Requirement;
- Intensive Supervision and Surveillance (based on the current ISSP);
- Intensive Fostering.

The YRO, which courts are not obliged to impose if another penalty (eg custody) is thought more appropriate, replaced various community sentences such as supervision orders, community rehabilitation orders, and community punishment orders. The intention is to have available a range of options to suit the situation of the juvenile that may be used several times (possibly with increased levels of severity) when in the past custody would have been likely for a repeat offender. The requirements attached to the YRO should be only those necessary to address the risk of serious harm to others and reduce the likelihood of reoffending, and should be proportionate to the offence. The individuals involved must indicate willingness to comply. Section 81–84 of LASPO makes some amendments to the YRO regime.

Pre-sentence reports from YOTs will be crucial in deciding whether an individual is suitable for a YRO, in particular whether he or she would benefit from some of the treatments and interventions involved (see s. 156(3) of the CJA).

The pre-sentence report will have to specify the supervision and other arrangements, and where cooperation from others (eg family or work with other agencies) is needed, confirmation that their cooperation is available.

When a YRO is imposed, an officer in charge of an individual's YRO will be appointed from a YOT or, for 16- and 17-year-olds, the probation service through a private firm may be the responsible officer if the only requirement is electronic monitoring for a curfew. If an attendance centre requirement is the only imposition, the responsible officer will be whoever is in charge of the centre.

Breach of a YRO

The officer in charge will deal with failure to comply with a YRO under Schedule 2 to the Criminal Justice and Immigration Act 2008. Two warnings may be given and on the third failure within a 12-month warned period the matter should be referred back to court unless the responsible officer/YOT manager considers that there are exceptional circumstances. If not, they lay an information seeking a summons or warrant for the individual's arrest. A court may fine someone up to £2,500 (under LASPO assuming it is in force—formerly only £250 for a child under 14, £1,000 for someone older); impose another tougher YRO including imposing an ISS even if the original offence would not have warranted it; and re-sentence on the basis of other sentences that would have been available originally, including imprisonment. The young person or responsible officer may seek a revocation of a YRO if good progress has been shown. They may apply for variation if circumstances require it (eg if the individual subject to a residence order moves home). If the young person reoffends during the period of a YRO, it may be revoked and the individual may be re-sentenced for the original offence as well as the new one.

Binding parents over

When a court convicts a juvenile of under 16, it must normally also bind over the parents (but it cannot bind over the local authority where the child is in care). If the juvenile is over 16, it can still choose to do this. This means the parent or guardian promises to exercise proper control over the child to prevent reoffending (PCCSA, s. 150). A sum is fixed by the court, which can be forfeited if a further offence is committed. The maximum sum is £1,000, and the period during which the parent is at risk lasts up to three years, or the offender's eighteenth birthday. The court should take into account whether the parents could have had or will have any influence over the juvenile's behaviour in deciding whether to use its power not to bind over. For more guidance see LAC (92) 5, para. 41.

A parent can refuse to be bound over, but if the court thinks a refusal is unreasonable, it can fine the parents up to £1,000 on top of any fine imposed for the juvenile's offence.

Deferred sentence

Under s. 1, a court can defer (ie postpone) the decision on sentence for up to six months. It should do so only if some change is imminent—for example, leaving school and taking up employment—which the court ought to take into account. The offender must consent, and the court can impose conditions with which the offender must comply pending the return to court. Compliance will usually be monitored by a probation officer, though the court can appoint another person. Breach of any conditions can lead to arrest and return to the court. All going well, however, a day is fixed for the return to court and the court will sentence in the light of the new circumstances—conduct after conviction including any appropriate reparations that may have been made and compliance with requirements regarding conduct imposed by the court. It will not normally be appropriate to order custody after deferment if the offender's circumstances are now looking more stable. The court can only order what the court could have ordered at the time of deferment—so if the offender is now 18, the court cannot use adult powers of sentencing.

Discharge

This is an option where in all the circumstances (the offence and the offender's past history) no punishment is appropriate. It is governed by ss. 12–15. If the offender had been prepared to admit the offence before charge, it might with hindsight have been more appropriate to reprimand or warn the offender. If the court orders an absolute discharge then, apart from showing on the offender's record, it does not count as a conviction. A discharge can be conditional for a period of up to three years. If the offender commits an offence within that period, the court can sentence for the original offence as well as the new offence. A conditional discharge is available only in exceptional circumstances if an offender has already had a warning in the last two years (CDA, s. 66) or, presumably, a youth caution under LASPO.

Compensation orders

Any person found guilty of an offence can be ordered to pay compensation to the victim. (This is one reason why a caution is sometimes inappropriate—there must be a conviction for a compensation order.) Indeed, a court must consider making such an order if appropriate, or give its reasons for not doing so (PCCSA, s. 130(3)). This order can stand alone, without the court making any other order against the offender, or it can accompany any other order made by the court. As with a fine, the juvenile's means are taken into account; and the parents can be ordered to pay the compensation (but not where they were not in control of the juvenile at the time of the offence—eg the child was in local authority accommodation—*A v DPP* (1996)). Where the offender has limited means, a compensation order should be made before a fine.

Parenting order

If the appropriate conditions apply, a sentencing court can order the parents of a convicted child to attend counselling sessions to receive support via a parenting order. They involve a parenting skills course or weekly counselling. There may be other conditions applied by the court over a period of up to 12 months, for example that the parent ensures the child is at home during set hours or ensures that the child attends school on time.

Sex offender orders—Crime and Disorder Act 1998, s. 2

These enable the police to apply to a court to restrict the activities of convicted sex offenders. The police can apply at any point after conviction. In that sense it is not a sentencing power.

These orders could be confused with the sex offenders' register, whereby all convicted sex offenders must register with the police who can use the information to monitor their activities and keep relevant agencies informed. By contrast, the sex offender order is not about monitoring—it addresses an identified risk. The idea is to keep an individual sex offender away from an area where he may commit offences. So a convicted sex offender who represents a danger to schoolchildren can be ordered to stay away from school gates. As a social worker you may be involved in asking the police to seek such an order. You may also be in a situation where you have a statutory responsibility to work with a child or adult who is subject to an order.

There are two grounds both of which the police must establish before the court when applying for an order under s. 2(1) of the CDA:

  (a) the person is a convicted sex offender under the Sex Offenders Act 1997, which can mean anyone over 10 years old (without a conviction there can be no order, whatever the risk);

(b) he has behaved in a way that gives reasonable cause to believe an order is necessary to protect the public or any individuals from serious harm from him.

As these are civil proceedings, the magistrates' court will apply the civil standard of the balance of probabilities (not 'beyond reasonable doubt'). This is not a human rights transgression, since an offender has by definition been convicted in a criminal court using a criminal standard of proof (*B v Chief Constable of Avon and Somerset* (2001)). Proving reasonable *belief* that the order is necessary is easier than proving that it is actually necessary. No one needs to give evidence except the officer who has that belief.

The sex offender order lasts for a minimum of five years and there is no upper time limit. The order specifies activities which the offender must not do. For example, the offender must not go near school gates or a defined area. The order cannot require the person to do anything, such as obtain treatment (though that result might be obtained through an appropriate sentence in the earlier criminal proceedings).

Breach of the order is a criminal offence and can lead to a fine or imprisonment.

EXERCISES

Consider the statutory responsibilities of a social worker and appropriate actions you might take in each of the following situations:

1 Jennifer, who is 14, is currently in local authority accommodation because her mother cannot cope. You feel you have established quite a good relationship with her, and having begun to gain her trust you have been able to talk to her about her life, which has included recent shop-lifting and drug use. The police inform you that they have arrested her for supplying cannabis and wish to question her.

2 You have arrived at Sunderfield police station following a request to be present as appropriate adult for the questioning of Abdul, who is 16 and is suspected of arson at a local school. The police sergeant tells you that Abdul has refused legal advice and therefore they are ready to interview him. He has been in the police station for 20 hours, and when you see him you can see he is tired. The police have not told you what evidence they have to connect Abdul with the offence, but Abdul tells you that he was with a group of friends and someone, perhaps himself, did accidentally drop a lighted match onto some paper. Abdul tells you the police have told him he will not be allowed to leave until he admits it.

3 Assume Abdul has been charged. You know he has no past history of offending and comes from what you believe to be a stable family. Consider his right to bail and what will happen if bail is refused.

4 We have not provided detail on sentences for different offences. Using one of the research tools indicated in the reading list, find out what the penalty for arson is.

5 If Abdul is found guilty, what opportunity would a social worker have to influence the court, and what approach might a court or courts take when deciding the appropriate sentence?

ONLINE RESOURCE CENTRE

For guidance on how to answer these exercises, visit the Online Resource Centre at www.oxfordtextbooks.co.uk/orc/socialwork13e/.

WHERE DO WE GO FROM HERE?

We have completed our discussion of the statutory duties of social workers in relation to children. You will realize that when other measures are impossible, social workers and other agencies have to use the courts. In relation to children, this means child protection proceedings and criminal prosecution of abusers. You need to know how to use the courts. That means getting your evidence together. See the **Appendix**, 'The Social Worker's Toolkit', p 539 for some hints on evidence.

ANNOTATED FURTHER READING

If you are really interested in the up-to-date and full details of a particular aspect of how the criminal process works, one of the standard reference works can provide the answer, if you use the contents or index carefully. The following are published annually: *Stone's Justices' Manual* (Butterworths) deals with the work of the youth courts; *Blackstone's Criminal Practice* (Oxford University Press) deals with all aspects of criminal law and practice, as does *Archbold's Criminal Pleading, Evidence and Practice* (Sweet & Maxwell). *Current Sentencing Practice* (Sweet & Maxwell), a loose-leaf encyclopaedia edited by D. Thomas, is very useful for the detail on sentencing, including how the courts approach particular offences.

A. Edwards, *Advising a Suspect in the Police Station* (7th edn, Sweet & Maxwell, 2009). The author, Anthony Edwards, is a leading writer and practitioner, and this book is of value to anyone working as an appropriate adult, though it covers all suspects who are being questioned.

C. Taylor and J. Krish, *Advising Mentally Disordered Offenders* (2nd edn, Law Society Publications, 2009). This volume is particularly useful for those attending the police station.

B. Goldson and J. Muncie, *Youth Crime and Juvenile Justice* (Sage Publications, 2009) has a range of pieces exploring this issue from many perspectives.

M. Stephenson, H. Giller, and S. Brown, *Effective Practice in Youth Justice* (2nd edn, Routledge, 2011) is a practical guide covering most of the topics you will deal with.

The Youth Justice Board is an agency with a statutory responsibility to prevent offending by children. Its website is usefully and accessibly organized, for example to take you through custodial and community sentences one at a time www.justice.gov.uk/about/yjb.

NACRO (National Association for the Care and Resettlement of Offenders) has an excellent list of publications, too long for inclusion here, but worth visiting: www.nacro.org.uk.

Part 3

Responsibilities towards adults

Part 3 Responsibilities towards adults

This part of the book concentrates on the law which governs adult social care. Adult social care is in general organized by local authorities. Their role can be summarized in a relatively straightforward way. Councils are required to assess the needs of vulnerable individuals for social care services, plan and then ensure the required services are delivered to meet those needs, and finally review and adjust provision to ensure the needs are met. Nonetheless, it is clearly more complicated than this; the Local Government Ombudsman and the Health Services Ombudsman receive complaints which demonstrate the difficulties that local authorities and health services have in meeting their legal responsibilities. The failure to assess service users' needs properly, the use of flawed criteria for assessments and for making decisions, the failure to follow government guidance, and the failure to provide services to meet assessed needs figure prominently in the complaints. These are serious issues for the individuals involved. If local authorities fail to make appropriate provision, there are consequences, not only for those individuals but for their families. There are a number of interlinked reasons for these failures. The limited resources available to local government to meet an increasing need for services is a major cause. The complexity of the legal framework and the lack of clarity in the policy drivers for social care also play significant roles. Since the last edition of this book, Parliament has been considering a bill to reform the legal basis of the provision of adult social care. The Care Act 2014 received Royal Assent on 14 May 2014. At the time of writing we do not know when its provisions will be implemented. The hope is that with the modernization of the law, and the removal of some complexities, local authorities will make better, in the sense of more lawful, decisions about service provision. Here we provide you with a summary of the new legislation, alongside explanations of the pre-existing legal framework.

Chapter 11 sets the scene by considering the legal and political context of adult social care and explains the principles and main provisions of the Care Act 2014. It also discusses the impact of some overarching legal requirements, such as human rights, and equalities legislation and policy approaches such as dignity and citizenship. Chapter 12 sets out the framework of the law relating to adult social care. The term 'framework' suggests a coherence that unfortunately does not exist. By the end of the chapter we are sure you will understand why the Care Act 2014 is necessary.

Chapter 13 is concerned with the responsibilities placed upon local authorities to manage adult care services. Local authorities have to assess the needs of those wanting services, prioritize and plan for those needs, and then arrange delivery of the most pressing of those needs. What is critical in the chapter is the pressure on local authorities to ration resources, and we will examine some responses from the courts to cuts in provision. The final part of the chapter looks at the mechanisms that exist to improve the quality of care services. It considers the role of the Care Quality Commission in ensuring quality services, and the role of the Local

Government Ombudsman as well as complaints procedures. We refer to the provisions of the Care Act 2014 where necessary.

The focus of **chapter 14** is the adult social care user. The chapter sets out the law on mental capacity. The Mental Capacity Act 2005 provides an excellent example of a careful balancing exercise between the right to autonomy and the need to be protected. The chapter looks at the role of the Court of Protection. It then turns to and explains current statutory and policy framework for safeguarding vulnerable adults—again, this area of law has been changed by the Care Act 2014. The chapter provides an overview of a specialized area of law—mental health.

Adult social care

11

OVERVIEW AND OBJECTIVES

The chapter provides an introduction to the legal and policy framework for the provision of adult social care. It starts by setting out the need for, and the scope of, adult social services. It then considers the Care Act 2014, explaining the legal and policy context of what is arguably the most important reform of the law relating to vulnerable adults since the implementation of the National Assistance Act 1948. Finally, it considers legal obligations that are overarching, such as human rights and anti-discrimination legislation, including the public sector equality duty.

CASE STUDY

C v A Local Authority (2011), Court of Protection

The court was required to make declarations about the treatment by a residential special school of an 18-year-old man (C), who suffered from severe autism and severe learning disabilities. C's challenging behaviour included severe anxiety, sensory impairment, aggressive and destructive traits, significant self-harm, and harm to his carers. One aspect of his sensory problems was a tendency towards nakedness. His behaviour management at the school included the use of a 'blue room', a small, specially constructed, padded room with a secure door and window. C was taken there whenever he was aggressive or naked. The amount of time C spent in the blue room had significantly increased because the school maintained that his behaviours were becoming increasingly uncontrolled. The Court of Protection was required to consider various issues including: (a) its decision-making process under the Mental Capacity Act 2005; (b) best practice regarding the approach to C's nakedness; (c) best practice regarding the use of seclusion and restraint, particularly the use of the blue room, and its impact on C's right not to be subjected to inhuman or degrading treatment, his right to liberty, and his right to respect for private life.

The court decided that the school's policies and procedures needed to better acknowledge C's sensory needs and choices. It was in his best interests to be clothed in communal areas, but there should be minimal restrictions on his choice to be naked; nakedness was not to be punished with seclusion. Staff had to be trained in strategies to allow C to be naked in their presence and to encourage him to be naked in areas of his accommodation where it was acceptable to others. Further, in order to be lawful, seclusion had to comply with statutory guidance, and when used to control aggressive behaviour, it should be used only so long as necessary and proportionate, and it had to be the least restrictive option. It had to be exercised in accordance with an intervention and prevention plan designed to safeguard C's psychological and physical health. That plan, together with guidance for use of the blue room, had to be written up into a protocol forming C's care plan and all staff had to be trained in a manner that was specific to C. Seclusion was not to be used solely for nakedness, for punishment, as part of behaviour management, or as a way of dealing with self-harming. The blue room could be used when C chose to go there, but he had to be free to leave.

WHAT DOES THIS CASE TELL YOU ABOUT SOCIAL CARE LAW AND PRACTICE?

This case demonstrates the interface between managing challenging behaviour and the law, and the difficult issues that you as a social worker have to manage. There is a lot of guidance available to you, but it must be read and followed. Moreover, seclusion, which may be explained as a way of protecting a service user's dignity, can all too quickly become punitive and a deprivation of liberty. The questions that you have to ask of a scheme designed to manage an adult service user's behaviour derive from human rights (see **chapter 3**): is it a necessary action, is it proportionate, and is it the least restrictive option?

The scope of adult social care

The extensive statutory responsibilities that local social services authorities have for adults and their carers are summed up in the term 'adult social care'. The services that may be provided under the umbrella of adult social care range from community-based services such as home care, meals provision, the provision of equipment and adaptations, to residential care. The providers of services may be social service departments, health authorities, voluntary sector organizations, or commercial enterprises. Service user categories include older people, people with learning disabilities, physically disabled people, people with mental health problems, and carers. Age UK describes social care as follows:

> Social care is any service designed to help people with support needs to live well. This could be someone coming in to your home to help with tasks like washing, dressing, getting in and out of bed and going to the toilet, right up to 24/7 support in a care home. Care services should protect people who are vulnerable, enable a decent quality of life, support independence and encourage people to remain active.

(Age UK, *Care in Crisis 2014*)

An indication of the extent of adult social care provision in England during 2012–13 is provided by **Box 11.1**, which replicates the key facts set out at the beginning of *Community Care Statistics: Social Services Activity, England—Councils with Adult Social Services Responsibilities* tables. These useful statistics can be found on the website of the Health and Social Care Information Centre (HSCIC) information centre, www.hscic. gov.uk/catalogue/PUB13148.

 BOX 11.1 Key facts, adult social care 2012–13

- The number of contacts from new clients in 2012–13 was 2.1 million (down less than 1 per cent from 2011–12 and up 1 per cent from 2007–08). Of these, 1 million required a further assessment or commissioning of ongoing service (a fall of 4 per cent from 2011–12) while 1.1 million were dealt with at the point of contact (a rise of 2 per cent from 2011–12).

- There were 603,000 assessments for new clients in 2012–13 (down less than 1 per cent from 2011–12 and down 9 per cent from 2007–08). Following assessment, 67 per cent of these clients went on to receive services as a result of their assessment (this is a decrease of less than one percentage point from 2011–12). There were 878,000 completed reviews for existing clients in 2012–13 (13 per cent less than in 2011–12 and 35 per cent less than in 2007–08). There were 878,000 completed reviews for existing clients in 2012–13 (13 per cent less than in 2011–12 and 35 per cent less than in 2007–08). Of these, 1.1 million received community based services (a fall of 10 per cent from 2011–12), 209,000 received residential care (a fall of 2 per cent from 2011–12) and 87,000 received nursing care (which is less than a 1 per cent change from 2011–12).

- The number of people receiving self-directed support was 611,000 (an increase of 16 per cent from 2011–12). Of these, 143,000 received a direct payment—up 8 per cent from 2011–12. 148,000 clients received a direct payment as one of their community-based services at some point during the reporting year (an increase of 7 per cent from 2011–12). The number of carers receiving self-directed support was 103,000 (an increase of 32 per cent from 2011–12). Of these, 71,000 received a direct payment, up 17 per cent from 2011–12.
- Of those receiving community based services not in the form of direct payments in 2012–13, 485,000 received home care, 373,000 received equipment, 196,000 received professional support, 141,000 received day care, 66,000 received short-term residential care (excluding respite care), 42,000 received meals, and 82,000 received other services.

The number of carers receiving services was 354,000 (2 per cent less than in 2011–12 but 5 per cent more than in 2007–08). Of these, 48 per cent of carers received a carer-specific service and 52 per cent received information only. This is the same distribution as in 2011–12.The statistics reveal the extraordinary scale of service provision. Perhaps something that is not so clear is that the need for social care is, in part, determined by socio-economic circumstances. Statistics produced by the Office for National Statistics (ONS) suggest that in the most deprived areas of England healthy life expectancy was 18.4 years lower for men and 19.0 years lower for women than in the least deprived areas. This inequality is almost twice as wide as the difference seen in full life expectancy at 9.2 years for men; for women it is almost three times wider than the difference in life expectancy at 6.8 years. Source: ONS statistical bulletin March 2014.

Age UK has no doubt that the provision of services for the elderly has reached a crisis point. In 2014 it published a report, *Care in Crisis—What next for adult social care.*

Age UK argues that:

> In real terms, spending on social care has fallen by around £770m since 2010/11 and we have seen a steep rise in the length of time people are waiting for care home places, home care and home adaptations. The role of local social services authorities.

It is important to remember exactly what it is that local social services authorities are responsible for. Their role as provider of services is secondary and shared with other providers from the private and voluntary sectors. The primary role of local authorities with community care responsibilities is to ensure that:

- adult social care is delivered effectively;
- service users' wishes are taken into account; and
- services are delivered safely.

Therefore social services authorities' responsibilities embrace planning for adult social care services, assessing individual needs for those services, promoting service user independence through direct payments, and maintaining appropriate safeguards for those using their services. These significant managerial responsibilities are the subject of the next two chapters. This chapter concentrates on the Care Act 2014 which sets out the legal framework that underpins adult social care.

Community care

Services provided for adults are described as community care services. Community care services are defined in s. 46(3) of the National Health Service and Community Care Act 1990. The subsection is set out in **Box 11.2.**

BOX 11.2 Community care services—s. 46(3) of the National Health Service and Community Care Act 1990

'Community care services' means services which a local authority may provide or arrange to be provided under any of the following provisions—

(a) Part III of the National Assistance Act 1948;

(b) section 45 of the Health Services and Public Health Act 1968;

(c) section 254 of, and Schedule 20 to, the National Health Service Act 2006, and section 192 of, and Schedule 15 to, the National Health Service (Wales) Act 2006;

(d) section 117 of the Mental Health Act 1983.

What is immediately apparent from reading this section of the statute is that community care services derive from a wide range of statutes. What is less clear from the face of the provision is that residential services are covered by the umbrella term 'community care'. They are provided under the auspices of Part III of the National Assistance Act 1948—referred to in s. 46(3) of the National Health Service and Community Care Act 1990.

The scope of adult social care services is to be changed by s. 8 of the Care Act 2014. This is discussed in **The Care Act 2014—a summary**, p 394.

The health/social care divide

One important limit to the scope of community care services is that they are not health services. This is made clear in s. 21(8) of the National Assistance Act 1948.

> Nothing in this section shall authorise or require a local authority to make any provision authorised or required to be made (whether by that or by any other authority) by or under any enactment not contained in this Part of this Act or authorised or required to be provided under the National Health Service Act 2006 or the National Health Service (Wales) Act 2006.

What this means is that it is unlawful for local authorities to provide services which can be provided by the National Health Service (NHS). One important distinction between health and social care services is that health services are free at the point of delivery, whereas charges can be made for social care services. Deciding whether services are health or social care services is therefore critical to the affordability of those services. Unfortunately, the divide is not clear, and causes confusion for local authorities, and considerable stress and anxiety for those who consider that the services they require are health services and yet are assessed as needing social care rather than health services.

The issue was litigated in *R v North and East Devon Health Authority, ex p Coughlan* (2002). This case is important, although technical. Miss Pamela Coughlan was tetra-plegic. She was moved from hospital to a purpose-built facility that she was promised would be her home for life. She judicially reviewed the decision to close the purpose-built facility. She was successful; her nursing care had to be provided free by the NHS and could not be provided by the local authority on a means-tested basis where appropriate, and the Health Authority was in breach of its promise by closing the facility. The crucial paragraphs of the Court of Appeal decision are set out in **Box 11.3**.

 BOX 11.3 The health care divide—extract from the Court of Appeal decision, para. 30

(d) The fact that some nursing services can be properly regarded as part of social services care, to be provided by the local authority, does not mean that all nursing services provided to those in the care of the local authority can be treated in this way. The scale and type of nursing required in an individual case may mean that it would not be appropriate to regard all or part of the nursing as being part of 'the package of care' which can be provided by a local authority. There can be no precise legal line drawn between those nursing services which are and those which are not capable of being treated as included in such a package of care services.

(e) The distinction between those services which can and cannot be so provided is one of degree which in a borderline case will depend on a careful appraisal of the facts of the individual case. However, as a very general indication as to where the line is to be drawn, it can be said that if the nursing services are (i) merely incidental or ancillary to the provision of the accommodation which a local authority is under a duty to provide to the category of persons to whom section 21 of the 1948 Act refers and (ii) of a nature which it can be expected that an authority whose primary responsibility is to provide social services can be expected to provide, then they can be provided under section 21. (This is known as the 'quantity and quality test' and is now enshrined in the Care Act 2014 s. 22(1).) It will be appreciated that the first part of the test is focusing on the overall quantity of the services and the second part on the quality of the services provided.

(f) The fact that care services are provided on a means tested contribution basis does not prevent the Secretary of State declining to provide the nursing part of those services on the NHS. However, he can only decline if he has formed a judgment which is tenable and consistent with his long-term general duty to continue to promote a comprehensive free health service that it is not necessary to provide the services. He cannot decline simply because social services will fill the gap.

In summary, what the Court of Appeal decided was that it is wrong to say that if any nursing care is provided for a service user then he or she is receiving health services which are the sole responsibility of the NHS and therefore free at the point of delivery. However, when the degree of nursing care that Miss Coughlan required was carefully examined, it was clear that her needs were far beyond what social services could provide. Therefore she was not someone to whom a local authority could lawfully provide the nursing services she needed.

Gaps in provision

One of the consequences of the *Coughlan* case was that it left gaps in provision. The needs of the service user could be greater than social care support could provide for, yet fall below what the Department of Health specified as necessary to qualify for NHS continuing support. The legality of the gap was considered in *R (Grogan) v Bexley NHS Care Trust* (2006). The judge was critical of the Department of Health Guidance of the time which led to serious problems in decisions about the provision of care. What he decided was that a gap could not be legal, and that as the definition of social care was statutory, that is, within s. 21 of the National Assistance Act 1948, and the definition of health care was provided in policy, the threshold for the provision of health care services had to fall to meet the upper limit of social care provision.

The National Framework for NHS Continuing Healthcare and NHS-funded Nursing Care in England

The current divide between health and social care provision is determined by the *National Framework for NHS Continuing Healthcare and NHS-funded Nursing Care in England*. This says (in answer to the question 'Is there an authoritative definition of "beyond the responsibility of the Local authority"?'):

> Whilst there is not a legal definition of a healthcare need (in the context of NHS continuing healthcare), in general terms it can be said that such a need is one related to the treatment, control or prevention of a disease, illness, injury or disability, and the care or aftercare of a person with these needs (whether or not the tasks involved have to be carried out by a health professional).
>
> In general terms (not a legal definition) it can be said that a social care need is one that is focused on providing assistance with activities of daily living, maintaining independence, social interaction, enabling the individual to play a fuller part in society, protecting them in vulnerable situations, helping them to manage complex relationships and (in some circumstances) accessing a care home or other supported accommodation.
>
> Social care needs are directly related to the type of welfare services that LAs [local authorities] have a duty or power to provide. These include, but are not limited to: social work services; advice; support; practical assistance in the home; assistance with equipment and home adaptations; visiting and sitting services; provision of meals; facilities for occupational, social, cultural and recreational activities outside the home; assistance to take advantage of educational facilities; and assistance in finding accommodation (e.g. a care home), etc. CCGs [clinical commissioning groups] should be mindful that where a person is eligible for NHS continuing healthcare the NHS is responsible for meeting their assessed health and social care needs.

We have provided an extract from the Framework in **Box 11.4** which indicates how the social care/health care issue is to be decided in individual cases. What is important is whether an individual's primary need is a health need. If so, then they are eligible for NHS continuing health care.

 BOX 11.4 *The National Framework for NHS Continuing Healthcare and NHS-funded Nursing Care*

Primary Health Need

33 To assist in deciding which treatment and other health services it is appropriate for the NHS to provide under the National Health Service Act 2006, and to distinguish between those and the services that LAs may provide under section 21 of the National Assistance Act 1948, the Secretary of State has developed the concept of a 'primary health need'. Where a person's primary need is a health need, they are eligible for NHS continuing healthcare. Deciding whether this is the case involves looking at the totality of the relevant needs. Where an individual has a primary health need and is therefore eligible for NHS continuing healthcare, the NHS is responsible for providing all of that individual's assessed needs—including accommodation, if that is part of the overall need.

34 There should be no gap in the provision of care. People should not find themselves in a situation where neither the NHS nor the relevant LA (subject to the person meeting the relevant means test and having needs that fall within their eligibility criteria for adult social care) will fund care, either separately or together. Therefore, the 'primary health need' test should be applied, so that a decision of ineligibility for NHS continuing healthcare is only possible where, taken as a whole, the nursing or other health services required by the individual:

(a) are no more than incidental or ancillary to the provision of accommodation which LA social services are, or would be but for a person's means, under a duty to provide; and

(b) are not of a nature beyond which an LA whose primary responsibility it is to provide social services could be expected to provide.

35 There are certain limitations to this test, which was originally indicated in *Coughlan*: neither the PCT [primary care trust] nor the LA can dictate what the other agency should provide. Instead, a practical approach to eligibility is required—one that will apply to a range of different circumstances, including situations in which the 'incidental or ancillary' test is not applicable because, for example, the person is to be cared for in their own home. Certain characteristics of need—and their impact on the care required to manage them—may help determine whether the 'quality' or 'quantity' of care required is more than the limits of an LA's responsibilities, as outlined in *Coughlan*:

Nature: This describes the particular characteristics of an individual's needs (which can include physical, mental health or psychological needs) and the type of those needs. This also describes the overall effect of those needs on the individual, including the type ('quality') of interventions required to manage them.

Intensity: This relates both to the extent ('quantity') and severity ('degree') of the needs and to the support required to meet them, including the need for sustained/ongoing care ('continuity').

Complexity: This is concerned with how the needs present and interact to increase the skill required to monitor the symptoms, treat the condition(s) and/or manage the care. This may arise with a single condition, or it could include the presence of multiple conditions or the interaction between two or more conditions. It may also include situations where an individual's response to their own condition has an impact on their overall needs, such as where a physical health need results in the individual developing a mental health need.

Unpredictability: This describes the degree to which needs fluctuate and thereby create challenges in managing them. It also relates to the level of risk to the person's health if adequate and timely care is not provided. Someone with an unpredictable healthcare need is likely to have either a fluctuating, unstable or rapidly deteriorating condition.

Each of these characteristics may, alone or in combination, demonstrate a primary health need, because of the quality and/or quantity of care that is required to meet the individual's needs. The totality of the overall needs and the effects of the interaction of needs should be carefully considered.

It is clear that there is still potential for disagreement about decisions made about the health/social care divide. However, the framework provides the most recent statement of that divide and the one you will be required to work with.

This discussion has already highlighted the legal complexities involved. We are now going to consider the legal framework of social care itself. Resolving the health/social care divide was one of the aims of the Care Act 2014. However, as we shall see in the next section, there was a broader social and political context. A range of problems with the provision of adult social care stimulated legislative reform.

The context of the Care Act 2014—a crisis in adult social care?

The Coalition Government took office in 2010. It published a statement of its intentions for adult social care, *A Vision for Adult Social Care: Capable Communities and Active Citizens*, in November of that year. Its priorities—not remarkably different from those of the previous government—are set out in **Box 11.5**.

 BOX 11.5 *A Vision for Adult Social Care: Capable Communities and Active Citizens*

The Vision for a modern system of social care is built on seven principles:

• Personalisation: individuals not institutions take control of their care. Personal budgets, preferably as direct payments, are provided to all eligible people. Information about care and support is available for all local people, regardless of whether or not they fund their own care.

- Partnership: care and support delivered in a partnership between individuals, communities, the voluntary and private sectors, the NHS and councils—including wider support services, such as housing.
- Plurality: the variety of people's needs is matched by diverse service provision, with a broad market of high quality service providers.
- Protection: there are sensible safeguards against the risk of abuse or neglect. Risk is no longer an excuse to limit people's freedom.
- Productivity: greater local accountability will drive improvements and innovation to deliver higher productivity and high quality care and support services. A focus on publishing information about agreed quality outcomes will support transparency and accountability.
- People: we can draw on a workforce who can provide care and support with skill, compassion and imagination, and who are given the freedom and support to do so. We need the whole workforce, including care workers, nurses, occupational therapists, physiotherapists and social workers, alongside carers and the people who use services, to lead the changes set out here.

The priorities set out in the vision statement are not consistent with the legal framework that preceded the Care Act 2014. The law relating to the provision of adult social care was based on the immediate post-war welfare settlement. While this was a progressive vision at the time, as the years have gone by, its paternalism and the way in which it was expected that ordinary citizens would defer to the authority of experts, passively accepting what was offered to them, has become increasingly at odds with societal expectations of public services. As the Dilnot Commission (see later in this section) put it:

> Expectations have changed, people want more choice and control over their lives and care and support needs to change to meet this expectation.

The Care Act 2014 starts with a statement of principles which reflect much more clearer contemporary values—**The Care Act 2014—a summary**, p 394.

Perhaps of greater political significance, a series of scandals about the provision of adult social care erupted in 2011. These included the collapse of Southern Cross, a private provider of residential care, leaving 31,000 vulnerable residents at risk of losing their homes. This raised the issue of how law and regulation can protect service users from the consequences of business failure by private providers—something that was not an issue when the state was the direct provider of services. The Care Act 2014 gives the Care Quality Commission specific responsibility for overseeing financial probity of private providers—see **The Care Act 2014—a summary**, p 394. The physical safety of vulnerable adults has also become an issue. For example, in 2011 the BBC broadcast secret filming of the treatment of patients with learning difficulties and autism in a private hospital, Winterbourne View, which led to four arrests and an unreserved apology from the Care Quality Commission. Again, the difficulties that law and regulators face in protecting vulnerable adults from unacceptable behaviour became apparent. Nor were the failures of the system limited to institutional care. The Equality and Human Rights Commission published a report, *Close to Home*, detailing a lack of attention to human rights and dignity by many councils in their provision of domiciliary care. We discuss the provisions of the Care Act 2014 designed to improve adult safeguarding in the following section.

The current funding system for care and support in England and Wales is confusing, unfair, and unsustainable for a variety of reasons.

- The demographic time bomb—the population of older people is projected to grow by 50 per cent over the next 20 years as a result of longer life expectancy, while the proportion of the working-age adult population is falling. This means that there will be a considerable shortfall in money available to pay for increased demand for care and support.

- Means testing—the current system means that those with high care costs are required to support themselves in residential care until their assets are reduced to £23,250, leaving little to pass on to their families.

- The postcode lottery—local councils set local eligibility thresholds designed to reflect local priorities. This means that people with identical support needs can receive quite different levels of support depending upon where they live.

The Commission on Funding of Care and Support (the Dilnot Commission) was set up by the Coalition Government on 20 July 2010. The Commission published its report on 4 July 2011. Its recommendations included the following:

> Individuals' lifetime contributions towards their social care costs—which are currently potentially unlimited—should be capped. After the cap is reached, individuals would be eligible for full state support. This cap should be between £25,000 and £50,000. We consider that £35,000 is the most appropriate and fair figure.
>
> The means-tested threshold, above which people are liable for their full care costs, should be increased from £23,250 to £100,000.
>
> National eligibility criteria and portable assessments should be introduced to ensure greater consistency.
>
> All those who enter adulthood with a care and support need should be eligible for free state support immediately rather than being subjected to a means test.

The report estimated that its proposals for change would cost the government an initial £1.7bn a year—0.25 per cent of total public spending. The government's response to the Dilnot proposals is set out in the Care Act 2014—see the following section.

There was another problem the Care Act 2014 was designed to overcome—the complex legal framework which comprises a multiplicity of statutes with overlapping provisions and significant gaps. This law is described in the next chapter because you will need some familiarity with it until the Care Act 2014 is fully implemented. In summary the legal limitations concerned:

- the lack of legislative provision for preventive measures;
- inadequacies in the legal framework in connection with carers' needs.

The Care Act 2014—a summary

In this section we summarize the provisions of the Care Act 2014. At this stage we cannot provide the details of implementation—the necessary regulations and guidance have not yet been published. This means that the pre-existing law and in particular the regulatory guidance continues to be relevant. That law is explained in the subsequent chapters. Within those chapters we indicate where the Care Act 2014 will change the current position.

The Care Act 2014 is in five parts. It is the first part that concerns you most closely. The other parts relate to care standards and health provision, in part providing a legislative response to the Mid Staffordshire NHS Foundation Trust Public Inquiry.

The government policy that informs the legislation is set out in the White Paper *Caring for our future: reforming care and support* (Cm 8378, July 2012). Other important background information is contained in the Report of the Commission on the Funding of Care and Support, chaired by Andrew Dilnot, and the recommendations of the Law Commission in its report *Adult Social Care* (Law Com 326, HC 941, May 2011).

Part 1 of the Act sets out the legal framework for the provision of care and support. It applies in general to England only as the Welsh government has its own legislative proposals. Once these are enacted we will set out a summary of the provisions on the Online Resource Centre.

Section 1 of the Care Act 2014 is particularly important. It sets out the principle that underpins the legislation—the responsibility of the state, and in particular local authorities, to promote individual well-being.

Box 11.6 sets out the general duty, which is provided for in s.1 (1) of the Act, and the meaning of well-being for the purposes of the legislation—s. 1(2).

 BOX 11.6 Section 1(1) and (2)

(1) The general duty of a local authority, in exercising a function under this Part in the case of an individual, is to promote that individual's well-being.

(2) 'Well-being', in relation to an individual, means that individual's well-being so far as relating to any of the following—

    (a) personal dignity (including treatment of the individual with respect);

    (b) physical and mental health and emotional well-being;

    (c) protection from abuse and neglect;

    (d) control by the individual over day-to-day life (including over care and support, or support, provided to the individual and the way in which it is provided);

    (e) participation in work, education, training or recreation;

    (f) social and economic well-being;

    (g) domestic, family and personal relationships;

    (h) suitability of living accommodation;

    (i) the individual's contribution to society.

Note that this duty is a general duty—that means that it is not directly enforceable as an individual right, but may well be taken into account when decisions are challenged via judicial review.

The matters that a local authority must take into account when making decisions about individual service provision are set out in s. 1(3) of the Act and listed in **Box 11.7** .

 BOX 11.7 Section 1(3)

- the importance of beginning with the assumption that the individual is best placed to judge the individual's well-being;
- the individual's views, wishes, feelings, and beliefs;
- the need to ensure that decisions about the individual are made having regard to all the individual's circumstances (and are not based only on the individual's age or appearance or any condition of the individual's or aspect of the individual's behaviour which might lead others to make unjustified assumptions about the individual's well-being);
- the importance of the individual participating as fully as possible in decisions relating to the exercise of the function concerned and being provided with the information and support necessary to enable the individual to participate;
- the importance of achieving a balance between the individual's well-being and that of any friends or relatives who are involved in caring for the individual;
- the need to protect people from abuse and neglect;
- the need to ensure that any restriction on the individual's rights or freedom of action that is involved in the exercise of the function is kept to the minimum necessary for achieving the purpose for which the function is being exercised.

Section 2 of the Act ensures that local authorities provide, or arrange to be provided preventative services. This responds to particular concerns that previous legislation failed to provide for the need for services which prevented or delayed the need for care and support services. Section 3 requires that local authorities ensure the integration of the health and support needs of service users—so the need for 'joined-up' thinking is specifically legislated for. Subsequent sections place a duty to cooperate with other providers of health and social care services on the local authorities (ss. 6 and 7) and require the local authority to promote diversity (meaning a range of providers) and quality in services for care and support (s. 5).

Section 8 provides an indicative list of the sort of services that can be made available to service users. This is set out in **Box 11.8** .

 BOX 11.8 Section 8—How to meet needs

(1) The following are examples of what may be provided to meet needs under sections 18 to 20—
    (a) accommodation in a care home or in premises of some other type;

(b) care and support at home or in the community;

(c) counselling and other types of social work;

(d) goods and facilities;

(e) information, advice and advocacy.

(2) The following are examples of the ways in which a local authority may meet needs under sections 18 to 20—

(a) by arranging for a person other than it to provide a service;

(b) by itself providing a service;

(c) by making direct payments.

Sections 9–13 set out the legislative process for the assessment of needs. We will look at these provisions more closely in **chapter 13**. For the time being note that the sections clarify and consolidate existing duties to assess, including duties to assess carers' needs.

The next set of sections set out the new charging regime for adult social care. They are the government's response to the recommendations of the Dilnot Committee. Local authorities will continue to charge for social care costs, following a means test. However what ss. 14–17 do is to cap the costs, limiting what people will be required to pay for care during their lifetime, and for the level of that cap to be reassessed annually. Although the details of the system will be provided for in regulations, the government intends that the cap will be £72,000 when it is introduced in April 2016.

This cap does not include 'living costs'. People in residential care will be expected to pay for costs such as utility bills and food. This is to equalize provision between those who are cared for in their own homes and those who are cared for in residential settings.

Sections 34–36 provide for payments for care to be deferred, meaning that people in residential care will not have to sell their homes during their lifetime to pay for social care. Note that there is no requirement for a home to be sold if the service user's partner is living in the family home. The details of the scheme will be fleshed out in regulations.

The duties on, and powers available to, local authorities to meet needs for care and support are set out in ss. 18–23 . These sections replace previous duties and powers which were dispersed through a variety of statutes. The sections apply as much to carers as to service users. Note that at s. 22 there is an exclusion for the provision of health care services, with the 'quality and quantity' test provided for in *Coughlan* (discussed in **The health/social care divide**, p 387) being set out in statutory form. People subject to immigration control are excluded from the provisions.

The next steps after assessment are provided for in ss. 24–33. These steps include planning care and support for service users and planning support for carers. The plans must be kept under review. There can be reassessments where circumstances indicate a need. The sections also provide for care accounts, personal budgets, and direct payments. We consider the details of the provisions more closely in **chapter 13**.

The need to ensure continuity of care and support is provided for in ss. 37–41. The sections provide a very clear statement of responsibilities upon each authority involved, in a move to ensure no one falls through the net.

Sections 42–47 provide a strengthened statutory framework for adult safeguarding. These provisions are considered more closely in **chapter 14**. Note that s. 46 of the Act abolishes the power within s. 47 of the National Assistance Act 1948 to remove someone in need of care from their home against their will.

The Act contains interesting responses to the problems posed by the collapse of Southern Cross, discussed in **The context of the Care Act 2014—a crisis in adult social care?**, p 391. Section 48 provides that in the event of the business failure of a private provider of care services the local authority has a temporary duty to step in and make provision for the service users. Sections 53–57 require the Care Quality Commission to have market oversight of private providers. Some commentators have raised doubts about whether the Care Quality Commission has the capacity to do this.

Sections 58–66 address gaps in the existing legislation relating to child carers and the transition of service users from child to adult.

The Act also makes provision for independent advocacy, including placing a duty on local authorities to arrange for independent advocates where, without one, the person in question would experience substantial difficulty in understanding relevant information, retaining that information, using or weighing that information, or communicating their views, wishes or feelings (s. 67(4)). The duty does not apply if the local authority thinks there is someone, not a paid carer, who is able to discharge that function.

The final two provisions we draw your attention to in this summary are important ones, added at relatively late stages in the bill's progress through Parliament. The first, at s. 72, provides for internal appeals against decisions made by local authorities in relation to Part 1 of the Act. It will be interesting to see what happens as a result of this provision. On the one hand, it will provide a facility for people to cheaply and simply challenge the local authority in relation to the provision of care and support. On the other hand, it will prevent local authority decision making in this area being scrutinized by judicial review.

Section 73 of the Act extends the Human Rights Act to the private provision of care either in residential or domiciliary settings when that care is funded or arranged by local authorities. This important extension of the Human Rights Act particularly to care services provided in the home reminds us of the importance of human rights and other overarching legal requirements in connection with adult social care.

Overarching legal responsibilities

There are a number of statutes which are overarching in the sense that provisions of other statutes have to be interpreted consistently with their requirements. We considered some of these in **chapter 3**. They comprise equalities legislation, such as the Equality Act 2010, and information legislation, such as the Freedom of Information Act 2000. All social care legislation has to be read bearing in mind the obligations set out in these statutes.

The most important overarching obligations upon the state are those contained in the Human Rights Act 1998. Individuals have challenged the services that the state provides to them in a number of cases which have had important consequences for the delivery of services. Some examples are set out in **Box 11.9**.

BOX 11.9 Human rights and adult social care

Case	Article	
Rabone and another v Pennine Care NHS Trust (2012)	Article 2—right to life	Failure to take reasonable steps to protect an informal patient under the Mental Health Act from the risk of suicide was a breach of Article 2
R (Limbuela) v Home Secretary (2006)	Article 3—right not to be subject to inhuman and degrading treatment	Failure to provide adequate means of support for asylum seekers was unlawful
R (A & B) v East Sussex (Manual Handling) (2003)	Article 8—right to respect for family and private life	A blanket ban on manual handling of disabled service users for health and safety reasons was a breach of Article 8. What is required are policies which strike a balance between the health and safety of carers and the rights of severely disabled people to be treated with dignity
R v Enfield London Borough Council, ex p Bernard (2002)	Article 8—right to respect for the home	The failure of the local authority to provide adaptations to the home of a severely disabled woman, despite it having assessed those adaptations as necessary, was unlawful
HL v UK (2004)	Article 5—right not to be deprived of liberty	The informal detention of a mentally incapacitated adult in a psychiatric hospital without any means of challenging that the detention was unlawful

---

The non-discrimination provisions of Article 14 of the European Convention on Human Rights must also be considered to have potential for litigation which may well prove productive for disabled people and other users of adult social care services.

United Nations Convention on Disability Rights

The UK government ratified the United Nations Convention on Disability Rights on 8 June 2009. The Convention is designed to promote, protect, and ensure the human rights, freedom, and dignity of disabled people. It explicitly sets out the rights that disabled people have and should be able to enjoy on the same basis as other people—for example, the right to dignity, freedom, equality, and justice. It also provides direction on how human rights should be interpreted from the perspective of disabled people all over the world. The government reported upon its compliance with the Convention in 2011. This contains useful statistics on the extent of its compliance: http://webarchive. nationalarchives.gov.uk/20130812104657/http://odi.dwp.gov.uk/docs/disabled-people-and-legislation/uk-initial-report.pdf.

The UK has implemented the optional protocol to the Convention. This provides two additional procedures in respect of implementation and monitoring of the Convention, including an avenue that enables individuals who feel their rights have been breached to bring petitions to the UN Committee, set up to monitor implementation of the Convention.

Equalities legislation

We discussed the scope of the Equality Act 2010 in **chapter 3**. The discussion of disability discrimination in that chapter is of particular relevance for adult social care. Here we focus on the public sector equality duty which has proved a productive legal tool to challenge cuts in provision of adult social care.

Duties on public authorities

As we indicated in **chapter 3**, the imposition of a positive duty upon public bodies to take action to eliminate discrimination and advance equality of opportunity has been one of the most significant legal advances of recent years. The duty known as the public sector equality duty is set out in s. 149 of the Equality Act 2010 and is fully discussed in **chapter 3**. Here we discuss some of the litigation in connection with the public sector equality duty that has become particularly pertinent because of financial cuts.

The public sector equality duty and financial cuts

There is no doubt that the financial crisis and cuts in public sector funding have reduced the resources available for adult social care. Local authorities are facing difficult choices about which services to cut, and where to increase contributions from users. The question arises: What role can the public sector equality duty play in ensuring that local authority decision making does not impact disproportionately upon the most vulnerable groups? In January 2013 the Equality and Human Rights Commission (EHRC) published useful non-statutory guidance on the public sector equality duty. At the time of writing this guidance was under review. When an update is provided we will provide a link to it on the Online Resource Centre. Meanwhile in **Box 11.10** we provide two extracts from the old guidance—which may be interesting to compare or contrast with the new guidance when it is published.

 BOX 11.10 *Using the Equality Duties to make Fair Financial Decisions* (pre-2014 guidance)

The equality duties do not prevent you from making difficult decisions such as reorganisations and relocations, redundancies, and service reductions nor do they stop you from making decisions which may affect one group more than another. What the equality duties do is enable you to demonstrate that you are making financial decisions in a fair, transparent and accountable way, considering the needs and the rights of different members of your community. This is achieved through assessing the impact that changes to policies, procedures and practices could have on different equality groups.

Assessing the impact of proposed changes to policies, procedures and practices is not just something the law requires, it is a positive opportunity for you as public authority leaders to ensure you make better decisions based on robust evidence.

. . .

By law, your assessments of impact on equality must:

- Contain enough information to enable a public authority to demonstrate it has had 'due regard' to the aims of the equality duty in its decision-making

- Consider ways of mitigating or avoiding any adverse impacts.

Such assessments do not have to take the form of a document called an equality impact assessment. If you choose not to develop a document of this type, then some alternative approach which systematically assesses any adverse impacts of a change in policy, procedure or practice will be required.

Assessing impact on equality is not an end in itself and it should be tailored to, and be proportionate to, the decision that is being made.

Whether it is proportionate for an authority to conduct an assessment of the impact on equality of a financial decision or not depends on its relevance to the authority's particular function and its likely impact on people from the protected groups.

We recommend that you document your assessment of the impact on equality when developing financial proposals. This will help you to:

• Ensure you have a written record of the equality considerations you have taken into account.

• Ensure that your decision includes a consideration of the actions that would help to avoid or mitigate any impacts on particular protected groups. Individual decisions should also be informed by the wider context of decisions in your own and other relevant public authorities, so that particular groups are not unduly affected by the cumulative effects of different decisions.

• Make your decisions based on evidence: a decision which is informed by relevant local and national information about equality is a better quality decision. Assessments of impact on equality provide a clear and systematic way to collect, assess and put forward relevant evidence.

• Make the decision-making process more transparent: a process which involves those likely to be affected by the policy, and which is based on evidence, is much more open and transparent. This should also help you secure better public understanding of the difficult decisions you will be making in the coming months.

• Comply with the law: a written record can be used to demonstrate that due regard has been had. Failure to meet the equality duty may result in authorities being exposed to costly, time-consuming and reputation-damaging legal challenges.

Litigation and the public sector equality duty

Three court decisions provide useful guidance on the legal expectations that arise from the public sector equality duty (PSEDs). The first is *R (Rahman) v Birmingham City Council* [2011] EWHC 944 (Admin). This was a judicial review of the decision of Birmingham City Council to close a number of legal advice centres in the city. It was accepted that the closure of the centres would disproportionally affect ethnic minority and disabled users. Whilst an Equality Impact Needs Assessment was prepared in connection with the decision, it was not provided to the councillors who make that decision. Following the issue of the court proceedings, to avoid potential difficulties with the lawfulness of the decision-making process, the relevant councillors were asked to take the decision again, this time with the benefit of the Equality Impact Needs Assessment. They affirmed their previous decision. This, the judge, Mr Justice Blake, said, was not adequate. There were substantial defects in the Equality Impact Needs

Assessment (EINA) that had been prepared in November 2010. It was inadequate in its examination of the evidence and its compliance with the approach recommended by Birmingham City Council's own guidance code for such documents. As the judge put it, in para. 35 of his judgment:

> In a number of respects the content of that EINA seem to have been driven by the hopes of the advantages to be derived from a new policy rather than focusing upon the assessment of the degree of disadvantage to existing users of terminating funding arrangements until new arrangements can be put in place.

Moreover, the duty is not merely to have regard to the EINA but to have due regard to the PSED duty. Paragraph 46 of the judgment makes the requirements clear.

> Even where the context of decision making is financial resources in a tight budget, that does not excuse compliance with the PSEDs and indeed there is much to be said for the proposition that even in the straightened times the need for clear, well-informed decision making when assessing the impacts on less advantaged members of society is as great, if not greater.

The judge refers positively to the original non-statutory guidance produced by the EHRC set out in **Box 11.10**.

The second case that it is useful to note is *R (W) v Birmingham City Council* [2011] EWHC 1147 (Admin). Here the judicial review challenged the defendant local authority's decision to reduce its budget for adult social care by restricting the provision of support for people with disabilities to those whose needs were assessed to be critical. The claimants were all severely disabled adults. They argued that the prospective change was unlawful since the local authority had failed to have due regard to the disability equality duty set out in s. 49A of the Disability Discrimination Act 1995 (the duty which preceded s. 149 of the Equality Act 2010). The local authority argued that the courts should be careful not to intervene in questions involving the balancing of competing claims, which were matters for expertise, specialist knowledge, local policy, and democratic accountability. The judge, Mr Justice Walker, upheld the claim. At para. 176 he stated:

> It is difficult to see how, in the circumstances of the present case, 'due regard' could be paid to the matters identified in s. 49A without some attempt at assessment of the practical impact on those whose needs in a particular respect fell into the 'substantial' band but not into the 'critical' band.

He concluded:

> that there was a failure . . . to address the questions which arose when considering whether the impact on the disabled of the move to 'critical only' was so serious that an alternative which was not so draconian should be identified and funded to the extent necessary by savings elsewhere.

He pointed out that:

> These cases indicate that the public sector equality duty may prove a very useful tool to protect the resources available for adult social care. What it requires is that local authorities take into account the potential. It is not that the cuts cannot go ahead, but they should

only go ahead when the potential impact of decisions to cut services on those people with protected characteristics has been fully assessed and faced up to. However both these cases are High Court decisions.

The third—and most recent case—is a Court of Appeal case—*Bracking v Secretary of State for Work and Pensions* [2013] EWCA Civ 1345 and therefore more authoritative. The legal challenge arose as a result of the decision to close the Independent Living Fund (ILF) from March 2015. The ILF, set up in 1988 as an interim measure pending the implementation of community care legislation and the reform of disability benefits, is funded by the Department for Work and Pensions (DWP) to provide services and direct payments to disabled people which help them to lead independent lives in the community. It has a complex bureaucratic history. Although wound up in 1993, its popularity meant that commitments were made to maintain funding to its existing recipients, and a new fund was established for applications made between 1993 and 2007. At the time of the Court of Appeal hearing it was estimated that more than 19,000 people were in receipt of assistance through the ILF which cost the DWP over £350mn. The government considered the system was unsustainable and in July 2012 the DWP launched its consultation on a new model of provision. This made clear that closure was the preferred option, with funding being transferred to local government in England and the devolved administrations in Scotland and Wales. In December 2012, the government announced its decision to close the ILF from 2015. It published an Equality Impact Assessment (EIA) which concluded that any negative impact was 'justified by the policy aims of providing greater equity and fairness in the social care system and delivering this funding at a local level in a way which is accountable to local people through the electoral system' (quoted at para. 19).

The four claimants, each of whom had severe disabilities and were current recipients of ILF payments, made two substantive challenges to the lawfulness of the decision to close the fund. First, they argued that the consultation that preceded the decision was inadequate and, second, that the minister had failed to discharge the PSED. At the High Court Mr Justice Blake, remarking upon the legal limits of the duty to consult, determined that the consultation process was fit for purpose, and was nothing 'other than candid and open, having regard to what it was: a desire to know the consequences of a provisional decision to close the ILF'. He also determined that the PSED had been met. There was one caveat: the duty was a continuing one and in particular the government needed to continue to have regard to the express terms of the UN Convention on the Rights of Persons with Disabilities 2006, ratified by the UK in June 2009.

The claimants appealed to the Court of Appeal. Lord Justice McCombe upheld Mr Justice Blake's decision on the adequacy of the consultation. However, his review of the documentation presented to the minister in connection with the discharge of the PSED led him to conclude that there was insufficient evidence 'to demonstrate to the court that a focused regard was had to the potentially very grave impact upon individuals in this group of disabled persons, within the context of a consideration of the statutory requirements for disabled people as a whole' (para. 61). He therefore allowed the appeal and quashed the decision to close the fund. This decision seems to promise that the Court of Appeal will take the duty seriously.

Note: **chapter 3** considers the case of *Blake and others v London Borough of Waltham Forest* [2014] EWHC 1027 (Admin) on the council's termination of a soup kitchen licence. The judge set out principles relating to the PSED and the process by which it must be fulfilled.

Just as equality has ethical and legal dimensions so does dignity, another mechanism for enhancing services to adult service users.

Human rights and dignity

The Department of Health, as part of a drive to improve services for vulnerable adults, has actively promoted the concept of dignity. The Social Care Institute for Excellence (SCIE) has produced a practice guide on dignity which you may find useful. It can be downloaded from www.scie.org.uk/publications/guides/guide15. It contains the Dignity Challenge, accepted by the NHS, explaining what the concept of dignity can offer. It is set out in **Box 11.11**.

BOX 11.11 The Dignity Challenge

High quality care services that respect people's dignity should:

1) have a zero tolerance of all forms of abuse
2) support people with the same respect you would want for yourself or a member of your family
3) treat each person as an individual by offering a personalised service
4) enable people to maintain the maximum possible level of independence, choice and control
5) listen and support people to express their needs and wants
6) respect people's right to privacy
7) ensure people feel able to complain without fear of retribution
8) engage with family members and carers as care partners
9) assist people to maintain confidence and a positive self-esteem
10) act to alleviate people's loneliness and isolation.

Box 11.12 sets out a useful working definition of dignity taken from the SCIE practice guide.

BOX 11.12 What is dignity?

Dignity consists of many overlapping aspects, involving respect, privacy, autonomy and self-worth. The provisional meaning of dignity used for this guide is based on a standard dictionary definition: a state, quality or manner worthy of esteem or respect; and (by extension) self-respect. Dignity in care, therefore, means the kind of care, in any setting, which supports and promotes, and does not undermine, a person's self respect regardless of any difference. While 'dignity' may be difficult to define, what is clear is that people know when they have not been treated with dignity and respect. Helping to put that right is the purpose of this guide.

SCIE also points out the factors that might indicate failure to treat people with appropriate dignity, which we have set out in **Box 11.13**.

BOX 11.13 Factors that diminish dignity—extract from SCIE dignity guide

Factors that have been held responsible for the absence of dignity in care include bureaucracy, staff shortages, poor management and lack of leadership, absence of appropriate training and induction and difficulties with recruitment and retention leading to overuse of temporary staff.

There are also wider societal issues, including ageism, other forms of discrimination and abuse. A great deal of work is needed to tackle negative attitudes towards older people, to bring about a culture change and to ensure that such attitudes have no place in the health and social care sectors.

The idea of dignity is deeply embedded within human rights. Article 1 of the preamble to the Convention to the Universal Declaration of Human Rights, proclaims that:

All human beings are born free and equal in dignity and rights. They are endowed with reason and conscience and should act towards one another in a spirit of brotherhood.

In the UK some judges refer to the importance of individual dignity when evaluating service provision. Perhaps the approach is best epitomized within the judgment of Mr Justice Munby in the case of *R (on the application of A & B) v East Sussex County Council* (2003). We looked more closely at this case on manual handling in **chapter 3** in connection with the Human Rights Act 1998. Here we want to use the case to demonstrate the legal importance of dignity. Mr Justice Munby, in his decision, made it clear that human dignity lies at the heart of the law—not just human rights law, but the common law as well. His judgment on this is well worth reading. We have set out paras 86 and 87 in **Box 11.14**.

BOX 11.14 Dignity and the law—paras 86 and 87 from *R (on the application of A & B) v East Sussex County Council* [2003] EWHC 167 (Admin)

86 The recognition and protection of human dignity is one of the core values—in truth *the* core value—of our society and, indeed, of all the societies which are part of the European family of nations and which have embraced the principles of the Convention. It is a core value of the common

law, long pre-dating the Convention and the Charter. The invocation of the dignity of the patient in the form of declaration habitually used when the court is exercising its inherent declaratory jurisdiction in relation to the gravely ill or dying is not some meaningless incantation designed to comfort the living or to assuage the consciences of those involved in making life and death decisions: it is a solemn affirmation of the law's and of society's recognition of our humanity and of human dignity as something fundamental. Not surprisingly, human dignity is extolled in article 1 of the Charter, just as it is in article 1 of the Universal Declaration. And the latter's call to us to 'act towards one another in a spirit of brotherhood' is nothing new. It reflects the fourth Earl of Chesterfield's injunction, 'Do as you would be done by' and, for the Christian, the biblical call (Matthew ch 7, v 12): 'all things whatsoever ye would that men should do to you, do ye even so to them: for this is the law and the prophets'.

87 Dignity interests are also, of course, at the core of the rights protected by article 3. Whether a particular set of circumstances constitutes 'inhuman or degrading treatment' is a matter of fact and degree. As the Court said in *A v United Kingdom* (1998) 27 EHRR 611 at 629 (para [20]):

'The Court recalls that ill-treatment must attain a minimum level of severity if it is to fall within the scope of Article 3. The assessment of this minimum is relative: it depends on all the circumstances of the case, such as the nature and context of the treatment, its duration, its physical and mental effects and, in some instances, the sex, age and state of health of the victim.'

What Mr Justice Munby makes clear is that the law will not step in to protect a claimant from *any* claim that their dignity has been violated. Life is not that straightforward. Article 3, as we explained in **chapter 3**, has a relatively high threshold which must be crossed before the courts will intervene. Moreover, there are circumstances where one person's dignity has to be breached in order to protect another's dignity. In the circumstances of *A & B v East Sussex County Council* the conflict was between the rights of the service users and the rights of those who were employed to care for them. Mr Justice Munby considers this conflict in his judgment. The relevant paragraphs are set out in **Box 11.15**. They contain a useful reminder of the value of compassion and the human touch as a prerequisite of humanity and dignity.

BOX 11.15 Dignified ends and undignified means, paras 120–122 of *A & B v East Sussex County Council*

120 I recognise of course that the compassion of the carer is itself a vital aspect of our humanity and dignity and that at a very deep level of our instinctive feelings we value and need the caring touch of the human hand. That no doubt is one of the reasons why the nobility of compassionate carers as different in their ways as Florence Nightingale, Leonard Cheshire and Mother Teresa resonates so strongly with us. . . . Even those who do not believe in any God know that a human being is more than a machine consisting of a few rather basic chemicals operated by electric currents

controlled by some animalistic equivalent of a computer located in the skull—and that, no doubt, is why we have an instinctive and intuitive preference for the touch of the human hand rather than the assistance of a machine. As disabled persons or invalids our instinctive preference is to be fed by a nurse with a spoon rather than through a naso-gastric or gastrostomy tube.

121 But, and this is the first point, insistence on the use of dignified means cannot be allowed to obstruct more important ends. On occasions our very humanity and dignity may itself demand that we be subjected to a certain amount—sometimes a very great deal—of indignity. Dignified ends may sometimes demand the use of undignified means. The immediate dignity of a person trapped in a blazing building is probably the very last thing on his mind or in the mind of the fireman who bundles him undignified out of the window to save his life. And one thinks of the gross violence and indignity of the methods necessarily used by the crash team in its desperate efforts to save life in the Accident and Emergency Department. But this does not mean that means must be allowed to triumph over ends. There is a balance to be held—and it is often a very difficult balance to strike. . . . Modern medical law and ethics illustrate the excruciating difficulty we often have in achieving the right balance between using undignified means in striving to achieve dignified ends.

122 The other point is this. One must guard against jumping too readily to the conclusion that manual handling is necessarily more dignified than the use of equipment. A disabled person or invalid may prefer manual handling by a relative or friend to the use of a hoist but at the same time prefer a hoist to manual handling by a stranger or a paid carer. The independently minded but physically disabled person might prefer to hoist himself up from his bath or chair rather than to be assisted even by his devoted wife. Dignity in the narrow context in which it has been used during much of the argument in this case is in truth part of a much wider concept of dignity, part of a complicated equation including such elusive concepts as, for example, (feelings of) independence and access to the world and to others. Hoisting is not inherently undignified, let alone inherently inhuman or degrading . . . It all depends on the context.

Munby J's words are moving and demonstrate the complexity of achieving dignity. There is never a clear answer which will protect dignity in all circumstances. You must be able to carry out the necessary balancing exercise, as described in **chapter 3**, and determine what the priorities are in particular circumstances. Neither should we get carried away with the idea that the law will intervene to protect the dignity of the service user regardless of resource implications. The decision of the Supreme Court in *R (McDonald) v Royal Borough of Kensington and Chelsea* (2011) made that absolutely clear. We will discuss this case further in **chapter 13**. For our purposes what you need to know is that Ms McDonald argued that requiring her to use incontinence pads when she was not incontinent was a breach of her dignity. Whilst Lord Brown, giving the leading judgment, acknowledged the positive obligation under Article 8 to respect a person's private life, he considered that the consultation process and the attempts to reach agreement with Ms McDonald were sufficient to demonstrate RBKC's respect for Ms McDonald's dignity and autonomy. Not only did he determine that there was no interference by RBKC with Ms McDonald's Article 8 rights, he added (at para. 19) that even if he were wrong any interference which was in accordance with the law would be justified:

> on the grounds that it is necessary for the economic well-being of the respondents [ie the council and its taxpayers] and the interests of their other service-users and is a proportionate response to the appellant's needs because it affords her the maximum protection from injury, greater privacy and independence, and results in a substantial costs saving.

In May 2014 the European Court of Human Rights (ECtHR) heard Ms McDonald's challenge to the Supreme Court decision. Whilst the outcome was not very positive for Ms McDonald (see the discussion in **chapter 13**), the ECtHR did make it clear that dignity is to be given serious consideration in decisions about adult social care. It will be interesting to see how authorities and courts in England and Wales respond to the judgment.

The reluctance of the English and Welsh courts to take a strong stand of human rights is also seen in the litigation on the closure of care homes.

Care homes and the right to a home

The closure of care homes by local authorities has stimulated extensive litigation on behalf of residents of those homes, their carers, and those who use the homes as respite facilities. Their advocates have mounted human rights arguments in efforts to prevent closures. The relevant Articles of the European Convention which may be engaged by the closure of a residential home are Article 8—the right to respect for the home; Article 3—the right not to be subject to degrading treatment; and Article 2—the right to life. In *Dudley Whitbread and others v East Sussex County Council* (2003) the local authority had gone through a consultation exercise with all of those interested in the future of the home and had decided to close it. What the judgment in that case demonstrates is that where the proper processes have been completed, including a proper consideration of human rights arguments, the courts will be reluctant to interfere on the basis of breach of human rights. The issue was revisited in *R (on the application of Verna Wilson and others) v Coventry City Council* and *R (on the application of Victor Thomas and others) v London Borough of Havering* (2008). The main argument here concerned Article 2. The claimants' argument was that the published medical literature, buttressed by two expert reports produced to the court on behalf of the claimants, established that there was a statistically demonstrable increase in the rate of mortality of residents in care homes who are elderly and/or who suffer from dementia when they are moved from care homes where they have lived for a number of years, unless they are moved as a group from one home to another with the staff that have always looked after them. Therefore if a decision was taken to close a care home without the decision-maker being aware of these risks, the authorities had acted in breach of Article 2 of the European Convention on Human Rights in taking the decision. That argument was dependent upon demonstrating that the officers concerned had failed to take the relevant evidence into consideration. The judge rejected the argument following an interesting analysis of the medical evidence which does not appear to have been quite as clear-cut as claimed, and decided that officials had thought very carefully and followed established protocols about the minimization of risk to residents prior to making the decision to close the home. The judge did concede that the claimants had a potentially arguable point about the necessity for careful timing of individual assessment of risk. The claimants had suggested that the decision was flawed because individual assessments of the residents had not been carried out prior to the decision to close the home. If those individual assessments were carried out subsequently and on a piecemeal basis, there was a risk that residents and staff would be split up, increasing the risk of a rise in mortality rates. However, there was no evidence in this case that this was going to happen, so such an argument would have to wait until a challenge based upon those particular facts.

What the cases demonstrate is that human rights arguments will not prevail in home closure cases as long as they are properly considered during the process of decision making. Officers must ensure that not only is consultation properly carried out but also that risks are properly managed via competent assessment procedures, that agreed protocols are followed, and that there is clear justification for closure decisions.

See also *YL v Birmingham City Council* (2007) considered in **chapter 3**.

Asylum seekers

Judges may have been reluctant to extend the remit of the Human Rights Act in order to protect the dignity of publicly funded elderly residents of private care homes, however they have demonstrated much greater activism in response to the needs of asylum seekers. This is an interesting area of law—20 years ago no one would have imagined that you would have to show your passport in order to claim welfare benefits. The combination of the state's increasing reluctance to provide generous benefits, global migration, and the devastation that conflict and disease have caused to particular parts of the world have meant that the individual needs of the asylum seeker in the UK have become a political minefield. This account will only provide a brief outline of this area.

The term 'asylum seeker' is statutorily defined. The definition is set out in **Box 11.16**.

 BOX 11.16 Statutory definition of asylum seeker

Immigration and Asylum Act 1999, s. 94(1):

> a person who is not under 18 and has made a claim for asylum which has been recorded by the Secretary of State but which has not been determined.

The meaning of a 'claim for asylum' is again statutorily defined. This is set out in **Box 11.17**.

BOX 11.17 A claim for asylum

Immigration and Asylum Act 1999, s. 94(1):

> claim that it would be contrary to the United Kingdom's obligations under the Refugee Convention, or under Article 3 of the Human Rights Convention, for the claimant to be removed from, or require to leave, the United Kingdom.

The basic position is that asylum seekers are entitled to accommodation and financial support whilst they are in the UK. However, for a long time the UK has been concerned that the generosity of its provisions to asylum seekers has made the UK disproportionately attractive to asylum seekers. Since 1996 there have been legislative efforts to reduce the benefits that are available to them. A distinction was made between those asylum seekers who made their claim for asylum at their port of entry on their arrival in the UK and those who made their claim later, whilst in the country. Those who made their claim later were excluded from benefits and from homelessness provisions. The Immigration and Asylum Act 1999 set up the National Asylum Support Service (NASS) and from that time until March 2007 the needs of asylum seekers were to be provided for by this agency. In March 2007 NASS was replaced by the New Asylum Model (NAM)—designed to provide a more effective service. Despite the intentions of the government, however, neither NASS nor NAM actually provide for all of the needs of asylum seekers. Through particularly complex legal gymnastics, some asylum seekers with community care needs have those needs provided by local authorities. It is as a result of this that social workers become involved in asylum cases. We will try to summarize the legal journey below, before explaining the current position.

Clearly, those asylum seekers who claimed asylum too late to be entitled to benefits were in great difficulties. They used their destitution to make claims under the National Assistance Act 1948 (NAA 1948). Their entitlement to accommodation under the NAA 1948 was acknowledged by the Court of Appeal in *R v Hammersmith LBC, ex p M* (1997). Whilst this provided access to local authority support for those asylum seekers who met the criteria set out in the Act, it provided huge difficulties for local authorities, especially in London. The government therefore amended the NAA 1948 to exclude asylum seekers from its remit. The provision is substantially re-enacted within s. 21 of the Care Act 2014 This is set out in **Box 11.18**.

 BOX 11.18 Section 21 of the Care Act 2014

A local authority may not meet the needs for care and support of an adult to whom section 115 of the Immigration and Asylum Act 1999 ('the 1999 Act') (exclusion from benefits) applies and whose needs for care and support have arisen solely—

(a) because the adult is destitute, or

(b) because of the physical effects, or anticipated physical effects, of being destitute.

Destitution itself is not a straightforward requirement. The government is seeking to ensure that as few people as possible are defined as destitute in order to limit its financial commitment. The meaning of destitution is set out in s. 95(3) of the Immigration and Asylum Act 1999 in **Box 11.19.**

BOX 11.19 Destitution

For the purposes of this section, a person is destitute if—

(a) he does not have adequate accommodation or any means of obtaining it (whether or not his other essential living needs are met); or

(b) he has adequate accommodation or the means of obtaining it, but cannot meet his other essential living needs.

The approach to destitution is amplified by the Asylum Support Regulations 2000 which require that when assessing whether or not an individual is destitute: (a) the whole family's circumstances must be taken into account; and (b) any other resources which the person might reasonably have access to must also be taken into account. So, for instance, community support for the individual, as long as it will provide essential needs for the next 14 days, must be taken into account.

Asylum seekers who are destitute, and their dependants, receive support, not through the NAA 1948, but through NAM managed by the Borders Agency.

The destitute and infirm asylum seeker

The 1999 amendment to the NAA 1948 used the word 'solely' in describing which asylum seekers are excluded from its remit. In *Westminster City Council v NASS* (2002) the House of Lords distinguished between destitute able-bodied asylum seekers and those who are destitute but infirm. It decided that those who have needs arising from infirmities over and beyond their destitution must have those needs provided for via the local authority. So the government's efforts to ensure that local authorities have no responsibility to provide for asylum seekers failed. The local authority still has duties to asylum seekers to provide community care services when:

(a) the asylum seeker is destitute;

(b) in addition the asylum seeker has a need for support services for infirmities caused other than by destitution;

(c) there is no other support available to the asylum seeker, including from NAM.

In these circumstances the local authority will have to assess the asylum seeker's needs.

In 2008, the House of Lords in *R(M) v Slough Borough Council*, considered whether an asylum seeker who was HIV positive, and required medication which needed refrigeration and a doctor's appointment every three months, was entitled to accommodation under s. 21 of the NAA 1948. Overruling the Court of Appeal, it decided that the applicant was not in need of the 'care and attention' that was an essential prerequisite to the provision of accommodation under the NAA 1948. In the opinion of Baroness Hale, the natural and ordinary meaning of 'care and attention' is 'looking after'. This means doing something for the person being cared for which he cannot or should not be expected to do for himself. It does not include the provision of medical care, and therefore the applicant's need for HIV medicine did not amount to a need for care and attention.

In *R (SL) v Westminster City Council* (2011), the Court of Appeal gave further consideration to the meaning of care and attention which was considered by the House of Lords in *Slough*. SL was a failed asylum seeker who had been granted indefinite leave to remain. He had been homeless and was later admitted to a psychiatric hospital where he was diagnosed as suffering from mental health problems. Following his discharge, the local authority provided him with assistance in the form of regular weekly meetings with a care coordinator who provided advice and encouragement, monitored his condition and progress, and helped to arrange contact with counselling groups and a 'befriender'. SL also received medical attention. Westminster City Council refused to provide SL with residential accommodation on the basis that he was not in need of care and attention within the meaning of s. 21(1)(a). The Court of Appeal disagreed. It decided that SL was in need of care and attention, and that the judge at the High Court who had rejected SL's claim for judicial review had underestimated the support provided by his care coordinator. It would be absurd for it to provide assistance through a care coordinator without providing stable accommodation. However, Westminster City Council appealed the case to the Supreme Court, which overturned the decision of the Court of Appeal. The decision is reported at [2013] UKSC 27. In essence, the Supreme Court decided that the local authority was entitled to conclude that SL was not in need of 'care and attention' which was not 'otherwise available' to him such as to require the provision of residential accommodation.

Lord Carnwath concluded:

> the present case is clearly distinguishable on the facts from the [*Westminster v*] *NASS* case. That case had been argued on the footing that the applicant's need for care and attention had arisen not solely because she was destitute 'but also (and largely) because she (was) ill' (Lord Hoffmann, para 49); and it was common ground that she had access to no other accommodation in which she could receive that care and attention (Lord Hoffmann, para 43). Furthermore, her needs affected both the nature and the location of the accommodation. In the present case, by contrast, care and attention can be, and is provided, independently of SL's need for accommodation or its location. Indeed, it was not in dispute that similar support services could be provided anywhere in the country.

Human rights and late asylum claims

There is a further complexity caused by the requirement for asylum seekers to claim asylum as soon as reasonably practicable after their arrival in the UK. If they fail to do so then those applicants who do not have dependent children can be excluded from support under s. 55 of the Nationality, Immigration and Asylum Act 2002 (NIAA

2002). Moreover, those who if they had claimed in time would have been entitled to community care services under the NAA 1948 are excluded as a result of amendments made to s. 21 of the NAA 1948 by s. 54 of and Schedule 3 to the NIAA 2002. However, the government is required to 'secure to everyone within their jurisdiction' the rights contained within the European Convention on Human Rights. This includes failed asylum seekers. The government's responsibility is recognized within s. 55(5)(a), which provides that the Secretary of State is not prevented from making provision to the extent necessary to prevent a breach of an applicant's human rights.

In *R (Adam, Limbuela and Tesema) v SSHD* (2005) the House of Lords considered the severity of the consequences of denial of support that an asylum seeker must suffer in order for there to be a violation of his or her human rights. Lord Bingham, the senior Law Lord at the time of the judgment, indicated when such a situation would arise. The relevant paragraphs of his opinion are set out in **Box 11.20**.

 BOX 11.20 Lord Bingham in *R (Adam, Limbuela and Tesema) v SSHD* (2005)

Treatment is inhuman or degrading if, to a seriously detrimental extent, it denies the most basic needs of any human being. As in all Art. 3 cases, the treatment, to be proscribed, must achieve a minimum standard of severity, and I would accept that in a context such as this, not involving the deliberate infliction of pain or suffering, the threshold is a high one. A general public duty to house the homeless or provide for the destitute cannot be spelled out of Art. 3. But I have no doubt that the threshold may be crossed if a late applicant with no means and no alternative sources of support, unable to support himself, is, by the deliberate action of the state, denied shelter, food or the most basic necessities of life. It is not necessary that treatment, to engage Art. 3, should merit the description used, in an immigration context, by Shakespeare and others in *Sir Thomas More* when they referred to 'your mountainish inhumanity'.

When does the Secretary of State's duty under s. 55(5)(a) arise? The answer must in my opinion be: when it appears on a fair and objective assessment of all relevant facts and circumstances that an individual applicant faces an imminent prospect of serious suffering caused or materially aggravated by denial of shelter, food or the most basic necessities of life. Many factors may affect that judgment, including age, gender, mental and physical health and condition, any facilities or sources of support available to the applicant, the weather and time of year and the period for which the applicant has already suffered or is likely to continue to suffer privation.

It is not in my opinion possible to formulate any simple test applicable in all cases. But if there were persuasive evidence that a late applicant was obliged to sleep in the street, save perhaps for a short and foreseeably finite period, or was seriously hungry, or unable to satisfy the most basic requirements of hygiene, the threshold would, in the ordinary way, be crossed.

It is unfortunate that the test cannot be stated simply. Nonetheless, the position of failed asylum seekers who are in need of accommodation under s. 21 of the NAA 1948 will receive those services if failure to provide them would mean that the government would be in breach of its obligations under the European Convention on Human Rights. Moreover, the judges appear to be determined to hold the government to account over its human rights responsibilities to asylum seekers.

Citizenship

So far in this chapter we have considered the concept of dignity as a driver to improve standards of service for the adult service user. There is another concept, citizenship, which is also used as a way of reminding service providers that decent services are an entitlement of service users, and not a privilege. Citizenship is an aspect of human rights, as Mr Justice Munby reminded us in his decision in *A & B v East Sussex County Council* (see **Box 11.21**).

BOX 11.21 Citizenship and social inclusion. Extract from the decision in *A & B v East Sussex County Council*

The other important concept embraced in the 'physical and psychological integrity' protected by article 8 is the right of the disabled to participate in the life of the community and to have what has been described (see below) as 'access to essential economic and social activities and to an appropriate range of recreational and cultural activities'. This is matched by the positive obligation of the State to take appropriate measures designed to ensure to the greatest extent feasible that a disabled person is not 'so circumscribed and so isolated as to be deprived of the possibility of developing his personality'.

This aspect of article 8 appears from *Botta* [v Italy: ECtHR case 153/1996/772/973] itself, where the claim was brought by a physically disabled man who went on holiday to a seaside resort but was unable to gain access to a private beach and the sea because they were not equipped with disabled facilities. As the Court explained at 255 (para [27]):

'The applicant complained, firstly, of impairment of his private life and the development of his personality resulting from the Italian State's failure to take appropriate measures to remedy the omissions imputable to the private bathing establishments of Lido degli Estensi (Comacchio), namely the lack of lavatories and ramps providing access to the sea for the use of disabled people. He relied on Article 8 of the Convention . . . The applicant asserted that he was unable to enjoy a normal social life which would enable him to participate in the life of the community and to exercise essential rights, such as his non-pecuniary personal rights, not because of interference by the State but on account of its failure to discharge its positive obligations to adopt measures and to monitor compliance with domestic provisions relating to private beaches.'

The Court dismissed the complaint, but the grounds on which it did so are revealing (at 257 paras [34]–[35]):

'[34] The Court has held that a State has obligations of this type where it has found a direct and immediate link between the measures sought by an applicant and the latter's private and/or family life . . .

[35] In the instant case, however, the right asserted by Mr Botta, namely the right to gain access to the beach and the sea at a place distant from his normal place of residence during his holidays, concerns interpersonal relations of such broad and indeterminate scope that there can be no conceivable direct link between the measures the State was urged to take in order to make good the omissions of the private bathing establishments and the applicant's private life.'

I have also been referred to the opinion of the Commission in *Botta* and, in particular, to the concurring opinion of, amongst others, Mr N Bratza (as he then was) at 250–252. His opinion, if I may say so, is important and merits quotation at some length: 'As the majority have recalled, although "the object of Article 8 is essentially that of protecting the individual against arbitrary interference by the public authorities", thereby imposing primarily negative obligations [i.e. not to interfere with a person's rights rather than actively to enhance them] on the Contracting States, this provision may nonetheless, in certain cases, impose on those States positive obligations inherent in an effective respect for private life. These positive obligations "may involve the adoption of measures designed to secure respect for private life even in the sphere of the relations of individuals between themselves".'

We believe this to be the case. Such positive obligations may exceptionally arise in the case of the handicapped in order to ensure that they are not deprived of the possibility of developing social relations with others and thereby developing their own personalities. In this regard, the Commission observes that there is no water-tight division separating the sphere of social and economic rights from the field covered by the Convention.

In the case of the physically handicapped, the above-mentioned positive obligations require appropriate measures to be taken, to the greatest extent feasible, to ensure that they have access to essential economic and social activities and to an appropriate range of recreational and cultural activities. The precise aim and nature of the measures undertaken may vary from place to place, and according to the priorities of facilitating access to sanitary facilities, footpaths, transport, entrances to buildings, historical sites, areas of natural beauty, and areas of recreational use. In the case of the mentally handicapped, the measures would necessarily be different. This is an area in which a wide discretion must inevitably be accorded to the national authorities. Nevertheless, the crucial factor is the extent to which a particular individual is so circumscribed and so isolated as to be deprived of the possibility of developing his personality.

As Mr Justice Munby indicates, citizenship is generally understood as the right to participate in the life of the community.

Ideas of citizenship are promoted by the government. This is evident in the statement, *A Vision for Adult Social Care: Capable Communities and Active Citizens*, published in November 2010, which we discussed earlier (**The context of the Care Act 2014—a crisis in adult social care?**, p 391). The vision claims to be a new direction but it continues the personalization agenda, the use of direct payments and the empowerment of carers. There are also critical perspectives on these initiatives, which point out that the vision is a very consumer-orientated view of citizenship, attempting to transform the user of social care services into an effective participant in a market system. This may limit the effectiveness of citizenship as a driver for change.

The EHRC takes a different approach. Its understanding of citizenship is very much based upon the human rights of individuals. In a paper setting out its approach to the reform of adult social care, *From Safety Net to Springboard: A New Approach to Care and Support for all Based on Equality and Human Rights*, published in February 2009, it provides seven principles which it considers should underpin any reform. These are:

- Care and support based on clear outcomes and founded on human rights and equality.
- Access to publicly funded care and support based on clear, fair and consistent criteria.
- Individuals and families in control of their care and support.
- The right balance between safety and risk to promote choice and independence.
- Local strategic partnerships that play a central role in developing and maintaining local care and support.
- Funding that balances affordability and sustainability with fairness.
- Equality and human rights law and practice re-calibrated to respond to our ageing society.

These principles provide a very useful framework for you to evaluate the Care Act 2014 and other legal developments relating to adult social care.

EXERCISES

1 To what extent does the Care Act 2014 resolve the crisis of adult social care?

2 Find the latest statistics on adult social care provision. Does your local area have particular plans for cuts in adult social care provision? What do you think the impact of cuts will be?

3 Locate responses to the passing of the Care Act 2014. What do pressure groups think of the new legislation?

ONLINE RESOURCE CENTRE

For guidance on how to answer these exercises, visit the Online Resource Centre at www. oxfordtextbooks.co.uk/orc/socialwork13e/.

WHERE DO WE GO FROM HERE?

This chapter has provided an introduction to adult social care, setting current provision in a legal and political context, in particularly introducing and summarizing the Care Act 2014. **Chapter 12** focuses on the existing law. We must spend some time describing the complex and incoherent statutory basis of adult social care services as it may be another two to three years before the Care Act is fully implemented.

ANNOTATED FURTHER READING

The Equality and Human Rights Commission contains extensive information on age and disability issues. Age UK campaigns actively for improved outcomes for older people. Its policy pages provide information about dignity in care, equality and human rights, and adult safeguarding—www.ageuk.org.uk. You can obtain Age UK's 2014 edition of *Care in Crisis* from www.ageuk.org.uk/Documents/EN-GB/Campaigns/CIC/Care_in_Crisis_report_2014. pdf?epslanguage=en-GB?dtrk%3Dtrue.

Other charities connected with adult social care run useful and informative websites. Mencap, for instance, is the leading campaign organization for learning disability—www. mencap.org.uk.

For something more academic, although with up-to-the-minute commentary on legal and policy developments on community care, we recommend the Small Places blog—http:// thesmallplaces.wordpress.com. It is authored by Lucy Series, a research assistant at Cardiff Law School who has a background working in mental health.

For those of you who enjoy the legal approach, here are two pieces on the public sector equality duty written by a practising barrister and a judge respectively:

> T. Dyke, 'Judicial review in an age of austerity' (2011) *JR* 16(3): 202
>
> Mr Justice Sales, 'The public sector equality duty' (2011) *JR* 16(1): 1.

A more academic and critical approach is taken in the following article:

> S. Fredman, 'The public sector equality duty' (2011) *Industrial Law Journal* 40(4): 405.

One particular article which focuses on the law and dignity is L. Clements, 'Disability, dignity and the *cri de coeur*' (2011) 6 EHRLR 675. This suggests that the judges treat the dignity of the prisoner with far greater respect than the dignity of the recipient of adult social care.

> At the time of writing there are no authoritative commentaries on the Care Act 2014. As they become available we will note them on the Online Resource Centre: www. oxfordtextbooks.co.uk/orc/social work13e/.

Finally, BBC Radio 4 has produced a number of programmes which cover the care crisis in the UK: www.bbc.co.uk/radio4/features/you-and-yours/care-in-the-uk-2010. They are well worth listening to.

The legal framework of adult social care

12

OVERVIEW AND OBJECTIVES

This chapter explains the main statutory provisions that relate specifically to adult social care which will remain in force until the Care Act 2014 is implemented. It begins by considering the duties and powers in a range of statutes beginning with the National Assistance Act 1948. It then provides a brief account of the multiplicity of statutes that have elaborated, reformed, and restricted the provision of services for adult social care since that date. The chapter includes an account of legal responsibilities towards carers. We will also provide some details of how the Care Act 2014 will change the law.

Our case study in this chapter may surprise you. Despite the focus on the law, we have chosen to look at complaints made to the Local Government Ombudsman. This serves as a timely reminder that the courts hear only a tiny percentage of disputes relating to adult social care.

CASE STUDY

Below we set out the results of two complaints reported during 2011 in connection with adult social care services to the Local Government Ombudsman and reported on its website www.lgo.org.uk/.

Leeds City Council (10 012 561): adult social care maladministration causing injustice, 29 November 2011

Leeds City Council wrongly kept a daughter from visiting her elderly mother in a care home. The Ombudsman said the Council's fault deprived the woman 'of the opportunity to speak with her mother before they were separated forever by death.'

She added: 'Relatives and friends have the right to visit and see each other without undue interference and the right to respect for family life is enshrined in law. Ms B was told unexpectedly—and without there being any evidence—that she was regarded as a threat to her own mother, denied access to her, made to hand over a Christmas gift outside the home and made to wait for over a month for the Council's processes before finally being told that she could see her mother.'

Ms B was estranged from her family. Shortly before Christmas she learned that her mother was in a care home and not likely to live long. Her brother wrote to the home saying that Ms B would try to remove their mother from the home and would upset her by talking about money. The home passed the information on to Council officers and told Ms B that she could not visit her mother.

A couple of days later an officer asked Ms B's brother about his allegations. He withdrew them but said he was concerned that his mother would be upset by seeing Ms B. A manager says that the officer concerned was told that Ms B could not be prevented from seeing her mother and that, because of the concern that her mother (Mrs B) might be distressed, staff should assess Mrs B's capacity to decide whether or not to see her daughter.

In the event: the home continued to tell Ms B that she could not visit her mother.

Ms B had to stand outside the home and hand a Christmas gift for her mother to staff, and the officer arranged for a specialist to assess Mrs B's capacity and this took a month.

By the time that the assessment was done and Ms B could visit, her mother had had a stroke and was unable to recognise or communicate with her daughter. Sadly, she died the next day.

The Ombudsman found maladministration in the Council: preventing Ms B from seeing her mother for over a month, and failing to review the situation after any of the nine contacts from Ms B. The Ombudsman found that the nature and scale of this injustice was difficult to express or quantify. The Council accepted her recommendation (made after consulting Ms B) that it should:

- make a full written apology to Ms B
- pay for a bench with an inscribed plaque in a location of Ms B's choice
- help Ms B to find out where her mother is buried or was cremated, and
- pay Ms B £5,000 in recognition of the distress caused to her.

There has been comprehensive staff training since the events in Ms B's complaint and so the Ombudsman has not recommended any further action.

Newcastle City Council (08 003 256): adult social care maladministration
causing injustice, 23 November 2011

An investigation by two Ombudsmen highlighted significant failings in the care provided to a man in Newcastle who had Down's syndrome. Their report describes how Mr J's basic human rights were ignored after he was detained unnecessarily in hospital for months and was then moved into inappropriate locked accommodation until his death.

The Health Service Ombudsman and Local Government Ombudsman conducted a joint investigation into complaints made by Mr J's brother about the care and treatment provided by Northumberland, Tyne and Wear NHS Foundation Trust, Newcastle City Council and the Coquet Trust.

Mr J had been an active, outgoing and sociable man, living independently in rented accommodation with his wife. He had day-to-day support from the Council, and his family, who he was close to, supported his wish to be as independent as possible. When health professionals became concerned about a significant deterioration in his skills and health, Mr J was admitted to hospital for a short assessment. He was diagnosed with dementia and epilepsy, but in spite of being declared ready for discharge, he was kept in hospital for a further five months. Rather than returning home, which was now considered to be unsuitable accommodation, Mr J and his wife were moved to a self-contained flat at a care home for older people. The flat was kept locked to restrict Mr J's access to the outside, for safety reasons. Although this was supposed to be temporary accommodation, Mr J and his wife were still living there ten months later when Mr J became ill with a chest infection. He was admitted to hospital, where he died. He was 53.

The Ombudsmen found significant failings by both the NHS Trust and the Council. Mr J's basic human rights, to liberty and to family life, had not been given appropriate consideration when decisions were being made about his care needs. The importance of Mr J's family in his life was not appreciated and as a result they were not fully involved in plans for his care. Opportunities to ensure that Mr J's wishes and best interests were fully taken into account were therefore missed. There was a lack of any properly co-ordinated and documented health and care plan for Mr J, and no-one from either the NHS Trust or the Council took a leadership role and had responsibility for co-ordinating his care and representing his interests. Action was not taken quickly enough to find permanent suitable accommodation for Mr J and his wife, and contact with his family had been restricted.

Following the Ombudsmen's investigation, the NHS Trust and the Council agreed to provide Mr J's family with a full acknowledgement of the serious mistakes they made, together with an apology. They also agreed to pay £2,000 in recognition of the distress caused, which the family have said they will donate to charity. The Ombudsmen have also asked the Trust and the Council to prepare, and report progress on, an action plan setting out what they have done (or will do) to ensure that these mistakes are not repeated in future.

Health Service Ombudsman, Ann Abraham, said:

> 'Mr J's rights, best interests, and family relationships were not taken into account when the Trust and the Council made plans for his care. This was highly likely to have had some impact on the quality of his life, and hence his well-being, in the last 18 months or so of his life. Mr J's family were also wrongly denied the opportunity to be involved and will never know if they could have made a difference to his quality of life in those last months, which must be a cause of significant and ongoing distress for them. It is shocking that the events described in this report happened in the 21st century. I hope the lessons from Mr J's story will be understood by public bodies and thereby help to drive improvements in public services.'

Local Government Ombudsman, Anne Seex, said:

> 'The failures in Mr J's case show how public authorities can neglect a vulnerable person's wishes and basic human rights to liberty and family life. The Ombudsmen's joint investigation brought serious service failures to light. As a result, the authorities concerned will make changes so that other families are not treated this way.'

WHAT DO THESE COMPLAINTS TELL YOU ABOUT SOCIAL CARE PRACTICE?

These complaints did not hit the headlines, nor are they cases where anyone had any bad intentions; they are just two examples of the sort of treatment that can be suffered by the recipients of adult social care. They show how easy it is for social care practitioners to overlook the dignity and human rights of vulnerable adults within their care. The best of intentions or a perceived need to follow prescribed procedures can have extremely distressing consequences. Human rights are not something which are remote and esoteric. The right to have contact with your family, for your family to be involved in decisions about your care, for your liberty and autonomy to be respected are rights which impact directly upon the quality of life of ordinary people in receipt of care. The reports also demonstrate the value of complaints—reflecting upon the consequences of decisions and additional training that can help practitioners to improve outcomes for individuals in the future. You need to ask yourself, had you been aware of either of these situations, what you would have done to alert service providers to the probable outcomes of their decisions, and how you can use the idea of human rights to improve service delivery.

Principal statutory provisions

There are around 30 statutes that contain provisions which are relevant to adult social care. In this chapter we set out the key features of the most relevant statutes for your practice. Remember, as you read our descriptions, that it is important to note which statutes impose duties, and what strength of duty is imposed. Remember too that statutes need to be read taking into account the overarching obligations upon the state imposed by the Human Rights Act. However, what we really want you to note from our account is the piecemeal development of legislation, and its incoherence. It is difficult to reconcile the duties and powers and categories of service users between the various pieces of legislation. Having read the chapter you will understand the force of the Law Commission's criticisms of the law—that it is incoherent and piecemeal and why the Care Act 2014 was so necessary.

Part III of the National Assistance Act 1948 (NAA 1948)

This Act was one of the founding statutes of the post-war welfare state and the only one that remains in force. During the war the government had set up an interdepartmental committee chaired by Sir William Beveridge. It had published its report *Social Insurance and Allied Services* in 1942. Its recommendations were designed to ensure that the state would provide health services, education, and welfare for all British citizens who had need of those services. In the mid-1940s, the Labour Government, keen to sweep away the vestiges of Victorian Poor Law and to demonstrate that the victory of the Second World War would result in a better society for everyone, passed legislation designed to put the Beveridge recommendations into effect. The statutes passed included the Education Act 1944, the National Health Service Act 1946, and the Children Act 1948. Part III of the NAA 1948 was particularly totemic—it finally abolished the loathed workhouses. Instead, local authorities were given powers to provide a broad range of services to disabled people. Particularly important is s. 21 of the NAA 1948, reproduced in **Box 12.1**, which sets out the duty of local authorities to provide accommodation for particular categories of people.

 BOX 12.1 Section 21 of the National Assistance Act 1948—duty of local authorities to provide accommodation

(1) Subject to and in accordance with the provisions of this Part of this Act, a local authority may with the approval of the Secretary of State, and to such extent as he may direct shall, make arrangements for providing—

    (a) residential accommodation for persons who by reason of age, illness, disability or any other circumstances are in need of care and attention which is not otherwise available to them; and

    (aa) residential accommodation for expectant and nursing mothers who are in need of care and attention which is not otherwise available to them.

This duty will be replaced by s. 18 of the Care Act 2014 set out in **Box 12.2**.

BOX 12.2 Duty to meet needs for care and support—s. 18 of the Care Act 2014

A local authority, having made a determination under section 13(1) [on eligibility criteria], must meet the adult's needs for care and support which meet the eligibility criteria if—

(a) the adult is ordinarily resident in the authority's area or is present in its area but of no settled residence,

(b) the adult's accrued costs do not exceed the cap on care costs, and

(c) there is no charge under section 14 for meeting the needs or, in so far as there is, condition 1, 2 or 3 is met.

Section 29 of the NAA 1948, set out in **Box 12.3**, gives local authorities powers to provide services in the circumstances set out in the section.

BOX 12.3 Section 29(1) of the NAA 1948—welfare arrangements for blind, deaf, dumb, and crippled persons, etc

A local authority may, with the approval of the Secretary of State, and to such extent as he may direct in relation to persons ordinarily resident in the area of the local authority shall make arrangements for promoting the welfare of persons to whom this section applies, that is to say persons who are blind, deaf or dumb, or who suffer from mental disorder of any description and other persons who are substantially and permanently handicapped by illness, injury, or congenital deformity or such other disabilities as may be prescribed by the Minister.

The new power to provide services under the Care Act is set at s. 19 set out in **Box 12.4**.

BOX 12.4 Section 19—Power to meet needs for care and support

A local authority, having carried out a needs assessment and (if required to do so) a financial assessment, may meet an adult's needs for care and support if—

(a) the adult is ordinarily resident in the authority's area or is present in its area but of no settled residence, and

(b) the authority is satisfied that it is not required to meet the adult's needs under section 18 [duty to meet needs].

The Law Commission refers to the NAA 1948 as 'the bedrock of adult social care law'. It gained an almost constitutional significance. Lord Woolf MR referred to it in *R v Westminster City Council, ex p M* (1997) as:

> A prime example of an Act which is 'always speaking' and so should be construed 'on a construction that continuously updates its wording to allow for changes since the Act was initially framed'.

Like all legislation, the Act reflects not only the hopes but the limitations of its times. Now it is criticized for its emphasis on institutional care and for the limited and uncertain provisions to provide community and domiciliary services. You are also likely to find the language used by the Act out of date and even offensive. Nonetheless, it has played a crucial part in ensuring that adults have access to the services they need.

Health Services and Public Health Act 1968 (HSPHA 1968)

This Act was designed to respond to the perceived failures of the NAA 1948. It gave local authorities a discretionary power to provide services 'promoting the welfare of older people'. It did not do this by amending the NAA 1948 but by introducing a new statutory power, at s. 45 of the Act, to provide services similar to those provided by the NAA 1948. As the Law Commission points out, 'This marked the beginning of a trend that has characterised the development of adult social care law up until the present day.' There is no consolidation of legislation, but duplication of and amendments to existing service provision. This confuses everyone who is required to use the legislation. The Act includes a power to provide home help for older people. Sections 18 and 19 of the Care Act on duties and powers to meet needs will replace these duties once implemented.

The Chronically Sick and Disabled Persons Act 1970 (CSDPA 1970)

This Act marks the beginnings of another significant trend in legislation relating to adult social care—the intervention of Members of Parliament (MPs) via private members' bills. These bills were pushed through Parliament as a result of the emergence of the disability rights movement which lobbied for changes in the law. The CSDPA 1970 began life as a private member's bill sponsored by Alf Morris MP and promoted the civil rights of the disabled to services in contrast with the safety net philosophy of the NAA 1948. Alf Morris's interest in disabled people's rights was stimulated by his own background with a father unemployable after being disabled in the First World War and a family 'amongst the poorest of Manchester's poor', according to his biographer Derek Kinrade.

Section 2 of the CSDPA 1970 imposes a duty on local authorities to provide a range of community services including home help and laundry services for those who are owed duties under s. 29 of the NAA 1948. The duty can be enforced by individual disabled people. The section is set out in full in **Box 12.5** because it has been of great importance to adult service users. Most services received by disabled adults (and children) prior to the implementation of the Care Act arise from this statutory provision.

BOX 12.5 Section 2(1) of the CSDPA 1970

Where a local authority having functions under section 29 of the National Assistance Act 1948 are satisfied in the case of any person to whom that section applies who is ordinarily resident in their area that it is necessary in order to meet the needs of that person for that authority to make arrangements for all or any of the following matters, namely—

(a) the provision of practical assistance for that person in his home;

(b) the provision for that person or, or assistance to that person in obtaining, wireless, television, library or similar recreational facilities;

(c) the provision for that person of lectures, games, outings or other recreational facilities outside his home or assistance to that person in taking advantage of educational facilities available to him;

(d) the provision for that person of facilities for, or assistance in, travelling to and from his home for the purpose of participating in any services provided under arrangements made by the authority under the said section 29 or, with the approval of the authority, in any services provided otherwise than as aforesaid which are similar to services which could be provided under such arrangements;

(e) the provision of assistance for that person in arranging for the carrying out of any works of adaptation in his home or the provision of any additional facilities designed to secure his greater safety, comfort or convenience;

(f) facilitating the taking of holidays by that person, whether at holiday homes or otherwise and whether provided under arrangements made by the authority or otherwise;

(g) the provision of meals for that person whether in his home or elsewhere;

(h) the provision for that person of, or assistance to that person in obtaining, a telephone and any special equipment necessary to enable him to use a telephone, then, subject to the provisions of section 35(2) of that Act (which requires local authorities to exercise their functions under Part III of that Act in accordance with the provisions of any regulations made for the purpose) [and to the provisions of s. 7(1) of the Local Authority Social Services Act 1970 (which requires local authorities in the exercise of certain functions, including functions under the said s. 29, to act under the general guidance of the Secretary of State)] it shall be the duty of that authority to make those arrangements in exercise of their functions under the said section 29.

The duty will be replaced by ss. 18 and 19 of the Care Act.

The Mental Health Act 1983

This Act comes from quite a different direction entirely. As you will see in **chapter 15**, its concerns are the rights and protections available to those who are compulsorily detained under mental health powers. What the Act does in relation to community care services is to impose a duty set out in s. 117 of the Act upon local authorities and health bodies to provide for the after-care needs of those discharged from compulsory detention under the Act. Local Government Ombudsman reports indicate that people discharged from compulsory detention face particular difficulties in ensuring that they get the services to which they are entitled. Note that the service user cannot be required to pay for these services. Section 117 is amended by s. 75 of the Care Act which, instead of imposing a duty to 'provide' after-care services, says 'provide or arrange for the provision of' such services—to allow for a 'diversity' of providers including private firms. Section 75 offers clarity about the provision of after-care needs. Section 75(5) is set out in **Box 12.6**.

 BOX 12.6 Section 75(5) of the Care Act 2014

In this section, 'after-care services', in relation to a person, means services which have both of the following purposes—

(a) meeting a need arising from or related to the person's mental disorder; and

(b) reducing the risk of a deterioration of the person's mental condition (and, accordingly, reducing the risk of the person requiring admission to a hospital again for treatment for mental disorder).

The Health and Social Services and Social Security Adjudication Act 1983 (HASSASSA)

This Act enables local authorities to charge for some domiciliary services that they provide. The relevant section is s. 17 which is set out in **Box 12.7**.

 BOX 12.7 Section 17 of HASSASSA—charges for local authority services in England and Wales

(1) Subject to subsection (3) below, an authority providing a service to which this section applies may recover such charge (if any) for it as they consider reasonable.

(2) This section applies to services provided under the following enactments—

    (a) section 29 of the National Assistance Act 1948 (welfare arrangements for blind, deaf, dumb and crippled persons etc.);

    (b) section 45(1) of the Health Services and Public Health Act 1968 (welfare of old people);

    (c) Schedule 20 to the National Health Service Act 2006 or Schedule 15 to the National Health Service (Wales) Act 2006 (care of mothers and young children, prevention of illness and care and after-care and home help and laundry facilities);

    (d) section 8 of the Residential Homes Act 1980 (meals and recreation for old people); and

    (e) paragraph 1 of Part II of Schedule 9 to this Act other than the provision of services for which payment may be required under section 22 or 26 of the National Assistance Act 1948;

    (f) section 2 of the Carers and Disabled Children Act 2000.

(3) If a person—

    (a) avails himself of a service to which this section applies, and

> (b) satisfies the authority providing the service that his means are insufficient for it to be reasonably practicable for him to pay for the service the amount which he would otherwise be obliged to pay for it,
>
> the authority shall not require him to pay more for it than it appears to them that it is reasonably practicable for him to pay.
>
> (4) Any charge under this section may, without prejudice to any other method of recovery, be recovered summarily as a civil debt.
>
> (5) This section has effect subject to any regulations under section 15 of the Community Care (Delayed Discharges etc.) Act 2003 (power to require certain community care services and services for carers to be free of charge).

It is important to note that local authorities must have procedures for reducing or waiving charges when it is not reasonably practicable for the user to pay the full charge. Additional policy and practice guidance is available to local authorities to ensure that their procedures are reasonable. The power to charge for care and support services is set out in the Care Act at s. 14.

The Disabled Persons (Services, Consultation and Representation) Act 1986 (DP(SCR)A 1986)

This Act was another that started as a private member's bill which sought to promote a rights-based agenda and to close loopholes in existing legislation. The problem was that the CSDPA 1970, although it obliged the local authority to provide services to a disabled person when it is satisfied that the services are necessary, did not put an express obligation upon the local authority to assess those needs. The DP(SCR)A 1986 addressed that problem. It created another one, however, which is a multiplicity of provisions that overlap but also differ from each other and which require an applicant for services to be assessed.

The Care Act consolidates all previous statutory powers and duties to assess in ss. 9–13. We discuss those sections in **chapter 13**.

The National Health Service and Community Care Act 1990 (NHSCCA 1990)

This Act marked a change in the direction of the provision of adult social care services. From a position where the state, via local authorities, accepted responsibility for the direct provision of services to those it acknowledged were in need, the Act moved to a position where the local authority role was to plan for responsive services which were to be provided by a 'mixed economy of care'. As the Law Commission Scoping Report puts it, 'The consumerist and managerial principles behind the NHSCCA 1990 are in marked contrast to the welfare state ideology that underpins the NAA 1948.' Baroness Hale, in her dissenting opinion in *YL v Birmingham City Council* (2007), clearly explains the transformative effect of the NHSCCA 1990 on the existing statutory framework. The relevant paragraphs are set out in **Box 12.8**.

BOX 12.8 Extract from the opinion of Baroness Hale in *YL v Birmingham City Council* (2007)

Section 21(1)(a) of the National Assistance Act 1948 originally required each local authority to provide 'residential accommodation for persons who by reason of age, infirmity or any other circumstances are in need of care and attention which is not otherwise available to them'. Accommodation could be provided either in homes owned and run by the authority, or by another local authority (section 21(4)), or by a voluntary organisation (section 26), but not by private persons. Residents were required to pay for their local authority accommodation according to their ability to pay: section 22. Where accommodation was arranged with a voluntary organisation, the local authority was liable to pay for it and could then recoup a means-tested contribution from the resident: section 26(2)(3). Schemes were later replaced with ministerial approval and directions (section 195(3) of the Local Government Act 1972) and the relevant words of section 21(1) amended to read 'a local authority may with the approval of the Secretary of State, and to such extent as he may direct shall, make arrangements for providing ...' [s. 195(6) of and para. 2(1) of Schedule 23 to the 1972 Act]. Ministerial directions required that provision be made for people ordinarily resident in the area: DHSS Local Authority Circular 13/74.

But supply was never able to match demand. Many older people were accommodated in private residential homes but paid for by the state, through the means-tested benefits system rather than by local authorities. This was widely regarded as inefficient and expensive, because there was no professional assessment of whether the resident really needed this expensive form of care, rather than to be helped to remain in her own home, nor was there any systematic control of the cost: see Audit Commission, 'Making a Reality of Community Care' (1986) and Griffiths, 'Community Care: Agenda for Action: A Report to The Secretary of State for Social Services' (1988). The result was Part III of the National Health Service and Community Care Act 1990. Under this, each local authority must prepare and publish a strategic plan for the provision of community care services in their area: section 46. They were instructed to develop a 'mixed economy of care' making use of voluntary, not for profit and private providers whenever this was most cost-effective. They were to move away from the role of exclusive service provider and into the role of service arranger and procurer: Department of Health 'Caring for People: Community Care in the Next Decade and Beyond' (1989) (Cm 849). To this end, section 26 of the 1948 Act was amended to allow them to place residents with private providers as well as with voluntary organisations. The charging arrangements remained broadly the same, primary liability remaining with the local authority.

At the same time, local authorities were placed under a duty to carry out an assessment of the need for community care services of any person who might be in need of them (section 47(1)(a) of the 1990 Act) and then to decide whether those needs called for the provision by them of any such services: section 47(1)(b). 'Community care services' include arranging or providing accommodation under section 21(1) of the 1948 Act: section 46(3). If the person may also need health care under the National Health Service Act 1977, the local authority must invite the relevant health body to assist in the assessment. A large slice of the social security budget was transferred to local authorities to enable them to meet these new responsibilities.

We will return to the planning and assessment responsibilities upon local authorities in **chapter 13**. What is important to note at this point is that the Act did not consolidate or codify local authority responsibilities. Previous statutory entitlements to service provision and assessments remained in force. The complexity caused by overlapping and incoherent provision therefore continues until the Care Act is implemented.

The Community Care (Direct Payments) Act 1996 (CC(DP)A 1996)

This Act marked a new departure in the provision of services for adults. In response to the demands of the disability rights movement for increasing control over the services provided to them, the Act empowered local authorities to make direct payments to people who have been assessed as needing services to make their own arrangements to meet their needs. The legislative framework dealing with direct payments is contained in ss. 57 and 58 of the Health and Social Care Act 2001. The Care Act 2014 provides a much more straightforward statutory scheme for direct payments which we set out in **Box 12.9**.

 BOX 12.9 Direct payments—ss. 31 and 32 of the Care Act 2014

31 Adults with capacity to request direct payments

(1) This section applies where—
  (a) a personal budget for an adult specifies an amount which the local authority must pay towards the cost of meeting the needs to which the personal budget relates, and
  (b) the adult requests the local authority to meet some or all of those needs by making payments to the adult or a person nominated by the adult.

(2) If conditions 1 to 4 are met, the local authority must, subject to regulations under section 33, make the payments to which the request relates to the adult or nominated person.

(3) A payment under this section is referred to in this Part as a 'direct payment'.

(4) Condition 1 is that—
  (a) the adult has capacity to make the request, and
  (b) where there is a nominated person, that person agrees to receive the payments.

(5) Condition 2 is that—
  (a) the local authority is not prohibited by regulations under section 33 from meeting the adult's needs by making direct payments to the adult or nominated person, and
  (b) if regulations under that section give the local authority discretion to decide not to meet the adult's needs by making direct payments to the adult or nominated person, it does not exercise that discretion.

(6) Condition 3 is that the local authority is satisfied that the adult or nominated person is capable of managing direct payments—
  (a) by himself or herself, or
  (b) with whatever help the authority thinks the adult or nominated person will be able to access.

(7) Condition 4 is that the local authority is satisfied that making direct payments to the adult or nominated person is an appropriate way to meet the needs in question.

32 Adults without capacity to request direct payments

(1) This section applies where—

    (a) a personal budget for an adult specifies an amount which the local authority must pay towards the cost of meeting the needs to which the personal budget relates, and

    (b) the adult lacks capacity to request the local authority to meet any of those needs by making payments to the adult, but

    (c) an authorised person requests the local authority to meet some or all of those needs by making payments to the authorised person.

(2) If conditions 1 to 5 are met, the local authority must, subject to regulations under section 33, make the payments to which the request relates to the authorised person.

(3) A payment under this section is referred to in this Part as a 'direct payment'.

(4) A person is authorised for the purposes of this section if—

    (a) the person is authorised under the Mental Capacity Act 2005 to make decisions about the adult's needs for care and support,

    (b) where the person is not authorised as mentioned in paragraph (a), a person who is so authorised agrees with the local authority that the person is a suitable person to whom to make direct payments, or

    (c) where the person is not authorised as mentioned in paragraph (a) and there is no person who is so authorised, the local authority considers that the person is a suitable person to whom to make direct payments.

(5) Condition 1 is that, where the authorised person is not authorised as mentioned in subsection (4)(a) but there is at least one person who is so authorised, a person who is so authorised supports the authorised person's request.

(6) Condition 2 is that—

    (a) the local authority is not prohibited by regulations under section 33 from meeting the adult's needs by making direct payments to the authorised person, and

    (b) if regulations under that section give the local authority discretion to decide not to meet the adult's needs by making direct payments to the authorised person, it does not exercise that discretion.

(7) Condition 3 is that the local authority is satisfied that the authorised person will act in the adult's best interests in arranging for the provision of the care and support for which the direct payments under this section would be used.

(8) Condition 4 is that the local authority is satisfied that the authorised person is capable of managing direct payments—

    (a) by himself or herself, or

    (b) with whatever help the authority thinks the authorised person will be able to access.

(9) Condition 5 is that the local authority is satisfied that making direct payments to the authorised person is an appropriate way to meet the needs in question.

Further details of direct payments under the Care Act will be provided when the appropriate regulations are published.

The Care Standards Act 2000 (CSA 2000)

This Act reflects contemporary concerns with the quality of service provision. It created a regulatory framework for care homes, domiciliary services, and social care staff. The Health and Social Care Act 2008 reforms the regulatory system established by the CSA 2000 by creating the Care Quality Commission through the merger of the Commission for Social Care Inspection, the Health Care Commission, and the Mental Health Act Commission. Part 2 of the Care Act contains provisions relating to Care Standards, including provisions designed to increase the independence of the Care Quality Commission. We will look more closely at the regulatory framework in **chapter 13**.

The Community Care (Delayed Discharges etc) Act 2003 (CC(DD)A 2003)

The focus of this Act is to ensure that National Health Service (NHS) patients are given community care assessments by local authorities in a timely manner, thus ensuring a greater efficient use of health resources. The Act sets out timescales and provides for fines or reimbursements if a delay in discharge is caused by social services. The Act has only been implemented in England.

Whilst there is some statistical evidence that the procedures have improved the rate of discharge from hospital, concern has also been raised that the results of the requirements are that some people are discharged prematurely or placed in unsuitable residential accommodation in order that local authorities can avoid paying charges. In 2007 the Joint Committee on Human Rights reported that the premature or inappropriate discharge of older people could lead to their readmission shortly after and recommended that the regulations be made more flexible in order to ensure that the Article 8 rights of older people are protected. New provisions relating to discharge from hospital are provided for in Schedule 3 to the Care Act 2014.

▮ Carers

The welfare state of the immediate post-war years did not consider the needs of carers. Most care was provided within the family. It was assumed that men in paid employment would provide for the material needs of the family and that women would work within the home to provide for the family's physical and emotional needs. That model of care provision was not sustainable for a variety of reasons. Women increasingly either had to or wanted to work, advances in medical care meant that the population of people who were in need of services grew, and there was a growing realization that being an unpaid carer led to social exclusion. **Box 12.10** sets out the origins of the movement for rights for carers as explained on the Carers UK website.

BOX 12.10 Civil rights for carers

In 1965 the National Council for the Single Woman and her Dependants (NCSWD) was founded by the Reverend Mary Webster who, in keeping with contemporary views on the duty of unmarried daughters, had sacrificed her career to care for her ageing parents. After both had died, she became aware of the effect that caring for them had had on her. She began writing to newspapers, journals, MPs, and peers drawing attention to the isolation and financial hardship that women carers were suffering. Her letters received a huge response from hundreds of women in similar situations. According to Baroness Seear, then a lecturer in the London School of Economics and a founder member of the NCSWD, 'nobody knew anything about caring. The clergy didn't know, the doctors didn't know ... it was a hidden problem. And the characteristic situation that Mary found was that women who were caring fell out of society into a kind of black hole. Nobody pushed them: they just fell.'

In 2001, the UK Census asked a question about whether, and if so, how much informal care was being provided for a family member or a friend. What the answers revealed is set out in **Box 12.11**.

BOX 12.11 Carers in the UK 2001 Census results

The resulting picture overall was one of a considerable amount of such care being provided— 5.2 million carers in England and Wales, including over a million providing more than 50 hours a week. The more detailed picture shows some interesting facts about this contribution. For instance, over 225,000 people providing 50 or more hours of unpaid care per week state they are in 'not good health' themselves. More than half of the people providing this much care are over the age of 55, and it is at these ages that the 'not good health' rate is highest.

However, there are nearly 80,000 people aged 54 and under providing more than 50 hours of unpaid care per week, who state that their health is not good.

The age group where the largest proportion of people provide care is in the fifties. More than one in five of people aged 50–59 are providing some unpaid care. About one in four (24.6 per cent) women in this age group are providing some care compared with 17.9 per cent of men.

Many of the people providing care do paid work as well. Of the 15.2 million employees aged 16–74 in full-time work, 1.6 million are providing at least some unpaid care—144,000 providing 50 or more hours a week. For full-time workers providing 50 or more hours care there is a larger proportion of men.

Of the nearly two million people aged 16–74 who are permanently sick or disabled, over a quarter of a million (273,000) provide some unpaid care for other people and 105,000 provide 50 or more hours care.

Further, and regularly updated, statistics can be obtained from the website of Carers UK www.carersuk.org.

Legislative responses to the needs of carers have been slow. In 1986 the DP(SCR)A 1986—at s. 8—required local authorities to have regard to the ability of a carer 'to continue to provide substantial care on a regular basis' to a disabled person when assessing whether the disabled person's needs call for the provision of services. Although useful, this requirement falls short of a duty to assess the carer's needs. Once more, the disability rights agenda was only pushed forward by a private member's bill. Malcolm Wicks MP sponsored the Carers (Recognition and Services) Act 1995 (C(RS)A), which required local authorities to assess a carer's needs, if he or she requested such an assessment, when carrying out an assessment of an adult under the NHSCCA 1990 or the assessment of a child under the Children Act 1989 or the CSDPA 1970.

The provision of direct payments was extended to cover the carers and parents of disabled children by virtue of the Carers and Disabled Children Act 2000 (CDCA 2000). Provisions on direct payments, as we noted earlier (**The Community Care (Direct Payments) Act 1996 (CC(DP)A 1996)**, p 428), are now contained in the Health and Social Care Act 2001. In addition, the CDCA 2000 provides carers with a free-standing right to an assessment. That solved a problem within the C(RS)A. If the person cared for refused an assessment, then there was no power for the local authority to assess the needs of the carer. However, the right is in addition to those within the C(RS)A and needs to be read in conjunction with it. Another private member's bill, which became the Carers (Equal Opportunities) Act 2004 (C(EO)A) tried to do more for carers than simply facilitating their caring role. Its aim was to address the social exclusion of carers. It required local authorities to take into account the carer's wish to undertake education, training, or any leisure activity and to enter into employment when carrying out the assessment of their needs.

The Care Act 2014 fully integrates the needs of carers into the statutory scheme. The duty to assess carers' needs is set out in s. 1 of the Care Act. We discuss this more fully in **chapter 13**. Two other problems are addressed within the legislation. A 'carer' is clearly defined, within s. 1 set out in **Box 12.12**, and there is provision for the assessment of the needs of children who care for vulnerable adults as they reach 18 (see s. 58 of the Care Act).

BOX 12.12 Defining carers—s. 10(3), (9), and (10)

(3) 'Carer' means an adult who provides or intends to provide care for another adult (an 'adult needing care'); but see subsections (9) and (10).

. . .

(9) An adult is not to be regarded as a carer if the adult provides or intends to provide care—
   (a) under or by virtue of a contract, or
   (b) as voluntary work.

(10) But in a case where the local authority considers that the relationship between the adult needing care and the adult providing or intending to provide care is such that it would be appropriate for the latter to be regarded as a carer, that adult is to be regarded as such (and subsection (9) is therefore to be ignored in that case).

▦ 'Personalisation'

Legislation deals with what can be provided. It is only concerned to a limited extent with how it is to be provided. The 'how' provision is often beset by conflicting and seemingly irresolvable policy concerns. The overriding tension is between quality services and affordability. The demand for adult social care services is estimated to rise and there seems little willingness fully to fund this rise in demand. At the same time, people's expectations of service delivery are increasing. One solution which aims to reconcile the conflicts is personalization—allowing people to choose services which suit their needs. It also includes moves towards early intervention and prevention services. The need and significance of personalization is explained in LAC (DH) (2008) 1, an extract from which is set out in **Box 12.13**.

 BOX 12.13 'Personalisation' of social care services extract from LAC (DH) (2008) 1

15 The wider government approach to personalisation can be summarised as 'the way in which services are tailored to the needs and preferences of citizens. The overall vision is that the state should empower citizens to shape their own lives and the services they receive' . . .

16 If personalisation is a cornerstone of the modernisation of public services, what does it mean for social care? What it means is that everyone who receives social care support, regardless of their level of need, in any setting, whether from statutory services, the third and community or private sector or by funding it themselves, will have choice and control over how that support is delivered. It will mean that people are able to live their own lives as they wish, confident that services are of high quality, are safe and promote their own individual requirements for independence, well-being and dignity.

17 To do this will require a common assessment of individual social care needs, emphasising the importance of self-assessment. The role of social workers will be focused on advocacy and brokerage, rather than assessment and gate keeping. This move is from the model of care, where an individual receives the care determined by a professional, to one that has person centred planning at its heart, with the individual firmly at the centre in identifying what is personally important to deliver his or her outcomes. With self-directed support, people are able to design the support or care arrangements that best suit their specific needs. It puts people in the centre of the planning process, and recognises that they are best placed to understand their own needs and how to meet them. They will be able to control or direct the flexible use of resources (where they wish to), building on the support of technology (eg telecare), family, friends and the wider community to enable them to enjoy their position as citizens within their communities.

18 Direct payments and individual budgets (currently being evaluated) are an existing way to foster this transformation in the community. Individual budgets (IBs) build on what works with direct payments and, like direct payments, they give people more choice and control. IBs can bring a number of income streams together to give the individual a more joined-up package of support. Critically they allow the person to plan how to achieve outcomes, which meet their needs within a clear allocation of resources.

19 In the future, all individuals eligible for publicly-funded adult social care will have a personal budget (other than in circumstances where people require emergency access to provision); a clear, upfront allocation of funding to enable them to make informed choices about how best to meet their needs, including their broader health and well-being. Having an understanding of what is available will enable people to use resources flexibly and innovatively, no longer simply choosing from an existing menu, but shaping their own menu of support. A person will be able to take all or part of their personal budget as a direct payment, to pay for their own support either by employing individuals themselves or for purchasing support through an agency. Others may wish, once they have decided on their preferred care package, to have the council continue to pay for this directly. The approach, which may be a combination of both, will depend on what works best for them. The term personal budget will describe this transparent allocation of resources.

20 Importantly, the ability to make choices about how people live their lives should not be restricted to those who live in their own homes. It is about better support, more tailored to individual choices and preferences in all care settings.

Many provisions in the Care Act reflect the personalization agenda, remedying a key defect in the previous law. So, for instance, s. 1(3) provides that:

In exercising a function under this Part in the case of an individual, a local authority must have regard to the following matters in particular—

(a)   the importance of beginning with the assumption that the individual is best-placed to judge the individual's well-being;

(b)   the individual's views, wishes, feelings and beliefs;

EXERCISES

1 Some years ago your department provided John, who is disabled, with a radio following an assessment of his needs under s. 2 of the Chronically Sick and Disabled Persons Act 1970. John's ability to hear the radio has now declined. What provisions in the Care Act 2014 enable you to provide John with an audio-headphone?

2 Hackbury Council has a policy that no domestic assistance can be provided to the disabled or the elderly unless it is accompanied by a need for personal care. Is that position lawful?

ONLINE RESOURCE CENTRE

For guidance on how to answer these exercises, visit the Online Resource Centre at www.oxfordtextbooks.co.uk/orc/socialwork13e/.

WHERE DO WE GO FROM HERE?

Now we have provided you with an outline of the law relating to the provision of adult social care and provided you with a map explaining how the old law is consolidated and clarified in the Care

Act, we can turn in **chapter 13** to the very important question of delivery of services. Local authorities have strategic responsibilities to plan for the provision of care services in their areas. They are also required to assess individual needs for service provision, to plan for these, and to deliver them. Both of these elements of delivery of adult social care services are considered in the chapter. The final matter that is considered is ensuring that services are delivered at an appropriate level of quality. Here we consider the work of the Care Quality Commission as well as complaints procedures and the work of the Local Government Ombudsman.

 ANNOTATED FURTHER READING

General

L. Clements and P. Thompson, *Community Care and the Law* (Legal Action Group, 2011). Professor Luke Clements is a nationally recognized authority on community care law. Pauline Thompson is a policy adviser on care finance for Age Concern England. This book is therefore authoritative and comprehensive. It is best used by those of you who enjoy the technical side of the law, and wish to become experts in this area. For everyone, however, it is an invaluable source of reference. No doubt the authors are working on an update following the introduction of the Care Act. However, it will not be available until after the relevant regulations and guidance are produced. Professor Clements has also published an article criticizing the personalization agenda. 'Social care law developments: a sideways look at personalisation and tightening eligibility criteria' (2011) *Elder Law* 1: 47. His views on the reform of care law have been published in (2013) *Elder Law* 219.

There are other useful books. *Elderly People and the Law* by G. Ashton and published by Butterworths is a good example. The second edition, published in 2011, has been considerably expanded and draws on the author's extensive legal experience.

Community Care Practice and the Law by M. Mandelstam, published by Jessica Kingsley, provides a thorough account of the law for social work practitioners. The latest edition of this book is a little dated now though—the fourth edition was published in 2008.

A more recent publication from Michael Mandelstam is *Quick Guide to Community Care Practice and the Law*, also published by Jessica Kingsley. This provides a very useful introduction to this complex subject and is recommended if you are struggling with the law.

J. Morris, 'Independent living and community care: a disempowering framework' (2004) *Disability and Society* 19: 427. This article explains the emergence and importance of a rights-based approach to the delivery of services.

Carers

The most useful account of the law for carers written by L. Clements is available for free at www.lukeclements.co.uk/downloads/update1-jan2011.pdf. The fourth edition was published in 2011 by Carers UK. Lots of other useful information about carers is available for free on the Carers UK website, www.carersuk.org.

13 Managing adult social care

This chapter looks at an individual's journey through the care and support system. It looks at the process of assessing someone's needs for care and support, establishing what a person is entitled to receive, care planning, and the provision of care and support. It explains the current regulatory framework for these procedures, but also alerts you to the role of the Care Act 2014. It then looks at some of the mechanisms for ensuring that adult social care services are of sufficient quality. It considers complaints to both the care provider and the local authority, the role of the Care Quality Commission (including its dealings with whistle-blowers) and the Local Government Ombudsman.

CASE STUDY

R v Gloucestershire County Council and another, ex p Barry [1997]
2 WLR 459 (House of Lords)

The facts are taken from the opinion of Lord Lloyd.

Mr. Michael Barry lives in Gloucestershire. He was born in 1915, so he is coming up for his eighty-second birthday. In the summer of 1992 he spent a short spell in Gloucestershire Royal Hospital suffering from dizzy spells and nausea. He was told that he had suffered a slight stroke. He has also had several heart attacks, and cannot see well. After discharge from hospital, he returned home, where he lives alone. He gets around by using a Zimmer frame, as a result of having fractured his hip several years ago. He has no contact with any of his family. But two friends call from time to time to do things for him. On 8 September 1992 he was referred to the Social Services Department of Gloucestershire County Council. On 15 September his needs were assessed as: 'Home care to call twice a week for shopping, pension, laundry, cleaning. Meals on wheels four days a week.' The council arranged to provide these services. Nearly a year later, on 3 August 1993 Mr. Barry received a routine visit from the Social Services Department. His needs were assessed as being the same.

Then on 29 September 1994 Mr. Barry received a letter from the council regretting that they would no longer be able to provide Mr. Barry with his full needs as assessed. Cleaning and laundry services would be withdrawn. The reason given was that the money allocated to the council by central government had been reduced by £2.5m. and there was 'nowhere near enough to meet demand.' It is only fair to add that the letter was sympathetic in tone.

Mr. Barry, and other residents, commenced proceedings for judicial review. His case is that his needs are the same as they always were. Parliament has imposed a duty on the council to do what is necessary to meet those needs, and it is no answer that they are short of money, as no doubt they are. The council's case is that in assessing Mr. Barry's *needs* they are entitled to have regard to their overall financial resources.

Decision

The Divisional Court of the Queen's Bench Division held that a local authority under s. 2(1) of the Act of 1970 [Chronically Sick and Disabled Persons Act] was entitled to take account of its resources in assessing needs and in deciding whether it was necessary to make arrangements to meet those needs, but granted the applicant a declaration that the council had acted unlawfully in withdrawing services previously provided to him without a reassessment of his needs. The Court of Appeal by a majority allowed an appeal by the applicant, holding that a local authority was not entitled to take account of its resources when assessing or reassessing whether it was necessary to make arrangements to meet an applicant's needs. The council appealed to the House of Lords. It allowed the appeal but with two of the Law Lords dissenting. It decided that in assessing an applicant's need for a service, the degree of that need, and the necessity to make arrangements to meet it, a local authority had to balance the severity of the applicant's disabling condition against the cost of those arrangements and the availability of resources. Therefore resources may, accordingly, be a proper consideration in deciding whether to meet needs.

Lord Clyde explains the decision as follows:

> The right given to the person by section 2(1) of the Act of 1970 was a right to have the arrangements made which the local authority was satisfied were necessary to meet his needs. The duty only arises if or when the local authority is so satisfied. But when it does arise then it is clear that a shortage of resources will not excuse a failure in the performance of the duty. However neither the fact that the section imposes the duty towards the individual, with the corresponding right in the individual to the enforcement of the duty, nor the fact that consideration of resources is not relevant to the question whether the duty is to be performed or not, means that a consideration of resources may not be relevant to the earlier stages of the implementation of the section which lead up to the stage when the satisfaction is achieved. ...

> The words 'necessary' and 'needs' are both relative expressions, admitting in each case a considerable range of meaning. They are not defined in the Act and reference to dictionary definitions does not seem to me to advance the construction of the subsection. In deciding whether there is a necessity to meet the needs of the individual some criteria have to be provided. Such criteria are required both to determine whether there is a necessity at all or only, for example, a desirability, and also to assess the degree of necessity. Counsel for Mr. Barry suggested that a criterion could be found in the values of a civilised society. ...

> In the framing of the criteria to be applied it seems to me that the severity of a condition may have to be matched against the availability of resources. Such an exercise indeed accords with everyday domestic experience in relation to things which we do not have. If my resources are limited I have to need the thing very much before I am satisfied that it is necessary to purchase it. It may also be observed that the range of the facilities which are listed as being the subject of possible arrangements, 'the service list', is so extensive as to make it unlikely that Parliament intended that they might all be provided regardless of the cost involved. It is not necessary to hold that cost and resources are always an element in determining the necessity. It is enough for the purposes of the present case to recognise that they may be a proper consideration. I have not been persuaded that they must always and necessarily be excluded from consideration. Counsel for Mr. Barry founded part of his submission on the claim that on the appellants' approach there would be an unmet need. However once it is recognised that criteria have to be devised for assessing the necessity required by the statutory provision it will be possible to allege that in one sense there will be an unmet need; but such an unmet need will be lawfully within what is contemplated by the statute. On a more exact analysis, whereby the necessity is measured by the appropriate criteria, what is necessary to be met will in fact be met and in the strict sense of the words no unmet need will exist.

What the decision makes clear is that eligibility criteria for the provision of services are lawful.

Lord Lloyd in his dissent makes pertinent observations about the rationing of resources based upon a local authority's financial position. He observes that needs cannot be determined by resources because that would mean that a person with needs in a place with sufficient resources would get those needs met, but he or she would not get them met in a place with fewer resources.

> The point can be illustrated by a simple example. Suppose there are two people with identical disabilities, living in identical circumstances, but in different parts of the country. Local authority A provides for his needs by arranging for meals on wheels four days a week. Local authority B might also be expected to provide meals on wheels four days a week, or its equivalent. It cannot, however, have been Parliament's intention that local authority B should be able to say 'because we do not have enough resources, we are going to reduce your needs.' His needs remain exactly the same. They cannot be affected by the local authority's inability to meet those needs. Every child needs a new pair of shoes from time to time. The need is not the less because his parents cannot afford them.

Second, he makes it clear that insufficient resources are provided by central government to meet the needs of adults who require social care services.

> This brings me, last of all, to the wretched position in which the council now find themselves, through no fault of their own. I have read the affidavits of Mr. Deryk Mead, the Director of Social Services, and Mr. Honey, Chief Executive, with something approaching despair. Equally depressing is the evidence of Margaret Newland, chair of Age Concern, Gloucestershire, and the numerous letters written by the council to the Secretary of State. Most depressing of all are the minutes of the community care sub-committee of the social services committee, especially those of the meeting held on 14 October 1994, in which members expressed their abhorrence at the choices which the Social Services Department was being required to make. The chairman commented:
>
> > 'It was deplorable that there was no other way forward apart from the exclusion of certain people from access to community care through the device of rationing services.'
>
> By your Lordships' decision today the council has escaped from the impossible position in which they, and other local authorities, have been placed. Nevertheless, I cannot help wondering whether they will not be regretting today's decision as much as Mr. Barry. The solution lies with the Government. The passing of the Act of 1970 was a noble aspiration. Having willed the end, Parliament must be asked to provide the means.

Richard Mullender in an article for the Law Quarterly Review (1997) 113: 545–8, comments as follows:

> In the *Barry* case, we are confronted by the reality of a welfare state in which high aspirations are mocked by modest means. The Act of 1970 is, of course, a product of an age in which the pressures that attend resourcing the welfare state were felt less keenly than now. Hence, it seems reasonable to suggest that the existing legislation should be replaced by a provision in which frank acknowledgment is made of both the inevitability of having to draw up a schedule of more or less urgent needs and the necessity (in the absence of adequate resources) of having to leave less pressing needs unmet. Plainly, such a statutory regime would be far from perfect. It would,

however, obviate the need for judges to render decisions capable of providing support for the Panglossian proposition that, in circumstances where there are no resources, it can legitimately be concluded that there are no needs.

WHAT DOES THIS CASE TELL YOU ABOUT SOCIAL CARE LAW?

Most of the cases we have considered at the start of chapters have been very recent. In contrast the *Barry* case was decided in 1997. Nevertheless, it is very important in your practice as a social worker and is the leading case about the role of resources in the provision of services. The case illustrates the operation of s. 2 of the Chronically Sick and Disabled Persons Act 1970 (CSDPA 1970). It demonstrates the importance of assessment of individual needs for services. But it also shows how assessment of needs forms part of the rationing of services, because local authorities cannot meet all needs—it would not be affordable.

In 2012 the Supreme Court declined an opportunity to reconsider *Barry* in its decision, *R on the Application of KM (By His Mother and Litigation Friend JM) v Cambridgeshire County Council* (2012). We will discuss the judgment in *KM* in the context of resource allocation systems later (see **Legal challenges**, p 454). However, Lord Wilson's explanation in *KM* of the process of assessing needs and the role of resources in determining which needs are met provides a useful restatement of the law. What he said was that:

> when a local authority is required to consider whether it is 'necessary in order to meet the needs of that person for that authority to make arrangements for' the provision of any of the matters on the service list, it is required to ask itself three questions and should do so in three separate stages:
>
> (i)   What are the needs of the disabled person?
> (ii) In order to meet the needs identified at (i), is it necessary for the authority to make arrangements for the provision of any of the listed services?
> (iii) If the answer to question (ii) is affirmative, what are the nature and extent of the listed services for the provision of which it is necessary for the authority to make arrangements?

Resources become significant at the second stage. Lord Wilson explains:

> One important aspect of the question raised at the second stage is to ask whether the presenting needs of the disabled person can reasonably be met by family or friends (which I will describe as natural support) or by other organs of the state, such as the NHS, or by charities etc, or indeed out of the person's own resources. But it will by now be clear that the question at the second stage goes far further and, in particular, encompasses consideration of the relationship between the scale of the local authority's resources and the weight of other demands upon it, in other words the availability of its resources.

So Wilson points out that the decision in *Barry* was that the availability of resources was relevant to the question at the second stage. Despite this restatement of the law the decision in *Barry* remains controversial, as Baroness Hale's observations in *McDonald*

(2011) (see **chapter 11**) and in *KM* make clear. Before you can make your mind up about the state of the law and whether the decision in *Barry* needs revisiting, you need to have an understanding of how adult social care is managed. We start by looking at the duty on local authorities to inform the public of the care and support services they provide.

Strategic planning

Local authorities have a duty to inform the public of the services they provide. Currently this duty is set out in s. 1(2)(a) of the CSDPA 1970, which says that each local authority 'shall cause to be published from time to time at such times and in such manner as they consider appropriate general information as to the services provided under arrangements made by the authority under the said section 29 [of the National Assistance Act 1948] which are for the time being available in their area'. Furthermore, users of the services should be informed of any other services relevant to their needs. From the implementation of s. 4 of the Care Act this duty will be replaced by a more expansive duty. This is set out in **Box 13.1**.

BOX 13.1 Providing information and advice—s. 4 of the Care Act 2014

(1) A local authority must establish and maintain a service for providing people in its area with information and advice relating to care and support for adults and support for carers.

(2) The service must provide information and advice on the following matters in particular—
   (a) the system provided for by this Part and how the system operates in the authority's area,
   (b) the choice of types of care and support, and the choice of providers, available to those who are in the authority's area,
   (c) how to access the care and support that is available,
   (d) how to access independent financial advice on matters relevant to the meeting of needs for care and support, and
   (e) how to raise concerns about the safety or well-being of an adult who has needs for care and support.

(3) In providing information and advice under this section, a local authority must in particular—
   (a) have regard to the importance of identifying adults in the authority's area who would be likely to benefit from financial advice on matters relevant to the meeting of needs for care and support, and
   (b) seek to ensure that what it provides is sufficient to enable adults—
      (i) to identify matters that are or might be relevant to their personal financial position that could be affected by the system provided for by this Part,

> (ii) to make plans for meeting needs for care and support that might arise, and
>
> (iii) to understand the different ways in which they may access independent financial advice on matters relevant to the meeting of needs for care and support.
>
> (4) Information and advice provided under this section must be accessible to, and proportionate to the needs of, those for whom it is being provided.

The duty is much more detailed than the duty it replaces. Note in particular the emphasis on financial advice, and the need to provide advice and information for carers.

There is another new duty that will be imposed upon the local authority by the Care Act—the duty to promote diversity (meaning multiple providers) and quality in the provision of services. This is provided for in s. 5 of the Care Act which is set out in **Box 13.2.**

 BOX 13.2 Section 5—Promoting diversity and quality in provision of services

(1) A local authority must promote the efficient and effective operation of a market in services for meeting care and support needs with a view to ensuring that any person in its area wishing to access services in the market—

(a) has a variety of providers to choose from who (taken together) provide a variety of services;

(b) has a variety of high quality services to choose from;

(c) has sufficient information to make an informed decision about how to meet the needs in question.

(2) In performing that duty, a local authority must have regard to the following matters in particular—

(a) the need to ensure that the authority has, and makes available, information about the providers of services for meeting care and support needs and the types of services they provide;

(b) the need to ensure that it is aware of current and likely future demand for such services and to consider how providers might meet that demand;

(c) the importance of enabling adults with needs for care and support, and carers with needs for support, who wish to do so to participate in work, education or training;

(d) the importance of ensuring the sustainability of the market (in circumstances where it is operating effectively as well as in circumstances where it is not);

(e) the importance of fostering continuous improvement in the quality of such services and the efficiency and effectiveness with which such services are provided and of encouraging innovation in their provision;

(f) the importance of fostering a workforce whose members are able to ensure the delivery of high quality services (because, for example, they have relevant skills and appropriate working conditions).

The strategic local planning for care and support which has been a feature of adult social care provision since the implementation of the National Health Service and Community Care Act 1990 (NHSCCA 1990) has been dismantled and replaced with a market-oriented system which depends for quality upon variety, choice, and information.

The duty to assess

The duties on local authorities to ensure a variety of quality provision and a well-informed public are accompanied by duties to assess individual service users' needs. The legal framework surrounding this is complex but about to be simplified by the Care Act. The Law Commission, in its Scoping Paper, points out the consequences of the pre-Care Act position:

> In order to carry out a comprehensive community care assessment and carer's assessment, a social care professional would need to have regard to: four separate sets of general assessment guidance; four separate sets of guidance on carers' assessment; specific user group assessment guidance; and directions. Added to this are: the National Service Frameworks; targets; performance indicators; and auditing regimes.

Currently the duties to assess are set out in s. 47(1) of the NHSCCA 1990, s. 2 of the CSDPA 1970, and s. 4 of the Disabled Persons (Services, Consultation and Representation) Act 1986. These duties will be replaced by one statutory duty, a duty to carry out a needs assessment. This important duty, contained in s. 9 of the Care Act 2014 is set out in **Box 13.3**. Notice how the needs assessment must place what the person wishes to achieve in everyday life at the centre of the process.

BOX 13.3 Section 9 of the Care Act 2014—Assessment of an adult's needs for care and support

(1) Where it appears to a local authority that an adult may have needs for care and support, the authority must assess—
 (a) whether the adult does have needs for care and support, and
 (b) if the adult does, what those needs are.

(2) An assessment under subsection (1) is referred to in this Part as a 'needs assessment'.

(3) The duty to carry out a needs assessment applies regardless of the authority's view of—
 (a) the level of the adult's needs for care and support, or
 (b) the level of the adult's financial resources.

(4) A needs assessment must include an assessment of—
 (a) the impact of the adult's needs for care and support on the matters specified in section 1(2),
 (b) the outcomes that the adult wishes to achieve in day-to-day life, and

(c) whether, and if so to what extent, the provision of care and support could contribute to the achievement of those outcomes.

(5) A local authority, in carrying out a needs assessment, must involve—

(a) the adult,

(b) any carer that the adult has, and

(c) any person whom the adult asks the authority to involve or, where the adult lacks capacity to ask the authority to do that, any person who appears to the authority to be interested in the adult's welfare.

(6) When carrying out a needs assessment, a local authority must also consider—

(a) whether, and if so to what extent, matters other than the provision of care and support could contribute to the achievement of the outcomes that the adult wishes to achieve in day-to-day life, and

(b) whether the adult would benefit from the provision of anything under section 2 or 4 or of anything which might be available in the community.

Notice that all that is required to trigger an assessment is that the authority has some awareness of someone's circumstances that indicates that they may have need of community care services. The threshold of knowledge required is very low—see *Bristol City Council, ex p Penfold* (1998) (**Box 13.4**). Local authorities must ensure that they have the necessary infrastructure to ensure that vulnerable individuals are referred for assessment as appropriate.

Notice also that all that is required is that the person *may* have needs—local authorities cannot refuse to carry out an assessment because they do not consider there is any likelihood that any assessed needs will be met. Again, *Bristol City Council, ex p Penfold* provides a useful illustration. The details are set out in **Box 13.4**.

BOX 13.4 *Bristol City Council, ex p Penfold* [1998] CCL Rep 315

Ms Penfold was a 52-year-old single mother of a dependent teenage daughter. She suffered from anxiety and depression, and received help and care from her family. Ms Penfold applied to Bristol City Council (BCC) for housing under the homelessness provisions of the Housing Act 1985. The council decided that it had an obligation to provide her with suitable accommodation and made two offers of housing, both of which were rejected by Ms Penfold as unsuitable. Ms Penfold then applied to be assessed for entitlement to community care services under s. 47 of the NHSCCA 1990, and for her daughter to be assessed under the Children Act 1989. The application was rejected on the basis that there was no prospect of her being granted any community care service because she did not 'appear' to be a person who required any of the services which the council's resources would enable it to give.

The judge held that under the 1990 Act, local authorities did not have the discretion to refuse to carry out an assessment simply on the basis that a lack of resources would mean that the authority would be unable to provide services to the applicant. On the facts, there had not been any assessment of Ms Penfold's needs or those of her daughter. There was an obligation to carry out an assessment once she had crossed the threshold test that there may be some need for a service which BCC might be able to provide. BCC had no authority to refuse to carry out such an assessment based on a reasonable belief that no service could be provided in fact. Further, BCC's failure was unlawful on the basis that it did not comply with the policy guidance and because there had been no assessment of Ms Penfold's daughter under s. 21 of the Carers (Recognition and Services) Act 1995.

The important question of what the local authority should do if someone refuses an assessment is dealt with in s. 11 of the Care Act. This is set out in **Box 13.5**. The normal position is to accept the individual's right to refuse an assessment, but you will see in the section two important exceptions.

BOX 13.5 Refusal of assessment

(1) Where an adult refuses a needs assessment, the local authority concerned is not required to carry out the assessment (and section 9(1) does not apply in the adult's case).

(2) But the local authority may not rely on subsection (1) (and so must carry out a needs assessment) if—
  (a) the adult lacks capacity to refuse the assessment and the authority is satisfied that carrying out the assessment would be in the adult's best interests, or
  (b) the adult is experiencing, or is at risk of, abuse or neglect.

The assessment process

Regulations determine the details of the assessment process. The current position is set out in the 2010 Department of Health Guidance *Prioritising need in the context of 'Putting people first': a whole system approach to eligibility for social care* headed 'Response to the first contact and assessment'.

The guidance makes it clear that staff should:

- work in partnership with individuals and their carers at all stages of the assessment process, beginning with the assumption that people are best placed to judge their own well-being, and should be provided with the information and support necessary to participate as fully as possible in decisions relating to their welfare;

- explain how the assessment process for care and support works, advise on the likely timescale, and tell people and carers how they can track progress in the meantime;
- ensure that knowledge about the individual's and carer's health conditions, health care needs, and NHS support informs the assessment process;
- apply the principles of personalization to:
  - maximize individuals' and carers' choices and control over their lives, and prioritize the outcomes they value;
  - recognize individuals' and carers' expert contributions to assessment;
  - explore solutions that lie within the individual's own network or via local community resources;
  - signpost or provide information and advice on support from universal services, other agencies and community resources;
- draw on the results of self-assessment to inform the assessment process;
- carry out capacity assessments where necessary, and Best Interests decision making if individuals are assessed as lacking the mental capacity to make a particular decision themselves;
- ensure that the scope of the assessment process is proportionate to the person's need and fit for purpose;
- collect sufficient evidence to make a sound judgement about eligibility within the *Fair Access to Care Services* bandings and criteria, agree outcomes, support the individual to identify and manage risks, and address any safeguarding issues.

New regulations in connection with carrying out the needs assessment will be issued in due course under the Care Act. Section 12 provides that the regulations will deal with, among other things:

- the requirement to have regard to the needs of the family of the adult to whom the assessment relates;
- the need to ensure that the assessment is carried out in an appropriate and proportionate manner;
- the involvement where necessary of people with sufficient expertise in particular conditions;
- the requirement to refer a person to the NHS for assessment of their health needs;
- the circumstances in which joint or self-assessments can take place, and the ability of a local authority to require a third party to carry out the assessment.

There is an important new duty within s. 12(3) of the Care Act, designed to protect service users. It is the duty to provide a written record of a needs assessment to the adult to whom the assessment relates, any carer that the adult has, if the adult asks the authority to do so, and any other person to whom the adult asks the authority to give a copy.

Eligibility criteria

Once a person has had their needs for care and support assessed, a local authority has to determine which of those needs it will meet. Currently *Fair Access to Care Services* (FACS) sets out the eligibility criteria that a local authority must use in reaching these important decisions about service provision. FACS is the national eligibility framework in England for prioritizing the use of adult social care resources fairly, transparently, and consistently. It was first introduced by the Department of Health in 2002. Revised policy guidance on assessment and eligibility for adult social care was issued in 2010, accompanied by a practice guide prepared by the Social Care Institute for Excellence (SCIE).

The Care Act will replace FACS, removing the current banding system described in that guidance. It will be replaced with a single set of criteria to describe a minimum threshold for eligible needs of those needing care, and a single set of criteria for carers. The government will produce and consult on draft regulations and more detailed statutory guidance about assessment and eligibility processes. Until that time 2010 policy guidance will remain in place. SCIE has, however, updated its practice guide to reflect changes in practice, and to anticipate the new approaches to assessment and eligibility contained in the Act. The aim is to assist councils with adult social services responsibilities to determine eligibility for adult social care, in a way that is fair, transparent, and consistent, accounting for the needs of local communities as a whole as well as individuals' need for support.

In what follows we explain the relevant provisions of FACS, drawing on the updated practice guide as appropriate, and set out the new statutory framework that will apply once the Care Act is implemented.

FACS 2010

FACS 2010 sets a national framework for criteria against which each local authority must assess a person's presenting needs in order to decide which of these are eligible needs. The eligibility criteria are not based on how much a service will cost, but on the seriousness of risk posed to a person's independence by a need for care services that is not being met. The eligibility framework is graded into four bands, which describe the seriousness of the risk to independence and well-being or other consequences if needs are not addressed. The eligibility criteria are set out in **Box 13.6**. These bands are applied nationally—every social services authority must use the banding and the exact wording of the band, although they are allowed to introduce, for instance, additional bullet points.

 BOX 13.6 FACS bandings and eligibility criteria for the individual

Critical—when:

• life is, or will be, threatened; and/or

• significant health problems have developed or will develop; and/or

- there is, or will be, little or no choice and control over vital aspects of the immediate environment; and/or
- serious abuse or neglect has occurred or will occur; and/or
- there is, or will be, an inability to carry out vital personal care or domestic routines; and/or
- vital involvement in work, education or learning cannot or will not be sustained; and/or
- vital social support systems and relationships cannot or will not be sustained; and/or
- vital family and other social roles and responsibilities cannot or will not be undertaken.

Substantial—when:

- there is, or will be, only partial choice and control over the immediate environment; and/or
- abuse or neglect has occurred or will occur; and/or
- there is, or will be, an inability to carry out the majority of personal care or domestic routines; and/or
- involvement in many aspects of work, education or learning cannot or will not be sustained; and/or
- the majority of social support systems and relationships cannot or will not be sustained; and/or
- the majority of family and other social roles and responsibilities cannot or will not be undertaken.

Moderate—when:

- there is, or will be, an inability to carry out several personal care or domestic routines; and/or
- involvement in several aspects of work, education or learning cannot or will not be sustained; and/or
- several social support systems and relationships cannot or will not be sustained; and/or
- several family and other social roles and responsibilities cannot or will not be undertaken.

Low—when:

- there is, or will be, an inability to carry out one or two personal care or domestic routines; and/or
- involvement in one or two aspects of work, education or learning cannot or will not be sustained; and/or
- one or two social support systems and relationships cannot or will not be sustained; and/or
- one or two family and other social roles and responsibilities cannot or will not be undertaken.

The SCIE practice guide points out that:

- Whether eligible or not under the FACS criteria, individuals in need of support have the same rights as everybody else to access universal services, such as the NHS and public transport. They are protected by the Equality Act 2010 from discrimination on grounds of disability or age in the provision of goods and services.
- Both those assessed eligible for publicly funded care and support and those ineligible can use universal services to complement support from their own family, friends, neighbours and community groups.

- Individuals who do not meet the threshold for publicly funded support may use information and advice to combine their own support network with private sector and/or third sector resources to improve the quality of their lives.
- The provision of equipment, telecare and telehealth can enable individuals and their carers to retain control over their lives and delay or minimise their need for formal care and support.

The SCIE practice guide also points out important changes in adult social care provision since the Collation Government took power in 2010. These are set out in **Box 13.7**.

 BOX 13.7 Changes in policy, terminology, practice, and resourcing since 2010—SCIE practice guide

Policy

- Government policies promoting localism, restructuring benefits and encouraging greater integration between the NHS and social care all influence the opportunities available to individuals and carers, the pressures placed on them and the outcomes they can achieve.

- Government has further emphasised the value and benefit of employment, both for individuals needing care and support and for their carers.

- Social care has felt the impact of a wider policy debate about the balance of responsibilities between the individual, the family and the state: arguments around the Dilnot Report on funding long-term care are a particular example.

- The government wishes to build the capacity of the community to provide more care and support, as seen in policies on volunteering, supporting carers and encouraging dementia-friendly and mental-health-friendly communities.

Terminology

Policy change has often been accompanied by new terminology.

'**Personalisation**' and '**co-production**' remain key concepts in social care, with some capacity to challenge traditional patterns of service provision and shift the balance of power between professionals and individuals/carers receiving support.

'**Integration**' within and between the NHS and social care has been a long-standing and much debated policy objective, but the notion remains ill-defined, and the term is applied in widely divergent ways.

'**Wellbeing**' is the overarching principle of the Care Act. The term has become widely used as shorthand for a range of beneficial personal, psychological and social outcomes, which may be enjoyed by individuals, families and communities. In the new NHS and local authority structures, health and wellbeing boards and health and wellbeing strategies are crucial mechanisms for coordinating the activities and plans of adults' and children's social care, the NHS and public health, housing and a wide range of local public services such as education, transport, parks, leisure, policing and the environment.

Practice

- In the changing adult social care scene, social work has not always found it easy to define its distinctive role and professional contribution. In many local authorities, the stress on personalisation has left social workers uncertain about what they have to offer.

- Some employers have been slow to grasp the importance of social work and social care knowledge and expertise. This is vital for supporting and safeguarding the growing numbers of disabled and older people, in complex and often vulnerable circumstances, with multiple physical, sensory and mental health conditions, affected by poverty and poor housing, and often neglected or harassed by neighbours.

- Assessment in these areas is underpinned by the Mental Capacity Act 2005, which requires local authorities to use a human rights framework, and assessments in these cases must consider people's 'liberty', 'family life' and protection from harm.

Resources for care and support

The effects of the economic downturn have tended to outweigh other factors in the thinking of many in central and local government. The Association of Directors of Adult Social Services (ADASS) calculates that between April 2011 and March 2013, £1.89 billion was removed from local authority social services budgets. While all authorities have experienced significant resource constraints, there are wide variations in how they are managing the consequences. Some have adopted a 'retrenchment' approach, applying eligibility criteria more strictly, reducing levels of support to individuals, withdrawing services and increasing charges. Others have preferred to look at alternative ways to use the resources they have available, working with the NHS to transform commissioned services, investing in early intervention and prevention to reduce demand for higher-dependency care and support, and working with voluntary and community sector bodies and with a wider range of commercial and private sector services to spread scarce resources further.

Once a person's needs have been categorized according to FACS, each local authority must set its own threshold that a service user *must* pass to become eligible for services. This presents a difficult balancing exercise. If the criteria are set too broadly this could result in a significant increase in expenditure. If the criteria are set too narrowly there is a risk of legal challenge. Those who fall into lower bands *may* be provided with services, but only if funding allows. Those who fall into the critical band must be provided with services. However, an authority may decide only to fund those whose needs fall in the critical band. Nonetheless, decisions to restrict eligibility in this way are fraught with legal dangers as the decision of the High Court in *R (on the application of JM) v Isle of Wight Council* [2011] makes clear.

R (on the application of JM) v Isle of Wight Council [2011] EWHC 2911 (Admin)

The claimants, who were two disabled adults, challenged changes that the local authority had made to the eligibility criteria for access to adult care services. The council decided that it would continue to meet fully the needs of all people who had been assessed as 'critical'. However, for those assessed as having needs defined as 'substantial', only needs that placed them at greatest risk of not being able to remain at home and of not being safe would be met. The claimants argued that the local authority had acted unlawfully by (a) failing to comply with the requirements of the statutory guidance and (b) failing to comply with the public sector equality duty in s. 49A of the Disability Discrimination Act 1995 (discussed in **chapter 11**).

The application succeeded. When the local authority prioritized the risk factors of not being able to remain at home and not being safe ahead of other risk factors within the 'substantial' band, it had created a 'hierarchy of needs' and restricted eligibility in a way that was contrary to the guidance. Further, in the 'eligibility review' it had carried out, the local authority had introduced criteria based on the likelihood that a particular risk would occur and how frequently it might occur. That had the effect of downgrading the needs of users with fluctuating and/or long-term conditions and was contrary to the guidance. Second, the local authority had not conducted the rigorous analysis and consideration required to satisfy s. 49A of the 1995 Act (as amended in the Disability Discrimination Act 2005), principally because it did not gather the information required to do so properly. The consultation document prepared by the local authority provided insufficient information to enable those consulted 'to give intelligent consideration and an intelligent response'. It did not provide any detail about the number of users whose support would be reduced or about the costs and potential savings, nor did it explain what types of services would or would not be included under the revised criteria. Further, there was no consultation in relation to the revised criteria adopted in the eligibility review, which was used as the basis for the reassessment of users. The local authority members were therefore deprived of important information as to the potential impact of the proposed changes, which meant that they had insufficient information when they were discharging their s. 49A duties. Moreover, there were flaws in the equality impact assessment which the local authority had conducted. Among other things, it contained no evidence-based information about the specific impact on disabled people of the proposals; it did not explain the nature of the 'substantial' needs that would be excluded from funding by the revised eligibility criteria or what the detriment would be to disabled people; it did not state how many disabled people would be detrimentally affected; and the suggestions made in it for mitigating the effects of the proposal were therefore made without a proper understanding of the potential detriment. Thus, although the assessment was provided to members, it did not provide the analysis and the information which they needed to discharge adequately their s. 49A duty.

Resources

Following the House of Lords decision in *R v Gloucestershire County Council, ex p Barry*, which we discussed earlier, it is clear that the local authority can take account of the resources available to it when setting its eligibility criteria. However, resources cannot be the sole factor in deciding what services to provide in fulfilling its duties—otherwise there would be no distinction between powers and duties. Moreover, resources shape eligibility criteria and not assessment, and the threshold requirements of the Human

Rights Act cannot be ignored. Nonetheless, because each local authority has different budgetary considerations and therefore decides its eligibility criteria differently, the system results in a postcode lottery: someone in Kent who has identical needs to someone in Sussex is unlikely to receive the same services. Perhaps even more important are the difficulties caused by the overly restrictive nature of the critical band. These concerns have informed the provisions of the Care Act, which we discuss later.

Resource allocation systems

The growth of direct payments (discussed in **chapter 12**) has meant that local authorities are increasingly required to provide money to enable service users to purchase the services they need. When the adult service user qualifies for direct payments a fourth question has to be added to the questions that local authorities answer when deciding whether and what needs are to be met: What is the reasonable cost of securing provision of the services which have been identified as being those for which the authority must make arrangements? Systems—known as resource allocation systems—have had to be devised to calculate the level of those payments. Non-statutory guidance, published in 2009 by the Association of Directors of Adult Social Services, *Common Resource Allocation Framework*, provides advice about how to develop legally robust resource allocation systems. It explains resource allocation systems as follows:

> The aim of a resource allocation system (RAS) linked to the allocation of personal budgets is to provide a clear and rational way to calculate how much money a person is likely to need to arrange support. ... A RAS cannot give a precise estimation of the cost of everybody's needs in every circumstance, but it should be sufficient to produce a ballpark figure for the majority of users that can be adjusted up or down, depending on those individual circumstances.

Some of the advice set out in the guidance which is designed to ensure that a RAS complies with statutory duties and guidance is summarized below.

(a) A short self-directed questionnaire should comply with the duty to assess provided it is supplemented with information gathered as part of the support planning process. Therefore the views of the person, family members, and professionals should be taken into account, the person's situation as a whole (including health and housing needs) should be considered, and basic data such as the information needed to meet statutory equality duties should be collated.

(b) Eligibility under FACS must be established at an early stage, but will need to be checked at any subsequent assessment or review. Councils should provide information about eligibility criteria, how the council has applied these to the person's situation, and how to challenge the council's decision.

(c) A RAS may enhance equal opportunities provided it is operated in a way that challenges rather than maintains the existing patterns of spending.

(d) Councils should exercise careful judgement when deciding the final amount of the personal budget, particularly when making decisions about people with high support needs.

(e) The RAS should be regularly reviewed to take account of actual support costs, so that over time it becomes possible to make indicative allocations that are better able to predict the costs for people with high support needs.

It is good practice at an early stage of the self-directed support process to tell the person how much money it is likely to cost to obtain the support their needs require. This is described as the indicative allocation. The final amount of the personal budget should only be agreed once there is a completed support plan that meets eligible social care needs and addresses risks. The guidance suggests that if councils take the view that the indicative allocation is a final figure with no flexibility, this could be open to legal challenge. The decision on the final amount of the personal budget therefore requires judgement on the part of the council, taking into account the person's overall circumstances including that of family carers. Otherwise the RAS will become the final figure. This could be a very onerous requirement legally and could work against transparency. Councils can operate a relatively crude RAS providing that there are good checks and balances in place.

The Care Act 2014—a new national approach to eligibility

The Care Act for the first time puts the system for determining eligibility for care and support services into statutory form. Section 13 of the Care Act—in **Box 13.8** sets out the basics of the national scheme.

 BOX 13.8 The eligibility criteria—s. 13 of the Care Act 2014

(1) Where a local authority is satisfied on the basis of a needs or carer's assessment that an adult has needs for care and support or that a carer has needs for support, it must determine whether any of the needs meet the eligibility criteria (see subsection (7)).

(2) Having made a determination under subsection (1), the local authority must give the adult concerned a written record of the determination and the reasons for it.

(3) Where at least some of an adult's needs for care and support meet the eligibility criteria, the local authority must—
    (a) consider what could be done to meet those needs that do,
    (b) ascertain whether the adult wants to have those needs met by the local authority in accordance with this Part, and
    (c) establish whether the adult is ordinarily resident in the local authority's area.

(4) Where at least some of a carer's needs for support meet the eligibility criteria, the local authority must—
    (a) consider what could be done to meet those needs that do, and
    (b) establish whether the adult needing care is ordinarily resident in the local authority's area.

> (5) Where none of the needs of the adult concerned meet the eligibility criteria, the local authority must give him or her written advice and information about—
>
> (a) what can be done to meet or reduce the needs;
>
> (b) what can be done to prevent or delay the development of needs for care and support, or the development of needs for support, in the future.

Regulations will be published which will flesh out the details of the assessment process, including how a local authority must go about determining whether an adult's needs meet the eligibility criteria and which needs are 'eligible' needs.

The regulations will prescribe the minimum level of needs that local authorities must meet. Local authorities will be able to decide to arrange services to meet needs at a lower level than the prescribed minimum. The government's decision about the minimum level will be crucial. Commentators are concerned that the level will be set at 'substantial', excluding adults with moderate needs from provision.

Legal challenges

The complexity of the pre-existing assessment regime and RASs, together with the increasing constraints imposed upon the budgets for adult social care, have made legal challenges inevitable. Here we consider three very important legal decisions. In the first, *R (on the application of McDonald) v Royal Borough of Kensington and Chelsea* (2011), the Supreme Court supported the local authority's decision to reduce the resources available to the adult service user and dismissed the argument that the failure to provide in the way that Ms McDonald wished was a breach of her human rights. The second case the court considered, *Savva v Kensington and Chelsea* (2010) challenged the allocation of monies via a RAS. The final case is *R on the Application of KM (By His Mother and Litigation Friend JM) v Cambridgeshire County Council* (Supreme Court, 2012). Like *Savva*, this challenged the amount awarded following an assessment of needs and its computation via RAS into a sum of money. We discussed the decision in *KM* in the case study at the beginning of the chapter, in relation to its restatement of the principles of *Barry*. Here we discuss the substantive issues raised. These cases are considered at some length because of their importance to your understanding of the legal framework. The issues raised will remain relevant even after the Care Act is implemented.

R (on the application of McDonald) v Royal Borough of Kensington and Chelsea [2011] UKSC 33

Elaine McDonald, a former ballerina with the Scottish Royal Ballet, was 67 years old at the time of the case. She had suffered a stroke in 1999 that left her with disabilities including severely limited mobility. She fell in April 2006, breaking her hips, and was hospitalized as a consequence for four months. Subsequently, and relatively rapidly, she suffered two more falls leading to further hospitalization. In addition to her impaired mobility, Ms McDonald suffered from a small and neurogenic bladder causing her to urinate two or three times during the night. Ms McDonald considered that it was the lack of support at night in using the commode that had led to her falls.

Following Ms McDonald's third serious fall, her local authority, the Royal Borough of Kensington and Chelsea (RBKC), assessed her needs and, from March 2007 upon her discharge from hospital, as part of an interim package of care, provided a carer to help her during the night to access a commode when necessary. This provision was to be temporary only, pending an application to the Independent Living Fund for full financial support for her day- and night-time needs. Unfortunately, the application failed, in part because Ms McDonald ceased to be eligible for assistance, having reached 65 years of age.

In a care plan formalized in April 2007, following her discharge from hospital, RBKC's assessment of Ms McDonald's needs and how those needs were to be met was recorded. In particular, meeting her assessed needs included 'assistance with toileting, when it's required during the night. 10 hours over night care'. An assessment completed in January 2008, following a meeting at Ms McDonald's home, recorded Ms McDonald's need as 'assistance to manage continence at night'. This need was classified as a 'Substantial Need', giving it priority in terms of resource allocation. Subsequently, however, the need was redefined as assistance at night to use the commode and was reclassified as a 'Moderate Need'. A further needs assessment was carried out in February 2008, recording 'Miss McDonald needs assistance to use the commode at night Substantial Need.' Yet another needs assessment, current at the outset of the court proceedings, was started on 2 July 2008 and completed on 28 October 2008. It repeated the conclusion of the previous assessment—'Miss McDonald needs assistance to use the commode at night Substantial Need. Consistent with this a Care Plan dated 17 November 2008 continues to record Ms McDonald's need as assistance to use the commode at night', and, consistently with that, states the total weekly cost of the care package to be provided at £703.

Despite the specificity of the care plan, RBKC considered that it would be preferable for Ms McDonald to use incontinence pads or special absorbent sheeting which would avoid the need for a night-time carer and reduce the cost of Ms McDonald's care by more than £20,000 a year. At a meeting on 17 October 2008, during the course of the final needs assessment, Ms McDonald was told that her 'care would need to be changed to reflect your needs', and that as a result the allocated funding would be reduced to £450 a week. Ms McDonald was unconvinced of the advantages of incontinence provisions over using a commode despite RBKC arguing that they provided greater safety, independence, and privacy. She strongly resisted RBKC's proposals; her argument was that she was not incontinent and did not wish to be treated as if she was. To suggest otherwise was an affront to her dignity. Nonetheless, RBKC implemented its change in provision.

Ms McDonald applied to judicially review the decision of RBKC to reduce the resources allocated to her in December 2008. RBKC chose not to implement the revised provision whilst the judicial review proceedings were ongoing. Instead it agreed a temporary compromise: to fund a night-time carer for four nights per week; on the other three nights, Ms McDonald's partner, who lived elsewhere, was to stay with her to provide support for her continued use of the commode for night-time urination. Of significance for the Court of Appeal decision in October 2010, following the High Court decision on 5 March 2009, which Ms McDonald lost, RBKC carried out a further care plan review on 4 November 2009. This reached the following conclusion:

> it remains Social Service's view that the use of incontinence pads is a practical and appropriate solution to Ms McDonald's night-time toileting needs. There does not see[m] to be any reason why this planned reduction to provide care should not go ahead ...
>
> (Para. 11)

A further review confirmed its previous decision. An alternative, Extra Care Sheltered Housing, was suggested to Ms McDonald but she refused to consider it. The Deputy High Court Judge, who heard the application, understood the question narrowly. She asked whether the need recorded in the care plan of July 2008 was to be read literally or whether, as RBKC argued, it was permissible to examine its underlying rationale and treat it as a need for safe urination at night. Accepting RBKC's position, she held that it was open to the local authority to meet the need for safe urination at night in the more economical manner; that is, by the provision of incontinence pads. She therefore refused permission for leave. On appeal, Ms McDonald was given permission to apply for judicial review and the case was reserved to the Court of Appeal. There the arguments were expanded. RBKC argued that its subsequent care plan reviews of 4 November 2009 and 15 April 2010 should be taken into account. Ms McDonald invoked Article 8 of the European Convention on Human Rights (this had been raised in the High Court proceedings but only ancillary to the primary ground) and also sought to rely on s. 21E of the Disability Discrimination Act 1995.

The Court of Appeal overruled the High Court. Its decision was that RBKC was in breach of its statutory duty at the time that proceedings were commenced. It disagreed with the High Court judge that the deliberately chosen language of the needs assessment of 2 July 2008 could be read as a more general need to manage Ms McDonald's night-time urination. However, it also held that since the December 2008 decision was not put into operation and since the need had been reassessed in the care plan reviews of November 2009 and April 2010, Ms McDonald had no substantial complaint. In other words, by the time the care package was reduced the necessary procedures had been complied with—there was no case for RBKC to answer. The Court of Appeal also rejected Ms McDonald's claim under Article 8 and the Disability Discrimination Act 1995. Ms McDonald appealed to the Supreme Court. The parties identified four questions for consideration.

(a) Are the 2009 and 2010 care plan reviews to be read as including a reassessment of Ms McDonald's community care needs?

(b) Did RBKC's decision to provide incontinence pads interfere with the appellant's Article 8 rights and, if so, was such interference justified and proportionate?

(c) Was RBKC operating any relevant policy or practice for the purposes of s. 21E(1) of the Disability Discrimination Act 1995 (now substantially re-enacted in the Equality Act 2010)?

(d) Has RBKC failed to have due regard to the needs specified in s. 49A of the Disability Discrimination Act 1995 ('the general disability equality duty' which is now contained in s. 149 of the Equality Act 2010) when carrying out their functions in this case?

Lord Brown delivered the leading judgment. In answer to the first question he was clear. The lengthy documentation of the reviews of 2009 and 2010 and the clarity of the conclusions reached, together with the extensive consultation with Ms McDonald and her partner, were a demonstration that those reviews included a reassessment of Ms McDonald's needs. Once that conclusion had been reached there was no more to be said—RBKC was entitled to reduce provision to the level required to meet Ms McDonald's reassessed needs (subject of course to consideration of Article 8 or disability discrimination provisions).

As far as Article 8 was concerned, Lord Brown was dismissive. He accepted that Article 8 has the potential in certain circumstances to impose positive obligations on a state to provide support in the form of community care to vulnerable individuals. However, he considered that a wide margin of appreciation is enjoyed by states when striking the necessary balance between the competing interests of the individual and of the community, most particularly in the context of the allocation of resources, and concluded that in this instance the Article 8 argument was hopeless. He was scathing about Ms McDonald's reliance on *R (Bernard) v Enfield London Borough Council* [2002] EWHC 2282 (Admin), pointing to the huge contrast between her circumstances and the facts found in *Bernard*, where Mrs Bernard was forced to defecate and urinate on the living-room floor and was unable to look after her children. Whilst he acknowledged the positive obligation under Article 8 to respect a person's private life, he considered that the consultation process and the attempts to reach agreement with Ms McDonald were sufficient to demonstrate RBKC's respect for Ms McDonald's dignity and autonomy. Not only did he determine that there was no interference by RBKC with Ms McDonald's Article 8 rights, he added that even if he were wrong, any interference which was in accordance with the law (thus excepting the period prior to the 2009 review) would be justified:

> on the grounds that it is necessary for the economic well-being of the respondents and the interests of their other service-users and is a proportionate response to the appellant's needs because it affords her the maximum protection from injury, greater privacy and independence, and results in a substantial costs saving.
>
> (Para. 19)

The provisions of the Disability Discrimination Act 1995 relied upon by counsel for Ms McDonald were given even shorter shrift than Article 8. For Lord Brown, the argument on both points was hopeless. He agreed with the Court of Appeal's scepticism about RBKC's procedures falling within the ambit of s. 21E(2) and even if they did, its actions were capable of justification under s. 21D. There was no more to be said.

Baroness Hale dissented. For her the decision of the local authority was 'irrational in the classic *Wednesbury* sense' because it characterized the appellant as 'having a different need from the one which she in fact has' (para. 78). She was concerned about the consequences of the local authority's decision. She argued that the logical conclusion of its decision could be the withdrawal of all assistance with mobility, during the day as well as at night, and, if Ms McDonald's physical condition deteriorated so that her bowels were affected, allowing her to lie in faeces until carers came in the morning. She echoed Lord Lloyd's dissent in *Barry*:

> In the United Kingdom we do not oblige people who can control their bodily functions to behave as if they cannot do so, unless they themselves find this the more convenient course. We are, I still believe, a civilized society. I would have allowed this appeal.
>
> (Para. 79)

Ms McDonald appealed to the European Court of Human Rights in Strasbourg. Its decision was handed down in May 2014. The Court held, unanimously, that the decision to reduce the amount allocated for Ms McDonald's care interfered with her right to respect for her family and private life, in respect of the period between 21 November 2008 and 4 November 2009 because the interference with her rights had not been in accordance with domestic law during this period. It held the complaint concerning the period after 4 November 2009 inadmissible as manifestly ill-founded because the state had considerable discretion when it came to decisions concerning the allocation of scarce resources and, as such, the interference with Ms McDonald's rights had been 'necessary in a democratic society'. She was awarded only €1,000 compensation and legal costs. However, the European Court decision may have more influence than the limited compensation suggest, as the judgment recognizes that a failure to consider a person's dignity can be a breach of human rights, which may lead to other challenges on this issue in future.

Savva v Kensington and Chelsea [2010] EWCA Civ 1209 (Court of Appeal)

The applicant, Mrs Savva, was 70 years old. She suffered from diabetes, heart and respiratory problems, and was arthritic with poor eyesight. She had had a stroke ten years previously and since then had been in receipt of adult social care services. In July 2009, Mrs Savva completed a Personal Budget Supported Self-Assessment Questionnaire (SAQ) with the support of her social worker. Using RAS Mrs Savva was allocated 16 points. This translated into a monetary value of £82.91 per week. The funding was adjusted to £132.56, and this was then increased to £170.45. The claimant completed another SAQ on 19 November 2009, after her discharge from hospital. This gave her 28 points which translated to a monetary value of £112.21. This sum, of course, was an increase from the £82.91 generated subsequent to the July SAQ. This sum was then adjusted to £142.02 per week. The local authority RAS then considered that the 'indicative budget' of £142.02 per week was too low and did not properly meet the claimant's needs particularly in terms of meal preparation. Therefore the panel increased the indicative figure and allocated a weekly budget of £170.45 to the claimant. Mrs Savva did not accept that this budget was reasonable to meet her assessed need. Her judicial review made three claims.

(a) The defendant's system for calculating budgets was inadequate to discharge the statutory duty to provide care services adequate to meet an individual's assessed needs.

(b) The defendant's reasons were inadequate to discharge the duty to provide adequate reasons for the decision to allocate the claimant a personal budget of £170.45 per week.

(c) The defendant assessed the claimant's needs to have increased substantially between July 2009 and December 2009, yet decided to keep the personal budget constant, at £170.45 per week. This, she argued, in the absence of a proper explanation, is irrational.

The judge at the High Court rejected the challenge based on the defendant's system of calculation but allowed the claim based on the failure to give adequate reasons. Mrs Savva appealed to the Court of Appeal on the lawfulness of Kensington and Chelsea's system of calculation and it cross-appealed on its duty to give reasons. The Court of Appeal decided that local authorities are entitled to use a RAS based on service users' assessed eligible needs and those of others in the area, as long as the figures reached were used only as a starting point for calculating the level of payments required to meet the service users' needs. In this case the court found that the local authority had not lost sight of its absolute duty to meet the recipient's needs or to provide a budget with which to meet them. It rejected the cross-appeal, pointing out that while neither the CSDPA 1970 nor the Community Care, Services for Carers and Children's Services (Direct Payment) (England) Regulations 2009 imposed a duty on the defendant to provide reasons for the panel's decision, the common law required reasons to be given as a matter of fairness. Mrs Savva was entitled to be told how the sum assessed to meet her eligible needs had been calculated in order to satisfy herself either that it had been properly calculated or to challenge the decision, which could be achieved with reasonable brevity by the defendant listing the required services and assumed timings together with the assumed hourly cost. Anxious to avoid imposing too much of a burden on local authorities, the Court indicated that, as a matter of common sense, decision letters which include an offer of the provision of reasons on request would satisfy legal requirements.

KM (By His Mother and Litigation Friend JM) v Cambridgeshire County Council [2012] UKSC 23

KM suffered from physical and mental disabilities and required significant support in his everyday life. The local authority was responsible for the provision of KM's care. Under the Health and Social Care Act 2001 (HSCA 2001), support could be provided to an individual by way of direct payments: entitling the individual to decide how to spend his care funds. KM's needs were assessed by an independent social worker. The local authority then determined the level of funding required by using a RAS calculation. That figure was then checked against KM's care assessment to ensure that the funding level would reasonably meet his assessed needs. In particular, the RAS indicated that KM's need would exceed the upper limit of funding allowed by that system; the local authority utilized a second indicative tool called an Upper Banding Calculator (UBC). It reflected, in effect, three factors which, in Cambridgeshire's experience, often greatly elevate the requisite level of services, namely a requirement for a carer to remain awake at night, for two carers to operate simultaneously, and for a carer to have specialist expertise. The social worker later reassessed KM's needs and also produced an addendum report setting out services which he assessed as necessary to meet those needs and their cost in the sum of £157,060. The local authority accepted the later needs assessment but it stated that the services assessment suggested unnecessary services and awarded KM £84,678 a year. KM sought to claim judicial review of the sum awarded to him but the High Court refused him permission to seek judicial review on the basis that the local authority had properly arrived at the sum that it had awarded KM and that it had given adequate intelligible reasons for how the figure was arrived at. KM contended that the amount of the assessed direct payment did not fulfil the local authority's obligation to provide him with care, that it had not given adequate reasons, and that its decision was irrational. The High Court refused permission for judicial review and its decision was upheld by the Court of Appeal.

The applicant appealed to the Supreme Court. It was asked to decide whether RASs are a legitimate means for local authorities to apply to determine funding to be made available to persons in need by means of direct payment, and whether adequate reasons were given for the decision that it reached. Legal commentators were excited by the fact that the Supreme Court also accepted as a question to be considered on appeal whether *Barry* was correctly decided. In the event, the judges avoided considering *Barry*, pointing out that the question of whether the local authority was entitled to consider its resources to meet KM's needs was not relevant. Cambridgeshire had agreed to meet KM's needs which were all decided to be critical.

The Supreme Court rejected KM's appeal. It was rational to use the RAS and the UBC provided that the result was cross-checked. The judges considered that the challenge to the adequacy of the *reasons* for the offer was more arguable. They suggested that Cambridgeshire should have made a more detailed presentation to KM of how in its opinion he might reasonably choose to deploy the offered sum than in the plans put forward in January and April 2010. In particular, Cambridgeshire should have made a presentation of its own assessment of the reasonable cost of the principal item of the appellant's future expenditure, namely the cost of paying for carers for him. Nevertheless, in the light of the amplification of Cambridgeshire's reasoning in the evidence filed in response to the application for judicial review, it would be a pointless exercise of discretion to order that it should be quashed so that the appellant's entitlement might be considered again, perhaps even to his disadvantage.

▨ The assessment of carers' needs

Under the law prior to the implementation of the Care Act there is a duty to assess a carer's needs under the Carers (Recognition and Services) Act 1995 (C(RS)A), when an assessment is carried out of an adult under s. 47 of the NHSCCA 1990, or a child under s. 2 of the CSDPA 1970, or Part III of the Children Act 1989, and the carer requests such an assessment. However, there is no explicit legal power to provide services under that Act to carers other than carrying out the assessment. The Carers and Disabled Children Act 2000 (CDCA) extended the rights of carers to include the right to support services. The Carers (Equal Opportunities) Act 2004 (C(EO)A) introduces a statutory obligation on social services to inform carers of their rights and requires that carers' assessments consider whether the carer works or wishes to work and/or is undertaking or wishes to undertake education, training, or any leisure activity.

The Care Act places carers at the centre of the system of support for vulnerable adults. Under s. 10 of the Act a local authority must assess a carer's needs for support. That assessment must take into account the following:

- whether the carer is able, and is likely to continue to be able, to provide care for the adult needing care;
- whether the carer is willing, and is likely to continue to be willing, to do so;
- the impact of the carer's needs for support;
- the outcomes that the carer wishes to achieve in day-to-day life; and
- whether, and if so to what extent, the provision of support could contribute to the achievement of those outcomes.

The local authority must also take into account whether the carer works or wishes to do so, and whether the carer is participating in or wishes to participate in education, training, or recreation. The carer must be involved in the assessment, alongside any other person the carer wishes to involve.

Eligibility criteria for carers

FACS sets out eligibility criteria for meeting carers needs. These are set out in **Box 13.9**.

 BOX 13.9 Levels of risk for sustainability of the caring role

Critical—when:

- their life may be threatened
- major health problems have developed or will develop
- there is, or will be, an extensive loss of autonomy for the carer in decisions about the nature of tasks they will perform and how much time they will give to their caring role

- there is, or will be, an inability to look after their own domestic needs and other daily routines while sustaining their caring role
- involvement in employment or other responsibilities is, or will be, at risk
- many significant social support systems and relationships are, or will be, at risk

Substantial—when:

- significant health problems have developed or will develop
- there is, or will be, some significant loss of autonomy for the carer in decisions about the nature of tasks they will perform and how much time they will give to their caring role
- there is, or will be, an inability to look after some of their own domestic needs and other daily routines while sustaining their caring role
- involvement in some significant aspects of employment or other responsibilities is, or will be, at risk
- some significant social support systems and relationships are, or will be, at risk

Moderate—when:

- there is, or will be, some loss of autonomy for the carer in decisions about the nature of tasks they will perform and how much time they will give to their caring role
- there is, or will be, some inability to look after their own domestic needs and other daily routines while sustaining their caring role
- several social support systems and relationships are, or will be, at risk

Low—when:

- there is, or will be, some inability to carry out one or two domestic tasks while sustaining their caring role
- one or two social support systems and relationships are, or will be, at risk

The eligibility criteria set out in s. 13 of the Care Act 2014 apply equally to carer's assessments as they do to the vulnerable adult so the local authority must meet the support needs which satisfy the eligibility criteria.

Care planning

Once the decision has been made that a person is eligible for particular community care services, then those services must be arranged. This is described as care planning. Good practice requires that care plans are provided to service users which set out what services the individual is entitled to and all other necessary information. The 2002 FACS guidance on care planning is set out in **Box 13.10**.

BOX 13.10 Guidance on care planning from FACS 2002

Care planning

47 If an individual is eligible for help then, together with the individual, councils should develop a care plan. The written record of the care plan should include as a minimum:

- A note of the eligible needs and associated risks.
- The preferred outcomes of service provision.
- Contingency plans to manage emergency changes.
- Details of services to be provided, and any charges the individual is assessed to pay, or if direct payments have been agreed.
- Contributions which carers and others are willing and able to make.
- A review date.

48 Appropriate services should be identified with reference to the statements of purpose requested from providers and, where appropriate, with reference to local continuing care agreements. Wherever applicable, the use of direct payments should also be considered and a decision made about their use.

49 Councils should aim to agree care plans with the service user, and should provide them with a copy of the care plan. Service users should be made aware of the arrangements for review and, where appropriate, advised that services may be withdrawn or changed as a result of the review.

The Care Act contains statutory provisions about care planning. Section 24—set out in **Box 13.11**—desribes the next steps the local authority must take.

BOX 13.11 Section 24 of the Care Act 2014

The steps for the local authority to take

(1) Where a local authority is required to meet needs under section 18 or 20(1), or decides to do so under section 19(1) or (2) or 20(6), it must—
   (a) prepare a care and support plan or a support plan for the adult concerned,
   (b) tell the adult which (if any) of the needs that it is going to meet may be met by direct payments, and
   (c) help the adult with deciding how to have the needs met.

(2) Where a local authority has carried out a needs or carer's assessment but is not required to meet needs under section 18 or 20(1), and does not decide to do so under section 19(1) or (2) or 20(6), it must give the adult concerned—
   (a) its written reasons for not meeting the needs, and
   (b) (unless it has already done so under section 13(5)) advice and information about—
     (i) what can be done to meet or reduce the needs;
     (ii) what can be done to prevent or delay the development by the adult concerned of needs for care and support or of needs for support in the future.

> (3) Where a local authority is not going to meet an adult's needs for care and support, it must none-theless prepare an independent personal budget for the adult (see section 28) if—
>
> (a) the needs meet the eligibility criteria,
>
> (b) at least some of the needs are not being met by a carer, and
>
> (c) the adult is ordinarily resident in the authority's area or is present in its area but of no settled residence.

Section 25 of the Care Act provides some detail as to what a care or support plan should contain—see **Box 13.12**.

BOX 13.12 Section 25 of the Care Act 2014—Care and support plans

(1) A care and support plan or, in the case of a carer, a support plan is a document prepared by a local authority which—

(a) specifies the needs identified by the needs assessment or carer's assessment,

(b) specifies whether, and if so to what extent, the needs meet the eligibility criteria,

(c) specifies the needs that the local authority is going to meet and how it is going to meet them,

(d) specifies to which of the matters referred to in section 9(4) the provision of care and support could be relevant or to which of the matters referred to in section 10(5) and (6) the provision of support could be relevant,

(e) includes the personal budget for the adult concerned (see section 26), and

(f) includes advice and information about—

(i) what can be done to meet or reduce the needs in question;

(ii) what can be done to prevent or delay the development of needs for care and support or of needs for support in the future.

In preparing the plan the local authority must involve the vulnerable adult, the carer, and any other person that the carer or the vulnerable adult wish to involve. Section 27 of the Act requires that local authorities keep plans under review.

Managing quality

So far, in this chapter, we have considered how local authorities aided by the social care professionals that they employ, decide upon service provision. In this section of the chapter we consider how the quality of that provision is managed. Local authorities are clearly concerned that the services that they provide are delivered to a good and safe standard. In the immediate post-war welfare state, local authorities provided services themselves and they could be held accountable for any defects in those services via the ballot box. Now responsibility for the delivery of services has been dispersed and services are more likely to be provided by the private or voluntary sector than by local authorities themselves. However, local authorities retain responsibility for the quality of those services. Democratic accountability is not (if it ever was) an appropriate mechanism. Instead local authorities use a range of techniques to ensure quality and manage risks. For instance, when they contract with a private or a voluntary sector provider they will put terms into the contract which require particular standards to be met. Another example is the use that local councils make of liaison groups, where adult social service users and their families meet council officers in an informal setting to discuss service provision. We look at three more formal means of ensuring quality. The first is located in the local authority itself—the requirement for local authorities to have a statutory complaints procedure. The second is the Local Government Ombudsman. The third is the Care Quality Commission, which is the national regulator of standards in health and social care. Each mechanism plays a part in ensuring that services do not fall below an acceptable level.

Statutory complaints procedure

The previous regime for local authority complaints about adult social care services was criticized for its bureaucracy and its inflexibility. Some complaints took a long time to resolve, and there was no system to ensure that complaints led to service improvement. Moreover, and in common with most complaint services, there was evidence that some people did not complain because they either did not know how to or they believed that doing so would be pointless.

From 1 April 2009, a single complaints system was introduced which covers all health and adult social care services in England. The aim of the new arrangements, known as 'making experiences count', is to encourage a flexible approach that aims to resolve complaints more effectively and ensure that opportunities for services to learn and improve are not lost.

The Local Authority Social Services and National Health Service Complaints (England) Regulations 2009 set out the procedures. What they require (in reg. 3(2) of the regulations) is that:

(a) complaints are dealt with efficiently;
(b) complaints are properly investigated;
(c) complainants are treated with respect and courtesy;
(d) complainants receive, so far as is reasonably practical—
    (i) assistance to enable them to understand the procedure in relation to complaints; or
    (ii) advice on where they may obtain such assistance;
(e) complainants receive a timely and appropriate response;
(f) complainants are told the outcome of the investigation of their complaint; and
(g) action is taken if necessary in the light of the outcome of a complaint.

The process for investigating complaints is set out in reg. 14 of the regulations: see **Box 13.13**.

BOX 13.13 Investigating complaints (extract) from the Local Authority Social Services and National Health Service Complaints (England) Regulations 2009

(1) A responsible body to which a complaint is made must—

   (a) investigate the complaint in a manner appropriate to resolve it speedily and efficiently; and

   (b) during the investigation, keep the complainant informed, as far as reasonably practicable, as to the progress of the investigation.

(2) As soon as reasonably practicable after completing the investigation, the responsible body must send the complainant in writing a response, signed by the responsible person, which includes—

   (a) a report which includes the following matters—

     (i) an explanation of how the complaint has been considered; and

     (ii) the conclusions reached in relation to the complaint, including any matters for which the complaint specifies, or the responsible body considers, that remedial action is needed; and

   (b) confirmation as to whether the responsible body is satisfied that any action needed in consequence of the complaint has been taken or is proposed to be taken;

   (c) where the complaint relates wholly or in part to the functions of a local authority, details of the complainant's right to take their complaint to a Local Commissioner under the Local Government Act 1974; and

   (d) except where the complaint relates only to the functions of a local authority, details of the complainant's right to take their complaint to the Health Service Commissioner under the 1993 Act.

Complainants have 12 months within which to make their complaint, although that time can be extended if it is reasonable to do so. Organizations must appoint someone, described as a complaints manager, to take responsibility for complaints; they must publicize their arrangements for handling complaints; and they must report annually on complaints received and their responses.

The Local Government Ombudsman

The Local Government Ombudsman considers complaints about councils and all types of care service for adults in England. This includes complaints about independent care providers as well as local authority provision. It does not matter whether the money for the service provided comes from the local authority or from private funds.

The Local Government Ombudsman produces a useful leaflet about how to complain which can be downloaded from www.lgo.org.uk/adult-social-care. Following investigations of complaints, the Local Government Ombudsman produces reports, two of which provided the case study at the beginning of **chapter 12**. These can be easily located on its website.

The Care Quality Commission

The Care Quality Commission (CQC) is the national body which was set up by the Health and Social Care Act 2008 (HSCA 2008) to regulate the quality and safety of health and care service provision in England regardless of whether the services are provided by the public, the private, or the voluntary sector. The CQC manages quality through a range of activities.

Registration

The primary activity of the CQC is to register providers of health and social care services. From April 2010 all health and adult social care providers are required by law to register with CQC if they provide 'regulated activities'. Failure to register is a criminal offence. Regulated activities are listed in Schedule 1 to the Health and Social Care Act 2008 (Regulated Activities) Regulations 2010. They include, for instance, the provision of personal care, provision of accommodation for people who require nursing or personal care, and accommodation for persons who require treatment for substance misuse. The CQC provides guidance on registration (as it is required to do by statute) at www.cqc.org.uk/content/guidance-providers.

The CQC explains the advantages of registration as follows:

- People who use services can expect all registered health and adult social care providers to meet essential standards of quality and safety and respect their dignity and rights.
- The same set of standards will apply right across the care sector, making it easier for one provider to be compared to another and for providers to work together.
- It is an outcomes based system of regulation.
- Continual monitoring and checking will make sure that potential problems are identified early and that swift action is taken where services are failing people.

Monitoring and inspection

Once providers are registered their activities are monitored through self-evaluation and inspection. There are three types of inspection:

- Scheduled—these are inspections carried out on a rolling programme. Providers are not told the date of a scheduled inspection.

- Responsive—these are carried out when concerns are raised over a provider's compliance with the standards.

- Themed—these are carried out when the CQC reviews a particular type of service (eg learning disability services) or a specific set of standards (eg the use of medication in care homes). The results of thematic inspections will be published as a national report on the specific theme.

Enforcement

One purpose of the reforms set out in the HSCA 2008 was to provide a more rigorous enforcement regime than the previous one under the Care Standards Act 2000. The CQC can require providers to deliver a plan of action or it can use its enforcement powers. These powers include:

- issuing a warning notice requiring improvements within a short period of time;
- restricting the services that the provider can offer;

- stopping admissions into the care service;
- issuing fixed penalty notices;
- suspending or cancelling the service's registration;
- prosecution.

Box 13.14 summarizes the enforcement policy of the CQC.

BOX 13.14 The enforcement policy of the CQC

Our overarching concern and priority is to protect and promote the health, safety and welfare of people who use the services we regulate, and to improve the quality of care they receive.

We will be proportionate in how we work with registered persons and others to achieve compliance with the Act and regulations:

- We will assess any risks to people using, working in and visiting services, and where necessary, take formal regulatory or enforcement action that is proportionate to those risks.
- Where a service fails to comply with legal requirements, we will take formal regulatory or enforcement action.
- Where legal requirements are not being met, we will choose the most proportionate way of achieving sustained compliance or we will remove the person's ability to provide or manage care if we consider that compliance could not be promptly achieved or sustained.
- Where legal requirements continue not to be met despite formal regulatory action being taken (compliance actions), we may escalate to enforcement action.

Criticism of the CQC

The performance of the CQC has been criticized by a number of bodies, particularly since BBC's *Panorama* revealed abuse at Winterbourne View. The conclusions of a Department of Health review of the performance and capability of the CQC published in February 2012, an extract from which is set out in **Box 13.15**, led to the resignation of its chief executive. Other critical reports include the report of the Public Accounts Committee published in March 2012 available at www.publications.parliament.uk/pa/cm201012/cmselect/cmpubacc/1779/177902.htm.

BOX 13.15 Extract from Department of Health review into the performance and capability of the CQC

CQC is the independent regulator of health and adult social care in England. CQC provides assurance that health and care provision meets government standards of quality and safety. It was established in April 2009 and formed by the merger of three previous regulators.

CQC's achievements are considerable and should not be underestimated. CQC has set the essential platform from which tougher regulatory action can be taken when needed if and where standards fall below acceptable levels. Yet, CQC has faced operational and strategic difficulties. Delays to provider registration, shortcomings in compliance activity and, at times, a negative public profile have seriously challenged public confidence in its role. With hindsight, both the Department and CQC underestimated the scale of the task. Even so, CQC could have done more to manage operational risks while its roles and functions changed.

Progress has been made over the last six to nine months. CQC is getting on a more stable footing. However, looking forward, CQC will need to learn lessons from its early years to ensure it has the capability and capacity to respond to patient, public and Parliamentary expectations.

Anna Dixon from the King's Fund attempted to put the criticism into context in April 2012:

The Commission had a troubled beginning, exacerbated by a lack of clarity about its role. Politicians must bear some responsibility for this—it is no good preaching the virtues of light touch regulation, and then blaming the regulator for not taking a more intervention-ist approach when problems emerge. They are also responsible for giving it such an enor-mous and complex task. As well as undertaking inspections, the Commission has registered 23,000 organisations in 40,000 locations since it was established and will embark on regis-tering 10,000 GP practices later this year.

(See www.kingsfund.org.uk/blog/cqc.html)

The CQC response has been to promise more focused inspections and better follow-up on the actions required by those inspections.

Part 2 of the Care Act 2014 is concerned with care standards and contains provi-sions which extend the remit of the CQC, introduce new criminal offences for bod-ies that provide false or misleading information about care services, and increase the independence of the CQC from government. In s. 55 of the Care Act the CQC is given the responsibility of overseeing the financial sustainability of private providers. This follows the financial problems suffered by private care firms particularly the failure of Southern Cross. Some commentators are sceptical about the ability of the CQC to take on this additional responsibility.

EXERCISES

1 Mrs Akuffo is about to be discharged from hospital where she has been receiving treatment for bipolar disorder. She has chronic diabetes and severe arthritis and she has difficulty managing stairs and much of her personal care. She has no income or savings. She has no home to return to as her private landlord terminated her tenancy shortly before her hospital admission, as she was said to have been shouting abusive comments to neighbours. How would you assess her needs for social care services?

2 Mr O'Keefe is dissatisfied with the assessment of his care needs. How can he complain about this? What will change under the Care Act?

3 The funding available for domiciliary services has been cut in your local authority area. How does that impact upon your service users who have a care plan in place?

4 Why do you think that the government is constantly revisiting and reforming its mechanisms to ensure that adult social care services are of an adequate quality? Do you think that the current arrangements will be effective?

ONLINE RESOURCE CENTRE

For guidance on how to answer these exercises, visit the Online Resource Centre at www.oxfordtextbooks.co.uk/orc/socialwork13e/.

WHERE DO WE GO FROM HERE?

This chapter has concentrated on the strategic planning of adult social care services and the assessment and planning of individuals' community care packages. It has also considered mechanisms for ensuring the quality of service provision. **Chapter 14** addresses two key issues of autonomy and protection for adult social care users, mental capacity, and adult safeguarding.

ANNOTATED FURTHER READING

There are a number of relevant chapters in L. Clements and P. Thompson's book, *Community Care and the Law* (Legal Action Group, 2011). Chapters 2, 3, and 4 are particularly important.

Resource allocations systems

L. Clements and L. Series, 'Putting the cart before the horse: resource allocation systems and community care' (2013) *Journal of Social Welfare and Family Law* 35(2): 207. The English Care Bill provides for all eligible community care service users to have a personal budget—and councils were required to ensure that 70 per cent of such users had one by April 2013. Almost all English authorities are experimenting with resource allocation systems (RASs) as a way of calculating these budgets. The article describes and critically analyses the nature of the RASs being used and the increasing body of case law they are attracting—in particular the Supreme Court's 2012 judgment in *R (KM) Cambridgeshire County Council*. The article draws on research involving 20 local authorities concerning their use of RASs and represents the first in-depth legal examination of the claims made by proponents of the use of RASs. It challenges many of the claims made concerning such systems—in particular that they are 'more transparent', 'more equitable', 'simpler', and less discretionary than the traditional social work-led community care assessment process.

The *KM* and *Barry* cases are also considered in 'R (KM) v Cambridgeshire— care and confusion: thinking legally': https://thinkinglegally.wordpress. com/2012/06/11/r-km-v-cambridgeshire-care-case-carers-rights.

Independent living

T. Collingbourne, 'Administrative justice? Realising the right to independent living in England: power, systems, identities' (2013) *Journal of Social Welfare and Family Law* 35(4): 475. Under Article 19 of the UN Convention on the Rights of Persons with Disabilities, disabled people have a right to live independently and to be included in the community. This article considers the potential for realization of that right through the English administrative justice system. It discusses models of administrative justice, and examines practical examples of the exercise of discretionary power in social care decision making, administration, and delivery. While some aspects of the current reconstruction in social care provision have succeeded in producing emancipatory outcomes, examples of continuing oppressive use of discretionary power still occur: in decision making, in the design of assessment questionnaires, and in the assessment experience. The article concludes that there is further to go before practice is aligned with meaningful, Convention-compliant change. Until then, realization in England of the right to independent living will remain partial, and the emancipatory purpose of the Convention compromised.

Complaints procedures

J. Gulland, 'Independence in complaints procedures: lessons from community care' (2009) *Journal of Social Welfare and Family Law* 31(1): 59. This article looks at internal complaints procedures and considers the role of independent elements in procedures that are designed to be simple, informal, and low cost. Taking the example of local authority community care services as a case study, it discusses research which looked at the views of complainants, potential complainants, and those who run the procedure. Most people do not make formal complaints at all and very few people seek an independent review of their complaint. When they do seek such a review, they expect it to be transparently independent of the body complained about. The article concludes that the current system of local authority complaints review panels or committees does not provide the independent element that complainants seek.

Ensuring quality

A. Stewart, 'Choosing care: dilemmas of a social market' (2005) *Journal of Social Welfare and Family Law* 27(3–4): 299. This article uses the lens of a personal experience of caring to reflect upon the provision of care services in England. It does so within the wider context of recent debates on the potential for a human rights culture within community care. The concept of independence, expressed as user choice in a social market of care, is central to government policy. The author, however, argues that this is a flawed approach and concludes that the starting point for policy and legal development should be the necessary interdependence of individuals.

14 Mental capacity and adult safeguarding

The focus of this chapter is the adult service user—or at least two of the most important legal and regulatory mechanisms that are in place to ensure that he or she is empowered and protected. The first part of the chapter considers the Mental Capacity Act 2005. It is designed to ensure that the wishes of the service user are taken into account as far as is possible, and where that is not possible, to set in place mechanisms to ensure that the best interests of the service user are protected. The second part of the chapter considers the various safeguards to protect service users from abuse.

CASE STUDY

A Local Authority v H [2012] EWHC 49 (COP)

A local authority sought a declaration from the Court of Protection on the capacity of H to consent to sexual relations. H, who was 29 years old, had mild learning difficulties, atypical autism, and an IQ of 64, and her history demonstrated a very early and a deep degree of sexualization. The local authority became aware of her sexual activities, vulnerability, and disinhibition. When interviewed, she gave an extensive and confused history of her willingness to have sex with strangers and indicated that she was engaging in sex with multiple partners at the same time, including a group of much older men. She saw herself as obligated to submit to what amounted to rape. H was compulsorily admitted to hospital under the Mental Health Act 1983 for nearly two years. After her discharge from hospital she lived in private accommodation provided by the local authority, but was supervised both in and out of the property at all times on a one-to-one basis. A deprivation of liberty safeguard standard authorization (see **Restraint and Deprivation of Liberty Safeguards,** p 482) under the Mental Capacity Act 2005, Schedule A1 was in force and a renewal was sought. The Court of Protection made the following judgment:

(1) For the purposes of s. 3(1) of the 2005 Act, a person was unable to make a decision for himself if he was unable

(a) to understand the information relevant to the decision;
(b) to retain that information;
(c) to use or weigh that information as part of the process of making the decision, or
(d) to communicate his decision.

In this case the court had to apply s. 3(1) with the question of sexual relations specifically in mind. Clearly, a person had to have a basic understanding of the mechanics of the physical sexual act and that intercourse could lead to pregnancy. Moreover, it seemed that capacity required some grasp of sexual health issues. It would suffice if a person understood that sexual relations might lead to significant ill-health and that those risks could be reduced by precautions such as condoms. The question to ask was whether the person whose capacity was in question understood that they had a choice and that they could refuse sexual relations. That was an important aspect of capacity and was as far as it was possible to go over and above an understanding of the physical component. Learning difficulties impaired memory and H was no exception. She had difficulty retaining information but with patient explanation and repetition would be able to retain basic information. The court was reluctant to conclude that she lacked capacity on that basis. The question of using and weighing the relevant information was a difficult concept in the context of human sexual relations since choices were made more by emotional drive and instinct than by rational choice. What was at issue was whether a person was able to deploy general knowledge into a specific decision-making act. H would struggle partly through an incomplete knowledge base and partly through an inability to deploy the knowledge she had when she was sexually aroused.

(2) H lacked capacity to consent to sexual relations on two specific bases: first, she did not understand the health implications of sexual relations, a matter made more serious by her history of multiple partners indiscriminately accommodated; and second, she could not effectively deploy the information she had into the decision-making process (para. 31).

(3) To protect H's best interests the court made a restrictive consequential order amounting to the deprivation of liberty.

WHAT DOES THIS CASE TELL YOU ABOUT SOCIAL CARE LAW AND PRACTICE?

This case illustrates the difficult task facing those concerned with both empowering vulnerable adults and protecting them. The Mental Capacity Act 2005 provides the tools with which this can be done, and the Court of Protection plays a very important role in making sure the necessary balancing act is carried out appropriately. The freedom to engage in sexual relationships is an important part of our identity as adults, and people with learning difficulties are as entitled to that freedom as others. However, if relationships appear to be abusive and an individual lacks capacity to consent to those relationships then the authorities may be obliged to intervene. The Court of Protection has an important and controversial role in sanctioning the deprivation of liberty in particular cases.

Mental capacity

The capacity of service users to make decisions about their lives can often be an issue. For instance, is Mrs Smith able to refuse to go into a care home or refuse to be assessed for services? Can Mr Jones decide to give his savings to his grandson or gamble them away? The common law and best practice provided principles upon which the capacity of individuals to make decisions could be assessed. These principles have now been reformed and codified within statute.

There are two important tools that you require in order to understand how the law regulates mental capacity. The first is the Mental Capacity Act 2005; the second is the Code of Practice to the Mental Capacity Act.

The Mental Capacity Act 2005 (MCA)

The Mental Capacity Act 2005 has its basis in the Law Commission Report No 231 on Mental Incapacity, which was published in 1995 after extensive consultation. The Act basically deals with three areas.

- It sets out the legal rules that are used to determine whether an individual has sufficient mental capacity to make a particular decision.

- It sets out the principles upon which decisions are to be made when an individual is assessed as lacking capacity.

- It enables people to make decisions to refuse medical treatment if they lose capacity in the future.

The Code of Practice

The Code of Practice provides guidance on how the MCA works on a day-to-day basis. It has useful case studies and explains the law in more detail.

Certain categories of people have a legal duty to have regard to the Code. These include:

- professionals and anyone who is paid for the work they do in relation to people who lack capacity. Clearly this includes social workers as well as doctors, nurses, care managers, solicitors, police officers, ambulance crew, and paid carers;

- attorneys appointed to act on someone's behalf under a Lasting Power of Attorney (LPA) or Enduring Power of Attorney (EPA); (we discuss these terms in **Lasting Powers of Attorney**, p 489);

- deputies appointed by the Court of Protection.

Family, friends, and unpaid carers do not have a duty to 'have regard' to the Code but they will still find the guidance helpful when they are caring for people who may lack capacity. The consequences of failure to comply with the Code are set out in **Box 14.1**.

 BOX 14.1 What happens if people don't comply with the Code of Practice?

There are no specific sanctions for failure to comply with the Code. But a failure to comply with the Code can be used in evidence before a court or tribunal in any civil or criminal proceedings, if the court or tribunal considers it to be relevant to those proceedings. For example, if a court or tribunal believes that anyone making decisions for someone who lacks capacity has not acted in the best interests of the person they care for, the court can use the person's failure to comply with the Code as evidence. That's why it's important that anyone working with or caring for a person who lacks capacity to make specific decisions should become familiar with the Code.

How the MCA works

The MCA is underpinned by five principles set out in s. 1 of the Act. These are set out in **Box 14.2**. We examine these principles later.

BOX 14.2 The statutory principles underpinning the Mental Capacity Act 2005

- A presumption of capacity—every adult has the right to make his or her own decisions and must be assumed to have capacity to do so unless it is proved otherwise.
- Individuals being supported to make their own decisions—a person must be given all practicable help before anyone treats them as not being able to make their own decisions.
- Unwise decisions—just because someone makes what might be seen as an unwise decision, they should not be treated as lacking capacity to make that decision.
- Best interests—an act done or decision made under the Act for or on behalf of a person who lacks capacity must be done in their best interests.
- Least restrictive principle—anything done for or on behalf of a person who lacks capacity should be the least restrictive possible to their basic rights and freedoms taking into account whether it is as effective as the proposed alternative.

Assessing capacity

A person lacks capacity if they meet the criteria of s. 2(1) of the MCA:

> For the purposes of this Act, a person lacks capacity in relation to a matter if at the material time he is unable to make a decision for himself in relation to the matter because of an impairment of, or a disturbance in the functioning of, the mind or brain.

The Act sets out a clear test for assessing whether a person lacks capacity to make a particular decision at a particular time. That test is in s. 3 of the MCA set out in **Box 14.3**.

BOX 14.3 Section 3 of the Mental Capacity Act 2005—Inability to make decisions

(1) For the purposes of section 2, a person is unable to make a decision for himself if he is unable—
   (a) to understand the information relevant to the decision,
   (b) to retain that information,
   (c) to use or weigh that information as part of the process of making the decision, or
   (d) to communicate his decision (whether by talking, using sign language or any other means).

(2) A person is not to be regarded as unable to understand the information relevant to a decision if he is able to understand an explanation of it given to him in a way that is appropriate to his circumstances (using simple language, visual aids or any other means).

(3) The fact that a person is able to retain the information relevant to a decision for a short period only does not prevent him from being regarded as able to make the decision.

(4) The information relevant to a decision includes information about the reasonably foreseeable consequences of—
   (a) deciding one way or another, or
   (b) failing to make the decision.

As the statutory principles make clear, people must be helped to make their own decisions. Only if all appropriate help has been given should anyone conclude that someone cannot make their own decisions.

The presumption of capacity

The MCA states clearly that a person must be assumed to have capacity unless it is established that he lacks capacity—MCA, s. 1(2). What that means is that you cannot treat someone as if they lack capacity unless you have proof. The standard of proof is balance of probabilities—that it is more likely than not that the individual lacks capacity. The MCA makes it clear that lack of capacity cannot be established merely by reference to a person's age or appearance, or a condition of his, or an aspect of his behaviour, which might lead others to make unjustified assumptions about his capacity—MCA, s. 2(3).

Significantly, capacity is tested on the basis of the decision which has to be made. A person may have the capacity to decide what they want to wear, or whether they wish to buy new clothes, but not have the capacity to buy a house. This is set out in s. 2(1) of the MCA.

For the purposes of this Act, a person lacks capacity in relation to a matter if at the material time he is unable to make a decision for himself in relation to the matter because of an impairment of, or a disturbance in the functioning of, the mind or brain.

Note that this test is a legal test and not a medical test. Doctors should only make decisions about capacity if they understand the law. What the section means in practice is illustrated by a scenario delineated in the Code of Practice which is set out in **Box 14.4**.

BOX 14.4 Scenario: assessing a person's capacity to make decisions

When planning for her retirement, Mrs Arnold made and registered a Lasting Power of Attorney (LPA)—a legal process that would allow her son to manage her property and financial affairs if she ever lacked capacity to manage them herself. She has now been diagnosed with dementia, and her son is worried that she is becoming confused about money.

Her son must assume that his mother has capacity to manage her affairs. Then he must consider each of Mrs Arnold's financial decisions as she makes them, giving her any help and support she needs to make these decisions herself.

Mrs Arnold's son goes shopping with her, and he sees she is quite capable of finding goods and making sure she gets the correct change. But when she needs to make decisions about her investments, Mrs Arnold gets confused—even though she has made such decisions in the past. She still doesn't understand after her son explains the different options.

Her son concludes that she has capacity to deal with everyday financial matters but not more difficult affairs at this time. Therefore, he is able to use the LPA for the difficult financial decisions his mother can't make. But Mrs Arnold can continue to deal with her other affairs for as long as she has capacity to do so.

The statutory principles make it clear that people need to be supported in making decisions. An example of how this can be done is set out in the Code of Practice provided for you in **Box 14.5**.

BOX 14.5 Scenario: taking steps to help people make decisions for themselves

Mr Jackson is brought into hospital following a traffic accident. He is conscious but in shock. He cannot speak and is clearly in distress, making noises and gestures.

From his behaviour, hospital staff conclude that Mr Jackson currently lacks the capacity to make decisions about treatment for his injuries, and they give him urgent treatment. They hope that after he has recovered from the shock they can use an advocate to help explain things to him.

However, one of the nurses thinks she recognises some of his gestures as sign language, and tries signing to him. Mr Jackson immediately becomes calmer, and the doctors realise that he can communicate in sign language. He can also answer some written questions about his injuries.

The hospital brings in a qualified sign-language interpreter and concludes that Mr Jackson has the capacity to make decisions about any further treatment.

Best interests

The law requires that decisions made in respect of individuals who lack capacity are made in the best interests of that person. 'Best interests' does not mean what you might think it means. Common sense would probably suggest that acting in someone's best interests means doing what is best for them objectively. However, the law is more complex; acting in someone's best interests has a subjective element—what would the person have decided to do for themselves if they had capacity. The relevant section of the MCA, s. 4, is set out in **Box 14.6**. What it does is provide a checklist to ensure that people act in someone's best interests.

BOX 14.6 Acting in a person's best interests—s. 4 of the MCA

(1) The person making the determination must consider all the relevant circumstances and, in particular, take the following steps.

(2) He must consider—
  (a) whether it is likely that the person will at some time have capacity in relation to the matter in question, and
  (b) if it appears likely that he will, when that is likely to be.

(3) He must, so far as reasonably practicable, permit and encourage the person to participate, or to improve his ability to participate, as fully as possible in any act done for him and any decision affecting him.

(4) Where the determination relates to life-sustaining treatment he must not, in considering whether the treatment is in the best interests of the person concerned, be motivated by a desire to bring about his death.

(5) He must consider, so far as is reasonably ascertainable—
   (a) the person's past and present wishes and feelings (and, in particular, any relevant written statement made by him when he had capacity),
   (b) the beliefs and values that would be likely to influence his decision if he had capacity, and
   (c) the other factors that he would be likely to consider if he were able to do so.

(6) He must take into account, if it is practicable and appropriate to consult them, the views of—
   (a) anyone named by the person as someone to be consulted on the matter in question or on matters of that kind,
   (b) anyone engaged in caring for the person or interested in his welfare,
   (c) any donee (person who has been given) of a lasting power of attorney granted by the person, and
   (d) any deputy appointed for the person by the court, as to what would be in the person's best interests and, in particular, as to the matters mentioned in subsection (6).

Notice that 'best interests' is not defined. Explanatory notes to the Act said: 'Best interests is not a test of "substituted judgement" (what the person would have wanted), but rather it requires a determination to be made by applying an objective test as to what would be in the person's best interests'. What is required is that anyone acting on behalf of someone else goes through a rigorous process of decision making. This is inevitably going to be complex. Is it, for instance, in the best interests of someone who lacks capacity for the decision-maker to make an unwise financial decision simply because that person habitually made unwise financial decisions when they had capacity? Perhaps not surprisingly the Court of Protection in *Re P* [2009] EWHC 163 (Ch) decided that it was not. In **Box 14.7** we set out the judge's explanation of the process that a decision-maker must follow. It demonstrates what a complex process acting in someone's best interests is. Even judges do not agree!

BOX 14.7 Making decisions in someone's best interests

The goal of the enquiry is not what P [meaning 'a person' here, not specifically the P of the court case] 'might be expected' to have done; but what is in P's best interests. This is more akin to the 'balance sheet' approach than to the 'substituted judgment' approach.

The previous guidance [before the 2005 Act] was concerned with deciding what P would have wanted if he were not mentally disordered. But the 2005 Act requires the decision maker to consider P's *present* wishes and feelings, which … are wishes and feelings entertained by a person who lacks mental capacity in relation to the decision being made on his behalf.

The same structured decision making process applies to all decisions to be made on P's behalf, whether great or small … Moreover, it is a decision making process which must be followed, not only by the court, but by anyone who takes decisions on P's behalf.

In making his decision the decision maker must consider 'all relevant circumstances'. The Act expressly directs the decision maker to take a number of steps before reaching a decision. These include encouraging P to participate in the decision. The decision maker must also 'consider' P's past and present wishes, and his beliefs and values and must 'take into account' the views of third parties as to what would be in P's best interests.

Having gone through these steps, the decision maker must then form a value judgment of his own giving effect to the paramount statutory instruction that any decision must be made in P's best interests. In my judgment this process is quite different to that which applied under the former Mental Health Acts.

That is not to say that P's expressed wishes should be lightly overridden. On the contrary, the Act expressly requires them to be considered; and for particular consideration to be given to wishes expressed by P when he had capacity. In *Re S and S (Protected Persons)* (unreported 25 November 2008) His Honour Judge Marshall QC ... pointed out the stress that the Act lays on the ascertainment of P's wishes and feelings and on involving him in the decision making process. She concluded:

'55. In my judgment it is the inescapable conclusion from the stress laid on these matters in the Act that the views and wishes of P in regard to decisions made on his behalf are to carry great weight. What, after all, is the point of taking great trouble to ascertain or deduce P's views, and to encourage P to be involved in the decision making process, unless the objective is to try to achieve the outcome which P wants or prefers, even if he does not have the capacity to achieve it for himself?

'56. The Act does not of course say that P's wishes are to be paramount, nor does it lay down any express presumption in favour of implementing them if they can be ascertained. Indeed the paramount objective is that of P's best interests. However, by giving such prominence to the above matters, the Act does in my judgment recognise that having his views and wishes taken into account and respected is a very significant aspect of P's best interests. Due regard should therefore be paid when doing the weighing exercise of determining what is in P's best interests in all the circumstances of the case.

'57. As to how this will work in practice, in my judgment, where P can and does express a wish or view which is not irrational (in the sense of being a wish which a person of full capacity might reasonably have), is not impractical as far as its physical implementation is concerned, and is not irresponsible having regard to the extent of P's resources (i.e. whether a responsible person of full capacity who had such resources might reasonably consider it worth using the necessary resources to implement his wish) then that situation carries great weight, and effectively gives rise to a presumption in favour of implementing those wishes, unless there is some potential sufficiently detrimental effect for P of doing so which outweighs this.

'58. That might be some extraneous consequence, or some other unforeseen, unknown or unappreciated factor. Whether this further consideration actually should justify overriding P's wishes might then be tested by asking whether, had he known of this further consideration, it appears (from what is known of P) that he would have changed his wishes. It might further be tested by asking whether the seriousness of this countervailing factor in terms of detriment to P is such that it must outweigh the detriment to an adult of having one's wishes overruled, and the sense of impotence, and the frustration and anger, which living with that awareness (insofar as P appreciates it) will cause to P. Given the policy of the Act to empower people to make their own decisions wherever possible, justification for overruling P and "saving him from himself" must, in my judgment, be strong and cogent. Otherwise, taking a different course from that which P wishes would be likely to infringe the statutory direction in s [1(6)] of the Act, that one must achieve any desired objective by the route which least restricts P's own rights and freedom of actions.'

I agree with the broad thrust of this, although I think that HH Judge Marshall QC may have slightly overstated the importance to be given to P's wishes. First, section 1(6) is not a statutory direction that one 'must achieve' any desired objective by the least restrictive route. Section 1(6) only requires that before a decision is made 'regard must be had' to that question. It is an important question, to be sure, but it is not determinative. The only imperative is that the decision must be made in P's best interests. Second, although P's wishes must be given weight, if, as I think, Parliament has endorsed the 'balance sheet' approach, they are only one part of the balance. I agree that those wishes are to be given great weight, but I would prefer not to speak in terms of presumptions. Third, any attempt to test a decision by reference to what P would hypothetically have done or wanted runs the risk of amounting to a 'substituted judgment' rather than a decision of what would be in P's best interests. But despite this risk, the Act itself requires some hypothesising. The decision maker must consider the beliefs and values that would be likely to influence P's decision if he had capacity and also the other factors that P would be likely to consider if he were able to do so. This does not, I think, necessarily require those to be given effect.

The Code of Practice provides extensive assistance here. **Box 14.8** provides a scenario which illustrates how to follow the checklist.

 BOX 14.8 Scenario: following the checklist

Martina, an elderly woman with dementia, is beginning to neglect her appearance and personal hygiene and has several times been found wandering in the street unable to find her way home. Her care workers are concerned that Martina no longer has capacity to make appropriate decisions relating to her daily care. Her daughter is her personal welfare attorney and believes the time has come to act under the Lasting Power of Attorney (LPA). She assumes it would be best for Martina to move into a care home, since the staff would be able to help her wash and dress smartly and prevent her from wandering. However, it cannot be assumed *simply on the basis of her age, condition, appearance or behaviour* either that Martina lacks capacity to make such a decision or that such a move would be in her best interests. Instead, steps must be taken to assess her capacity.

If it is then agreed that Martina lacks the capacity to make this decision, all the relevant factors in the best interests checklist must be considered to try to work out what her best interests would be.
Her daughter must therefore consider:

- Martina's past and present wishes and feelings;
- the views of the people involved in her care;
- any alternative ways of meeting her care needs effectively which might be less restrictive of Martina's rights and freedoms, such as increased provision of home care or attendance at a day centre.

By following this process, Martina's daughter can then take decisions on behalf of her mother and in her best interests, when her mother lacks the capacity to make them herself, on any matters that fall under the authority of the LPA.

The Code of Practice also suggests that written records be kept of the decision-making process involved in working out what is in someone's best interests. This is important: demonstrably acting in someone's best interests protects a person from liability for what might otherwise be unlawful acts (eg touching or entering their home without permission) when they carry out care and treatment in connection with a person who lacks capacity. This is set out in s. 5 of the MCA, the effects of which are explained in the Code of Practice—see **Box 14.9**.

BOX 14.9 What protection do people have when caring for those who lack capacity to consent? Extract from the Code of Practice

6.1 Every day, millions of acts are done to and for people who lack capacity either to:

- take decisions about their own care or treatment, or

- consent to someone else caring for them.

Such acts range from everyday tasks of caring (for example, helping someone to wash) to life-changing events (for example, serious medical treatment or arranging for someone to go into a care home). In theory, many of these actions could be against the law. Legally, people have the right to stop others from interfering with their body or property unless they give permission. But what happens if someone lacks capacity to give permission? Carers who dress people who cannot dress themselves are potentially interfering with someone's body without their consent, so could theoretically be prosecuted for assault. A neighbour who enters and cleans the house of a person who lacks capacity could be trespassing on the person's property.

6.2 Section 5 of the Act provides 'protection from liability'. In other words, it protects people who carry out these actions. It stops them being prosecuted for acts that could otherwise be classed as civil wrongs or crimes. By protecting family and other carers from liability, the Act allows necessary caring acts or treatment to take place as if a person who lacks capacity to consent had consented to them. People providing care of this sort do not therefore need to get formal authority to act.

6.3 Importantly, section 5 does not give people caring for or treating someone the power to make any other decisions on behalf of those who lack capacity to make their own decisions. Instead, it offers protection from liability so that they can act in connection with the person's care or treatment. The power to make decisions on behalf of someone who lacks capacity can be granted through other parts of the Act (such as the powers granted to attorneys and deputies, which are explained in chapters 7 and 8 [of the Code of Practice]).

Restraint and Deprivation of Liberty Safeguards

There are some limitations on the protections offered by s. 5 of the MCA set out in s. 6 of the Act. These concern acts of 'restraint' which are defined in s. 6(4).

(4)   For the purposes of this section D restrains P if he—

    (a)   uses, or threatens to use, force to secure the doing of an act which P resists, or

    (b)   restricts P's liberty of movement, whether or not P resists.

Simple everyday acts like using a seat belt or stopping someone from crossing the road or leaving the house are acts of restraint. Restraint can only be applied to someone if two conditions are met. These are set out in s. 6(2) and (3):

(2) The first condition is that D reasonably believes that it is necessary to do the act in order to prevent harm to P.

(3) The second is that the act is a proportionate response to—

  (a) the likelihood of P's suffering harm, and

  (b) the seriousness of that harm.

Once more the Code of Practice contains helpful advice. An extract from this is set out in **Box 14.10**.

BOX 14.10 Restraint—extract from the Code of Practice

When might restraint be 'necessary'?

6.44 Anybody considering using restraint must have objective reasons to justify that restraint is necessary. They must be able to show that the person being cared for is likely to suffer harm unless proportionate restraint is used. A carer or professional must not use restraint just so that they can do something more easily. If restraint is necessary to prevent harm to the person who lacks capacity, it must be the minimum amount of force for the shortest time possible.

What is 'harm'?

6.45 The Act does not define 'harm', because it will vary depending on the situation. For example,

- a person with learning disabilities might run into a busy road without warning, if they do not understand the dangers of cars

- a person with dementia may wander away from home and get lost, if they cannot remember where they live

- a person with manic depression might engage in excessive spending during a manic phase, causing them to get into debt

- a person may also be at risk of harm if they behave in a way that encourages others to assault or exploit them (for example, by behaving in a dangerously provocative way).

6.46 Common sense measures can often help remove the risk of harm (for example, by locking away poisonous chemicals or removing obstacles). Also, care planning should include risk assessments and set out appropriate actions to try to prevent possible risks. But it is impossible to remove all risk, and a proportionate response is needed when the risk of harm does arise.

What is a 'proportionate response'?

6.47 A 'proportionate response' means using the least intrusive type and minimum amount of restraint to achieve a specific outcome in the best interests of the person who lacks capacity. On occasions when the use of force may be necessary, carers and healthcare and social care staff should use the minimum amount of force for the shortest possible time. For example, a carer may need to hold a person's arm while they cross the road, if the person does not understand the dangers of roads. But it would not be a proportionate response to stop the person going outdoors at all. It may be appropriate

> to have a secure lock on a door that faces a busy road, but it would not be a proportionate response to lock someone in a bedroom all the time to prevent them from attempting to cross the road.
>
> 6.48 Carers and healthcare and social care staff should consider less restrictive options before using restraint. Where possible, they should ask other people involved in the person's care what action they think is necessary to protect the person from harm. For example, it may be appropriate to get an advocate to work with the person to see if they can avoid or minimise the need for restraint to be used.

If the restraint involves the deprivation of someone's liberty then different procedures apply. The Code of Practice provides guidance on the distinction between restraint and deprivation of liberty. What it says is:

> It is difficult to define the difference between actions that amount to a restriction of someone's liberty and those that result in a deprivation of liberty. In recent legal cases, the European Court of Human Rights said that the difference was 'one of degree or intensity, not one of nature or substance'. There must therefore be particular factors in the specific situation of the person concerned which provide the 'degree' or 'intensity' to result in a deprivation of liberty. In practice, this can relate to:
>
> • the type of care being provided
> • how long the situation lasts
> • its effects, or
> • the way in a particular situation came about.

The case that the Code of Practice refers to is *HL v UK* (45508/99) [2004] ECHR 471. In this case the UK was found to have breached Article 5 of the European Convention on Human Rights (ECHR)—deprivation of liberty—because there were no procedural protections available for patients who were informally detained in care settings. The case had been taken to the European Court of Human Rights in Strasbourg after the House of Lords (now Supreme Court) had ruled in *R (L) v Bournewood NHS Trust* [1998] UKHL 24 that an autistic man without capacity who was admitted into a psychiatric unit had not been unlawfully detained under English common law since the authorities acted reasonably in his best interests (see **chapter 3** for a definition of '*Wednesbury* reasonableness' and its limitations in terms of human rights). The Strasbourg judges, in contrast, said the UK had no 'procedure prescribed by law' to protect his Article 5 right to liberty so admitting him to the unit without his consent was a breach of Article 5. This lack of procedure became known as the *Bournewood* gap. There was also a contravention of Article 5(4) of the ECHR ('Everyone who is deprived of his liberty by arrest or detention shall be entitled to take proceedings by which the lawfulness of his detention shall be decided speedily by a court and his release ordered if the detention is not lawful'). HL had no means of applying quickly to a court to see if the deprivation of liberty was lawful.

In response to the judgment, the Deprivation of Liberty Safeguards system was introduced (DoLS) in 2009 in an amendment to the MCA. A DoLS authorization is applied when someone does not have the mental capacity to make a decision about going into a care home or hospital for treatment (whether for mental or physical illness or injury) or their own well-being. The principle is that a person should only be deprived of their liberty without consent if:

- they lack capacity to make decisions;
- it is in their best interests;
- it is 'proportionate' (not excessive given the danger it is intended to avoid, eg taking account of the likelihood of an individual suffering harm and the seriousness of that harm);
- there is no reasonable alternative.

An application is made to a supervisory body—a local authority (or primary care trust for keeping someone in a hospital). This body must:

- ensure the person is over 18;
- ensure that he or she has no one who can make the decision for them;
- assess whether they can make the decision themselves;
- assess whether they have a mental incapacity;
- check whether someone would meet the requirement to be detained instead under the Mental Health Act 1983;
- make sure the deprivation of liberty is necessary, proportionate, and in the best interests of the person.

The order can last for 12 months but should be for the shortest time possible to deal with the issue.

The supervisory body will make a 'standard authorization' within 21 days of the application unless there is an emergency (in which case an 'urgent authorization' can be sought for immediate deprivation of liberty which can last for seven days). The assessments are made by at least two people. Crucially they can be challenged in the Court of Protection (described in the following section). The managing authority must monitor the detention to ensure it is not continuing unnecessarily. Detention is unlawful once the period authorized is over, though a new authorization can be applied for in advance.

In the Court of Protection the lawfulness of the authorization can be challenged on one or more of the following grounds:

- whether the relevant person meets one or more of the qualifying requirements for deprivation of liberty;
- the period for which the standard authorization is to be in force;
- the purpose for which the standard authorization is given;
- the conditions subject to which the standard authorization is given.

An urgent authorization can also be challenged on:

- whether the urgent authorization should have been given;
- the period for which the urgent authorization is to be in force;
- the purpose for which the urgent authorization has been given.

See the *Mental Capacity Act 2005: Deprivation of Liberty Safeguards—Code of Practice to supplement the main Mental Capacity Act 2005 Code of Practice*, issued 2008, now archived at: http://webarchive.nationalarchives.gov.uk/20130107105354/http://www.dh.gov.uk/en/Publicationsandstatistics/Publications/PublicationsPolicyAndGuidance/DH_085476. There is also a useful Social Care Institute for Excellence (SCIE) guide published in 2011, *At a Glance 43: The Deprivation of Liberty Safeguards*, available at www.scie.org.uk/publications/ataglance/ataglance43.asp.

There are two important public bodies set up to help protect those who may lack capacity. The first of these is the Court of Protection, the second the Public Guardian.

The Court of Protection

The Court of Protection is the court which has jurisdiction relating to the MCA. It is the final arbiter on whether a person has capacity to make a particular decision for themselves. In addition it can:

- make declarations, decisions, or orders on financial or welfare matters affecting people who lack capacity to make these decisions;
- appoint a Deputy to make ongoing decisions for people lacking capacity to make those decisions;
- decide whether an LPA or EPA is valid;
- remove Deputies or Attorneys who fail to carry out their duties;
- hear cases concerning objections to register an LPA or EPA.

It is a court of record and its decisions have precedent value—that is, they bind lower courts. The Code of Practice provides information about how and when someone can make an application to the Court of Protection.

The Court of Protection has an important role in the DoLS. It is the legal forum through which challenges to the DoLS can be made. *London Borough of Hillingdon v Steven Neary* provides a useful illustration of its role and how it can help local authorities protect the liberties of vulnerable adults.

London Borough of Hillingdon v Steven Neary [2011] EWHC 1377 (COP)

This case, which gained a good deal of media attention, provides salutary lessons for social workers seeking to admit people without capacity into care. Steven Neary was a 21-year-old with autism and a severe learning disability. He was cared for by his father. The local authority, Hillingdon, arranged care services to support Steven at home and provided respite care. In January 2010 Steven was placed in a support unit for a short period of respite care at the request of his father. Hillingdon started an assessment of Steven's needs and concluded that he could not get those needs met at home owing to his behaviour. There was concern food was used to control his behaviour and so Steven had gained a lot of weight. There was evidence that 'he can become moody and anxious … He can lash out, not in malice but rather in the manner of a small child.' The local authority refused to return Steven to the care of his father. Hillingdon said it was in his best interests to keep him beyond a period of respite care, that they had his father's permission at least until April 2010, and that he had not in fact been deprived of his liberty. From April to December DoLS authorizations granted by Hillingdon to itself allowed the local authority to keep him in care.

Steven's father challenged Hillingdon but was informed that he could take the matter to the Court of Protection if he wanted to dispute the DoLS authorizations. In October 2010 the authority took the case to the Court of Protection itself. The judge, Mr Justice Peter Jackson, found Hillingdon had deprived Steven of his liberty throughout the year. 'It acted as if it had the right to make decisions about Steven, and by a combination of turning a deaf ear and *force majeure* [irresistible compulsion], it tried to wear down Mr Neary's resistance, stretching its relationship with him almost to breaking point. It relied upon him coming to see things its way, even though, as events have proved, he was right and it was wrong. In the meantime, it failed to activate the statutory safeguards that exist to prevent situations like this arising.' In particular Hillingdon should not have left it to Steven's father to bring the matter to the Court of Protection but should have done so itself at the earliest opportunity. The four months without court oversight was far too long. Jackson concluded that the local authority had breached Stephen Neary's right to respect for family life (Article 8, ECHR), and had unlawfully deprived him of his liberty in contravention of Article 5(1) ECHR. The court made clear that the local authority has a responsibility to bring deprivation of liberty cases to court in a timely fashion whenever there is any doubt regarding the DoLS, best interests, or proportionality.

The case provides useful lessons for social workers. Jackson said the DoLS regime 'is not to be used by a local authority as a means of getting its own way on the question of whether it is in the person's best interests to be in [a particular place] at all'. It follows that the local authority, acting as the supervisory body over its own adult social care department, has an obligation to scrutinize an assessment like the department's regarding the Nearys' 'with independence and a degree of care that is appropriate to the seriousness of the decision and to the circumstances of the individual case that are or should be known to it'. Instead it had offered authorization based on 'perfunctory scrutiny of superficial best interests assessments'.

So the report of the Best Interests Assessor authorizing the DoLS order should 'consider whether any care or treatment the person needs can be provided effectively in a way that is less restrictive of their rights and freedom of action'. The report flagged this up as an issue but it was not followed through. No doubt the local authority wanted a quick result. By now, looking at whether to return Steven home would have involved a quite complex inquiry. But in law that is no excuse for a 'perfunctory' assessment. Proper regard to keeping him at home was not given: 'Nowhere in their very full records of Steven's year in care is there any mention of the supposition that he should be at home, other things being equal, or the disadvantages to him of living away from his family, still less an attempt to weigh those disadvantages against the supposed advantages of care elsewhere.'

The criticisms made by the Court of Protection of the DoLS have been echoed by House of Lords Select Committee on the MCA. In its report published in March 2014 and available at http://socialwelfare.bl.uk/subject-areas/government-issues/legislation/tso/160248139.pdf it concluded that the DoLS are not 'fit for purpose'. It recommend their replacement with legislation that is in keeping with the language and ethos of the MCA as a whole. In addition, whilst the Committee considered that the ethos of the Act was good, what is needed is a change in attitudes and practice across the health and social care sector to reflect the empowering ethos of the Act. It therefore recommended that overall responsibility for the Act be given to an independent body whose task will be to oversee, monitor, and drive forward implementation.

Deputies

The appointment of Deputies is another role of the Court of Protection. What the Code of Practice has to say about deputies is set out in **Box 14.11**.

BOX 14.11 What are the rules for appointing deputies?

8.31 Sometimes it is not practical or appropriate for the court to make a single declaration or decision. In such cases, if the court thinks that somebody needs to make future or ongoing decisions for someone whose condition makes it likely they will lack capacity to make some further decisions in the future, it can appoint a deputy to act for and make decisions for that person. A deputy's authority should be as limited in scope and duration as possible (see paragraphs 8.35–8.39 below).

How does the court appoint deputies?

8.32 It is for the court to decide who to appoint as a deputy. Different skills may be required depending on whether the deputy's decisions will be about a person's welfare (including healthcare), their finances or both. The court will decide whether the proposed deputy is reliable and trustworthy and has an appropriate level of skill and competence to carry out the necessary tasks.

8.33 In the majority of cases, the deputy is likely to be a family member or someone who knows the person well. But in some cases the court may decide to appoint a deputy who is independent of the family (for example, where the person's affairs or care needs are particularly complicated). This could be, for example, the Director of Adult Services in the relevant local authority (but see paragraph 8.60 below) or a professional deputy. The OPG [Office of the Public Guardian] has a panel of professional deputies (mainly solicitors who specialise in this area of law) who may be appointed to deal with property and affairs if the court decides that would be in the person's best interests.

When might a deputy need to be appointed?

8.34 Whether a person who lacks capacity to make specific decisions needs a deputy will depend on:

• the individual circumstances of the person concerned

• whether future or ongoing decisions are likely to be necessary, and

• whether the appointment is for decisions about property and affairs or personal welfare.

There will usually be no need to appoint a deputy if the only income of a person who lacks capacity is social security benefits and they have no property or savings. Their benefits can be managed by an *appointee*, appointed by the Department for Work and Pensions. An appointee must, of course, act in the best interests of the person lacking capacity.

The Public Guardian

The Public Guardian is a role created by the MCA to protect people who lack capacity by:

- setting up and managing a register of LPAs;
- setting up and managing a register of EPAs;
- setting up and managing a register of court orders that appoint Deputies;
- supervising Deputies, working with other relevant organizations (eg social services, if the person who lacks capacity is receiving social care);
- instructing Court of Protection Visitors to visit people who may lack mental capacity to make particular decisions and those who have formal powers to act on their behalf such as Deputies;
- receiving reports from Attorneys acting under LPAs and from Deputies; and
- providing reports to the Court of Protection, when requested, and dealing with cases where there are concerns raised about the way in which Attorneys or Deputies are carrying out their duties.

Lasting Powers of Attorney

An LPA enables someone who has capacity to choose who they want to make decisions on their behalf when they lack mental capacity to make the decision themselves in advance of them losing mental capacity. It only comes into effect if and when the person making the LPA—the donor—loses capacity. Until that date they continue to make decisions themselves. If they lose capacity, the LPA is 'registered' with the Office of the Public Guardian. From this point on—the other people—the attorney or attorneys are able to make decisions on the donor's behalf.

There are two types of LPA:

- health and welfare (allowing decisions on treatment, care, medication, where you live, etc);
- property and financial affairs (allowing an attorney to make decisions about paying bills, dealing with the bank, collecting benefits, selling your house, etc).

Different attorneys can be appointed to make decisions under the different powers of attorney.

LPAs replaced Enduring Powers of Attorney as a result of the MCA. The important difference between LPAs and EPAs is the ability to appoint an attorney to make decisions concerning personal welfare matters. Although no new EPAs can now be created, you will come across EPAs made before the implementation of the MCA.

The Code of Practice provides advice on personal welfare LPAs which is set out in **Box 14.12**.

 BOX 14.12 Personal welfare LPAs—para. 7.21 of the Code of Practice

LPAs can be used to appoint attorneys to make decisions about personal welfare, which can include healthcare and medical treatment decisions. Personal welfare LPAs might include decisions about:

- where the donor should live and who they should live with
- the donor's day-to-day care, including diet and dress
- who the donor may have contact with
- consenting to or refusing medical examination and treatment on the donor's behalf
- arrangements needed for the donor to be given medical, dental or optical treatment
- assessments for and provision of community care services
- whether the donor should take part in social activities, leisure activities, education or training
- the donor's personal correspondence and papers
- rights of access to personal information about the donor, or
- complaints about the donor's care or treatment.

The types of action that may be carried out by an attorney with a property and affairs LPA are set out in **Box 14.13**.

 BOX 14.13 Property and affairs LPA—para. 7.36 of the Code of Practice

If a donor does not restrict decisions the attorney can make, the attorney will be able to decide on any or all of the person's property and financial affairs. This might include:

- buying or selling property
- opening, closing or operating any bank, building society or other account
- giving access to the donor's financial information
- claiming, receiving and using (on the donor's behalf) all benefits, pensions, allowances and rebates (unless the Department for Work and Pensions has already appointed someone and everyone is happy for this to continue)
- receiving any income, inheritance or other entitlement on behalf of the donor
- dealing with the donor's tax affairs
- paying the donor's mortgage, rent and household expenses

- insuring, maintaining and repairing the donor's property
- investing the donor's savings
- making limited gifts on the donor's behalf (but see paragraphs 7.40–7.42 below)
- paying for private medical care and residential care or nursing home fees
- applying for any entitlement to funding for NHS care, social care or adaptations
- using the donor's money to buy a vehicle or any equipment or other help they need
- repaying interest and capital on any loan taken out by the donor.

Advance decisions to refuse treatment

The MCA sets out statutory rules with built-in safeguards which allow people to make a decision in advance to refuse treatment if they should lose capacity in the future. If the advance decision is to refuse life-sustaining treatment, it must comply with the formalities set out in **Box 14.14** which are taken from the Code of Practice.

BOX 14.14 The formalities required of advance decisions to refuse life-sustaining treatment

Advance decisions to refuse life-sustaining treatment *must* meet specific requirements:

- They must be put in writing. If the person is unable to write, someone else should write it down for them. For example, a family member can write down the decision on their behalf, or a healthcare professional can record it in the person's healthcare notes.
- The person must sign the advance decision. If they are unable to sign, they can direct someone to sign on their behalf in their presence.
- The person making the decision must sign in the presence of a witness to the signature. The witness must then sign the document in the presence of the person making the advance decision. If the person making the advance decision is unable to sign, the witness can witness them directing someone else to sign on their behalf. The witness must then sign to indicate that they have witnessed the nominated person signing the document in front of the person making the advance decision.
- The advance decision must include a clear, specific written statement from the person making the advance decision that the advance decision is to apply to the specific treatment even if life is at risk.
- If this statement is made at a different time or in a separate document to the advance decision, the person making the advance decision (or someone they have directed to sign) must sign it in the presence of a witness, who must also sign it.

More information on advance directives, and indeed on all aspects of the law, can be found in the Code of Practice. We recommend you become very familiar with it. The law in connection with mental capacity reflects the complexity of balancing the right of an individual to autonomy and the need to protect those who need protection. The next section of the chapter concentrates on recent developments to improve the law in connection with the safeguarding of adults.

Safeguarding adults

The televising of abuse in the private hospital Winterbourne, run by Castlebeck, by the BBC *Panorama* programme in summer 2011 highlighted the problem of abuse of vulnerable adults. Awareness of the issue has been growing for the last ten years. A report from the House of Commons Health Select Committee published in 2004 about the extent of abuse and the lack of coherent responses to it provides useful background. Some paragraphs from the introduction to that report are set out in **Box 14.15**.

BOX 14.15 Extract from House of Commons Health Select Committee Report 2004

1 'The voice of older people is rarely heard by those who have a responsibility for commissioning, regulating and inspecting services.' This remark was made to us by Gary Fitzgerald, representing the charity Action for Elder Abuse. Mr Fitzgerald pointed out that many people would be familiar with the case of Victoria Climbié, a child tortured and murdered in the care of a relative, but few knew about Margaret Panting, a 78-year-old woman from Sheffield who died after suffering 'unbelievable cruelty' while living with relatives. After her death in 2001, a post-mortem found 49 injuries on her body including cuts probably made by a razor blade and cigarette burns. She had moved from sheltered accommodation to her son-in-law's home—five weeks later she was dead. But as the cause of Margaret Panting's death could not be established, no one was ever charged. An inquest in 2002 recorded an open verdict.

15 The prevalence of elder abuse is difficult to quantify for a number of reasons. Abuse is frequently hidden, may not be obvious even to the victim, and is likely to be under-reported. The Association of Directors of Social Services quoted research to suggest that 'reported alleged abuse is but a small proportion of the overall experience.' Moreover, a lack of staff awareness of what constitutes abuse (including poor practice), and inadequate knowledge and training in how to detect abuse can also lead to under-reporting of cases of abuse. Overall therefore, robust evidence is very hard to obtain.

34 A number of submissions drew particular attention to the potential for abuse to occur 'behind closed doors,' in situations where services were provided in a 'one-to-one situation', and where an older person was entirely dependent on the district nurse, or care worker, who came into their home. Gary Fitzgerald for AEA told us that it was almost impossible to quantify the level of 'unknown abuse' that occurred in such settings, but in terms of calls to his organisation's helpline it was clear that a great deal of reported abuse took place in people's own homes. Such concerns were also recently highlighted by the BBC Panorama programme broadcast in November 2003 which used an under cover reporter to investigate the vulnerability of older people cared for in their own homes.

Defining abuse has proved problematic. Important guidance on the abuse of adult service users, *No Secrets,* published jointly by the Department of Health and the Home Office, suggests a particular approach to defining abuse which proceeds from an understanding of abuse as a violation of an individual's human rights. The relevant paragraphs are set out in **Box 14.16**.

BOX 14.16 Defining abuse—*No Secrets*

2.5 What constitutes abuse? In drawing up guidance locally, it needs to be recognised that the term 'abuse' can be subject to wide interpretation. The starting point for a definition is the following statement:

Abuse is a violation of an individual's human and civil rights by any other person or persons.

In giving substance to that statement, however, consideration needs to be given to a number of factors.

2.6 Abuse may consist of a single act or repeated acts. It may be physical, verbal or psychological, it may be an act of neglect or an omission to act, or it may occur when a vulnerable person is persuaded to enter into a financial or sexual transaction to which he or she has not consented, or cannot consent. Abuse can occur in any relationship and may result in significant harm to, or exploitation of, the person subjected to it.

2.7 A consensus has emerged identifying the following main different forms of abuse:

- physical abuse, including hitting, slapping, pushing, kicking, misuse of medication, restraint, or inappropriate sanctions;

- sexual abuse, including rape and sexual assault or sexual acts to which the vulnerable adult has not consented, or could not consent or was pressured into consenting;

- psychological abuse, including emotional abuse, threats of harm or abandonment, deprivation of contact, humiliation, blaming, controlling, intimidation, coercion, harassment, verbal abuse, isolation or withdrawal from services or supportive networks;

- financial or material abuse, including theft, fraud, exploitation, pressure in connection with wills, property or inheritance or financial transactions, or the misuse or misappropriation of property, possessions or benefits;

- neglect and acts of omission, including ignoring medical or physical care needs, failure to provide access to appropriate health, social care or educational services, the withholding of the necessities of life, such as medication, adequate nutrition and heating; and

- discriminatory abuse, including racist, sexist, that based on a person's disability, and other forms of harassment, slurs or similar treatment.

Any or all of these types of abuse may be perpetrated as the result of deliberate intent, negligence or ignorance.

2.8 Incidents of abuse may be multiple, either to one person in a continuing relationship or service context, or to more than one person at a time. This makes it important to look beyond the single incident or breach in standards to underlying dynamics and patterns of harm. Some instances of abuse will constitute a criminal offence. In this respect vulnerable adults are entitled to the protection of the law in the same way as any other member of the public. In addition, statutory offences have been created which specifically protect those who may be incapacitated in various ways. Examples of actions which may constitute criminal offences are assault, whether physical or psychological, sexual assault and rape, theft, fraud or other forms of financial exploitation, and certain forms of discrimination, whether on racial or gender grounds. Alleged criminal offences differ from all other non-criminal forms of abuse in that the responsibility for initiating action invariably rests with the state in the form of the police and the Crown Prosecution Service (private prosecutions are theoretically possible but wholly exceptional in practice). Accordingly, when complaints about alleged abuse suggest that a criminal offence may have been committed it is imperative that reference should be made to the police as a matter of urgency. Criminal investigation by the police takes priority over all other lines of enquiry.

2.9 Neglect and poor professional practice also need to be taken into account. This may take the form of isolated incidents of poor or unsatisfactory professional practice, at one end of the spectrum, through to pervasive ill treatment or gross misconduct at the other. Repeated instances of poor care may be an indication of more serious problems and this is sometimes referred to as institutional abuse.

The definition of abuse developed by Action on Elder Abuse may prove particularly useful in your own practice. It is set out in **Box 14.17**.

BOX 14.17 Defining Abuse—Action on Elder Abuse definition

A single or repeated act or lack of appropriate action occurring within any relationship where there is an expectation of trust, which causes harm or distress to an older person.

The extent of abuse is also problematic. It is inevitably hidden. The Select Committee's report on elder abuse recommended that further research should be carried out. In response, King's College London (KCL) (Institute of Gerontology and Social Care Workforce Research Unit) and the National Centre for Social Research were commissioned by Comic Relief and the Department of Health to carry out the UK Study of Abuse and Neglect of Older People. This was the first dedicated study of its kind in the UK. More robust statistics have now been collated and were published by the NHS information centre for the first time in March 2012. The statistical report covers data collected about vulnerable adults aged 18 and over in England for whom social services have been made aware, by means of either a safeguarding alert or a safeguarding referral, of their being at risk of abuse/harm or actually being abused/harmed. The most recent statistics are set out in **Box 14.18**.

BOX 14.18 Extract from key facts from *Abuse of Vulnerable Adults* statistics 2012–13

In 2012–13, a total of 173,000 safeguarding alerts and 112,000 safeguarding referrals were reported for vulnerable adults aged 18 and over in England.

For councils who reported on referrals in 2011–12 and in 2012–13, the number of referrals has increased by 4 per cent (4,000 referrals).

61 per cent of safeguarding referrals were for women and 61 per cent were for vulnerable adults aged 65 or over. Half of the referrals (50 per cent) were for adults with a physical disability. The rate of referrals per 100,000 population was highest in the West Midlands (320), North West (300) and London (295) regions in 2012–13.

Physical abuse and neglect were the most common types of abuse reported in referrals, accounting for 28 per cent and 27 per cent respectively of all allegations.

The alleged abuse was more likely to occur in the vulnerable adults own home (accounting for 39 per cent of all locations cited) or a care home (36 per cent) than in other locations.

The source of harm was most likely to be cited as a social care worker (31 per cent of all perpetrators) or a family member (a combination of the Partner and Other Family Member categories, 23 per cent).

Guidance

The protections for adult service users are set out in both policy guidance and in the law. We have already referred to the guidance *No Secrets* published jointly by the Department of Health and the Home Office in 2000. The Welsh equivalent of the guidance published by the Welsh Assembly is *In Safe Hands*, published in 2000 and updated in 2011. The guidance, which is issued under s. 7 of the Local Authority Social Services Act 1970, is largely about establishing effective inter-agency procedures to respond to abuse of those it defines as vulnerable. Clements and Thompson in *Community Care and the Law* (Legal Action Group, 2011) recognize the value of this but also observe that it shows 'how powerless social service are when faced with cases of abuse where there is not enough evidence to prosecute' (p 710). The guidance has been also criticized for its limited ambit—it only extends to those who are or may be in need of community care services and who are unable to protect themselves from significant harm or exploitation. The Association of Directors of Adult Social Services (ADASS) published a national framework of standards for good practice in adult protection work, *Safeguarding Adults*, in 2005. The framework moves away from definitions of vulnerability and protection to a language of safeguarding.

For the team of academics who published the survey into the prevalence of abuse among older people, *Safeguarding Adults* is important; it reflects the experience of those charged with implementing the guidance and was drawn up in consultation and partnership with key organizations that included the Association of Chief Police Officers, the Commission for Social Care Inspection, the Department of Health, and the Public Guardianship Office.

You should note that the ethos behind *Safeguarding Adults* derives explicitly from human rights. The introduction to the national framework points out that 'All persons have the right to live their lives free from violence and abuse.' This right is underpinned by the duty on public agencies under the Human Rights Act 1998 to intervene proportionately to protect the rights of citizens. These rights include Article 2: 'Right to life'; Article 3: 'Freedom from torture' (including humiliating and degrading treatment); and Article 8: 'Right to family life' (one that sustains the individual). The Executive Summary of the guidance is set out in **Box 14.19**.

 BOX 14.19 Executive Summary of *Safeguarding Adults* (ADSS 2005)

This national framework is comprised of eleven sets of good practice standards. We believe their implementation in every local area will lead to the development of consistent, high quality adult protection work across the country.

Standard 1 Each local authority has established a multi-agency partnership to lead 'Safeguarding Adults' work.

Standard 2 Accountability for and ownership of 'Safeguarding Adults' work is recognised by each partner organisation's executive body.

Standard 3 The 'Safeguarding Adults' policy includes a clear statement of every person's right to live a life free from abuse and neglect, and this message is actively promoted to the public by the Local Strategic Partnership, the 'Safeguarding Adults' partnership, and its member organisations.

Standard 4 Each partner agency has a clear, well-publicised policy of Zero-Tolerance of abuse within the organisation.

Standard 5 The 'Safeguarding Adults' partnership oversees a multi-agency workforce development/training sub-group. The partnership has a workforce development/training strategy and ensures that it is appropriately resourced.

Standard 6 All citizens can access information about how to gain safety from abuse and violence, including information about the local 'Safeguarding Adults' procedures.

Standard 7 There is a local multi-agency 'Safeguarding Adults' policy and procedure describing the framework for responding to all adults '*who is or may be eligible for community care services*' and who may be at risk of abuse or neglect.

Standard 8 Each partner agency has a set of internal guidelines, consistent with the local multi-agency 'Safeguarding Adults' policy and procedures, which set out the responsibilities of all workers to operate within it.

Standard 9 The multi-agency 'Safeguarding Adults' procedures detail the following stages:

Alert, Referral, Decision, Safeguarding assessment strategy, Safeguarding assessment, Safeguarding plan, Review, Recording and Monitoring.

Standard 10 The safeguarding procedures are accessible to all adults covered by the policy.

Standard 11 The partnership explicitly includes service users as key partners in all aspects of the work. This includes building service-user participation into its: membership; monitoring, development and implementation of its work; training strategy; and planning and implementation of their individual safeguarding assessment and plans.

Safeguarding Adults Boards

One particular mechanism for safeguarding vulnerable adults mentioned in the *No Secrets* guidance is local adult safeguarding boards. These are multi-agency partnerships made up of a wide range of statutory agencies and voluntary organizations. They are aimed at facilitating joint working in adult protection, and their responsibilities include ensuring that multi-agency policies and procedures are in place, conducting serious case reviews, and providing training and information. Until the relevant sections of the Care Act 2014 (ss. 42–47) are implemented there is no statutory basis for Safeguarding Adults Boards. Safeguarding Adults Boards will be required to conduct Safeguarding Adults Reviews into certain cases in specific circumstances. The aim of a review is to ensure that lessons are learned from such cases, not to allocate blame but to improve future practice and partnership working, and to minimize the possibility of its happening again.

The legal framework for safeguarding adults

In theory, there should be no need to have additional legal protections for adult service users. The normal provisions of both civil and criminal law on assault and trespass to the person should adequately protect all citizens, regardless of their particular characteristics. However, increasing knowledge of the prevalence of abuse, and the particular problems of those who lack capacity, has required the law to respond.

Criminal provisions specifically relating to the victimization of adult service users who lack capacity have therefore increased in recent years. **Box 14.20** summarizes these.

BOX 14.20 Criminal offences and vulnerable adults

Provision	Offence
Fraud Act 2006, s. 4	It is an offence for a person who occupies a position where he or she is required to safeguard, or not act against, the financial interests of another person, to dishonestly abuse that position, with the intent of self-benefit or to benefit others
Mental Capacity Act 2005, s. 44	It is an offence for someone who has the care of a person who lacks capacity; a donee of a Lasting or Enduring Power of Attorney; or a deputy to ill-treat or wilfully neglect that person. The maximum penalty is five years' imprisonment
Domestic Violence, Crime and Victims Act 2004, s. 5	It is an offence to cause or allow the death of a child or vulnerable adult. A vulnerable adult is defined as a person aged 16 or over whose ability to protect himself or herself from

Provision	Offence
	violence, abuse, or neglect is significantly impaired through physical or mental disability or illness, through old age, or otherwise. This applies if:
	(a) the person lived in the same household and had frequent contact with the victim;
	(b) there was significant risk of serious physical harm and the person either caused the victim's death, or was or ought to have been aware of the risk and failed to take steps to protect the victim; and
	(c) the act occurred in circumstances that the person foresaw or ought to have foreseen.
	The maximum penalty is 14 years' imprisonment
Criminal Justice Act2003, s. 146	Imposes a duty on the criminal courts to increase the sentence for any offence aggravated by hostility based on the victim's disability or perceived disability
Sexual Offences Act2003	Establishes a number of criminal offences arising from sexual abuse. Specifically these relate to:
	(a) the inability of a person with a mental disorder to refuse sexual activity where he or she lacks capacity or is unable to communicate refusal;
	(b) where a person with a mental disorder is induced, threatened, or deceived into sexual activity where the perpetrator knows or could reasonably be expected to know that the person is suffering from a mental disorder; and
	(c) situations involving care workers and sexual activity with mentally disordered people
Mental Health Act 1983	Creates three offences of ill-treatment or neglect of mentally disordered persons by:
	an employee or manager of a hospital or care home;
	a guardian or some other person who has custody or care;
	any person in respect of a person subject to supervised discharge.
	The maximum penalty was extended from two to five years' imprisonment as a result of the Mental Health Act 2007

Conviction of the perpetrators of offences against vulnerable adults has been made easier by measures which enhance the ability of the victims of crime who have impaired mental capacity to give evidence in court proceedings. The special measures that may be available include:

- giving evidence through a TV link;
- video-recorded evidence: the witnesses evidence is videotaped and played to the court;

- screens around the witness box;

- removal of wigs and gowns;

- evidence given in private, in the courtroom;

- use of communication aids such as an alphabet board;

- examination through an intermediary who can help a witness to understand questions that they are being asked, and can make his or her answers understood by the court.

The specific criminal offences set out in **Box 14.20** are enhanced by two particular pieces of legislation. The Public Interest Disclosure Act 1998 is designed to provide protection from dismissal or other disciplinary victimization for workers who raise concerns about abuse and malpractice in the workplace. These provisions are particularly useful for those who work in a care setting who suspect that abuse is occurring.

The Safeguarding Vulnerable Groups Act 2006 is a significant piece of legislation which directly impacts upon your practice as a social worker.

Safeguarding Vulnerable Groups Act 2006 (SVGA)

Whilst there have been statutory procedures since 2000 to prevent unsuitable people from working with vulnerable adults, they were criticized by the Bichard Inquiry arising from the Soham murders in 2002, when the schoolgirls Jessica Chapman and Holly Wells were murdered by Ian Huntley (a school caretaker). One recommendation of the Inquiry Report was that a single agency should be established to vet all individuals who want to work or volunteer with children or vulnerable adults and to bar unsuitable people from doing so. This was done in the SVGA. However, the Coalition Government considered the provisions of the SVGA to be too extensive. The Home Secretary announced a review, which reported in February 2011. Among other things, the report recommended that the requirement on those working with children and vulnerable adults to be monitored under the scheme should be dropped. The recommendations were put into legislative form in the Protection of Freedoms Act 2012.

The SVGA set up the Independent Safeguarding Authority (ISA). Some of its role survives the Protection of Freedoms Act. In particular, the requirement to make referrals are made to the ISA when an employer or an organization, for example a regulatory body, has concerns that a person has caused harm or poses a future risk of harm to children or vulnerable adults. In these circumstances, the employer or regulatory body must make a referral to the ISA. The range of organizations which are able to make referrals include:

- regulated activity providers;

- personnel suppliers;

- local authorities;

- Education and Library Boards;

- Health and Social Care (HSC) bodies;
- keepers of registers named in the legislation; and
- supervisory authorities named in the legislation.

Regulated activities covers a range of specified activities that involve close contact with children or vulnerable adults, other activities in key settings such as schools and care homes which provide an opportunity for contact, and key positions of responsibility such as the Children's Commissioner and the Director of Adult Social Services. It is a criminal offence if a barred individual engages in regulated activities.

If an organization dismisses or removes a member of staff/volunteer from working with children and/or vulnerable adults in a regulated activity because they have harmed a child or vulnerable adult, then that organization has a legal duty to inform the ISA. An organization that knowingly employs someone who is barred is breaking the law. A person barred from working with children or vulnerable adults is breaking the law if they work/volunteer or seek to work/volunteer with these groups.

EXERCISES

1 Legislation relating to the abuse of adults has been categorized by Clements and Thompson in four different ways.

  (a) That which bars certain individuals from working with vulnerable people.

  (b) That which involves setting up protocols and procedures to prevent abuse.

  (c) That which imposes duties to act in a person's best interests and restricts the actions they can take in relation to people who lack capacity.

  (d) That which might act as a deterrent by criminalizing certain actions in relation to vulnerable adults.

Produce a table that sets out which legislation falls into which category. Which approach do you consider to be most effective?

2 Fiona Adair is 55 and has early onset Alzheimer's. She is living with her 19-year-old son Bill, having divorced her husband some years ago. She receives a teacher's pension, having retired early on health grounds, and the lowest rate of the care element of disability living allowance. She recently had a relationship with George but that ended with allegations that George had subjected her to violence. Her sister Lillian, who does not live locally, has contacted social services because she is concerned that Mrs Adair is at risk of exploitation. There is evidence that Bill is misusing her credit card to make internet purchases, that George has started visiting her again and may have access to her bank account, and that she is becoming increasingly at risk by leaving things on the stove and letting strangers into the house. Mrs Adair, George, and Bill all tell you and Lillian that Mrs Adair is coping fine and this is none of your business. What should you do?

3 John is 25 and lives in a residential home since a serious car accident left him brain damaged. He is unable to communicate other than through gestures. His parents would like him to have a further brain scan because they are convinced that brain surgery would alleviate his condition. John gets very agitated when he has to leave the care home, and when he is in confined spaces.

Medical advice suggests that there is nothing to be gained from a further brain scan. The care home agrees to him having the further scan. Is their decision lawful?

4 Do you think there is a need to reform the Mental Capacity Act 2005? Give reasons for your answer.

ONLINE RESOURCE CENTRE

For guidance on how to answer these exercises, visit the Online Resource Centre at www. oxfordtextbooks.co.uk/orc/socialwork13e/.

WHERE DO WE GO FROM HERE?

This chapter and the two that preceded it have focused on the responsibilities of local authorities towards adult social care users who are in the community or residential care. The next chapter retains the focus on adults, but turns to the more specialized area of mental health. It examines the legal rights of the mentally ill, and the responsibilities that social workers have to ensure that those rights are respected.

ANNOTATED FURTHER READING

Mental capacity

There are a number of useful books covering the law on mental capacity—though the Code of Practice is an excellent starting point. These include the *Mental Capacity Act Manual* (3rd edn, Sweet & Maxwell, 2008) by R. Jones (targeted at lawyers) and *The Mental Capacity Act 2005: A Guide for Practice (Post-Qualifying Social Work Practice)* by R. Brown, P. Barber, and D. Martin (Learning Matters, 2009).

The Court of Protection has been the focus of media attention. One useful article by Amelia Hill in the *Guardian* was published on 6 November 2011: 'The court of protection: defender of the vulnerable or shadowy and unjust?' (www.theguardian.com/law/2011/nov/06/court-protection-defender-vulnerable-unjust). On the same date the *Guardian* published an interview with the president of the Court of Protection, Sir Nicholas Wall: 'Court of protection should be open to public scrutiny, says leading judge' (www.guardian.co.uk/law/2011/nov/06/court-of-protection-public-scrutiny).

The Small Places blog contains useful discussions of these issues: thesmallplaces.blogspot.co.uk/.

Adult safeguarding

D. Galpin, 'Policy and the protection of older people from abuse' (2010) *Journal of Social Welfare and Family Law* 32(3): 247.

T. Spencer-Lane, 'Reforming the legal framework for adult safeguarding: the Law Commission's final recommendations on adult social care' (2011) *Journal of Adult Protection* 13(5): 275.

These articles describe in useful detail the current state of the law and proposals for reform.

S. Hussein, et al., 'Accusations of misconduct among staff working with vulnerable adults in England' (2009) *Journal of Social Welfare and Family Law* 31(1): 17. This article examines explanations and mitigation provided in response to accusations of misconduct amongst care staff.

J. Manthorpe, 'Local responses to elder abuse: building effective prevention strategies' in A. Wahidin and M. Cain (eds), *Ageing, Crime and Society* (Willan Publishing, 2006), 139–153. This chapter of an edited collection discusses local responses to the problems of elder abuse.

The *Journal of Adult Protection* provides regular articles and digests of information about practice and law in this area.

Mental health and the law

15

OVERVIEW AND OBJECTIVES

The state, acting mainly through social workers and doctors, has considerable powers over the lives of people with mental disorder. The law lays down the circumstances and procedures in which those powers can be exercised. If you step outside it, your actions are unlawful. This chapter tells you about those circumstances and procedures.

Unless there is a need for compulsory powers over a patient, your involvement with mental disorder will be under community care legislation, as discussed in the previous three chapters. This chapter deals with the problems when community care is not enough and compulsion is needed.

These are the important issues:

- In what circumstances do doctors, social workers, and relatives have the power to override the wishes of people with a mental disorder?

- How does the Mental Health Act 1983 (MHA) (as amended by the Mental Health Act 2007) work to enable or require people to obtain assessment, treatment in hospital, treatment in the community, and after-care following discharge?

- To what extent are patients' rights safeguarded by tribunals and courts?

- How can people who lack the consent to make their own decisions be deprived of liberty and treated?

 CASE STUDY

Re S-C (Mental Patient: Habeas Corpus) (1996)

S-C had a history of mental disorder. He had been in hospital at least once before. As we will see later in the chapter, a specialist mental health social worker can apply to have a person detained (sectioned) under the MHA. The Act lays down a procedure for the application. Under s. 11(4)(a) and (b) the social worker cannot apply if the nearest relative objects and cannot apply without consulting the nearest relative (unless this is impossible).

The Act defines who is the nearest relative, and, where there are many family members, how to identify the right one, because in law only one person can be the nearest relative at any one time.

In this case the social worker misled the court. She said the mother of the patient was the nearest relative, that the mother had been consulted, and that she did not object. In fact the father was the nearest relative. He had not been consulted, because the social worker knew he would object.

Having been sectioned, the patient applied for an order from the High Court for habeas corpus—a legal order requiring a person to be released immediately from unlawful detention. So it was not an application to review the grounds for detention or whether the required nature or degree of mental disorder had been established. It was an application to require that the rights of the patient to liberty be restored because they had been taken away without due process of law.

The words of Sir Thomas Bingham MR should be carefully noted:

> As we are all well aware, no adult citizen of the United Kingdom is liable to be confined in any institution against his will, save by the authority of law. That is a fundamental constitutional principle, traceable back to . . . Magna Carta . . . (1215). There are, of course, situations in which the law sanctions detention. The most obvious is in the case of those suspected or convicted of crime. Powers then exist to arrest and detain. But the conditions in which those powers may be exercised are very closely prescribed by statute and the common law. . . .
>
> [Mental patients] present a special problem since they may be liable, as a result of mental illness, to cause injury either to themselves or to others. But the very illness which is the source of the danger may deprive the sufferer of the insight necessary to ensure access to proper medical care, whether the proper medical care consists of assessment or treatment, and, if treatment, whether in-patient or out-patient treatment.
>
> Powers therefore exist to ensure that those who suffer from mental illness may, in appropriate circumstances, be involuntarily admitted to mental hospitals and detained. But, and it is a very important but, the circumstances in which the mentally ill may be detained are very carefully prescribed by statute. Action may only be taken if there is clear evidence that the medical condition of a patient justifies such action, and there are detailed rules prescribing the classes of person who may apply to a hospital to admit and detain a mentally disordered person. The legislation recognises that action may be necessary at short notice and also recognises that it will be impracticable for a hospital to investigate the background facts to ensure that all the requirements of the Act are satisfied if they appear to be so. Thus we find in the statute a panoply of powers combined with detailed safeguards for the protection of the patient. The underlying issue in the present appeal is whether those powers were properly exercised and whether the appellant was lawfully detained. One reminds oneself that the liberty of the subject is at stake in a case of this kind, and that liberty may be violated only to the extent permitted by law and not otherwise.

> **WHAT DOES THIS CASE TELL YOU ABOUT SOCIAL WORK PRACTICE?**
>
> This case serves as a further reminder that you can only act to intervene in people's lives if you have their consent or if you act with legal authority. It is not enough justification to believe that you are acting in the best interests of the service user—no doubt that is what the social worker in this case thought. If the law requires that you consult with the nearest relative, then that is what you must do, however unpalatable that may be.

Is mental health law just for specialist social workers?

We will see shortly that a social services department must appoint specialists to deal with hospital and guardianship admissions. But non-specialist social workers also need to be aware of mental health law.

For example, what are you going to do about a mentally disordered service user who threatens to jump off a window ledge, or to attack you? What about the service user who denies having a mental disorder and refuses appropriate care or medication? The question you face may be within the realm of consent, dealt with in **chapter 2**, but it may fall into the realm of compulsion. At the very least you need to be able to contact the right person, sometimes urgently; that involves knowing who does what, whether using MHA powers to detain and treat in a hospital, to treat or care for released patients, or to make guardianship orders. It also helps to know what help you can get from the police.

Powers to detain and treat people who cannot consent can involve social workers who are not Approved Mental Health Professionals (AMHPs), even where the detention and treatment is for mental disorders.

Statutory framework of the Mental Health Act 1983

There are two distinct features of the MHA:

* decisions under the MHA are first and foremost medical decisions, though they may have social care consequences;
* the MHA gives the doctors, social workers, and relatives the possibility of using compulsory powers.

The Mental Health Act in its historical context

The 1983 Act is derived from the 1959 Mental Health Act, as amended in 1982. The 1959 Act was 'revolutionary' according to Brenda Hoggett (now the Supreme Court justice Baroness Hale) in *Mental Health Law* (Sweet & Maxwell, 2010). Modern treatments, particularly medication, were to replace reliance on detention and restraint. Patients would obtain hospital treatment with as little fuss as any other medical treatment. Doctors would only use compulsory powers for exceptional circumstances. Patients who could not benefit from hospital treatment would be treated in the community. And criminals with mental disorder would receive the same medical care as anyone else.

This can be described as a medical model. It puts the state's powers of compelling individuals into the hands of doctors and, to a lesser extent, social workers. It is doctors, generally aided by social workers or other health professionals, and sometimes by relatives, who have powers to detain patients. It is usually doctors who decide to release patients.

Legal powers and constraints are grafted onto this medical model: criminal courts can send an offender to hospital for treatment, and in the case of dangerous offenders can restrict the power of doctors to release the patient; after detention has commenced a patient can apply to a Mental Health Tribunal for release, and the hospital must then prove that the detention remains justified in law.

A key concept of the 1959 and 1983 legislation was that compulsory treatment should be for the benefit of the patient. If the condition cannot be treated, the patient should not be detained. As we shall see, that concept has been watered down, so that a patient now can be detained if appropriate treatment is available, even if it cannot be shown that it will benefit the patient.

For almost ten years the government planned to replace the whole of the legislation, but opposition from the medical profession and mental health organizations against the proposed powers of compulsory treatment in the community and preventive detention of those with psychopathic disorder eventually led to less ambitious plans. The Mental Health Act 2007 amended the 1983 legislation with effect from November 2008 and what we describe is not radically different from the previous regime. The core difference is that the definitions of mental disorder are not set out so narrowly, that new powers now exist to treat a patient in the community following release from detention, and that detention for treatment is not dependent on the treatment alleviating the condition.

Statutory duties

Section numbers below are from the 1983 Act. Any reference to regulations is to the Mental Health Regulations 2008 unless we indicate otherwise. Any reference to the Code is to the May 2008 version of the Code of Practice Mental Health Act 1983.

The MHA confers statutory powers on social workers in three ways, all of which will be explored in more detail.

First, it creates specialist mental health professionals who make decisions alongside doctors. Previously called Approved Social Workers (ASWs), the 2007 amendments changed their name and broadened the number of professions able to exercise these powers. Their new name is Approved Mental Health Professionals (AMHPs): members of other professions can be approved under the MHA, including nurses, occupational therapists, and psychologists. The panel of AMHPs is in the control of (but need not be employed by) social services authorities (s. 114), which must appoint enough AMHPs to provide 24-hour cover for admissions of mental patients and their treatment (DoH Circular LAC (93) 10 and Mental Health Act 1983 Code of Practice, para. 4.33). The AMHP exercises his or her powers personally, not under the direction of their employer.

The AMHP has powers, working with doctors, to detain for assessment or treatment or to admit to guardianship. The AMHP plays no statutory role in decisions to discharge, but social services are likely to be heavily involved in preparing for discharge and advising whether community facilities are ready and appropriate for the patient's discharge.

Second, a social services authority has statutory powers and duties relating to guardianship. It must either itself take on the role of guardian, or it must approve the appointment of an individual as guardian.

Third, the authority has duties under s. 117 to plan and provide after-care following discharge. We touched on that when looking at community care.

The scale

Statistics published by Mind (www.mind.org.uk) indicate that 30 per cent of the population experiences a mental health problem in any year. Most of these do not involve specialist help, though 10 per cent of the population are diagnosed with a specific condition each year. Government statistics, published in October 2013 and set out in **Box 15.1**, indicate the scale of use of formal powers under the legislation.

BOX 15.1 Key facts—Annual report on formal detentions under the MHA

The total number of people subject to detention or CTO [Community Treatment Order] restrictions under the MHA at year end has remained similar to the number during 2011/12. On the 31st March 2013, this figure stood at 22,207 people, 60 fewer than in the previous year. This decrease is less than 1 per cent.

Of the number subject to the Act:

• 16,989 people were detained in hospital (a decrease of 514 or 3 per cent). This corresponds with a reported fall in the number of available NHS beds.

• 5,218 people were subject to a CTO (an increase of 454 or 10 per cent).

These figures include detentions and CTOs for both NHS and independent sector providers. There were a total of 50,408 detentions in NHS and independent hospitals during 2012/13. This number was 4 per cent (1,777) greater than during the 2010/11 reporting period. Of this total:

- All detentions in independent sector hospitals increased by 17 per cent; a large proportion of this increase was attributable to a 31 per cent increase (313) in uses of Part II Section 2 on detention to hospital.

- Detentions on admission to NHS and independent hospitals increased by 4 per cent (1,324) overall.

- Detentions under Part III (Court and Prison disposals) decreased by 16 per cent.

There were 4,647 CTOs made during 2012/13, an increase of 427 (10 per cent) since last year:

- 190 more CTO recalls were made during 2012/13 than during 2011/12 (a 9 per cent rise) and 41 per cent of CTOs which ended were by revocation (down from 46 per cent during 2011/12).

- The number of CTO revocations has increased by 40 (3 per cent) since the previous year; this increase is small compared with the observed increase between the 2010/11 and 2011/12 reporting years (44 per cent).

- The number of CTO discharges has increased by 450 (an increase of 26 per cent).

There were 14,296 uses of place of safety orders (Sections 135 and 136) in hospitals; this figure is 6 per cent (944) lower than during 2011/12.

- More males than females were subject to place of safety orders in hospitals (8,354 compared to 5,942). The fall in uses was larger for females (9 per cent) than for males (4 per cent).

The need for compulsory powers over a patient is comparatively rare. By comparison with the numbers of people with some form of mental health problem, even voluntary admissions to hospital are rare. Out-patient hospital treatment, help from a GP or community mental health teams, social services support in the community, or simply coping without professional help, are how the bulk of mental health problems are dealt with.

▓ 'No health without mental health'

As with community care generally, mental health services involve a range of agencies. To ensure that the service user does not experience disjointed provision, the government has published 'No health without mental health', a cross-government mental health outcomes strategy for people of all ages. This approach and how it is distinct from the previous government's approach is explained as follows:

> This mental health outcomes strategy will demonstrate how the Government's localised approach, together with the reforms to health and other public services and action across all government departments, will deliver improvements by:
>
> - lifting the burden of bureaucracy;
> - empowering communities to do things their way;
> - personalising the production and delivery of services and support;
> - increasing local control of public finance;

- diversifying the supply of public services;
- opening up the Government to public scrutiny;
- promoting social action, social inclusion and human rights; and
- strengthening accountability to local people.

The six key objectives of the strategy are set out in **Box 15.2**.

 BOX 15.2 'No health without mental health'—six objectives

(i)   More people will have good mental health

More people of all ages and backgrounds will have better wellbeing and good mental health.

Fewer people will develop mental health problems—by starting well, developing well, working well, living well and ageing well.

(ii) More people with mental health problems will recover

More people who develop mental health problems will have a good quality of life—greater ability to manage their own lives, stronger social relationships, a greater sense of purpose, the skills they need for living and working, improved chances in education, better employment rates and a suitable and stable place to live.

(iii) More people with mental health problems will have good physical health

Fewer people with mental health problems will die prematurely, and more people with physical ill health will have better mental health.

(iv) More people will have a positive experience of care and support

Care and support, wherever it takes place, should offer access to timely, evidence-based interventions and approaches that give people the greatest choice and control over their own lives, in the least restrictive environment, and should ensure that people's human rights are protected.

(v)   Fewer people will suffer avoidable harm

People receiving care and support should have confidence that the services they use are of the highest quality and at least as safe as any other public service.

(vi) Fewer people will experience stigma and discrimination

Public understanding of mental health will improve and, as a result, negative attitudes and behaviours to people with mental health problems will decrease.

In July 2012 the government published best practice guidance on implementing its strategy. The guidance was developed by a range of organizations including the Centre for Mental Health, the Department of Health, Mind, NHS Confederation Mental Health Network, Rethink Mental Illness, and Turning Point. It includes examples of good practice. The implementation framework is available at www.gov.uk/government/uploads/system/uploads/attachment_data/file/216870/No-Health-Without-Mental-Health-Implementation Framework-Report-accessible-version pdf.

Suggestions made for action by local authorities are set out in **Box 15.3**.

BOX 15.3 What local authorities can do

- Appoint an elected member as 'mental health champion'.

  This role might include raising awareness of mental health issues, including the impact of stigma and discrimination, across the full range of the authority's work and with other elected members, including lead members for children. It can also link to the work of the OSC [Overview and Scrutiny Committee] and health and wellbeing board.

- Assess how its strategies, commissioning decisions and directly provided services support and improve mental health and wellbeing.

  Almost all areas of a local authority's responsibility have the potential to contribute to good mental health and wellbeing, or to lead to poor mental health. Decisions about employment, housing, planning, transport, leisure and green spaces and other community services all directly affect mental health.

- Involve the local community, including those with mental health problems, their families and carers, in the co-production of service pathways and in service design.

  This includes providing clear and accessible communication regarding how people's views and priorities have been taken into account.

- Consider using 'whole place' or community budgets to improve the quality and efficiency of support offered to people with multiple needs including a mental health problem.

- Use the Local Government Association's Knowledge Hub allowing members and staff to share innovative approaches and good practice.

- Sign up to the Time to Change campaign to raise the profile of mental health across the authority and address stigma among staff.

- Authorities can also develop local initiatives to make tackling stigma 'business as usual'.

Accountability to the Care Quality Commission

Those working in social care generally are accountable through complaints procedures (see **chapter 14**), through the courts (we look at some of the mental health case law later) and through the normal channels of democratic and media scrutiny. The Care Quality Commission, made up of laypeople, lawyers, doctors, nurses, social workers, psychologists, and other specialists (as we discussed in **chapter 14**), also has responsibilities under the MHA. It is required to:

- review MHA powers of detention;
- visit patients detained under the Act;
- investigate complaints;
- review decisions to withhold the mail of patients detained in high security hospitals;

- appoint medical practitioners and others to give second opinions;
- monitor the implementation of the Code of Practice.

The Commission's performance has been criticized by Members of Parliament (MPs) on the Public Accounts Committee which accused it of 'insufficient focus on both the quality and consistency of inspectors' work' (*The Care Quality Commission: Regulating the Quality and Safety of Health and Adult Social Care*, PAC, 12 March 2012). The Commission insists that it has since increased inspections. During 2013 the Commission consulted on changing the way it monitors Mental Health Act provision. Changes to its practices will be published shortly.

Accountability to the courts

It is a fundamental principle of health and social care law that service users and patients can choose whether they accept or refuse services or treatment. Only if they lack mental capacity does the law allow others to make decisions in their best interests (see **chapter 2**). However, compulsory detention under the MHA operates independently of capacity questions. The MHA allows health professionals to assess, detain, and treat patients, or impose guardianship or community treatment, even where they have adequate mental capacity to refuse.

This gives mental health professionals and, unless they have been barred from involvement (see **Barring discharge from hospital by the nearest relative**, p 531), nearest relatives, a power to override the wishes of mentally disordered adults with mental capacity. Such powers have to be exercised with respect for human rights. The European Convention provides, in particular, the right to liberty. Article 5 states:

> No one shall be deprived of his liberty save in the following cases and in accordance with a procedure prescribed by law . . . [including] the lawful detention . . . of persons of unsound mind, alcoholics or drug addicts, or vagrants.

An example of the application of Article 5 in a mental health detention case was *K v UK* (1998). Mr Kay had been convicted of manslaughter and was subject to a hospital order with restriction. We will describe this later. Mr Kay was conditionally discharged from hospital in 1985 (the conditional release meant he was still subject to recall); he offended again, but this time was sentenced to prison, not sent to hospital. While in prison he obtained evidence showing he was no longer suffering from a mental disorder. Yet he was still liable to recall under the hospital order because of the restriction imposed on his previous conviction. A Mental Health Review Tribunal (MHRT) accepted that he had no mental disorder but refused to discharge the restriction order. The hospital then recalled him just before his release from prison, with the result that he was detained under the hospital order as soon as he left prison.

The European Court of Human Rights (ECtHR) said that if he was to be detained for treatment for mental disorder, the state must prove both that he had the mental disorder and that he needed the treatment. Deprivation of liberty was otherwise unlawful.

We will see later that MHRTs are routinely involved where patients wish to challenge their continuing detention.

Mental Health Act 1983 Code of Practice

The Mental Health Act 1983 Code of Practice (Department of Health and Welsh Office 2008) is essential reading. It is available at http://webarchive.nationalarchives.gov.uk/20130107105354/http://www.dh.gov.uk/en/Publicationsandstatistics/Publications/PublicationsPolicyAndGuidance/DH_084597. Extracts from the Code are set out in **Box 15.4**. The Code must (s. 118) conform to the following statutory principles:

(a) respect for patients' past and present wishes and feelings,

(b) minimising restrictions on liberty,

(c) involvement of patients in planning,

(d) developing and delivering care and treatment appropriate to them,

(e) avoidance of unlawful discrimination,

(f) effectiveness of treatment,

(g) views of carers and other interested parties,

(h) patient wellbeing and safety, and

(i) public safety.

 BOX 15.4 Principles set out in the 2008 Code of Practice

1 Decisions under the Act must be taken with a view to minimising the undesirable effects of mental disorder, by maximising the safety and wellbeing (mental and physical) of patients, promoting their recovery and protecting other people from harm.

Least restriction principle

1.3 People taking action without a patient's consent must attempt to keep to a minimum the restrictions they impose on the patient's liberty, having regard to the purpose for which the restrictions are imposed.

Respect principle

1.4 People taking decisions under the Act must recognise and respect the diverse needs, values and circumstances of each patient, including their race, religion, culture, gender, age, sexual orientation and any disability. They must consider the patient's views, wishes and feelings (whether expressed at the time or in advance), so far as they are reasonably ascertainable, and follow those wishes wherever practicable and consistent with the purpose of the decision. There must be no unlawful discrimination.

Participation principle

1.5 Patients must be given the opportunity to be involved, as far as is practicable in the circumstances, in planning, developing and reviewing their own treatment and care to help ensure that it is delivered in a way that is as appropriate and effective for them as possible. The involvement of carers, family members and other people who have an interest in the patient's welfare should be encouraged (unless there are particular reasons to the contrary) and their views taken seriously.

Effectiveness, efficiency and equity principle

1.6 People taking decisions under the Act must seek to use the resources available to them and to patients in the most effective, efficient and equitable way, to meet the needs of patients and achieve the purpose for which the decision was taken.

Independent mental health advocates

Mental patients are often unable to articulate their own views adequately. Independent mental health advocates (IMHAs) have a role independent of all other professionals to help the patient voice their wishes and concerns. Any detained patient (except detained in an emergency for six or 72 hours or in a place of safety) is entitled to this assistance, and to be told of its availability. The IMHA should have access to the patient and to records at all reasonable times. Clearly, as they aim to be the voice of the patient, what they say must be carefully listened to at all times. The Code provides more detail at Chapter 20.

Assessment of mental disorder with a view to admission

The MHA uses the word 'patient' for any person suffering from mental disorder. But it is not necessary to be an in-patient or even an out-patient for the MHA to apply.

A patient can be of any age for MHA powers to be available, except that for admission to guardianship the child must be at least 16. Of course, unless circumstances are exceptional, doctors and social workers are more likely to rely on Children Act powers where children have mental health problems.

The legal definition of mental disorder is simple: 'Any disorder or disability of the mind' (s. 1). Those with a learning disability are not considered to be suffering from a mental disorder unless 'that disability is associated with abnormally aggressive or seriously irresponsible conduct' (s. 1(2A)). Section 1(3) provides that 'dependence on alcohol or drugs is not to be considered a mental disorder'.

It is for mental health professionals to assess who has and who does not have a mental disorder. Courts and tribunal will not overrule such diagnoses, since they are matters of professional judgement. However, an MHRT considering grounds for continuing detention must itself identify the nature and degree of the mental disorder where this triggers statutory powers to detain, so in theory the tribunal can disagree on clear evidence of a misdiagnosis.

Although mental disorder must not be diagnosed solely on grounds of alcohol or drug abuse (s. 1(3)), alcohol or drug abuse can be symptomatic of or can cause mental disorder and can lead to mental disorder. Anorexia nervosa has been found by a court to be a mental illness (*Re KB (Adult) (Mental Patient: Medical Treatment)* (1994)).

Assessment of the patient for MHA purposes should be carried out where possible by the doctors and the AMHP at the same time, but the conclusions are to be reached by each professional independently. While the AMHP acts on behalf of the local social services authority, they exercise their own judgement, deciding independently whether to apply for a patient to be detained on the basis of the medical evidence and whether there are alternatives (Code, para. 4.51). The AMHP must not defer to the doctor. It is for the AMHP to provide the social perspective, and also to consult the nearest relative and others, such as a carer, before reaching a conclusion (Code, Pt 4).

A diagnosis cannot be founded on unwise or irrational behaviour. *St George's NHS Trust v S* (1998) involved a woman who was refusing a caesarean section, even though she was, on the evidence, putting herself and her baby at grave risk. To get round the lack of consent the hospital had her sectioned. This left her powerless, so she accepted the caesarean. Afterwards she applied to the court for a declaration that this use of MHA powers had been unlawful. No evidence was put forward that she had a mental disorder. The Court of Appeal ruling makes clear that the Act should be used to deal with mental health issues and not for social control.

The professional assessment can be reviewed by courts, for example where 'seriously irresponsible conduct' has to be identified. In *Re F (Mental Health Act: Guardianship)* (2000), the Court of Appeal disagreed with an assessment by doctors that a 17-year-old girl who chose to return to an unhappy, abusive home was behaving seriously irresponsibly, for the purpose of diagnosing mental impairment (now called learning disability).

MHA criteria for admission, as we shall shortly see, require that the patient 'is suffering'. However, a person can be liable to mental disorder, but presently symptom free, perhaps because the treatment is working. Does that person have the required mental disorder? In *R (on the application of P) v Mental Health Review Tribunal* (2002), the court agreed with the doctors that disorder (in this case psychopathic disorder) still exists while there is a risk of recurrence.

The Code contains extensive guidance on communicating with the patient and others. **Box 15.5** contains a flavour of this.

 BOX 15.5 Extracts from the Code of Practice concerning assessment and communication

Communicating with patients

2.2 Effective communication is essential in ensuring appropriate care and respect for patients' rights. It is important that the language used is clear and unambiguous and that people giving information check that the information that has been communicated has been understood.

2.7 Wherever possible, patients should be engaged in the process of reaching decisions which affect their care and treatment under the Act. Consultation with patients involves assisting them in understanding the issue, their role and the roles of others who are involved in taking the decision. Ideally decisions should be agreed with the patient. Where a decision is made that is contrary to the patient's wishes, that decision and the authority for it should be explained to the patient using a form of communication that the patient understands.

Confidentiality

18.2 In common law, a duty of confidence arises when one person discloses information to another in circumstances where it is reasonable to expect that the information will be held in confidence. Certain situations, such as discussions with a health professional or social worker, are generally presumed to be confidential.

However, there are circumstances in which it is both justifiable and important to share otherwise confidential patient information with people outside the immediate team treating a patient.

Before considering such disclosure of confidential patient information, the individual's consent should normally be sought.

If a person lacks the capacity to consent to the disclosure, it may nonetheless be acceptable and appropriate to disclose the information in the person's best interests.

Otherwise, confidential patient information should be disclosed outside the team only:

- with the person's consent (where the person has capacity to consent);
- if there is a specific legal obligation or authority to do so; or
- where there is an overriding public interest in disclosing the information.

▓ The nearest relative

Doctors and AMHPs have to work with the nearest relative. At any given moment a particular patient can have only one nearest relative. Section 26 sets out how this person is identified, and this is summarized in **Box 15.6**.

 BOX 15.6 The nearest relative, in order of priority

The following order of priority is the starting point:

- spouse or civil partner (but not a spouse or partner who has deserted the patient or been separated by court order or formal agreement);
- cohabitee of six months' standing;
- son or daughter;
- parent;
- brother or sister;
- grandparent;
- grandchild;
- uncle or aunt;
- niece or nephew;
- any other person who has lived with the patient for at least five years (if there is no spouse).

A relative who actually lives with and cares for the patient takes precedence over someone higher up the list. Anyone who lives abroad is ignored altogether. And, conversely, if the patient reasonably objects to the nearest relative (in *R (on the application of M) v Secretary of State for Health* (2003) where the patient had no relationship of trust with her adoptive father) that person cannot be a nearest relative. Where there is more than one person competing for the position on the same level in the list (eg a brother and a sister; two parents) then the oldest takes precedence. Relationships of the whole blood take precedence over those of half blood (eg a sister comes before a half-sister).

If a child is in care under the Children Act 1989, the nearest relative is the authority named in the care order, even if the child is accommodated at home (s. 27).

The nearest relative can give written authorization to allow another person to discharge their role (reg. 14).

▓ Discharge or replacement of nearest relative

Consulting with the family is important. But there may be no family, or no family willing to play the role. Alternatively the nearest relative may, you think, be standing in the way of the patient's best interests, or of the interests of public safety. That was the problem, as the social worker saw it, in the case study at the beginning of the chapter.

Let us assume that it was entirely appropriate for S-C to be sectioned, and the father's objections were standing in the way of appropriate help being given. The correct approach would be to apply to the County Court to displace the nearest relative.

In either of these situations—unsuitability or unwillingness—any relative, any person with whom the patient normally resides, or an AMHP can apply to the County Court to be appointed or to have someone else appointed. The doctors, incidentally, cannot themselves make this application. They are reliant on the AMHP. The patient him or herself (since 2008) can also apply to the court to displace the nearest relative.

A decision to make an application to displace the existing nearest relative itself raises human rights issues. It is a determination of the nearest relative's responsibilities and it triggers Article 6 of the Convention, so there must be a proper and fair process. In particular, the nearest relative who does not agree with being displaced has a right to see relevant documents: *R (on the application of S) v Plymouth City Council* (2002).

The court can make the s. 29 displacement order only if one of the following grounds is established:

(a) no nearest relative can be found; or

(b) the present nearest relative is incapable of acting because of mental disorder or other illness; or

(c) the nearest relative unreasonably refuses to consent to an application for admission to hospital or guardianship under the MHA; or

(d) the nearest relative has unreasonably exercised his or her power to discharge the patient without taking into account the public interest or the welfare of the patient (s. 26(3)).

(e) that the nearest relative is otherwise not a suitable person to act as such: *R (on the application of M) v Secretary of State for Health* (2003).

As soon as a s. 29 application is submitted—before any order is made—the current nearest relative loses the power to discharge the patient. This is the only means available to an AMHP to prevent a discharge. The doctors, as we will see, have other ways of preventing discharge by the nearest relative.

The nearest relative has the right, at any time, to appoint an independent doctor to visit the patient in hospital and look at relevant records. This is important, for the nearest relative (even if displaced) has rights to apply to the Mental Health Tribunal, and, if not displaced, to discharge a detained patient, and needs the best information before making that decision.

Informal admission to hospital

Some 70 per cent of mental health admissions are not compulsory. Section 131 and the Code of Practice (para. 4.9) explicitly encourage informal admissions. In fact there is no power to detain a person in hospital under ss. 2–5 if the patient genuinely consents to be admitted and to remain.

Any person of 16 or over can become an informal patient, regardless of the wishes of his or her parent or guardian. Below that age the informal admission requires consent of the parent or guardian (s. 131(2)). The local authority can admit a child informally, against the child's will, even if there are no grounds for a compulsory MHA admission: *R v Kirklees MBC, ex p C (A Minor)* (1993). Before admitting a child informally, the question of competence must be addressed. In *Kirklees* the Court of Appeal accepted that if the child had been 'competent' she would have been entitled to refuse informal admission.

Before the 2007 amendments, the legal framework included something which had come to be called the '*Bournewood* gap'. The gap has been dealt with by amendments which came into force in April 2009. A brief explanation will, however, help you to understand the 'deprivation of liberty safeguards' (DoLS) created under the amended MHA. The gap was identified by the long-running case which started out as *R v Bournewood Community and Mental Health NHS Trust, ex p L* (1998). Mr L was severely autistic with a 30-year history of in-patient treatment, though he had more recently been looked after by devoted carers in the community. On one occasion they brought him in to the hospital for professional help as L was getting agitated. They were then prevented from removing him from the hospital, even though he was not detained by any sectioning decision. L himself was not capable of objecting to remaining in hospital. His carers sought judicial review of the refusal to release him, arguing that if he was not free to go, he should be sectioned: this would trigger statutory reviews of detention, time limits, and automatic referral to the tribunal. The Court of Appeal ruled that L was being unlawfully detained, but the House of Lords (now Supreme Court) disagreed.

L's carers took the case to the ECtHR (*HL v UK* (2005)) where the Strasbourg judges ruled that L had been unlawfully detained since there was no power to review the lawfulness of his admission and continuation in the hospital. The gap in the mental health legislation was the arbitrary nature of his deprivation of liberty and the absence of a route to challenge informal detention (which is what the ECtHR recognized it to be) where patients lacked capacity to discharge themselves.

A new Schedule A1 to the Mental Capacity Act 2005 (MCA) creates an authorization procedure to enable managers of the care home or hospital to prevent a resident who lacks capacity to decide for him or herself from leaving. Relatives, carers, or friends will be able to request an assessment for the purpose of authorization, and detention will have to be shown to be in the interests of the resident: that means necessary to avoid harm to the patient, and proportionate to the risk of harm. The authorizing body is the primary care trust or the Welsh Assembly. There is no power to refer a detention to the tribunal, but the Court of Protection can hear appeals against the DoLS, and the High Court could be asked to judicially review the lawfulness of an authorization.

Authorization cannot, however, be given to detain a patient informally if he or she has given an advance directive (see **chapter 14**) refusing consent, or where the patient has given a Lasting Power of Attorney covering health and welfare decisions (see **chapter 14**) and the donee has withheld consent.

Detention in these circumstances must be under the powers of the MHA, or not at all. In fact, such a patient should have been admitted under the MHA and not the MCA (Code, para. 4.18).

Application for compulsory admission to hospital—'sectioning'

The compulsory route of most importance for social workers will be compulsory admission, or sectioning, for assessment or for treatment under ss. 2 and 3 of the MHA.

Applicants should remind themselves of the least restriction principle set out in the Code. Liberty should only be restricted by compulsory admission in the absence of a suitable less restrictive approach. A full discussion of the problematic nature of DoLS is included in **chapter 14**.

Who is the applicant? An AMHP is usually a better person to make the application than the nearest relative, 'given an AMHP's professional training and knowledge of the legislation and local resources, together with the potential adverse effect that an application by the nearest relative might have on their relationship with the patient' (Code, para. 4.28). The AMHP must first consult with whoever appears to be the nearest relative (s. 11(4)). Consultation need not take place if it is 'not reasonably practicable or would involve unreasonable delay'. Knowingly consulting the wrong relative makes the ensuing admission and detention unlawful (*Re S-C (Mental Patient) (Habeas Corpus)* (1996), the **Case Study**, p 504). Unilaterally deciding that it would be too difficult to consult the nearest relative before admitting the patient also amounted to unlawful detention, in circumstances where such consultation could have been arranged and had been deliberately avoided to secure the patient's admission: *GD v (1) Hospital Managers of the Edgware Community Hospital (2) Barnet LBC* (2008).

An application must be supported by two (or, in an emergency, one) doctors' statements.

The application is addressed to the managers of the proposed hospital (s. 11); this means the health authority or, if it is a private mental nursing home, the person registered with the Care Quality Commission to run it, or, if the hospital is secure (eg Broadmoor), the Secretary of State for Health.

An AMHP *must* make an application where in his or her professional opinion that is the appropriate course (s. 13(1)). This is a matter for the AMHP; it is not a departmental decision. And he or she must reach the decision independently, even if it is a different decision from that of the doctors. This was spelled out in *St George's Healthcare NHS Trust v S* (1998), where the Court of Appeal stated that the approved social worker (predecessor to the AMHP) should have realized that a woman refusing a caesarean was not suffering from a mental disorder.

Before making the application, the AMHP must interview the patient 'in a suitable manner', and must be satisfied that compulsory admission is the most appropriate way of providing the care and medical treatment that the patient needs (s. 13(2)). A suitable manner means taking into account any language barriers, hearing difficulties, and other potential communication obstacles such as cultural differences. Guidance is given in the Code, paras 4.28 onwards. As soon as the AMHP has made a decision—to apply or not to apply for compulsory admission—he or she must explain the decision to the patient, the doctors, the nearest relative (if possible), the patient's key worker and doctor (Code, para. 4.78).

Patients do not always cooperate with an assessment. An assessment can be valid for admission purposes even if there is no conversation: *M v South West London and St George's Mental Health NHS Trust* ((2008).

Certain pre-application requirements must be satisfied. The applicant for a compulsory admission must have seen the patient within the previous 14 days. The application must be supported by the signed medical recommendations of two doctors, one from a Department of Health-approved mental health specialist, the other, if possible, from a doctor who knows the patient. Both doctors must have examined the patient within five days of each other. They must sign the recommendations before the applicant signs the application, otherwise the application is invalid.

The five-day and 14-day time periods are shortened in the case of an emergency admission (which is discussed in **Compulsory admission for assessment**, p 521): the applicant must have seen the patient not more than 24 hours before making the application, and the admission must be carried out within 24 hours of the medical examination (s. 6(2)(b)).

Neither the managers nor the hospital doctors who receive the application actually consider its merits. They only consider whether they have space. Indeed, once the application for admission has been completed, even before it is delivered to the hospital, it gives rise to compulsory MHA powers: the applicant or his or her authorized agent is now empowered to take the patient to the named hospital. However, the detention ceases to be lawful if the hospital managers realize that the facts stated in the forms are untrue (*R v Central London County Court, ex p London* (1999)). Unless there is a clear abuse of process, in which case proceedings can be commenced, the detention can only be challenged through the Mental Health Tribunal, but a hearing will take time to arrange and until then the section continues to be lawful.

The power to convey the patient to hospital lapses 14 days after the last of the two medical examinations (s. 6(1)), so the medical information will be reasonably up to date at the time of the admission.

Once a patient is compulsorily detained, hospital managers must inform the patient of the grounds for detention, and their rights to a discharge and to apply to the Mental Health Tribunal. If the application was by an AMHP, the nearest relative must be similarly informed unless the patient objects (s. 132).

Where the application was by a nearest relative, the managers must notify the patient's local social services department; a social worker (who does not have to be an AMHP) must then interview the patient and provide the hospital with a social circumstances report (s. 14). The report should set out not only the history of the patient and the disorder, but also state whether alternative methods of dealing with the patient are available and appropriate. Alternative methods mean looking after the patient in the community—can anything be organized under the powers described in the Code at Chapters 17 and 18?

Compulsory admission for assessment

Application for an admission for assessment is under s. 2. It is possible even if the nearest relative objects since there is no statutory requirement to consult the nearest relative. This is in contrast to an application for treatment under s. 3. (It remains good practice to consult, of course.) Note that there is a statutory requirement to inform the nearest relative that an application for detention under s. 2 is to be or has been made.

For compulsory admission for assessment under s. 2, the doctors must certify on the application that they are satisfied that the patient (s. 2(2):

(a) he is suffering from mental disorder of a nature or degree that warrants the detention of the patient in a hospital for assessment (or for assessment followed by medical treatment) for at least a limited period;

(b) he ought to be so detained in the interests of his own health or safety or with a view to the protection of other persons.

A correctly completed application gives the applicant immediate powers to convey the patient to hospital. The hospital may detain the patient for up to 28 days (s. 2(4)). After that, the patient must be discharged unless he or she remains as an informal patient, or detention is authorized for treatment under s. 3 (see **Compulsory admission to hospital for treatment**, p 522).

In an emergency, s. 4 enables a brief detention on just one medical recommendation. The applicant must certify that the need for admission for assessment is urgent and that obtaining two recommendations would involve undesirable delay (s. 4(2)). The doctor should, if possible, be someone who knows the patient. The doctor must confirm that admission for assessment is a matter of urgency. The Code (para. 5.5) advises that urgency is more than a matter of administrative convenience. There must be evidence of at least one of the following:

- immediate and significant risk of mental or physical harm to the patient or others
- danger of serious harm to property
- need for physical restraint of the patient.

Once the s. 4 application is completed the patient can be detained for up to 72 hours. During these 72 hours, if the second doctor's recommendation is received by the managers, the detention is converted into a s. 2, 28-day admission, starting from the day of the admission. Otherwise, at the end of the 72-hour period the patient is free to leave.

▓ Compulsory admission to hospital for treatment

If the applicant is an AMHP, he or she must consult the person who appears to be the nearest relative before making the application for admission for treatment (s. 11(1)), unless it is 'not reasonably practicable or would involve unreasonable delay'. The nearest relative can then block the application (s. 11(4)), which means the AMHP may have to apply to the County Court to displace the nearest relative (see **Discharge or replacement of nearest relative**, p 517).

Medical grounds for admission for treatment are more rigorous than for assessment, which is not surprising given that the doctors are now, by definition, satisfied that treatment is appropriate. Mental disorder on its own is not enough. The doctors' recommendations must confirm that:

- the patient's 'mental disorder is of a nature or degree which makes it appropriate for him to receive medical treatment in a hospital';
- it is 'necessary for the health or safety of the patient or the protection of other persons' that he or she receives such treatment;
- the treatment cannot be provided without the detention; and
- appropriate medical treatment must be available.

Let us look at some of these requirements. Having a mental disorder is not sufficient if it can be treated entirely in the community; however, if the treatment has to be in or organized by the hospital, the patient may be allowed by the doctors to live in the community. The question is whether the patient would agree without compulsory powers to receive the treatment. A mental disorder can be cyclical, or the patient can be well when compliant with medication, but not otherwise. So the nature of the condition must be such that detention for treatment is appropriate even if at this particular moment the patient is not necessarily unwell. A patient may therefore need treatment in a hospital under compulsory powers, even if not at present showing signs of severe disorder.

Popplewell J explained the distinction between nature and degree in *R v MHRT, ex p Smith* (1999) 47 BMLR 104. 'Nature' refers to the 'particular mental disorder from which the patient suffers, its chronicity, its prognosis, and the patient's previous response to receiving treatment for the disorder' and that it is not a static condition. 'Degree' refers to the 'current manifestation of the patient's disorder' and therefore allows the detention to be justified in relation to the current severity of the disorder. Degree and nature can be alternative grounds for assessing the patient as requiring admission—they do not both need to be satisfied for admission for treatment to be lawful.

Treatment must be available and appropriate. Treatment is a broad concept. Section 145 defines 'medical treatment' as including 'nursing, psychological intervention and specialist mental health habilitation, rehabilitation and care', and goes on to say that 'any reference in this Act to medical treatment, in relation to mental disorder, shall be construed as a reference to medical treatment the purpose of which is to alleviate, or prevent a worsening of, the disorder or one or more of its symptoms or manifestations'.

Force-feeding can be treatment where the patient is refusing to eat (*B v Croydon Health Authority (No 2)* (1996)). Group therapy is treatment, even if the patient is unwilling to participate: *B v Croydon Health Authority (No 2)* (1996). If the patient refuses available treatment, he or she is nevertheless treatable under the old legislation, and treatment would be available under the new legislation (*R v Canons Park MHRT, ex p A* (1994)).

The MHA was, as we mentioned earlier, designed on a medical model. Treatment for mental health was to be no different from treatment for other health problems. But what if there was no treatment to alleviate the condition? Formerly the power to detain for compulsory treatment under s. 3 did not apply if the patient was diagnosed as suffering from a 'minor' disorder—mental impairment or pyschopathic disorder—unless the doctors certified that treatment was likely to alleviate the condition or stop it getting worse. The thinking was that, since the disorders were 'minor', no one should compulsorily be sent to hospital for treatment unless he or she would benefit from it. It was felt that even an untreatable psychopathic patient who was dangerous was not a problem that doctors should be required to solve.

In a controversial change opposed by psychiatrists and mental health organizations, the 'treatability test' for the patient has ceased to be a requirement. The government wanted to detain people in hospital even though there was no effective treatment for them so the requirement, under the new s. 3(2)(d), is the availability of 'appropriate medical treatment', meaning 'treatment which is appropriate in his case, taking into account the nature [the particular mental disorder] and degree [the current manifestation] of the mental disorder and all other circumstances of his case'. The definition in s. 145(4) is 'medical treatment the purpose of which is to alleviate or prevent a worsening of the disorder or one or more of its symptoms or manifestations'. The treatment must actually be available to the patient. It need not be the best possible treatment, and it need only be available at this time, even if the long-term availability is unknown. Detention on its own cannot count as treatment.

On top of the required diagnosis of a disorder, the doctors must confirm that treatment is necessary 'for the health or safety of the patient or for the protection of other persons'—that is, the patient is a risk to him or herself or others—and that 'it cannot be provided unless he is admitted under this section'. So if the patient could be treated in the community, or be admitted voluntarily, the s. 3 grounds would not be established.

There is no emergency admission for treatment.

Detention for treatment then lasts up to six months unless it is renewed (see **Detaining the patient who is already in hospital**, p 528).

Getting the patient to hospital following admission

The completion of the admission procedures gives the applicant (usually, as we have seen, the AMHPs) power to convey the patient to hospital or to delegate that power. Chapter 11 of the Code, Conveyance of Patients, provides helpful guidance including the need to be aware of any local agreements between social service departments, the ambulance service, and the police. Taking a patient in your car without an escort is discouraged. If the task is delegated to police or ambulance staff, the AMHP is still in charge (Code, paras 11.13 onwards).

Admission to hospital for treatment from a criminal court

Home Office Circular 66/90, *Mentally Disordered Offenders*, makes clear that police and Crown Prosecutors should avoid prosecution of a mentally disordered suspect unless this would be in the public interest. The circular also states that courts should if possible impose sentences that are therapeutic not punitive.

The power to make a hospital order arises under s. 37 but only if the crime is one that would have led to a prison sentence. It requires that there has been a conviction, or if there is no conviction, the magistrates' court has to be satisfied that the accused did the act, otherwise there will have to be unqualified acquittal. Section 37 requires that the offender must be 'suffering from a mental disorder of a nature or degree which makes it appropriate for him to be detained in a hospital for medical treatment and appropriate medical treatment is available for him', and that:

> the court is of the opinion, having regard to all the circumstances including the nature of the offence and the character and antecedents of the offender, and to the other available methods of dealing with him, that the most suitable method of disposing of the case is by means of an order under this section.

The court can make this order where the offender is a child of 10 or more (since children under 10 cannot come before criminal courts).

A medical report is required by the court, and evidence that a hospital bed is available. The court must weigh up the likely effect of any custodial sentence on the offender's mental disorder (Criminal Justice Act 2003, s. 157(3)(b)).

There is no need for proof of a connection between the mental disorder and the criminal offence.

Once the offender is in the hospital, he or she is now a patient, and will be treated the same as any other patient. This means the detention expires after six months unless renewed (see **Detaining the patient who is already in hospital**, p 528). To avoid this risk of early release, the Crown Court can add to a hospital order a restriction order designed to protect the public from serious harm (MHA, s. 41). A youth court or magistrates' court does not have this particular power, but can commit an offender of 14 or over to the Crown Court in the expectation that the Crown Court will decide that such an order with restriction should be made.

The restriction period is indefinite. The result is that until it is discharged the detainee cannot be released, even for leave of absence, without an order of the Secretary of State for Justice or the Mental Health Tribunal. This is in contrast to other detained patients, who can and should be released by the hospital if the doctors think release is appropriate. The restriction will only apply until the earliest release date of the transferred prisoner, whereafter the restriction part of the order will lapse. If the patient remains in hospital, he or she will continue to be detained as if on a hospital order without restrictions from that date (called a 'notional s. 37'). We will consider restriction orders again when looking at discharge from hospital.

Transfer of mentally disordered offenders from prison to hospital is possible under s. 47 by a 'transfer direction' issued by the Home Secretary on the basis of reports from at least two medical practitioners. There is no role for the AMHP to be involved. The appropriate treatment must be available. Once admitted, the patient is treated like any other s. 2 patient, unless the Home Secretary places a restriction on the patient similar in effect to the restriction imposed by the Crown Court.

Admission from a police station

There is no special procedure for admission from a police station. We saw in **chapter 10** that a doctor should be called to assess a detainee in the police station when mental disorder is suspected. From there, informal or formal admission under the ss. 2–4, can take place. The decision whether to continue with any criminal proceedings will be taken by the police and Crown Prosecution Service. They should charge a mentally disordered suspect only if it is in the public interest.

Temporary detention by a police officer

At the beginning of the chapter, we talked about someone threatening suicide or violence. Your instinct may be to call the police. That is correct. The police can arrest someone, whether or not there is mental disorder, who is committing any kind of offence that is likely to be threatening, and in particular a person committing a breach of the peace. What then happens will be decided at the police station—see **Admission from a police station**, above.

Section 136 also enables a police officer to detain in a place of safety any person found in a public place who appears to be mentally disordered. This power of detention lasts only 72 hours, and any longer detention requires an admission for assessment or treatment. A public place is defined in case law as somewhere to which the public have access (eg the landings in a block of flats—*Knox v Anderton* (1983)). The officer must consider that detention is necessary in the interests of the mentally disordered person or to protect another person. The place of safety can be a police station, a hospital, Part III accommodation provided by the local authority (see Code, Chapters 16–18), a nursing home, or any other suitable place. The Code provides guidance at Chapter 10 and makes clear that the patient should be assessed as soon as possible after removal to the place of safety.

Any person, not just a suspect, detained in a police station has the right to a lawyer under s. 58 of the Police and Criminal Evidence Act 1984 (PACE) and to the presence of an appropriate adult under PACE Code C (see **chapter 10**).

The power to detain in a place of safety is not given to a social worker, even an AMHP. You must call the police if you cannot yourself deal safely with the situation. But the police authority must agree its policy on use of this power with social services and the health authority (Code, para. 10.16).

Searching out and protecting the mentally disordered

The power of removal to a place of safety does not extend to entering property. Section 135 enables a magistrates' court to issue a warrant for the police to enter premises, by force if necessary, and remove a mentally disordered person to a place of safety for up to 72 hours. The magistrate must believe, on the basis of information on oath from an AMHP, that there is evidence that either:

(a) a person suffering from a mental disorder has been or is being ill-treated, neglected, or kept otherwise than under proper control, or is living alone and unable to look after him or herself; or

(b) you are being denied access to a patient who has absconded from hospital or the place the patient is required to live by the guardian; or in respect of whom the proper admission procedures have been completed.

When the police officer executes the warrant he or she should be accompanied by an AMHP and a doctor.

Admission to guardianship

We have seen that a person should not be compelled to go to hospital for treatment if they can be treated in the community. But this can leave a gap in terms of having some control of the mentally disordered person's life in the community. Applying the principles of the Code of Practice set out earlier (**Mental Health Act 1983 Code of Practice**, p 513), guardianship can be a less restrictive option than detention.

A guardian can be either an individual or a social services department. If the patient is under 16, however, MHA guardianship is not available: a person with parental responsibility is automatically the guardian.

The application procedure differs only slightly from that for admission for treatment. The application is submitted to a local authority social services department, either for the area where the proposed guardian lives or to the authority which is named as the proposed guardian (s. 11; Regulations, reg. 5). The application must be accepted before it is effective, unlike s. 3 applications for admission.

Procedures for an application for guardianship are otherwise the same as those for admission for treatment. The applicant is the AMHP or nearest relative, and must have seen the patient within the previous 14 days. If the AMHP is the applicant, the nearest relative must be consulted unless consultation is not practicable. An AMHP may not make an application if the nearest relative objects.

There must be two medical recommendations. The requirements (s. 7) are slightly different from those for admission to hospital. The patient must still be suffering from mental disorder, to a nature or degree that warrants reception into guardianship. The doctors must confirm that guardianship will either benefit the welfare of the patient or protect other persons. This is not such a stringent requirement as the need to show that detention is necessary for the health or safety of the patient under s. 3, which we saw is needed for admission for treatment. If the doctors think that guardianship would improve the quality of the patient's life, that is enough for guardianship.

As an alternative to the hospital order, s. 37 empowers any criminal court to make a guardianship order on the offender. The guardian will be nominated by social services and may well be the AMHP. The local authority will have to provide the court with details of how the guardian will exercise his or her powers. A guardianship order imposed by a court, once made, is identical in effect to any other guardianship order—see the following section.

Powers and duties of the guardian (s. 8 and Regulations, reg. 22)

If the local authority accepts the application, the guardian assumes certain powers over the patient: to specify where the patient shall live, to require the patient to go for medical treatment, to become involved in occupation, education, or training, and to require whoever the patient lives with to give access to a doctor, AMHP, or other named person. The particular place the patient might be required to live could well be Part III of the National Assistance Act accommodation (see Code, Chapters 16–18). Any imposition of a requirement must be compatible with human rights, for example the right to family life. In *Re Connor's Application for Judicial Review* (2005) the patient had been subject to a condition that she must live in a particular institution, which meant that she could not live with her husband. The court held that such a requirement could be imposed if it was necessary and proportionate, but in this case the alternatives had not been considered.

There is no sanction against a patient who breaches these requirements, except the power discussed later to fetch back an absconding patient (see **Leave of absence and patients who abscond from detention or guardianship**, p 529). If the patient will not comply with the requirements then guardianship is not appropriate and the order should be discharged (Code, para. 26.35).

Social services must see the patient every three months, and ensure that a doctor does so at least every 12 months (reg. 23).

Guardianship lasts initially for six months. The nominated doctor must review the guardianship during the last two months and report to the social services authority whether he or she is satisfied that the conditions for continuation of guardianship are fulfilled, including that appropriate medical treatment is available. If so, the guardianship is automatically renewed for six months on the first occasion, and each time after that for 12 months (s. 20).

Transfer from guardianship to hospital or vice versa

A patient under guardianship can be admitted to hospital as an informal patient, but if necessary can be sectioned. The application procedure is similar to the s. 2 and s. 3 admission procedures, and in particular the same medical recommendations are required (s. 79). A transfer from a hospital section into guardianship, either to an individual or to a social services authority, is more straightforward. If the proposed guardian and the relevant social services department agree, the hospital managers simply authorize the transfer (s. 19; reg. 7). Readmission to hospital after such a transfer would either be informal or require an application under s. 2, 3, or 4.

Detaining the patient who is already in hospital

If hospital managers wish to detain an informal patient, the nearest relative or AMHP should be asked to make an application under s. 3 for treatment, or consider applying to the primary care trust or Welsh Assembly for authorization to detain a patient lacking mental capacity.

But if time is short—the patient is packing his or her bags, the taxi is waiting—the informal patient can be temporarily detained using s. 5 or s. 6 powers. The psychiatrist responsible for the patient, called in the legislation the 'responsible clinician' (RC), or his or her delegate, can detain any existing hospital patient by delivering a report to the hospital managers stating that such detention is necessary. This report creates a 72-hour power of detention and a breathing space for the authorities to consider a s. 3 application. If the doctor is unavailable and there is a crisis, a nurse (who must be registered for mental disorder work under the Nurses, Midwives and Health Visitors Act 1979) can detain for up to six hours. In this case the power of detention begins as soon as the report is completed. Again, no second opinion is required.

Incidentally, these powers can apply to any hospital patient, not just a patient admitted informally for mental disorder. Although the nurse has to be a mental health specialist, any type of hospital doctor can exercise the 72-hour power of detention.

MHA detentions all have time limits. After the time limit expires, detention is unlawful unless compulsory powers are exercised to renew it. The possibilities for renewal or upgrading are:

- a six-hour nurse's detention can become a 72-hour detention on receipt of the report of the doctor treating the patient;

- a 72-hour doctor's detention can become an admission for treatment (or in theory assessment) under s. 3 or s. 2 by obtaining the second medical recommendation;

- the 28-day detention for assessment can become a six-month detention for treatment by making an application under s. 3.

In all of these cases, any time already spent detained counts towards the new detention period.

None of the powers of detention we have looked at so far last more than the six months allowed for treatment under s. 3 (except a Crown Court hospital order with restriction). However, s. 20 provides a procedure for review and, if appropriate, renewal of detention for treatment. Review must take place in the last two months of a s. 3 detention, or the last two months of an unrestricted s. 37 detention. The RC must do two things: first, examine the patient and, second, consult at least one other person who has been professionally concerned with the patient's medical treatment—such as a hospital social worker.

The doctor must then report to the managers stating whether he or she is satisfied that the requirements for continued detention apply. These requirements mirror the requirements for admission for treatment set out earlier: mental disorder of a nature or degree that makes it appropriate to be detained for treatment which is necessary for the health or safety of the patient or the protection of others. The renewal does not take effect until the expiry of the previous period of detention.

When the managers receive the signed report, they can detain the patient for treatment for a further six months on the first occasion, and on future occasions for 12 months at a time. The review must be repeated during the last two months of each new period of detention.

Leave of absence and patients who abscond from detention or guardianship

The RC (or the Secretary of State for Justice in the case of restricted patients) can give leave of absence under s. 17, and can recall a patient from such leave. The leave often is defined very closely: for example, it must be accompanied; it is limited to one hour a day; etc.

A patient absent without leave for less than six months, or a person subject to guardianship who disappears from the address specified by their guardian, can be detained and brought back by an AMHP, a member of the hospital staff, a police constable, or any person authorized by the hospital managers (s. 18).

Discharge of a detained patient

Except where there is a restriction order, it is good practice to discharge a patient if the criteria for detention in hospital no longer apply. Patients must be discharged if they are found not to be suffering from a mental disorder (*Kynaston v Secretary of State for Home Affairs* (1981)).

The power to discharge arises under s. 23 and can be exercised by hospital managers, the RC, or the nearest relative. However, the nearest relative has less power to discharge than the doctor or managers: this is because he or she has no power of discharge during the period of a hospital order made by a criminal court (s. 23 and Sch. 1); and because the nearest relative must give 72 hours' notice of intention. During that period the discharge can be barred by the RC (**Barring discharge from hospital by the nearest relative**, p 531).

The criteria for an 'order for discharge' are not stated in s. 23, but it implies that the RC should constantly be checking that the admission criteria are met; they should not wait until the automatic s. 20 review, which occurs towards the end of the detention period. The discharge does not have to be immediate (eg if after-care needs to be arranged), but must be within a reasonable time.

If the patient is subject to a restriction order imposed by the Crown Court, the release has to be approved by the Secretary of State unless discharge is ordered by the tribunal.

Discharge under Community Treatment Order (CTO)

Discharge may be absolute or subject to supervised treatment in the community. The CTO replaces what used to be called supervised after-care and its framework is set out in ss. 17A–17G. A CTO cannot be imposed unless the patient is currently detained under s. 3 or s. 37 without restrictions.

If a CTO is appropriate, it is—by definition—no longer necessary to detain the patient in hospital. The RC must consult with an AMHP and the AMHP must agree.

The criteria for discharge subject to the CTO are set out in s. 17A(5) and (6):

(5)   The relevant criteria are—
   (a)   the patient is suffering from mental disorder of a nature or degree which makes it appropriate for him to receive medical treatment;
   (b)   it is necessary for his health or safety or for the protection of other persons that he should receive such treatment;
   (c)   subject to his being liable to be recalled as mentioned in paragraph (d) below, such treatment can be provided without his continuing to be detained in a hospital;
   (d)   it is necessary that the responsible clinician should be able to exercise the power under section 17E(1) to recall the patient to hospital; and
   (e)   appropriate medical treatment is available for him.

(6) In determining whether the power of recall is required, the RC shall, in particular, consider, having regard to the patient's history of mental disorder and any other relevant factors, what risk there would be of a deterioration of the patient's condition if he were not detained in a hospital (as a result, for example, of his refusing or neglecting to receive the medical treatment he requires for his mental disorder).

There can be requirements, enforced by the power of recall, imposed on patients in the community to ensure that they stay in contact with mental health services and practitioners can monitor them for signs of deteriorating health, and if necessary decide that they must be recalled to hospital. The patient can be recalled by the RC if the RC considers that he or she requires hospital treatment for mental disorder and there would be a risk of harm to the patient's health or safety or to others if not recalled. The recall will be for up to 72 hours during which time the RC will have to decide if the CTO should be revoked or the patient sent out again on the CTO. If the RC decides to revoke, he or she must do so in writing with the agreement of an AMHP. The effect of revocation is that the original s. 3 or s. 37 is revived from the date of revocation (ie no need to do a fresh MHA assessment).

Conditions can be imposed under s. 17B(2) to ensure that the patient receives medical treatment, to prevent risk of harm to the patient's health or safety, or to protect others. The RC must agree these requirements with the AMHP. If treatment against a patient's will becomes clinically necessary, a patient can be recalled to hospital for treatment.

Renewal of the CTO occurs along the same time frame as renewal of detention under s. 3—that is, after six months from the time a patient leaves hospital, at one year and then at yearly intervals. Renewal is via a report to the hospital managers in the same way as renewal of detention.

Discharge by Parole Board

Section 74(5A) permits mental patients held under a restriction order to apply to the Parole Board for release, like any other prisoner. If the Parole Board orders release, the restriction order lapses.

Discharge from guardianship

Guardianship can be terminated before the end of the six- or 12-month period by the nearest relative, the social services authority, or the RC (s. 23)—but not by the guardian unless he or she is also the nearest relative.

Where guardianship was ordered by a criminal court, discharge under s. 23 can be made only by the social services department, not by the RC or the nearest relative (Sch. 1, Pt I, paras 2 and 8).

Barring discharge from hospital by the nearest relative

The doctors may not agree with the nearest relative that the patient should be discharged from hospital. The nearest relative must give 72 hours' notice of intention to discharge. The RC who wishes to bar this discharge must submit a report to the hospital managers stating that the patient would, if discharged, be a danger to him or herself or to others. The barring order, once signed by the RC, bars the nearest relative discharge.

The case must then be considered by the managers who decide if they should discharge the patient. Assuming the managers agree with the RC, the nearest relative is barred from discharging the patient for the next six months.

Neither the 72-hour notice period nor the barring order procedure apply to a discharge from guardianship by the nearest relative because the nearest relative has an absolute right to discharge the patient.

An AMHP can also block discharge by the nearest relative from hospital and from guardianship. But to do this the AMHP must apply to the County Court to displace the nearest relative (see **Discharge or replacement of nearest relative**, p 517). Under s. 29, once an application is filed with the court (which would have to be during the 72-hour notice period) discharge from hospital is blocked until the court makes its decision. It will probably be too late to use this power to block discharge from guardianship as there is no 72-hour notice requirement.

Discharge by the First Tier Tribunal (Mental Health)

The tribunal (known as a Mental Health Tribunal) can order a discharge from hospital, from guardianship, or from CTO (MHA, Pt V). Procedures are governed by the Tribunal Procedure (First-tier Tribunal) (Health, Education and Social Care Chamber) Rules 2008.

Although first tier tribunals, as we saw in **chapter 1**, are in theory less orientated towards formal legal procedures than courts, in mental health cases it is recognized that applicants need free specialist legal representation. It is a good idea if the representative is a member of an approved panel of specialists for there will be a need to marshal evidence of fact and medical opinion, and cross-examine witnesses, including experts in mental health. However, there is no need for the patient's representative to be a panel member; the patient can appoint who they wish provided it is not another detained patient. Hospitals keep lists of local panel members. The AMHP does not have a statutory role, but a report with detailed plans and recommendations for the patient if discharged must be provided, and social services are likely to be involved in providing this information.

Who can apply to the tribunal? The applicant will usually be the patient, but it may be the nearest relative if he or she has been barred from discharging the patient. Patients detained for treatment or in guardianship can apply once in each period of detention (ie first six months, second six months, and each subsequent period of 12 months).

If a patient detained under s. 3 is detained beyond six months and no one has made an application to the tribunal, the hospital managers must themselves refer the case to the tribunal within the first year. Subsequent references must be made if three years (or one year if the patient is under 18) have elapsed since the case was last considered by a tribunal. CTO patients must be referred to the tribunal if there has been no application in the six months since their original detention under s. 3. See **Box 15.7**.

BOX 15.7 Time limits for applications to the tribunal (MHA, ss. 66 and 68)

Application by the nearest relative

Discharge of patient blocked by the RC	28 days from the date of being informed
Nearest relative displaced by county court order	12 months from order, then once every 12 months
Patient detained under a hospital order; patient under a restriction order	not before 6 months; once during the second 6-month period, then once in every 12-month period

Application by the patient

Admission for assessment	14 days
Admission for treatment/reception into guardianship	6 months
Patient under CTO	no time limit

The tribunal hearing requires an up-to-date social circumstances report. The exact contents are specified in para. 12 of the First Tier Tribunal Health Education and Social Care Chamber Practice Direction on Statements and Reports in Mental Health Cases (2012) set out in **Box 15.8**.

BOX 15.8 Requirements for a social circumstances report submitted to the tribunal

This report must include the following information:

(a) the patient's home and family circumstances and the housing facilities available;

(b) in so far as it is practicable, and except in restricted cases, a summary of the views of the patient's nearest relative, unless (having consulted the patient) the person compiling the report thinks it would be inappropriate to consult the nearest relative;

(c) so far as it is practicable, the views of any person who plays a significant part in the care of the patient but is not professionally concerned with it;

(d) the views of the patient, including his concerns, hopes and beliefs;

(e) the opportunities for employment available to the patient;

(f) what (if any) community support or after-care is being or would be made available to the patient and the author's views as to its likely effectiveness were the patient to be discharged from hospital;

(g) the patient's financial circumstances (including entitlement to benefits);

(h) an assessment of the patient's strengths and any other positive factors of which the Tribunal should be aware;

(i) an assessment of the extent to which the patient or other persons would be likely to be at risk if the patient were to be discharged from hospital, and how any such risks could be managed effectively.

The tribunal must consider whether the criteria for continued detention, guardianship, or CTO are justified. The criteria are almost identical to the admission criteria so we have not repeated them. The tribunal has a judge, and a lay member (often with mental health professional experience, such as a nurse), and also a medically qualified member (invariably a psychiatrist). This member must examine the patient before the hearing and report findings to the hearing.

Unless it considers that the criteria for detention remain satisfied, a tribunal must order the discharge of the patient—either now or at a future date (s. 72). As noted already, these criteria are that the patient must be suffering from mental disorder of a nature or degree which warrants the patient's detention in hospital for assessment or treatment; if detained, for appropriate treatment which must be available.

The facts leading to the decision on whether the section is to be lifted are determined on the balance of probabilities. An attempt by a patient to argue that grounds for detention, as in criminal cases, should be proved beyond reasonable doubt did not succeed: *R (on the application of N) v Mental Health Review Tribunal (Northern Region)* (2005). Failure to order discharge where there is no continuing mental disorder was declared unlawful by the ECtHR: *Johnson v UK* (1997). Such discharge need not necessarily be immediate.

Discharge can also be ordered—though it rarely happens—even if the original admission criteria continue to be satisfied. In unrestricted (but not restricted) cases, the tribunal also has an overriding discretion to discharge even if the criteria for detention are still satisfied (ie even if it is not obliged to discharge).

If a patient has been transferred from prison to hospital under s. 47 (ie is still a serving prisoner), the MHRT is allowed only to make a recommendation to the Secretary of State for Justice and cannot direct release. However, the patient can apply for release to the Parole Board (see **Discharge by Parole Board**, p 531).

Discharge by the tribunal does not prevent a compulsory readmission taking place under s. 3—but, unless the professionals are now aware of factors of which the tribunal was not aware and which would have affected its decision, this is an abuse of the patient's right to liberty: *R (on the application of Von Brandenburg) v East London and the City Mental Health NHS Trust* (2003). According to Sedley LJ at the Court of Appeal stage in, at para. 32:

In such circumstances I do not see how an [AMHP] can properly be satisfied, as required by section 13, that 'an application ought to be made' unless aware of circumstances not known to the tribunal which invalidate the decision of the tribunal. In the absence of such circumstances an application by the AMHP should, on an application for judicial review, be held unlawful on the ground of irrationality.

Lord Bingham made the key point at para. 8 of his judgment: 'the rule of law requires that effect should be loyally given to the decisions of legally constituted tribunals in accordance with what is decided'.

If the hospital thinks the tribunal decision is wrong it should, instead, appeal to the Upper Tribunal. In this case it was, the court agreed, wrong to discharge the patient, since the patient was discharged in the absence of suitable after-care facilities.

If a discharge is ordered, the tribunal can make it conditional on suitable after-care arrangements being made. It will not necessarily be a breach of the patient's human rights (Art 5, ECHR, right to liberty) if detention continues because the arrangements cannot in fact be made. In *R (on the application of W) v Doncaster MBC* (2004), the local authority did not have suitably trained staff to supervise the applicant in the hostel to which he would be discharged, so detention was prolonged for another seven months. The Court of Appeal held that this was a rational and lawful reason for refusing discharge. Additionally, the local authority was not responsible for detaining the patient, only for dealing with after-care, so the court could not make any order against it in relation to the detention itself.

The tribunal can defer an order for discharge in restricted cases under s. 73(7) until arrangements for after-care are in place; the tribunal can reconvene the hearing and reach a different decision if the arrangements it considers appropriate are not put into place within a reasonable time. In unrestricted cases, an order for discharge can be delayed to a specific date. Tribunals in unrestricted cases have powers of recommendation if they do not order discharge, for instance if the patient is transferred to another hospital or into guardianship or is given leave or the RC considers making a CTO. There is no direct power of enforcement of recommendations, but the tribunal can reconvene if its recommendation is not complied with within a specified time.

The tribunal hearing an application for discharge following the barring of a nearest relative's power to discharge must discharge if it is not satisfied that the patient would be likely on discharge to act in a manner dangerous to others or to him or herself. Evidence submitted to the tribunal must, among other things, address the dangerousness criterion as well as the need to detain the patient because of the nature or degree of the disorder. If the patient disputes the accuracy of allegations of events in the past, it will be essential to marshal reliable evidence to show them: vague file notes, sometimes based on vague information, are not a basis for detaining a person when what is at stake is not clinical judgement but proof of disputed facts.

Treatment in hospital for the mental disorder

The MHA and the Code of Practice provide detailed powers to treat a person for mental disorder where they are refusing consent to such treatment. As you are unlikely to be formally involved in the exercise of these powers, we have not described them here.

After-care following detention

Where a patient is discharged from detention in hospital or from guardianship, s. 117 imposes the duty jointly on the health authority and social services to provide after-care services for as long as they are needed. The authorities should cooperate with suitable voluntary agencies. Section 75 of the Care Act 2014 makes some clarifications and amendments to s. 117 of the MHA. The changes remove anomalies in determining the responsible local authority in relation to the provision of after-care services under the 1983 Act to people who have been detained in hospital for treatment of mental disorder and the provision of care and support services to which the Act applies. The section also inserts a new s. 117A into the 1983 Act. This is about enabling a person to express a preference for particular accommodation to be provided under s. 117. All discharged patients must have an individual care plan drawn up with an identified key worker who will ensure that it is implemented. There is no statutory definition of what level of after-care is required. The decision on provision is made under community care law (see previous chapters), with the important difference that it must be paid for by the NHS.

Miscellaneous powers outside the MHA to control mentally disordered people

You would be forgiven for thinking that the powers of compulsory intervention in the lives of vulnerable people would be clearly set out in the legislation. Two interesting cases, taken together, cast doubt on this. They both concern the same mentally incapacitated young woman. She was 17 years old at the time of the first hearing—too old for a care order. The local authority tried guardianship as its preferred way of removing her from a sexually abusive home environment. There was no doubt that she suffered from a mental disorder under s. 1 of the MHA but her wish to return home, according to the Court of Appeal, did not amount to 'seriously irresponsible conduct', which also has to be shown in cases of learning disability. So guardianship was not available (*Re F (Mental Health Act: Guardianship)* (2000)).

The local authority then tried another approach by resurrecting the common law doctrine of 'necessity'. The Court of Appeal in *Re F (Adult Patient)* (2000) held that it had the power to make a declaration as to the living arrangements to be made for a mentally incapacitated person, allowing the local authority control. It could do so if it was in F's best interests. The result is that the courts can declare it lawful for the state (the local authority in this case) to take control over a person's life even where there are no statutory powers.

EXERCISE

Steven, aged 20, has a developmental age of around 4 or 5. As a child, he spent a significant amount of time in residential care, provided or paid for by the local authority, though he never required care under a care order. His parents struggled to cope, but managed. Recently his mother, to whom he was very attached, died. Now he is an adult and, though he receives day care, is living at home with his father, Cyril. Since his mother died, Steven has become quite aggressive towards Cyril, who finds it difficult to maintain a safe environment at home for Steven; also Steven tends to wander off, talk with strangers, and stay out for long periods, sometimes having to be brought home by police or others. Recently Cyril hit Steven. A social services assessment of Steven's needs and those of Cyril as his carer, which involved obtaining psychiatric evidence, now recommends that Steven should be accommodated elsewhere as Cyril cannot cope. Cyril is strongly opposed to Steven being removed from his care and, insofar as it can be determined, Steven does not want to live away.

In the light of community care and mental health law, what options should the various agencies responsible for Steven's welfare consider?

ONLINE RESOURCE CENTRE

For guidance on how to answer this exercise, visit the Online Resource Centre at www.oxfordtextbooks.co.uk/orc/socialwork13e/.

WHERE DO WE GO FROM HERE?

You have finished reading *Law for Social Workers*. After a short celebration, we suggest you keep it handy as a reference source. If you have any comments please contact OUP. Your feedback may make the next edition even more useful. Thank you for reading our book, and good luck.

ANNOTATED FURTHER READING

Mental health

R. Jones, *Mental Health Act Manual* (14th edn, Sweet & Maxwell, 2011). This is used as a handbook by lawyers and members of the MHRT.

P. Bartlett, L. Gostin, P. Fennell, J. McHale, and R. MacKay, *Principles of Mental Health Law* (Oxford University Press, 2010). A collection of essays by leading academics in the field.

Two other good books are:

B. Hale, *Mental Health Law* (5th edn, Sweet & Maxwell, 2012).

P. Fennell, *Mental Health: Law and Practice* (2nd edn, Jordans, 2011).

Mind, www.mind.org.uk—access to a range of helpful materials to help those with mental health problems.

Department of Health, www.gov.uk/government/organisations/department-of-health—not an easy site to navigate, but you will need it to locate press releases and official documents.

Appendix: The Social Worker's Toolkit

Appendix: The Social Worker's Toolkit

In this Toolkit we provide you with some quick reference points to guide you during your first years in practice. Undoubtedly the most testing experience in practice occurs when one has to attend court to give evidence but we begin with you as an employee. This chapter also provides quick reference tips on working with lawyers, report writing, whistle-blowing, and your responsibilities as an employed social worker.

You as an employee

Negligence and accountability

Many social workers are concerned that they may be personally liable if they make mistakes. There is no doubt that if things go wrong you will have to explain your decisions. If you have taken reasonable care, kept your written records properly, and acted within an acceptable level of professional competence then you will be able to do this. If you do make a professional misjudgement there may be several consequences:

- First, the case may become the subject of an inquiry and you may be personally blamed in the report. Many feel that such an emphasis on individual social workers is unfair. The Laming Report on the death of Victoria Climbié made this point:

  It is not to the handful of hapless, if sometimes inexperienced, front line staff that I direct most criticism for the events leading up to Victoria's death. Whilst the standard of work done by those with direct contact with her was generally of very poor quality, the greatest failure rests with the managers and senior members of the authorities whose task it was to ensure that services for children like Victoria were properly financed, staffed, and able to deliver good quality support to children and families. (para. 1.23)

- Second, you are subject to the risk that you will be disciplined, and even dismissed, as a result of your mistake. The incompetent social worker will always take this risk. As Laming points out, the risk to you is almost always greater than the risk to senior managers.

- Finally, the person who suffers may be able to sue for compensation for the effects of your mistake. He or she is far more likely to sue the local authority than you, and even if you are sued you will be indemnified by your employer.

Your rights as an employee

- You have obligations, as does any employee, to do the best you can for your employer. This may produce conflicts arising in individual cases. As an employee you are legally required to follow the instructions of your employer. However, your employer has hired you because you are a professional, and the exercise of professional judgement is part—a major part—of your duties to the employer. We hope conflict occurs rarely, but it remains a real possibility.

- In the event of irreconcilable conflict, you must do what the employer tells you to do, but this does not mean keeping quiet about your professional opinion. In fact, to express as your opinion a belief that you actually do not hold is itself a breach of your professional duty. If expressed in court it would be close to perjury (false testimony). It is, of course, rare that opinions differ in an irreconcilable way.

'Whistle-blowing' under the Public Interest Disclosure Act 1998

The Act is designed to encourage people to raise genuine concerns about malpractice in the workplace by providing legal protection against dismissal or victimization. If a social worker makes a disclosure in good faith to a manager or an employer, he or she will be protected as a whistle-blower if he or she has a reasonable suspicion that the malpractice has occurred, is occurring, or is likely to occur. The Act also protects disclosures made in good faith to prescribed regulatory bodies where the whistle-blower reasonably believes that the information and any allegation in it are substantially true. Wider disclosures (eg to the police, the media, MPs, and non-prescribed regulators) are protected if, in addition to the test for regulatory disclosure, they are reasonable in all the circumstances and:

- they are not made for personal gain;
- the whistle-blower must have reasonably believed that he or she would be victimized if he or she raised the matter internally or with a prescribed regulator; and
- reasonably believed that a cover-up was likely and there was not a prescribed regulator, or had already raised the matter internally or with a prescribed regulator.

If the concern is exceptionally serious, a disclosure will be protected if it meets the test for regulatory disclosures and is not made for personal gain. The disclosure must also be reasonable, having particular regard to the identity of the person to whom it was made.

Where the whistle-blower is victimized in breach of the Act, he or she can bring a claim to an employment tribunal for compensation.

Information sharing

Information sharing is a balancing act. The British Association of Social Workers (BASW's) Code of Ethics is worth remembering.

> Social workers should respect the principles of confidentiality that apply to their relationships and ensure that confidential information is only divulged with the consent of the

person using social work services or the informant. Exceptions to this may only be justified on the basis of a greater ethical requirement such as evidence of serious risk or the preservation of life. Social workers need to explain the nature of that confidentiality to people with whom they work and any circumstances where confidentiality must be waived should be made explicit. Social workers should identify dilemmas about confidentiality and seek support to address these issues.

It is worth bearing in mind the following questions when considering whether to share information or not:

1　Is there a clear and legitimate purpose for you or your agency to share the information?

2　Does the information enable a living person to be identified?

3　Is the information confidential?

4　If the information is confidential, do you have consent to share?

5　If consent is refused, or there are good reasons not to seek consent to share confidential information, is there a sufficient public interest to share the information?

6　If the decision is to share, are you sharing information appropriately and securely?

7　Have you properly recorded your information-sharing decision?

For more detail on information sharing see **chapter 4**. You can also download further guidance on information sharing at http://webarchive.nationalarchives. gov.uk/20130401151715/http://www.education.gov.uk/publications/standard/ Integratedworking/Page1/DCSF-00807-2008.

Writing a report

Tips for report writing

- Use the appropriate template for your report to the court.
- Prepare the evidence carefully beforehand including the completion of a comprehensive chronology.
- Leave plenty of time so that your report is not rushed and to allow you the opportunity to re-read the report before submission.
- Use straightforward sentences, the shorter the better.
- Ensure you have addressed the central question; for example, has the child suffered significant harm?
- Read the report out loud (you might want to do this in private). A badly written report is very difficult to read. If you stumble over reading it, it probably needs rewriting or editing.
- Supervision sessions are good places to reflect on and analyse evidence. Ensure you have discussed your report in supervision before completing it.

Since the judgment in *Re B* (see **chapter 8**) there has been renewed focus on the need for reports for courts to be analytical and evidence-based. In that particular case the local authority report and the report written by the children's guardian came in for some considerable criticism because they had not provided reasoned arguments for the various options open to the court in its decision making. Michael Jones's commentary of the implications of that case suggests that evidence should address the following:

- The use of a pro-forma or 'balancing sheet' in respect of the available placement options is advisable.

- The contents of any such document must, however, be detailed in its analysis of the alternative options available and must carefully reason why each option is or is not suitable for the subject child.

- In the event that a care plan of adoption is sought, then the local authority should evidence that no other placement option available would be sustainable in the long term and that it is necessary to dispense with parental consent to adoption.

- The local authority should detail any support services which could be provided to the family and, if appropriate, why the provision of such services would not be sufficient to sustain any placement within the family.

- The local authority should be able clearly to evidence that it has had regard to concurrent care planning in each case.

- The evidence should acknowledge the gravity and the draconian nature of not just an adoptive care plan, but also of the making of a care order and why this is necessary in the circumstances.

- This advice is obviously specific to cases involving the adoption of a child but generalizations are also appropriate.

- Reports for court should clearly demonstrate the evidence on which decision making is proposed.

- Reasoned arguments for alternative options should be very clearly set out.

- Such arguments should try to explain what has happened, why it has happened, and what is likely to follow as a consequence.

Such explanations are likely to draw on both theory and empirical evidence. For example, it is possible to explain how a child's insecure avoidant attachment style has developed as a result of the care given by her clinically depressed mother (see D. Howe, *Child Abuse and Neglect: Attachment, Development and Intervention* (Palgrave Macmillan, 2005) for a discussion of how insecure attachments occur and C. Martins and E. Gaffan, 'Effects of early maternal depression on patterns of infant–mother attachment: a meta analytic investigation' (2000) *Journal of Child Psychology and Psychiatry* 41(6): 737, for research evidence on the impact of maternal depression on attachment styles). The consequences of living with an insecure attachment style can include an increased incidence of depression and anxiety in adolescence and adulthood (see A. Lee and B. Hankin (2009) 'Insecure attachment, dysfunctional attitudes, and low self-esteem predicting prospective symptoms of depression and anxiety during adolescence' (2009) *Journal of Clinical Child and Adolescent Psychology* 38(2): 219).

Working with lawyers

- Lawyers belong to a professional body, the Law Society or the Bar Council dependent upon whether they are solicitors or barristers, and are bound by a code of conduct.

- The code of conduct for solicitors focuses on less complex dilemmas, such as not acting for people where you have a conflict of interest, and having to hold money that belongs to clients in a separate account from your own money.

- Lawyers have a more straightforward relationship with their clients than you have with the service user. If the lawyer and the client disagree on what is the best course of action then the client can sack the lawyer.

- Lawyers are committed to the rule of law, which includes the right of all to have the best professional help to argue their case on an equal footing.

- Lawyers' skills lie in the interpretation of complex statutes and cases and in defending the interests of their clients through negotiation and advocacy.

- Lawyers are interested in achieving for the client what he or she wants, and the question of whether it should be what they want is wholly irrelevant.

- The local authority lawyer's role is to advise the social worker as to the legal strengths and weakness of the case.

- The local authority lawyer, however, may not always do as the social worker suggests since their 'client' is in fact the local authority.

Going to court

Giving evidence in court is a vital part of the role of a social worker. The role of the court is to determine the truth so far as this can be ascertained and to agree plans for the future. These are fundamental processes for the social work task.

See **Figure 1.1**, p 23 for a reminder of the court system.

What will happen at court?

Figure A, a flow diagram of the procedure in family proceedings, is a useful way of understanding what happens in court.

The making or refusing of the order ends the proceedings, unless there is an appeal (see **Appeal hearings**, pp 28–30 in **chapter 1**).

Preparing for court

The best advice for going to court is to be prepared. You should know the case inside out and back to front. It is important to have thought carefully about the evidence you

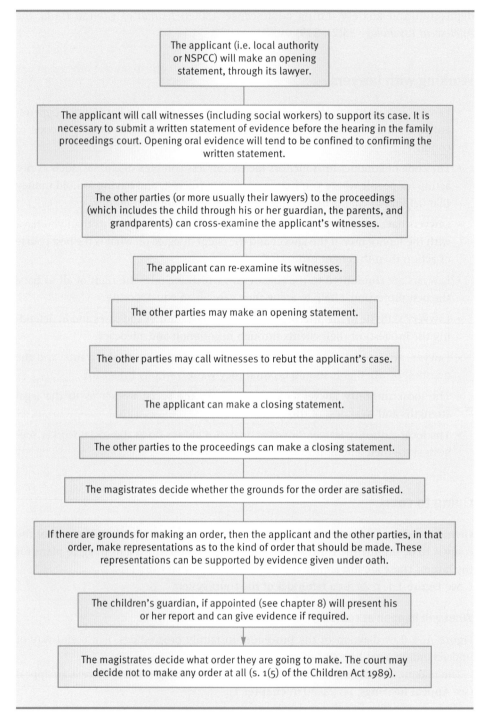

FIGURE A   The procedure in family proceedings

have for the threshold criteria and reasons for your care plan. Something to avoid is finding yourself being cross-examined on aspects of the statement that were drafted in the lawyer's words, not your own. Courts will be angry if you express doubts about what is in your statement. Before you sign it, read your statement and ask yourself if you are ready to be cross-examined on it. It is worth anticipating very hard questions on any opinions you have stated in your evidence; if you cannot justify them, perhaps they are unjustifiable, or perhaps you are the wrong person to call as the witness on this point.

Tips for presenting

- You are likely to be nervous and most nervous people speak faster than usual. Try to slow down deliberately.
- Face the magistrate or judge when speaking even though the question put to you will have come from one of the lawyers who will be in a physically different part of the court.
- If you do not understand the question, ask for clarification.
- Where smart but comfortable clothes.

Be prepared for the apparently friendly question which softens you up for the sharp follow-up question. You may wonder what the questioner is getting at. If you are unsure, then the best advice is to answer the question in as matter-of-fact a way as you can, and let the questioner reveal the strategy. Long, complex answers, given under pressure, may well contain things that you are not confident about, or even that contradict your earlier evidence. But giving evidence is an art, and giving short answers may itself allow a false picture to be constructed. Consider the following exchange:

Q: You were concerned about June?
A: Yes.
Q: Very concerned?
A: Yes.
Q: Did you discuss this with your management?
A: Oh yes, we had many meetings and case conferences.
Q: There was considerable concern throughout the department?
A: Yes.
Q: June was a constant preoccupation?
A: Yes.
Q: Then why did you visit only twice before you applied for a protection order?

How should the witness have answered these questions? Perhaps he or she was too eager. There is no correct answer except what you consider to be the truth. A skilled cross-examiner will know how to trip you up. You will say something which you think on reflection is wrong. The immediate temptation is to cover your tracks. But you risk digging a deeper hole, and a good cross-examining lawyer will allow you to dig deep before pointing out the inconsistencies in what you have just said. We suggest: 'I think I have just said something which gives the wrong impression', or even 'I made a mistake when I said that; what I meant to say was . . .'

Evidence

Social workers' evidence is largely about what they have seen and heard in the families in question or in relation to the context of family life, or what other professionals have said or done. This evidence is normally put together as a statement for the court. You might be drawing on more formal documents like assessments completed.

We would argue that in compiling a statement, and indeed in giving evidence in court, a useful question to bear in mind is, how can I assist the court to make a decision? For example, in care proceedings, the primary question for the court is, has this child been significantly harmed and is the harm attributable to the parent's care? Your statement should answer this question. You will inevitably draw on evidence from other people including other professionals and you may have commissioned assessment reports to help you to analyse what is happening in the family. The following sources of evidence may be used.

Sources of evidence

Child development dimensions

Description of harm	Examples of evidence
Indications of poor health for which there is no organic explanation	Paediatric assessment
Delayed speech and language	Speech and language therapy assessment
Physical injuries	Paediatric assessment
Behavioural problems	Systematic social work observations including attachment styles
	Psychiatric assessment
Sexual abuse	ABE interview disclosure
	Paediatric assessment
Emotional harm	Social work interviews with child
	Systematic social work observations including attachment styles
	Psychiatric assessment
Poor education development	School reports
	Educational psychology assessments

Parenting capacity dimensions

Parenting omissions and commissions	Evidence
Neglect	Assessment of parenting activities
Alcohol/drug misuse	Assessment of what, where, when, and how of alcohol or drug use plus the affect on the parenting. Psychiatric assessment
Parental mental health	Psychiatric assessment Social work assessment
Domestic violence	Assessment of what, where, when, and how of domestic violence plus the affect on the parenting.
Learning disabilities	Assessment of impact of learning abilities on parenting Educational psychology assessment

Family and environmental dimensions

Family history and functioning	Psycho-social history
	Assessment of adult attachment styles
	Assessment of relationship quality
Wider family and support	Assessment of who is available to help with practical and emotional support
Income, housing, community services	Social work assessment of the likely impact of wider society

Evidence FAQ

Can anyone help me with my evidence?

The simple answer is 'No'. Once in the witness box, you are on your own. Preparation of your evidence gives some assistance, as long as it is still your own evidence and truthful. There is nothing to prevent you discussing what you will say (so long as no one coaches you).

Can I refuse to answer questions?

No, unless the answer would incriminate you—that is, leave you personally vulnerable to criminal charges. Since s. 98 of the Children Act, you are unlikely to see a witness being allowed to refuse to answer a question on this ground, for the rule of self-incrimination no longer applies in a case involving children.

Can I refer to notes?

You may refresh your memory from notes, if you made these notes when the events were fresh in your mind. Before being allowed to refresh your memory, you will be asked a few questions about when you made the note.

The cross-examining lawyer is entitled to take a look at the note and if it is, as is normal, in a file, the whole file becomes open to inspection. Suddenly you may get a totally unexpected question: ('But it says here that . . .')

There are two safe options. One is to rely on memory only. This is advisable only if your memory is clear, for it will be fully tested under cross-examination. The other (recommended) option is to use the whole file. You should, as a matter of course, have prepared every entry in the knowledge that it may be the subject matter of skilled cross-examination. Every opinion must then be justifiable, every fact accurately recorded, with the name of the person making the note (and the time and place) also recorded. Your legal department should already, as a matter of course, have informed any other parties of material within the files which is helpful to them.

Can I refer to other people's notes?

If something is recorded on the file which is of particular importance but of which you cannot give first-hand evidence, then calling the witness, if necessary using a summons, should be considered.

Otherwise, as we saw when discussing hearsay, file notes and other records compiled by others are admissible, and will help you, in your own evidence, to give the court a full picture. You must make it clear, in oral testimony or in your statement, what part of any evidence is not derived from your own observations. You must explain the source, and the date, and circumstances in which any file record was created or other information supplied. The more careful the record keeping, the more likely the hearsay content is to be useful as evidence.

Can I withhold information from my file?

Even if you do not choose to bring your file to court, as you will see in **chapter 5**, a person called a children's guardian can inspect your file, take copies, and produce the contents in court whether you like it or not. There is, as we discussed in **chapter 4**, no concept of privilege for what social workers put in their files, and if potentially relevant, a court will not allow it to be withheld.

What if my opinion is different from that of my employer?

As an employee of your agency, you must abide by directions given to you by your managers. If you are told to instruct your lawyers to commence care proceedings, you do so. Of course, as a professional, you make it plain that in your view this is not the best course. If you testify in the case, you answer all questions truthfully, giving your opinion professionally and honestly, regardless of what your colleagues and managers say: the alternative is perjury.

Am I allowed into court when I am not giving evidence?

If a local authority social services department is party to the case, it is represented through the social worker in charge of the case, who must be allowed to remain in court even if also called as a witness. But this is subject to the court's overall discretion to allow witnesses and non-parties to be present and also to exclude people, even the social worker who personifies the agency.

If you are a witness in a criminal trial you will certainly have to remain outside court until you have given your evidence.